Scripture in the Theologies of W. Pannenberg and D. G. Bloesch
An Investigation and Assessment of its Origin, Nature and Use

Frank Hasel

Scripture in the Theologies of W. Pannenberg and D. G. Bloesch

An Investigation and Assessment of its Origin, Nature and Use

Wipf & Stock
PUBLISHERS
Eugene, Oregon

Wipf and Stock Publishers
199 West 8th Avenue, Suite 3
Eugene, Oregon 97401

Scripture in the Theologies of W. Pannenberg and D.G. Bloesch
By Hasel, Frank M.
Copyright©1996 by Hasel, Frank M.
ISBN: 1-59244--571-3
Publication date 3/1/2004
Previously published by Peter Lang, 1996

To the memory of
my grandfather

FRANZ HASEL

May 3, 1899 - April 18, 1991
A diligent student of Scripture
and a lover of the Word of God
who inspired me to follow his footsteps

FOREWORD

Usually forewords are skipped over in order to move on to the "real thing." But these pages are actually meant to be read. The role of Scripture in Christian theology has been hotly debated in the history of theology and has received renewed attention in very recent scholarly discussions, particular in systematic theology. Coming from a theological tradition that has always upheld the Protestant scripture principle, where Scripture alone (*sola scriptura*) is accepted as final and decisive norm and authority for faith and practice, I have increasingly become interested in the role Scripture plays in the construction of Christian theology. It appears that a proper understanding of the the Protestant principle of *sola scriptura* is crucially important for any Protestant identity. In this dissertation I am engaging in the discussion by exploring the role of Scripture in the ongoing work of two theological leaders of our time, namely Wolfhart Pannenberg of Germany and Donald G. Bloesch of the United States. I believe, that this study is valuable not only for those interested in the theologies of Pannenberg and Bloesch but beyond in the role of Scripture in the history of theology from the days of the 16th century Protestant Reformation up to the present. I have chosen Pannenberg and Bloesch because their understanding of the role of Scripture has paradigmatic implications far beyond their personal theologies.

This publication is my dissertation which was presented in partial fulfillment for a Ph.D. in theological studies (Field: Systematic Theology) in July 1994 to the theological faculty of Andrews University. It was accepted without revisions. Except for a few bibliographical entries that have been incorporated in the footnotes, where recent publications have contributed and added to the discussion, nothing has been changed.

A dissertation like this would not have been written without the support, help, and encouragement of numerous individuals. I would like to thank especially my parents, Kurt and Berbel Hasel, and my parents-in-law, Ulli and Uschi Fuhr, who have carried my family and me during this long and demanding task not only in their daily prayers but have lifted the burden with their unconditional emotional support and have eased the strains of a tight budget with their unsolicited financial contributions. I also extend a warm "thank you" to my aunt and my uncle, Brunhilde and Gerhard Mogwitz, without whose very generous and unexpected financial backing the publication of this dissertation would have been greatly hampered and delayed.

I wish to thank my dissertation chairman, Professor Dr. Fernando L. Canale, who introduced me to the world of philosophical thinking and its impact on theological discourse, for his guidance and constructive criticism which challenged me for higher excellence, and to Professor Dr. Raoul Dederen, who offered constructive criticism and shared valuable insights for improvement. In addition, I would like to thank Drs. Norman Miles and Miroslav Kiš, the other members of my committee, for their helpful suggestions and timely return of my submissions. A particular thanks is extended to Professor Dr. Carl E. Braaten, distinguished and widely recognized Lutheran scholar and respected expert on Pannenberg, who teaches at the Lutheran School of Theology, at Chicago, Illinois, and currently is also the executive director of the Center for Catholic and Evangelical Theology in Northfield, Minnesota. I appreciate his willingness to be the external examiner for the defense of this dissertation and for his genuine interest in this topic.

I would also like to express a sincere word of appreciation to Professor Wolfhart Pannenberg whom I had the opportunity to get to know better on a personal basis during his visit at Earlham College, Indiana, in April 1992. His friendly correspondence helped to clarify a number of questions in his thinking. Similarly, I am grateful to Professor Donald G. Bloesch, for his personal interest in this project and for the opportunity to become better acquainted with him on a personal basis on a number of occasions, not only as a scholar and theologian but as a genuine Christian and laborer in Christ. His willingness to share even unpublished material has been greatly appreciated. Both Pannenberg and Bloesch have been generously attentive to my concerns and questions, even when my analysis has led me to stand at a distance from some of their key theses. But even where I genuinely disagree with them, it is done in the context of deep appreciation.

I am also thankful to Joyce Jones and Bonnie Proctor, the former and current dissertation secretaries, without whose help my English would not have been as readable. They have both helped to bring the dissertation to a high level of conformity with the Andrews standards for written work. Furthermore, I am indebted to the staff of the James White Library at Andrews University, and here especially to Mrs. Sandra White from the Inter-Library-Loan department, who went out of her way to obtain hard-to-find books and articles--even from the other side of the Atlantic--which were essential for my research. I would also like to thank the Joseph Regenstein Library of the University of Chicago, Illinois, the Hesburgh Library of the University of Notre Dame, Indiana, and the Lilly Library of Earlham College, Richmond, Indiana, for letting me use their facilities for my research.

A special thanks goes to the Euro-Africa Division of the Seventh-day Adventist church for the trust they have extended and the financial support which they have given me, without which this project would not have been started nor completed. A sincere word of appreciation also goes to the South German Union, the Baden-Württemberg Conference, and the church members in Mannheim, Germany, who have so patiently waited for my return.

I am grateful for the many students and faculty at Andrews University who have enriched my life, broadened my perspective, challenged my conventional thinking, humbled my knowledge, stimulated me to search for better answers, inspired me through their example, and deepened my understanding of the riches of God's Word.

It was the unfailing love and unwavering faithfulness of my companion and friend for life, my wife Ulrike, that ever so often cheered me on and provided timely encouragement. She was not only a present helper in "times of trouble" but a genuine partner in the many theological discussions that have enriched my life and thinking and shaped the outlook of this dissertation. I thank her for her love, care, and support that has kept me going and has kept our family together. And I would like to thank my two sons, Jonathan and Florian, who were born while this project was in the making, for graciously allowing me to finish this "big book."

Most of all, I want to thank God for His gentle yet persistent love and His sustaining care during all this time which made HIM even more precious to me than before. "Not to us, O Lord, not to us but to Your name give glory, for Your mercy *and* loving-kindness and for the sake of Your truth *and* faithfulness!" (Ps 115:1; The Amplified Bible).

Berrien Springs, Michigan, U.S.A.,	1994	
Hockenheim, Germany	1995	Frank M. Hasel

TABLE OF CONTENTS

LIST OF ABBREVIATIONS 13

Chapter
I. INTRODUCTION 21

    Statement and Justification of the Problem 23
    Purpose and Scope of the Study 27
    Research Methodology and Limitations 29
    Outline of the Study 30

II. SCRIPTURE IN THEOLOGY: A TYPOLOGICAL OVERVIEW . . . 31

    Introduction 31
    Scripture from Above 34
        The Protestant Reformation 35
            Martin Luther 38
            John Calvin 47
            Ulrich Zwingli 51
        Protestant Orthodoxy 55
        Evangelicalism 61
    Summary 67
    Scripture from Below 69
        The Impact of the Enlightenment 70
        Johann Salomo Semler 76
        Johann Philipp Gabler 78
        Friedrich Daniel Ernst Schleiermacher 80
        Neo-Orthodoxy 85
    Summary 90
    Conclusion 92

III. SCRIPTURE IN W. PANNENBERG'S SYSTEMATIC THEOLOGY 95

    Introduction 95
    W. Pannenberg--The Man and Theologian 96
    A Description of the Concept of Scripture in
    Pannenberg's Systematic Theology 104
        The Origin of Scripture 105
            How Scripture Did Not Originate 105
            How Scripture Is Perceived to Have Originated. 109
        The Nature of Scripture 113
            What Scripture Is Not 113
            What Scripture Is Perceived to Be 116
        The Use of Scripture 120
            How Scripture Is Not Used 120
            How Scripture Is Suggested to Be Used 122
    An Analysis of Presuppositions which Influence
    Pannenberg's Concept of Scripture 128

	Theological Presuppositions	130
	Anthropological Presuppositions	144
	Conclusion	154
IV.	SCRIPTURE IN D. G. BLOESCH'S SYSTEMATIC THEOLOGY	159

Introduction 159
D. G. Bloesch--The Man and Theologian 159
A Description of the Concept of Scripture
  in Bloesch's Systematic Theology 172
  The Origin of Scripture 172
    How Scripture Is Perceived to Have Originated 172
    How Scripture Did Not Originate 177
  The Nature of Scripture 179
    What Scripture Is Perceived to Be 179
    What Scripture Is Not 187
  The Use of Scripture 191
    How Scripture Is Used 191
    How Scripture Is Not Used 201
An Analysis of Presuppositions which Influence
  Bloesch's Concept of Scripture 202
  Theological Presuppositions 203
  Anthropological Presuppositions 210
Conclusion 213

V.	EVALUATION AND CONCLUSION	217

Introductory Remarks 217
Pannenberg's and Bloesch's Concept of Scripture:
  A Comparison 217
  The Origin of Scripture 218
  The Nature of Scripture 221
  The Use of Scripture 224
Pannenberg's and Bloesch's Concept of Scripture:
  An Evaluation 226
  Pannenberg's View of Scripture 226
    Strengths 227
    Weaknesses 229
  Bloesch's View of Scripture 242
    Strengths 242
    Weaknesses 244
  Conclusion and Final Suggestions 255

SELECTED BIBLIOGRAPHY 263

LIST OF ABBREVIATIONS

AARAS	American Academy of Religion Academy Series
AARSR	American Academy of Religion Studies in Religion
AsbTJ	**The Asbury Theological Journal**
ATSOP	Adventist Theological Society Occasional Papers
AUSS	**Andrews University Seminary Studies**
AUSDDS	Andrews University Seminary Doctoral Dissertation Series
BDS	Bonner Dogmatische Studien
BEvTh	Beiträge zur evangelischen Theologie
BGBH	Beiträge zur Geschichte der biblischen Hermeneutik
BJRL	**Bulletin of the John Rylands Library**
BJSUCSD	Biblical and Judaic Studies from the University of California, San Diego
BÖR	Beihefte zur Ökumenischen Rundschau
BÖTh	Beiträge zur ökumenischen Theologie
BQT	Wolfhart Pannenberg, **Basic Questions in Theology**
BRTh	Beiträge zur Religionstheologie
BSac	**Bibliotheca Sacra**
BTFT	**Bijdragen, Tijdschrift voor Filosofie en Theologie**
Cath	**Catholica**
CBQ	**Catholic Biblical Quarterly**
CC	**The Christian Century**
CD	Karl Barth, **Church Dogmatics**
CHB	**Cambridge History of the Bible**, vol. 3, Stanley Lawrence Greenslade, ed.
ChM	**The Churchman**

CivCatt	Civiltà Cattolica
CJT	Canadian Journal of Theology
CoTh	Collectanea Theologica
CovQ	Covenant Quarterly
Criterion	Criterion: A Publication of the Divinity School of the University of Chicago
CSR	Christian Scholars Review
CT	Christianity Today
CTHDD	Jaroslav Pelikan, The Christian Tradition: A History of the Development of Doctrine
CTJ	Calvin Theological Journal
CTQ	Concordia Theological Quarterly
CTSAP	Catholic Theological Society of America Proceedings
CTSSR	College Theology Society Studies in Religion
DdK	Dialog der Kirchen. Veröffentlichungen des Ökumenischen Arbeitskreises evangelischer und katholischer Theologen
DDSR	Duke Divinity School Review
DG	The Drew Gateway
DR	The Downside Review
DSTS	Duquesne Studies Theological Series
DtPfrBl	Deutsches Pfarrerblatt
EE	Estudios Eclesiásticos
EET	Donald G. Bloesch, Essentials of Evangelical Theology
EKL(2)	Evangelisches Kirchenlexikon, 2d edition
EKL(3)	Evangelisches Kirchenlexikon, 3d edition
ESt	Eichstätter Studien. Neue Folge
ETL	Ephemerides Theologicas Lovanienses

EvK	Evangelische Kommentare
EvQ	Evangelical Quarterly
EvT	Evangelische Theologie
ExpTim	The Expository Times
FaF	Faith and Freedom
FCI	Foundations of Contemporary Interpretation
FGLP	Forschungen zur Geschichte und Lehre des Protestantismus
FiT	First Things
FKDG	Forschungen zur Kirchen- und Dogmengeschichte
FSÖTh	Forschungen zur systematischen und ökumenischen Theologie
FSThR	Forschungen zur systematischen Theologie und Religionsphilosophie
FThS	Freiburger Theologische Studien
FZPT	Freiburger Zeitschrift für Philosophie und Theologie
Greg	Gregorianum
GTA	Göttinger Theologische Arbeiten
GTJ	Grace Theological Journal
HBT	Horizons in Biblical Theology: An International Dialogue
HDB	Harvard Divinity Bulletin
HDG	Handbuch der Dogmengeschichte, Michael Schmaus and Alois Grillmeier, eds.
HDTh	Handbuch der Dogmen- und Theologiegeschichte, Carl Andresen, ed.
HerKorr	Herder-Korrespondenz
HeyJ	Heythrop Journal
HFT	Handbuch der Fundamentaltheologie, Walter Kern, Hermann J. Pottmeyer, and Max Seckler, eds.

HibJ	The Hibbert Journal
HSRII	Donald G. Bloesch, **Holy Scripture: Revelation, Inspiration & Interpretation**
HTR	Harvard Theological Review
HWP	**Historisches Wörterbuch der Philosophie**, Joachim Ritter, ed.
IDB	**The Interpreters Dictionary of the Bible**, George Arthur Buttrick, ed.
IDBSup	**The Interpreters Dictionary of the Bible: Supplementary Volume**, Keith Crim, ed.
IDZ	Internationale Dialog Zeitschrift
Int	Interpretation
ITS	Innsbrucker theologische Studien
ITQ	Irish Theological Quarterly
JAAR	Journal of the American Academy of Religion
JATS	Journal of the Adventist Theological Society
JBT	Jahrbuch für Biblische Theologie
JCQ	The Japan Christian Quarterly
JES	Journal of Ecumenical Studies
JETS	Journal of the Evangelical Theological Society
JMRS	Journal of Medieval and Renaissance Studies
JR	The Journal of Religion
JRT	The Journal of Religious Thought
JTSA	Journal of Theology for Southern Africa
KKThS	Konfessionskundliche und Kontroverstheologische Studien
KRP	**Kolloquium Religion und Philosophie**, Willi Oelmüller, ed.
KSJAMI	Konfessionskundliche Schriften des Johann-Adam-Möhler-Instituts
KuD	Kerygma und Dogma

KuK	Kirche und Konfession: Veröffentlichungen des Konfessionskundlichen Instituts des Evangelischen Bundes
LCC	**Library of Christian Classics**
LQ	**The Lutheran Quarterly**
LThK	**Lexikon für Theologie und Kirche**, Josef Höfer and Karl Rahner, eds.
LTJ	**Lutheran Theological Journal**
LuJ	**Lutherjahrbuch**
LW	American Edition of Luther's Works. Jaroslav Pelikan and Helmut Lehmann, eds. (Philadelphia and St. Louis, 1955-)
ModM	**Moody Monthly**
ModT	**Modern Theology**
MQR	**The Mennonite Quarterly Review**
MThZ	**Münchner Theologische Zeitschrift**
NDThT	New Directions in Theology Today
NOR	**New Oxford Review**
NZSTh	Neue Zeitschrift für Systematische Theologie
NZSTR	Neue Zeitschrift für Systematische Theologie und Religionsphilosophie
Pacifica	**Pacifica: Australian Theological Studies**
Perspective	Perspective: **A Journal of Pittsburgh Theological Seminary**
PG	Philosophie und Geschichte
PLAS	Publications of Luther-Agricola Society
Princ S B	**The Princeton Seminary Bulletin**
Prism	**Prism: A Theological Forum for the United Church of Christ**
PRS	**Perspectives in Religious Studies**
PrSt	Process Studies

QD	Quaestiones Disputatae
Ref	Reformatio. Evangelische Zeitschrift für Kultur, Politik, Kirche
RefR	Reformed Review
Renovatio	Renovatio. Zeitschrift für das interdisziplinare Gespräch
ResQ	Restoration Quarterly
RevExp	Review and Expositor
RGG	**Die Religion in Geschichte und Gegenwart**, 3d edition, Kurt Galling, ed.
RJ	The Reformed Journal
RL	Religion in Life
RLM	Reformed Liturgy and Music
RS	Religious Studies
RSR	Religious Studies Review
SBLDS	Society of Biblical Literature Dissertation Series
SBT	Studies in Biblical Theology
SBT(2)	Studies in Biblical Theology, 2d series
SDGSTh	Studien zur Dogmengeschichte und systematischen Theologie
SEv	**Studia Evangelica**
SJT	**Scottish Journal of Theology**
SKAB	Schriften der Katholischen Akademie in Bayern
SLG	Schriftenreihe der Luthergesellschaft
Spfdr	**The Springfielder**
SWJT	**Southwestern Journal of Theology**
SyTh/E	Wolfhart Pannenberg, **Systematic Theology**, English Text
SyTh/G	Wolfhart Pannenberg, **Systematische Theologie**, German Text

TaH	**Theology as History**, New Frontiers in Theology, vol. 3. James M. Robinson and John B. Cobb, Jr., eds.
TB	**Theologische Beiträge**
TEH	Theologische Existenz Heute
Theol	**Theology**
ThExH	Theologische Existenz Heute
ThF	Theologische Forschung
ThRv	**Theologische Revue**
ThSt	Theologische Studien
TJ	**Trinity Journal**
TKTG	Texte zur Kirchen- und Theologiegeschichte
TLZ	**Theologische Literaturzeitung**
TPS	Wolfhart Pannenberg, **Theology and the Philosophy of Science**
TRE	**Theologische Realenzyklopädie**, Gerhard Krause and Gerhard Müller, eds.
TRS	Text-Reader Series
TRu	**Theologische Rundschau**
TS	**Theological Studies**
TSF Bulletin	**Theological Students Fellowship Bulletin**
TSR	**Trinity Seminary Review**
TSSTh	Tübinger Studien zur systematischen Theologie
TST	Toronto Studies in Theology
TTh	**Tijdschrift voor Theologie**
TThS	Tübinger Theologische Studien
TToday	**Theology Today**

TWP	The Theology of Wolfhart Pannenberg: Twelve American Critiques, with an Autobiographical Essay and Response, Carl E. Braaten and Philip Clayton, eds.
TWS	Donald G. Bloesch, A Theology of Word and Spirit: Authority and Method in Theology
TynBul	Tyndale Bulletin
TZ	Theologische Zeitschrift
USQR	Union Seminary Quarterly Review
VF	Verkündigung und Forschung
VIEG	Veröffentlichungen des Instituts für europäische Geschichte Mainz
WA	D. Martin Luthers Werke. Kritische Gesamtausgabe (Weimar: Bohlau, 1883-1983)
WADB	D. Martin Luthers Werke. Deutsche Bibel (Weimar: Bohlau, 1906-)
WATr	D. Martin Luthers Werke. Tischreden (Weimar: Bohlau, 1912-)
W2	D. Marin Luthers Sämtliche Schriften. Johann Georg Walch, ed., 2d edition, St. Louis: Concordia, 1918-1930
WesTJ	Wesleyan Theological Journal
WSFTh	Würzburger Studien zur Fundamentaltheologie
WTJ	Westminster Theological Journal
Z	Huldreich Zwinglis Sämtliche Werke. Corpus Reformatorum vol. 88-. Emil Egli, et al., eds. Zurich: Theologischer Verlag, 1905-
ZAW	Zeitschrift für die alttestamentliche Wissenschaft
ZKG	Zeitschrift für Kirchengeschichte
ZKT	Zeitschrift für Katholische Theologie
ZTK	Zeitschrift für Theologie und Kirche
ZWT	Zeitschrift für wissenschaftliche Theologie
ZZ	Zwischen den Zeiten

CHAPTER I

INTRODUCTION

For centuries, the Bible, considered as the Word of God to man, has played an authoritative role in Christian theology. In the past, Scripture was generally used to support the teachings (doctrines and dogmas) of the church.[1] The role and significance of Scripture in theology, however, has never been, and still is not, the same in all confessions and theological systems.[2]

In addition to Scripture and tradition, systematic theology commonly uses two other sources, namely experience and reason.[3] The persistent question has been and

---

[1] So J. J. Mueller, **What Are They Saying about Theological Method?** (New York: Paulist Press, 1984), 2. Richard A. Muller writes that "Scripture, variously understood . . . has been the foundation of Christian doctrine throughout all ages of the church" (**Post-Reformation Reformed Dogmatics**, vol. 2, **Holy Scripture: The Cognitive Foundation of Theology** [Grand Rapids, MI: Baker Book House, 1993], 5). Thus, "in the early medieval period, *sacra doctrina*, *sacra scriptura*, and *sacra* or *divina pagina* were the customary terms for the discipline [of theology]. They expressed the primacy of the Christian Scriptures in Christian doctrine" (Francis Schüssler Fiorenza, "Systematic Theology: Task and Methods," in **Systematic Theology: Roman Catholic Perspectives**, 2 vols., ed. Francis Schüssler Fiorenza and John P. Galvin [Minneapolis: Fortress Press, 1991], 1:6); cf. also Kenneth Hagen, "The History of Scripture in the Church," in **The Bible in the Churches: How Different Christians Interpret the Scriptures**, ed. Kenneth Hagen (New York: Paulist Press, 1985), 3-34; and Christopher Evans, **Is 'Holy Scripture' Christian? And Other Questions** (London: SCM Press, 1971), 21-36.

[2] Cf. for instance David H. Kelsey, **The Uses of Scripture in Recent Theology** (Philadelphia: Fortress Press, 1975); idem, "Appeals to Scripture in Theology," JR 48/1 (1968): 1-21; William Newton Clarke, **The Use of the Scriptures in Theology** (Edinburgh: T. & T. Clark, 1907); Kenneth Hagen, ed., **The Bible in the Churches: How Different Christians Interpret the Scriptures** (New York: Paulist Press, 1985); Donald K. McKim, **What Christians Believe about the Bible** (Nashville, TN: Thomas Nelson Publishers, 1985); Robert K. Johnston, ed., **The Use of the Bible in Theology: Evangelical Options** (Atlanta: John Knox Press, 1985); Klaus Reinhardt, **Der dogmatische Schriftgebrauch in der Katholischen und Protestantischen Christologie von der Aufklärung bis zur Gegenwart** (Munich: Verlag Ferdinand Schöningh, 1970); Avery Dulles, "Scripture: Recent Protestant and Catholic Views," TToday 37/1 (1980): 7-26; and idem, **The Craft of Theology: From Symbol to System** (New York: Crossroad, 1992), 69-85.

[3] "In older usage, the question was put as that of 'authorities'; modern usage tends rather to speak of 'sources'. These are often grouped under four heads: Scripture, tradition, reason and experience" (Geoffrey Wainwright, "Method in Theology," **The Blackwell Encyclopedia of Modern Christian Thought**, ed. Alister E. McGrath [Oxford: Basil Blackwell, 1993], 369); John Macquarrie speaks of "formative factors" and mentions six: experience, revelation, Scripture, tradition, culture, and reason (**Principles of Christian Theology**, 2d ed. [New York: Charles Scribner's Sons, 1977], 4-17); more recently he has listed only revelation, Scripture, tradition, culture, and experience (idem, "Systematic Theology," **A New Handbook of Christian Theology**, ed. Donald W. Musser and Joseph L. Price [Nashville, TN: Abingdon, 1992], 471-473); cf. also

will be: Which of these sources, or combination of them, has priority and how are they used in relationship to each other? The priority given to any source or sources will determine the direction of the entire theological enterprise. With regard to Scripture, it is particularly interesting to look at Protestant theology because "the Bible and Protestantism are entwined in a common history after the early sixteenth century."[1] It is well known that the Protestant Reformers raised the "battle cry" of *sola scriptura*," which elevated the role of Scripture to the sole standard and source for theology.[2]

Kenneth Cauthen, **Systematic Theology: A Modern Protestant Approach**, TST 25 (Lewiston, NY: Edwin Mellen Press, 1986), 27-55; and Louis Berkhof, **Introduction to Systematic Theology** (Grand Rapids, MI: Baker Book House, 1979), 59-67. On the meaning of the term "source," see Gerhard Ebeling, **Dogmatik des christlichen Glaubens**, 3 vols. (Tübingen: J. C. B. Mohr, 1979), 1:24-25, 35-42.

[1]Martin E. Marty, **Protestantism** (New York: Holt, Rinehart and Winston, 1972), 119.

[2]It has been said that the phrase *sola scriptura*, by Scripture alone, summarizes the Scripture principle (**The Blackwell Encyclopedia of Modern Christian Thought**, ed. Alister E. McGrath [Oxford: Basil Blackwell, 1993], s.v. "Scripture Principle," 667). On the Scripture principle, see Gerhard Gloege, "Schriftprinzip," **RGG**, 5:1540-1543; Friedrich Kropatscheck, **Das Schriftprinzip der lutherischen Kirche: geschichtliche und dogmatische Untersuchungen**, vol. 1 (Leipzig: A. Deichertsche Verlagsbuchhandlung, 1904); and Karl Barth, "Das Schriftprinzip der Reformierten Kirche," **ZZ** 3 (1925): 215-245. See also Markus Barth, "Sola Scriptura," in **Scripture and Ecumenism: Protestant, Catholic, Orthodox and Jewish**, DSTS 3, ed. Leonard J. Swidler (Pittsburgh, PA: Duquesne University Press, 1965), 75-94; Graham Cole, "Sola Scriptura: Some Historical and Contemporary Perspectives," **ChM** 104/1 (1990): 20-34; Gerhard Ebeling, "'Sola Scriptura' and Tradition," in Gerhard Ebeling, **The Word of God and Tradition: Historical Studies Interpreting the Divisions of Christianity**, trans. S. H. Hooke (Philadelphia: Fortress Press, 1968), 102-147; Harry William Eberts, Jr. "'Sola Scriptura': Then and Now," **RLM** 18 (1984): 64-69; Klaus Haaker, "Sola Scriptura: Zur Bedeutung der Bibel für die Kirche heute," **TB** 24/3 (1993): 130-139; Heinz Liebing, "Sola Scriptura--die reformatorische Antwort auf das Problem der Tradition," in **Sola Scriptura: Ringvorlesung der theologischen Fakultät der Philipps-Universität**, ed. Carl-Heinz Ratschow (Marburg: N. G. Elwert Verlag, 1977), 81-95; David W. Lotz, "Sola Scriptura: Luther on Biblical Authority," **Int** 35 (1981): 258-273; Reinhard Slenczka, "Was heißt und was ist schriftgemäß?" **KuD** 34 (1988): 304-320; James I. Packer, "'Sola Scriptura' in History and Today," in **God's Inerrant Word: An International Symposium on the Trustworthiness of Scripture**, ed. John Warwick Montgomery (Minneapolis, MN: Bethany Fellowship, 1974), 43-62; and Jörg Baur, "Sola Scriptura--historisches Erbe und bleibende Bedeutung," in **Sola Scriptura: Das reformatorische Schriftprinzip in der säkularen Welt**, ed. Hans Heinrich Schmid and Joachim Mehlhausen (Gütersloh: Gerd Mohn, 1991), 19-43.

Statement and Justification of the Problem

The development of historical criticism[1] increasingly challenged the authority of the Bible and with it its role as source and norm of theology.[2] As a consequence the earlier role of Scripture in theology became more and more problematic for Protestant theology.[3] Wolfhart Pannenberg holds that "the development of historical research led to the dissolution of the Scripture principle"[4] which "constitutes a crisis at the very foundation of modern Protestant theology."[5] Recently theologians have voiced serious doubts about an authoritative role of Scripture in theology.[6] In a major

---

[1] For a concise description of the historical-critical method, see Edgar Krentz, **The Historical-Critical Method** (Philadelphia: Fortress Press, 1975); for a historical analysis of the rise of modern critical theology, see Henning Graf Reventlow, **The Authority of the Bible and the Rise of the Modern World**, trans. John Bowden (Philadelphia: Fortress Press, 1984); and Klaus Scholder, **The Birth of Modern Critical Theology: Origins and Problems of Biblical Criticism in the Seventeenth Century**, trans. John Bowden (London: SCM Press, 1990).

[2] Reinhardt, 426. Cf. also more recently Reinhard Slenczka's perceptive analysis in "Die Auflösung der Schriftgrundlage und was daraus folgt," **TRu** 60/1 (1995): 96-107.

[3] It has been said that "a consequence of the close bond between Protestantism and the Bible is that they often share a common fate" (Marty, **Protestantism**, 120). The German theologian Gerhard Ebeling once suggested that the history of Christianity is simply the history of the interpretation of the Bible ("Church History Is the History of the Exposition of Scripture," in Gerhard Ebeling, **The Word of God and Tradition: Historical Studies Interpreting the Divisions of Christianity**, trans. S. H. Hooke [Philadelphia: Fortress Press, 1968], 11-31). In some respects this seems to be true especially of Protestantism.

[4] Wolfhart Pannenberg, "The Crisis of the Scripture Principle," in **BQT**, 1:6.

[5] Ibid., 4; also idem, **SyTh/G**, 3:167-169.

[6] Cf. Gordon Kaufman's article "What Shall We Do With the Bible?" **Int** 25 (1971): 95-112; idem, "Doing Theology from a Liberal Christian Point of View," in **Doing Theology in Today's World: Essays in Honor of Kenneth S. Kantzer**, ed. John D. Woodbridge and Thomas Edward McComiskey (Grand Rapids, MI: Zondervan Publishing House, 1991), 399; Ninian Smart and Steven Konstantine recently wrote: "Because we need to change the message in order to repeat it, and because we are not always solely interested in repeating it, since the Church from the earliest times may have taken wrong turnings, our attitudes sit fairly loosely to Biblical or other authority. It happens that critical enquiry into the Biblical texts has reached such a point that there is no general agreement on precisely what Jesus said, or what the early Church believed about him. The liberal-academic solvents have gnawed away at the rusts of Biblical certainty. It therefore seems nonsense to pretend that the Bible has doctrinal or narrative authority" (**Christian Systematic Theology in a World Context** (Minneapolis: Fortress Press, 1991], 47); cf. also the radical theses in John Doran, "A New Reformation," **FaF** 44/3 (1991): 119-122, where he states that "everything in the Christian system, Scripture, Sacrament, Authority is for human persons, not the other way round. . . . In our secular and democratic West the individual's rights and convictions themselves, whether Scriptural or otherwise, are the ultimate court of appeal for all the children of God" (ibid., 119). Carl E. Braaten, therefore, is right on target when he states that "there is a crisis of authority in the church today" where traditional authority structures, including the authority of Scripture, have collapsed ("The Gospel and the Crisis of Authority," **Dialog** 31/4 [1992]: 302).

recent introductory textbook for theology, Edward Farley and Peter C. Hodgson claim that:

> It is our thesis that the scripture principle and the 'way of authority' associated with it are actually inappropriate to 'ecclesiastical existence' when properly understood, but this critique by no means entails a rejection of scripture as such.[1]

The intense discussion on the role of Scripture in theology that developed during the aftermath of the Enlightenment within Protestant[2] and Roman Catholic theology[3] appears to have produced only greater uncertainty about the proper role of Scripture in theology. This seems to be reflected in new discussions over theological methodology,[4] where a pluralism with regards to method has taken over.[5]

---

[1]Edward Farley and Peter C. Hodgson, "Scripture and Tradition," in **Christian Theology**, 2d ed., ed. Peter C. Hodgson and Robert H. King (Philadelphia: Fortress Press, 1985), 62.

[2]Cf. Paul Gennrich, **Der Kampf um die Schrift in der Deutsch-Evangelischen Kirche des Neunzehnten Jahrhunderts** (Berlin: Verlag von Reuther and Reichard, 1898), with further bibliographic references; Eginhard Peter Meijering, "'Sola Scriptura' und die historische Kritik," in **Sola Scriptura: Das reformatorische Schriftprinzip in der säkularen Welt**, ed. Hans Heinrich Schmid and Joachim Mehlhausen (Gütersloh: Gerd Mohn, 1991), 44-60; cf. Carl-Heinz Ratschow, "Einleitende Analyse der Themenfrage," in **Sola Scriptura: Ringvorlesung der theologischen Fakultät der Philipps-Universität**, ed. Carl-Heinz Ratschow (Marburg: N. G. Elwert Verlag, 1977), 1-21; cf. also Wilton Donald Ernst, "The Place of the Scriptures in the Lutheran Churches in America from the End of the First World War to the Middle of the Twentieth Century" (Ph.D. dissertation, Temple University, 1962).

[3]Catholic theologians point out that since Vatican II an increasing interest in the Bible has been shown in Catholic theology. Cf. Roland E. Murphy and Carl J. Peter, "The Role of the Bible in Roman Catholic Theology," **Int** 25 (1971): 78-94; Walter Kasper, **The Methods of Dogmatic Theology**, trans. John Drury (New York: Paulist Press, 1969), 2; Hans Küng, **Theology for the Third Millennium: An Ecumenical View**, trans. Peter Heinegg (New York: Doubleday, 1988), 47-63; Robert Bruce Robinson, **Roman Catholic Exegesis Since Divino Afflante Spiritu: Hermeneutical Implications**, SBLDS 111 (Atlanta, GA: Scholars Press, 1988), 1-27.

[4]In 1967 Walter Kasper could still write that "methodology is not discussed too frequently in present-day theology" (**The Methods of Dogmatic Theology**, 1). This, however, has changed radically in the meantime. Since then a number of significant studies on theological methodology have appeared. Cf. Bernard J. F. Lonergan, **Method in Theology** (New York: Seabury Press, 1972); Gordon D. Kaufman, **An Essay on Theological Method** (Missoula: Scholars Press, 1975); David Tracy, **Blessed Rage for Order: The New Pluralism in Theology** (New York: Seabury Press, 1975); Wolfhart Pannenberg, TPS; Koloman N. Micskey, **Die Axiom-Sytax des evangelisch-dogmatischen Denkens: Strukturanalysen des Denkprozesses und des Wahrheitsbegriffes in den Wissenschaftstheorien (Prolegomena) zeitgenössiser systematischer Theologen**, FSÖTh 35 (Göttingen: Vandenhoeck & Ruprecht, 1976); Helmut Peukert, **Science, Action, and Fundamental Theology: Toward a Theology of Communicative Action**, trans. James Bohman (Cambridge, MA: MIT Press, 1984); Clodovis Boff, **Theology and Praxis: Epistemological Foundations**, trans. Robert R. Barr (Maryknoll, NY: Orbis Books, 1987); Elisabeth Schüssler Fiorenza, **In Memory of Her: A Feminist Theological Reconstruction of Christian Origins** (New York: Crossroad, 1983); Rosemary Radford Ruether, **Sexism and God-**

Even though today opinions vary sharply as to the exact authority and role of Scripture in theology,[1] Christian theologians almost without exceptions agree that

---

Talk: Toward a Feminist Theology (Boston, MA: Beacon Press, 1983); George A. Lindbeck, **The Nature of Doctrine: Religion and Theology in a Postliberal Age** (Philadelphia: Westminster Press, 1984); cf. also David H. Kelsey, "Method, Theological," in **The Westminster Dictionary of Christian Theology**, ed. Alan Richardson and John Bowden (Philadelphia: Westminster Press, 1983), 363-368; and Reinhard Slenczka, **Kirchliche Entscheidung in theologischer Verantwortung: Grundlagen--Kriterien--Grenzen** (Göttingen: Vandenhoeck & Ruprecht, 1991). A helpful overview can be found in David F. Ford, ed., **The Modern Theologians: An Introduction to Christian Theology in the Twentieth Century**, vol. 2 (Oxford: Basil Blackwell, 1989); John B. Cobb, Jr. "Theologie in den Vereinigten Staaten: Woher und Wohin," EvT 48/2 (1989): 200-213; Ted Peters, "Methode und System in der heutigen amerikanischen Theologie," **KuD** 29/1 (1983): 2-46; C. John Weborg, "Of the Making of Theologies There Is No End: A Bibliographic Report," **CovQ** 44/4 (1986): 25-39; and George A. Lindbeck, "Theologische Methode und Wissenschaftstheorie," **ThRv** 74/4 (1978): 265-280.

[5]J. J. Mueller, **What are They Saying about Theological Method?** 2. Paul Holmer has described the state of academic theology as a Babel of conflicting voices, verging on anarchy (Paul L. Holmer, **The Grammar of Faith** [San Francisco: Harper and Row, 1978], 1-2); similarly Jack Rogers has described the future of the "hopelessly fragmented" theology of the sixties to be *"pluralistic"* in the 1980s ("The Search for System: Theology in the 1980s," **JRT** 37/1 (1980): 8-10. See also David Tracy, **Plurality and Ambiguity: Hermeneutics, Religion, Hope** (San Fransisco: Harper and Row, 1987); and Lonnie D. Kliever, **The Shattered Spectrum: A Survey of Contemporary Theology** (Atlanta: John Knox Press, 1981).

[1]Cf. Francis Schüssler Fiorenza, "The Crisis of Scriptural Authority: Interpretation and Reception," **Int** 44 (1990): 353-368; Darrell Jodock, **The Church's Bible: Its Contemporary Authority** (Minneapolis: Fortress Press, 1989); idem, "The Reciprocity Between Scripture and Theology: The Role of Scripture in Contemporary Theological Reflection," **Int** 44 (1990): 369-382; John M. Frame, "Uses of Scripture in Recent Theology," **WTJ** 39 (1977): 328-358; Leonard W. Doolan, "Scripture: The Supreme Court of Divine Authority" (Ph.D. dissertation, The Southern Baptist Theological Seminary, 1901); Wilmer Roy Kensinger, "Certain Outstanding Theological and Philosophical Movements of the Past Two Centuries in Relation to their Bearing Upon the Doctrine and Use of Scripture" (Ph.D. dissertation, New York Theological Seminary, 1941); Robert Hyman Ayers, "A Study of the Problem of Biblical Authority in Selected Contemporary American Theologians" (Ph.D. dissertation, Vanderbilt University, 1958); Arnold Withrow Hearn, "The Problem of Biblical Authority: A Critical Study of Some Recent and Contemporary American Protestant Theologians Representative of Evangelical Liberalism, Contemporary Orthodoxy, and Neo-Reformationism" (Ph.D. dissertation, Columbia University, 1961); Denis E. Nineham, "The Use of the Bible in Modern Theology," **BJRL** 52 (1969): 178-199; Maurice Wiles, "The Use of 'Holy Scripture'," in **What about the New Testament? Essays in Honour of Christopher Evans**, ed. Morna Hooker and Colin Hickling (London: SCM Press, 1974), 155-164; William Countryman, **Biblical Authority or Biblical Tyranny?** (Philadelphia: Fortress Press, 1981); Charles R. Blaisdell, **Conservative, Moderate, Liberal: The Biblical Authority Debate** (St. Louis, MO: CBP Press, 1990); Colin E. Gunton, "Using and Being Used: Scripture and Systematic Theology," **TToday** 47/3 (1990): 248-259; Robert P. Carroll, **Wolf in the Sheepfold: The Bible as a Problem for Christianty** (London: SPCK, 1991); and the discussion in John D. Woodbridge and Thomas Esward McComiskey, **Doing Theology in Todays's World: Essays in Honor of Kenneth S. Kantzer** (Grand Rapids, MI: Zondervan Publishing House, 1991); John Goldingay, **Models for Scripture** (Grand Rapids, MI: Eerdmans, 1994); and more recently idem, **Models for Interpretation of Scripture** (Grand Rapids, MI: Eerdmans, 1995); Slenczka, "Die Auflösung der Schriftgrundlage und was daraus folgt," 96-107. Cf. also Armin Wenz, **Das Wort Gottes--Gericht und Rettung. Untersuchungen zur Autorität**

Christian systematic theology has to make use of Scripture to some degree. Still, there is no indication of a consensus of opinion on the role of Scripture in theology, which has led some to affirm that the question that is most troublesome for contemporary dogmatics is the problem of the use of Scripture.[1] Thus, the "present crisis in theology"[2] that seems to be reflected in the current "disarray" in systematic theology[3] appears to be due to quite some extent to an uncertainty about the proper role of Scripture in theology.[4] This disorientation invites a fresh investigation of the contemporary understanding of the role of Scripture in theology, which is an issue that lies at the very center[5] of the contemporary debate about the sources of theology.[6]

---

der Heiligen Schrift in Bekenntnis und Lehre der Kirche (Göttingen: Vandenhoeck & Ruprecht, forthcoming). Although new approaches are currently flowering in systematic theology it has been also noticed that there is a strange silence of the Bible in the Church (James D. Smart, **The Strange Silence of the Bible in the Church: A Study in Hermeneutics** [Philadelphia: Westminster Press, 1970], 15-27).

[1]Reinhardt, 1.

[2]William J. Abraham, "Oh God, Poor God--the State of Contemporary Theology," **RJ** 40 (1990): 22.

[3]Gabriel Fackre, "The State of Systematics: Research and Commentary," **Dialog** 31 (1992): 54. According to Thor Hall the following two varieties can be supported: "either that theology is 'in the doldrums', 'between times', 'without leadership', or 'floundering', or that it is 'in upheaval', 'characterized by experimentation', 'confusing', or 'confused'.
. . . When one looks at contemporary theology, attempting to identify not individual leaders but current trends, one is faced with a literal profusion of perspectives, orientations, methodologies, and language games" (**Systematic Theology Today: The State of the Art in North America**, part 1 [Washington, DC: University Press of America, 1978], 3); cf. also Hall's article: "Does Systematic Theology Have a Future?" **CC** 93 (1976): 253-256. John Macquarrie has said that we find ourselves today in a "situation of theological pluralism" that stems from the fact that "a plurality of theologies have been systematized on different principles," that emphasize different aspects of Christianity and are "not easily harmonized" ("Systematic Theology," 473). Gerhold Becker, **Theologie in der Gegenwart: Tendenzen und Perspektiven** (Regensburg: Verlag Friedrich Pustet, 1978), 11, says that the general crisis of orientation in society is reflected in theology.

[4]Abraham, "Oh God, Poor God," 22; cf. Heinz Kruse, **Die heilige Schrift in der theologischen Erkenntnislehre: Grundfragen des Katholischen Schriftverständnisses**, KSJAMI 5 (Paderborn: Verlag Bonifatius Druckerei, 1964), 16.

[5]Cf. Reinhardt, 1. James Barr states that it is "in the relations between the Bible and theology that the most crucial problems are to be found" (**The Bible in the Modern World** [London: SCM Press, 1973], 89).

[6]The question of the role of Scripture in theology belongs to the area of "Fundamental theology," where the proper source(s) of theology are discussed and determined (Matthias Petzholdt, "Sola Scriptura--brauchbares Prinzip zur Rechenschaft über den Glauben?" in **Sola Scriptura: Das reformatorische Schriftprinzip in der säkularen Welt**, ed. Hans Heinrich Schmid and Joachim Mehlhausen (Gütersloh: Gerd Mohn, 1991), 293. On the history of the term "Fundamental theology" and its development as a discipline in Roman Catholic and Protestant

Purpose and Scope of the Study

Since Scripture has been at the very heart of Protestant theology from its beginning[1] it seems appropriate to limit the study of the concept of Scripture to contemporary Protestant theology where the dissolution of the traditional doctrine of Scripture through historical criticism has let to a crisis at the very foundation of modern Protestant theology.[2] In this context this dissertation investigates the role of Scripture in two[3] contemporary Protestant systematic theologians who represent significantly different theological approaches. In order to discover the reasons for the variety in the use of Scripture in theology, the undergirding presuppositional structure is investigated, on the basis of which the specific role of Scripture is determined.

The theologians chosen for study are Wolfhart Pannenberg and Donald G. Bloesch. Both are recognized as established scholars in their field. They are both at the zenith of their theological career and have published widely.[4] Each has a

---

theology, see Heinrich Stirnimann, "Erwägungen zur Fundamentaltheologie: Problematik, Grundfragen, Konzept," **FZPT** 24 (1977): 291-365; Harald Wagner, "Fundamentaltheologie," **TRE**, 11:738-752; Gerhard Ebeling, "Erwägungen zu einer evangelischen Fundamentaltheologie," **ZTK** 67 (1970): 479-524; Randy L. Maddox, **Toward an Ecumenical Fundamental Theology**, AARAS 47 (Chico, CA: Scholars Press, 1984), 1-119; Max Seckler, "Fundamentaltheologie: Aufgaben und Aufbau, Begriff und Name," **HFT**, 4:450-514; and René Latourelle, "Théologie Fondamentale," in **Dictionnaire de Theologie Fondamentale**, ed. René Latourelle (Montréal: Éditions Bellarmin, 1992), 1352-1362.

[1]It has been said that "'*sola scriptura*' represents the battle-cry raised in answer to the Catholic formula 'Scripture and Tradition'" (Ebeling, "'Sola Scriptura' and Tradition," 102). While "Scripture alone" is not the essence of Christianity (Bernard Ramm, "Is 'Scripture Alone' the Essence of Christianity?" in **Biblical Authority**, ed. Jack Rogers [Waco, TX: Word Books, 1977], 107-123), it certainly is "of crucial importance" for Protestant theology (R. C. Sproul, "Sola Scriptura: Crucial to Evangelicalism," in **The Foundation of Biblical Authority**, ed. James Montgomery Boice [Grand Rapids, MI: Zondervan Publishing House, 1978], 114, 111). It has been said, not without reasons, that *sola scriptura* "shows the essential motivation and concern, theological and religious, of the entire Reformation movement" (Packer, "'Sola Scripura' in History and Today," 44).

[2]Reinhard Slenczka, "Schriftautorität und Schriftkritik," in **Verbindliches Zeugnis: Kanon--Schrift--Tradition**, DdK 7, ed. Wolfhart Pannenberg and Theodor Schneider (Freiburg: Herder, 1992), 316-318; Pannenberg, "The Crisis of the Scripture Principle," 4, 6; Ebeling, "'Sola Scriptura' and Tradition," 102.

[3]More than two representatives could be chosen, but time and space limitations make it necessary to restrict the discussion at this point.

[4]A comprehensive bibliography on Pannenberg's publications has been put together by Bernd Burkhardt, "Bibliographie der Veröffentlichungen von Wolfhart Pannenberg 1953-1987," in **Vernunft des Glaubens: Wissenschaftliche Theologie und kirchliche Lehre. Festschrift zum 60. Geburtstag von Wolfhart Pannenberg, mit einem bibliographischen Anhang**, ed. Jan Rohls and Gunther Wenz (Göttingen: Vandenhoeck & Ruprecht, 1988), 693-718; and Wolfgang Steck,

significantly different understanding of Scripture that stems from a distinct theological approach. Both are sensitive to their own theological background and are open to dialogue and interaction with different positions. Pannenberg, standing in the Lutheran tradition, takes up the discussion where the Enlightenment left it off, with its rejection of all external authority and its emphasis on reason.[1] He has inaugurated a new program in theology that attempts to go beyond that of Karl Barth and much of Kerygmatic theology.[2] Bloesch, on the other hand, represents a refined Evangelical theological view that builds on the neo-orthodox position.[3] He is commited to a high view of Scripture which is characteristic of an Evangelical perspective.[4] Yet, in contrast to the rationalistic stream in American Evangelicalism,[5] Bloesch stresses the priority of faith over reason.

Thus, Pannenberg and Bloesch exemplify a fundamental tension that exists in any understanding of Scripture, namely whether the role of Scripture is to be determined ultimately "from below" or "from above." Finally, the study of two contemporary, living, theologians is interesting because it deals with current attempts to determine the role of Scripture in theology where earlier theological and philosophical ideas are taken up and developed further into new proposals.

"Von Personen: Laudatio Wolfhart Pannenberg," **TLZ** 118/10 (1993): 887-888. The most comprehensive English bibliography on Pannenberg today is Philip Clayton, "A Pannenberg Bibliography," in **TWP**, 337-352; the most comprehensive bibliography of Donald Bloesch can be found in: Donald G. Bloesch, **Theological Notebook**, vol. 2, **1964-1968** (Colorado Springs: Helmers & Howard, 1991), 181-197.

[1]William Carl Placher recently classified Pannenberg "as a theologian of reason, a theologian of the Enlightenment" ("Revealed to Reason: Theology as 'Normal Science'," **CC** 109/6 [1992]: 192).

[2]Nancey C. Murphey has described Pannenberg's program as "the boldest attempt in this generation to establish the credibility of the Christian belief vis-à-vis the canon of probable reasoning" **(Theology in the Age of Scientific Reasoning** [Ithaca: Cornell University Press, 1990], 19).

[3]Lance A. Wonders has said that Bloesch promises to develop "a Post-fundamentalist, neo-Barthian evangelicalism" that attempts to go beyond the shortcomings of both ("Review of **A Theology of Word and Spirit: Authority and Method in Theology**, by Donald G. Bloesch," **CovQ** 51/2 [1993]: 48).

[4]Bloesch has recently labeled himself as "a Reformed theologian as well as an evangelical theologian." Donald G. Bloesch, To Frank M. Hasel, October 14, 1994, 1.

[5]Here one thinks of such scholars as Carl F. H. Henry, Gordon Clark, R. C. Sproul, Norman L. Geisler, Ronald H. Nash, and others. For a discussion and analysis of Evangelical Rationalism, see Nicholas F. Gier, **God, Reason, and the Evangelicals: The Case Against Evangelical Rationalism** (Lanham, MD: University Press of America, 1987).

Research Methodology and Limitations

This dissertation is a phenomenological description and systematic analysis of the concept of Scripture in Pannenberg's and Bloesch's theology. For the purpose of this study, the term "theology" is limited to the systematic theologies of Pannenberg[1] and Bloesch.[2] It is here that they bring together in a systematic fashion what they have proposed earlier. While this inquiry is limited primarily to their systematic theologies, I have also branched out into other writings that are relevant to the issue under investigation. In this investigation first their understanding of the origin, nature, and use of Scripture are described and analyzed and thus their concept of Scripture determined. Next, the presuppositions that may have influenced their understanding of Scripture are examined. Third, both positions are compared and assessed. To keep the scope of this dissertation within reasonable bounds, certain limitations are unavoidable. The focus of this study is to explore the understanding of the role of Scripture in Pannenberg's and Bloesch's theology. While those aspects of both theologians' overall theological system that impinge on the topic under discussion are included, no comprehensive treatment of their entire theology and theological method is attempted. Thus, this investigation deals with such issues as revelation and inspiration, the authority of Scripture, the relationship of faith and reason, and hermeneutical questions only insofar as they are helpful for a better understanding of Pannenberg's and Bloesch's view of Scripture. These most important questions deserve a separate and fuller treatment in their own right.

---

[1] Wolfhart Pannenberg, **Systematische Theologie**, 3 vols. (Göttingen: Vandenhoeck & Ruprecht, 1988-1993); an English translation of the first volume is available, the second volume is in preparation (idem, **Systematic Theology**, vol. 1, trans. Geoffrey W. Bromiley [Grand Rapids, MI: Eerdmans, 1991]).

[2] The first two volumes of his new systematic theology have appeared: Donald G. Bloesch, **A Theology of Word and Spirit: Authority and Method in Theology** (Downers Grove, IL: InterVarsity Press, 1992); and idem, **Holy Scripture: Revelation, Inspiration and Interpretation** (Downers Grove, IL: InterVarsity Press, 1994). Cf. also idem, **Essentials of Evangelical Theology**, vol. 1, **God, Authority, and Salvation** (San Francisco: Harper and Row, 1978); and idem, **Essentials of Evangelical Theology**, vol. 2, **Life, Ministry, and Hope** (San Francisco: Harper and Row, 1978).

Outline of the Study

Before beginning this investigation into the understanding of Scripture in Pannenberg and Bloesch in chapter 3 an issue-oriented historical survey of the role of Scripture in theology is presented in chapter 2. This should contribute to a clearer grasp of key issues, which since the Protestant Reformation have set the stage for the current discussion.

Chapter 3 examines Pannenberg's understanding of Scripture by focusing on his perception of its origin, nature, and use. After this more descriptive task, we turn to an analysis of some fundamental presuppositions that may have influenced his concept of Scripture. Here particular attention is given to the theological and anthropological presuppositions, both foundational in one's account of Scripture.

A similar investigation is undertaken in chapter 4 with Donald G. Bloesch's understanding of Scripture. Again a description of his perception of Scripture's origin, nature, and use precedes an analysis of what appears to be his theological and anthropological presuppositions.

The final chapter presents an evaluative comparison of both positions. First the understanding of Scripture in our two theologians is contrasted which is followed by an evaluation of their strengths and weaknesses, based essentially on the internal consistency of their views and assumptions.

CHAPTER II

SCRIPTURE IN THEOLOGY: A TYPOLOGICAL OVERVIEW

Introduction

The question of the role of Scripture in theology is a crucial one. It has occupied the attention of theologians for centuries. Even though opinions vary sharply as to the exact role of Scripture in theology, virtually all Christian theologians within the full spectrum of opinion agree that Scripture has to play some part in Christian theology.[1] The problem, however, is that the question as to what role Scripture should precisely play in theological deliberation "remains unresolved"[2] and stands out as a pressing current theological issue.[3]

Certain notions or concepts about Scripture have defined and shaped its status and have had a direct bearing on how Scripture was used in doing theology.[4] Among these concepts are the question of Scripture's origin, touching upon the issue of revelation and inspiration; its nature, entailing such derivatory aspects as the transcultural and universalistic value of its message; and its being an external authority and norm[5] for the church.

---

[1]John Leith categorically states that "Christian theology has always been done 'in accordance with Scripture'. . ." although he adds that "the role of Scripture in the theological task . . . has rarely been spelled out in a precise way" (John H. Leith, "The Bible and Theology," **Int** 30 [1976]: 227).

[2]Ted Peters, "Editorials: Seven Pressing Theological Issues," **Dialog** 32/2 (1994): 82. Cf. Farley and Hodgson, "Scripture and Tradition," 61.

[3]Cf. also the discussion in the recently published dissertations by Matthias Haudel, **Die Bibel und die Einheit der Kirchen: Eine Untersuchung der Studien von 'Glauben und Kirchenverfassung'**, KuK 34 (Göttingen: Vandenhoeck & Ruprecht, 1993); Martin Hamel, **Bibel--Mission--Ökumene: Schriftverständnis und Schriftgebrauch in der neueren ökumenischen Missionstheologie** (Giessen: Brunnen Verlag, 1993); also Gunter Wenz, "Sola Scriptura? Erwägungen zum reformatorischen Schriftprinzip," in **Vernunft des Glaubens: Wissenschaftliche Theologie und kirchliche Lehre. Festschrift zum 60. Geburtstag von Wolfhart Pannenberg, mit einem bibliographischen Anhang**, ed. Jan Rohls and Gunther Wenz (Göttingen: Vandenhoeck & Ruprecht, 1988), 540-567.

[4]Roger Haight, **Dynamics of Theology** (New York: Paulist Press, 1990), 90.

[5]By authority we mean the legal or rightful power and right to command and determine action. By norm we mean a rule or authoritative standard by which everything is evaluated and measured. Bernard Ramm has stated that "the concept of authority has become one of the most controversial notions of modern times" (**The Pattern of Religious Authority** [Grand Rapids, MI:

In order to better understand and situate the current discussion of the role of Scripture, as exemplified in Pannenberg and Bloesch, this chapter briefly examines the role of Scripture in the history of theology. However, rather than giving a strictly historical overview that exhaustively covers every position, it attempts to engage in an issue-oriented, historical survey that is done specifically from the perspective of this dissertation. By focusing on characteristics that are typical of particular positions, it is easier to identify certain key issues that are crucial for the role of Scripture in theology. This is also helpful in evaluating the position of Pannenberg and Bloesch.

A conducive way to organize the historical material on the role of Scripture is through the classification of different approaches into types or models.[1] It has been

---

Eerdmans, 1968], 9). Ramm goes on to define authority as "that right or power to command action or compliance, or to determine belief or custom, expecting obedience from those under authority, and in turn giving responsible account for the claim to right or power" (ibid., 10). James Barr has pointed out that "'authority' is the term which has been most widely used in recent studies of the status of the Bible. It is a relational or hierarchical concept; it tries to order and grade the various powers, or sources of ideas, that may influence us. . . . The notion of authority defines the priority of one such force over another" (**The Bible in the Modern World**, 23). Barr then compares the terms "authority" and "norm" with respect to Scripture, saying that "the conception of 'norm' is more or less the same thing. If we say that scripture is 'normative', it means that it is the final court of appeal, the highest of the tests, to which Christian thoughts and actions have to be subjected. There may be various grades of things having some sort of authority, but that which is normative has the highest and final authority. 'Authority' and 'norm' thus define relations. They define (i) the relation between the Bible and ourselves, so that the Bible may be seen as something binding upon us, something to which we have to submit ourselves; and (ii) the relation between the Bible and other documents or sources of knowledge which might also influence our minds or actions at the same time." On the question of the authority of Scripture in theology, see also the discussion in David L. Bartlett, **The Shape of Scriptural Authority** (Philadelphia: Fortress Press, 1983), 1-9; Schubert M. Ogden, "The Authority of Scripture for Theology," **Int** 30 (1976): 224-261; James D. Smart, **The Strange Silence of the Bible in the Church**, 90-101; Darrell Jodock, **The Church's Bible: Its Contemporary Authority**; John Barton, **People of the Book? The Authority of the Bible in Christianity** (Louisville, KY: Westminster/John Knox Press, 1988); J. Christiaan Beker, "The Authority of Scripture: Normative or Incidental?" **TToday** 49/3 (1992): 376-382; Robert Harry Bryant, "The Authority of the Bible" (Ph.D. dissertation, Yale University, 1956); idem, **The Bible's Authority Today** (Minneapolis: Augsburg Publishing House, 1968); Andrew Dooman Chang, "Crisis of Biblical Authority: A Critical Examination of Biblical Authority in Contemporary Theology with Special Reference to Functionalist" (Th.D. dissertation, Dallas Theological Seminary, 1985); and Carl F. H. Henry, **God, Revelation and Authority** (Waco, TX: Word, 1979), 4:7-102.

[1]The literature on "ideal types" and on "models" is vast. We are not attempting to enter in the more technical discussion of models as in Max Black, **Models and Metaphors** (Ithaca: Cornell University Press, 1962); Mary Hesse, **Models and Analogies in Science** (Notre Dame: University of Notre Dame Press, 1966); Ian Ramsey, **Models and Mystery** (London: Oxford University Press, 1956); Ian G. Barbour, **Myths, Models and Paradigms: A Comparative Study in Science and Religion** (New York: Harper and Row, 1974); Robert P. Scharlemann, "Theological Models and Their Construction," **JR** 53 (1973): 65-82; and others. For our purpose it suffices to note that the idea of "models" or "types" has been used in theology by other

noted that models can be useful in guiding investigations, framing hypotheses, and writing descriptions.¹ According to Ian Barbour, a model is an "organizing image" which gives a particular emphasis, enabling one to notice and interpret certain aspects of experience.² In organizing different approaches into types or models, one is able to investigate and discover more clearly the role Scripture has played and continues to play in theology. This helps us at the same time to "situate" the contemporary discussion about the role of Scripture in theology in its own historical-theological thought context.

In light of the fact that the role and use of Scripture seems to hinge upon its nature, which in turn is dependent on its origin,³ one must investigate those areas in order to come to an appropriate understanding of the role of Scripture in theology. Since two agents are involved in any account of Christian Scripture, namely, God and man, it appears that the role of Scripture in theology is influenced to a considerable degree by the question whether Scripture is understood to have originated "from above," i.e., from God, or "from below," i.e., from man. Within those two basic categories is room for differences in emphasis and variation in detail, but it seems that the different roles of Scripture can be illumined best by grouping them in these most

---

theologians for similar purposes in the recent past. Here we think of Avery Dulles, **Models of the Church** (Garden City, NY: Doubleday, 1974); idem, **Models of Revelation** (Garden City, NY: Doubleday, 1985); idem, "Models of Faith," in **Fides Quaerens Intellectum. Beiträge zur Fundamentaltheologie**, ed. Michael Kessler, Wolfhart Pannenberg, and Hermann Josef Pottmeyer (Tübingen: Francke Verlag, 1992), 405-413; David Tracy, **Blessed Rage for Order**, 22-34; Sallie McFague, **Metaphorical Theology: Models of God in Religious Language** (Philadelphia: Fortress Press, 1982); idem, **Models of God: Theology for an Ecological, Nuclear Age** (Philadelphia: Fortress Press, 1987); and most recently the post-humously published book by Hans W. Frei, **Types of Christian Theology**, ed. George Hunsinger and William C. Placher (New Haven: Yale University Press, 1992). For a critical perspective on the use of models in Avery Dulles, see Terrence Merrigan, "Models in the Theology of Avery Dulles: A Critical Analysis," **BTFT** 54 (1993): 141-161; cf. also John Goldingay, "Models for Scripture," **SJT** 44 (1991): 19-37; and A. A. Glenn, "Criteria for Theological Models," **SJT** 25 (1972): 296-308.

¹Lonergan, **Method in Theology**, 284-285.

²Barbour, **Myths, Models, and Paradigms**, 16; cf. also his recent book **Religion in an Age of Science**, The Gifford Lectures 1989-1991, vol. 1 (San Francisco: Harper and Row, 1990), 31-65.

³Cf. Moisés Silva, **Has the Church Misread the Bible? The History of Interpretation in the Light of Current Issues**, FCI 1 (Grand Rapids, MI: Zondervan Publishing House, 1987), 38.

general categories, i.e., whether Scripture is seen to originate ultimately "from below" or whether it is thought to be a book "from above."[1]

The analysis of the following material, therefore, is issue-oriented rather than strictly historical. As the first organizing type for this investigation into the role of Scripture[2] in theology, we consider examples that exemplify a "high view" of Scripture, i.e., where Scripture is understood to have come ultimately "from above."

Scripture from Above

While a full-blown historical study on the role of Scripture in theology is outside the scope of this dissertation, nevertheless, one needs to begin at one point in history. Since Pannenberg and Bloesch, who are at the center of this investigation, both stand within the Protestant tradition, it seems appropriate to begin with the Protestant Reformation of the sixteenth century.[3] The Reformation seems to be an appropriate

---

[1] One could give those "models" other names, like "liberal" and "conservative," but since those terms carry a theological "backage" they are not always helpful for discussing the issue under investigation. With respect to the role of Scripture, "Liberalism" has been defined by its rejection of religious belief based on authority alone and by a deep respect for the authority of reason and experience in religion. For "Liberals" the Bible is the work of writers who were limited by their times. It "is neither supernatural nor an infallible record of divine revelation, and thus does not possess absolute authority." R. V. Pierard, "Liberalism, Theological," **Evangelical Dictionary of Theology**, ed. Walter A. Elwell (Grand Rapids, MI: Baker Book House, 1984), 632. See also John P. Crossley, Jr., "Liberalism," in **A New Handbook of Christian Theology**, ed. Donald W. Musser and Joseph L. Price (Nashville, TN: Abingdon, 1992), 285-287; Donald E. Miller, "Liberalism," **The Westminster Dictionary of Christian Theology**, ed. Alan Richardson and John Bowden (Philadelphia: Westminster Press, 1983), 324-325; and Manfred Jacobs, "Liberale Theologie," **TRE**, 21:47-68, esp. 51. James I. Packer has said that "'Conservatism', when used, signifies a rejection of the liberal outlook as a provincial aberration, neither objective nor scientific nor rational in any significant sense, and with this a conservationist purpose of handing on the doctrines and disciplines of historic Christianity intact and undiluted. . . . Conservatism in this sense implies no particular political stance or eschatological expectation, though the contrary is often alleged" ("Liberalism and Conservatism in Theology," **New Dictionary of Theology**, ed. Sinclair B. Ferguson and David F. Wright [Downers Grove, IL: InterVarsity Press, 1988], 385).

[2] It might help to define the term "Scripture" as it is used here. "Scripture" refers to the canonical writings of both testaments. It is used by us in essentially the same sense in both the singular and the plural. "The Scriptures," plural, denote all the items that make up the Bible, which is viewed as being divinely inspired and carrying divine content. "Scripture," singular, denotes the same material viewed as one organic unit of divine origin. As such Scripture is the Word of God, expressing His will by which He wants mankind to live. Hence, Scripture is called "canonical," i.e., a rule, measure, or standard. Cf. James I. Packer, "Scripture," **New Dictionary of Theology**, ed. Sinclair B. Ferguson and David F. Wright (Downers Grove, IL: InterVarsity Press, 1988), 627-628.

[3] In using the word "Reformation" we refer to the Reformation of the Protestant Reformers in the sixteenth and early seventeenth centuries, unless otherwise noted. Commonly, the following names are associated with the continental Reformation: Martin Luther (1483-1546), John Calvin

starting point not only because of the two contemporary theologians who are examined in more detail below but also because it was here that the question of the role of Scripture came to the forefront with new intensity and precision.

The Protestant Reformation

During the Protestant Reformation, the issue of the role of Scripture in theology was taken up with a new emphasis and vigor that was not present before and that has exercised a pervasive influence for all Christian theology ever since. Whereas Protestant theologians differed little from their Roman Catholic counterparts with respect to the question of the divine inspiration and nature of Scripture,[1] they differed sharply in their understanding of the role of Scripture in theology. Catholic theology has been characterized as having a "both-and" character, in contrast to Protestantism's "either-or."[2] It has been keenly observed by a Catholic and Protestant scholars alike

---

(1509-1564), and Zwingli (1484-1531). However, several forerunners of the Reformation emphasized the normative role of Scripture for theology. Individuals like John Wycliffe (1330-1384) and John Huss (1372-1415) and the Waldensies could be mentioned. One could also point to the Humanists (Reuchlin, Erasmus et al.) whose program can be summarized by the slogan: "ad fontes," i.e., back to the (original) sources. Cf. Alister E. McGrath, **Reformation Thought: An Introduction** (Oxford: Basil Blackwell, 1988), 32-48, 99-101; idem, **The Intellectual Origins of the European Reformation**, 127. On Wyclif's understanding of Scripture, see Thomas Geoffrey Oey, "Wyclif's Doctrine of Scripture Within the Context of His Doctrinal and Social Ideas" (Ph.D. dissertation, Vanderbilt University, 1991); Paul de Vooght, "Wyclif et la *scriptura sola*," ETL 39 (1963): 50-86; Jack B. Rogers and Donald K. McKim, **The Authority and Interpretation of the Bible: An Historical Approach** (San Francisco: Harper and Row, 1979), 73-75. On Huss and other forerunners of the Reformation, see George H. Tavard, **Holy Writ or Holy Church: The Crisis of the Protestant Reformation** (New York: Harper and Brothers, 1959), 48-51, and passim; Karl Holzhey, **Inspiration der heiligen Schrift in der Anschauung des Mittelalters: Von Karl dem Grossen bis zum Konzil von Trient** (Munich: J. J. Lentner'sche Buchhandlung, 1895), esp. 125-128; and Muller, **Post-Reformation Reformed Dogmatics**, 2:41-42.

[1]Recent scholarship has pointed out, contrary to popular belief, that there existed significant continuity between the Later Middle Ages and the Reformation with regards to the origin and nature of Scripture. Cf. Muller, **Post-Reformation Reformed Dogmatics**, 2:4, 9, 11-50, 540-543; Heinrich Karpp, **Schrift, Geist und Wort Gottes. Geltung und Wirkung der Bibel in der Geschichte der Kirche: Von der Alten Kirche bis zum Ausgang der Reformationszeit** (Darmstadt: Wissenschaftliche Buchgesellschaft, 1992), 82-87; Miikka Ruokanen, **Doctrina Divinitus Inspirata: Martin Luther's Position in the Ecumenical Problem of Biblical Inspiration**, PLAS 14 (Helsinki: Luther-Agricola Society, 1985), 27-48; Hans-Jochen Kühne, **Schriftautorität und Kirche: Eine kontroverstheologische Studie zur Begründung der Schriftautorität in der neueren katholischen Theologie** (Berlin: Evangelische Verlagsanstalt, 1979), 36-43; Hermann Schüssler, **Der Primat der Heiligen Schrift als theologisches und kanonistisches Problem im Spätmittelalter**, VIEG 86 (Wiesbaden: Franz Steiner Verlag, 1977); Robert E. McNally, **The Bible in the Early Middle Ages** (Westminster, MD: Newman Press, 1959, reprint, Atlanta, GA: Scholars Press, 1986); McGrath, **The Intellectual Origins**, 122-123.

[2]Richard P. McBrien, **Catholicism** (Minneapolis, MN: Winston Press, 1981), 1174;

that "while a key word in Protestantism is the intensive *solus* (alone), Catholicism's word is the comprehensive *et* (and)."[1] In other words, when any human authority, whether living or dead, was put besides or above Scripture, Protestants declared Scripture alone to have authority as the sole source of its own exposition.

It is well known that several forerunners of the Reformation attempted to emphasize the normative role of Scripture for theology prior to the Protestant Reformation in the sixteenth century.[2] But not everything in the Reformation understanding of Scripture can be comprehended as a more or less natural development of medieval theology. This is especially the case with the *sola Scriptura* principle,[3]

Stephen Bevans, "Reaching for Fidelity: Roman Catholic Theology Today," in **Doing Theology in Today's World: Essays in Honor of Kenneth S. Kantzer**, ed. John D. Woodbridge and Thomas Edward McComiskey (Grand Rapids, MI: Zondervan Publishing House, 1991), 324; Kruse, 14-16; Avery Dulles, **The Reshaping of Catholicism: Current Challenges in the Theology of Church** (San Francisco: Harper and Row, 1988), 72. Dulles recently stated that Catholic theologians "never accepted the idea that the Bible alone is the source of Christian truth" (idem, **The Craft of Theology**, 72, 88-89).

[1]Bevans, 324. Karl Barth has called this the "damned Catholic And" (Das Erste Gebot als theologisches Axiom," **ZZ** 11 [1933]: 308).

[2]For an overview of the role of Scripture prior to the Protestant Reformation, see Holzhey, **Die Inspiration der Heiligen Schrift in der Anschauung des Mittelalters; Christian Pesch, De Inspiratione Sacrae Scripturae** (Freiburg: Herder, 1906); Beryl Smalley, **The Study of the Bible in the Middle Ages** (Oxford: Basil Blackwell, 1952); Paul de Vooght, **Les sources de la Doctrine Chrétienne d'après les Théologiens du XIVe Siècle et du Début du XVe Avec le Texte Integral des XII Premieres Questions de la Summa Inedite de Gerard de Bologne** (Bruges: Desclée de Brouwer, 1954); Tavard, **Holy Writ or Holy Church** (1959); McNally, **The Bible in the Early Middle Ages**; Heiko Augustinus Oberman, **The Harvest of Medieval Theology: Gabriel Biel and Late Medieval Nominalism** (Cambridge, MA: Harvard University Press, 1963); Hermann Schüssler, **Der Primat der Heiligen Schrift**; Ruokanen, 27-48; Karpp, **Schrift, Geist und Wort Gottes**, 63-142, esp. 99ff; idem, "Bibel IV. Die Funktion der Bibel in der Kirche," TRE, 6:49-70; Muller, **Post-Reformation Reformed Dogmatics**, 2:3-50.

[3]Stephan H. Pfürtner, "Das reformatorische 'Sola Scriptura'--theologischer Auslegungsgrund des Thomas von Aquin?" in **Sola Scriptura: Ringvorlesung der theologischen Fakultät der Philipps-Universität**, ed. Carl-Heinz Ratschow (Marburg: N. G. Elwert Verlag, 1977), 48-80, has tried to show that the formal principle of the Reformation, i.e., *sola scriptura*, was practiced already by Thomas Aquinas. In a similar vein, Kropatscheck, **Das Schriftprinzip der lutherischen Kirche**, 439-440, calls the *sola Scriptura* formula "vulgärkatholisch." Gerhard Gloege, "Zur Geschichte des Schriftverständnisses," in Gerhard Gloege, **Verkündigung und Verantwortung: Theologische Traktate** (Göttingen: Vandenhoeck & Ruprecht, 1967), 2:274-275, follows Kropatschek's assessment. Cf. also Hermann Schüssler, **Der Primat der Heiligen Schrift**, 48-52. It should be noted, however, that despite statements which might seem to point towards something like a "Scripture principle" in the later Protestant sense, Thomas Aquinas, as does Bonavantura and Duns Scotus, differ with the later Protestant Reformers on their understanding of the role of Scripture for theology. Thus, even Pfürtner, 72-73, admits that the greatest dissimilarity in the historical situation between the High Middle Ages and the Reformation is to be seen in the critical function of the *sola scriptura* over against the church. Cf. also McGrath who writes: "For many theologians of the later medieval period, the material sufficiency of

i.e., the call to judge all faith and practice by Scripture alone,[1] which became one of the great catch cries of the Protestant Reformation.[2] Thus, this systematic investigation into the role of Scripture begins by looking at the origin and nature of Scripture in the Protestant Reformers who asserted the divine authority of Scripture over against all human authority.[3] Because it was Martin Luther who set the stage, so to speak, for the subsequent understanding of Scripture among Protestants, he is considered first and in more depth than others.

---

scripture as a theological source was tantamount to the assertion that theology was essentially nothing other than the exposition of **scripture within the sphere of the church**" (**The Intellectual Origins**, 148), (emphasis supplied). Against the position of Kropatschek and Gloege, Oberman has conclusively shown that the Nominalists as discussed by him "can by no means be praised for, or accused of having reintroduced the *sola scriptura* principle. . . . Occam, d'Ailly, and Gerson attack the curial position, not on grounds of Scripture alone, nor of Scripture as interpreted by the doctors of Scripture, but on grounds of the superior authority of the Church which derives its knowledge of revealed truths from two sources: Scripture and Tradition" (**The Harvest of Medieval Theology**, 390-391). McNally contends that during the early Middle Ages the Bible was more a norm for the spiritual life than a source of dogmatic theology and that the excessive respect for tradition was not condusive to the growth of new ideas and methods (**The Bible in the Early Middle Ages**, 63). Bernhard Lohse claims that the principle of "Scripture alone" was never advocated before Luther (**Martin Luther: An Introduction to His Life and Work**, trans. Robert C. Schulz [Philadelphia: Fortress Press, 1986], 153-154). Cf. also Hermann Schüssler, 5, who points out that the testimonies for an early scholastical Scripture principle are not to be interpreted in a manner that is foreign to its time. Nowhere is Scripture being used critically over against the church fathers.

[1]According to Markus Barth, the "words *sola Scriptura* are preferably to be interpreted not as a nominative but as an instrumental ablative, 'by the Scripture alone.' Thus the formula describes an efficient and normative instrument which God uses and puts into the hands of the church." Markus Barth, "Sola Scriptura," 75. In a similar manner Gordon J. Spykman writes that the central question is: "By what unimpeachable standard is Christian faith to be evaluated? What is our central criterion of judgment? The answer is *sola Scriptura*, which in the ablative case, means 'by Scripture alone.' This password of the Reformation conveys the idea of means or agency. That is, by the light of Scripture alone we are to judge all things and 'hold fast to what is good'" (**Reformational Theology: A New Paradigm for Doing Dogmatics** [Grand Rapids, MI: Eerdmans, 1992], 77).

[2]So Cole, "Sola Scriptura," 21. Gerhard Ebeling calls it the "battle-cry" of the Reformation ("'Sola Scriptura' and Tradition," 102). Cf. also Heiko Augustinus Oberman, **Luther: Man between God and the Devil**, trans. Eileen Walliser-Schwarzbart (New Haven: Yale University Press, 1989), 221, who writes: "In the early days of the Reformation the principle of the Scriptures alone (*sola scriptura*) was such a convincing battle cry that it must be numbered among the factors that enable us to understand how a scholastically trained monk from a university at the edge of civilization could, despite these obstacles, find such enthusiastic acceptance. The thesis of the sufficiency of Scripture alone had the immediate ring of truth. . . ." Yet, Oberman also holds, that "for us in the twentieth century, his [Luther's] answer cannot be convincing . . ." (ibid., 220).

[3]Cf. Roland H. Bainton, "The Bible in the Reformation," in **CHB**, 3:1-37.

Martin Luther

As far as the role of Scripture in Martin Luther's (1483-1546) theology is concerned,[1] one faces the difficulty of dealing with his multifaceted teaching concerning Scripture[2] that allows almost everyone to claim Luther as an ally for his or her position.[3] Nevertheless, some aspects stand out clearly and point in an indubitable direction.

---

[1] While a full-blown study of the role of Scripture in Luther's theology and thought is outside the scope of this dissertation, we would like to refer to a number of works that have dealt with this issue in more detail: T. Stork, **Luther and the Bible** (Philadelphia: Lutheran Board of Publications, 1873); Johannes Preuss, **Die Entwicklung des Schriftprinzips bei Luther bis zur Leipziger Disputation** (Leipzig: Chr. Herm. Tauchnitz, 1901); Otto Scheel, **Luthers Stellung zur Heiligen Schrift** (Tübingen: J. C. B. Mohr, 1902); Karl Thimme, **Luthers Stellung zur Heiligen Schrift** (Gütersloh: C. Bertelsmann Verlag, 1903); Paul Schempp, **Luthers Stellung zur Heiligen Schrift**, FGLP 3 (Munich: Chr. Kaiser, 1929); Karl Holl, **Gesammelte Aufsätze zur Kirchengeschichte: Luther**, vol. 1 (Tübingen: J. C. B. Mohr, 1932), 544-582; Heinrich Bornkamm, **Das Wort Gottes bei Luther**, SLG 7 (Munich: Chr. Kaiser Verlag, 1933); J. M. Reu, **Luther and the Scriptures** (Columbus, OH: Wartburg Press, 1949); H. Østergaard-Nielsen, **Scriptura Sacra et Viva Vox: Eine Lutherstudie**, FGLP 10 (Munich: Chr. Kaiser, 1957); Theodore Mueller, "Luther and the Bible," in **Inspiration and Interpretation**, ed. John F. Walvoord (Grand Rapids, MI: Eerdmans, 1957), 87-114; Willem Jan Kooiman, **Luther and the Bible**, trans. John Schmidt (Philadelphia: Muhlenberg Press, 1961); Friedrich Beisser, **Claritas Scripturae bei Martin Luther**, FKDG 18 (Göttingen: Vandenhoeck & Ruprecht, 1966); A. Skevington Wood, **Captive to the Word. Martin Luther: Doctor of Sacred Scripture** (Grand Rapids, MI: Eerdmans, 1969); Eugene F. Klug, **From Luther to Chemnitz: On Scripture and the Word** (Grand Rapids, MI: Eerdmans, 1971); idem, "Word and Scripture in Luther Studies since World War II," TJ 5NS (1984): 3-46; Gerhard Ebeling, "Luther und die Bibel," in **Lutherstudien**, ed. Gerhard Ebeling, vol. 1 (Tübingen: J. C. B. Mohr, 1971), 286-301; Robert D. Preus, "Luther and Biblical Infallibility," in **Inerrancy and the Church**, ed. Martin D. Hannah (Chicago: Moody Press, 1984), 99-142; idem, "The View of the Bible Held by the Church: The Early Church through Luther," in **Inerrancy**, ed. Norman L. Geisler (Grand Rapids, MI: Zondervan Publishing House, 1979), 357-382, esp. 372-382; Werner Führer, **Das Wort Gottes in Luthers Theologie**, GTA 30 (Göttingen: Vandenhoeck & Ruprecht, 1984), with a helpful summary and overview of the discussion on pages 16-22; Martin Brecht, "Zu Luthers Schriftverständnis," in **Die Autorität der Schrift im ökumenischen Gespräch**, BÖR 50, ed. Karl Kertelge (Frankfurt am Main: Verlag Otto Lembeck, 1985), 9-29; Silvia Hell, **Die Dialektik des Wortes bei Martin Luther: Die Beziehung zwischen Gott und dem Menschen**, ITS 35 (Innsbruck: Tyrolia Verlag, 1992).

[2] On the one hand, one finds derogatory statements about the books of James, Hebrews, Revelation, Esther, etc., and a seeming impatience and criticism with certain statements in the Scriptures. On the other hand stand his continuous affirmations concerning the divine authority, origin, and truthfulness of Scripture. For a concise summary of different attempts to solve such seemingly contradictory statements in Luther, see Preus, "Luther and Biblical Infallibility," 104-109.

[3] Muller has pointed out that altogether too much of the discussion of Luther's understanding of the role of Scripture has approached the subject from theologically biased perspectives and it seems with the specific intention of justifying one or another contemporary view of Scripture (**Post-Reformation Reformed Dogmatics**, 2:54); also Preus, "Luther and Biblical Infallibility," 105.

Although Luther rarely spoke of inspiration as such,[1] one can safely say that he firmly affirmed the divine origin of Scripture.[2] For him Scripture is the Holy Spirit's book.[3] In contrast to all human books, Scripture is God's book--God's letter[4] to us. Because all Scripture is attributed to the Holy Spirit,[5] the words of Scripture are not the words of men but God's Word. Of course, human authors wrote the Scriptures as God's spokespersons and instruments, but their words are the Spirit's Word, representing God's thoughts and His message to humankind.[6] Thus, God is understood as the primary author of Scripture, and Scripture as the Word of God,[7] to the point where Luther equates the Word of God with Scripture.[8] According to Muller

---

[1] So Preus, "The View of the Bible Held by the Church," 377. Klug thinks that "perhaps Luther does not express the doctrine of inspiration in the customary terms of the later dogmaticians, but he most certainly appears to hold a teaching . . . which corresponds closely, if indeed not exactly, to the formal statements on the locus of Scripture in the writings of men like Chemnitz . . . as well as in the second generation after the Reformation with theologians like Gerhard, Quenstedt, and the like" (**From Luther to Chemnitz**, 17).

[2] "Very often Luther spoke of the 'divine Scripture' (*göttliche Schrift, scriptura divina*), thus referring either to its divine origin, or more likely, to its divine form as God's Word, or perhaps to its divine origin and saving message" (Preus, "Luther and Biblical Infallibility," 116-117). Cf. Martin Luther, W2 1:924; 4:876; 7:1086; 10:927, 1570.

[3] WA 48, 43, 55, 1.

[4] Stressing the divine authorship of Scripture, Luther called Scripture "God's letter" to us, "our letter from God" (W2 9:1808; 1:1069).

[5] WA 54, 35, 2-3.

[6] During the years 1532 to 1533 Luther lectured on the *Psalmi Gradum* where he writes: "Not only the words but also the diction used by the Holy Ghost and the Scripture is divine (*Non solum enim vocabula, sed et phrasis est divina, qua Spiritus sanctus et scriptura utitur*)" (WA 40, 254, 23-24). The translation is taken from Reu, **Luther and the Scriptures**, 58.

[7] "scriptura sancta est verbum dei" WA 2, 649, 15.

[8] This is seen by different Luther scholars, such as Bernhard Lohse, **Martin Luther**, 156; Lewis W. Spitz, "Luther's *Sola Scriptura*," in **Crisis in Lutheran Theology: The Validity and Relevance of Historic Lutheranism vs. Its Contemporary Rivals**, vol. 2, ed. John Warwick Montgomery (Minneapolis, MN: Bethany Fellowship, 1967), 124; and Preus, "Luther and Biblical Infallibility," 116-120. Klug, **From Luther to Chemnitz**, 28, calls the identification of Scripture and the Word of God in Luther "his regular modus operandi." We share this interpretation against Emil Brunner who asserts that Luther did not identify the letters and words of Scriptures with the Word of God. Cf. Emil Brunner, **Theology of Crisis** (New York: Charles Scribner's Sons, 1929), 19-20. Even Adolph von Harnack had to acknowledge this identification, although he deplored the fact that Luther placed Scripture and the Word of God on the same level in which von Harnack saw a remnant of Roman Catholicism (**History of Dogma**, trans. William M'Gilchrist [London: Williams & Northgate, 1894-1899], 7:246-247).

Perhaps the most remarkable testimony to this strict view of verbal inspiration can be found in connection with the sacramentarian controversy and the interpretation of the words: "*Hoc est corpus meum*" ("This is my flesh"). Luther maintained that these words were spoken by the mouth

Luther clearly identifies Scripture itself, in the words of the text, as the authoritative Word of God, making no distinction like that found in the neo-orthodox writers of this century, between Christ alone as Word and Scripture as derived Word or witness to the Word.[1]

Because God, through the Holy Spirit, is the ultimate author of Scripture and Scripture is formally God's Word, it carries with it divine authority.[2] That Scripture is authoritative meant that it alone is the source and norm of doctrine.[3] It is obvious that neither reason,[4] nor philosophy, nor experience, nor pope, nor church council can be regarded as an independent authority. Scripture is the queen which must rule over

---

of God and insisted that every word in the sentence is divine and, therefore, the *est* is inescapable (WA 26, 448, 18-19). Cf. also Brian A. Gerrish, "Biblical Authority and the Continental Reformation," **SJT** 10 (1957), 344. Luther also deliberately drew an analogy between the Bible and the person of Jesus Christ (cf. Kooiman, 225-239). For Luther, Scripture can be seen "just like the Son of God" (A. Skevington Wood, **Captive to the Word**, 176). More explicitly he writes: "The Holy Scripture is God's Word, written, and so to say 'in-lettered,' just as Christ is the eternal Word of God incarnate in the garment of his humanity. And just as it is with Christ in the world, as he is viewed and dealt with, so it is also with the written Word of God" (WA 48, 31, 4-6).

[1]Muller, **Post-Reformation Reformed Dogmatics**, 2:55. Professor David Lotz of Union Theological Seminary has pointed to the distortion which Luther's views have suffered so often because of over simplification. Speaking on the issue of Biblical authority, Lotz writes: "Luther never hesitates to speak of Scripture as God's Word. Nor may one give the impression that he makes this identification only rarely, or reluctantly, or in some sense improperly. Scripture for Luther *is* God's Word since it has God the Holy Spirit as its ultimate author. Thus he can use such traditional phrases as 'the words of God' (*verba Dei*) or 'divine words' (*verba divina*) to designate Scripture (WA 7, 97-98; WA 40, III, 254) One may not invoke Luther's authority in defense of such familiar formulas as 'Scripture witnesses to the Word of God', or 'Scripture becomes God's Word when heard in faith', or 'Scripture is the record of God's revelation'--*if* such formulas are taken to mean that for Luther himself Scripture is only a fallible, human word which first becomes an infallible, divine Word when 'animated' by the Spirit of Christ, or that Scripture is not as such God's true Word and authentic revelation. These formulas have their provenance in modern theology, chiefly in Protestant Neo-Orthodoxy. They can be attributed to Luther only by reading them back into his theology in an anachronistic, hence erroneous, fashion" (Lotz, "Sola Scriptura," 263). This fact is not adequately taken into consideration by Rogers and McKim, **The Authority and Interpretation of the Bible**. Cf. John D. Woodbridge, **Biblical Authority: A Critique of the Rogers/McKim Proposal** (Grand Rapids, MI: Zondervan Publishing House, 1982), especially 49-56.

[2]Preus, "The View of the Bible Held by the Church," 481.

[3]WA 18, 147, 23-27. Cf. also J. F. Johnson, "Lutheran Tradition, The," **Evangelical Dictionary of Theology**, ed. Walter A. Elwell (Grand Rapids, MI: Baker Book House, 1984), 667.

[4]On Luther's understanding of the role of reason, see Bernhard Lohse, **Ratio und Fides: Eine Untersuchung über die Ratio in der Theologie Luthers**, FKDG 8 (Göttingen: Vandenhoeck & Ruprecht, 1958); idem, "Reason and Revelation in Luther." SJT 13 (1960): 337-365; Brian A. Gerrish, **Grace and Reason: A Study in the Theology of Luther** (Oxford: Clarendon Press, 1962); and Siegbert W. Becker, **The Foolishness of God: The Place of Reason in the Theology of Martin Luther** (Milwaukee, WI: Northwestern Publishing House, 1982).

all and to which all must submit and obey.[1] It is the *norma normans* (the ruling or determining norm), not a *norma normata* (the ruled or determined norm). To be such a "ruling norm" Luther assumes the unity[2] as well at the clarity of Scripture.[3] Scripture is an actively shining light[4] that illumens human understanding, penetrates human consciousness, and actively enlightens the many dark shadows of life including sinful human reason.[5]

This ruling function as source and norm of theology is expressed in the principle of *sola Scriptura*.[6] The appeal to *sola Scriptura*, therefore, acknowledges the unique authority of Scripture. In brief, the logic of '*sola*' has to do with the exclusion of rivals.[7] The *sola Scriptura* was intended to safeguard the authority of Scripture from its dependence upon the church which, in fact, made Scripture inferior to the church.[8] Its character as the sole and final authority precluded the possibility that the standard

---

[1] WA 40 I, 120, 20-24; LW 26, 58: "This queen must rule, and everyone must obey, and be subject to her. The Pope, Luther, Augustine, Paul, or even an angel from heaven--these should not be masters, judges, or arbiters but only witnesses, disciples, and confessors of Scripture."

[2] "A fundamental assumption of Luther's criticism and of his exegetical work generally . . . is the unity of the Bible" (Jaroslav Pelikan, "Luther's Works on the New Testament," LW 21, xiii). Cf. also A. Skevington Wood, **Captive to the Word**, 149-158; and Beisser, **Claritas Scripturae**, 129.

[3] Luther discusses the clarity of Scripture particularly in **The Bondage of the Will**, WA 18, 609, 653ff. On the meaning of the clarity of Scripture in Luther's theology, see the major studies by Beisser, **Claritas Scripturae**; Bernhard Rothen, **Die Klarheit der Schrift. Teil 1: Martin Luther. Die wiederentdeckten Grundlagen** (Göttingen: Vandenhoeck & Ruprecht, 1990); and Rudolf Hermann, **Von der Klarheit der Heiligen Schrift. Untersuchungen und Erörterungen über Luthers Lehre von der Schrift in *De servo arbitrio*** (Berlin: Evangelische Verlagsanstalt, 1958); Ernst Wolf, "Über 'Klarheit der Heiligen Schrift' nach Luthers 'De Servo Arbitrio'," TLZ 92 (1967): 721-730.

[4] WA 18, 653, 30.

[5] Rothen, **Die Klarheit der Schrift, Teil 1: Martin Luther**, 19, 144.

[6] Heiko Oberman has said that "there can be no doubt that one of the most essential aspects, even the very foundation of Luther's theology is the *sola scriptura* principle" ("Quo Vadis, Petre? The History of Tradition from Irenaeus to *Humanis Generis*," **HDB** 26/4 [1962]: 14). It has been pointed out that "*Sola Scriptura*, the Reformation principle of Scripture's authority, was linked intimately and absolutely with its divine inspiration" (Klug, **From Luther to Chemnitz**, 24).

[7] Cole, 24-25; Gerhard Ebeling, **Evangelische Evangelienauslegung: Eine Untersuchung zu Luthers Hermeneutik** (Darmstadt: Wissenschaftliche Buchgesellschaft, 1962), 405-406.

[8] So Timothy George, **Theology of the Reformers** (Nashville, TN: Broadman Press, 1988), 81.

of its interpretation could come from outside Scripture.¹ Hence, Scripture is the sole source of its own exposition.² Thus one can say with Paul Althaus that "all [of] Luther's theological thinking presupposes the authority of Scripture."³

The *sola Scriptura* principle as proposed by Luther raises the important question of the relationship between Scripture and tradition.⁴ It is sometimes thought that Luther had a total disregard for the tradition of the church and eliminated everything but the Bible from theological consideration. But this does not adequately reflect his position. Although Luther maintained that the tradition was full of concessions to philosophy, for him and later Lutherans the *sola Scriptura* principle did not rule out a respectful listening to the testimony of the Fathers. Luther frequently consulted the Fathers of the Church in order to substantiate his position. Eminent Luther scholar Jaroslav Pelikan, while commenting on Luther's work as expositor, concludes by saying that

> . . . in opposition to traditionalism . . . Luther claimed to be opposing, not the tradition itself, or even the proper use of the tradition in theology, but the abuse of the tradition. He took the position of defending the tradition against its abusers; not they, but he, should be classified on the side of tradition.⁵

---

¹Paul Althaus, **The Theology of Martin Luther**, trans. Robert C. Schultz (Philadelphia: Fortress Press, 1966), 76; see also Beisser, **Claritas Scripturae**, 168-169.

²Ebeling, "'Sola Scriptura' and Tradition," 130-131. The self-interpretation of Scripture is expressed in such formulas as *"scriptura sacra sui ipsius interpres,"* *"Scripturam ex Scriptura explicandum esse,"* *"Scriptura Scripturam interpretatur."* Cf. Richard A. Muller, **Dictionary of Latin and Greek Theological Terms: Drawn Principally from Protestant Scholastic Theology** (Grand Rapids, MI: Baker Book House, 1985), 277. Cf. Luther, WA 7, 97, 20-26. In a sermon in 1522 Luther says: "Also ist die schrifft ir selbs ain aigen liecht. Das ist dann fein, wenn sich die schrift selbs ausslegt . . ." (WA 10, III, 238, 10f).

Walter Mostert, "Scriptura sacra sui ipsius interpres. Bemerkungen zum Verständnis der Heiligen Schrift durch Luther" (**LuJ** 46 [1979]: 60-96, esp. 61, 69, 74, 79, 83-95), and Gerhard Ebeling, **Luther: An Introduction to His Thought**, trans. R. A. Wilson (Philadelphia: Fortress Press, 1970), 93-109, esp., 97-101, attempt to interpret Luther's Scripture principle along existentialistic hermeneutical lines. It seems, however, that such a position does not sufficiently account for Luther's repeated referral to Scripture as the very Word of God. So Ernst-Wilhelm Kohls, "Luthers Aussagen über die Mitte, Klarheit und Selbstätigkeit der Heiligen Schrift," **LuJ** 40 (1973): 46-75, Beisser, **Claritas Scripturae**; Rothen, **Die Klarheit der Schrift, Teil 1: Martin Luther**, and others. Rothen has aptly raised the question: "Wie ist es möglich, die Wörter 'in, mit und unter', mit denen Luther die Präsenz des Leibes Christi in den Abendmahlselementen beschreibt, auf die 'gesammte Lebenserfahrung' zu beziehen--auch wenn dies nur in einer Allusion geschieht?" (ibid., 216, n. 131).

³Althaus, **The Theology of Martin Luther**, 3.

⁴On this issue, cf. the important article by Gerhard Ebeling, "'Sola Scriptura' and Tradition," 102-254.

⁵Jaroslav Pelikan, LW, Companion Volume: Luther the Expositor (St. Louis: Concordia

Thus, the Bible was not the only object of theological reflection for Luther. When Luther spoke of *sola Scriptura*, he was not suggesting that the creeds and the tradition of the church were without value. Rather, he was arguing a case of *relative* clarity and weight. In other words, if a conflict arises in the interpretation of faith, then Scripture has an authority that transcends and judges any of the church's tradition.[1] Although Luther's view of Scripture took away the hermeneutical function of tradition over Scripture, Luther himself was not closed to the need of a guiding norm in the sense of a confession.[2] The historical irony of this is that the Lutheran Confessions, which also asserted the primacy of Scripture in the church, later became themselves hermeneutic standards and guides to the interpretation of Scripture.[3]

Publishing House, 1959), 81. For a more detailed discussion of the role of tradition and its influence on Luther's theology, see Friedrich Beisser, **Claritas Scripturae bei Martin Luther**, 144-158; and Alister E. McGrath, **The Genesis of Doctrine: A Study in the Foundations of Doctrinal Criticism** (Oxford: Basil Blackwell, 1990), 123-130.

[1]Graeme Garrett, "Scripture, Inspiration and the Word of God," **Pacifica** 6/1 (1993): 95.

[2]Gerhard Ebeling, **Evangelische Evangelienauslegung**, 406. This, of course, has specific implications for the interpretation of Scripture as Ralph A. Bohlmann ("Principles of Biblical Interpretation in the Lutheran Confessions," in **Crisis in Lutheran Theology: The Validity and Relevance of Historic Lutheranism vs. its Contemporary Rivals**, vol. 2, ed. John Warwick Montgomery [Minneapolis, MN: Bethany Fellowship, 1967], 157), has pointed out.

[3]"Lutherans have sometimes elevated other writings to the same level as the Scriptures. They have not done so deliberately, but especially in the heat of the controversy they have treated the Confessions or the writings of Luther as though they *were* Scripture. . . . They have also at times treated Luther's writings as this kind of exegetical authority, insisting that the Confessions or, lacking a treatment of a passage in the Confessions, the writings of Luther, provide the ultimate authority for the interpretation of a biblical passage" (Warren A. Quanbeck, "The Confessions and Their Influence upon Biblical Interpretation," in **Studies in Lutheran Hermeneutics**, ed. John Reumann [Philadelphia: Fortress Press, 1979], 181). David P. Scaer has described the Lutheran approach to theology in these words: "Lutheran theology is derived from Holy Scripture, but it is also normed or regulated by the ancient catholic creeds and the Lutheran confessions from the sixteenth century" ("How Do Lutheran Theologians Approach the Doing of Theology?" in **Doing Theology in Today's World: Essays in Honor of Kenneth S. Kantzer**, ed. John D. Woodbridge and Thomas Edward McComiskey [Grand Rapids, MI: Zondervan Publishing House, 1991], 197). Jaroslav Pelikan has keenly observed that in connection with the status of the Reformation confessions "the charge of self-contradiction" arose because "the elevation of the confessions . . . to the status of an enforcable 'norm' of public teaching appeared to be inconsistent with 'sola Scriptura'" (**CTHDD**, vol. 4, **Reformation of Church and Dogma (1300-1700**, 340). Already Bellarmine put it to the followers of the Protestant Reformation "that they could not have it both ways: Either they had to enforce 'sola Scriptura' in relation to their own confessions, or they had to admit that they too were elevating tradition to a position alongside Scripture" (ibid.). The Catholic author Brian Gaybba has said with regards to modern Protestant theology in general that "there seems to be a strong tendency, especially among the continental, to take the fact of *'scriptura nunquam sola'*! seriously enough to give confessional traditions some normative function in the interpretation of Scripture" (***The* Tradition: An Ecumenical Breakthrough?** [Rome: Herder, 1971], 216).

Despite Luther's affirmations of the authority of Scripture, it is well known that he made a number of rather critical remarks about it.[1] Here Luther's famous preface to the epistle of James comes to mind where he claims that whatever does not point to Christ or draws out Christ (was Christum treibet) is not apostolic, even though Peter or Paul would teach it. On the other hand, whatever "drives home" Christ is apostolic, even though it would come from Judas, Annas, Pilate, and Herod.[2] Thus, the *content* of Scripture is Christ,[3] and from this fact, he seems to repeatedly assign its authority.[4] Christ is the *punctus mathematicus sacrae scripturae*.[5] All Scripture revolves around Him as its authentic center. This "christological concentration" can be seen as the decisive element in Luther's interpretation and use of Scripture. For Luther, it seems, there is no *sola Scriptura* without a *solus Christus*.[6] Scripture must be understood in favor of Christ, not against Him.[7] This means that Christ is at once the center of Scripture and the Lord of Scripture. If Scripture is queen, Christ is King--even over Scripture![8] This means that if a passage of Scripture seems to be in conflict with

---

[1] A list of critical comments by Luther is given by Reinhold Seeberg, **Text-Book of the History of Doctrines**, 2 vols., trans. Charles E. Hay (Grand Rapids, MI: Baker Book House, 1952), 2:300; see also Holl, 560-565, 573-576, who gives additional examples and comments on Luther's freedom to point to discrepancies in the story of the baptism and resurrection by saying that 50 years later Luther probably would have been disfellowshiped from his own church for those comments. Holl, 574. Others, however, have tried to defend an infallibilistic stance of Luther and have interpreted those passages differently. Cf. Reu, 65-102; already earlier Wilhelm Rohnert, **Die Inspiration der heiligen Schrift und ihre Bestreiter. Eine biblisch-dogmengeschichtliche Studie** (Leipzig: Verlag von Georg Böhme, 1889); and Wilhelm Walther, **Die normale Stellung zur heiligen Schrift** (Leipzig: A. Deichertsche Verlagsbuchhandlung, 1917); more recently Woodbridge, **Biblical Authority**, 49-56; Preus, "Luther and Biblical Infallibility," 99-142; and idem, "The View of the Bible Held by the Church," 372-380.

[2] LW 35, 396; WADB 7, 385. Cf. Scheel, 47; and Timothy George, "'A Right Strawy Epistle': Reformation Perspectives on James," **RevExp** 83 (1986): 369-382.

[3] Ruokanen has argued that for Luther, the content of revelation is a salvific message where God communicates Himself, His presence, His properties, and His promises. The essence of prophetic inspiration is the reception of a salvific message, of which Christ is the nucleus and the essence of the promises (Ruokanen, 76, 79, 84, 86, 89, 91, 111).

[4] Cf. Gerrish, "Biblical Authority," 342.

[5] WATr. 2, 439, as quoted in Gerrish, "Biblical Authority," 343.

[6] So Lotz, 262, 270-273; Klug, **From Luther to Chemnitz**, 46.

[7] Cf. WA 18, 607.

[8] In his 1535 **Lectures on Galatians**, for example, Luther says of Scripture: "This queen must rule, and everyone must obey, and be subject to her. The pope, Luther, Augustine, Paul, an angel from heaven--these should not be masters, judges, or arbiters but only witnesses,

Luther's Christ-centered interpretation, his interpretation becomes "gospel-centered criticism of Scripture."[1] Christ and Scripture can be set over against each other[2] because Luther ranked the personal Word (Christ), the spoken Word (Gospel), and the written Word (Scripture).[3] This distinction and ranking leads to a canon within the canon,[4] where Christ becomes the hermeneutical key to a proper understanding of Scripture. This, however, seems to compromise the strength of the Scripture principle, where Scripture is the sole source of its own exposition. For

> if Scripture is interpreted either by an doctrinal center or by a tradition it is no longer Scripture that is interpreting itself--rather it is **we** who are interpreting Scripture by means of a doctrine or tradition, to which Scripture is in practice, being subjected.[5]

Thus, it is not surprising that Luther's Christological method "sharpened into a tool of theological criticism,"[6] that it only inaugurated a new set of problems that have engaged scholarly minds ever since.

There appears to be a certain tension, if not an unsolved discrepancy, in Luther's understanding of Scripture,[7] namely, between his affirmation of the divine authority

---

disciples, and confessors of Scripture" (WA 40, I, 120, 20-23; LW 26, 58). Yet while replying to opponents who adduce Biblical passages stressing works and merits, Luther stresses the following point in these very same lectures: "You are stressing the servant, that is, Scripture--and not all of it at that or even its most powerful part, but only a few passages concerning works. I leave this servant to you. I for my part stress the Lord, who is the King of Scripture" (WA 40, I, 459, 14-16); also LW 26, 295. In the same year Luther again underscored Scripture's servant status relative to Christ: "Briefly, Christ is the Lord, not the servant, the Lord of the Sabbath, of law, and of all things. The Scriptures must be understood in favor of Christ, not against him. For that reason they must either refer to him or must not be held to be true Scriptures. . . . Therefore, if the adversaries press the Scriptures against Christ, we urge Christ against the Scriptures. We have the Lord, they have the servants; we have the Head, they the feet or members, over which the head necessarily dominates and takes precedence. If one of them had to be parted with, Christ or the law, the law would have to be let go, not Christ. For if we have Christ, we can easily establish laws and we shall judge all things rightly. Indeed, we would make new decalogues, as Paul does in all the epistles, and Peter, but above all Christ in the gospel" (LW 34, 112, 40-53).

[1]Althaus, **The Theology of Martin Luther**, 81.

[2]LW 34, 112.

[3]Lotz, 264.

[4]Ebeling, "'Sola Scriptura' and Tradition," 118. See also Inge Lønning, **"Kanon im Kanon": Zum dogmatischen Grundlagenproblem des neutestamentlichen Kanons**, FGLP 43 (Munich: Chr. Kaiser, 1972), 72-213.

[5]Gaybba, 221.

[6]Werner Georg Kümmel, **The New Testament: The History of the Investigation of Its Problems**, trans. S. McLean Gilmour and Howard C. Kee (Nashville, TN: Abingdon, 1972), 24.

[7]In light of these tensions some Luther scholars have argued that Luther is not without

and the binding force of Scripture because of its divine inspiration and his Christological criticism of Scripture. It should be noted, however, that despite Luther's critical remarks on some parts of Scripture a truly historical-critical use of Scripture as widely practiced since the Enlightenment, is not possible from Luther's perspective because he still accepts Scripture as the divinely inspired Word of God.[1]

Despite his own ambiguities, Luther had established a theological starting point with the *sola Scriptura* principle which became basic to all Protestants.[2] As a matter of fact, Luther's new understanding of the role of Scripture for theology, with its strengths and problems, was to influence and shape most of the subsequent discussion on this issue even to the present time.

---

contradictions in his use of Scripture. Scheel, 24, for instance, has said that "Luthers Anschauung von der Schrift, mag auch eine bestimmte Grundüberzeugung heraustreten, nicht klar und geschlossen ist." Furthermore, "die Doppelseitigkeit seiner Stellung zur Schrift ist vielmehr zu jeder Zeit seines Lebens zu konstatieren, vor 1517 sowohl wie in der grossen reformatorischen Epoche und in den letzen Jahren seines Lebens" (ibid., 76).

[1]Cf. Gerhard Ebeling, "The Significance of the Critical Historical Method for Church and Theology in Protestantism," in Gerhard Ebeling, **Word and Faith**, trans. James W. Leitch (Philadelphia: Fortress Press, 1963), 42: "It leads only to obscuring the nature of the problem when the critical historical method is held to be a purely formal scientific technique, entirely free of presuppositions, whose application to the historical objects in the theological realm provokes no conflicts and does no hurt to the dogmatic structure. . . . For historical criticism is more than lively historical interest. Even the early and medieval churches concerned themselves more or less with history and the study of its sources, and therefore also always provided a certain measure of criticism where legends and falsifications of history were concerned. . . . And yet that was all merely accompaniment, but was not of revolutionary significance for the church's teaching and the generally recognized traditional picture of the world and of history. It was **not** what we know today as the critical historical method. For the latter is not concerned with the greatest possible refinement of the philological methods, but with subjecting the tradition to critical examination on the basis of new principles of thought" (emphasis supplied). In this programmatic and influential article Ebeling, however, also argues for the legitimacy of the historical-critical method and claims that the historical exegesis of the Reformers "becomes critical theology" (ibid., 36). For a careful analysis of Ebeling's theses as propagated in the above mentioned article, see Joachim Cochlovius, "Ist die 'historisch-kritische Methode' reformatorisch? Kritische Fragen and Gerhard Ebelings Programmaufsatz," in **Evangelische Schriftauslegung: Ein Quellen- und Arbeitsbuch für Studium und Gemeinde**, ed. Joachim Cochlovius and Peter Zimmerling (Wuppertal: R. Brockhaus Verlag, 1987), 228-234; cf. also Slenczka, **Kirchliche Entscheidung in theologischer Verantwortung**, 98-102. That the historical-critical method did not originate with the Reformers is also pointed out by Victor Paul Furnish, "The Historical Criticism of the New Testament: A Survey of Origins," **BJRL** 56 (1974): 336-370; Kendrick Grobel, "Biblical Criticism," **IDB**, 1:408; S. J. de Vries, "Biblical Criticism, History of," **IDB**, 1:413; and more recently by Ulrich H. J. Körtner, "Schrift und Geist: Über Legitimität und Grenzen allegorischer Schriftauslegung," **NZSTh** 36 (1994): 12.

[2]Bainton, "The Bible in the Reformation," **CHB**, 3:4.

John Calvin

John Calvin (1509-1564) has been called Luther's greatest pupil.[1] Even though the "literature on Calvin and the Scriptures is immense,"[2] one can safely say that Calvin tried to formulate his theology according to the Reformation principle of *sola Scriptura*.[3] Just like Luther before him, Calvin affirmed the supernatural origin of Scripture.[4] Scripture is produced by the inspiration of the Holy Spirit.[5] For Calvin, the Biblical writers put forward nothing of their own[6] and "obediently followed the

---

[1] Hanns Rückert, "Calvin," in Hans Rückert, **Vorträge und Aufsätze zur historischen Theologie** (Tübingen: J. C. B. Mohr, 1972), 167.

[2] So Donald K. McKim, "Calvin's View of Scripture," in **Readings in Calvin's Theology**, ed. Donald K. McKim (Grand Rapids, MI: Baker Book House, 1984), 43, n. 1. James I. Packer, "Calvin's View of Scripture," in **God's Inerrant Word: An International Symposium on the Trustworthiness of Scripture**, ed. John Warwick Montgomery (Minneapolis, MN: Bethany Fellowship, 1974), 95, states similarly: "The biggest problem facing anyone who attempts a paper on Calvin's view of Scripture is simply *embarrass de richesse*. Far more material presents itself than can be properly treated in space available." On Calvin's view of Scripture, the most useful bibliography seems to be that of Richard Stauffer, **Dieu, la Creation et la Providence dans la Predication de Calvin** (Berne: Peter Lang, 1978), 72, n. 1. For further references to bibliographies on Calvin, see James I. Packer, "John Calvin and the Inerrancy of Holy Scripture," in **Inerrancy and the Church**, ed. John D. Hannah (Chicago, IL: Moody Press, 1984), 151, n. 19; and Muller, **Post-Reformation Reformed Dogmatics**, 2:62-63, n. 33 and 34. See also H. Jackson Forstman, **Word and Spirit: Calvin's Doctrine of Biblical Authority** (Stanford, CA: Stanford University Press, 1962), 52-60.

[3] Calvin's own viewpoint on Scripture is carefully put together in the first book of the **Institutes of the Christian Religion**. References to the **Institutes** are from the **Library of Christian Classics**, hereinafter **LCC**, vols. XX and XXI, ed. John T. McNeill, trans. Ford Lewis Battles [as quoted in Leith, John Calvin, 331]. It should be noted that in the earliest edition of Calvin's **Institutes** (1536) there was no formal statement of a doctrine of Scripture. Calvin's understanding of Scripture was subsumed under the heading of "Faith" in his second chapter. In the final Latin version of the **Institutes** (1559), however, Calvin dealt with the doctrine of Scripture in three separate sections. On this point, cf. the discussion in Rogers and McKim, **The Authority and Interpretation of the Bible**, 102-103. See also the article by John H. Leith, "John Calvin--Theologian of the Bible," **Int**, 25 (1971): 329-344.

[4] Kenneth S. Kantzer, "Calvin and the Holy Scriptures," in **Inspiration and Interpretation**, ed. John F. Walvoord (Grand Rapids, MI: Eerdmans, 1957), 137-142.

[5] On Calvin's view of inspiration, see Michael Carl Armour, "Calvin's Hermeneutic and the History of Christian Exegesis" (Ph.D. dissertation, University of California, Los Angeles, 1992), 317-355.

[6] "This is a principle which distinguishes our religion from all others, that we know that God hath spoken to us, and are fully convinced that the prophets did not speak at their own suggestion, but that, being organs of the Holy Spirit, they only uttered what they had been commissioned from heaven to declare. Whoever then wishes to profit in the Scriptures, let him, first of all, lay down this as a settled point, that the law and the prophets are not a doctrine delivered according to the will and pleasure of men, but dictated by the Holy Spirit" (John Calvin,

Spirit as their guide, who ruled in their mouth as in his own sanctuary."[1] From his account of God's authorship,[2] it is obvious that the intent is to represent God's Word as "spoken directly from heaven and in all respects identical with the canonical Scriptures of the Old and New Testaments."[3] Hence, the whole Bible is the "Word of God."[4] It seems that Calvin is in basic agreement with Luther when he affirms the authority of Holy Scripture because of its divine origin.[5] Since Calvin identifies Scripture as the inspired and revelatory Word of God, it is the source of doctrinal truths about God and everything it touches upon.[6] Because God is the author of Scripture, the unity of the Bible is a fundamental theological axiom for Calvin.[7] As with Luther, Calvin insisted that Scripture must be interpreted by Scripture so that obscure passages are interpreted by the clearer passages. Perhaps nowhere has the binding authority of Scripture been described more clearly by Calvin than in his concluding remarks to chapter xviii of book I: "Our true wisdom is to embrace with meek docility, and without reservation, whatever the Holy Scriptures have delivered."[8] The point which is maintained with extraordinary consistency throughout the **Institutes** is Calvin's insistence on the absolute sufficiency of Scripture as guide to belief and conduct for the

---

Commentaries on the Second Epistle to Timothy, trans. William Pringle [Grand Rapids, MI: Eerdmans, 1948], 248-249).

[1] John Calvin, **Commentaries on the Second Epistle of Peter**, trans. John Owen (Grand Rapids, MI: Eerdmans, 1948), 391.

[2] Cf. **Institutes**, I.vi.1, where Calvin writes that in the Scriptures God "opens His own sacred mouth." Or ibid., I.vii.5, where he says that we are sure that the Scriptures came to us "from the very mouth of God." The real author of Scripture is God Himself (ibid., I.vii.4).

[3] Rupert E. Davies, **The Problem of Authority in the Continental Reformers: A Study in Luther, Zwingli, and Calvin** (London: Epworth Press, 1946), 146; Richard C. Prust, "Was Calvin a Biblical Literalist?" **SJT** 20 (1967): 312-328.

[4] Gerrish, "Biblical Authority," 353.

[5] Cf. Armour, 317-355.

[6] Armour, 322-351; Kantzer, "Calvin and the Holy Scriptures," 137-152.

[7] "He [God] is the Author of the Scriptures: he cannot vary and differ from himself. Hence, he must ever remain just as once he revealed himself there" (Calvin, **Institutes**, I.ix.2). Cf. Leith, "John Calvin," 338-340.

[8] The Latin text reads as follows: "Nam sapere nostrum nihil aliud esse debet quam mansueta dcilitate amplecti, et quidem sine exceptione, quicquid in sacris Scripturis traditum est." Gerrish has pointed out that *Exceptione* could be rendered "exception" and taken with the phrase "*quicquid . . . est*": i.e., "everything without any exception . . ." ("Biblical Authority," 350, n. 1).

Christian.¹ Hence, Calvin subscribed to the Reformation tag that "Scripture interprets Scripture."²

The authority of Scripture rests upon its character as the verbally inspired Word of God that was given through the Holy Spirit.³ This made Scripture the source for all doctrine and the norm for all practice. The authority of Scripture, however, although something intrinsic, is recognized for what it is only when the Holy Spirit illuminates the mind.⁴ More than Luther, Calvin highlights the role of the Holy Spirit in confirming Biblical authority to us. This stress of the inner witness of the Holy Spirit is characteristic of Calvin. The ability "to recognize" the Bible as the Word of God, then, was not something that could be acquired through academic study; it was rather a gift of God.⁵ Calvin maintained the unity of Word and Spirit against two opposing errors. On the one hand, the Roman Catholics down-played the role of the Holy Spirit by subordinating Scripture to the interpretation of the church.⁶ On the other hand, some of Calvin's contemporaries so elevated the role of the Spirit that they saw little need for the written Word. For Calvin, the Holy Spirit did not bypass the Scriptures but was recognized in His agreement with them.⁷ Thus, Scripture remains the sole authoritative norm.

Calvin is concerned to point out that the authority of the Bible cannot be produced by means of reasonable arguments or rational proofs or any other human judgment. Scripture, rather, is "self-authenticated."⁸ Calvin's concept of the Spirit's

---

¹So Gerrish, "Biblical Authority," 352.

²Packer, "John Calvin and the Inerrancy of Holy Scripture," 173.

³This is admitted by scholars of different persuasion. Cf. Gerrish, "Biblical Authority," 355; Davies, **The Problem of Authority**, 114. As far as the term "verbal inspiration" is concerned, Packer has pointed out that the proper comments are: verbal--yes; mechanical--no ("John Calvin and the Inerrancy of Holy Scripture," 159, n. 39).

⁴Richard A. Muller, "The Foundation of Calvin's Theology: Scripture as Revealing God's Word," **DDSR** 44/1 (1979): 22.

⁵This does not mean that Calvin was opposed to a serious and in-depth investigation of Scripture. His whole academic education, his familiarity with the ancient languages, his intellectual skill and expertise testifies amply to the contrary. Cf. Rogers and McKim, 89-96.

⁶To this, Calvin was utterly opposed, cf. **Institutes**, I.1.7.2.

⁷Cf. George, **Theology of the Reformers**, 197-198.

⁸"Let this point therefore stand: that those whom the Holy Spirit has inwardly taught truly rest upon Scripture, and that Scripture indeed is self-authenticated; hence it is not right to subject

authenticating witness was his counter to the idea that the authority of Scripture strictly and properly depended on the church.[1]

Calvin also regarded Jesus Christ as the "scope" of all Scripture and wrote that people should read Scripture with the purpose of finding Christ.[2] Christ, however, never became a canon within the canon as for Luther.[3] Calvin also saw no conflict between the Law and the Gospel as did Luther.

Although Calvin was committed to the authority of Scripture in his theology, it does not follow that all of the content of his theology, as well as his style, is necessarily derived from Scripture alone. As others have shown, Calvin regarded the common experience of nature as a source of theological knowledge and displayed a greater openness for reason and the ability of man to know God from nature than Luther.[4]

---

it to proofs and reasoning. And the certainty it deserves with us, it attains by the testimony of the Spirit. For even if it wins reverence for itself by its own majesty, it seriously affects us only when it is sealed upon our hearts through the Spirit. Therefore, illumined by his power, we believe neither by our own not by anyone else's judgment that Scripture is from God; but above human judgment we affirm with utter certainty (just as we were saying upon the majesty of God himself) that it has flowed to us from the very mouth of God by the ministry of men. We seek no proofs, no marks of genuineness upon which our judgment may lean; but we subject our judgment and wit to it as to a thing far beyond any guesswork! This we do, not as persons accustomed to seize upon some unknown thing, which, under closer scrutiny, displeases then, but fully conscious that we hold the unassailable truth! Nor do we do this as those miserable men who habitually bind over their minds to the thralldom of superstition; but we feel that the undoubted power of his divine majesty lives and breathes there. By this power we are drawn and inflamed, knowingly and willingly, to obey him, yet also more vitally and more effectively than by mere human willing or knowing!" (Calvin, **Institutes**, I.vii.5). Similarly: "Unless this certainty, higher and stronger than any human judgment, be present, it will be vain to fortify the authority of Scripture by arguments, to establish it by common agreement of the church, or to confirm it with other helps. For unless this foundation is laid, its authority will always remain in doubt. Conversely, once we have embraced it devoutly as its dignity deserves, and have recognized it to be above the common sort of things, those arguments--not strong enough before to engraft and fix the certainty of Scripture in our minds--become very useful aids" (ibid., I,viii,1).

[1]"As to their question--How can we be assured that this has sprung from God unless we have recourse to the degree of the church?--it is as if someone asked: Whence will we learn to distinguish light from darkness, white from black, sweet from bitter? Indeed, Scripture exhibits fully as clear evidence of its own truth as white and black things do of their color, or sweet and bitter things do of their taste" (Calvin, **Institutes**, I.vii.2).

[2]A repeated affirmation of Calvin is that one knows God only through Christ yet, the only way to discern Jesus Christ from the false "christs" is through the Scriptures. Cf. E. David Willis, **Calvin's Catholic Christology: The Function of the So-Called Extra Calvinisticum in Calvin's Theology** (Leiden: E. J. Brill, 1966), 105, 119.

[3]Leith, "John Calvin," 341.

[4]For a concise overview over the debate on the question of natural theology in Calvin, see Susan Elizabeth Schreiner, "The Theater of His Glory: Nature and the Natural Order in the Thought of John Calvin" (Ph.D. dissertation, Duke University, 1983), ix-xv. In support of

Hence, despite his subjection to the authority of Scripture, his theology contains elements that must be credited not to Scripture but to ancient philosophy.[1]

Ulrich Zwingli

As with Luther and Calvin, the Bible stood at the center of the Zwinglian Reformation and played a dominant theological role.[2] Just as with Luther and Calvin, the Bible is the Word of God for Zwingli.[3] It is the Word of God "because it was spoken by God and because he [God] speaks through it."[4] That God or the Spirit is the author of Scripture was taken for granted by Zwingli and needed no proof.[5] Zwingli's view of inspiration is not mechanical,[6] although he believes that everything

---

Calvin's openness to natural theology, see Günter Gloede, **Theologia Naturalis bei Calvin**, TSSTh 5 (Stuttgart: Kohlhammer, 1935); Victor L. Nuovo, "Calvin's Theology: A Study of Its Sources in Classical Antiquity" (Ph.D. dissertation, Columbia University, 1964), 58-75; Gerald Postema, "Calvin's Alleged Rejection of Natural Theology," **SJT** 24 (1971): 423-434; and Willis, 101-131. For a different interpretation, see Peter Barth, **Das Problem der natürlichen Theologie bei Calvin**, TEH 18 (Munich: Chr. Kaiser, 1935); Wilhelm Niesel, **The Theology of John Calvin**, trans. Harold Knight (London: Lutterworth Press, 1956), 39-53; T. H. L. Parker, **Calvin's Doctrine of the Knowledge of God** (Grand Rapids, MI: Eerdmans, 1959).

[1]Joseph C. McLelland, "Calvin and Philosophy," **CJT** 11 (1965): 42-53; Nuovo, 1-2, claims that Calvin's theology is in some of its content and its style dependent upon Classical Antiquity. As examples he lists Calvin's teaching on divine providence and human immortality. Cf. also Rogers and McKim, 100-101; and Charles Partee, **Calvin and Classical Philosophy** (Leiden: E. J. Brill, 1977), 146, who says that "without doubt Calvin's knowledge of classical philosophy influences his thinking."

[2]Important studies on Zwingli's view of the Bible are: Ernst Nagel, **Zwingli's Stellung zur Schrift** (Freiburg: J. C. B. Mohr, 1896); Christof Gestrich, **Zwingli als Theologe: Glaube und Geist beim Zürcher Reformator**, SDGSTh 20 (Zurich: Zwingli Verlag, 1967), 42-87; Gottfried W. Locher, **Zwingli's Thought: New Perspectives** (Leiden: E. J. Brill, 1981); W. P. Stephens, **The Theology of Huldrych Zwingli** (Oxford: Clarendon Press, 1986), 51-79; Davies, **The Problem of Authority in the Continental Reformers**, 62-92; and Ulrich Gäbler, **Huldrych Zwingli im 20. Jahrhundert: Forschungsbericht und annotierte Bibliographie 1897-1972** (Zurich: Theologischer Verlag, 1975), 68-78, with further literature. There has been a great deal of argument as to whether Zwingli was dependent upon Luther or not. Some scholars as Seeberg, **History of Doctrines** 2:308, n. 1, consider Zwingli's dependence upon Luther as a settled historical fact. Zwingli himself, however, refused to be called a pupil of Luther and insisted that he had begun to preach the Gospel in 1516. See the balanced discussion in J. L. Neve, **A History of Christian Thought**, 2 vols. (Philadelphia: Muhlenberg Press, 1946), 1:241-242.

[3]Davies, **The Problem of Authority in the Continental Reformers**, 71-73.

[4]Stephens, 55.

[5]Zwingli refers quite naturally to the Spirit speaking in Paul and to Paul. Z I, 205, 25-28; 207, 21-22.

[6]Stephens, 56.

must yield to the Scriptures because they come from the dictation of the Spirit.[1] According to Stephens, "it is precisely the fact that the scriptures are God's word and not man's that gives them their authority"[2] and their preeminence as the source for Zwingli's theology.[3]

Since the Scriptures derive from the Spirit, who is the Spirit of Concord, they are to be in harmony with each other.[4] This meant that for Zwingli the Word of God "is certain and powerful."[5] It contains no contradictions,[6] and it is intrinsically clear.[7] As for Luther and Calvin, Scripture is its own interpreter. Zwingli could say: "I understand Scripture only in the way it interprets itself by the Spirit of God. It does not require any human opinion."[8] The true teacher is not the learned scholar, pope, or council, but "God reveals himself by his own Spirit. He will enlighten all who seek with humility."[9] Therefore, Scripture or the Spirit speaking in Scripture is its own judge.[10] The Word of God in the historical and concrete form of the canonical Scriptures is the sole authoritative source of religious truth.[11] At least in principle, Scriptural authority relativized all extra-biblical practices and sources for Zwingli's theology. To guard against a subjective misuse of Scripture, Zwingli stressed the so-called "natural sense" of Scripture (*sensus literalis or naturalis*), more than it was done in tradition or even with Erasmus.[12]

Yet, Zwingli was aware that the simple presence or absence of something in Scripture was not always decisive for one's theology, since his opponents also quoted

---

[1] Z I 260, 21-23.

[2] Stephens, 57.

[3] See the helpful presentation in Stephens, 55-58, with further references.

[4] Z, V 735, 21-23; cf. Z IV 841, 18-22.

[5] Z, I 353, 358.

[6] Z V 853.

[7] On this, cf. the discussion in Geoffrey W. Bromiley, **Historical Theology: An Introduction** (Grand Rapids, MI: Eerdmans, 1978), 215-216.

[8] Z I 559.

[9] LCC, 24, 82.

[10] Z, I 558, 2-5; 561, 7-30; cf. Z, IV 757, 19-20.

[11] Davies, **The Problem of Authority in the Continental Reformers**, 89.

[12] Gestrich, 75.

Scripture for their position. This situation leads one to look more closely at one of Zwingli's fundamental principles, namely, the necessity of the Spirit in understanding and using Scripture.[1] Gestrich has shown convincingly that for Zwingli one already has to believe in order to understand correctly.[2] Thus, there exists a spirit-originated belief that is already pre-given ("geistgewirkte Vorgabe-Glaube") before one approaches Scripture. Therefore, the believer has an unfailing "feeling" ("Empfinden") of what interpretation of Scripture is correct or not.[3] This means, however, that besides Scripture the pre-given Spirit is necessary. Although Scripture has authority, it needs to be interpreted and for this the Holy Spirit needs to be placed as a second authority next to the Scriptures. As Gestrich points out, strictly spoken, Zwingli even puts the Spirit above Scripture because only he guarantees the correct interpretation.[4] Zwingli held that God had written His Law already on the heart and mind of the believer and therefore the believer could know whether the letter of Scripture is according to the divine teaching or not. In holding to this position, Zwingli paved the way, so to speak, to an autonomous elevation of the inner experience of the interpreter over the letter because God already has given the believer the inner Word of faith. Thus, the criteria for right faith are not contained in Scripture alone but rather in the "inner" knowledge of the believer.[5] Put differently, Zwingli did his exegesis from a strong theological presupposition, namely, the movement from the experience of the inner faith towards Scripture rather than the other way around.[6] This might also explain why it was impossible for the Anabaptists to come to an agreement with him on the basis of Scripture alone.[7] With Gestrich, one has to raise the question in what

---

[1]According to Gäbler, 77, Christof Gerstich's important monograph remains the most helpful discussion on this important aspect of Zwingli's theology. In my analysis, I follow Gerstich's presentation.

[2]Gestrich, 70-71.

[3]Ibid., 71.

[4]Ibid., 72.

[5]Ibid., 83.

[6]"Zwingli hat also stark von einem theologischen Grundverständnis aus Exegese betrieben, er pflegte bei der Auslegung von dem auszugehen, was er als christlich und richtig ansah, so dass bei ihm tatsächlich die Komponente vom 'inneren Glauben' zur Schrift hin weit stärker betont ist als die Komponente von der Schrift zum eigentlichen Verstehen hin" (ibid., 78-79).

[7]Gestrich observes: "Deshalb haftet dem hermeneutischen Zirkel bei Zwingli ein Mangel an. Deshalb was es auch für die Täufer unmöglich, sich mit Zwingli auf dem Boden der Schrift

sense it is still meaningful to argue on the ground of Scripture alone, taking Zwingli's position.[1] Indeed, the key question seems to be whether one should interpret Scripture on the basis of what one knows already, be that the "pre-given faith" or some other source of knowledge, or whether Scripture should judge critically any pre-knowledge one has.[2] It seems that Zwingli's position, with regards to the role of the Spirit and Scripture, is not without contradictions. As Stephens has pointed out, Zwingli's appeal to Scripture was not a denial that God had also spoken elsewhere.[3] Thus, even though in some sense Zwingli "took more literally than Luther the *sola* in *sola scriptura*,"[4] he used and introduced other ideas that were not derived from Scripture alone.

Now that these three major Protestant reformers[5] have been considered it is time

---

zu einigen. Denn was die Schrift an strittigen Stellen eigentlich sagen wollte, daß sah vom 'inneren Glauben' und von der überlegenen Bildung Zwinglis her allemal anders aus als die Aussage, welche die Täufer hier wahrnehmen wollten" (ibid., 79). Also: "Wir haben zwar alle die dieselbe heilige Schrift, schreibt Zwingli, aber manche leihen einem anderen Geist als dem göttlichen ihr Ohr. [Z, VIII, 317,26-31] Das bedeutet: Wer anders denkt als Zwingli lehrt, besitzt den Geist Gottes nicht" (ibid., 83).

[1]Ibid., 84.

[2]Cf. ibid., 86.

[3]Stephens, 57. This is especially evident in his use of pagan writers in **The Providence of God** which "seems almost to use the bible in support of a position built up by philosophical argument" (ibid., 55).

[4]So George, **Theology of the Reformers**, 160. McGrath thinks that a certain degree of variation can be detected among the mainstream Reformers on the Scripture principle, esp. over against tradition. McGrath, therefore, concludes that "Zwingli is closer to the radical position than Calvin is, while Luther is closer to the catholic position. But none, it must be emphasized, was prepared to abandon the concept of a traditional interpretation of scripture, in favor of the radical alternative" (**Reformation Thought**, 109).

[5]We have not included other Protestant Reformers like Bullinger, Bucer, or even the so-called "Radical Reformation" (George Hunston Williams, **The Radical Reformation** [Philadelphia: Westminster Press, 1962]) in our discussion because they do not seem to go significantly beyond the covered positions. On Bucer and Bullinger, see the discussion in Muller, **Post-Reformation Reformed Dogmatics**, 2:58-61. On the Radical Reformation, which is characterized neither by doctrinal homogeneity nor organizational efficiency (so George, **Theology of the Reformers**, 256), see the helpful list of references mentioned in Reventlow, **The Authority of the Bible and the Rise of the Modern World**, 450-451, n. 50, 51, 53, 57a. For further primary and secondary works, see Wilhelm Wiswedel, "Bible," **The Mennonite Encyclopedia**, ed. Harold S. Bender and C. Henry Smith (Hillsboro, KS: Mennonite Brethren Publishing House, 1955), 1:322-328. Cf. also idem, "The Inner and the Outer Word: A Study in the Anabaptist Doctrine of Scripture," **MQR** 26 (1952): 171-191; John C. Wenger, "The Biblicism of the Anabaptists," in **The Rediscovery of the Anabaptist Vision: A Sixtieth Anniversary Tribute to Harold S. Bender**, ed. Guy F. Hershberger (Scottdale, PA: Herald Press, 1957), 167-179; and the essays in Willard M. Swartley, ed., **Essays on Biblical Interpretation: Anabaptist-Mennonite Perspectives**, TRS 1 (Elkhart, IN: Institute of Mennonite Studies, 1984).

to turn our attention to Protestant Orthodoxy. In contrast to the towering Protestant leaders discussed above, one is faced with a multitude of Orthodox theologians who continue the Lutheran and Reformed traditions. For the purpose of this study, it is most effective to treat these theologians collectively rather than on an individual basis.

Protestant Orthodoxy

It often is believed that the period following the original Reformers[1] represents a period of hardening of their original theological positions by casting them into an Aristotelian mold of thinking as used by their opponents.[2] This, so it is often thought, was especially true with regard to the doctrine of Scripture. The changes in method during this period also involved distortions of the Reformers original doctrine.[3] A careful study of the theology of the theologians of the Protestant Orthodoxy seems to

---

[1] For this period, see especially the following important literature: Heinrich Schmid, **The Doctrinal Theology of the Evangelical Lutheran Church, Exhibited and Verified from the Original Sources**, trans. Charles A. Hay and Henry E. Jacobs (Philadelphia: Lutheran Publication Society, 1876); Johannes Reinhard, **Die Prinzipienlehre der lutherischen Dogmatik von 1700 bis 1750: Beitrag zur Geschichte der altprotestantischen Theologie und zur Vorgeschichte des Rationalismus** (Leipzig: A. Deichertsche Verlagsbuchhandlung, 1906); Hans Emil Weber, **Die analytische Methode der lutherischen Orthodoxie** (Naumburg a. S.: Lippert & Co., 1907); idem, **Die philosophische Scholastik des deutschen Protestantismus im Zeitalter der Orthodoxie** (Leipzig: Quelle & Meyer, 1907); idem, **Reformation, Orthodoxie und Rationalismus**, 3 vols. (Gütersloh: C. Bertelsmann Verlag, 1937-51); idem, **Der Einfluss der protestantischen Schulphilosophie auf die orthodox-lutherische Dogmatik** (Darmstadt: Wissenschaftliche Buchgesellschaft, 1969); Karl Heim, **Das Gewissheitsproblem in der systematischen Theologie bis zu Schleiermacher** (Leipzig: J. C. Hinrichsche Buchhandlung, 1911); Paul Althaus, **Die Prinzipien der deutschen reformierten Dogmatik im Zeitalter der aristotelischen Scholastik** (Leipzig: A Deichert'sche Verlagsbuchhandlung, 1914, reprint: Darmstadt: Wissenschaftliche Buchgesellschaft, 1967); Heinrich Heppe, **Reformed Dogmatics: Set Out and Illustrated from the Sources**, rev. and ed. Ernst Bizer, trans. G. T. Thomson (London: George Allen & Unwin, 1950); Bengt Hägglund, **Die Heilige Schrift und ihre Deutung in der Theologie Johann Gerhards: Eine Untersuchung über das altlutherische Schriftverständnis** (Lund: CWK Gleerup, 1951); Emanuel Hirsch, **Geschichte der neueren Evangelischen Theologie im Zusammenhang mit den allgemeinen Bewegungen des europäischen Denkens**, 5 vols. (Gütersloh: Gerd Mohn, 1964); Robert D. Preus, **The Inspiration of Scripture: A Study of the Theology of the Seventeenth Century Lutheran Dogmaticians** (London: Oliver and Boyd, 1957); idem, **The Theology of Post-Reformation Lutheranism: A Study of Theological Prolegomena**, 2 vols. (St. Louis, MO: Concordia Publishing House, 1970-1972); Carl-Heinz Ratschow, **Lutherische Dogmatik zwischen Reformation und Aufkärung**, 2 vols. (Gütersloh: Gütersloher Verlagshaus Gerd Mohn, 1964); Rogers and McKim, **The Authority and Interpretation of the Bible**, 147-198, Woodbridge, **Biblical Authority**, 69-83; Richard A. Muller, **Post-Reformation Reformed Dogmatics**, vol. 1, **Prolegomena to Theology** (Grand Rapids, MI: Baker Book House, 1987); and idem, **Post-Reformation Reformed Dogmatics**, vol. 2.

[2] So Rogers and McKim, 148, 187, among others.

[3] So Rogers and McKim, 185.

reveal, however, that the actual situation was much more complex and the development more subtle than often believed.¹ Noted church historian Bromiley concludes his discussion on the role of Scripture during this period by saying that

> what change there has been is more in style, or, materially, in elaboration. The substance of the Reformation doctrine of scripture has not yet been altered, let alone abandoned.²

This conclusion is supported by the careful and in-depth studies of Preus and Muller who have shown that the orthodox Lutheran and Reformed theologians had the same basic concern in their treatment of Scripture as did Luther and Calvin: they wanted to maintain the principle of *sola Scriptura*, i.e., by Scripture alone can articles of faith be established.³ With Luther and Calvin, the early seventeenth century Protestant orthodox theologians held that God is the author (*causa prinicpalis*) of Scripture and the prophets and apostles are the instruments (*causa instrumentalis*) which God employed in their production.⁴ Hence, the origin of Scripture is ascribed to a peculiar agency of God by means of which God communicated to the Biblical writers "both the matter and the form of that which was to be written."⁵ Through inspiration, God

> supernaturally communicated to the intellect of those who wrote not only the correct conception of all that was to be written, but also the conception of the words themselves and of everything by which they were to be expressed.⁶

Thus, "the Sacred Scriptures are the Word of God recorded in the sacred writings."⁷

---

¹"Altogether too much of the discussion of the Reformation and Protestant orthodox doctrines of Scripture has approached the subject from theologically biased perspectives and with the specific intention of justifying one or another twentieth-century view of Scripture" (Muller, **Post-Reformation Reformed Dogmatics**, 2:4, cf. 540-543). See also Preus, **The Theology of Post-Reformation Lutheranism**, 1:306-309; idem, **The Inspiration of Scripture**, 134-146; and Richard H. Popkin, **The History of Scepticism from Erasmus to Descartes**, rev. ed. (Assen: Van Gorcum & Comp., 1964).

²Bromiley, **Historical Theology**, 328.

³Preus, **The Theology of Post-Reformation Lutheranism**, 1:256-263; Muller, **Post-Reformation Reformed Dogmatics**, 2:123-125, 149-156.

⁴Schmid, 56; see also Bong Rin Ro, "The Inspiration of Scripture Among Seventeenth-Century Reformed Theologians," in **The Living and Active Word of God: Studies in Honor of Samuel J. Schultz**, ed. Morris Inch and Ronald Youngblood (Winona Lake, IN: Eisenbrauns, 1983), 207-221.

⁵Schmid, 56.

⁶Ibid., 57.

⁷Ibid., 56. Hence, there is no difference between Luther and Calvin and the later Orthodox theologians in identifying Scripture as the word of God as Heppe, 16, claims when he says that "at the root of the original Reformed doctrine of inspiration lay the distinction *between*, at the root of the later Church doctrine the identification *of* the concepts 'Word of God' and 'Holy

Since Scripture really is the Word of God, it follows that the church is bound to yield to it as the only source of truth from which all theology is to be drawn.[1] As the only source of truth, Scripture must contain it entirely and clearly.[2] Furthermore, since Orthodox theologians recognized the divine origin of Scripture, they ascribed to it the attributes of *authority, perfection or sufficiency, perspicuity efficiency, and unity*.[3] Scripture, therefore, stands above the church and any (unwritten) tradition,[4] as well as religious experience, because of its divine origin and nature and because it is self-authenticating.[5] The importance of the authority of Scripture for the orthodox Lutheran theologians of the seventeenth century, therefore, cannot be overestimated. It has been said that their entire theological position against Rome and the rationalistic Socinians stood or fell with the *sola Scriptura* principle.[6]

Despite this outward similarity, however, one can detect a subtle but crucial shift in the argumentation of the divine authority of Scripture for theology. It is a slight shift towards an underpinning of the authority and divinity of Scripture on rationalistic terms.[7] It seems that this initially small but crucial shift reflects a more rationalistic

---

Scripture'[sic]." We have corrected the typological error "'Word of God' and 'H. Spirit'." For a detailed refutation of Heppe's view, see Muller, **Post-Reformation Reformed Dogmatics**, 2:239-270, esp. 249-253. Gottfried Hornig, **Die Anfänge der historisch-kritischen Theologie: Johann Salomo Semlers Schriftverständnis und seine Stellung zu Luther**, FSThR 8 (Göttingen: Vandenhoeck & Ruprecht, 1961), 43, also points out that the identification of the Word of Scripture with the Word of God gave Holy Scripture a unique position that distinguished it from all other books.

[1]Preus, **The Theology of Post-Reformation Lutheranism**, 1:256; Schmid, 68.

[2]Preus, **The Theology of Post-Reformation Lutheranism**, 1:257; Schmid, 68.

[3]Cf. Muller, **Post-Reformation Reformed Dogmatics**, 2:313-388; Preus, **The Theology of Post-Reformation Lutheranism**, 1:296-300, 309-315, 362-378; Schmid, 68.

[4]Preus, **The Inspiration of Scripture**, 118-130.

[5]Preus sees in this important point no difference between the early dogmaticians of the seventeenth century and Luther (**The Theology of Post-Reformation Lutheranism**, 1:302). Similarly Hägglund, **Die Heilige Schrift und Ihre Deutung in der Theologie Johann Gerhards**, 143, about Johann Gerhard and his theology.

[6]Preus, **The Inspiration of Scripture**, 93-94

[7]Preus, **The Theology of Post-Reformation Lutheranism**, 1:302. Reid seems to overstate the case when he claims that "a landslide takes place towards rationalism and rationalization of the faith" (John Kelman Sutherland Reid, **The Authority of Scripture: A Study of the Reformation and Post-Reformation Understanding of the Bible** [London: Methuen and Company, 1957], 94). Bromiley thinks that "tendencies may be discerned in the presentation which give evidence of some movement away from the Reformation emphases. The movement, however, has not yet proceeded very far" (**Historical Theology**, 328).

approach to Scripture that was slowly gaining prominence among the Protestant theologians of the seventeenth century.[1] The authority of Scripture is by no means surrendered, but a shift occurred that eventually and decisively affected the role of Scripture in theology. Although Scripture--and the theology founded upon it--was not exactly rational in the sense that all arose from reason, Orthodoxy increasingly acknowledged a form of "natural theology" based on God's "general revelation" in nature and in human conscience. This "natural" or rational branch of theology, however, was given only an introductory task in relation to "revealed theology,"[2] but Scripture was increasingly regarded as being understandable and openly intelligible in the sense that it lies open to the judgment of reason.[3]

It seems that due to the critical attacks on Scripture by their opponents, who tried to undermine the confidence in Scripture by pointing to its defects, the Protestant dogmaticians of this period tried to ascribe new reliability to Scripture by means of rational argument. They adopted the prevailing scholastic methods of their opponents and began structuring theology as a logical system[4] of belief in reliance on Aristotelian philosophy and syllogistic reasoning.[5] External criteria by which the divine authorship

---

[1] Bromiley, **Historical Theology**, 317.

[2] Ragnar Holte, "Rationality and the Christian Tradition," in **Belief in God and Intellectual Honesty**, ed. Ruurd Veldhuis, Andy F. Sanders and Heine J. Siebrand (Assen/Maastricht: Van Gorcum, 1990), 84. See also Schmid, 45-55, on the role of reason as handmaid of theology.

[3] So Reid, **The Authority of Scripture**, 79.

[4] On the history and use of the term "system" and "systematic method," see Alois von der Stein, "Der Systembegriff in seiner geschichtlichen Entwicklung," in **System und Klassifikation in Wissenschaft und Dokumentation**, ed. A. Diemer (Meisenheim am Glan: Verlag Anton Hain, 1968), 1-13; and the in-depth study by Otto Ritschl, **System und systematischen Methode in der Geschichte des wissenschaftlichen Sprachgebrauchs in der philosophischen Methodologie** (Bonn: A. Marcus and E. Webers Verlag, 1906), which despite its age is still the most comprehensive discussion. Cf. also idem, "Literarhistorische Beobachtungen über die Nomenklatur der theologischen Disziplinen im 17. Jahrhundert," in **Studien zur systematischen Theologie. Festschrift für Theodor Haering zum 70. Geburtstag**, ed. Friedrich Traub (Tübingen: J. C. B. Mohr, 1918), 76-85. Although the expression "systematic" was in use for quite some time, it seems that it was the Reformed theologian Batholomaeus Keckermann who in 1600 first applied the analytical method in a systematic fashion in his **Systema sacrosanctae theologiae**. Otto Ritschl, **System und systematischen Methode**, 25-30. See also Hans Emil Weber, **Der Einfluss der protestantischen Schulphilosophie auf die orthodox-lutherische Dogmatik**, 20ff; and Althaus, **Die Prinzipien der deutschen reformierten Dogmatik**, 20-36.

[5] Muller, **Post-Reformation Reformed Dogmatics**, 1:28-40, 36; Althaus, **Die Prinzipien der deutschen reformierten Dogmatik**, 230-273; Ernst Bizer, **Frühorthodoxie und**

of Scripture might be known increasingly were emphasized to a point where Scripture was judged in the light of reason to a degree which was not the case with Luther and Calvin.[1] In the attempt to make the authority of Scripture reasonable and knowable, we have, as Preus has aptly stated, "one of the most unfortunate concessions to rationalism in the theology of Lutheran orthodoxy."[2] Reason, however, was not as yet given the right to criticize Scripture.[3] Nevertheless, history seems to justify the comment of Koehler, that "reason in theology has always had the tendency to change from minister (Diener) to magister (Herr)."[4] This inconsistency between criteria and the self-validation of Scripture through the Spirit would eventually have far-reaching consequences for Protestant theology.[5]

Rationalismus, ThSt 71 (Zurich: EVZ Verlag, 1963); Rogers and McKim, **The Authority and Interpretation of the Bible**, 185-186.

[1]Cf. Bromiley, **Historical Theology**, 318; Althaus, **Die Prinzipien der deutschen reformierten Dogmatik**, 201-273; Heim, 282, 298. Reid has described the shift as follows: "the primacy of faith gives way, first to an equality of faith with reason: faith must at least be intelligible. But the equality is difficult to maintain. The faith is intellectually conceived, and then it is reason and not faith that moves up into the dominant position. The authority of Scripture is compromised and made equivocal" **(The Authority of Scripture**, 94). This recourse to external criteria "reveals a certain concession to rationalism which is inherent in their theological method . . . and betrays a certain inconsistency with their rigid adherence to the $\alpha\dot{\nu}\tau o\pi\iota\sigma\tau\dot{\eta}\alpha$ of Scripture and to their principles of *sola scriptura* and *sola fide*. The witness of the Spirit which is *sola fides* and which is the result of *sola gratia* simply rules out the necessity and the validity of any observable criteria" (Preus, **The Inspiration of Scripture**, 114). Werner Elert traces the practice to use external "testimonies" for Scripture back to Melanchton and concludes that by doing this Melanchton "trod a path which later became disastrous for establishing the basis of the authority of Scripture" **(The Structure of Lutheranism**, vol. 1, **The Theology and Philosophy of Life of Lutheranism Especially in the Sixteenth and Seventeenth Centuries**, trans. Walter A. Hansen [St. Louis, MS: Concordia Publishing House, 1962], 197). For a list of some of the external and internal criteria for the divine authority of Scripture, see Preus, **The Theology of Post-Reformation Lutheranism**, 1:301; idem, **The Inspiration of Scripture**, 106-108.

[2]Preus, **The Theology of Post-Reformation Lutheranism**, 1:303.

[3]Bizer, 65; Holte, 84; cf. also Hornig, 45, 52.

[4]Cf. Walther Koehler, **Dogmengeschichte als Geschichte des christlichen Selbstbewusstseins: Das Zeitalter der Reformation** (Zurich: Max Niehans Verlag, 1951), 2:135.

[5]Hans-Martin Barth, **Atheismus und Orthodoxie: Analysen und Modelle christlicher Apologetik im 17. Jahrhundert** FSÖTh 26 (Göttingen: Vandenhoeck & Ruprecht, 1971), 314-315, concludes his fascinating study about the Christian apologists of the seventeenth century in their debate with atheists by saying: "Die Apologeten des 17. Jahrhunderts hatten versucht, mit ihrem Gegner in der Auseinandersetzung über den Atheismus eine gemeinsame Ebene zu finden. . . . Diese ihre Überzeugung von der Selbstverständlichkeit des Glaubens machte sie ihren Gegnern gegenüber verständnislos. Gerade ihr so eifriger Versuch, mit dem Gegner auf eine Ebene zu kommen, endete damit, daß sie ihm ferner standen, als sie sich überhaupt vorstellen konnten. Sie verstanden ihn nicht und waren deshalb nicht in der Lage, ihm zum Verstehen zu helfen. . . . Sie meinten, für Gott zu kämpfen, und kämpften doch nur für ein philosophisches System, das von nun

It should be noted that in this context the Creeds came to be regarded in a new light and with fresh importance.[1] They not only expounded intellectually what Scripture says, at greater length, but also tried to define it. Thus, as Koehler has pointed out, the creeds which were intended as defenders of right doctrine against the attacks from outside became their own inner justification and, finally, achieved a position alongside of Holy Scripture.[2] As the Lutheran scholar Quanbeck has pointed out, one function of the creeds has been a hermeneutic one: they serve as standards and guides to the interpretation of the Bible in the church.[3] Thus, Scripture has been domesticated by dogmatics in orthodox theology, even though it so strongly emphasized the Scripture principle.[4]

This development had far-reaching consequences. In that the Scripture principle had become rational, it was now rationally refutable.[5] Therefore, theology increasingly was challenged rationally, historically, and otherwise during the following

---

an prinzipiell der Vergangenheit angehören sollte. Sie wollten im Namen Gottes die Aufklärung stoppen--und standen damit in Wahrheit nicht der Aufklärung, sondern Gott im Wege. Statt sich auf die *theologische* Fragestellung nach der Existenz Gottes und auf *biblische* Antworten zu besinnen, machten sie den Glauben an Gott zu einer scheinbar rational einsichtigen Angelegenheit. . . . Sie wiesen damit die Christenheit auf einen Weg, der in den Theologien des Todes Gottes endete. Ihrem Ansatz ist es zur Last zu legen, wenn die Theologie noch im 20. Jahrhundert die Probleme noch nicht bewältigt hat, die ihr die Aufklärung vor 300 Jahren stellte."

[1]So Reid, **The Authority of Scripture**, 94, who draws from Koehler, 136.

[2]Koehler, 136; cf. Reid, **The Authority of Scripture**, 95. According to John Dillenberger and Claude Welch, **Protestant Christianity Interpreted Through Its Development** (New York: Charles Scribner's Sons, 1954), 97, "Orthodox theology now tended to be the custodian of biblical truth. Theology came before the Bible, as the key to its interpretation, rather than after it, as its explication."

[3]Quanbeck, 177, 181. Hayes and Prussner concur when they say that "it is certainly not too much to say that dogmatic systems completely outweighed any other form of religious authority, even overshadowing that of the Bible or of personal religious experience. What the Protestant churches did was to create their own tradition, in the form of dogmas summarized in the so-called 'symbolic books' (confessions and credal statements), which came to have its own authority" (John H. Hayes and Frederick Prussner, **Old Testament Theology: Its History and Development** [Atlanta: John Knox Press, 1985], 13).

[4]Ebeling, **Dogmatik des Christlichen Glaubens**, 1:33. Hornig, 51, speaks of a secret dominance of the already fixed dogmatic teachings which resulted in a dogmatically bound exegesis, which provided dogmatics with many new dicta probantia but was not able to correct or even question its teachings. Similarly F. Lau, "Orthodoxie, altprotestantische," **RGG**, 4:1724.

[5]So Otto Weber, **Foundations of Dogmatics**, trans. Darrell L. Guder (Grand Rapids, MI: Eerdmans, 1981), 1:119-120.

period.¹ Orthodoxy did not produce the Enlightenment, as Otto Weber has pointed out, but "Orthodoxy prepared the way for rationalism as the preferred and characteristic thought structure of the Age of Enlightenment, especially theological Rationalism."²

Evangelicalism

Evangelicalism, which claims its roots go back at least as far as the Protestant Reformation,³ is marked by a surprising and fascinating diversity⁴ that transcends denominational and confessional boundaries.⁵ Despite its wide diversity, both

---

¹One such challenge came from the Socinians who challenged, among other things, the doctrine of the Trinity and the substitutionary atonement on rational grounds. Although the Socinians tried to provide a new certainty by recourse to the secure and undisputable norms of reason, they still accorded the Bible a central place in their system and were convinced that they were putting forward more consistently the Protestant principle of Scripture as the sole authority and norm of faith. This has been shown nicely by Scholder, **The Birth of Modern Critical Theology**, 32-34. That the Socinian system came into being before the great philosophical and mathematical movements of the seventeenth century is indicated by the fact that the Socinians had no hesitation in acknowledging Biblical miracles like the famous passage about the standing still of the sun in Jos 10:12f. Scholder, 42-43. On the Socinians, see also P. Wrzecionko, "Vernunft und Wahrheit im Denken der Sozinianer und der altprotestantischen Orthodoxie," **NZSTR** 14 (1972): 172-196; and J. H. S. Kent, "The Socinian Tradition," **Theol** 78 (1975): 131-140.

²Otto Weber, **Foundations of Dogmatics**, 1:129.

³Cf. Donald G. Bloesch, "Evangelicalism," in **A New Handbook of Christian Theology**, ed. Donald W. Musser and Joseph L. Price (Nashville, TN: Abingdon, 1992), 168-169; idem, **The Future of Evangelical Christianity: A Call for Unity Amid Diversity** (Colorado Springs: Helmers & Howard, 1988); R. V. Pierard, "Evangelicalism," **Evangelical Dictionary of Theology**, ed. Walter A. Elwell (Grand Rapids, MI: Baker Book House, 1984), 380-383; Bernard Ramm, **The Evangelical Heritage** (Waco, TX: Word Books, 1973).

⁴"There are three indisputable facts about the evangelical tradition in America. First, it is important. Second, it is understudied. Third, it is diverse" (Leonard I. Sweet, "The Evangelical Tradition in America," in **The Evangelical Tradition in America**, ed. Leonard I. Sweet [Macon, GA: Mercer University Press, 1984], 1). On the rich diversity of Evangelicalism, see the contributions in Donald W. Dayton and Robert K. Johnston, eds., **The Variety of American Evangelicalism** (Downers Grove, IL: InterVarsity Press, 1991); and Mark Ellingsen, **The Evangelical Movement: Growth, Impact, Controversy, Dialog** (Minneapolis: Augsburg Publishing House, 1988); cf. also Robert W. Yarbrough, "Evangelical Theology in Germany," **EvQ** 65/4 (1993): 329-353.

⁵"Evangelicalism" is used by us as a broad umbrella term to refer to contemporary "theologically conservative Protestantism" which encompasses "a wide variety of religious and denominational traditions." As such it includes, but is not synonymous with "Fundamentalism" which is viewed "as a faction *within* Evangelicalism and not as a movement *distinct from* Evangelicalism" (James Davison Hunter, **Evangelicalism: The Coming Generation** [Chicago: University of Chicago Press, 1987], 3-4); see also idem, **American Evangelicalism: Conservative Religion and the Quandary of Modernity** (New Brunswick, NJ: Rutgers University Press, 1983). Millard J. Erickson also describes Evangelicalism as "conservative in its theology, maintaining that

sociologically and theologically, the Evangelical movement is united around a cluster of salient themes and doctrines, among which the divine authority and primacy of Scripture features very prominently.¹

As far as the origin of Scripture is concerned, one can safely say that all Evangelicals affirm its supernatural origin. God's normative revelation, which is propositional in nature,² is preserved in the teachings of the Bible. Thus, Scripture is regarded as "the divinely inspired record of God's revelation."³

The Evangelical view of inspiration can be expressed by means of the terms "verbal," "plenary," and "confluent."⁴ It is "verbal" in that the very words of

---

there has been a once-for-all or normative revelation by God in his Word, and that the teachings of the Bible must therefore be preserved from any erosion of modern thinking" ("Evangelicalism: USA," **The Blackwell Encyclopedia of Modern Christian Thought**, ed. Alister E. McGrath [Oxford: Basil Blackwell, 1993], 188). Alister A. McGrath, "Evangelicalism," **The Blackwell Encyclopedia of Modern Christian Thought** (Oxford: Basil Blackwell, 1993), 183 thinks that Evangelicalism "has now become a *trend within the mainstream denominations*." See also Ellingsen, **The Evangelical Movement**, 136-200. For a comprehensive survey of materials relating to Evangelicalism, see Edith L. Blumhofer and Joel A. Carpenter, eds., **Twentieth-Century Evangelicalism: A Guide to the Sources** (New York: Garland, 1990); Norris A. Magnuson and William G. Travis, **American Evangelicalism: An Annotated Bibliography** (West Cornwall, CT: Locust Hill Press, 1990); and Robert D. Shuster et al., **Researching Modern Evangelicalism: A Guide to the Holdings of the Billy Graham Center, with Information of Other Collections** (Westport, CT: Greenwood, 1990).

¹Other basic assumptions of Evangelicalism are the uniqueness of redemption through the death of Christ upon the cross, often linked with a substitutionary theory of atonement; the need for personal conversion; and the necessity, propriety and urgency of evangelism. See McGrath, "Evangelicalism," 183; Pierard, "Evangelicalism," 379-380; Donald A. Hagner, "What Is Distinctive about 'Evangelical' Scholarship?" **TSF Bulletin** 7/3 (1984), 5; Kenneth S. Kantzer and Carl F. H. Henry, eds., **Evangelical Affirmations** (Grand Rapids, MI: Zondervan Publishing House, 1990), 27-38. For a helpful bibliography on Evangelical views of the Bible, see John R. Muether, "Evangelicals and the Bible: A Bibliographic Postscript," in **Inerrancy and Hermeneutic: A Tradition, A Challenge, A Debate**, ed. Harvie M. Conn (Grand Rapids, MI: Baker Book House, 1988), 253-264.

²Carl F. H. Henry, who has been called "the most prominent evangelical theologian of the second half of the twentieth century" (Stanley J. Grenz and Roger E. Olson, **20th Century Theology: God and the World in a Transitional Age** [Downers Grove, IL: Inter Varsity Press, 1992], 288), describes God's revelation as "rational communication conveyed in intelligible ideas and meaningful words, that is, in conceptual-verbal form" (**God, Revelation and Authority**, 3:248-487, 248); see also Ronald H. Nash, **The Word of God and the Mind of Man: The Crisis of Revealed Truth in Contemporary Theology** (Grand Rapids, MI: Zondervan Publishing House, 1982).

³Pierard, "Evangelicalism," 379. James I. Packer has said that "the Word of God consists of *revealed truths*" (**'Fundamentalism' and the Word of God: Some Evangelical Principles** [Grand Rapids, MI: Eerdmans, 1958], 91).

⁴John Jefferson Davis, **Foundations of Evangelical Theology** (Grand Rapids, MI: Baker Book House, 1984), 174. Ellingson has pointed out that there is "some evidence which indicates

Scripture are the subjects of the Holy Spirit's special influence.[1] It is plenary, i.e., it extends to all parts of the canon,[2] and the process of inspiration is "confluent" in that the divine and human elements in the origin of Scripture "flow together."[3] While the human element in the writing down of Scripture is not denied, the words of Scripture are wholly God's. Thus, Evangelicals hold the Bible to be God's Word.[4]

As such, it is "the final and authoritative source of all doctrine."[5] Because Scripture in its entirety is given by the inspiration of the Holy Spirit, it speaks the truth and all presence of error is denied. Thus, there is an intimate connection between the understanding of the divine inspiration of Scripture and the affirmation of the Bible's

---

that the most crucial, if not the first affirmation typically made by Evangelicals is to establish their own position concerning the confession of the verbal and plenary inspiration of the Bible, of its infallibility and inerrancy (in the autographs [original manuscripts])" (**The Evangelical Movement**, 205). Ellingson concludes his survey of the Evangelical understanding of the inerrancy of Scripture by saying: "In any case, despite the reticence of a few Evangelicals, many analysts maintain, and this book will confirm, that the doctrine of biblical inerrancy (or at least an affirmation that the Bible is reliable and authoritative in all its parts) is the principal affirmation which provides the Evangelical movement with unity and a distinctive character" (ibid., 207). Thus, as late as 1975, Martin E. Marty, could still insist that so far as the doctrine of the inerrancy of Scripture is concerned there was no difference between the two groups ("Tensions Within Contemporary Evangelicalism: A Critical Appraisal," in **The Evangelicals: What They Believe, Who They Are, Where They Are Changing**, ed. David F. Wells and John D. Woodbridge [Nashville, TN: Abingdon, 1975], 173, 180). This might have been an exaggeration. Other Evangelical scholars, like Donald G. Bloesch, have pointed out later that the issue of inerrancy has been incorrectly identified as the distinctive characteristic of Evangelicalism (**The Future of Evangelical Christianity**, 11, 13). Nevertheless, Marty's assessment made in 1975 "highlights a point of some importance: until fairly recently, the infallibility or inerrancy of Scripture was one of the self-identifying flags of Evangelicalism, recognized by friend and foe alike" (Donald A. Carson, "Recent Developments in the Doctrine of Scripture," in **Hermeneutics, Authority, and Canon**, ed. D. A. Carson and John D. Woodbridge [Grand Rapids, MI: Zondervan Publishing House, 1986], 10). Cf. also Mark A. Noll, **Between Faith and Criticism: Evangelicals, Scholarship, and the Bible in America**, 2d ed. (Grand Rapids, MI: Baker Book House, 1991), esp. 143; and idem, "Evangelicals and the Study of the Bible," **RJ** 34/4 (1984): 11-22.

[1] Davis, **Foundations of Evangelical Theology**, 174. John Barton, in an informative article on verbal inspiration has aptly pointed out that "so long as we are talking about the inspiration of scripture, it is hard to see how we can avoid calling the inspiration verbal, since the Bible, being a book or collection of books, is composed of words. There is a considerable paradox in saying that a book is divinely inspired while denying that the inspiration extends to the words which comprise it" ("Verbal Inspiration," **A Dictionary of Biblical Interpretation**, ed. R. J. Coggins and J. L. Houlden [London: SCM Press, 1990], 721).

[2] This is held in contrast to view of "partial inspiration." Davis, **Foundations of Evangelical Theology**, 175.

[3] Ibid., 176.

[4] Kantzer and Henry, 38.

[5] Ibid., 37.

inerrancy and infallibility among Evangelicals.¹ However, a heated debate has occurred among Evangelicals about the interpretation and implication of Biblical inerrancy and the scope of the authority of Scripture.² While one group seems to come to the issue of inerrancy more deductively from a certain perception of God and His sovereignty,³ the other side tries to approach this question more inductively from the phenomena of Scripture and has been more open for the idea of human limitations.⁴ The latter group still tries to combine a high view of scriptural authority, which, however, is usually coupled with a "willingness to accept the principle of historical criticism" and, consequently, has been termed "neo-evangelical theology."⁵

---

¹Ellingsen, **The Evangelical Movement**, 206.

²This is not the place to enter into a detailed discussion of the history of this debate among Evangelicals. It suffices to notice that Robert K. Johnston thinks that this issue is at an "impasse" among Evangelicals and acknowledges four types of inerrancy: detailed, partial, irenic, and complete inerrancy (**Evangelicals at an Impasse: Biblical Authority in Practice** [Atlanta, GA: John Knox Press, 1979], 19). Robert McNair Price discusses five major approaches under the terms "limited inerrancy," "partial infallibilitists," "pluriform canonists," "cultural deabsolutizing," and the rejection of *sola Scriptura* in favor of ecclesiastical and creedal authority ("The Crisis of Biblical Authority: The Setting and Range of the Current Evangelical Crisis" (Ph.D. dissertation, Drew University, 1981, 99-243). Gabriel Fackre has classified the options in the question of the authority of Scripture as "The Oracular View"; "The Inerrancy View," in which he distinguishes "Transmissive Inerrancy," "Trajectory Inerrancy," and "Intentional Inerrancy"; "The Infallibilist View," in which he distinguishes between "Unitive Infallibility," "Essential Infallibility," and "Christocentric infallibility" (**The Christian Story: A Pastoral Systematics, vol. 2, Authority: Scripture in the Church for the World** [Grand Rapids, MI: Eerdmans, 1987], 62-73).

³We are aware that this is an oversimplification that might not do justice to all the nuances of each position. It is well known, for instance, that Benjamin Warfield explicitly claims to apply the inductive method in establishing the Biblical doctrine of inspiration. Cf. Peter Maarten van Bemmelen, **Issues in Biblical Inspiration: Sanday and Warfield**, AUSDDS 13 (Berrien Springs, MI: Andrews University Press, 1988), 321. Other proponents of this group have argued for the incorporation of inductive and deductive processes, calling this interplay "adduction," "abduction," or "retroduction," respectively. See Arthur F. Holmes, "Ordinary Language Analysis and Theological Method," **JETS** 11 (1968): 131-138; John Warwick Montgomery, "The Theologians Craft: A Discussion of Theory Formation and Theory Testing in Theology," in **The Suicide of Theology** (Minneapolis: Bethany Fellowship, 1970), 267-313; and Paul D. Feinberg, "The Meaning of Inerrancy," in **Inerrancy**, ed. Norman L. Geisler (Grand Rapids, MI: Zondervan Publishing House, 1979), 265-304, 468-471.

⁴Here prominent Evangelical scholars like Clark H. Pinnock, Bernhard Ramm, and Donald G. Bloesch come to mind.

⁵The term neo-evangelicalism or new-evangelicalism can be traced back to the formation in 1942 of the National Association of Evangelicals and seems to have been popularized by Harold Ockenga in 1957. So George M. Marsden, **Reforming Fundamentalism: Fuller Seminary and the New Evangelicalism** (Grand Rapids, MI: Eerdmans, 1987), 3. Cf. also Bloesch, "Evangelicalism," 170; and McKim, **What Christians Believe about the Bible**, 82-94.

While the line that distinguishes Evangelicals from their fellow Fundamentalists[1] is not clear cut and, in fact, appears to be somewhat blurred,[2] it seems that "Fundamentalism represents the right wing of the evangelical movement"[3] that is characterized by propagating its belief in the inerrancy of Scripture, at times militantly.[4] A number of

---

[1]From the abundance of literature on Fundamentalism, see especially the helpful overviews and discussion in the recent issues of **Concilium** (1992/3) and **RevExp** 79/1 (1982), and especially the articles by Miroslav Volf, "The Challenge of Protestant Fundamentalism," **Concilium** (1992/3): 97-106; and Bill J. Leonard, "The Origin and Character of Fundamentalism," **RevExp** 79/1 (1982): 5-17. See also Morris Ashcraft, "The Theology of Fundamentalism," **RevExp** 79/1 (1982): 31-44; idem, "The Strengths and Weaknessess of Fundamentalism," in **The Proceedings of the Conference on Biblical Inerrancy 1987** (Nashville, TN: Broadman Press, 1987), 531-541; and Timothy P. Weber, "The Two-Edged Sword: The Fundamentalist Use of the Bible," in **The Bible in America: Essays in Cultural History**, ed. Nathan O. Hatch and Mark A. Noll (New York: Oxford University Press, 1982), 101-120. It has been pointed out that "fundamentalism was originally a broad coalition of antimodernists. From the 1920s to the 1940s, to be a fundamentalist meant only to be theologically traditional, a believer in the fundamentals of evangelical Christianity, and willing to take a militant stand against modernism. *Conservative* was sometimes a synonym. So to call oneself a fundamentalist did not necessarily imply, as it virtually does today, that one was either a dispensationalist or a separatist. Neither did it necessarily imply, despite efforts to the contrary by its detractors, that one was obscurantist, anti-intellectual, or a political extremist" (Marsden, **Reforming Fundamentalism**, 10). Fundamentalism seems to have received its name from the publication of **The Fundamentals: A Testimony to the Truth**, 12 vols. (Chicago: Testimony Publishing Co., 1910-1915). In them, five essential doctrines, which were under attack in the church, were affirmed: the inerrancy of Scripture, the virgin birth of Christ, the substitutionary atonement of Christ, Christ's bodily resurrection, and the historicity of the miracles (C. T. McIntire, "Fundamentalism," **Evangelical Dictionary of Theology**, ed. Walter A. Elwell [Grand Rapids, MI: Baker Book House, 1984], 433). The term "Fundamentalist" was probably first used in 1920 by Curtis Lee Laws in the Baptist **Watchman-Examiner** (ibid.).

[2]George Marsden claims that even in the late 1940s the distinction of later days between "evangelical" and "fundamentalist" has to be put aside because they "were not then separate entities" (**Reforming Fundamentalism**, 3); cf. William Vance Trollinger, Jr., "Fundamentalism," in **A New Handbook of Christian Theology**, ed. Donald W. Musser and Joseph L. Price (Nashville, TN: Abingdon, 1992), 195. Ellingsen, **The Evangelical Movement**, 97, speaks of an "organic interpenetration of the Evangelical movement and Fundamentalism," although he also points out that the two are not identical.

[3]Bloesch, **The Future of Evangelical Christianity**, 24. It seems that the term "Fundamentalist" eventually came to designate separatistic groups, whose principal mark was belief in the inerrancy of the Bible. James Barr, **Fundamentalism** (Philadelphia: Westminster Press, 1977), 1, and passim.

[4]According to George Marsden, "A Fundamentalist is an Evangelical who is angry about something. That seems simple and is fairly accurate," (**Understanding Fundamentalism and Evangelicalism** [Grand Rapids, MI: Eerdmans, 1991], 1, 4). "While militancy against modernism was the *key distinguishing* factor that drew fundamentalists together, militancy was not necessarily the *central* trait of fundamentalists. Mission, evangelism, prayer, personal holiness, or a variety of doctrinal concerns may often or usually have been their first interest. Yet, without militancy, none of these important aspects of the movement set it apart as 'fundamentalist'" (George M. Marsden, **Fundamentalism and American Culture: The Shaping of Twentieth-Century Evangelicalism: 1870-1925** [New York: Oxford University Press, 1980], 231, n. 4).

rationalistic-oriented Evangelicals[1] seem to have accepted inductive scientific rationalism to defend the trustworthiness of Scripture and have thereby implicitly accepted a rather modern approach to Scripture.[2] This scientific, rational, logical approach to Scripture has the tendency to judge the truth of the Bible in terms of its correspondence to scientifically established data. This means, however, as Mark Corner has aptly observed about Fundamentalism and which also applies to Evangelicalism, that

> despite its overt hostility to 'liberalism' it could be claimed that fundamentalism shares with its opponent a reductionistic, scientific mentality, and that in some ways both come from the same stable. One uses science to reject the Christian faith as traditionally perceived, the other uses it to prove it; neither is sufficiently aware of problems concerning the nature and limitations of its particular scientific approach.[3]

These presuppositions lead to a reductionistic view of Scripture where some parts, like the literal understanding of the creation story, have to be reinterpreted so that the Biblical data can be harmonized with current scientific data.[4]

In its attempt to give a rationalistic foundation for the belief in the divinity of Scripture, a sizeable number of Evangelical scholars show certain affinities with Protestant Orthodoxy.[5] Although Scripture seems to be the primary source in most of Evangelical theology, it hardly can be said to be the final norm in all areas. Rather, reason and human logic often appear to be the final arbiter. Thus, despite its commendable intentions to defend Scripture on rational grounds with modern means, in doing so these Evangelicals risk losing sight of the self-authentication of Scripture. No less problematic is the attempt of Neo-Evangelical scholars to use historical-critical methodologies moderately, even in defense of Scripture.[6] Again, Neo-Evangelicals

---

[1]Names like Norman L. Geisler, R. C. Sproul, Carl F. H. Henry, Ronald H. Nash, Gordon R. Lewis, and Bruce A. Demarest could be mentioned.

[2]What Miroslav Volf has said about Fundamentalists is equally applicable for Evangelicals (Volf, 101-102).

[3]Mark Corner, "Fundamentalism," **A Dictionary of Biblical Interpretation**, ed. R. J. Coggins and J. L. Houlden (London: SCM Press, 1990), 244. Jürgen Moltmann also recognizes that modernism and fundamentalism "really belong together in their deepest layers" ("Christianity in the Third Millennium," **TToday** 51/1 [1994]: 83).

[4]Wilfried Joest, "Fundamentalismus," in **TRE**, 11:736; Corner, 244.

[5]This is seen by Joest, "Fundamentalismus," 734; James Barr, "Fundamentalismus," **EKL**, 1:1404-1405.

[6]This recently and forcefully has been pointed out by former historical-critical scholar Eta

appear to work within modern parameters that ultimately seem to question the very thing they try to affirm, namely, the authority of Scripture alone.

Summary

Despite differences in emphasis and consistency, the above discussed positions share a commonality that unites them all. All of them affirm a divine origin of Scripture where some form of cognitive content is supernaturally communicated from God to man and where the writing down of this special revelation is supervised by God Himself. Hence, it is understandable that there is a common concern to define rather clearly the nature of Biblical inspiration and authority.[1] All the foregoing perspectives associate the authority of Scripture intimately with the words of the text. Thus, the way Scripture expresses itself as well as its content count as authoritative. Because the words of Scripture are God's words, Scripture carries inherently divine authority.[2] Thus, it seems not illegitimate to describe the position of this "type" as a form of "Biblicism."[3]

Linnemann who has completely abandoned the use of the historical-critical method because of its incompatibility with the supernatural claims of Scripture (**Historical Criticism of the Bible: Methodology or Ideology?**, trans. Robert W. Yarbrough [Grand Rapids, MI: Baker Book House, 1990]); see also Thomas C. Oden, **After Modernity--What? Agenda for Theology** (Grand Rapids, MI: Zondervan Publishing House, 1990). Cf. also the perceptive comment about the historical-critical methodology and American evangelicals' partially lighthearted use of it in Yarbrough, "Evangelical Theology in Germany," 335.

[1]Cf. Millard J. Erickson, "Immanence, Transcendence, and the Doctrine of Scripture," in **The Living and Active Word of God: Studies in Honor of Samuel J. Schultz**, ed. Morris Inch and Ronald Youngblood (Winona Lake, IN: Eisenbrauns, 1983), 200.

[2]Ibid., 200.

[3]Otto Ritschl has said that the position on Scripture, as held by the old Reformers, including Luther, can be described as "Biblicism" (Biblicismus) (**Dogmengeschichte des Protestantismus: Grundlagen und Grundzüge der theologischen Gedanken- und Lehrbildung in den protestantischen Kirchen, vol. 1, Prolegomena: Biblicismus und Traditionalismus in der altprotestantischen Theologie** [Leipzig: J. C. Hinrichsche Buchhandlung, 1908], 196). This certainly holds true for Protestant Orthodoxy as well as for Evangelicalism. The term "Biblicism" is frequently used pejoratively to describe a strong attachment to the Bible as the objectively authoritative Word of God and is used by some Evangelicals "to indicate their commitment to the absolute authority of the Bible in all matters of faith and practice" (J. J. Scott, Jr., "Biblicism, Bibliolatry," **Evangelical Dictionary of Theology**, ed. Walter A. Elwell [Grand Rapids, MI: Baker Book House, 1984], 152). The term "Bibliolatry" seems to go back at least as far as Gotthold Ephraim Lessing ("Bibliolatrie," in **Lessings Werke**, 25 vols., ed. Leopold Zscharnack [Berlin: Deutsches Verlagshaus Bong & Co., 1925], 23:307-312). See also Moisés Silva, **God, Language and Scripture: Reading the Bible in the Light of General Linguistics**, FCI 4 (Grand Rapids, MI: Zondervan Publishing House, 1990), 38.

Furthermore, although all affirm the confluence of the divine and the human element in the production of Scripture, all seem to stress the divine aspect of Scripture so that for all practical purposes the human element is made subservient to the divine-- at least as far as the freedom[1] of the Biblical writers in composing the divine message is concerned.[2] This seems to be more pronounced in the Reformed tradition where God's absolute sovereignty and complete control is emphasized to a greater degree. One gets the impression that the stronger the supernatural aspect of Scripture is emphasized, the greater the reservations become to the employment of critical methodology.[3]

While all are united in their attempt to apply the *sola Scriptura* principle to decide matters of faith and practice by Scripture alone, one can also detect certain differences. It seems that the Reformed tradition is more emphatic than Lutheranism in its iterated assertion of the Scripture principle because it is carried further.[4] The Lutheran tradition, in general, has retained in its worship those practices and customs not directly prohibited by Scripture. The Reformed tradition has tended to eliminate

---

[1]By freedom we think of what has often been termed "libertarian free will." According to one philosopher, this understanding of free will is expressed when a person is free with respect to performing an action if she "has it in her power to choose to perform action A or choose not to perform action A. *Both A and not A could actually occur*; which *will* actually occur has *not yet been determined*" (David Basinger, "Middle Knowledge and Classical Christian Thought," **RS** 22 [1986], 416), (emphasis supplied).

[2]This is most pronounced in the so-called "dictation" theory, especially of Protestant Orthodoxy, but also of Calvin. With regards to the former, it is often claimed that many proposed the view that even the vowel points of the Hebrew text were dictated by the Holy Spirit. On Calvin and the "dictation" theory, see the discussion in H. Jackson Forstman, 50-62; for a balanced account of the background to the problem of the vowel points in Protestant Orthodoxy, see Richard A. Muller, "The Debate over the Vowel Points and the Crisis in Orthodox Hermeneutics," **JMRS** 10/1 (1980): 53-72; idem, **Post-Reformation Reformed Dogmatics**, 2:418-437; Ludwig Diestel, **Geschichte des Alten Testaments in der Christlichen Kirche** (Jena: Mauke, 1869), 334-341; and Preus, **The Theology of Post-Reformation Lutheranism**, 1:307-309.

[3]Erickson has pointed out that while 'lower' or textual criticism is usually practiced, representatives of a high view of Scripture usually see "serious problems with different varieties of 'higher' criticism. In particular, these thinkers object to the philosophical presuppositions underlying or incorporated into the method. The negative criticism rests upon the premise of naturalism rather than supernaturalism. Consequently, instead of letting criticism judge the Bible they propose that higher criticism must be judged and corrected by the Biblical revelation" ("Immanence, Transcendence, and Scripture," 200-201).

[4]Otto Ritschl, **Dogmengeschichte des Protestantismus**, 196, has spoken of the tendency towards a formally more consistent use of Scripture in the Reformed Tradition.

what is not expressly commanded in Scripture.[1] This raises the question whether the *sola Scriptura* principle has really been put in force consistently in Protestant theology. Otto Ritschl's conclusion that Lutheranism, including Luther and Lutheran Orthodoxy, has practiced only "an eclective Biblicism" (eklektischen Biblizismus)[2] could equally well be extended to the Reformed tradition[3] and even to Evangelicalism. Thus it appears that most if not all representatives of this "model" have followed at some point presuppositions that were not derived and shaped by Scripture alone. Hence, no consistent application of the Scripture principle has been practiced so far. This leads one to the alternative model where Scripture is perceived to have come "from below."

Scripture from Below

The second aspect of this investigation into the role of Scripture in theology considers instances that exemplify a view where Scripture is understood to have come ultimately "from below." This constitutes a radically different model from the one discussed above in that man rather than God is ultimately involved in the origin of Scripture.[4] This "paradigm shift"[5] in the understanding of the origin of Scripture

---

[1]Cf. Norman Sykes, "The Religion of Protestants," in **CHB**, 3:176.

[2]Otto Ritschl, **Dogmengeschichte des Protestantismus**, 196.

[3]Several scholars have pointed out that the representatives of the so-called Radical Reformation tried to follow the original intentions of Luther, "only by carrying them out consistently" (Reventlow, **The Authority of the Bible**, 50). Noted church historian Fritz Blanke claims that the Anabaptists moved towards a more literal, more strict observance of Holy Scripture than Zwingli and says: "Die Autorität der Bibel ist für Zwingli und für die von ihm ausgehenden Täufer die Richtschnur, aber in der Anwendung dieser Richtschnur denken die Täufer im einzelnen buchstäblicher, biblizistischer. So entsteht zwischen dem Lehrer Zwingli und seinen ultrazwinglianischen Lehrlingen der Widerspruch. Man wird sagen dürfen, daß das Täufertum gerade in diesem Widerspruch, d.h. in seiner Berufung auf die heilige Schrift allein, eine--freilich eigenwillige--Tochter der Reformation geblieben ist" (**Brüder in Christo. Die Geschichte der ältesten Täufergemeinde** [Zurich: Zwingli Verlag, 1955], 56). Alister McGrath goes so far as to say that the Radical Reformation was "the only wing of the Reformation to have been utterly consistent in its application of the *scriptura sola* principle" (**Reformation Thought**, 108-109). This view is also shared by notable church historian Bainton, who writes: "Of all the parties in the Reformation, the Anabaptists were the most scriptural. They were the ones who formulated and adhered to the principle often attributed to Zwingli, that only that which is expressly allowed in the Bible is permissible" ("The Bible in the Reformation," 3:5). In that sense, one could say that the Radical Reformation was not only a "wing" or a side effect of the Reformation begun by Luther but, instead, a "reformation of the Reformation." Cf. J. A. Oosterbaan, "The Reformation of the Reformation: Fundamentals of Anabaptist Theology," **MQR** 51 (1977): 176.

[4]It has been said that "as for Scripture, theological liberalism understands the Bible, as it understands the person of the Redeemer, primarily in human categories. The Bible is essentially a human book whose message is *inspiring*--insofar as it is consonant with contemporary thought-

significantly changed its role in theology.¹ This new view flowered into full bloom during the Enlightenment² and it continues to impact theology even now. Therefore, this study briefly notes some pertinent aspects that caused this revolution in thought before dealing with some specific representatives of this model.

The Impact of the Enlightenment

The Enlightenment ushered in a period of considerable uncertainty for Christianity because traditional Christian thought was radically challenged. This challenge brought about a radical shift, among other things, in the understanding and role of Scripture.³ In a fundamental and significant way, Kant described the terms of the Enlightenment by saying: "Our age is the true age of criticism, to which all things

---

categories--but not *inspired* in the sense tha that the authors were guided in a unique way by God's Spirit in what they wrote" (Paul King Jewett, **God, Creation, and Revelation: A Neo-Evangelical Theology** [Grand Rapids, MI: Eerdmans, 1991], 12).

⁵Hans Küng has used the term "Paradigm Change," which he took over from Thomas Kuhn, to describe different periods in the history of theology. Thus, he speaks of a "Modern Enlightenment Paradigm" (**Theology for the Third Millennium**, 128). Cf. also the contributions in Hans Küng and David Tracy, eds., **Paradigm Change in Theology: A Symposium for the Future**, trans. Margaret Köhl (New York: Crossroad, 1989). For an analysis and critique of the concept of paradigm and paradigm change for theology, see Frank M. Hasel, "Scientific Revolution: An Analysis and Evaluation of Thomas Kuhn's Concept of Paradigm and Paradigm Change for Theology," **JATS** 2/2 (1991): 160-177.

¹On the changed role of Scripture that took place during the eighteenth century, see the excellent study by Hans W. Frei, **The Eclipse of Biblical Narrative: A Study in Eighteenth and Nineteenth Century Hermeneutics** (New Haven: Yale University Press, 1974).

²The term "Enlightenment" is a self-designation which was used by the followers of this movement in a positive sense. Yet, the term "Enlightenment" remains a loose term that defies precise definition because it embraces a cluster of ideas and attitudes. "Nevertheless, an emphasis upon the ability of human reason to penetrate the mysteries of the world is rightly regarded as a defining characteristic of 'Enlightenment'" (Alister E. McGrath, "Enlightenment," **The Blackwell Encyclopedia of Modern Christian Thought**, ed. Alister E. McGrath [Oxford: Basil Blackwell, 1993], 150-156). Out of the innumerable sources on the Enlightenment, see the overview given by Peter Gay, **The Enlightenment: An Interpretation: The Rise of Modern Paganism** (New York: Alfred A. Knopf, 1966); and Rainer Piepmeier, "Aufklärung: I. Philosophisch," **TRE** 4:575-594; and Martin Schmidt, "Aufklärung: II. Theologisch," **TRE** 4:594-608 with further literature.

³McGrath mentions six major areas of traditional Christian theology which were in conflict with the rational religion of the Enlightenment: miracles, revelation, original sin, the problem of evil, the status and interpretation of Scripture, and the identity and significance of Jesus Christ ("Enlightenment," 154-155). Cf. Bruce Demarest, "The Bible in the Enlightenment Era," in **Challenges to Inerrancy: A Theological Response**, ed. Gordon R. Lewis and Bruce Demarest (Chicago: Moody Press, 1984), 11-47.

must be subjected."[1] The motto of the Enlightenment, therefore, was *Sapere aude*, have courage to use your own understanding.[2] This meant that in the Enlightenment human reason replaced any external authorities as arbiters of truth and reason became the ultimate criterion for the exposition of Scripture.[3] One can see a number of stages in the development of the principle of the omnipotence of human reason.[4] But ultimately it was reason which determined what constitutes revelation.[5] The

---

[1] Immanuel Kant, **Critique of Pure Reason**, trans. J. M. D. Meiklejohn (London: J. M. Dent & Sons, 1959), v, as quoted in Karl Barth, **Protestant Thought: From Rousseau to Ritschl**, trans. Brian Cozens (New York: Simon and Schuster, 1969), 153.

[2] Immanuel Kant, **What Is Enlightenment?**, trans. and ed. Lewis White Beck (Indianapolis: Bobbs-Merrill, 1959): 85. In 1784 Immanuel Kant defined Enlightenment as the spirit's determination to exercise its intellectual faculties in unfettered integrity. Enlightenment is man's release from his self-incurred tutelage which is his inability to make use of his understanding without direction from another. It was man's rise from the immaturity which caused him to rely on such external authorities as the Bible, the church, tradition, etc., to tell him what to think and do (ibid.).

[3] So Reventlow, **The Authority of the Bible**, 277. "More than anything else the Enlightenment marks a revolt against authoritarianism and the emergence of individual reason and conscience as the primary arbiter of truth. . . . The ideal of the Enlightenment is the duty of not entertaining any belief that is not warranted by rational evidence, which means by the assent of autonomous reason rather than biblical or ecclesiastical authority. . . . For men of the Enlightenment, the will or law of God can only be followed autonomously--only when the divine commands can be transformed into general laws which can become universal, rational axioms of behavior" (James C. Livingston, **Modern Christian Thought: From the Enlightenment to Vatican II** [New York: Macmillan Company, 1971], 3). Hugh Ross Mackintosh, **Types of Modern Theology: Schleiermacher to Barth** (New York: Charles Scribner's Sons, 1937), 14, describes the spirit of the Enlightenment in similar terms when he writes that reason is put "on the seat of judgment, and . . . that every Christian doctrine must undergo trial in the court of reason. . . . Only what is rational can be accepted." Similarly David A. Pailin, "Enlightenment," **The Westminster Dictionary of Christian Theology**, ed. Alan Richardson and John Bowden (Philadelphia: Westminster Press, 1983), 179; and Grenz and Olson, 20.

[4] Karl Aner has shown the increasing dominance of the role of reason in relation to divine revelation by pointing out that in Wolffian rationalism one can still see the attempt to preserve reason and revelation; later one finds only reason and the concept of revelation but no longer any content of revelation; in rationalism, finally, one finds the identification of reason with the content of revelation without any concept of revelation (**Die Theologie der Lessingzeit** [Halle: Verlag von Max Niemeyer, 1929], 4). For a similar description, see also McGrath, "Enlightenment," 152, who says: "First, it was argued that the beliefs of Christianity were rational, and thus capable of standing up to critical examination. . . . The notion of divine revelation was thus maintained. Second, it was argued that the basic ideas of Christianity, being rational, could be derived from reason itself. . . . All so-called 'revealed religion' is actually nothing other that the reconfirmation of what can be known through rational reflection on nature. . . . 'Revelation' was simply a rational reaffirmation of moral truths already available to enlightened reason. Third, the ability of reason to judge revelation was affirmed."

[5] John Locke, **The Reasonableness of Christianity**, section 14, says: "Reason must be our last judge in everything," as quoted in H. D. McDonald, **Theories of Revelation: A Historical Study 1700-1960** (Grand Rapids, MI: Baker Book House, 1979), 41-42. Nothing

predictability of nature's working let many thinkers of this period to conclude that there is no supernatural power that enters the realm of nature and history. In particular, the idea of a supernatural communication of information was more and more questioned until special revelation was denied altogether.[1]

Going hand in hand with the collapse of special revelation was the decline in the belief in the divine (verbal) inspiration of Scripture as held by orthodox Christianity.[2] With respect to Scripture, this meant that the Bible no longer was regarded as a divinely inspired source of doctrine and morals.[3] Inspiration was either rejected altogether or attributed to the creativity of the human writer.[4] Thus, Scripture no longer was differentiated from other types of literature and was treated "as if it were any other book."[5] The Bible increasingly was seen as the work of many hands, a book demonstrating internal contradictions, a historically and culturally conditiond document, one that was open to precisely the same methods of interpretation as any other literary work.[6]

---

contrary to reason can be accepted on the supposed authority of revelation. Revelation itself must have the approval of reason so that reason alone is the true judge. Locke reiterates that "Revelation must be judged by reason," John Locke, **On Human Understanding**, 595, as quoted in McDonald, **Theories of Revelation**, 42.

[1]Demarest, 33; on the development of the concept of revelation, see also the detailed study by McDonald, **Theories of Revelation**, 1-148. Although men like Locke did not explicitly reject divine revelation, their critical standpoints effectively emptied Christianity of its supernatural content and prepared the way for Deism and the anti-Christian polemics of more uncompromising thinkers. Gerald Hanratty, "Enlightenment," **The New Dictionary of Theology**, ed. Joseph A. Komonchak, Mary Collins and Dermot A. Lane (Wilmington, DE: Michael Glazier, 1987), 323. For Lessing there was an "ugly great ditch" between history and reason that lead him to accept only those truth's about God that were timeless and open to the investigation of human reason. Gotthold Ephraim Lessing, "On the Proof of the Spirit and of Power," in **Lessing's Theological Writings**, trans. Henry Chadwick (Stanford, CA: Stanford University Press, 1957), 55.

[2]"It is not that liberal theology rejected Holy Scripture. It relocated its authority. . . . The liberal mind found the authority of Holy Scripture in the religious experiences the Bible inspired and not in its dogmatic content, its divine inspiration, nor in its nature as a special revelation from God" (Bernard Ramm, "The Fortunes of Theology from Schleiermacher to Barth to Bultmann," in **Tensions in Contemporary Theology**, 2d ed., ed. Stanley N. Gundry and Alan F. Johnson [Grand Rapids, MI: Baker Book House, 1983], 28); also Demarest, 35.

[3]McGrath, "Enlightenment," 155.

[4]Demarest, 35.

[5]Benjamin Jowett, "On the Interpretation of Scripture," in **Essays and Reviews** (London: John Parker and Sons, 1860), 330-433.

[6]Hans-Joachim Kraus, **Geschichte der historisch-kritischen Erforschung des Alten**

Ernst Troeltsch, the German theologian turned historian,[1] has been credited with the classical formulation of modern historical-critical methodology as originated during the Enlightenment.[2] According to Troeltsch, three foundational principles characterize the procedure of the historical-critical method.[3] The first is the principle of correlation, according to which the phenomena of man's historical life are so related and interdependent that no radical change can take place within the historical nexus without affecting a change in all that immediately surrounds it. The second principle is that of analogy which describes the fundamental homogeneity of all historical events. It enables the historian to interpret the unknown from what is known. The third principle is that of criticism, according to which our judgment of the past can claim no absolute truth but only a greater or lesser degree of probability which must always remain open to revision.[4]

The application of these historical-critical principles to theology had far-reaching consequences. Developed to deal with natural events, the historical-critical method is bound, if applied to the supernatural, to dissolve theology and Scripture into the natural and to interpret it as analogous to everything else. According to Troeltsch, the historical-critical method is like a leaven: it transforms everything and finally bursts the

---

Testaments, 3d rev. and enl. ed. (Neukirchen-Vluyn: Neukirchener Verlag des Erziehungsvereins, 1982); Kümmel, **The New Testament**.

[1]Brian Gerrish, "From 'Dogmatik' to 'Glaubenslehre': A Paradigm Change in Modern Theology," in **Paradigm Change in Theology: A Symposium for the Future**, ed. Hans Küng and David Tracy, trans. Margaret Köhl (New York: Crossroad, 1989), 161-173.

[2]In Troeltsch's shadow much of contemporary theology still functions. See Austin Van Harvey, **The Historian and the Believer: The Morality of Historical Knowledge and Christian Belief** (New York: MacMillan Publishing Co., 1966), 3-37; Krentz, **The Historical-Critical Method**, 85.

[3]Ernst Troeltsch, "Über historische und dogmatische Methode in der Theologie," in **Gesammelte Schriften** (Tübingen: J. C. B. Mohr, 1913), 2:729-753.

[4]Karl Girgensohn, **Der Schriftbeweis in der evangelischen Dogmatik einst und jetzt** (Leipzig: A. Deichertsche Verlagsbuchhandlung, 1914), 37-41, has described the nature of modern science with the following characteristics: (1) the autonomy of human reason; (2) the principle of immanent explanation; (3) the tendency towards a mechanistic-causalistic explanation of reality. Girgensohn concludes by saying that this scientific understanding necessarily had to lead to a dissolution of the authority of Scripture. Even if it is allowed only at one place the Biblical authority is in principle put on hold [43]. More recently the atheistic character of modern science has been exposed in a penetrating critique by Gerhard Noller, **Metaphysik und Theologische Realisation. Das Ende der metaphysischen Grundstellung der Neuzeit und die Neubesinnung auf die theologische Wirklichkeit der Bibel** (Zurich: Theologischer Verlag, 1990), 67, 69, and passim.

entire mold of previous theological methods.¹ It has been pointed out that "one of the most striking features of the development of biblical interpretation during the nineteenth century was the way in which philosophical presuppositions implicitly guided it."² It is no surprise, therefore, that the new historical methods led to increasing doctrinal revisions and restatements of Christianity, so that Scripture no longer enjoyed the same theological authority it had with the original Reformers. Scripture no longer represented an independent criterion of truth; instead, it was made subordinate to the concept of natural, rational religion in such a way that only those Biblical elements which coincided with the content of "natural religion" were credited with abiding validity. Hence, Scripture was used only in so far as it illustrated "natural" theological truths.³

Furthermore, whereas "at the beginning of the seventeenth century the Bible was the universal authority in all fields of knowledge, . . . by the end of the century that authority was eroded."⁴ The new scientific impetus that came through important discoveries in the natural and astronomical sciences made a lasting impact on the understanding and authority of Scripture. Science is no longer informed by Scripture, but Scripture is interpreted through the conclusions of science. Hence, "the Scriptures are authoritative only within their own *scopus*, the transmission of matters of faith,"⁵ and authority of the Scriptures is further diminished.

Lastly, one can say that Kant's revolution in the area of philosophy also brought about a crisis in the authority of the Bible. Kant argued that it was impossible for pure reason to find God. This premise led to the collapse of the traditional arguments for the existence of God⁶ and to the development of arguments for the existence of God

---

¹Troeltsch, "Über historische und dogmatischen Methode in der Theologie," 2:730. In a different article, Troeltsch observes that the historical-critical method, once it gains entrance, brooks no limit (idem, "Geschichte und Metaphysik," **ZTK** 8 [1898]: 5-6).

²Robert M. Grant with David Tracy, **A Short History of the Interpretation of the Bible**, 2d ed. (Philadelphia: Fortress Press, 1984), 111.

³The real criterion of truth consisted in a principle of rationality. Holte, 84, 86.

⁴Krentz, 11.

⁵Ibid., 13; cf. the detailed description in Scholder, 46-109.

⁶Immanuel Kant, **Critique of Pure Reason**, 336-372, 371-372.

on the basis of practical reason.[1] Kant's philosophical approach allowed the possibility of a distinct knowledge of the material world but made it impossible to know anything beyond it.[2] The implications for theology are obviously immense:

> If God is, in the strictest sense, unknowable, then the proper object and study for theology is not God but man's religious states and sentiments and their individual and communal expressions. Theology becomes anthropology.[3]

Thus, the theology produced by following Kant's philosophical presuppositions remains anthropocentric and leads inescapably to an emphasis on the divine immanence.[4] Today, it seems virtually impossible to do theology without taking Kant's views into account.[5]

With these briefly presented aspects of the Enlightenment paradigm in mind, one is in a position to consider some representatives of this approach.

---

[1] Immanuel Kant, **Critique of Practical Reason**, trans. Lewis White Beck (Indianapolis: Bobbs-Merrill, 1956), 128-136, 130.

[2] Karl-Heinz Michel, **Immanuel Kant und die Frage der Erkennbarkeit Gottes. Eine kritische Untersuchung der 'Transzendentalen Ästhetik' in der 'Kritik der reinen Vernunft' und ihrer theologischen Konsequenz** (Wuppertal: R. Brockhaus Verlag, 1987); idem, "Kants Vernunftkritik und ihre Folgen für die Theologie," in **Evangelische Schriftauslegung: Ein Quellen- und Arbeitsbuch für Studium und Gemeinde**, ed. Joachim Cochlovius and Peter Zimmerling (Wuppertal: R. Brockhaus Verlag, 1987), 370-375; and idem, "Erkenntnis und Idee Gottes in der Philosophie Immanuel Kants," in **Wer ist das--Gott? Christliche Gotteserkenntnis in den Herausforderungen der Gegenwart**, ed. Helmut Burkhardt (Wuppertal: R. Brockhaus, 1982), 107-119.

[3] M. D. Geldard, "Kant, Immanuel," **New Dictionary of Theology**, ed. Sinclair B. Ferguson and David F. Wright (Downers Grove, IL: InterVarsity Press, 1988), 363.

[4] Grenz and Olson, 31. Bromiley, **Historical Theology**, 361, thinks that "theology is thus swallowed up in moral anthropology."

[5] "Generally speaking, this [Kant's] influence is seen in the emphasis on religious experience in liberalism (moral intuition or mystical awareness of God, e.g.) and on the emphasis on personal encounter with God (the I-Thou meeting divinely initiated) in neo-orthodoxy and in the sharp distinction made between detached, theoretical thinking and involved, committed thought and action (faith and obedience) made by existentialist theologians. The common thread is that moral and religious truth is not discovered primarily by examining the objective processes of nature or by speculative thought. Instead, God is known by a unique, special kind of non-theoretical, non-cognitive apprehension or in personal value judgments, decisions, and faith. In all these perspectives, especially those that continue the Kantian anti-metaphysical bias, religious knowledge tends to be mediated to persons through some faculty of the self which in one way or another resembles Kant's idea of the practical reason" (Cauthen, 37).

Johann Salomo Semler

Johann Salomo Semler (1725-1791) has been called "the great founder of the historical-critical work of rationalism."[1] Since Semler had a significant influence upon contemporary theology,[2] it is imperative to be aware of his understanding of Scripture.[3]

Hans-Joachim Kraus thinks that Semler brought about the great transformation in the Protestant understanding of Scripture,[4] and Johann Gottfried Eichhorn has called Semler the first reformer of the new theology.[5] It has been pointed out, however, that this "reformation" by Semler did not originate as an understanding of Scripture as in Luther, Calvin, and other Reformers; it was aimed at new goals because it was committed to the rational conscience.[6]

In the spirit of the Enlightenment, which was critical of all external authorities and traditions, Semler rejected the orthodox doctrine of Scripture[7] as divine authority and with it the belief in the divine origin and inspiration of Scripture.[8] He vehemently rejected the orthodox belief that not only the content of Scripture but also the very words of Scripture, including the letters and even the Hebrew vowel points, were

---

[1] Martin Kähler, **Geschichte der protestantischen Dogmatik im 19. Jahrhundert**, 2d enl. ed. (Wuppertal: R. Brockhaus Verlag, 1989), 30, 33, (translation by author).

[2] Hornig, 14; according to Klaus Reinhardt, 16, no other theologian of the eighteenth century has contributed so much to the reform of theology and especially to the dogmatic use of Scripture than Semler.

[3] On Semmler and his critical theology, see the authoritative study by Hornig; Kraus, **Geschichte der historisch-kritischen Erforschung des Alten Testaments**, 103-113; Kümmel, **The New Testament**, 62-69; Reinhardt, 16-25; and Carl Mirbt, "Semler, Johann Salomo," **Realencyklopädie für protestantische Theologie und Kirche**, 3d enl. ed., ed. Albert Hauck (Leipzig: J. C. Hinrichsche Buchhandlung, 1906), 18:203-209.

[4] Kraus, **Geschichte der historisch-kritischen Erforschung des Alten Testaments**, 104.

[5] As quoted in Hornig, 56.

[6] Kraus, **Geschichte der historisch-kritischen Erforschung des Alten Testaments**, 107.

[7] Hornig, 66.

[8] Ibid., 73-74. Semler also denies the supernatural superintendence in the transmission of the Biblical material. Cf. Johann Salomo Semler, **Lebensbeschreibung**, Part II, 125, as quoted in Kraus, **Geschichte der historisch-kritischen Erforschung des Alten Testaments**, 108. Apparently Semler also rejected the belief that all Scripture is inspired by God because of the peculiar Lutheran distinction between Law and Gospel. If all Scripture is inspired, Semler saw the danger leveling out the old and the new covenant, the Old Testament claim of the Law and the New Testament offer of salvation. See Hornig, 64.

divine.[1] Yet, Semler apparently still believed that there existed supernatural revelations where truths were communicated that were not available to human reason in general.[2] The writing down of those revelations, however, was left completely to man. Thus, Scripture was written by men and was and is not divine.[3] Scripture is but the human witness to God's revelations.[4]

This distinction between the human form of Scripture and its divine content[5] let Semler to reject a direct identification between the Word of God and Scripture,[6] between revelation and the Bible.[7] Instead, Semler proposed that Holy Scripture contains the Word of God, here and there, but not through and through.[8] This distinction between Word of God and Scripture caused Semler to separate theology and religion[9] and led him to criticize the canon of Scripture,[10] its internal unity[11] as well as the content of Scripture (Sachkritik).[12] Because Semler did not accept the divine inspiration of Scripture, he regarded Scripture as a relative, past, human document in contrast to the Word of God, which is absolute and contemporary.[13] This view of Scripture allowed him to introduce secular historical criticism to the study of Scripture. Although Scripture was still regarded as an abiding foundation of theology,[14] it is to

---

[1] Hornig, 73-74.

[2] Ibid., 74, 108-109.

[3] Ibid., 73.

[4] Ibid., 74.

[5] Kraus, **Geschichte der historisch-kritischen Erforschung des Alten Testaments**, 108; Hornig, 74, 111.

[6] The identification *"scriptura sacra est verbum dei"* that was held by the Protestant Reformers and orthodox theologians was given up. Cf. Hornig, 84; Reinhardt, 18.

[7] Hornig, 100.

[8] Ibid., 84.

[9] Kraus, **Geschichte der historisch-kritischen Erforschung des Alten Testaments**, 112.

[10] Johann Salomo Semler, **Abhandung von freier Untersuchung des Canon** (1771-1776), ed. Heinz Scheible, TKTG 5 (Gütersloh: Gerd Mohn, 1967).

[11] Reinhardt, 18; Hornig, 90.

[12] Cf. Kraus, **Geschichte der historisch-kritischen Erforschung des Alten Testaments**, 109, Hornig, 87.

[13] Kraus, **Geschichte der historisch-kritischen Erforschung des Alten Testaments**, 111.

[14] Reinhardt, 22.

be interpreted only in such a way that the spirit of Christ is revealed in them.[1] One can say that Semler had voiced already significant aspects of modern scholarship when he understood theology not as explication of revealed truths in Scripture but saw Scripture as a pluralistic, time conditioned, human document, where God and His revelation can be grasped only in its moral significance.[2]

Johann Philipp Gabler

It has been said that Johann Philipp Gabler (1753-1826), the father of modern Biblical theology,[3] tried to complete what Semler had begun, namely, the call for a fundamental separation between Biblical theology and dogmatics.[4] Although Gabler appears to assume that "the Bible is divinely inspired as a means of providing sure guidance to men,"[5] Gabler himself seems much more cautious in his interpretation of this matter. He admits that the question of inspiration is "to be sure very difficult," and in his "opinion at least, rather incorrectly inferred from the sayings of the Apostles."[6] Echoing the rational criticism of the Enlightenment, Gabler cautions that one has to "deal with these things with reason and not with fear or bias, not to press those meanings of the Apostles beyond their just limits . . ."[7] In harmony with Semler and other Enlightenment thinkers, Gabler allows for the possibility that some opinions of the Apostles, "which have no bearing on salvation, were left to their own ingenuity."[8]

---

[1]Hornig, 89, 65.

[2]Cf. Reinhardt, 22. On the relationship and mutual influence of Semler and Kant, see ibid., 24-25.

[3]D. H. Wallace, "Historicism and Biblical Theology," **SEv** 3/2 (1964): 223.

[4]Horst Stephan and Martin Schmidt, **Geschichte der evangelischen Theologie in Deutschland seit dem Idealismus**, 3d ed. (Berlin: Walter de Gruyter, 1973), 13. Similarly John Sandys-Wunsch and Laurence Eldredge, who claim that "Gabler can be said to have done more than any other single figure to make biblical theology a separate discipline" ("J. P. Gabler and the Distinction between Biblical and Dogmatic Theology: Translation, Commentary, and Discussion of his Originality," **SJT** 33 [1980]: 150).

[5]So Sandys-Wunsch and Eldredge, 152.

[6]So Gabler in his famous inaugural address, **De Justo Discrimine Theologiae Biblicae et Dogmaticae Regundisque Recte Utriusque Finibus**, as trans. Sandys-Wunsch and Eldredge, 143, in which he continues that the Apostles "make mention of a certain divine inspiration, since these individual passages are very obscure and ambiguous."

[7]Sandys-Wunsch and Eldredge, 143.

[8]Ibid., 143.

Thus, it is not surprising that Gabler usually calls the Biblical writers "holy writers" or "sacred authors" rather than "divinely inspired writers,"[1] because inspiration does not destroy a "holy man's own native intelligence and his natural way of knowing things."[2]

Just as Semler did, so also Gabler separates the divine from the human in Scripture, in order to distinguish "those things which in the sacred books refer most immediately to their own times and to the men of those times from those pure notions which divine providence wished to be characteristic of all times and places."[3] Thus, he calls for an approach in exegesis and interpretation in which one should be able to differentiate the limited historical nature of the Biblical writings from what is eternally valid in them. The distinction between divine and human in Scripture led Gabler to the further step of distinguishing and separating Biblical theology from dogmatic theology.[4]

Because of this distinction between purely historical exegesis and a systematic presentation of the universal and changeless ideas of Biblical religion, a "total separation of biblical studies and church dogma and life occurred."[5] It is evident that Biblical theology, thus understood, became detached from the theological concern to speak to the present and to address the interpretation of truth in and for the present.[6]

---

[1]Cf. ibid., 137, 139.

[2]Ibid., 139.

[3]Ibid., 138.

[4]Gabler's definition of both disciplines is worth quoting in full: "There is truly a biblical theology, of historical origin, conveying what the holy writers felt about divine matters; on the other hand there is a dogmatic theology of didactic origin, teaching what each theologian philosophizes rationally about divine things, according to the measure of his ability or the times, age, place, sect, school, and other similar factors" (quoted in Sandys-Wunsch and Eldredge, 137). Cf. also Gerhard F. Hasel, "The Relationship between Biblical Theology and Systematic Theology," **TJ** 5NS (1984):113-116. It is a well-acknowledged fact that the separation of Biblical and systematic theology as distinct theological disciplines is a fairly recent development that did not occur until the eighteenth century. Until then all theology was considered to be Biblical. Cf. Hayes and Prussner, 15-30; and Wolfhart Pannenberg, **TPS**, 346-358.

[5]D. H. Wallace, 225.

[6]Gerhard F. Hasel, "Biblical and Systematic Theology," 115. This detachment of the Biblical message to speak to the present is expressed forcefully in Krister Stendahl's influential article on contemporary Biblical theology with the distinction between "what it meant and what it means" (Krister Stendahl, "Biblical Theology, Contemporary," **IDB**, 1:419). This separation has been severely criticized by scholars such as Ben C. Ollenburger, "What Krister Stendahl 'Meant'-- A Normative Critique of 'Descriptive Biblical Theology.'" **HBT** 8/1 (1986): 61-98; and Avery

For Gabler and those following his path, dogmatics cannot operate on the principle of *sola Scriptura*[1] because the contemporary statement of faith is based ultimately not on Scripture but on philosophy and the use of reason.[2] Thus, Biblical theology, and with it Scripture, had no longer a dogmatic theological function to provide authoritative theological statements for the present situation. Dogmatic or systematic theology still had a normative, albeit not authoritative function, which functions normatively, however, only for a limited period of time.[3] Scripture, in other words, is no longer seen as divine authority, but at best, as a document that has a temporary normative function within the community of faith. Thus, the role of Scripture is seen more in functional terms rather than being an authoritative source and norm for theology that stems from its divine origin and character.

Friedrich Daniel Ernst Schleiermacher

Friedrich Daniel Ernst Schleiermacher (1768-1834) is the undisputed father of modern liberal theology. He not only gave distinctive impulses to theology but also determined the direction that Protestant theology would follow to the present day either in continuity or by reaction or by dialog with his thought.[4] He is generally considered the dominant Protestant theologian between John Calvin and Karl Barth,[5] and it is said

---

Dulles, "Response to Krister Stendahl's 'Method in the Study of Biblical Theology,'" in **The Bible in Modern Scholarship**, ed. J. Philip Hyatt (Nashville, TN: Abingdon, 1965), 210-219; cf. also Langdon B. Gilkey, "The Roles of the 'Descriptive' or 'Historical' and of the 'Normative' in Our Work." **Criterion** 20/1 (1981): 10-17.

[1]Hayes and Prussner, 65. Says Gabler: "The manner and form of dogmatic theology should be varied, as Christian philosophy especially is, according to the variety both of philosophy and of every human point of view of that which is subtle, learned, suitable and appropriate, elegant and graceful . . ." (as quoted in Sandys-Wunsch and Eldredge, 144).

[2]Richard B. Gaffin, "Systematic Theology and Biblical Theology," **WTJ** 38 (1976): 283.

[3]It has been noted that a changing systematic theology that becomes normative through the current philosophical system that is adopted by the systematic theologian and accepted by the religious community is very "unlikely to persuade skeptics," (Robert Morgan and John Barton, **Biblical Interpretation** [Oxford: Oxford University Press, 1988], 198) and is certainly not designed for the demands of missions. Ernst Troeltsch, "Die Dogmatik der 'religionsgeschichtlichen Schule'," in **Gesammelte Schriften** (Tübingen: J. C. B. Mohr, 1913), 2:517-518.

[4]Paul Avis, **The Methods of Modern Theology: The Dream of Reason** (Hants: Marshall Pickering, 1986), 1.

[5]Schleiermacher has been hailed as a "Prince of the Church," and one of the few giants of Christian thought (Brian A. Gerrish, **A Prince of the Church: Schleiermacher and the**

that "he carried out a 'Copernican Revolution' in theology as consequential as Kant's revolution in philosophy."[1]

Just as Copernicus had shifted the focus of the center of astronomy from the earth to the sun, so Schleiermacher shifted the center of authority in theology from propositions in divine Scripture to human experience. Rather than viewing Scripture as a collection of divine truths "from above," Schleiermacher proposed that religious experience would become the true source of theological reflection. God is immediately known in the "feeling of absolute dependence."[2] "Feeling," however, is not so much a certain "emotion" but rather an intuition that could be described as divination, which means an immediate awareness of the divine.[3] It lies on the prereflective plane of consciousness, i.e., beneath and before explicit thought or sensation,[4] and since it is an immediate awareness of the divine, "all religious feelings are supernatural."[5] Thus,

---

Beginnings of Modern Theology [Philadelphia: Fortress Press, 1984], 20). He has been called the most influential theologian since John Calvin (Richard R. Niebuhr, **Schleiermacher on Christ and Religion** [London: SCM Press, 1965], 6). He is deemed the founder of modern religious and theological thought (Robert R. Williams, **Schleiermacher the Theologian: The Construction of the Doctrine of God** [Philadelphia: Fortress Press, 1978], 1) and has been classified among the "church-fathers" of the Protestant church (Friedrich Wilhelm Kantzenbach, **Programme der Theologie: Denker, Schulen, Wirkungen von Schleiermacher bis Moltmann** [Munich: Claudius Verlag: 1978], 14). In the words of Karl Barth, "He did not found a school but an era" (Barth, **Protestant Thought**, 306).

[1]Livingston, 96.

[2]Friedrich D. E. Schleiermacher, **The Christian Faith**, ed. H. R. Mackintosh and J. S. Steward (Philadelphia: Fortress Press, 1976), § I, 12-18. It has been noted that Schleiermacher's central principle of religious experience, the feeling of absolute dependence, was unduly influenced by his desire to harmonize his theology with the metaphysical principles he had worked out in the **Dialectic** and **Ethics**. Richard B. Brandt writes: "One is first of all struck with the similarity between his theological treatment and the philosophical one. The fundamental idea of God's timeless causation of the world of finite objects, based upon the religious 'feeling of dependence', is so similar to his metaphysical theory that God is the 'transcendent source' or ground of all finite being that one is led to suspect that Schleiermacher came to emphasize the 'feeling of dependence' in religious experience . . . chiefly for the reason that it enabled him to derive a theological doctrine, supposedly as the expression of religious experience, which was congenial to his metaphysical theory" **(The Philosophy of Schleiermacher: The Development of His Theory of Scientific and Religious Knowledge** [New York: Harper and Brothers, 1941], 249). Cf. also Terrence Nelson Tice, "Schleiermacher's Theological Method with Particular Attention to His Production of Church Dogmatics" (Ph.D. dissertation, Princeton, 1961); and W. Schultz, "Schleiermachers Theorie des Gefühls und ihre theologische Bedeutung," **ZTK** 53 (1956): 75-103.

[3]Paul Tillich, **A History of Christian Thought: From Its Judaic and Hellenistic Origins to Existentialism**, ed. Carl E. Braaten (New York: Simon and Schuster, 1967), 392.

[4]Grenz and Olson, 44.

[5]Friedrich Schleiermacher, **On Religion: Speeches to Its Cultured Despisers**, with an

Schleiermacher identifies religion as a universal human phenomenon of which Christianity was the highest moral and spiritual form.[1]

With respect to the origin of Scripture, this meant that "things like miraculous interventions of God, special inspirations and revelations are beneath the level of real religious experience."[2] The idea of "revelation" is interpreted as "a spiritual reality prior to its verbal expression" where "God makes himself known to mankind through our feeling of absolute dependence."[3] Thus, as Schleiermacher put it with apologetic fervor in his **Speeches**, "every original and new intuition of the universe is" revelation[4] because it signifies "the *originality* of the fact which lies at the foundation of a religious communion."[5] The central aspect of this religious communion is seen in Jesus Christ who is Himself that "original divine bestowal of all that the Holy Scriptures contain."[6] The sacred literature and doctrine of any religion are secondary to this experience.[7] In a similar manner, the concept of inspiration is of "a wholly subordinate significance."[8] For Schleiermacher, only those books were "inspired" that

---

Introduction, trans. Richard Crouter (Cambridge: Cambridge University Press, 1988), 134.

[1]Keith W. Clements, "Schleiermacher, Friedrich Daniel Ernst," **The Blackwell Encyclopedia of Modern Christian Thought**, ed. Alister E. McGrath (Oxford: Basil Blackwell, 1993), 591.

[2]Tillich, **A History of Christian Thought**, 395.

[3]Allan D. Galloway, "Nineteenth and Twentieth Century Theology," in **The History of Christian Theology, vol. 1, The Science of Theology**, ed. Paul Avis (Grand Rapids, MI: Eerdmans, 1986), 246.

[4]Schleiermacher, **On Religion**, 133.

[5]Schleiermacher, **Christian Faith**, § 10, postscript, 50.

[6]Ibid., **Christian Faith**, § 130, 1, 598. "Thus the speaking and writing of the Apostles as moved by the Spirit was simply a communication drawn from the divine revelation in Christ" (ibid.). It has been said that "the person of Jesus Christ, with all that flows immediately from it, is alone absolutely normative" (F. Lichtenberger, History of German Theology in the Nineteenth Century, trans. W. Hastie [Edinburgh: T. & T. Clark, 1889], 137).

[7]In Schleiermacher's concept of revelation, no cognitive content is given to man. Says Schleiermacher, "But I am unwilling to accept the further definition that it [revelation] operates upon man as a cognitive being. For that would make the revelation to be originally and essentially *doctrine*; and I do not believe that we can adopt that position . . ." (**Christian Faith**, § 10, postscript, 50). Furthermore, "if this is taken to mean that the sacred writers, being under inspiration, were informed of the content of what they wrote in a special divine manner, there is no foundation for any such statement, whether we consider the act of composing a sacred book itself or the excitation of thought preceding or underlying it" (ibid., § 130, 1, 598).

[8]Schleiermacher, **Christian Faith**, § 14, postscript, 75. In fact, Schleiermacher defines inspiration as "merely the religious name for freedom. Every free action that becomes a religious

communicated the spirit of Christ.¹ Since the writers of Scripture were not informed of the content of what they wrote, nor were they guided in the composition of the sacred books,² not everything in the canon can be attributed to the Holy Spirit.³ "Clearly, Schleiermacher did not consider the Bible supernaturally inspired or infallible."⁴

It is obvious that Schleiermacher has shifted the weight of authority away from Scripture, as revealed and attested to by God, to the authority of the self⁵ and its experience.⁶ Since the "actual experience"⁷ becomes the final norm of truth, it does not come as a surprise that he declares that

> every holy writing is merely a mausoleum of religion, a monument that a great spirit was there that no longer exists; for if it still lived and were active, why would it attach such great importance to the dead letter that can only be a weak reproduction of it?⁸

Hence, Scripture is no longer the source and norm of theology.⁹ In fact, the truly religious person is not one who trusts Scripture but who really needs no Scripture at all and might himself be able to create Scripture out of his own experience.¹⁰ This

---

act, every restoration of a religious intuition, every expression of a religious feeling that really communicates itself so that the intuition of the universe is transferred to others, took place upon inspiration . . ." (idem, **On Religion**, 133).

¹Bruce Vawter, **Biblical Inspiration** (Philadelphia: Westminster Press, 1972), 90; Robert Gnuse, **The Authority of the Bible: Theories of Inspiration, Revelation and the Canon of Scripture** (New York: Paulist Press, 1985), 99.

²Schleiermacher, **Christian Faith**, § 130, 1, 598.

³Reinhardt, 70-71.

⁴Grenz and Olson, 47.

⁵Royce Gordon Gruenler, **Meaning and Understanding: The Philosophical Framework for Biblical Interpretation**, FCI 2 (Grand Rapids, MI: Zondervan Publishing House, 1991), 49.

⁶Thomas A. Idinopolis thinks that Schleiermacher "set forth a vigorous brand of religious naturalism. Theological truth is truth about God, man, and the world from the point of view of man's experience. Thus, theology inescapably becomes anthropocentric. The Bible is no longer the source of theology. Rather it is understood as a manifestation of the religious consciousness--a record of a distinct type of religious experience" **(The Erosion of Faith: An Inquiry into the Origins of the Contemporary Crisis in Religious Thought** [Chicago: Quadrangle Books, 1971], 26).

⁷Schleiermacher, **Christian Faith**, § 132, 3, 611.

⁸Schleiermacher, **On Religion**, 134-135.

⁹Reinhardt, 72.

¹⁰"It is not the person who believes in a holy writing who has religion, but only the one

paradigm change in the nature of Scripture which was no longer exempt from the relativities of history is indicated by Schleiermacher's avoidance of the term "dogmatics" and his shift to the term "Glaubenslehre" in the title of his systematic theology.[1]

Although Scripture did not play the same central role in Schleiermacher's theology as it did in orthodox theology,[2] it nevertheless played an important role. Schleiermacher did not rely on Scripture to draw Christian doctrine from it. Instead "all doctrines properly so called must be extracted from the Christian religious self-consciousness, i.e., the inward experience of Christian people."[3] Scripture is special and still important for Schleiermacher because it records the religious experience of the earliest Christian communities[4] and thus preserves for succeeding generations the perfect God-consciousness of Jesus Christ and its impact on the earliest Christians.[5] In other words, Schleiermacher assigns Scripture a chronological priority because it is the first part in the development of the consciousness of the church.[6] Because Scripture is the product of men, no uniformity is ascribed to every part of it[7] and, consequently, no demonstration from Scripture in the traditional sense is possible.[8]

---

who needs none and probably could make one for himself" (Schleiermacher, **On Religion**, 135). Cf. also the stronger translation of the same passage in Gruenler, 49.

[1]Gerrish, "From 'Dogmatik' to 'Glaubenslehre'," 163-167.

[2]Schleiermacher deals with the doctrine of Scripture not in the prolegomena but only towards the end of his systematic theology under the general division of the church (Schleiermacher, **Christian Faith**, §§ 128-132, 591-611).

[3]Ibid., § 64, 1, 265.

[4]"The Bible and the creeds are important, but as records and interpretations of the experience of Christians. The Christian does not have faith in Christ because of the Bible; rather the Bible gains its authority from the believer's faith in Christ" (Dillenberger and Welch, 188).

[5]Grenz and Olson, 47.

[6]Schleiermacher, **Christian Faith**, § 129, 594; Reinhardt, 73.

[7]Schleiermacher, **Christian Faith**, § 129, 2, 596.

[8]"It follows that the scriptural norm is not to be simply identified with the letter of the New Testament, and that no exclusive appeal can be made to the Bible (no *scriptura sola*)" (Gerrish, "From 'Dogmatik' to 'Glaubenslehre,'" 165); similarly Harold O. J. Brown, "Romanticism and the Bible," in **Challenges to Inerrancy: A Theological Response**, ed. Gordon R. Lewis and Bruce Demarest (Chicago: Moody Press, 1984), 61; and Reinhardt, 73.

Because Scripture originates "from below," Schleiermacher allows no different sets of interpretive rules for its interpretation.[1]

With this new approach, Schleiermacher became "the principal creative sponsor of the whole revisionist and liberal enterprise."[2] But even those who reacted the strongest against him, like Karl Barth, could not evade his influence. Therefore, one must turn attention now to the neo-orthodox reaction to liberal theology.

Neo-Orthodoxy

The theological movement variously known as neo-orthodoxy[3] can most easily be understood as a theological response to the "liberalism" of nineteenth-century theology that had turned theology into anthropology. Neo-orthodox thinkers drew their theological ideas largely from Reformation sources, without the dogmatic rigidities of classical orthodoxy, however.[4] Hence, the movement can validly be called "neo-orthodox" or even "neo-Reformation."[5] Nevertheless, as Gilkey has pointed out with perceptive insight, neo-orthodoxy cannot be understood solely as a return to an "orthodox" perspective, as its name implies, for it is also genuinely "neo" in character.[6] It is increasingly recognized[7] that the movement not only reacted against

---

[1] For a brief introduction to Schleiermacher's hermeneutics, see Werner G. Jeanrond, **Theological Hermeneutics: Development and Significance** (New York: Crossroads, 1991), 44-55.

[2] David F. Ford, "Introduction to Modern Christian Theology," in **The Modern Theologians: An Introduction to Christian Theology in the Twentieth Century**, 2 vols. (Oxford: Basil Blackwell, 1989), 1:11.

[3] Sometimes the terms "dialectical theology" or "theology of crisis" are also used as a designation for what became known as neo-orthodoxy because they have common beginnings. Cf. James M. Robinson, ed., **The Beginnings of Dialectical Theology**, trans. Keith R. Crim and Louis De Grazia (Richmond, VA: John Knox Press, 1968); Wolfgang Trillhaas, "Die Evangelische Theologie im 20. Jahrhundert," in **Bilanz der Theologie im 20. Jahrhundert: Perspektiven, Strömungen, Motive in der christlichen und nichtchristlichen Welt**, ed. Herbert Vorgrimmler and Robert Vander Gucht, 2 vols. (Freiburg: Herder, 1970), 2:101-113; see also Langdon Gilkey, "Neoorthodoxy," in **A New Handbook of Christian Theology**, ed. Donald W. Musser and Joseph L. Price (Nashville, TN: Abingdon, 1992), 334-337.

[4] Dulles, "Scripture: Recent Protestant and Catholic Views," 8; Gilkey, "Neoorthodoxy," 335.

[5] Gilkey, "Neoorthodoxy," 335.

[6] Ibid. Wilhelm Pauck makes a valid point when he states that "Orthodox theologies give rise to more orthodoxies; liberal theologies give rise to neo-orthodoxies" (as quoted in Tracy, **Blessed Rage for Order**, 27).

[7] Gilkey, "Neoorthodoxy," 335; Tracy, **Blessed Rage for Order**, 27.

liberalism but also was its child, for it retained in a revised form many of the most important affirmations and principles of liberal theology.[1]

The towering figure in Christian theology who probably describes the characteristics of this movement best was without doubt Karl Barth (1886-1968).[2] His understanding of Scripture is important not only because almost every theologian from 1925 to 1960 can be said to have been influenced by neo-orthodox theology[3] but also because Pannenberg reacted with his approach against Barth's emphasis on the Word of God and Bloesch is trying to develop further Barth's concept of Scripture. This makes an investigation of Karl Barth's understanding of Scripture imperative.

---

[1] In the words of Langdon Gilkey, "Neoorthodoxy agreed with liberalism that the whole area of spatio-temporal fact and event is the valid object of scientific inquiry, with the result that the hypotheses of science in the areas of natural and historical events were regarded as authoritative if not exhaustive. . . . In other words, to neoorthodox thinkers theological doctrines were statements containing symbolic rather than literal, factual truth; they were propositions pointing to the religious dimensions of events rather than propositions containing factual information about events. . . . Second, neoorthodoxy affirmed with liberalism that all the activities and products of human religious life (scriptures, creeds, laws, church statements, acts and so forth) are historically conditioned. From these resources neoorthodox theology drew two 'liberal' conclusions: (1) These scriptures and institutions must be studied historically and critically in order to be understood, and (2) none of these products of human religious life is itself infallible or a direct, unmediated result of divine activity" ("Neoorthodoxy," 335-336).

[2] For the role of Scripture in Karl Barth's theology, see: Klaas Runia, **Karl Barth's Doctrine of Holy Scripture** (Grand Rapids, MI: Eerdmans, 1962); Gordon H. Clark, **Karl Barth's Theological Method** (Philadelphia: The Presbyterian and Reformed Publishing Company, 1963), esp. 151-184; Arnold B. Come, **An Introduction to Barth's Dogmatics for Preachers** (Philadelphia: Westminster Press, 1963), 168-198; Reinhardt, 221-239; Wolfhart Schlichting, **Biblische Denkform in der Dogmatik: Die Vorbildlichkeit des biblischen Denkens für die Methode der Kirchlichen Dogmatik Karl Barths** (Zurich: Theologischer Verlag, 1971); Walter Lindemann, **Karl Barth und die Kritische Schriftauslegung**, ThF 54 (Hamburg-Bergstedt: Evangelischer Verlag, 1973; Kelsey, **The Uses of Scripture in Recent Theology**, 39-50; Rogers and McKim, 406-426; Thomas Edward Provence, "The Hermeneutics of Karl Barth" (Ph.D. dissertation, Fuller Theological Seminary, 1980); Geoffrey W. Bromiley, "The Authority of Scripture in Karl Barth," in **Hermeneutics, Authority, and Canon**, ed. D. A. Carson and John D. Woodbridge (Grand Rapids, MI: Zondervan Publishing House, 1986), 271-294; Paul Charles McGlasson, "Karl Barth and the Scriptures: A Study of the Biblical Exegesis in *Church Dogmatics* I and II" (Ph.D. dissertation, Yale University, 1986); Christina A. Baxter, "The Nature and Place of Scripture in the Church Dogmatics," in **Theology beyond Christendom: Essays on the Centenary of the Birth of Karl Barth May 10, 1886**, ed. John Thompson (Allison Park, PA: Pickwick Publications, 1986), 33-62; idem, "Barth--a Truly Biblical Theologian?" **TynBul** 38 (1987): 3-27; David L. Mueller, "The Contributions and Weaknesses of Karl Barth's View of the Bible," in **The Proceedings of the Conference on Biblical Inerrancy 1987** (Nashville, TN: Broadman Press, 1987), 423-447; Werner G. Jeanrond, "Karl Barth's Hermeneutics," in **Reckoning with Barth: Essays in Commemoration of the Centenary of Karl Barth's Birth**, ed. Nigel Biggar (London: Mowbray, 1988), 80-97; Bernhard Rothen, **Die Klarheit der Schrift. Teil 2: Karl Barth. Eine Kritik** (Göttingen: Vandenhoeck & Ruprecht, 1990); and Frank M. Hasel, "The Christological Analogy of Scripture in Karl Barth," **TZ** 50 (1994): 41-49.

[3] Gilkey, "Neoorthodoxy," 337.

Karl Barth begins his **Church Dogmatics** with an exposition of the doctrine of the Word of God which is the norm of all Christian theology.[1] For Barth, the "Word of God" has a threefold form: the Word proclaimed, the Word written, and the Word revealed.[2] He goes on to define revelation as God's self-revelation. What is revealed, Barth maintained, is not information about God, but God Himself[3] who has revealed Himself in conclusive form in His son Jesus Christ.[4] Since revelation is seen as God's self-revelation in Jesus Christ, Scripture is not revelation in itself but only a witness to revelation.[5] In fact, Barth seems to advocate "an *actualistic* concept of revelation"[6] where the Bible again and again has to become the Word of God.[7] God's Word is God's own activity and as such something spiritual, something divine. However, this Word does not communicate itself to us except through certain signs which attest to it. In this way Barth points not only to the sacramental character of the communication of God's Word to humankind but also to the distinction that must be preserved between that Word and the medium of its communication.[8] The sign can never be identified with the Word itself for God retains His freedom to reveal or not to reveal through the medium, despite the existence of the medium.[9] This means, moreover, that for Barth the human language is inherently incapable of making any valid affirmation about God

---

[1] Karl Barth, **Church Dogmatics**, 13 vols., ed. G. W. Bromiley and T. F. Torrance (Edinburgh: T. & T. Clark, 1936-1969), I/1, 98-335.

[2] Ibid., 98-135.

[3] Thus, the "Word of God" is synonymous with God's self-revelation. Ibid., 339. Cf. Roger Nicole, "The Neo-orthodox Reduction," in **Challenges to Inerrancy: A Theological Response**, ed. Gordon R. Lewis and Bruce Demarest (Chicago: Moody Press, 1984), 123. Thus, it seems as if Barth goes back to earlier positions in affirming the reality of a special revelation, but he also remains genuinely "neo" in the sense that he does not allow for information to be revealed but rather restricts God's revelation to His self-revelation in Jesus Christ.

[4] According to Barth, "Revelation in fact does not differ from the person of Jesus Christ nor from the reconciliation accomplished in Him. To say revelation is to say 'The Word became flesh'" (**CD**, I/1, 134). Cf. also Rothen, **Die Klarheit der Schrift. Teil 2**, 72.

[5] Runia, 33.

[6] Ibid., 196.

[7] Barth, **CD** I/1, 127.

[8] Gaybba, 45.

[9] Barth, **CD**, I/1, 368-382.

whatsoever.[1] The sign can only *become* God's Word when God acts and decides to use it in His freedom but it never *is* the Word of God in a direct identification.[2]

This distinction between Scripture and the revelation of God Himself constitutes the Bible's limitation, because "a witness is not absolutely identical with that to which it witnesses."[3] To equate Scripture with God's revelation would be bibliolatry to Barth. Instead, Barth believes that in Scripture one meets with human words written in human speech[4] which seems to suggest that the origin of Scripture goes back to the human authors who are encountered by Jesus Christ.[5] In this encounter with Christ, the prophets and apostles have a personal relation to the perception of divine truth which, however, is not sufficient to convey it reliably to others.

It appears that "on the ground of his abstract-transcendence idea, Barth separates the divine and human in Scripture, opposing the divine perfection to the human imperfection of the Bible."[6] This distinction between the divine and the human implies

---

[1] Gaybba, 46.

[2] Runia, 196-197, 203; Gaybba, 51; William Young, "The Inspiration of Scripture in Reformation and Barthian Theology," **WTJ** 8 (1946): 28-29.

[3] Barth, **CD**, I/2, 463. Scripture can be seen as containing the Word, i.e., Jesus Christ, among the many words of Scripture (Barth, **CD**, I/1, 116-117; idem, **The Epistle to the Romans**, trans. Edwyn C. Hoskyns [Oxford: Oxford University Press, 1933], 8: "The Word ought to be exposed in the words;" similarly idem, "The Christian Understanding of Revelation," in **Against the Stream: Shorter Post-War Writings**, trans. E. M. Delacour and S. Godman, ed. R. G. Smith (London: SCM Press, 1954), 220: "The Word waits for us in the words of the prophets and apostles").

[4] Barth, **CD**, I/2, 463.

[5] Cf. Barth, **CD**, IV/3, 508, 83. On the aspect of encounter in Karl Barth, see also George Hunsinger, **How to Read Karl Barth: The Shape of His Theology** (New York: Oxford University Press, 1991), 152-184. Emil Brunner, another pioneer theologian of the neo-orthodox movement, developed the concept of revelation as a divine-human encounter in which he was influenced by Jewish philosopher and theologian Martin Buber, who in turn was influenced by the Christian existentialist Søren Kierkegaard. Cf. Emil Brunner, **The Divine-Human Encounter**, trans. Amadeus W. Loos (Philadelphia: Westminster Press, 1943). Brunner also thinks that revelation is a personal self-disclosure of God Himself, in which nothing is communicated. On Brunner's view of revelation, see Paul King Jewett, **Emil Brunner's Concept of Revelation** (London: James Clarke & Co., LTD, 1954), esp. 70-74; cf. also idem, "Emil Brunner's Doctrine of Scripture," in **Inspiration and Interpretation**, ed. John W. Walvoord (Grand Rapids, MI: Eerdmans, 1957), 210-238; and James L. Leavenworth, "The Use of the Scriptures in the Works of Emil Brunner" (Ph.D. dissertation, Yale University, 1950).

[6] Young, 33. Cf. also McKim, **What Christian Believe about the Bible**, 73; Runia, 189. Karl Barth is being quoted saying: "If I have a 'system', it consists in this, that I always keep in mind with the utmost vigor what Kierkegaard has called the 'infinite qualitative difference' between time and eternity, and that in both its positive and negative implications. 'God is in heaven and thou upon earth'" (as quoted in Jewett, **Emil Brunner's Concept of Revelation**, 7).

that at least from one point of view, Scripture is a fully human book.[1] It has been pointed out that the human words of Scripture belonged to the created order, and therefore were limited to all the conditions of time and space.[2] Since Barth rejects a mechanical conception of inspiration, the words of Scripture are always only human words[3] and, as such, can again and again become the Word of God.[4]

To acknowledge that the words of Scripture are human words is only the first step. Barth at once acknowledges that the Bible as human document is also a fallible document. Written by fallible men in human language, it is fallible in every respect.[5] Nevertheless, as a witness to revelation, it may be used by God if and when it pleases Him to encounter individuals. In other words, Scripture has a functional authority for Barth.[6] It is "not a book of oracles or an instrument of direct impartation. It is genuine witness."[7] As such, it is "to be interpreted from the standpoint of and with

---

[1] "Even here [i.e., in the presence of God in the word of the prophets and apostles] the human element does not cease to be human, and as such and in itself it is certainly not divine" (Barth, **CD**, I/2, 499). Barth also states on the same page: "Again it is quite impossible that there should be direct identity between the human word of Holy Scripture and the word of God, and therefore between the creaturely reality in itself and as such and the reality of God the Creator. It is impossible that there should have been a transmutation of one into the other or an admixture of the one with the other." Cf. Frank M. Hasel, "The Christological Analogy of Scripture in Karl Barth," 45.

[2] Rogers and McKim, 423.

[3] It has been pointed out that Barth does not reject the idea of inspiration but re-interprets it from his own presuppositions which are not derived from Scripture itself. Runia, 137. Moreover, Barth rejects the idea that inspiration is only a matter of the past, i.e., when the Biblical books were written. Instead, it comprises also a second moment, namely, when the books are read and heard. Barth, **CD**, I/2, 507-508. It has been pointed out convincingly by Runia, however, that according to Scripture and the Reformers inspiration does not refer to the understanding and receiving of Scripture but to its origin and being. The former traditionally has been called "illumination." Cf. Runia, 138-168.

[4] Ibid., 196-197.

[5] Karl Barth clearly states that "in our search for an absolute, unconditional, supreme source of divine revelation we inevitably come up against the fact of human relativity and limitations of the authors of the Bible" ("The Christian Understanding of Revelation," 221). This limitation of the Biblical authors goes beyond the limitations of culture and age and includes their theological understanding. "The vulnerability of the Bible, i.e., its capacity for error, also extends to its religious or theological content . . . they [the Biblical authors] are all vulnerable and therefore capable of error even in respect of religion and theology" (Barth, **CD**, I/2, 509-510).

[6] Kelsey, **The Uses of Scripture in Recent Theology**, 47; Bromiley, "The Authority of Scripture in Karl Barth," 283.

[7] Barth, **CD**, I/2, 507.

a view of its theme, and in conformity with that theme."[1] In other words, Barth is thoroughly Christological in his use of Scripture. Furthermore, as human documents, the Scriptures are to be understood in a human way by the scientific historical-critical study of the Bible.[2] Yet, although such study may clarify the human form of Scripture, it is incapable of bringing out the object of the human testimony, which is God's non-cognitive self-revelation.[3] In other words, Barth's theological reading of Scripture is independent from its historical analysis. Barth, therefore, can use historical-critical methods without being bogged down by their conclusions.[4] Historical criticism can knock out all the historical support for one's faith by showing that the object of one's faith is not accessible through historical knowledge. This, however, earned Barth the criticism of making theology immune against any historical findings or conclusions.[5] Thus, one can say that Barth uses Scripture Christologically, i.e., where he interprets Scripture in the light of its center, Jesus Christ.[6]

Summary

Although there are differences in emphasis, all the positions discussed above are united in their belief that Scripture is ultimately a human book that originates "from below." This is to say that all believe that no supernatural guidance or supervision is present in the process of writing the Biblical material. In other words, on the level of the actual coming into being of the Biblical text, Scripture is originated "from below" because this process is left to the human agent alone. Consequently, Scripture is

---

[1]Ibid., 521.

[2]Cf. Provence, 213-241.

[3]Bromiley, "The Authority of Scripture in Karl Barth," 281.

[4]The use and endorsement of the historical-critical method by Barth himself is discussed in detail by Provence, 213-287; cf. also Christina A. Baxter, "Barth--A Truly Biblical Theologian?" 3-27.

[5]Pannenberg, **TPS**, 265-276, esp. 272-273.

[6]It is an acknowledged fact that the decisive mark of Barth's theology is his christocentricity. In 1938 Barth himself spoke of the "Christological concentration" of his thinking which from 1932 on found expression in his **Church Dogmatics** (Karl Barth, "Parergon. Karl Barth über sich selbst," **EvT** 8 [1948/49]: 272). This has led some to speak of a "Christomonism" in Karl Barth. So Come, 133-142, 79-80. On Barth's Christological use of Scripture, see Reinhardt, 233-237, with specific examples. Cf. for example, Barth's Christological interpretation of creation; Johann Friedrich Konrad, **Abbild und Schöpfung: Untersuchungen zur Exegese von Genesis 1 und 2 in Barths Kirchlicher Dogmatik III, 1**, BGBH 5 (Tübingen: J. C. B. Mohr, 1962).

approached more from the perspective of the historical disciplines rather than from theology.[1] One can also notice the presence of a considerable positive attitude toward the employment of the historical-critical method.[2] Hence, little emphasis is placed on the words of Scripture being inspired and there exists a pervasive dislike of the concept or the idea of an inerrant or infallible Scripture.[3] It appears that for the representatives of this "type," the way Scripture expresses things is of secondary importance--at least they tend not to read and apply Scripture literally. Moreover, all stress the human element over against the divine.[4] The divine element, if present at all, is made subservient to the human. This seems especially evident after Kant, who radically questioned the very possibility of any knowledge of God as He is in Himself. Scripture, then, is not taken to be a textbook for doctrine where one can find God's revealed will, and thus it is no authoritative source nor the final norm for theology.

Despite these similarities, a number of differences are apparent. Some, and interestingly enough, most of the initial proponents of the historical-critical method, allow for the possibility that some form of supernatural revelation has taken place where truths were communicated. This view, however, has been increasingly questioned to the point where no content is believed to have been revealed, as for example in Schleiermacher. Revelation becomes every original and new intuition of the divine through feeling or is strictly restricted to the self-revelation of Jesus Christ that is appropriated in an non-cognitive existential encounter. The perennial problem that faces all representatives who maintain some form of divine revelation--but dismiss any divine supervision in the writing down of it--is the question of how to extract the unchanging eternal content from the changing and limited human form of Scripture. This is usually done by allowing some extra Scriptural criterion, be that reason or common human experience, to decide what is to be retained and what is to be dismissed. Here naturalistic and extra-Scriptural presuppositions are much more openly at work than in the previous model. Furthermore, all struggle with the quandary of why a historically conditioned and relatively human book should have any special

---

[1] Cf. Erickson, "Immanence, Transcendence, and Scripture," 199.

[2] Ibid.

[3] Ibid.

[4] In this they display characteristics that are typical for a liberal approach. Cf. Raymond Abba, **The Nature and Authority of the Bible** (London: James Clarke, 1958), 61.

authority and how authoritative claims can be made by a human document that is culturally and historically limited. It does not surprise that many, if not all representatives of this "model," emphasize the function of Scripture rather than the nature of the Bible per se.[1]

Conclusion

At the end of this issue-oriented historical survey on the role of Scripture in theology, one is prepared to single out some issues that are crucial for the role of Scripture in theology. It seems that in this old question, problems are still outstanding which had not been solved in the sixteenth century[2] and which remain unresolved even today.[3]

Our survey indicates that the question of the authority of Scripture and its role in theology is intricately connected with the question of its nature, which in turn is bound up with its origin.[4] Is Scripture to be understood to have originated basically "from above?" That is, does it have a divine origin, or did it originate basically "from below?" Does it have a human origin where there is no divine supervision in the process of what the Biblical writers put into words? The decision about the understanding of the nature of revelation shapes not only the formulations concerning the nature of Scripture but also influence its use.[5] What is the nature of revelation? Is there any supernatural revelation and, if so, is there any propositional truth that is being revealed or is no cognitive content communicated? What is the relationship

---

[1] Cf. Erickson, "Immanence, Transcendence, and Scripture," 199. On the functionalistic use of Scripture, see Kelsey, **The Uses of Scripture in Recent Theolog**; Chang; and earlier, Charles Manford Sharpe, "The Normative Use of Scripture by Typical Theologians of Protestant Orthodoxy in Great Britain and America" (Ph.D. dissertation, University of Chicago, 1912), 75.

[2] Ebeling, "'Sola Scriptura' and Tradition," 138.

[3] Peters, "Editorials: Seven Pressing Theological Issues," 82.

[4] Berkeley Mickelsen has pointed out that "during the last of the nineteenth century and throughout the twentieth century, the nature of the authority of the Bible has been intensely debated. Much of this debate has paralleled studies about how books of the Bible were written. . . . The time-honored axiom 'Because God is its author, the Bible is authoritative' came to be counterbalanced by some scholars with another axiom, "Because men are its authors, the Bible is not *intrinsically authoritative*': it has only an *illuminating, relational authority* . . . " ("The Bible's Own Approach to Authority," in **Biblical Authority**, ed. Jack Rogers [Waco, TX: Word Books, 1977], 78).

[5] Recently Nancey C. Murphy has come to a similar conclusion when she says "that the use of Scripture in theological research program is governed by a variety of *auxiliary hypotheses*-- usually doctrines of revelation" (170).

between revelation and the writing down of it? What is the nature and the role of the words of Scripture? Here is the general issue of the relationship between the divine and the human element in Scripture and particularly in the composition of it. If both elements are affirmed, how are they accounted for and what is considered to be permanent and what is seen as relative? Moreover, from where is the understanding of this crucial relationship informed and influenced, from Scripture alone--and here from all of Scripture (*tota Scriptura*)--or from selective passages and extra-Scriptural sources like philosophy?

Related to the question of the origin of Scripture is the issue of its nature. Is Scripture to be thought of in terms of a divinely inspired source--perhaps the only source--for theology, or is the Bible one source among a number of other sources, albeit with a higher ranking and with a certain priority, thus still functioning as a norm in theology? In other words, should the Scripture principle of the Protestant Reformation be understood in the sense of *sola Scriptura* or rather as *prima Scriptura*? In the latter case the Bible, although still a fundamental norm, is no longer the final authority and is neither "the only place where theological reflection originates nor the direct source from which all theological positions arise."[1]

Closely connected with the question of the nature of Scripture is the problem of the use of Scripture and the proper approach to it. Is there a special methodology in the use of Scripture? Or can and should one use historical-critical methods? Furthermore, the question emerges whether the *sola Scriptura* principle has been consistently applied in theology or whether there has been only a selective and functional use of Scripture in theology.

Why should Scripture be authoritative? Should one speak only of a normative function of Scripture? And if there is any normative claim to Scripture, why is it still normative? What makes Scripture unique and what is its role in theology?

These are some of the key issues that have emerged from the above overview. It appears that the tension that arises between the two basic perspectives of Scripture still continues to engage leading theologians of the present time. Pannenberg and Bloesch both have reacted against what they perceive as shortcomings in the understanding of Scripture in the above-mentioned "models." In an effort to advance

---

[1]Richard Rice, **Reason and the Contours of Faith** (Riverside, CA: La Sierra University Press, 1991), 87-88.

the discussion and to move beyond the perceived shortcomings of previous positions they have put forth their own proposal. Therefore, this discussion turns to Pannenberg and Bloesch in order to investigate their understanding of the origin, nature, and role of Scripture in theology.

CHAPTER III

SCRIPTURE IN W. PANNENBERG'S SYSTEMATIC THEOLOGY

Introduction

The systematic survey on the role of Scripture in theology in the previous chapter has served to provide the background for the current discussion of the understanding of Scripture in Pannenberg and Bloesch, which is at the center of our investigation. The present chapter intends first of all to examine Pannenberg's understanding of Scripture. In order to illumine his perception of Scripture and to arrive at a comprehensive perspective of his position we should give a brief discussion of Pannenberg's personal and theological background before we concentrate on his understanding of the origin, nature, and role of Scipture. After this more descriptive task we will turn to the second part of this chapter where an analysis of some fundamental presuppositions[1] that have influenced his concept of Scripture will be attempted.

The method adopted here is a systematic approach rather than a merely historical description. For that reason, special consideration is given to the mature Pannenberg as he is presented in his recently completed **Systematic Theology**.[2] It is here that he

---

[1] On the role of presuppositions in scholarship, see Paul Helm, "Understanding Scholarly Presuppositions: A Crucial Tool for Research?" **TynBul** 44/1 (1993): 143-154.

[2] All three volumes have appeared in German: Wolfhart Pannenberg, **SyTh/G**, 3 vols. (Göttingen: Vandenhoeck & Ruprecht, 1988-1993); the first volume has been translated into English: idem, **SyTh/E**, 1, trans. Geoffrey Bromiley (Grand Rapids, MI: Eerdmans, 1991).
For some of the major book reviews of Pannenberg's **Systematic Theology**, see Nicklaus Peter, "Geschichtstheologischer Auszug aus der Geschichte? Wolfhart Pannenberg, **Systematische Theologie**, vol. 1," **Ref** 37 (1988): 481-485; Eberhard Jüngel, "Nihil divinitatis, ubi non fides: Ist christliche Dogmatik in rein theoretischer Perspektive möglich? Bemerkungen zu einem theologischen Entwurf von Rang," **ZTK** 86 (1989): 204-235; Ulrich Ruh, "Den Glauben denken: Zu Wolfhart Pannenbergs 'Systematischer Theologie'," **HerKorr** 42 (1989): 180-184; Juan A. Martínez Camino, "La 'Teología Sistemática' de W. Pannenberg," **EE** 65 (1990): 215-225; Gerhard Ludwig Müller, "Pannenbergs Entwurf einer systematischen Theologie," **ThRv** 86/1 (1990): 1-9; idem, "Pannenbergs Entwurf einer systematischen Theologie (II)," **ThRv** 88/5 (1992): 353-360; Johannes Fischer, "Wie wird Geschichte als Handeln Gottes offenbar? Zur Bedeutung der Anwesenheit Gottes im Offenbarungsgeschehen," **ZTK** 88 (1991): 211-231; Hans-Peter Willi, "Dogmatik als Lehre von Gott: Ein Bericht über den ersten Band der 'Systematischen Theologie' von Wolfhart Pannenberg," **TB** 22/2 (1991): 102-110; idem, "Theologie der Menschwerdung: Ein Bericht über den zweiten Band der 'Systematischen Theologie' von Wolfhart Pannenberg," **TB** 22/6 (1991): 332-339; John O'Donnell, "Pannenberg's Doctrine of God," **Greg** 72/1 (1991): 73-98; Placher, "Revealed to Reason: Theology as 'Normal Science'," 192-195; W. D. Hudson,

brings together in a systematic fashion what he proposed earlier. Such a systematic investigation also includes earlier statements that are pertinent to the issue under investigation.

In our endeavor to uncover Pannenberg's understanding of Scripture we will touch upon a variety of theological themes and issues such as the concept of revelation and inspiration, the concept of history, hermeneutics, the doctrine of God, anthroplogy, etc. To scrutinize all of these aspects in detail is beyond the scope of this study, however, we will briefly deal with with them, in as much as they are important for helping to understand Pannenberg's concept of Scripture and help to clarify his position.

W. Pannenberg: The Man and Theologian

In order to better understand the views of Pannenberg, one should have at least some knowledge of his life and personal background. Before we turn our attention to Pannenberg's understanding of Scripture, therefore, we consider here a brief profile that includes biographical data,[1] the intellectual influences on his thought, and a short résumé of his place in the theological and philosophical spectrum.[2]

"God Revealed in Creation: Review Article," **ExpTim** 104/2 (1992): 47-48; the Symposium on Pannenberg's *Systematic Theology*, vol. 1, in **CTJ** 27 (1992): 304-325, with contributions by Brian J. Walsh, "Introduction," **CTJ** 27 (1992): 304-306; Stanley J. Grenz., "The Irrelevance of Theology: Pannenberg and the Quest for Truth," **CTJ** 27 (1992): 307-311; Rory A. A. Hinton, "Pannenberg on the Truth of Christian Discourse: A Logical Response," **CTJ** 27 (1992): 312-318; James H. Olthuis, "God as True Infinite: Concerns about Wolfhart Pannenberg's *Systematic Theology*, vol. 1," **CTJ** 27 (1992): 318-325; Richard Viladesau, "**Systematic Theology** 1: by Wolfhart Pannenberg," **TS** 54 (1993): 171-173; and Maurice Wiles, "**Systematic Theology**: vol. 1, Wolfhart Pannenberg," **Theol** 96/769 (1993): 57-59.

[1]Several works provide biographical information on Pannenberg. See James M. Robinson, "Revelation as Word and as History," in **TaH**, 3-12; Richard John Neuhaus, "Wolfhart Pannenberg: Profile of a Theologian," in Wolfhart Pannenberg, **Theology and the Kingdom of God** (Philadelphia: Westminster Press, 1969), 9-50; Don H. Olive, **Wolfhart Pannenberg**, Makers of the Modern Theological Mind, ed. Bob E. Patterson (Waco, TX: Word Books, 1973); Allan D. Galloway, **Wolfhart Pannenberg** (London: George Allen & Unwin, 1973); E. Frank Tupper, **The Theology of Wolfhart Pannenberg** (Philadelphia: Westminster Press, 1973), 21-27; Steck, 887-888. For an autobiographical account, see Wolfhart Pannenberg, "An Autobiographical Sketch," in **TWP**, 11-18; idem, "God's Presence in History," **CC** 98 (1981): 260-263.

[2]In addition to references cited in n. 1 above, see the following general references to Pannenberg's theology: J. Wirsching, "Ein neues theologisches System? Randbemerkungen zur Theologie Wolfhart Pannenbergs," **DtPfrBl** 64 (1964): 601-609; Daniel P. Fuller, "A New German Theological Movement," **SJT** 19 (1966): 160-175; William Hamilton, "The Character of Pannenberg's Theology," in **Theology as History**, New Frontiers in Theology, vol. 3, ed. James M. Robinson and John B. Cobb, Jr. (New York: Harper and Row, 1967), 176-196; Robert T.

Wolfhart Pannenberg was born on 2 October 1928, in Stettin, Germany (now Poland).¹ Although he was baptized into the Lutheran church, he was "raised as an atheist in the time of nihilism during the years of the Nazi regime."² On 6 January 1945, at the age of sixteen, he was on his way home from his music lessons when he experienced an extraordinary event: he found himself absorbed into an encounter with

---

Osborn, "Pannenberg's Programme," **CJT** 13/2 (1967): 109-122; Ignace Berten, **Geschichte, Offenbarung, Glaube: Eine Einführung in die Theologie Wolfhart Pannenbergs** (Munich: Claudius Verlag, 1970); Gian Luigi Brena, "La Theologia di Wolfhart Pannenberg," **CivCatt** 126 (1975): 368-386; Hans-Theodor Goebel, **Wort Gottes als Auftrag: Zur Theologie von Rudolf Bultmann, Gerhard Ebeling und Wolfhart Pannenberg** (Neukirchen-Vluyn: Neukirchener Verlag des Erziehungsvereins, 1972), 179-260; Clark H. Pinnock, "Pannenberg's Theology: Part 1: Reasonable Happenings in History; Part 2: No-Nonsense Theology: Pinnock Reviews Pannenberg," **CT** 21 (1976): 147-150 and 218-220; Charles Villa-Vicencio, "The Theology of Wolfhart Pannenberg," **JTSA** 16 (1976): 28-41; Kantzenbach, 289-314; Wilfried Härle and Eiler Herms, "Deutschsprachige protestantische Dogmatik nach 1945. II. Teil," **VF** 28 (1983): 43-53; Horst Georg Pöhlmann, **Gottesdenker: Prägende evangelische und katholische Theologen der Gegenwart, 12 Porträts** (Hamburg: Rowohlt Verlag, 1984), 146-165; Carl E. Braaten, "Wolfhart Pannenberg," in **A Handbook of Christian Theologians**, enl. ed., ed. Dean G. Peerman and Martin E. Marty (Nashville, TN: Abingdon Press, 1984), 639-659; Bernd Burkhardt, "Pannenberg," in **Argumente für Gott. Gott-Denker von der Antike bis zur Gegenwart: Ein Autoren-Lexikon**, ed. Karl-Heinz Weger (Freiburg: Herder, 1987), 270-272; Sebastian Greiner, **Die Theologie Wolfhart Pannenbergs**, BDS 2 (Würzburg: Echter Verlag, 1988); David P. Polk, **On the Way to God: An Exploration into the Theology of Wolfhart Pannenberg** (Lanham, MD: University Press of America, 1989); Christoph Schwöbel, "Wolfhart Pannenberg," in **The Modern Theologians: An Introduction to Christian Theology in the Twentieth Century**, ed. David F. Ford (Oxford: Basil Blackwell, 1989), 1:257-292; James M. Childs, Jr., "The Significance of Wolfhart Pannenberg for Contemporary Theology," **TSR** 13/2 (1991): 61-68; Hermann Fischer, **Systematische Theologie: Konzeptionen und Probleme im 20. Jahrhundert** (Stuttgart: W. Kohlhammer, 1992), 198-205; Grenz and Olson, 186-199; David L. Smith, **A Handbook of Contemporary Theology** (Wheaton, IL: Victor Books, 1992), 139-148; Gian Luigi Brena, **La Theologia di Wolfhart Pannenberg: Christianesimo e Modernità** (Casale Monferrato: Edizioni Piemme, 1993); Reginald Nnamdi, **Offenbarung und Geschichte: Zur hermeneutischen Bestimmung der Theologie Wolfhart Pannenbergs**, WSFTh 13 (Frankfurt/Main: Peter Lang, 1993). See also the two "Festschriften" in honor of Pannenberg's 60th birthday: Carl E. Braaten and Philip Clayton, eds., **TWP** (Minneapolis: Augsburg Publishing House, 1988); and Jan Rohls and Gunther Wenz, eds., **Vernunft des Glaubens. Wissenschaftliche Theologie und kirchliche Lehre. Festschrift zum 60. Geburtstag von Wolfhart Pannenberg, mit einem bibliographischen Anhang** (Göttingen: Vandenhoeck & Ruprecht, 1988).

¹Greiner, 14.

²These are the words of Pannenberg himself at the "Theta Phi Talkback Session with Wolfhart Pannenberg," **AsbTJ** 46/2 (1991): 38. Some have noted the relationship between Pannenberg's biography and his theology. According to John Scally, critical reflection has been a feature of his theology just as the skeptical and secular mentality had been present during his youth ("Faith at the Frontiers: Pannenberg's Theology of Faith," **ITQ** 58 [1992]: 135).

light. In retrospect, he believes this to have been the most important event in his life and compares it to a kind of vocational call.[1]

After World War II, Pannenberg studied philosophy in Berlin, and from 1948-1949, he studied in Göttingen under Friedrich Gogarten and Nicolai Hartmann. In 1950, he went to Basel to study under Karl Jasper and Karl Barth.[2]

The next year, Pannenberg went to Heidelberg. This proved to be a crucial step for him. A number of important scholars, engaged in different fields of study were instrumental in shaping his thought. This was a very formative stage of his career.[3] Pannenberg completed his doctorate in 1953 under Edmund Schlink.[4] Two years later, in 1955, he passed his *Habilitation* with his *Habilitationsschrift* (a kind of second dissertation) on the history of the idea of analogy between God and the world from early Greek philosophy to Thomas Aquinas.[5]

---

[1]Pannenberg, "An Autobiographical Sketch," 12; cf. idem, in "Theta Phi Talkback Session," 38-39; idem, "God's Presence in History," 261. James M. Robinson, however, seems to make a valid observation when he observes that Pannenberg's "own road to Christianity had been more one of rational reflection than of Christian nurture or a conversion experience" ("Revelation as Word and as History," 11, n. 31). Similarly, Clark H. Pinnock, who writes: "Like C. S. Lewis and Malcom Muggeridge, he [Pannenberg] traveled a path to Christ that entailed more rational reflection than Christian nurture or emotional crisis" (Pinnock, "Pannenberg's Theology," 147).

[2]Although Pannenberg greatly admired Karl Barth, and never ceased to do so, even in Basel he had become dissatisfied with the lack of philosophical rigor in Barth's thought. Pannenberg, "An Autobiographical Sketch," 14. Elsewhere Pannenberg writes that when he came to Basel to study under Barth [I] "was almost convinced of the appropriateness of his approach. On the other hand, I was troubled by the dualism involved in his revelational positivism. . . . Therefore, I felt that my philosophy and theology should not be permitted to separate, but that within their unity it should be possible to affirm the awe-inspiring otherness of God even more uncompromisingly than Barth had done, since he returned to reasoning by analogy" ("God's Presence in History," CC 98 [1981]: 261).

[3]Among them were the Lutheran theologians Edmund Schlink, who later became his "Doktorvater," as well as Peter Brunner, Günter Bornkamm, Heinrich Bornkamm, Hans von Campenhausen, Karl Löwith, and Gerhard von Rad. The latter exerted an important influence on Pannenberg's thought through his emphasis on the interpenetration of Israel's history as the history of transmission of traditions. On von Rad's influence on Pannenberg, see Gerhard F. Hasel, "The Problem of History in the Old Testament," AUSS 8 (1970): 23-50, especially 41-46.

[4]Pannenberg's dissertation, **Die Prädestinationslehre des Duns Skotus im Zusammenhang der scholastischen Lehrentwicklung** (Göttingen: Vandenhoeck & Ruprecht, 1954), was published the following year.

[5]Wolfhart Pannenberg, "Analogie und Offenbarung: Eine kritische Untersuchung der Geschichte des Analogiebegriffs in der Gotteserkenntnis," Ruprecht-Karls-University, Heidelberg, 1955; cf. idem, Analogy and Doxology," in **BQT**, 1:211-238; idem, "Analogie," in **RGG**, 1:350-353; idem, "Analogie," in **EKL**(2), 1:113-114. Elizabeth Ann Johnson has given careful attention to Pannenberg's early work on analogy in her unpublished dissertation "Analogy/Doxology and

From 1955 to 1958, Pannenberg was "Privatdozent" at the University of Heidelberg.[1] Probably the most important aspect of his experience at Heidelberg was his participation in a small discussion group of graduate students that met weekly to explore a range of questions encompassing the whole theological enterprise. This circle came to be known, against his own wishes, as the "Pannenberg Circle."[2] It gained worldwide recognition with its proposal of revelation as history.[3]

Their Connection With Christology in the Thought of Wolfhart Pannenberg" (Ph.D. dissertation, Catholic University of America, 1981); and more concisely in her article "The Right Way to Speak about God," Pannenberg on Analogy," **TS** 43 (1982): 673-692; on Pannenberg's understanding of analogy, cf. also Joachim Drumm, **Doxologie und Dogma: Die Bedeutung der Doxologie für die Wiedergewinnung theologischer Rede in der evangelischen Theologie**, BÖTh 22 (Paderborn: Ferdinand Schöningh, 1991), 191-292; Barbara Delp Alpern, "The Logic of Doxological Language: A Reinterpretation of Aquinas and Pannenberg on Analogy and Doxology" (Ph.D. dissertation, University of Pittsburgh, 1980), 1-14; and Franz Konrad, **Das Offenbarungsverständnis in der evangelischen Theologie**, BÖTh 6 (Munich: Max Hueber Verlag, 1971), 401-414.

[1]Andreas Bsteh, ed., **Dialog aus der Mitte christlicher Theologie**, BRTh 5 (Mödling: Verlag St. Gabriel, 1987), 243.

[2]Apparently the group had been formed already when Pannenberg was invited to join. Only subsequently, with the publication of the fruits of their joint labors in which Pannenberg contributed the introduction and focal essay, did it come to be known against his own wishes as the "Pannenberg Circle." Pannenberg himself calls it a "working circle." Wolfhart Pannenberg, **Jesus--God and Man**, 2d ed., trans. Lewis L. Wilkins and Duane A. Priebe (Philadelphia: Westminster Press, 1977), 12. The original participants were Klaus Koch and Rolf Rendtorff in Old Testament and Ulrich Wilckens and Dietrich Rössler in New Testament. Later, Martin Elze in Church History and the younger Rendtorff brother Trutz, in theology, joined the group. The circle ceased meeting regularly in 1969, apparently largely because of differences of opinion about the historicity and fundamental significance of Jesus' resurrection (Tupper, 23-24).

[3]Wolfhart Pannenberg, ed., **Revelation as History**, trans. David Granskou (London: Macmillan, 1968). The appearance of the German original in 1961 has been described "like the sound of ice breaking up on a frozen lake. . . ." Millard J. Erickson, "Pannenberg's Use of History as a Solution to the Religious Language Problem," **JETS** 17 (1974): 99. On Pannenberg's concept of revelation as history, cf. the discussion in Paul Althaus, "Offenbarung als Geschichte und Glaube: Bemerkungen zu Wolfhart Pannenbergs Begriff der Offenbarung," **TLZ** 87 (1962): 321-330; James Barr, "Revelation Through History in the Old Testament and in Modern Theology," **Int** 17 (1963): 193-205; Georg Muschalek and Arnold Gamper, "Offenbarung in Geschichte," **ZKT** 86 (1964): 180-196; Ignace Berten, **Geschichte, Offenbarung, Glauben**, 19-43; idem, "Openbaring in de Geschiedenis: De Theologie van Wolfhart Pannenberg," **TTh** 9/2 (1969): 151-177; Hans-Georg Geyer, "Geschichte als theologisches Problem: Bemerkungen zu W. Pannenbergs Geschichtstheologie," **EvT** 22 (1962): 92-104; Lothar Steiger, "Offenbarungsgeschichte und theologische Vernunft: Zur Theologie W. Pannenbergs," **ZTK** 59 (1962): 88-113; James M. Robinson, "Revelation as Word and as History," 1-100; Carl E. Braaten, "The Current Controversy on Revelation: Pannenberg and His Critics," **JR** 45 (1965): 225-237; idem, **History and Hermeneutics**, NDThT 2 (Philadelphia: Westminster Press, 1966); E. Gutwenger, "Offenbarung und Geschichte," **ZKT** 88 (1966): 393-410; G. G. O'Collins, "Revelation as History," **HeyJ** 7 (1966): 394-406; Jürgen Moltmann, **Theology of Hope: On the Ground and the Implications of a Christian Eschatology**, trans. James W. Leith (London: SCM Press, 1967), 76-84; Max Seckler, "Zur Diskussion um das Offenbarungsverständnis W. Pannenbergs,"

In 1958, Pannenberg accepted a call to the *Kirchliche Hochschule* in Wuppertal, where he together with Jürgen Moltmann taught systematic theology for three years.[1] In 1961, he was invited to the University of Mainz to become professor of systematic theology. Later (1968) he accepted a similar post at the University of Munich, where he stayed until his retirement.[2] Pannenberg has been a prominent figure in the Faith and Order Commission of the World Council of Churches and is a member of its

---

MThZ 19 (1968): 132-134; Felix Flückiger, **Theologie der Geschichte: Die biblische Rede von Gott und die neuere Geschichtstheologie** (Wuppertal: Brockhaus Verlag, 1970), 93-103; Franz Konrad, 277-426, especially 337-381; Edmund J. Dobbin, "Revelation as History: A Study of Wolfhart Pannenberg's Theology of Revelation" (Th.D. dissertation, University of Louvain, 1971); Tupper, 79-109; William Carl Placher, "History and Faith in the Theology of Wolfhart Pannenberg" (Ph.D. dissertation, Yale University, 1975); idem, "Pannenberg on History and Revelation," **RefR** 30 (1976): 39-47; Peter Eicher, **Offenbarung: Prinzip neuzeitlicher Theologie** (Munich: Kösel, 1977), 425-464; idem, "Geschichte und Wort Gottes: Ein Protokoll der Pannenbergdiskussion von 1961-1972," **Cath** 32 (1978): 321-354; Ekkehard Mühlenberg, "Gott in der Geschichte: Erwägung zur Geschichtstheologie von W. Pannenberg," **KuD** 24 (1978): 244-261; Rolf Rendtorff, "Offenbarung und Geschichte--Partikularismus und Universalismus im Offenbarungsverständnis Israels," in **Offenbarung im Jüdischen und Christlichen Glaubensverständnis**, QD 92, ed. Jakob J. Petuchowski and Walter Strolz (Freiburg: Herder, 1981), 37-49; Laurence Wood, "History and Hermeneutics: A Pannenbergian Perspective," **WesTJ** 16/1 (1981): 7-22; Denis Müller, **Parole et Histoire: Dialogue avec W. Pannenberg** (Geneva: Labor et Fides, 1983), 19-58; Krzysztof Góźdź, "Das theologische Verständnis der Geschichte bei Wolfhart Pannenberg," **CoTh** 54 (1984): 70-82; Dulles, **Models of Revelation**, 58-67; Kyuun-Jin Kim, "Offenbarung Gottes und die Geschichte Bei W. Pannenberg und J. Moltmann," in **Gottes Zukunft--Zukunft der Welt. Festschrift für Jürgen Moltmann zum 60. Geburtstag**, ed., Hermann Deuser, Gerhard Marcel Martin, Konrad Stock, and Michael Welker (Munich: Chr. Kaiser, 1986), 481-490; Kurt Koch, **Der Gott der Geschichte: Theologie der Geschichte bei Wolfhart Pannenberg als Paradigma einer Philosophischen Theologie in ökumenischer Perspektive**, TThs 32 (Mainz: Matthias Grünewald Verlag, 1988), and Timothy Bradshaw, "God's Relationship to History in Pannenberg," in **Issues in Faith and History: Papers Presented at the Second Edinburgh Conference on Dogmatics, 1987**, ed. Nigel M. de S. Cameron (Edinburgh: Rutherford House Books, 1989), 48-67.

[1]According to Tupper, 285, Pannenberg was the first of the eschatological theologians to conceive God as the power of the future. Cf. Wolfhart Pannenberg, "Der Gott der Hoffnung," in **Ernst Bloch zu Ehren: Beiträge zu seinem Werk**, ed. Siegfried Unseld (Frankfurt: Suhrkamp Verlag, 1965), 209-225. Four years later Jürgen Moltmann wrote the article "Die Zukunft als neues Paradigma der Transzendenz," **IDZ** 2 (1969): 2-13. David Polk is undoubtedly correct when he states that both men drew on the insights of the other during the three years they were colleagues in Wuppertal (**On the Way to God**, 10). Polk then adds the following observation: "In private conversations with me, each man [i.e., Moltmann and Pannenberg] minimized the contribution of the other towards his own work. There is reason to believe that this is somewhat less justified in Moltmann's case and that the borrowing of ideas was greater on his part (ibid., 18, n. 41).

[2]Since 1963 Pannenberg entered into dialogue with American currents of thought and lectured at the University of Chicago (Spring 1963), Harvard (1966), and Claremont (1967 and 1975).

standing commission.[1] Since 1964, he has been a founding member of the "Academie Internationale des Sciences Religioeuses" and a member of the "Bavarian Academy of Sciences."[2] While at the University of Munich, he received doctor of divinity degrees from the University of Glasgow (1972), the University of Manchester (1977), and the University of Dublin (1979).[3]

As impressive as Pannenberg's career might appear, it says little about Pannenberg as the theologian. Therefore, we must take a brief look at his theological and intellectual configurations.[4] Pannenberg has been characterized as a scholar whose originality of vision and insight, whose breadth of learning and power of constructive thinking across the whole range of theological issues makes him and his contributions "unparalleled in the contemporary non-catholic world."[5] His writings reveal an almost encyclopedic grasp of material on the most diverse subjects. He has been described aptly as a "comprehensive theologian,"[6] a "synthetic thinker flexible enough to incorporate widely differing insights avoiding extreme positions."[7]

Pannenberg probably became best known through a new theological approach[8]

---

[1]Bsteh, 243; Geoffrey Wainwright, "Pannenberg's Ecumenism," in **Theology and the Philosophy of Science**, trans. Francis McDonagh (London: Darton, Longman and Todd, 1976), 207.

[2]Steck, 887.

[3]Bsteh, 243.

[4]Richard John Neuhaus claims that a profile of Pannenberg "must be largely an intellectual profile, for he is a relentlessly intellectual man" ("Wolfhart Pannenberg: Profile of a Theologian," 14).

[5]Langdon Gilkey, "Pannenberg's **Basic Questions in Theology**: A Review Article," Perspective 14 (1973): 34. Paul Avis has said that "if Schleiermacher, as the founder of modern theology, represents (in terms of Hegelian dialectic) the *thesis* and Barth the *antithesis*, it is arguable that Wolfhart Pannenberg offers the *synthesis*. He is the third force in Protestant theology" (70).

[6]Minus Baskin Jackson, "An Interpretation of Wolfhart Pannenberg's Theory of Knowledge as Creative Subjectivity" (Th.D. dissertation, Union Theological Seminary, 1973, 23).

[7]Peter J. A. Cook, "Pannenberg: A Post-Enlightenment Theologian," **ChM** 90 (1976): 245.

[8]The early Pannenberg tried to distance himself from the term "system," preferring instead to speak about a theological sketch ["Entwurf"] (Wolfhart Pannenberg, "Nachwort zur zweiten Auflage," in **Offenbarung als Geschichte**, 3d ed. [Göttingen: Vandenhoeck & Ruprecht, 1965], 132, n. 1). In the foreword to his **SyTh/E**, 1:x-xi, however, Pannenberg consciously defends the term "systematic theology" for his presentation of Christian doctrine.

introduced in 1959. He proposed an eschatological method of theology[1] where history is the most comprehensive horizon of Christian theology.[2] In seeking to provide a new theological approach, he tried to combat what he perceives to be a widespread privatization of theology.[3] Such a "self-inflicted isolation of a higher glossolalia,"[4] as he calls it, occurs when faith is presented as a mere wager or a groundless commitment of an existential nature rather than a response to objectively sufficient evidence.[5] In contrast to the subjective "leap of faith" that, through Kierkegaard,

---

[1]It appears that with Pannenberg's new approach, a primary stimulus towards contemporary eschatological theology was given. Cf. Fuller, "A New German Theological Movement," 160-175. Klaus Koch says that "with Pannenberg the renaissance of apocalyptic in post-war theology begins" (**The Rediscovery of Apocalyptic**, SBT 22, trans. Margaret Köhl [Naperville, IL: A.R. Allenson, 1972], 101). According to Tupper, 20, this new movement was subsequently identified by its different emphases and spokespersons as "theology of hope," "theology of history," "theology of the future," "theology of the Kingdom of God," and "eschatological theology." According to Wirsching, 602, Pannenberg is the main Biblical-dogmatical founder and systematic leader of this new important approach.

[2]By pointing out that existentialistic kerygmatic theology dissolves history into the inward historicity of existence and *Heilsgeschichte* theology depreciates real history by fleeing from history to the realm of suprahistory or prehistory, Pannenberg exposed an underlying unity of the Barthians and Bultmannians who are usually seen in diametrical opposition to each other. For Pannenberg's interaction with Oscar Cullmann's concept of *Heilsgeschichte*, see Wolfhart Pannenberg, "Weltgeschichte und Heilsgeschichte," in **Probleme biblischer Theologie**, ed. Hans Walter Wolff (Munich: Chr. Kaiser, 1971), 349-366, 358ff; idem, **SyTh/G**, 3:539-540. On his understanding of history as the most comprehensive horizon of theology, see idem, "Redemptive Event and History," in **BQT**, 1:15; and idem, "Dogmatic Theses on the Doctrine of Revelation," in **Revelation as History**, ed. Wolfhart Pannenberg, trans. by David Granskou (New York: Macmillian, 1968), 124-158. James Barr thinks that "Pannenberg's position . . . contains many innovations as against earlier views and must be judged to be only partly in continuity with them" ("Revelation in History," in **IDBSupp**, 748). It appears that Pannenberg has not fundamentally changed his theological perspective since the above-mentioned essay in 1959. See his own evaluation in his article "God's Presence in History," 260.

[3]Pannenberg's position is put forth most stringently in **TPS**. From this position Pannenberg never departed. Compare also more recently idem, "Theology and Philosophy in Interaction with Science: A Response to the Message of Pope John Paul II on the Occasion of the Newton Tricentennial in 1987," in **John Paul II on Science and Religion: Reflections on the New View from Rome**, ed. Robert J. Russell, William R. Stoeger, and George V. Coyne (Vatican City State: Vatican Observatory Publications, 1990), 75; and idem, "Eine philosophisch-historische Hermeneutik des Christentums," in **In Verantwortung für den Glauben leben: Beiträge zur Fundamentaltheologie und Ökumenik. Festschrift für Heinrich Fries**, ed. Peter Neuner and Harald Wagner (Freiburg: Herder, 1992), 38.

[4]Wolfhart Pannenberg, "Types of Atheism and Their Theological Significance," in **BQT**, 2:189.

[5]Wolfhart Pannenberg, "Wahrheit, Gewissheit und Glaube," in **Grundfragen systematischer Theologie**, vol. 2 (Göttingen: Vandenhoeck & Ruprecht, 1980): 245. Carl Braaten has said that "Pannenberg is boldly trying to reverse the irrationalist trend in theology since Schleiermacher, which derives revelation from the experience of faith rather than from reason's

became so popular in Dialectical theology, Pannenberg does not want to shield faith from the potentially critical findings of reason.[1] Faith is not a separate way of knowing truth alongside rational inquiry; it is open to scientific inquiry and confirmation. Therefore, for him theology is a public discipline, subject to the same critical canons as are the other sciences.[2] Thus, his whole theology has been characterized as probably "the boldest attempt in this generation to establish the credibility of Christian belief vis-à-vis the canons of probable reasoning."[3]

Pannenberg's new approach has found a mixed reception.[4] It calls for a

---

knowledge of history" (**History and Hermeneutics**, 47). Although Braaten is certainly correct when he points out Pannenberg's opposition to irrational trends in theology, one can see a much closer similarity to Schleiermacher than sometimes thought. Cf. Avis, 86, 88.

[1]"The idea of the Word is not excluded, but restituted to a more modest and subordinate role within the context of revelation as history. **Instead of the authoritarian style of theological thought, the open rationality of the Enlightenment is preferred**, but combined with a concern for the substance of the Christian faith" (Wolfhart Pannenberg, "Preface to the American Edition," in **Revelation as History**, ed. Wolfhart Pannenberg, trans. David Granskou [London: Macmillan, 1968], ix), (emphasis supplied).

[2]Pannenberg, **TPS**, 326-345. Pannenberg has acknowledged that his criticism of the bifurcation of the supernatural and the natural and of the subjectivism in the revivalist tradition "emerges in the emphasis on reason and truth, in the use of critical rationalism in [his] appraisal of theological method, but also in [his] criticism of the shortcomings of secularization." Wolfhart Pannenberg, "A Response to My American Friends," in **TWP**, 316. Cf. idem, "Die Rationalität der Theologie," in **Fides Quaerens Intellectum: Beiträge zur Fundamentaltheologie**, ed. Michael Kessler, Wolfhart Pannenberg, and Hermann Josef Pottmeyer (Tübingen: Francke Verlag, 1992), 533-544.

[3]So, recently, Nancey C. Murphy, 19. Paul Avis has said that for Pannenberg "talk of rationality has the quality of a manifesto" (Avis, 72). William Placher classifies Pannenberg as "a theologian of reason, a theologian of the Enlightenment" ("Revealed to Reason: Theology as 'Normal Science'," 192). Pinnock, "Pannenberg's Theology," 147, claims that "Pannenberg's advocacy of a theology solidly based on reason is an identifying feature of his position." This Pinnock also maintains more recently when he writes that Pannenberg "commends reason as the tool for vindicating the historic faith," and "enlists reason as ally" (Clark H. Pinnock, **Tracking the Maze: Finding our Way Through Modern Theology From an Evangelical Perspective** [San Francisco: Harper and Row, 1990], 56). Already in 1968 Max Seckler described Pannenberg as advocate of autonomous and independent reason in theology ("Zur Diskussion um das Offenbarungsverständnis W. Pannenbergs," 134). Similarly, Josef Schmitz, who maintains that "Pannenberg macht sich in der Theologie zum Anwalt der mündigen Vernunft im Sinne der Aufklärung, der eine nur positiv gesetzte Autorität unerträglich ist" ("Die Fundamentaltheologie im 20. Jahrhundert," in **Bilanz der Theologie im 20. Jahrhundert: Perspektiven, Strömungen, Motive in der christlichen und nichtchristlichen Welt**, 4 vols., ed. Herbert Vorgrimmler and Robert Vander Gucht (Freiburg: Herder, 1969), 2:242. A sympathetic interpreter described Pannenberg's entire theological program as an attempt of a theology of reason (Neuhaus, "Wolfhart Pannenberg Profile of a Theologian," 43). See also the presentation by Stanley J. Grenz, "Reasonable Christianity: Wolfhart Pannenberg Turns 60," **CT** 32/7 (1988): 32-34.

[4]Carl E. Braaten summarized the reaction to Pannenberg's thought across the theological spectrum in the following words: "The neo-fundamentalists would enjoy his position on the

careful, and differentiating analysis. It has been claimed in regard to his theology that "the chief point of difficulty raised against Pannenberg in the past has centered on his understanding of Scripture."[1] Yet, so far, no comprehensive investigation of his understanding of Scripture has been made. It seems appropriate, therefore, that one should investigate more closely his understanding of Scripture.

A Description of the Concept of Scripture in Pannenberg's Systematic Theology

With the appearance of Pannenberg's massive **Systematic Theology**, one had hoped to find a systematic and in-depth treatment of the role of Scripture in theology. These hopes, however, have not materialized.[2] A reading of his **Systematic Theology** reveals that Pannenberg has not followed the order of the traditional theological foci to organize his systematic theology.[3] Instead of a prolegomenon on the role and function of Scripture in theology, one finds scattered statements on this question throughout **Systematic Theology**.[4] Nevertheless, several key passages in **Systematic Theology**

---

historical verifiability of the resurrection as a datable event of past history. The orthodox would like the sound of *noitia*, *assensus*, and *fiducia* but wouldn't know what to do about his antisupernaturalism. *Heilsgeschichte* theologians would endorse his stress on history but would generally not approve of eliminating the prophetic word from the definition of revelation. Historians would applaud his devotion to the facts, but few would succeed in reading revelation right off the facts of history. Those who see Pannenberg's theology as a revival of conservatism need only to meet his doctrine of scripture and of the confessions to be disabused of any illusions. Pannenberg's theology obviously escapes ready-made labels" ("The Current Controversy on Revelation," 233-234). For a helpful overview of the reception that Pannenberg has gained especially in the English-speaking world during the last twenty-five years, see Stanley J. Grenz, "The Appraisal of Pannenberg: A Survey of the Literature," in **TWP**, 19-52, and Kurt Koch, **Der Gott der Geschichte**, 45-53.

[1]Stanley J. Grenz, "Pannenberg and Evangelical Theology: Sympathy and Caution," **CSR** 20/3 (1990): 276.

[2]According to Grenz and Olson, 196, Pannenberg does not seem to have developed "a full-orbed doctrine of Scripture" yet.

[3]Stanley J. Grenz, **Reason for Hope: The Systematic Theology of Wolfhart Pannenberg** (New York: Oxford University Press, 1990), 7.

[4]In fact, at the very end of **SyTh/G**, 2:510-511, Pannenberg states that the statement about the inspiration of Scripture is no warranty for its truth because it assumes already the conviction about the truth of God's revelation in the person and history of Jesus on different grounds. Therefore, any statement about the divine inspiration of Scripture and its authority in the church belongs at the end, to the doctrine of reconciliation, and not at the beginnings of dogmatics. Professor Dr. Friedrich Mildenberger, who teaches systematic theology at the Friedrich-Alexander-Universität Erlangen-Nürnberg, Germany, stated to me, that in his opinion Pannenberg does not develop a teaching of Scripture (Schriftlehre) since he uses Biblical texts as historical sources

as well as other of his books and articles deal specifically with the issue under investigation.[1] These will all be taken into consideration in our investigation.

The Origin of Scripture

To better consider the question of the origin of Scripture, it is helpful, first of all, to examine statements in which Pannenberg tells us how Scripture did not originate. Then we concentrate on Pannenberg's understanding of how Scripture is perceived to have been originated.

How Scripture Did Not Originate

Pannenberg does not explicitly develop a full-fledged description of his understanding of the origin of Scripture. He is convinced that belief in the divine origin of Scripture as well as its divine inspiration might have been appropriate at the time of the older Protestant theology.[2] Today he says, "There can be no restoring of the older view of biblical inspiration."[3] In the modern age, he believes, the doctrine of the divine origin of Scripture--that is, the belief that Biblical writings are the product of divine revelation[4] written under divine inspiration[5]--is no longer tenable.[6] The

---

without giving them a special status over against other texts. Friedrich Mildenberger to Frank M. Hasel, June 26, 1992.

[1] In a letter to the author, Pannenberg referred specifically to his earlier article "The Crisis of the Scripture Principle," 1-14; his book **TPS**, especially pp. 344-345, his **SyTh/E**, 1:46, 50; and the last chapter of **SyTh/G**, 2:509-511; cf. also **SyTh/G**, 3:167-169, 176-177 (Wolfhart Pannenberg to Frank M. Hasel, June 23, 1992). I would point also to the following essays by Pannenberg: "Gibt es Prinzipien des Protestantismus, die im ökumenischen Dialog nicht zur Disposition gestellt werden dürfen?" in **Protestantische Identität Heute**, ed. Friedrich Wilhelm Graf and Klaus Tanner (Gütersloh: Gerd Mohn, 1992), 79-86; idem, "Hermeneutic and Universal History," in **BQT**, 1:96-136; idem, "On Historical and Theological Hermeneutic," in **BQT**, 1:137-181; idem, "What Is a Dogmatic Statement?" in **BQT**, 1:182-210, idem, "Schriftautorität und Lehrautorität," in **Mainzer Universitätsgespräche**, Sommersemester, 1962, 5-10, where the importance of Scripture and its use are discussed.

[2] Pannenberg, **SyTh/G**, 3:167.

[3] Pannenberg, **SyTh/E**, 1:45, idem, **SyTh/G**, 3:168-169.

[4] "By 'revelation' is generally meant the disclosure of what was previously unknown or only uncertainly apprehended. In theology such disclosure is normally regarded as caused by the agency of God . . . and as making known hidden aspects of the character and purposes of God, of humanity in its relationship with God and of what is to occur in the future through the providence of God. . . . God is the agent who reveals and human persons are the subjects who receive the revelation" (David A. Pailin, "Revelation," **The Westminster Dictionary of Christian Theology**, ed. Alan Richardson and John Bowden [Philadelphia: Westminster Press, 1983], 503). Pailin goes on to say that "traditionally revelation has been understood in terms of verbal or quasi-

challenge that Pannenberg faces in this context is to find a way to maintain the idea of revelation without at the same time subscribing to supernaturalism.[1]

According to Pannenberg, the content of Scripture is neither divinely revealed,[2] nor divinely inspired.[3] Scripture does not originate directly from God as His Word because revelation is not to be understood in the same sense as direct communication.[4] In fact, Pannenberg states that propositional revelation is to be rejected.[5]

---

verbal communications by God to recipients who then pass on what they have heard . . . the primary location of these revealed propositions, furthermore, is commonly held to be the Bible" (ibid., 505).

[5]"In theological language, inspiration signifies the operation of the Holy Spirit upon the writers of the Bible, by which the Bible becomes the expression of the will of God binding upon us, or the Word of God" (H. Cremer, "Inspiration," **The New Schaff-Herzog Encyclopedia of Religious Knowledge**, ed. Samuel Macauley Jackson [New York: Funk and Wagnalls Company, 1910], 6:12). Thus, inspiration signifies the special operation of the Holy Spirit on the origin of the Scriptures, which gives them unique power to impose obligation (ibid., 16).

[6]Pannenberg, **SyTh/E**, 1:120, idem, **SyTh/G**, 3:167-169. Already in 1961 Pannenberg stated that "the Enlightenment destroyed the old concept of revelation that belonged to seventeenth-century orthodox dogmatics, namely, the identification of revelation and the inspiration of Holy Scripture, the understanding of revelation as the transmission of supernatural and hidden truths" (Wolfhart Pannenberg, "Introduction," in **Revelation as History**, ed. Wolfhart Pannenberg, trans. by David Granskou [London: Macmillan, 1968], 4).

It should be noted, however, that this old concept of revelation and inspiration is much older than seventeenth-century Orthodoxy. It reaches back beyond the Protestant Reformers, medieval scholastic theology, and the early Christian church, right to the Biblical period itself. Cf. the detailed studies by Johannes Beumer, "Die Inspiration der Heiligen Schrift," in **HDG**, vol. 1, fasc. 3b (Freiburg: Herder, 1968); Vawter, 8-81; Alexander Sand, "Die biblischen Aussagen über die Offenbarung," in **HDG**, vol. 1, fasc. 1a (Freiburg: Herder, 1971), 1-26; Peter Stockmeier, "'Offenbarung' in der frühchristlichen Kirche," in ibid., 27-87; Michael Seybold, "Die Offenbarungsthematik in der Spätpatristik und Frühscholastik," in ibid., 88-115; Ulrich Horst, "Das Offenbarungsverständnis der Hochscholastik," in ibid., 116-143; Richard A. Muller, **Post-Reformation Reformed Dogmatics**, 2:1-69; cf. also Gnuse; and Karpp, **Schrift, Geist und Wort Gottes**.

[1]Eicher, **Offenbarung**, 431.

[2]According to Pannenberg, we have to "rid ourselves of the notion that only the communication of a primary knowledge of deity can be revelation. Nor should we expect that every form of revelation will have God himself as its content or even its author" (Pannenberg, **SyTh/E**, 1:195).

[3]Pannenberg, **SyTh/G**, 3:167-169. Pannenberg acknowledges here that the abandonment of the idea of divine inspiration has unavoidable consequences for the authority of Scripture, making it only a human document.

[4]Pannenberg, **SyTh/E**, 1:207; cf. Drumm, 203.

[5]Pannenberg, **SyTh/E**, 1:272, n. 45. Also: "But if we take into account the relevant biblical data in all their variety, we can hardly maintain that direct divine speaking is the basis" (ibid., 235); cf. 240-243. Already Franz Konrad, 284-286, has pointed out, however, that the exegetes Rolf Rentdorff and Ulrich Wilkens have taken over the concept of God's self-revelation

It is not surprising, then, to find Pannenberg stating that the catch-word "Word of God" can no longer be understood in the classical sense as the divinely inspired Word--the Bible.[1] According to Pannenberg, his "approach does not necessarily exclude the interpretation of the Bible as inspired by God," but it certainly involves "a very different account of the inspiration of scripture than that of premodern Christian thought."[2] Eventually, it is only in view of the function of the gospel and of the New Testament Scriptures as expression and document of the apostolic proclamation of the gospel that one can speak about Scripture as inspired by God's Spirit.[3]

In other words, Pannenberg does not hold to the supernatural explanation of the origin of Scripture[4] that lies at the basis of classical theology.[5] Instead, he regards the

---

from the same systematic theologian, i.e., Pannenberg, who appeals to them in support of his thesis. For Franz Konrad, it is unsatisfactory how Pannenberg eliminates Biblical concepts of revelation because they do not fit his theological claim of an indirect self-revelation of God. Even Rolf Rendtorff has distanced himself more recently from his earlier position and admitted that a dogmatic or philosophical presupposition had distorted the exegetical facts ("Offenbarung und Geschichte," 46). Rolf Knierim observes that "it is clear that Pannenberg's point of departure leads from the outset to a critical separation between texts that are suitable and unsuitable for the theme [of revelation]" ("Offenbarung im alten Testament," in **Probleme biblischer Theologie**, ed. Hans Walter Wolff [Munich: Chr. Kaiser, 1971], 206, n. 1). Already Kendrick Grobel, "Revelation and Resurrection," in **TaH**, 157 wrote: "Certainly any prospector has the right to decide what he is looking for, but he may in the process let gold or uranium glide by him." See also the criticism offered by the Old Testament scholar Franz Hesse, "Wolfhart Pannenberg und das Alte Testament," **NZSTh** 7 (1965): 174-199, especially 184ff, and the New Testament scholar Hans Hübner, **Biblische Theologie des Neuen Testaments**, vol. 1, **Prolegomena** (Göttingen: Vandenhoeck & Ruprecht, 1990), 101-239, especially 149-172.

[1]Pannenberg, **SyTh/G**, 2:45. This position is already put forth by Pannenberg in his article "On Historical and Theological Hermeneutic," 146. He goes on to say that theology must free itself today from such a pseudo-orthodox terminology which is but a flight from the full scope of the hermeneutical task that is posed for Christianity in this present situation (ibid., 147).

[2]Wolfhart Pannenberg, **An Introduction to Systematic Theology** (Grand Rapids, MI: Eerdmans, 1991), 15.

[3]Pannenberg, **SyTh/G**, 2:510-511. According to Pannenberg, every human word can be regarded as divinely inspired if "it rightly names the meaning of things and events, and thus brings out their truth . . . to the extent that the human word is apt and true, then, it no longer belongs to humanity alone; it is God's Word" (idem, **SyTh/E**, 1:254).

[4]Earlier Pannenberg wrote about the origin of the religion of Israel, which applies inter alia also for the origin of Scripture, that "the religion of Israel did not fall straight from heaven as a pure revelation. On the contrary, the beginnings of Israel and precisely that of the Israelite conception of God were closely interwoven with the Ancient Near Eastern religions and their history" (Wolfhart Pannenberg, "The Revelation of God in Jesus of Nazareth," in **TaH**, 105). For Pannenberg, it is clear that "revelation is not the starting point, but the end of a long path, which began with still indistinct and inadequate notions of God. *It is not true that the revelation, the self-disclosure of God, falls from heaven ready-made. Nor must it be the starting point of all*

Bible as essentially "*human* speech."[1] He has pointed out affirmatively that the historical critical "dissolution of the doctrine of inspiration had cut the ground from under the authority of scripture as a direct expression of divine revelation."[2] In accepting the epistemological constrains of modernity, Pannenberg stands in continuity rather than in apologetic opposition to the rational criticism of the Enlightenment.[3] Compared to the classical view of revelation and inspiration which understood the content of Scripture to be directly communicated from God, such an understanding of

---

knowledge of God, as if one could not otherwise know anything about him" (ibid., 118), (emphasis supplied).

[5]Cf. Vawter, 20-82; Gnuse, 6-41; Pesch; Holzhey.

[1]Pannenberg, **SyTh/E**, 1:254.

[2]Ibid., 1:224; idem, **SyTh/G**, 3:167-169. In his famous article "The Crisis of the Scripture Principle," 4, Pannenberg had stated that "The starting-point of the transformation of the foundations of Protestant theology which has been accomplished under the influence of historical consciousness is to be found here [i.e., in the historical-critical exposition of the Biblical writings]." In the same context Pannenberg observes that "the dissolution of the traditional doctrine of Scripture constitutes a crisis at the very foundation of modern Protestant theology." Similarly, idem, "Offenbarung und 'Offenbarungen' im Zeugnis der Geschichte," in **Handbuch der Fundamentaltheologie**, ed. Walter Kern, Hermann Josef Pottmeyer, and Max Seckler (Freiburg: Herder, 1985), 4:99. Earlier a comparable observation was reached by Girgensohn, 3, who speaks about the self-disintegration and dissolution of Protestantism through the historical-critical method; and Hans Emil Weber, **Historisch-kritische Schriftforschung und Bibelglaube: Ein Versuch zur theologischen Wissenschaftslehre**, 2d enl. ed. (Gütersloh: Bertelsmann, 1914), 43-213, especially 143, where Weber concludes that "Bibelglaube und 'moderne' historisch-kritische Forschung stehen in einem tief innerlichen Gegensatz." Cf. also Emil Pfenningsdorf, **Das Problem des theologischen Denkens: Eine Einführung in die Fragen, Aufgaben und Methoden der gegenwärtigen Theologie** (Leipzig: A. Deichertsche Verlagsbuchhandlung, 1925), 118-133; Paul Gennrich, **Der Kampf um die Schrift in der Deutsch-Evangelischen Kirche des Neunzehnten Jahrhunderts** (Berlin: Verlag von Reuther & Reichard, 1898), 18-24; and, more recently, the perceptive analysis and critique of the presuppositions and results of historical criticism in Gerhard Maier, **Biblische Hermeneutik**, 2d rev. ed. (Wuppertal: R. Brockhaus Verlag, 1991), especially 179-270.

[3]This has been accurately shown by Eicher, **Offenbarung**, 426-429. Eicher, 428, notes that Pannenberg does not justify his option in favor of the Enlightenment through a direct historical discussion of it but rather through the positive reception of its history of effects (Wirkungsgeschichte) for the understanding of freedom in philosophy, theology, and science. Pannenberg states in the untranslated "Nachwort zur zweiten Auflage," 137, that the rational criticism of the Enlightenment and its heirs has to be taken up positively by theology in order to be overcome.

Scripture constitutes nothing less than a paradigm change.[1] This brings us to the question of how Pannenberg explains the origin of Scripture.

How Scripture Is Perceived to Have Originated

We have noted that Pannenberg stands in continuation with the Enlightenment's rejection of a supernatural origin of Scripture;[2] i.e., where God reveals His will through propositional revelation and divine inspiration. Now we must find out what he means when he states that "God can be known only if he gives himself to be known."[3] Pannenberg himself immediately qualifies his statement that "the knowledge of God is possible only by revelation"[4] by arguing that "to say this is not to say what is the kind of revelation by which God makes himself known."[5] Even though Pannenberg thinks that the Bible does not originate through a direct communication from God, he recognizes that an explanation of its origin requires a "place where the reality of God may be encountered."[6]

He believes that this place of contact between the divine and the human in history is found in man's ecstatic nature which is open to the infinite through its capability for self-transcendence.[7] This openness to the infinite is characteristic of all

---

[1] "The theological paradigm shift has its roots . . . specifically in the collapse of the older Protestant scripture principle as formulated in the doctrine of inspiration" (Pannenberg, **SyTh/E**, 1:46). Yet, Pannenberg does not want to abandon completely the Scripture principle which is foundational for Protestantism. Instead, he tries to retain it in a modified form (Pannenberg, "Gibt es Prinzipien des Protestantismus," 79-80).

[2] Franz Konrad, 282, speaks of a "Abgrenzung gegen alles bloß Mirakelhafte." Similarly, Laurence W. Wood, "Above, Within or Ahead Of? Pannenberg's Eschatologicalism as a Replacement for Supernaturalism," **AsbTJ** 46/2 (1991): 53.

[3] Pannenberg, **SyTh/E**, 1:189; similarly, p. 194.

[4] Pannenberg, **SyTh/E**, 1:189.

[5] Ibid.

[6] Pannenberg, "Analogy and Doxology," 211.

[7] According to Pannenberg "the concept of human self-transcendence--like the concept of openness to the world which is to a great extent its equivalent--summarizes a broad consensus among contemporary anthropologists in their effort to define the special character of the human" (Wolfhart Pannenberg, **Anthropology in Theological Perspective**, trans. Matthew J. O'Connell [Philadelphia: Westminster Press, 1985], 63). This "exocentric structure of human living has . . . an openness that is not restricted to the things of the world . . . so that the real meaning of this openness to the world might be better described as an openness to God which alone makes possible a gaze embracing the world as a whole" (ibid., 68-69). Cf. also idem, **What Is Man? Contemporary Anthropology in Theological Perspective**, trans. Duane A. Priebe (Philadelphia: Fortress Press, 1970); idem, "Anthropology and the Question of God," in **BQT**, 3:80-98; and

human life¹ and constitutive of religion itself.² In order to fully comprehend Pannenberg's proposal of an origin of Scripture "from below,"³ one has to be aware that for him all human life is characterized by an ecstatic structure⁴ which includes

---

idem, **Human Nature, Election, and History** (Philadelphia: Westminster Press, 1977), 86-87, where Pannenberg describes religion as basic for human beings individually as well as for the social system in general. This anthropological orientation and foundation has been recognized by many, among which are Georg Kraus, **Gotteserkenntnis ohne Offenbarung und Glaube?** **Natürliche Theologie als ökumenisches Problem**, KKThS 50 (Paderborn: Verlag Bonifatius Druckerei, 1987), 359-363; Jafet Mencía González, "Das Göttliche als Begriff und als Wirklichkeit: Begrifflichkeit und Bewährung beim theologischen Ansatz Wolfhart Pannenbergs" (Ph.D. dissertation, Ludwig-Maximilians-University Munich, 1981, 115-146, especially 131ff); Kurt Koch, 133-210; also Franz Konrad, 286-326; Denis Müller, **Parole et Histoire**, 119-120.

¹Pannenberg, **SyTh/G**, 2:330-331.

²"In this regard one might speak of a religious 'disposition' which is inseparable from humanity" (Pannenberg, **SyTh/E**, 1:156). For Pannenberg, "an indication of the fact that in some form or other religion is a constitutive part of human nature is its universal occurrence from the very beginnings of humanity, and especially its basic importance for all cultures and probably also for the origin of speech" (ibid., 155). Cf. idem, "Religion und menschliche Natur," in **Sind wir von Natur aus religiös?**, SKAB 120, ed. Wolfhart Pannenberg (Düsseldorf: Patmos Verlag, 1987), 9-24; and idem, "Anthropologie in theologischer Perspektive: Philosophisch-theologische Grundlinien," in ibid., 87-105. The modern shift of the question of God to anthropology should not, according to Pannenberg, be regarded as a necessarily wrong development but rather as a further development of Biblical motives in the definition of the relationship between man and the world (idem, **SyTh/G**, 2:282). Consequently, dogmatics "cannot begin directly with the reality of God. More precisely, the reality of God is initially present only as a human notion, word, or concept" (idem, **SyTh/E**, 1:61). Earlier, William Hamilton, "The Character of Pannenberg's Theology," 178, concluded that Pannenberg's theology is that of a religious *a priori*.

³Cf. Werner Löser, "'Universale Concretum' als Grundgesetz der Oekonomia Revelationis," in **HFT**, 2:119, who speaks of Pannenberg's approach as a theology "from below." Pannenberg uses this expression to describe his Christological methodology. Pannenberg, **Jesus--God and Man**, 33-37. Gunton's observation on Pannenberg's theological approach merits attention when he says: "What begins below must, on certain epistemological assumptions, end there too. Method and content imply each other" (Colin E. Gunton, **Yesterday and Today: A Study of Continuities in Christology** [Grand Rapids, MI: Eerdmans, 1983], 62).

⁴Pannenberg builds on the recent phenomenological analyses of modern anthropology and emphasizes the ec-centric nature of man which manifests itself in the openness of man towards the world and beyond. Says Pannenberg, **Anthropology in Theological Perspective**, 524: "All life, then, is ecstatic and to that extent spiritual. But the ecstatic character found in all life reaches a new level of intensity, a new high point, in human beings. To the extent that human beings exist exocentrically, . . . and experience themselves from that vantage point, the life-giving power of the spirit, which raises them above their own finiteness, manifests itself in an intensified form." In their ecstatic nature "human personality is similar to the trinitarian persons" in that "it is constituted by its relation to a social context" (idem, **SyTh/E**, 1:430). Pannenberg has recently linked the ecstatic nature of man more explicitly to the participation of man in the life of God through the Spirit, the creative origin of all life, who lifts men out of their own finiteness into their being "in Christ" (idem, **SyTh/G**, 2:227, 498-499, 48; idem, **SyTh/G**, 3:24, 150, 206-207, 219).

imaginative inspiration.¹ This phenomenon of inspiration is "to be understood in the broader context of imagination and its efficacy in all human thought and perception."² Pannenberg's explanation of the relationship between the ecstatic nature of humankind, which includes inspirations,³ to Scripture and especially the transition and connection between the latter and the origin of Scripture is rather scant. From what we have gathered so far, however, it would appear that those imaginative inspirations, in which the true meaning of an event seems to be grasped, are ultimately responsible for the process of writing down those experiences with the divine and thus for the origin and formation of different traditions.⁴ From this account it appears that for Pannenberg "the history of the manifestations of God in the history of religions,"⁵ corresponds to the classical concept of revelation. Revelation, however, is not understood as a supernatural communication of some form of information but is defined by Pannenberg in his famous proposal as "Revelation as History,"⁶ where history is understood

---

¹Pannenberg, **SyTh/G**, 3:219; idem, "The Working of the Spirit in the Creation and in the People of God," in **Spirit, Faith, and Church**, ed. Wolfhart Pannenberg, Avery Dulles, and Carl E. Braaten (Philadelphia: Westminster Press, 1970), 18.

²Wolfhart Pannenberg, "Response to the Discussion," in **TaH**, 236-237.

³According to Pannenberg, imagination "constitutes the principal creative feature in human behavior" (**What Is Man?** 23) and "access to reality is opend up precisely through imaginative constructs" (ibid., 24). Yet, "something else always precedes all imaginative activity in the formation of religions, and for that reason religion is more than merely a creation of man" (ibid., 9-10).

⁴"If the history of religion is not just a history of human ideas and attitudes, if the issue in it is instead the truth of divine reality in the deities of the religions, this is because the history of religion can be read as that of the manifestation of divine reality and the process of criticism of inadequate human views of this reality" (Pannenberg, **SyTh/E**, 1:171).

⁵Pannenberg, **SyTh/E**, 1:171. Cf. also the following quotation: "The fact that history is the sphere of the self-demonstration of the deity of God was a discovery of Israel, into whose inheritance Christianity has stepped" (ibid.). Cf. also the earlier statements in idem, "The Revelation of God in Jesus of Nazareth," 104-105.

⁶Cf. the discussion in Pannenberg, ed., **Revelation as History**. It seems appropriate to briefly comment on Pannenberg's use of the term "history" or "Geschichte." In German theological language there is a technical distinction between "historisch" and "geschichtlich." Very roughly, Galloway has defined the distinction between the two by saying that *Historie* is the bare recounting of the facts, whereas *Geschichte* is history interpreted in its existential significance for us (Galloway, **Wolfhart Pannenberg**, 43). This distinction seems to go back at least to Martin Kähler and his famous lecture **Der sogenannte historische Jesus und der geschichtliche biblische Christus** (Leipzig: A. Deichert, 1896), (Eng. trans. **The So-called Historical Jesus and the Historic-Biblical Christ**, trans. Carl E. Braaten [Philadelphia: Fortress Press, 1964]); cf. also Georg Wobbermin, **Geschichte und Historie in der Religionswissenschaft: Über die Notwendigkeit in der Religionswissenschaft zwischen Geschichte und Historie strenger zu unterscheiden** (Tübingen: J. C. B. Mohr, 1911), 5, 6, 10, 14. The problem of rendering the

primarily in the sense of history as the transmission of traditions.¹ It is not difficult to see why Pannenberg considers the history of the transmission of traditions as the place where the very "origin of Scripture is to be conceived as a process of tradition."² Thus, anthropology has foundational significance for theology,³ in general, and for the

---

distinction between "historisch" and "Geschichtlich" into proper English has disturbed more than one translator. Carl E. Braaten, "Introduction: Revelation, History, and Faith in Martin Kähler," in Martin Kähler, **The So-called Historical Jesus and the Historic-Biblical Christ**, 21. Braaten has pointed out that "the contrast between the substantives *Historie* and *Geschichte* has been expressed in the following pairs of terms: objective history and existential history, outer history and inner history, or even writing history and making history" (ibid., 21). In their adjectival form one can maintain their distinction in English by translating *historisch* as "historical" and *geschichtlich* as "historic." For a concise account of the history and meaning of the terms "Historie" and "Geschichte," see O. Köhler, "Geschichte," **LThK**, 4:777-778; and Hans-Werner Bartsch, "Geschichte/ Historie," **Historisches Wörterbuch der Philosophie**, ed. Joachim Ritter (Basel: Schwabe & Co Verlag, 1974), 3:398-399. For a further discussion of Pannenberg's understanding of "Revelation as History," see below p. 136ff; and the evaluative critique in the final chapter.

¹Pannenberg thinks that history is essentially constituted by a process of "*Überlieferungsgeschichte*," i.e., a "history of the transmission of traditions." Thus, "historical process . . . is essentially a process of the transmission of tradition" (Wolfhart Pannenberg, "Kerygma and History," in **BQT**, 1:90). "So is history always even a history of the transmission of traditions" (Pannenberg, "Dogmatic Theses on the Doctrine of Revelation," 152; translation by author). Unfortunately, the English translation has weakened the force of the German original. Cf. idem, **Offenbarung als Geschichte**, 3d, ed., ed. Wolfhart Pannenberg [Göttingen: Vandenhoeck & Ruprecht, 1965], 112). Also idem, "Response to the Discussion," 257: ". . . history seen as the transmission of traditions is the deeper meaning of history in general." The German words *Tradtition* and *Überlieferung* retain some of the dual meaning of the Latin term *traditio*, which means both "tradition" and "transmission." Hence, it has been suggested that "one should translate *Traditions*--or *Überlieferungs*--as "transmission of traditions." Cf. the helpful discussion by James M. Robinson and John B. Cobb, Jr. "Editor's Preface," **TaH**, ix-x. It seems that Pannenberg has inherited the notion of "Traditionsgeschichte" through his contact with Gerhard von Rad. It is very close to Hans-Georg Gadamer's notion of "Wirkungsgeschichte" and has similar implications for hermeneutical and historical thinking. Theodore Frank Peters, "Method and Truth: An Inquiry into the Philosophical Hermeneutics of Hans-Georg Gadamer and the Theology of History of Wolfhart Pannenberg" (Ph.D. dissertation, University of Chicago, 1973), 208-209, 218-220. Kurt Koch thinks that the aspect of the "history of the transmission of traditions" is the key to Pannenberg's understanding of history (**Der Gott der Geschichte**, 82).

²Pannenberg, "What Is a Dogmatic Statement?" 186. In support of such a statement, Pannenberg quotes approvingly from the Danish Lutheran theologian Kristen E. Skydsgaard, "Schrift und Tradition: Bemerkungen zum Traditionsproblem in der neueren Theologie," **KuD** 1 (1955): 170, who writes that "before there was Scripture, there was tradition" (ibid., 186, n. 18). A similar statement is made more recently by James Barr, **Holy Scripture: Canon, Authority, Criticism** (Philadelphia: Westminster Press, 1983), 1. Cf. also Wolfhart Pannenberg, "Kerygma und Geschichte," in **Studien zur Theologie der alttestamentlichen Überlieferungen**, ed. Rolf Rendtorff and Klaus Koch (Neukirchen: Neukirchener Verlag der Buchhandlung des Erziehungsvereins, 1961), 136.

³Pannenberg, **TPS**, 422. Pannenberg has stressed that "we can know of divine revelation only through human mediation, which means through the mediation of the religious form of human experience of revelation" (ibid., 319).

explanation of the origin of Scripture, in particular. Anthropology, however, has only methodological priority rather than being materially the basis of theology.[1]

From what we have said so far, the picture that emerges for the origin of Scripture according to Pannenberg is as follows: the religious nature of man, which is constituted by his openness to the infinite beyond this world, is responsible for bringing forth religious literature. These human documents serve as primary documents for theology because in them the human awareness of the divine is reflected in the form of testimony. This fact, however, is applicable to all religious writings[2] and does not guarantee their truth.[3] Together with other religious texts, the Christian Bible originated as a phenomenon of religious experience. This leads us to an investigation of Pannenberg's understanding of the nature of Scripture.

The Nature of Scripture

In looking at Pannenberg's understanding of the nature of Scripture, we concentrate first on what Scripture is not. Then we turn to statements where he delineates what he perceives as the nature of Scripture.

What Scripture Is Not

Since Scripture is essentially a human product, it is no longer the basis of religion but is the cognitive expression of religion.[4] For Pannenberg God's self-revelation through history is indirect,[5] and therefore, the Bible is not the Word of God

---

[1] Pannenberg, **SyTh/E**, 1:157-158, n. 111. In the English translation the word "anthropology" has mistakenly been translated as "theology," thereby obfuscating the meaning when it reads that he is "not treating theology [sic] as materially the basis of theology."

[2] This is alluded to in **SyTh/E**, 1:178, where Pannenberg in passing mentions the fact that other religions also trace back their own knowledge of God to divine revelation.

[3] According to Pannenberg, it was the weakness of the orthodox position that it "handled the divine truth of scripture as the presupposition rather than the goal of theology" (**SyTh/E**, 1:35). Elsewhere Pannenberg has stated it this way: "It follows that religious traditions, with the variety of their assertions about divine reality and divine activity, must first be allowed to appear as religions and therefore as an expression of human experience and its processing. Only then can they be tested for reliability and truth" (**TPS**, 319). This is where Pannenberg's rationalism comes in.

[4] Pannenberg, **SyTh/E**, 1:120.

[5] This is repeatedly emphasized by Pannenberg. Cf. Pannenberg, **SyTh/E**, 1:191: "What is disclosed in the experience of a revelation is usually different from the deity that reveals." According to Pannenberg, **SyTh/E**, 1:243, the thesis of the indirectness of God's self-revelation has the systematic function of integrating the various experiences of revelation to which the Biblical

in direct identification with the letter of the text where the inspired text communicates direct supernatural verbal revelation from God.[1] Scripture, then, is not to be equated with divine revelation. By rejecting any claim to a supernatural origin of Scripture's cognitive contents, Pannenberg also dismisses its divine authority.[2] The special status of Scripture is no longer derived from its divine origin but from the church which quickly designated the Bible as a point of reference and the norm for Christian identity.[3]

Being essentially historical documents, Biblical testimonies are subject to the same historical limitations that characterize all human documents. Scripture contains pluralistic and conflicting ideas and its reliability is questionable.[4] In other words, Scripture does not carry divine authority; it lacks internal unity and sufficiency. Consequently, for Pannenberg, the nature of Scripture has changed from a principle of immediate divine authority to a principle of attaching Christianity to its historical origin as a permanent norm of its identity.[5] Pannenberg is fully aware of the significant implications of his proposal which changes the very nature of the Scripture principle itself.[6] In fact, the classical Scripture principle is modified to such a degree

---

writings bear witness. Cf. ibid., 240-241; and, earlier, idem, "Introduction," 8-15. Wolfhart Pannenberg, "Dogmatic Theses on the Doctrine of Revelation," 125-131. John B. Cobb, Jr. has explained that "a direct revelation would be one in which the content imparted directly coincides with the intention of the revealer and does not require any secondary interpretation. A direct self-revelation of God would be one which revealed directly the nature or character of God. Pannenberg's point is that when the Bible tells us of God's disclosures, the content of these disclosures is characteristically something about human events and actions, not directly information about himself. When elsewhere the Bible speaks directly of what God is like, it does so on the basis of interpretation of those events" ("Past, Present, and Future," in **TaH**, 207-208).

[1] Pannenberg maintains that taking into account all the relevant Biblical data in all their variety one cannot "maintain that direct divine speaking is the basis" (**SyTh/E**, 1:235).

[2] "There is thus something forced when theology must begin with the expectation that is implicit in the concept of the Word of God, i.e., in the demand that we take God seriously as a God who speaks. Instead, ideas of the Word and of a God who speaks stand in great need of interpretation. To assert them directly, arguing that what is communicated has an inescapable claim to supreme authority, is to make an authoritarian demand (Zumutung) outside the agreed consensus of the church's discourse. . . . In modern circumstances demands of this kind fortunately carry no weight by their very nature" (Pannenberg, **SyTh/E**, 1:242).

[3] Ibid., 1:50; cf. also idem, **SyTh/G**, 3:378; and idem, "Eine philosophisch-historische Hermeneutik des Christentums," 35-36.

[4] Pannenberg, **SyTh/G**, 3:167, 169.

[5] Pannenberg, "Gibt es Prinzipien des Protestantismus," 80; cf. idem, **SyTh/G**, 3:140.

[6] Pannenberg, "Gibt es Prinzipien des Protestantismus," 80.

that one wonders whether one can still speak of a Scripture principle in the traditional Protestant sense.[1]

Furthermore, having accepted the historical critical method and its results, Pannenberg has no place for the concept of a Biblical canon involving a material agreement among the Biblical writers.[2] Hence, the assertion of a doctrinal unity of Scripture is made impossible.[3] Through the historical critical approach to Scripture, the Protestant tenet of the clarity[4] and sufficiency of Scripture also becomes problematic.[5]

Accordingly, Scripture cannot be a source book for doctrine, nor is it the revealed truth as Protestant orthodoxy used to think. The truth and authority of Scripture are not qualities that can be presupposed because of divine inspiration; rather, they are the goals of theology which will be reached only at the end of the process of

---

[1] Cf. Gerhard Gloege, "Schriftprinzip," **RGG**, 5:1540-1543; Kropatscheck; and Karl Barth, "Das Schriftprinzip der Reformierten Kirche," 215-245. Recently, the Scripture principle has been defined as "the theory . . . that the practices and beliefs of the church should be grounded in Scripture. Nothing that could not be demonstrated to be grounded in Scripture could be regarded as binding upon the believer. The phrase *sola scriptura*, 'by Scripture alone', summarizes this principle" (Alister E. McGrath, ed., **The Blackwell Encyclopedia of Modern Christian Thought** [Oxford: Basil Blackwell, 1993], 667). Along similar lines, Richard A. Muller describes the term *sola Scriptura* as "the watchword of the Reformation in its establishment of the basis for a renewal and reformed statement of Christian doctrine. We find the concept *sola Scriptura*, Scriptura alone as the primary and absolute norm of doctrine at the foundation of the early Protestant attempts at theological system in the form of exegetical loci communes, or common places" (**Dictionary of Latin and Greek Theological Terms**, 284).

[2] Pannenberg, "The Crisis of the Scripture Principle," 7.

[3] Pannenberg, "What Is a Dogmatic Statement?" 194. This opinion is reiterated in his **SyTh/E**, 1:14-15, n. 23.

[4] On the clarity of Scripture in the theology of Martin Luther, see Beisser, **Claritas Scripturae bei Martin Luther**; Hermann; Rothen, **Die Klarheit der Schrift. Teil 1: Martin Luther. Die wiederentdeckten Grundlagen**; and Robert D. Preus, **The Theology of Post-Reformation Lutheranism**, 1:311-315.

[5] By *sufficiency* Lutheran theology meant that Scripture contains everything that one must believe to be saved and everything one must do to live a God-pleasing life. Robert Preus has pointed out that the clarity of Scripture "was a principle that was closely bound to the sufficiency of Scripture. The sufficiency of Scripture could not possibly be maintained if Scripture was a dark and obscure book" (**The Theology of Post-Reformation Lutheranism**, 1:311, 309). Cf. Pannenberg, "Hermeneutic and Universal History," 96.

history.[1] Hence, Scripture is not the final or ultimate authority of Christian faith. How, then, does Pannenberg see the nature of Scripture?

What Scripture Is Perceived to Be

In response to the two most common answers regarding the character of Scripture, which he perceives to be false alternatives, Pannenberg suggests his own proposal. Instead of understanding Scripture in normative terms--where the Biblical writings are applied in their immediate relevance of their statements to the present[2] or, alternatively, where they treat the Biblical texts strictly and exclusively as sources for the religious history of Israel and primitive Christianity[3]--Pannenberg perceives Scripture as *theologically* oriented texts to be understood within the context of the history of religions.

> In this context it is not just application to the present which gives the biblical texts their theological dimension. It is now the phenomena of the history of the Judeo-Christian religion themselves and their own context in that history which requires them to be interpreted as the self-manifestation of the divine power over everything, i.e., of the all-determining reality.[4]

One can say that for Pannenberg Scripture is a testimony to the religious experience of man's essential openness to the divine. This means Pannenberg considers Scripture as a collection of historical documents[5] that testify to God's indirect

---

[1]Pannenberg, **SyTh/E**, 1:35; idem, "Die Rationalität der Theologie," 542-543; and idem, "What Is Truth?" in **BQT**, 2:21. Cf. Pannenberg, **SyTh/E**, 1:242, 234-235, 21-22; idem, **SyTh/G**, 3:143. Although Pannenberg does not refer to Gadamer in this context, it is interesting to note that for Gadamer authority in a similar way is not blind obedience to a command but is connected with understanding and the use of reason. See the discussion in Bernd Jochen Hilberath, **Theologie zwischen Tradition und Kritik. Die philosophische Hermeneutik Hans-Georg Gadamers als Herausforderung des theologischen Selbstverständnisses** (Düsseldorf: Patmos Verlag, 1978), 201-205, especially 204.

[2]This is the first alternative which Pannenberg dismisses. For Pannenberg, **TPS**, 378, such an approach "must lead to unhistorical and forced interpretations . . . which disregards the history which lies between the primitive Christian writings and the situation of the interpreter, and the changes this history has produced in the content of religion. Not least among the failings of this approach is that it ultimately does not do justice to the present because it does not consider it in relation to its origins."

[3]This is the second false alternative that Pannenberg dismisses. In this case "the exegetical disciplines seem to lose their theological character because they now seem to be concerned only with historical phenomena in the study of which considerations of their present force is inadmissible" (**TPS**, 378).

[4]Pannenberg, **TPS**, 379; cf., idem, **SyTh/G**, 3:539.

[5]Pannenberg, **Introduction to Systematic Theology**, 15.

self-revelation which is "a reflex of his activity in history."[1] It is a place where one finds the history of the transmission of the Judeo-Christian tradition recorded.[2] The peculiar characteristic of the Biblical texts, in contrast to other texts, is that they speak about God and his action in specific events.[3] It is clear that Scripture is no longer to be perceived as a direct source for theology, in general. Instead, history as the history of the transmission of religious traditions, of which Scripture is part, replaces Scripture as the source for theological ideas.

Since the history of religions is the location of a dispute among rival religious truth claims,[4] Scripture must be seen within the broader framework of a historical theology of Christianity.[5] Christianity "describes one segment of the history of world religion" and, therefore, "the history of the religion of Israel, of Judaism and of primitive Christianity must be at the center of biblical theology."[6] For Pannenberg,

---

[1] Cf. Pannenberg, "Introduction," 14.

[2] Recently, Rolf Rendtorff, one of the founding members of the "Pannenberg circle," has pointed out that such a program is implicitly based on a substitutionary theory where the Christian church has replaced Israel. In Rendtorff's opinion this does not account for the fact that even today Judaism exists as a vital religion that lives in unbroken continuity with the traditions of the Old Testament. In other words, the program of "Revelation as History" does not belong to the interpretation of the Old Testament but to Christian appropriation ("Offenbarung und Geschichte," 39-40). Cf. Pannenberg, **TPS**, 387. See also Robert Spaemann's response to Pannenberg's presentation "Die Wahrheit Gottes in der Bibel und im christlichen Dogma," in **Wahrheitsansprüche der Religion heute**, KRP 2, ed. Willi Oelmüller (Paderborn: Ferdinand Schöningh), 294.

[3] Pannenberg, "Eine philosophisch-historische Hermeneutik des Christentums," 36.

[4] "Es geht ja im Wettstreit der Religionen darum, ob . . . die Realität der Welt und des Menschen angemessener und differenzierter erfaßt werden kann als von konkurrierenden Ansatzpunkten" (Pannenberg, SyTh/G, 2:10). Cf. idem, "Geschichte/Geschichtsschreibung/ Geschichtsphilosophie: VIII, Systematisch-theologisch," **TRE**, 12:669-670. One can see a certain affinity between Pannenberg and Schleiermacher on this point. Friedrich D. E. Schleiermacher, **The Christian Faith**, § 7,3, p. 33, was convinced of the "exclusive superiority of Christianity" and thought that in comparison with other similar religions "Christianity is, in fact, the most perfect of the most highly developed forms of religion" (ibid., § 8,4, p. 38). Edmund J. Dobbin has captured Pannenberg's approach in these words: "*Since it is in the religions that the theme of God comes to expression, religions are the subject matter of theology viewed as the science of God. Religions make claims to the experience of the all-determining Power. The task of theology as distinct from any other science which might study the religions is to test the truth of these claims 'against the full range of accessible experience'*" ("Seminar on Foundations: Pannenberg on Theological Method," **CTSAP** 32 [1977]: 212).

[5] Cf. Pannenberg, **TPS**, 386; idem, SyTh/E, 1:341.

[6] Pannenberg, **TPS**, 386. Carl F. H. Henry thinks that Pannenberg does not expound the implications of universal history for the history of the nations. He also wonders why Pannenberg

Scripture is the source book for this tradition.¹ Gunneweg has pointed out it is this early history of Christianity that has normative character for Pannenberg rather than the canon of Scripture and the *sola scriptura* principle.² Consequently, Scripture becomes only a historical document that is theological in orientation. Theology becomes the science of history.³

Such a historical understanding of Scripture implies that the Bible reflects only an ongoing process of the transmission of traditions, and the traditions witnessed to are constantly reinterpreted in light of later events, thus undergoing constant transformation.⁴ Such traditions precede the origin of Christianity and continue after it.⁵ Hence, "the boundaries between primitive Christianity and the history of the early church become fluid,"⁶ because the "formation of the canon is seen as a moment *within* the history of Christianity."⁷ In other words, Pannenberg's understanding of the nature of Scripture arises out of his understanding of revelation as history.⁸ Hence,

---

has chosen the particular history of Israel as opposed to exposing the revelation found in some other national history (**God, Revelation, and Authority**, 2:300).

¹Grenz, **Reason for Hope**, 37.

²Antonius H. J. Gunneweg, "Sola Scriptura. Theologische und methodologische Erwägungen zu einem akuten Problem," in **Sola Scriptura: Beiträge zu Exegese und Hermeneutik des Alten Testaments**, ed. Peter Höffken (Göttingen: Vandenhoeck & Ruprecht, 1983), 185; see also Pannenberg, "Gibt es Prinzipien des Protestantismus," 80.

³Gunneweg, 194. Galloway, **Wolfhart Pannenberg**, 44-45, thinks that "there is a sense in which Pannenberg does tend to turn his historians into theologians and his theologians into historians. According to him, the method and interest of the historian and the theologian are essentially the same. The only difference is that the historian is typically interested in interpreting the facts in relation to a specific, limited area or period. The theologian, on the other hand, is interested in the self-disclosure of the universal God in history. He is concerned with specific events and periods only in so far as they illuminate the meaning of history as a whole. . . . Pannenberg maintains that every judgment by a historian about the significance of events is made on the basis of some assumptions, however rudimentary and vague, about what human history is all about. This is the sense in which every historian is, in Pannenberg's view, a kind of crypto-theologian." Cf., Micskey, 158.

⁴Pannenberg, "Response to the Discussion," 258.

⁵Cf. Pannenberg, **TPS**, 387-388.

⁶Ibid., 375.

⁷Ibid., 375.

⁸Pannenberg has repeatedly been criticized for the weak scriptural foundations of his concept of "Revelation as History." His selective use of Biblical material is guided by dogmatic and philosophical demands. Cf. Horst Seebaß, **Biblische Hermeneutik** (Stuttgart: W. Kohlhammer Varlag, 1974), 83-88; Rolf Rendtorff, "Offenbarung und Geschichte," 40, 42, 45, 46; James Barr, "Revelation Through History," 197-203; Micskey, 156, has pointed out that it is

the canon of Scripture is essentially unclosed.¹ Given the pluralistic nature of the history of the tradition which Scripture reflects, Scripture also is considered quite a pluralistic document.² This idea is supported by the historical critical method, which Pannenberg endorses, and through which Scripture forever has lost its unity.³

Pannenberg, however, still wants to maintain that one can speak of a "unity of scripture relative to its central content."⁴ For him, Scripture has a normative function in theology--not by virtue of its divine authority or inspiration, but because of its function in the context of the life and teaching of the church⁵ which has as its "central content" the gospel of Jesus Christ.⁶ Scripture testifies to this unifying center because

---

typical for Pannenberg's thinking "daß er diese Geschichte nicht in ihrer Gegebenheit in den neutestamentlichen Zeugnissen sieht, sondern aus diesen Zeugnissen als ein auch ihnen vorgeordnetes theologisches Kriterium zu konstruieren anstrebt. **Die neutestamentlichen Zeugnisse rücken darin funktional von der Funktion des Kriteriums ab...**" (emphasis added). More recently John O'Donnell has remarked that "Pannenberg knows his exegesis but he is not a biblical theologian..." ("Wolfhart Pannenberg, **Systematische Theologie**, Band II," **Greg** 73/3 [1992]: 554). Similarly, Hermann Fischer, who comments on Pannenberg's **Anthropology in Theological Perspective**: "It amazes one in the new anthropology, viewed as a whole, how little Pannenberg argues theologically. The reader receives the impression that the theological voice is increasingly muffled for the sake of the project of mediating to the human consciousness" ("Fundamentaltheologische Prologomena zur theologischen Anthroplogie: Anfragen an W. Pannenbergs Anthropologie," **TRu** 50 [1985]: 60), (translation by author).

¹This is hinted at in a statement in **SyTh/G**, 2:510, where Pannenberg writes that the circumference of the canon is only a subordinate question with regards to the gospel and history of Jesus Christ. That the canon is essentially unclosed has been confirmed by Pannenberg himself in an answer to a question by the author at a question-and-answer session on "Central Themes in Christian Theology," 24 April 1992, Richmond, IN, Earlham School of Religion Classroom Building, Earlham College. Tape recording.

²Pannenberg can speak of "the varied and divergent witness of scripture" (Pannenberg, **SyTh/E**, 1:303). Cf. Pannenberg's treatment of conflicting statements in Scripture concerning creation, ibid., 2:56, and the resurrection accounts, ibid., 2:342.

³"Criticism of tradition by the Enlightenment ... sharpened Roman Catholic criticism of the older Protestant thesis of biblical unity and destroyed the basic scripture principle of Protestantism by drawing attention to contradictions and antitheses in biblical statements, by criticizing the traditional dates regarding authorship of the books of the Bible, and finally by demonstrating the historical relativism of many biblical concepts" (Pannenberg, **SyTh/E**, 1:26).

⁴Pannenberg, **SyTh/E**, 1:14. In n. 23 on the same page he writes: "In the light of the results of historico-critical investigation one can speak of a unity of scripture at least with respect to its central content, but not in the sense of a total consistency of all its detailed statements." A similar position has been maintained by Pannenberg earlier, cf. idem, "What Is a Dogmatic Statement?" 192-198.

⁵Wolfhart Pannenberg to Frank M. Hasel, January 21, 1994, 2.

⁶Pannenberg has delineated this stance in the very last section in **SyTh/G**, 2:510-511, where he states that the authority of Scripture is grounded in the gospel and only inasmuch as the words and sentences of Scripture testify to Jesus Christ do they have authority in the church. Cf.

Jesus Christ "is undoubtedly the focal point of revelation."[1] It is only from the gospel that Scripture derives its authority,[2] and it is from the *res* of Jesus Christ that it gains its unity and clarity.[3] Hence, Scripture possesses only secondary or relative authority. The ultimate authority and norm[4] is Jesus Christ himself,[5] who is the "central content," the "subject matter," and the "central theme of scripture."[6] This is so because **only** in the history of Jesus of Nazareth has the eschatological future, and with it the eternity of God, entered history.[7] Although the content of the gospel is accessible only through Scripture, Scripture needs to be judged by the gospel which is to be distinguished from the Bible.[8] This leads us to the next question, namely, how Scripture is used by Pannenberg.

The Use of Scripture

Next we study how Pannenberg does not use Scripture and then consider his proposal regarding the theological function of Scripture.

How Scripture Is Not Used

From our investigation thus far, it is obvious that Pannenberg does not use Scripture as a final norm and authority. His Post-Enlightenment perspective, which

---

idem, "Gibt es Prinzipien des Protestantismus," 83, 85; idem, "Eine Philosophisch-historische Hermeneutik," 36; idem, **SyTh/G**, 3:460, 463, where he uses the phrase "primacy of the gospel" [Primat des Evangeliums] and writes that the gospel is the foundational norm [Grundnorm] for theology. Pannenberg has maintained this position from as early as 1962, when he wrote that the real authority of Christian faith is Jesus Christ Himself (idem, "Schriftautorität und Lehrautorität," 5).

[1]Pannenberg, **SyTh/E**, 1:212 (translation by author). Bromiley has translated "Brennpunkt der Offenbarung" as "crux of revelation." But the meaning in the German original seems to be that Jesus Christ is the focal point of revelation.

[2]Pannenberg, **SyTh/G**, 2:510-511.

[3]Drumm, 261.

[4]This is the thesis of Góźdź.

[5]Pannenberg, "Schriftautorität und Lehrautorität," 5, 6, 8.

[6]Pannenberg, **SyTh/E**, 1:14-16. Earlier Pannenberg spoke of God's revelation in Christ as the "essential content" that allowed Christ to "become effective as the norm of all interpretation . . ." (Pannenberg, "On Historical and Theological Hermeneutics," 143). Thus, Jesus as the norm of all proclamation is a central "theological presupposition" for Pannenberg. Cf. ibid., 155.

[7]Pannenberg, **SyTh/G**, 3:650.

[8]Ibid., 2:511.

accepts the results of the historical critical approach to Scripture as an unquestioned given,[1] does not allow Scripture to function as the sole source of its own interpretation.[2] He maintains that today the established results of the historical critical method make the *sola scriptura* principle no longer tenable.[3] Consequently, he finds it impossible for him to maintain the foundational principle of the Protestant Reformation that Scripture is its own interpreter (*scriptura sui ipsius interpres; scripturam ex scriptura explicandam esse*).[4] Nor does he believe that Scripture can be used as a deposit of divine truths that can be applied directly to the contemporary situation. The concept of the clarity and unity of Scripture which are foundational for its ability to interpret itself has shifted, in Pannenberg's thought, to the concept of the clarity and unity of history.[5] Since Scripture is essentially a human document, it can be investigated historically-critically. In this context, any special approach that would

---

[1]"Seit dem Ende des Zeitalters der Vermittlung allen geschichtlichen Wissens durch Autorität kann man nun einmal das Bewußtsein eines geschichtlichen Glaubensgrundes nur noch haben, indem man die damit verbundene Relativität historisch-exegetischen Wissens auf sich nimmt samt der Bereitschaft, die geschichtlichen Grundlagen des Glaubens immer wieder zu prüfen und ihre vorhandenen Darstellungen wo nötig zu revidieren. . . . Die Entwicklung des historischen Bewußtseins und der historischen Hermeneutik hat zur Einsicht in die Situationsgebundenheit geschichtlicher Überlieferung geführt. Daraus ergeben sich Perspektivität und Relativität aller geschichtlicher Zeugnisse und Interpretationen. . . . Diese Einsicht gilt auch für den geschichtlichen Gegenstand des christlichen Glaubens, für die urchristlichen Zeugnisse von Person und Geschichte Jesu, sowie für alle späteren, darauf begründeten Lehraussagen und historischen Beschreibungen" (Pannenberg, **SyTh/G**, 3:176-177). It is surprising that Wirsching, 604, in an otherwise excellent analysis of Pannenberg's early theology, misinterprets some statements made by Pannenberg about the Protestant Reformation in a way that portrays Pannenberg himself as "submitting to the Reformation claim, that all theological statements have to be derived in principle from Scripture." Cf. Pannenberg, "What Is a Dogmatic Statement?" 184-191.

[2]Gerhard Ebeling, "'Sola Scriptura' and Tradition," 130-131. To start out with a historically and culturally conditioned Scripture, arriving at the authority of Scripture only at the end, as Pannenberg does, stands as a challenge to the classical Protestant approach as Grenz has recognized correctly. Grenz, **Reason for Hope**, 38. More recently, Grenz and Olson, 196, called it a "valid challenge to the classical Protestant approach," which seems to indicate a certain approval of Pannenberg's theological approach to the detriment of the classical Protestant Scripture principle.

[3]Pannenberg, "What Is a Dogmatic Statement?" 186. This is also seen by Carl E. Braaten, "Can We Still Hold to the Principle 'Sola Scriptura'?" **Dialog** 20 (1981): 191, who writes that the chief result of the historical critical method "as far as Christian theology is concerned, is undoubtedly that the authority of the Bible can no longer function as it did before the rise of the critical historical consciousness."

[4]Cf. Muller, **Dictionary of Latin and Greek Theological Terms**, 277.

[5]Cf. Ulrich Duchrow, "Die Klarheit der Schrift und die Vernunft," **KuD** 15 (1969): 4.

take into consideration its own claim to supernatural, divine authority is to be eliminated.¹

Acknowledging that Pannenberg basically rejects any approach that conceives Scripture as being the final norm and authority, we must turn our attention to his suggestion regarding how Scripture should be used in theology.

How Scripture Is Suggested to Be Used

Pannenberg's writings reveal that he supports the use of Scripture within the epistemological framework of the Enlightenment.² This stance towards Scripture probably expresses itself most clearly in his adamant opposition to all forms of external authority.³ Although Pannenberg admits in his later works that "there is indeed a spell of authority emanating from the Bible,"⁴ it is clear for him, that

> in the modern period . . . the initiative has gone over to the side of reason. It is no longer a question of whether the authority of the Christian source of revelation, viz., Scripture, can

---

[1] Cf. Schleiermacher, **The Christian Faith**, § 130,2, p. 600.

[2] "Until the Enlightenment, Christian theology was doubtless a theology of revelation in this sense [i.e., putting forth authoritarian truth], appealing to revelation as a supernatural authority. The authoritative revelation was found in the 'Word of God', i.e., in the inspired word of the Bible. As the product of the divine Spirit, this word was regarded in a strongly literal sense as the 'Word of God.' . . . **But for men who live in the sphere in which the Enlightenment has become effective, authoritarian claims are no longer acceptable**, . . ." (Pannenberg, "Response to the Discussion," 226), (emphasis supplied). Such authoritarian features are seen by Pannenberg "in the positivism of the Reformation's *sola scriptura*" (ibid., 228). For him, "the question concerning the revelation of God, as it has been reformulated on the basis of the enlightenment, is not seeking for some authoritarian court of appeal which suppresses critical questioning and individual judgment, but for a manifestation of divine reality **which meets the test of man's matured understanding as such**" (ibid., 229), (emphasis supplied). In this sense, Pannenberg has rightly been recognized as standing in the tradition of the Enlightenment: "Pannenberg is in the true sense a post-Enlightenment theologian" (Scally, 130); cf. also Peter J. A. Cook, 245-264; and Tupper, 33. Stanley J. Grenz, in writing about the first volume of Pannenberg's **Systematic Theology**, describes him as being fully modern. "He affirms the changed intellectual situation created by the Enlightenment" (**Reason for Hope**, 13-14).

[3] This is a consistent characteristic of Pannenberg's approach. Already in 1966, Pannenberg wrote in his article "Faith and Reason," in **BQT**, 2:51, that in the realm of modern thought, where even historical questions are no longer settled by appeals to authorities but by the new science of historical criticism, an insistence upon an authority is no longer convincing and takes on the character of an external coercion. Recently, Pannenberg has renewed this claim in SyTh/E, 1:242, where he states: "Today all such claims to authority inevitably involve faith subjectivism. There is thus something forced when theology must begin with the expectation that is implicit in the concept of the Word of God, i.e., in the demand that we take God seriously as a God who speaks." It was this perception which turned him away from the "theology of the Word of God" in which he saw only the modern expression of such an authoritarian theology of revelation (Pannenberg, "Response to the Discussion," 227).

[4] Pannenberg. **Introduction to Systematic Theology**, 17.

be accepted by reason without contradiction. In the modern period the question is instead whether reason, after it has shown that belief on the basis of authority is irrational, can still allow any room at all for the Christian faith.[1]

It is Pannenberg's conviction that the Biblical understanding of reality is still relevant to modern man.[2] In fact, for Pannenberg, modern thought appears to be closer to the Biblical understanding of God, freedom, and historical reality than much of the unhistorical view of Greek philosophy.[3] This perspective, together with the conviction that revelation takes place as history, might explain the unique parallelism in Pannenberg's theology between exegetical arguments on the one hand and insights gained from the history of philosophy and theology on the other. Thus, it is often **after** he has gone through the development of a thought during the history of philosophy or theology that he tries to show the Scriptural legitimacy of it, too.[4] This procedure, i.e., the **dual** evidence in support of a thesis, from Scripture **and** from modern thought,

---

[1] Pannenberg, "Faith and Reason," 50-51.

[2] Georg Kraus, 347, 366-369, observes a fundamental apologetic intention in Pannenberg's theology. According to Pannenberg, Christianity possesses a commanding view of reason that is superior to the shortcomings of secular culture (Wolfhart Pannenberg, **Christentum in einer säkularisierten Welt** [Freiburg: Herder, 1988], 76) and Scripture is believed to possess the most adequate understanding of historical reality. Eberhard Jüngel has raised the question whether such an argument for the rational superiority of faith and even the rational necessity of God independently from faith ends not in the conundrum that one might earn the applause from some shaken believers but does not win the support from those thinkers who do not believe in God (Das Dilemma der natürlichen Theologie und die Wahrheit Ihres Problems: Überlegungen für ein Gespräch mit Wolfhart Pannenberg," in **Denken im Schatten des Nihilismus. Festschrift für Wilhelm Weischedel zum 70. Geburtstag**, ed. Alexander Schwan [Darmstadt: Wissenschaftliche Buchgesellschaft, 1975], 436). Grenz has pointed out, however, that "Pannenberg's orientation toward giving a reasonable account is not to be confused with the apologetic theology exemplified by Tillich, in which theological assertions are related to questions external to theology. Pannenberg, in contrast, does not develop systematic theology as the answer to the question posed from the outside but appeals only to the coherence of the unfolding theology itself. As a result he entertains no difference between apologetics and dogmatics. The unfolding of Christian doctrine comprising his systematic theology constitutes at the same time the testing of the Christian conception of God found therein" (Grenz, **Reason for Hope**, 220, n. 9).

[3] Cf. Wolfhart Pannenberg, "The Appropriation of the Philosophical Concept of God as a Dogmatic Problem of Early Christian Theology," in **BQT**, 2:119-183.

[4] Pannenberg freely admits that in addition to "philosophical and historical criteria which have to be met by a theological hypothesis . . . the *conceptuality* of new theological theories is never directly derived by verbal agreement from their subject matter, for example, from the biblical writings, but depends for its formulation on the current state of discussion in theological theory" (Pannenberg, **TPS**, 243). Pannenberg specifically referred me to this page (Pannenberg to Hasel, 2). Cf. also idem, **Metaphysics and the Idea of God**, trans. Philip Clayton (Grand Rapids, MI: Eerdmans, 1990), xiii.

is a typical characteristic of Pannenberg's approach.[1] Such a **dual** evidence in support of a thesis stands in contrast to the *sola scriptura* principle, where Scripture **alone** is sufficient to determine a theological question.

Under the conditions of historical and critical consciousness, the content of Christian faith can be appropriated only in connection with its tradition. This means that systematic theology always has to reflect its content as historically mediated statements.[2] This explains why Pannenberg's **Systematic Theology** often reads more like a sophisticated textbook on the history of theology. At the same time, it seems to reveal a subtle commitment to the Christian Scriptures and the adequacy of their thought that stands in some tension to Pannenberg's claim that truth is derived only at the end of a historical process.[3]

In order to be able to use Scripture within the parameters of modernity, Scripture needs to be tested by criteria other than those of an authoritarian doctrinal tradition.[4] Biblical statements and concepts can be accepted only if they are "confirmed" scientifically[5] because of their "reasonableness" and adequacy for modern

---

[1]Drumm, 212.

[2]Trutz Rendtorff, "Überlieferungsgeschichte als Problem der systematischen Theologie: Anmerkungen zu den Möglichkeiten und Grenzen der Theologie" **TLZ** 90/2 (1965): 94; cf. Pannenberg, **TPS**, 341.

[3]That a faith commitment has influenced the structure of Pannenberg's historical argument in the question of Jesus' resurrection has been pointed out by David Holwerda, "Faith, Reason, and the Resurrection in the Theology of Wolfhart Pannenberg," in **Faith and Rationality: Reason and Belief in God**, ed. Alvin Plantinga and Nicholas Wolterstorff (Notre Dame: University of Notre Dame Press, 1983), 303-304.

[4]Neie has pointed out that Biblical statements are not accepted by Pannenberg just because they are in harmony with other Biblical statements. Herbert Neie, **The Doctrine of the Atonement in the Theology of Wolfhart Pannenberg** (Berlin: Walter de Gruyter, 1979), 10. Pannenberg is well aware that "the demand for control stands in opposition to the divine authority which theology has always recognized in Christian doctrine and especially in the Bible. It is also opposed to the dogmatic certainty which has been claimed for Christian doctrinal pronouncements on the basis of such authority. If it could be taken for granted from the start that Christian doctrine and the Bible embodied the authority of God, any claim to test these sources by human judgment could only be blatant arrogance and a refusal of the obedience due to God's majesty." Nevertheless, Pannenberg outrightly insists that "it is impossible to regard the question of the divine authority of the Bible and Christian doctrine as settled in advance. It is a disputed question and one which theology **must** treat as a problem. For this reason theology today must not avoid the demand for a means of testing its statements by criteria other than those of an authoritative doctrinal tradition" **(TPS**, 330).

[5]Pannenberg, **TPS**, 326-345.

humankind.¹ It seems that one key criteria for determining whether a religion speaks authentically about God is whether God can be conceived as that reality which brings about unity in the stream of historical events and in the universe as a whole.² Another sign of the adequacy of Biblical statements for today is when those passages anticipate the future and the completion of the world and humankind from the perspective of God. To the degree that the future destiny of mankind is expressed in Biblical statements and stories are they relevant for people in later centuries.³ Such a use of Scripture, however, implies that Pannenberg somehow seems to know the future, even apart from Scripture. This raises the question whether the future is genuinely open or somehow pre-determined.⁴ It seems that Scripture at best is able to confirm but never

---

¹Pannenberg argues, for instance, that in the modern situation the belief in the resurrection of Jesus and the resurrection of the dead in general is no longer possible in the same "mythological" way as it was in late antiquity (SyTh/G, 2:393-394); cf. also idem, "Dogmatische Erwägungen zur Auferstehung Jesu," **KuD** 14 (1968): 114-115, where he says that Jesus' ascension towards heaven is no longer intellectually acceptable for modern man and is reinterpreted to mean having communion with God. Through new anthropological insights into the nature of man, however, where man is seen as being open to God, beyond the world, and where man finds no adequate fulfillment if death is the absolute end, the idea of a resurrection is once more a plausible thought. Similarly, idem, "Eine philosophisch-historische Hermeneutik des Christentums," 42. Pannenberg's anthropological argument is delineated in **What Is Man?** especially 1-13, 41-53; idem, **Anthropology in Theological Perspective**, 43-79; cf. idem, "Constructive and Critical Functions of Christian Eschatology," **HTR** 77/2 (1984): 119-139. For a critical investigation of Pannenberg's understanding of Jesus resurrection, see Herbert Burhenn, "Pannenberg's Argument for the Historicity of the Resurrection," **JAAR** 50/3 (1972): 368-379; Gordon E. Michalson, Jr., "Pannenberg on the Resurrection and Historical Method," **SJT** 33 (1980): 345-359; D. Holwerda, "Faith, Reason, and the Resurrection in the Theology of Wolfhart Pannenberg," 265-316; William Lane Craig, "Pannenbergs Beweis für die Auferstehung Jesu," **KuD** 34 (1988): 78-104; idem, "On Doubts about the Resurrection," **ModT** 6 (1989): 53-75.

²"Unity is the most comprehensive characteristic of being . . . Everything that is, and everything conceivable, is by its very existence or conception 'one.' The quest for the ultimate unity which integrates and thus unifies everything is the question reaching for God, as that question has been asked since the beginning of Greek philosophy. For us, too, the way in which we must test any concept of God is by asking whether it can account for the unity of all reality. If an idea of God fails that test, it does not comprehend the power dominating everything and is, therefore, not a true concept of God" (Wolfhart Pannenberg, **Theology and the Kingdom of God** [Philadelphia: Westminster Press, 1969], 60).

³Pannenberg, **SyTh/G**, 3:367-368.

⁴Langdon Gilkey thinks that we have in Pannenberg "a kind of Calvinism set in temporal reverse gear" ("Pannenberg's **Basic Questions in Theology**, 53); Christopher B. Kaiser, **The Doctrine of God: An Historical Survey** (Westchester, IL: Crossway Books, 1982), 124, follows Gilkey's analysis and criticism. That there are fundamental tensions in Pannenberg's doctrine of divine causality has been pointed out by Polk, **On the Way to God**, 286ff.

to object or to truly challenge the results of historical reason and historical investigation.¹

Yet, Pannenberg quotes Scripture extensively and repeatedly refers to it in developing his arguments.² This is most likely the case because Scripture remains the norm of Christian identity by means of its relationship to the historical origin of Christianity.³ Consequently, Scripture should be used and studied only as a historical-literary document, but not under the perspective of a divine authority to which Scripture itself testifies.⁴ Thus, Scripture should be used for reconstructing the history of God's acts through which God is revealed.⁵ Such a view depends heavily upon extra-biblical categories, as Pannenberg himself recognizes.⁶ This means that Biblical

---

¹Cf. Wirsching's critique of Pannenberg, 609.

²One has only to consult the extensive Scripture indexes at the end of each volume of his **Systematic Theology** to see the considerable amount of Scripture passages that are taken up by Pannenberg.

³Pannenberg, "Gibt es Prinzipien des Protestantismus," 80; Pannenberg has also pointed this out in a letter to the author (Pannenberg to Hasel, June 23, 1992, 2).

⁴Fred Klooster has criticized Pannenberg for rejecting Scripture's own claim to its divine authority ("Historical Method and the Resurrection in Pannenberg's Theology," **CTJ** 11 [1976]: 22). Similarly, Seebaß, 83, who writes that "Die Theologie des Wortes Gottes muß, wie immer sie auch gefaßt sein mag, nach ihrer eigenen Logik Auslegerin der Schrift sein, während Pannenbergs System die Bibel nur als Spenderin des archimedischen Punktes benötigt." This goes contrary to James Barr, **Fundamentalism**, 78, who claims that "there is no such thing as 'the Bible's view of itself' from which a fully authoritative answer to these questions can be obtained." On Scripture's self-testimony, see Wayne A. Grudem, "Scripture's Self-Attestation and the Problem of Formulating a Doctrine of Scripture," in **Scripture and Truth**, ed. D. A. Carson and John D. Woodbridge (Grand Rapids, MI; Zondervan Publishing House, 1983), 19-59; John M. Frame, "Scripture Speaks for Itself," in **God's Inerrant Word: An International Symposium on the Trustworthiness of Scripture**, ed. John Warwick Montgomery (Minneapolis, MN: Bethany Fellowship, 1974), 178-200; and Sinclair B. Ferguson, "How Does the Bible Look at Itself?" in **Inerrancy and Hermeneutic: A Tradition, A Challenge, A Debate**, ed. Harvie M. Conn (Grand Rapids, MI: Baker Book House, 1988), 47-66.

⁵Kelsey, **The Uses of Scripture in Recent Theology**, 53, n. 84, sees in this point some similarity between Pannenberg's use of Scripture and G. Ernest Wright.

⁶"In particular, the *conceptuality* of new theological theories is never directly derived by verbal agreement from their subject-matter, for example, from the biblical writings, but depends for its formulation on the current state of discussion in theological theory" (Pannenberg, **TPS**, 342). Pannenberg continues by giving an illustration: "For example, the description of Jesus as the revelation or the revealer of God is not justified merely by the appearance of the notion of revelation in the biblical texts, but depends also on the discussion of the concept of revelation in subsequent theology, though this interpretation of revelation must fit the semantic implications of the biblical text. The interpretation must also be related to current philosophical discussion, as for example when the category 'revelation' is assigned to a prior knowledge of the whole of history in spite of the incompleteness of the historical process. Finally it must enable the various areas of experience to be combined from its particular point of view, by, for example, enabling the

writings no longer function prescriptively but should be used descriptivly, namely, by providing a meaningful unity to historical experience.[1]

This, of course, immediately raises the following question: If Scripture should be used only descriptively,[2] how should Scripture be used in relation to tradition? Pannenberg claims there is no longer any fundamental objection to the intertwining of Scripture and tradition.[3] Hence, besides Scripture and even prior to it, history as the transmission of its traditions should be used as sources of theological knowledge. It is the task of systematic theology, then, to combine these different aspects of the history of the transmission of traditions under the perspective of the reality of God and His dealings in the world.[4] According to Pannenberg,

> The only difficulty in this approach is that it requires the interpretation of scripture to be defined very broadly, in fact as equivalent to the process of tradition itself. . . . In other words, the interpretation of scripture should be regarded as only one typical structural element in the process of the Christian tradition.[5]

In closing, we can say that Pannenberg appears to suggest that for the study of one particular tradition, i.e., the history of the religion of Israel which leads to the advent of Christianity, the Bible should be used as the source book from which theological ideas are derived. Because of its chronological priority and universal reception in the Christian tradition through the centuries, Scripture retains its theological significance and value for the Christian today. It should not be abandoned or replaced by other texts as long as one is able to adhere to the intention behind its statements.[6]

---

totality of reality to be treated as the still incomplete process of a history" (ibid., n. 637); cf. also Pannenberg, "Eine philosophisch-historische Hermeneutik des Christentums," 42.

[1]Pannenberg, **Human Nature, Election, and History**, 88.

[2]Pannenberg accepts the fact that Scripture does not function as the final norm of theology and states that "the substantive sufficiency of Scripture seems no longer to be or need to be the chief thesis in the evangelical doctrine of Scripture" ("What Is a Dogmatic Statement?" 187).

[3]Ibid. Recently Reihard Slenczka has keenly pointed out that a "Geschichtsbedingtheit der Heiligen Schrift impliziert unweigerlich, daß nicht Gottes Wort die Geschichte, sondern die, wie auch immer verstandene, Geschichte menschlicher Erfahrung Gottes Wort bestimmt. Das 'sola scriptura' wird dann nicht nur zum Problem, sondern es wird aufgelöst in menschliche Meinungen, Erfahrungen und Überlieferungen" ("Die Auflösung der Schriftgrundlage und was daraus folgt," TRu 60/1 [1995]: 97). In the place of the Scripture-principle one finds a "tradition-principle (ibid., 99).

[4]Pannenberg, "Eine philosophisch-historische Hermeneutik des Christentums," 42-43.

[5]Pannenberg, **TPS**, 401.

[6]Pannenberg, SyTh/G, 3:141, 176; cf. idem, **The Apostles' Creed in the Light of**

Having described different aspects of Pannenberg's understanding of Scripture, we now analyze some important presuppositions that influence his concept of Scripture.

An Analysis of Presuppositions Which Influence Pannenberg's Concept of Scripture

In the previous section we have attempted to present Pannenberg's concept of Scripture as it expresses itself in his understanding of its origin, nature, and use. This, however, does not provide an answer to the question how Pannenberg arrives at these conclusions. In order to grasp the reasons why Pannenberg maintains this particular concept of Scripture, a further investigation of some of his theological presuppositions is needed. Any concept of Scripture that covers the issue of its origin and nature involves an interpretation of God and man, the two agents theologians consciously or unconsciously assume in any concept of Scripture.[1] Because one's understanding of God[2] and the interpretation of human nature[3] has direct implications for the

---

Today's Questions, trans. Margaret Köhl (Philadelphia: Westminster Press, 1972), 13. "That does not mean that it [theology] would have to hold on to the ancient conceptions of the world which have found expression in the biblical writings. Human beings' understanding of the world and themselves is relative to historical conditions; it is therefore changeable and also capable of progress in knowledge. . . . The mistake of the theology of demythologizing is not that it pointed out the historical relativity of the aspects of a world-view to be found in biblical statements, but that it disputes that faith in God has any relevance for understanding the world" (Wolfhart Pannenberg, **Christianity in a Secularized World**, trans. John Bowden [New York: Crossroad, 1989], 52-53).

[1]James I. Packer has pointed out that *"when you encounter a presentday view of Holy Scripture*, you encounter more than a view of Scripture. What you meet is a total view of God and the world, that is, a total theology, which is both an ontology, declaring what there is, and an epistemology, stating how we know what there is. . . . Every view of Scripture, in particular, proves on analysis to be bound up with an overall view of God and man" ("Encountering Present-Day Views of Scripture," in **The Foundation of Biblical Authority**, ed. James Montgomery Boice [Grand Rapids, MI: Zondervan Publishing House, 1978], 61-62). G. C. Berkouwer has called it the "'and-and' quality" of Scripture, i.e., being the Word of God and word of man (G. C. Berkouwer, **Holy Scripture**, trans. and ed. Jack B. Rogers [Grand Rapids, MI: Eerdmans, 1975], 197); cf. also Fernando Luis Canale, "Revelation and Inspiration: The Ground for a New Approach," **AUSS** 31/2 (1993): 91; and idem, "Revelation and Inspiration: Method for a New Approach," **AUSS** 31/3 (1993): 191.

[2]The systematic centrality of the doctrine of God has been recognized by many theologians. John Macquarrie, for instance, states that in Christian theology the doctrine of God "has a central place" that "underlies all the other doctrines" (**Principles of Christian Theology**, 187); similarly, Anders Nygren, **Meaning and Method: Prolegomena to a Scientific Philosophy of Religion and a Scientific Theology**, trans. Philip S. Watson (Philadelphia: Fortress Press, 1972), 357; see also Erickson, "Immanence, Transcendence, and the Doctrine of Scripture," 194; Pannenberg, TPS, 297; idem, **Introduction to Systematic Theology**, 8, 21; and idem, SyTh/E, 1:59.

[3]Millard J. Erickson has pointed out that "the doctrine of man is important because of its

understanding of Scripture,¹ it is crucial to examine those two "presuppositional structures"² in as much as they relate to one's concept of Scripture.

At this point, the question arises whether we should start with Pannenberg's anthropological or theological presuppositions? Pannenberg has stated often that anthropology has foundational significance for theology.³ One has to keep in mind, however, that for Pannenberg this fundamental theological rank of anthropology is to be seen only "as the basis of a theology of religion." He says, "I naturally have in view only a methodological priority and am not treating anthropology as materially the basis of theology."⁴

The importance and systematic priority of Pannenberg's idea of God is apparent in several statements. He points out that "Christian dogmatics in every part is the doctrine of God,"⁵ and adds that "[I] shall be expressing the subject matter of dogmatics in all its variety as the unfolding of the Christian idea of God."⁶ Hence,

> . . . in the systematic presentation of Christian teaching the world, humanity, and history are claimed as an expression of the deity of God and as testimony to it. . . . Even in discussing the world, humanity, and history, dogmatics has to do with the reality of God. Only in this way does it really deal with humanity and the world. God is the one all-embracing theme of theology as also of faith. Neither has any other theme besides him.⁷

---

relationship to other major Christian doctrines" and "has an unusual status" because it "will determine how we understand ourselves and, consequently, how we do theology, or even what theology is . . ." (**Christian Theology** [Grand Rapids, MI: Baker Book House, 1985], 456-457).

¹Cf. Canale, "Revelation and Inspiration: the Ground for an New Approach," 92, 98, whose statements on revelation and inspiration are also applicable to Scripture.

²Canale, "Revelation and Inspiration: Method for a New Approach," 191.

³Pannenberg, **TPS**, 319, 422; idem, **SyTh/E**, 1:157; idem, **SyTh/G**, 3:584; idem, "Anthropology and the Question of God," 93. Cf. William J. Hill, **The Three-Personed God: The Trinity as a Mystery of Salvation** (Washington, D.C.: The Catholic University of America Press, 1982), 156.

⁴Pannenberg, **SyTh/E**, 1:158, n. 111. Unfortunately in the English translation, the word "anthropology" has been translated mistakenly by "theology," thereby obfuscating the meaning when it reads that Pannenberg is "not treating theology [sic] as materially the basis of theology." Cf. the German original in idem, **SyTh/G**, 1:173-174, n. 120.

⁵Pannenberg, **SyTh/E**, 1:447; at the end of **SyTh/G**, 3:677, the same idea is reiterated.

⁶Pannenberg, **SyTh/E**, 1:x. Note that it is the "Christian idea of God," rather than the "Biblical idea of God" that is expressed by Pannenberg.

⁷Ibid., 1:59. Cf. idem, "An Autobiographical Sketch," in **TWP**, 16.

Therefore, it seems appropriate to begin with Pannenberg's Theological presuppositions first before we move to anthropological presuppositions as they are related to the doctrine of Scripture in his theology.

Theological Presuppositions

The pervasive influence of the idea of God in Pannenberg's thought[1] also has implications for his understanding of Scripture. The way God's nature is perceived affects, among other things, the manner in which God relates to the world and how He communicates with humankind. This in turn has significant repercussions for one's understanding of Scripture. Therefore, a grasp of Pannenberg's theological presuppositions is needed in order to understand why he arrives at his particular understanding of Scripture.

Pannenberg submits that the semantic minimum from which one can start to speak about God is the idea of "a power that determines everything."[2] This definition of God does not specifically suggest that God is personal in nature.[3] Although Pannenberg admits that "the God of the Bible is certainly personal, this is not necessarily a requirement of the idea of God in general, though the word 'God', because of its religious origin, carries personal connotations."[4] When recently asked to describe God, Pannenberg gave an answer that seems to support an impersonal concept of God. He said that

> God is a field of force without limits of extension or power, pervading all reality, and giving rise again and again to new creatures. This the Bible calls Spirit and is identified by Jesus Christ as fatherly love.[5]

---

[1]Cf. Pannenberg, **Introduction to Systematic Theology**, 8; idem, **TPS**, 297.

[2]Pannenberg, **Introduction to Systematic Theology**, 8. Also idem, **SyTh/G**, 3:546, where the idea of God as the all determining reality is said to be the minimal content of every monotheistic idea of God.

[3]Cf. Pannenberg, **Theology and the Kingdom of God**, 57-58; idem, "Theta Phi Talkback Session with Wolfhart Pannenberg," 39. Pannenberg even claims that "die Auffassung des einen göttlichen Wesens als Person im Sinne von Selbstbewußtsein als die Häresie des christlichen Theismus [zu] beurteilen [ist]" ("Die Subjektivität Gottes und die Trinitätslehre: Ein Beitrag zur Beziehung zwischen Karl Barth und der Philosophie Hegels," **KuD** 23 [1977]: 39); cf. also Jan Rohls, "Die Persönlichkeit Gottes und die Trinitätslehre," **EvT** 45 (1985): 127-128.

[4]Pannenberg, **Introduction to Systematic Theology**, 9.

[5]Wolfhart Pannenberg in Michael Bauman, **Roundtable: Conversations with European Theologians** (Grand Rapids, MI: Baker Book House), 52. Adrio König has chided Pannenberg for not writing more personalistic about God and proposes that a more biblical formulation would

This concept of God as a field of force has become much more prominent in his **Systematic Theology** than anywhere else.[1] Through it, Pannenberg is able to appropriate the concept of God's "person" in a creative new way as "the reciprocity of the divine Persons."[2] Here Pannenberg follows Hegel's defense of the personal character of God against Fichte's denial of it[3] by conceiving the essence of God's personality to exist in self-dedication to another person.[4] Thus, "in the vital movement

---

speak of God as "having" power over the future or as "keeping his promises." Adrio König, **Here Am I: A Christian Reflection on God** (Grand Rapids, MI: Eerdmans, 1982), 197.

[1]Pannenberg, **SyTh/E**, 1:382-383; idem, **SyTh/G**, 2:99-125. On the metaphysical origin of the term "field" in Stoic and pre-Socratic philosophy and its modern appropriation, see esp. 101-105. On the field theory, see also idem, "Schöpfungstheologie und moderne Naturwissenschaft," in **Gottes Zukunft--Zukunft der Welt. Festschrift für Jürgen Moltmann zum 60. Geburtstag**, ed. Hermann Deuser, Gerhard Marcel Martin, Konrad Stock, and Michael Welker (Munich: Chr. Kaiser, 1986), 282-288. Pannenberg gathers from the field theory insights into the role of the Spirit in the Biblical material. In the words of Grenz, **Reason for Hope**, 61, "Pannenberg suggests that the dilemma that gave rise to the patristic doctrine of God is no longer present. The Stoic doctrine of a physical pneuma, rejected in the patristic era in favor of the conception of God as spiritual mind, has itself developed into the noncorporal field theory of modern physics. In the connection between this newer scientific theory and the conception of God Pannenberg finds 'surprising possibilities' for a new delineation of the relationship between the trinitarian persons and the divine essence." For a concise discussion of the concept of "field theory," see Mary Hesse, "Action at a Distance and Field Theory," **The Encyclopedia of Philosophy**, ed. Paul Edwards (New York: Macmillan Company and the Free Press, 1967), 1:9-15; and Max Jammer, "Feld, Feldtheorie," in **HWP**, 2:923-926.

[2]Pannenberg, **Jesus--God and Man**, 181, 334-344.

[3]Johann Gottlob Fichte attempted to show that ideas of God as substance and person are contradictory because they are incompatible with the concept of the infinite. Johann Gottlob Fichte, "Über den Grund unseres Glaubens an eine göttliche Weltregierung," **Philosophisches Journal** 8 (1798): 1-20, especially 15ff., as quoted in Pannenberg, **SyTh/E**, 1:92, n. 92. Furthermore, Fichte directed his criticism of the idea of a personal God against the hypothesis of a divine self-consciousness because it always presupposes something beyond itself from which to distinguish itself. This means that we cannot conceive of it apart from limitation and finitude, so that if we attribute it to God we make him finite, a being like ourselves. Cf. Pannenberg, **SyTh/E**, 1:376. Hegel, in contrast, emphasized that God as Spirit is not substance but subject and thus defends the personality of God "which forms the context for Hegel's statements about God's inner-trinitarian Trinity of persons" (idem, **Jesus--God and Man**, 181-182, n. 155).

[4]Falk Wagner, a former pupil of Pannenberg criticized Pannenberg's developing doctrine of the Trinity by arguing that in spite of good intentions, Pannenberg finally cannot avoid the shadow of Triteism because the unity of the Trinity cannot be established when it is based solely on the presupposed persons and their relations. Falk Wagner, "Religiöser Inhalt und logische Form. Zum Verhältnis von Religionsphilosophie und Wissenschaft der Logik am Beispiel der Trinitätslehre," in **Die Flucht in den Begriff: Materialien zu Hegels Religionsphilosophie**, ed. Friedrich Wilhelm Graf and Falk Wagner (Stuttgart: Klett and Cotta, 1982), 216-217. On a similar note Michael Moxter and Ingolf U. Dalfert have criticized Pannenberg recently for not succeeding to offer "a Trinitarian solution to the problem of the unity of God which is more than an eschatological postponement. Rather he gets stuck in a dualist cul-de-sac: on the one hand he develops the difference of Father, Son and Spirit from his account of revelation in terms of

of such reciprocal dedication, the unity of Father, Son, and Spirit consummates itself in the historical process of the revelatory event."¹ Hence, the divine field of force is structured along trinitarian lines,² where the divine unity is conceptualized "as the spiritual *field* of lively fellowship between Father, Son and Spirit."³ Through the

---

Jesus' self-distinction from the God he calls Father; on the other hand he grounds the unity of God in a metaphysical concept of God's essence prior to and independent of revelation: the concept of God as Infinite" (Michael Moxter and Ingolf U. Dalfert, "Protestant Theology: Germany," **The Blackwell Encyclopedia of Modern Christian Thought**, ed. Alister E. McGrath [Oxford: Basil Blackwell, 1993], 503). It has been observed that Pannenberg's model of the Trinity has some resemblance to the social analogy. Cf. Roger E. Olson, "Wolfhart Pannenberg's Doctrine of the Trinity," **SJT** 43 (1990): 195-196, 202.

¹Pannenberg, **Jesus--God and Man**, 183. It has been said that the doctrine of the Trinity is taken up relatively seldom in Pannenberg's earlier writings. Grenz, **Reason for Hope**, 228, n. 3. In 1975 Herbert Burhenn could still write about Pannenberg's doctrine of God that "readers may be struck by the paucity of references here to the doctrine of the Trinity," and that "the Trinity cannot function for Pannenberg, as it does for Barth, as a structural principle of theology" ("Pannenberg's Doctrine of God," **SJT** 28 [1975]: 535, 536). On a similar note, Brian McDermott concluded in 1974 that Pannenberg's trinitarian theology remained sorely underdeveloped ("Pannenberg's Resurrection Christology: A Critique," **TS** 35 [1974]: 719). But this has thoroughly changed. In 1981 Wolfhart Pannenberg maintained that the Trinity is at the heart of the Christian doctrine of God ("God's Presence in History," **CC** 98 (1981): 263). Ten years later Pannenberg affirmed the importance of the trinitarian concept of God when he wrote: ". . . I think that the trinitarian conception of God has a good claim to be considered the specifically Christian idea of God. It is not a doctrine of only secondary importance in addition to some other basic concept of God. . . . It has been at the center of my own project of developing a systematic presentation of the Christian doctrine" ("The Christian Vision of God: The New Discussion on the Trinitarian Doctrine," **TSR** 13/2 [1991]: 53-54); and, almost identical, idem, "The Christian Vision of God: The New Discussion on the Trinitarian Doctrine," **AsbTJ** 46/2 [1991]: 27-36; cf. idem, "Problems of a Trinitarian Doctrine of God," **Dialog** 26/4 [1987]: 250-257; and idem, **SyTh/E**, 1:280-299, especially 294-295: "With the doctrine of the Trinity, however, God and his revelation are at the heart of Christian theology." It has been pointed out that contrary to Burhenn's comment quoted above, "Pannenberg **does** make the doctrine of the Trinity a structural principle of theology . . ." (Olson, "Wolfhart Pannenberg's Doctrine of the Trinity," 177). Cf. idem, "Trinity and Eschatology: The Historical Being of God in Jürgen Moltmann and Wolfhart Pannenberg," **SJT** 36 (1983): 213-227; and idem, "Trinity and Eschatology: The Historical Being of God in the Theology of Wolfhart Pannenberg" (Ph.D. dissertation, Rice University, 1984). It should be noted that Pannenberg fervently denies that sound doctrine of the Trinity can be constructed from Biblical teachings alone. He agrees with Maurice Wiles that in the light of recent historical-critical exegesis the Trinity cannot be considered a datum of revelation given in clear propositional form (Pannenberg, **SyTh/E**, 1:271-272).

²Pannenberg, **SyTh/G**, 2:104.

³Robert W. Jenson, "God," **The Blackwell Encyclopedia of Modern Christian Thought**, ed. Alister E. McGrath (Oxford: Basil Blackwell, 1993), 245. To use Pannenberg's words, "the personal community of the three divine Persons is the living subjectivity of the one personal God" (Pannenberg, **Jesus--God and Man**, 182, n. 155). Ted Peters recent comment on Pannenberg's concept of field seems somewhat imprecise when he states that Pannenberg "does not say that spirit *is like* a force field. He says spirit *is* a force field" ("Editor's Introduction: Pannenberg on Theology and Natural Science," in Wolfhart Pannenberg, **Toward a Theology of Nature: Essays on Science and Faith**, ed. Ted Peters [Louisville, KY: Westminster/John Knox

trinitarian concept of field, where God's essence is understood in relational terms,[1] Pannenberg tries to account for God's active presence in the reality of the world through His Spirit. Accordingly, "the essence of the one God is revealed by both Father and Son, and by their communion in a third, the Spirit, who proceeds from the Father and is received by the Son and given to the people."[2] As such, the Spirit is given to all humans at creation and is active in everything living, especially in the souls of humans.[3] In other words, Pannenberg see's "the Trinity as the answer to the

---

Press, 1993], 14). Cf. Pannenberg who specifically states that the *person* of the Holy Spirit is not itself to be understood as a field but rather as singular manifestation of the field of the divine essence (**SyTh/G**, 2:104). Peters, however, is undoubtedly correct when he observes that "there is a directness and a literalness here that seems to throw caution to the wind. One can admire his scholarly courage, but perhaps this assertion should retain its hypothetical status for a period to await confirmation or disconfirmation. Historians of science are quick to point out the dangers of trying to float a theological assertion aboard a scientific ship, because the intellectual weather can change suddenly. . . . How long will field theory stay afloat? If someday it should sink, will Pannenberg's theology of spirit sink with it?" (Peters, "Editor's Introduction," 14). Cf. similar concerns voiced by Hudson, 48; and Steven Toulmin, of the University of Chicago, who criticizes the general tendency of theologians "to assemble the more up-to-date scientific ideas of a post-Darwin, post-Einstein, post-Freud era into a novel cosmological construction that claims the same fundamental authority and permanence that were claimed for Aristotle and Newton earlier. That will simply lay up fresh trouble for theology a century or two down the road, when scientists have rethought the problems of their own disciplines, to the point of making radical changes for which theologians would once again be ill prepared. It may well be the case, that theology can hope for no secure and permanently reliable foothold in the natural sciences. . . . It will be better if they distance themselves from the ideas of science rather than embrace them too systematically and uncritically" ("The Historization of Natural Science: Its Implications for Theology," in **Paradigm Change in Theology: A Symposium for the Future**, ed. Hans Küng and David Tracy, trans. Margaret Köhl [New York: Crossroad, 1989], 237).

[1]This is not the place to enter into a full blown discussion of Pannenberg's understanding of the nature and essence of God. For our purposes it may suffice to note that Pannenberg defines God's "essence" in relational terms and see's the link between God's "essence" and his attributes in action. Cf. Pannenberg, **SyTh/E**, 1:359-361, 366-370; idem, **SyTh/G**, 2:106; idem, **SyTh/G**, 3:597. Thus, "the essence of the one God is revealed by both Father and Son, and by their communion in a third, the Spirit, who proceeds from the Father and is received by the Son and given to his people" (idem, **SyTh/E**, 1:358). This means that Pannenberg does not reject the question of essence as superfluous, although he does not adopt Aristotle's definition of essence as substance (ibid., 354). On Pannenberg's understanding of essence as relational term, see idem, **Jesus--God and Man**, 179-183, especially 182-183; and idem, "Person," in **RGG**, 5:230-235. On Pannenberg's understanding of the trinitarian relationship, see Goebel, 250-260; Hill, **The Three-Personed God**, 155-166; Olson, "Trinity and Eschatology: The Historical Being of God in the Theology of Wolfhart Pannenberg," 230-323; Kurt Koch, **Der Gott der Geschichte**, 171-180; Polk, **On the Way to God**, 280-284.

[2]Pannenberg, **SyTh/E**, 1:358. Thus, the Spirit "mediates the fellowship of the Father and the Son as he proceeds from the Father and is received by the Son. In this function the Spirit is a third form of the existence of the one divine essence alongside the Father and the Son" (ibid.).

[3]Pannenberg, **SyTh/G**, 3:21, 154.

question of how God and the world can be different in such a way that each is nevertheless not separated from the other."[1]

The idea of the trinitarian divine life as a dynamic field[2] sees the divine Spirit, who proceeds from the Father and is received by the Son, as uniting the three persons so that He is the force field of the divine fellowship[3] and also the principle of the relation of God to creation and the principle of the participation of creation in the divine life.[4] God is both immanent in the world, through His Spirit, and transcendent to it. God's immanence is given through the fact that humankind is animated by the immanent Spirit which raises them beyond themselves to participate in some measure in the divine life.[5] With this approach, Pannenberg has produced a model of God and the world which revises the upstairs-downstairs, supernatural--natural model.[6] At the same time, we touch upon a intricate interconnection between Pannenberg's concept of God and His relation to humankind.[7]

Pannenberg's concept of the Trinity is crucially important, even for his concept of Scripture, because with it God and His revelation are at the heart of Christian

---

[1] Wolfhart Pannenberg, **Christian Spirituality** (Philadelphia: Westminster Press, 1983), 105.

[2] Pannenberg, **SyTh/E**, 1:382-384; idem, **SyTh/G**, 2:96-138, especially 99-124; cf. idem, Schöpfungstheologie und moderne Naturwissenschaft," 276-291.

[3] Pannenberg, **SyTh/E**, 1:383. Pannenberg maintains that the Spirit as ungraspable field is at the same time a gift, but the Spirit is always more than gift, he is the quintessence of the ecstatic movement of the divine life (idem, **SyTh/G**, 3:19, 24).

[4] Grenz and Olsen, 193. Pannenberg states that the Holy Spirit is the medium through which each individual Christian is immediately connected with God (**SyTh/G**, 3:154); cf. idem, **Introduction to Systematic Theology**, 49. Yet, the believer is not simply absorbed in the dynamic of the divine effects by which they are filled through the divine spirit (idem, **SyTh/G**, 3:231).

[5] "The Spirit animates the creatures in raising them beyond themselves to participate in some measure in the life of the eternal God, who is Spirit" (Pannenberg, **Introduction to Systematic Theology**, 45). Pannenberg denies that such a statement carries pantheistic or panentheistic connotations "because the Spirit is always transcendent, and only by transcending themselves do the creatures participate in the spiritual dynamics" (ibid., 45-46). Despite this denial it remains questionable how Pannenberg can consistently avoid at least panentheistic thoughts from the structure of his argument. It should be noted in this context that Pannenberg recently has preferred to use the term "Intravenienz" rather than "Immanence" when he speaks about the contemporaniety of the divine Logos with the creation and its creatures (idem, **SyTh/G**, 2:82).

[6] Cf. Laurence W. Wood, "Above, Within, or Ahead Of?" 53, 62.

[7] Below we examine Pannenberg's anthropological presuppositions that allow for man's essential openness for the divine and the interaction between God's Spirit and the human mind.

theology.¹ The doctrine of the Trinity links constantly "the eternal essence of God to his historical revelation, since revelation cannot be viewed as extraneous to his deity."² This raises the question of what Pannenberg thinks is being revealed and how this revelation is taking place.

Pannenberg's impersonal concept of God and his Enlightenment framework of thinking³ excludes the possibility of any verbal or cognitive content to be revealed by God, be that about Himself or His will for humankind. Instead, Pannenberg adopts the modern notion that revelation is essentially God's self-revelation.⁴ This self-revelation

---

¹Pannenberg, **SyTh/E**, 1:292-293.

²Ibid., 1:328.

³It is well known that the rationalism of the Enlightenment radically questioned the possibility of supernatural revelation. Cf. H. D. McDonald, **Theories of Revelation**, 17-62; Gerald R. Cragg, **Reason and Authority in the Eighteenth Century** (Cambridge: At the University Press, 1964), 62-92; Max Seckler and Michael Kessler, "Die Kritik der Offenbarung," in **HFT** 2:29-59; Demarest, 11-47. It was Kant who argued that the intellect did not have the capability to reach into the timeless nature of ultimate reality but is limited to the spacio-temporal realm which does not allow for cognitive contact between man's reason and a timeless divine object. For an introduction to Kant's thought, specifically as it relates to our discussion, see Gruenler, 35-45. Gruenler points out that Pannenberg "stands within the Kantian hermeneutical circle" (ibid., 107). See also W. David Beck, "Agnosticism: Kant," in **Biblical Errancy: An Analysis of its Philosophical Roots**, ed. Norman L. Geisler (Grand Rapids, MI: Zondervan Publishing House, 1981), 53-78.

⁴"That appearance and essence belong together is expressed by the concept of 'revelation' as self-revelation. The concept of revelation is predominantly understood in this way in contemporary theology: revelation is not the communication of some 'truths' by supernatural means, by inspiration, for example, but is essentially God's 'self-disclosure', as Karl Barth says. . . . The restriction of the concept of 'revelation' to the strict sense of self-revelation is modern" (Pannenberg, **Jesus--God and Man**, 127); idem, "Introduction," 3-8; cf. idem, "Offenbarung und 'Offenbarungen' im Zeugnis der Geschichte," 85-107, especially 103-106, where Pannenberg points out that the term "self-revelation" has a long history that goes back until Philo and Plotinus but was newly introduced by Schelling and Hegel. "The idea of an indirect self-revelation of God through history in which God is active is not new. It has its source in German idealism, as does the exclusive conception of revelation as self-revelation" (idem, "Introduction," 19). Pannenberg is aware "that the Old Testament and the New Testament expressions that are translated by 'to reveal' and 'revelation' do not have this meaning at all [i.e., self-revelation], but were meant as the making known of the most varied sorts of information through inspiration or as the 'appearance' of God or of Jesus" (ibid., 127-128). Nonetheless, he continues to retain the concept of God's self-revelation (idem, **SyTh/E**, 1:242). This reveals that there are extra Biblical presuppositions that guide Pannenberg in his use of Scripture. This fact is recognized by others like Polk, **On the Way to God**, 141-142; and Rolf Rendtorff, "Offenbarung und Geschichte," 40, 44; especially 46. Alfred North Whitehead has very tellingly pointed out the difficulty in historical studies when he stated that "it is a delusion that the rock upon which our beliefs can be founded is a historical investigation. . . . history presupposes a metaphysics. . . . you can only deduce metaphysical dogmas from your interpretation of the past on the basis of a prior metaphysical interpretation of the present" (Alfred North Whitehead, **Religion in the Making** [New York: Macmillan, 1926], 84).

of God is closely connected with the divine action in history.¹ Pannenberg's clarion call to take history seriously is expressed forcefully in his famous statement that "history [Geschichte] is the most comprehensive horizon of Christian theology."² Here one is reminded of Pannenberg's famous proposal of "Revelation as History," which calls for a brief exposition. A clue to the connection between revelation and history [Geschichte] seems to be given by the word "as" in "Revelation *as* History."³ Revelation comes not merely *in* or from *above* history but occurs *as* history.⁴ In other words, revelation does not enter history from the outside, providing communication of some truths by supernatural means or through inspiration.⁵ Instead, it occurs through history [Geschichte] in as much as this history [Geschichte] is understood as a result of divine action [Handeln].⁶

---

¹Pannenberg, "Offenbarung und 'Offenbarungen' im Zeugnis der Geschichte," 102. Cf. also his earlier statement where he wrote that "the theme of 'history' is relevant for the question of the reality of God, to which the modern problem of revelation is related, insofar as history characterizes reality as a whole" (idem, "Response to the Discussion," 241). "In its very idea, history is constituted by the active presence of the infinite God . . ." (ibid., 253). Philip Clayton has correctly pointed out that history and God can be conceptualized in Pannenberg only in a reciprocal relationship ("The God of History and the Presence of the Future," **JR** 65 [1985]: 103).

²Pannenberg, "Redemptive Event and History," 15.

³Pannenberg denies that there is a direct identification of God with the process of history itself as William Hamilton thinks ("The Character of Pannenberg's Theology," 185); cf. Pannenberg's rejoinder in "Response to the Discussion," 250. Klaus Schwarzwäller, **Theologie oder Phänomenologie: Erwägungen zur Methodik theologischen Verstehens**, BEvTh 42 (Munich: Chr. Kaiser, 1966), 111, similarly interprets the meaning of the word "as" in the sense of an identification of revelation and history. It should be noted that for Pannenberg, revelation reveals God only indirectly, cf. Georg Kraus, 350; G. Muschalek and A. Gamper, 189; Eicher, "Geschichte und Wort Gottes," 331; Klaus Kienzler, **Logik der Auferstehung: Eine Untersuchung zu R. Bultmann, G. Ebeling und W. Pannenberg**, FThS 100 (Freiburg: Herder, 1976), 122. Neither is history seen as the field of a finitude which is enclosed within itself, an "immanence" to which one would have to oppose a "transcendence," as proposed by Schwarzwäller, 102, n. 315, and Martin J. Buss, "The Meaning of History," in **TaH**, 153-154. Instead, as Pannenberg puts it in his own words, "in its very idea, history is constituted by the active presence of the infinite God, and therefore one can only say that God reveals himself in history. At any rate he reveals *his divinity* through history . . ." ("Response to the Discussion," 253). That Pannenberg does not directly identify revelation with history but rather understands it more as "revelation *through* history" ("Offenbarung durch Geschichte") has been confirmed by Pannenberg (Pannenberg to Hasel, January 21, 1994, 1).

⁴Braaten, **History and Hermeneutics**, 27.

⁵Pannenberg, **SyTh/E**, 1:235, 242; idem, **Jesus--God and Man**, 127; idem to Hasel, January 21, 1994, 1.

⁶Ibid.

Furthermore, this history [Geschichte] is understood and defined as being primarily the history of the transmission of traditions [Überlieferungsgeschichte].¹ Hence, for Pannenberg, "God is immanent in history in the process of the transmission of his eschatological revelation, determining it in its totality from within."² Because God is **one** there can be only **one** self-revelation of Him, which means that only history in its totality reveals God.³ This accounts for Pannenberg's second⁴ fundamental

---

¹Ibid. Pannenberg thinks that history is essentially constituted by a process of "*Überlieferungsgeschichte,*" i.e., a "history of the transmission of traditions." Thus, "historical process . . . is essentially a process of the transmission of tradition" ("Kerygma and History," 90. More recently Pannenberg has stated that "in opposition to a mere history of political and economic facts, the thesis has thus been formulated that the process of the development and refashioning of the traditions by which human civilizations live has to be a theme of historical presentations, and in this broader sense history must be treated as a history of traditions" (idem, **SyTh/E**, 1:232, n. 104).

²Pannenberg, "On Historical and Theological Hermeneutic," 158.

³This is set forth succinctly in the second dogmatic thesis: "Revelation occurs not at the beginning but at the end of revelatory history" (Pannenberg, **Offenbarung als Geschichte**, 95), (translation by author). The English translation misses the force of the German statement and changes even its meaning when it says: "Revelation is not comprehended completely in the beginning, but at the end of the revealing history" (idem, "Dogmatic Theses on the Doctrine of Revelation," 131). Nevertheless, Pannenberg thinks that single events can anticipate the entirety of all events. "To this extent anticipatory revelations (or better: anticipations of the one revelation) . . . are thinkable. . . . I have spoken of such a provisional, anticipatory revelation also as a 'partial' revelation" (idem, "Response to the Discussion," 240). Peter Eicher comments on Pannenberg's concept of revelation by saying: "Solange der Lauf der Geschichte noch nicht vollendet ist, kann Offenbarung im strengen Sinne des Wortes nicht Ereignis werden; . . ." (Eicher, **Offenbarung**, 448); see also Kienzler, 123.

⁴Tupper, 96-107, recognizes two fundamental aspects of history, the history of the transmission of traditions and universal history. Others have seen a threefold distinction, adding the tension between promise and fulfillment. The threefold distinction seems to have been presented first in a systematic fashion by Helmut Harder, "Continuity Between Method and Content in Contemporary Theology: The Achievement of Wolfhart Pannenberg" (Th.D. dissertation, Toronto School of Theology, 1971), 36ff., and has appeared subsequently in an article by Helmut G. Harder and W. Taylor Stevenson, "The Continuity of History and Faith in the Theology of Wolfhart Pannenberg: Towards an Erotics of History," **JR** 51 (1971): 34-56, especially 38-41; and in Theodore Peters's dissertation, 196-237. Pannenberg himself, however, has called attention to a "material shift" in his thinking, "away from my original effort to establish a theological understanding of history as constituted by the tension of promise and fulfillment." This shift occurred according to Pannenberg's own words "because as a rule the promises do not enter so literally into a fulfillment as one would assume that they would if they were the word of God effecting history. . . . Rather, history has 'overtaken' promises understood in this sense . . . so that their 'fulfillment' could be affirmed in a way that deviates from their original literal meaning. . . . Now we can only grasp the continuity of 'fulfillment' with the preceding promise or threat in terms of the history of the transmission of traditions" ("Response to the Discussion," 259-260). Similar formulations by Pannenberg occur repeatedly elsewhere. Cf. idem, **What Is Man?** 133; idem, "The God of Hope," in **BQT**, 2:245; idem, "On Historical and Theological Hermeneutics," 180; idem, The Biblical Understanding of Reality," in **Faith and Reality**, trans. John Maxwell (Philadelphia: Westminster Press, 1977), 12. James M. Robinson has raised a

aspect of history, namely, universal history.¹ For Pannenberg universal history seems to encompass not so much all events that ever happened or will happen in this world but rather a unification of the world through the development of an all-embracing history. Such a unification is made possible for the first time from the ancient Mediterranean area in which the Christian church has entered.² By creatively appropriating the philosophical insights of such thinkers as Georg Wilhelm Friedrich Hegel (1770-1831),³ Wilhelm Dilthey (1833-1911),⁴ and Robin George Collingwood

---

significant objection to Pannenberg's employment of the principle of promise and fulfillment by calling attention to the fact that this was yet another instance of an unhistorical structure being imposed on the data of history ("The Historicity of Biblical Language," in **The Old Testament and Christian Faith**, ed. Bernhard W. Anderson [New York: Herder, 1969], 128). Wilhelm Weischedel has pointed out the problematic relationship in Pannenberg's concept of promise and fulfillment and its recourse to universal history in order to maintain unity in history (**Der Gott der Philosophen: Grundlegung einer philosophischen Theologie im Zeitalter des Nihilismus**, 2 vols. [Darmstadt: Wissenschaftliche Buchhandlung, 1971], 2:82-84). This leaves Tupper's classification essentially intact.

¹Pannenberg, "Hermeneutic and Universal History," 96-136, 129; idem, "Dogmatic Theses on the Doctrine of Revelation," 135.

²"There is a world history that embraces mankind only from the perspective of the biblical discovery of history. The unity of humanity in world history cannot come into view from its beginning. The first human cultural developments apparently emerged independently of one another, and grew together only subsequently. The unification of the world . . . in the sense of an all-embracing history, has emanated from the ancient Mediterranean area. In this development the Christian church has entered into the inheritance of the old Mediterranean culture, and the movement toward the unification of the whole world has emaneated from the Christian West. Thus, along with the consciousness of history and inseparable from it, the development of a unified world history has emanated from the God of the Bible and his revelation in Jesus Christ. The pre-Christian nations share in this unity of world history only through the historical connections they have with the Christ-event. In part these connections are formed only relatively late, through the Christian mission. . . . Through the Christian tradition antiquity, modern times, and their future are embraced in the unity of one history. Without this unifying bond, they must fall apart as blocks that are without connection" (Pannenberg, **What Is Man?** 146-148).

³Pannenberg himself refers directly to Hegel when he explains his concept of revelation as universal history (Universalgeschichte). This concept was transmitted to him by his teachers Karl Barth and Heinrich Vogel ("Introduction," 4-6). To simply categorize Pannenberg as a Hegelian, as has been done by Horst Georg Pöhlmann, **Abriß der Dogmatik: Ein Kompendium**, 4th rev. and enl. ed. (Gütersloh: Gerd Mohn, 1985), 24, whose graph draws a straight line of influence from Hegel to Pannenberg and acknowledges no other influences on him, seems not to do justice to his careful discussions of his similarities to and disagreements with Hegel. On Pannenberg's interaction with Hegel, cf. for instance, Pannenberg, SyTh/E, 1:228-229; idem, "Hermeneutic and Universal History," 134-136; idem, "The Significance of Christianity in the Philosophy of Hegel," in **BQT**, 3:144-177. More recently, Pannenberg has insisted that one aspect of his thought that continues to be misunderstood is his supposed Hegelianism. He emphatically claimed: "I am not a Hegelian. I just happen to think that [Georg] Hegel was one of the outstanding minds in the history of modern thought, one whose work sets a high standard for us to follow. That is why I believe that theology after Hegel should strive to rise to his level of sophistication and rigor. But very few of my ideas did I actually get from Hegel--very few"

(1889-1943),[1] Pannenberg thinks that each event in history gains its significance and its ultimate meaning only in relation to other events with which it is connected. Thus, the immediate context is progressively broadened to encompass the whole of history, i.e., universal history from where alone the ultimate meaning of an individual event can be evaluated. Until that totality of history, that absolute future has arrived, history [Geschichte] reveals God only partially and indirectly as the all-encompassing reality[2]

(Pannenberg in Bauman, 48). On Hegel's influence on Pannenberg, see Neie, 94-98; Greiner, 200-203; Galloway, **Wolfhart Pannenberg**, 25-27, 112-115; Polk, **On the Way to God**, 34-35.

[4]Pannenberg is indebted to the so-called historicist school, and here especially to Wilhelm Dilthey. Cf. Pannenberg, **SyTh/E**, 1:54; idem, **SyTh/G**, 3:177, 193, 333; idem, "On Historical and Theological Hermeneutic," 162-166; idem, **TPS**, 103-116; and idem, **Metaphysics and the Idea of God**, 7-8, 74-75, 104-105, 162-167. Pannenberg stressed his dependence on Dilthey's thought in his understanding of history in a letter to the author in which he states that Dilthey's influence on his thinking has had a much greater impact than that of Hegel (Pannenberg to Hasel, January 21, 1994, 1). Pannenberg has been criticized that he "reads the Hebrew tradition too strongly through an influence from Hegel that results in too quick an appropriation of Dilthey's and Löwith's thesis that an anticipated whole and therefore end of history is a necessary condition for meaning in and of history" (Polk, **On the Way to God**, 78). In other words, there seems to be a superimposing of extra Biblical philosophical concepts present in Pannenberg's understanding of history.

[1]John P. Hogan has shown that "Pannenberg uses Collingwood's doctrine of the historical imagination for his projection of the totality: a universal history." Yet, he "makes selective use of Collingwood, and ends up expecting too much from the historical method" (**Collingwood and Theological Hermeneutics**, CTSSR 3 [Lanham, MD: University Press of America, 1989], 185, 195). Pannenberg's relationship to Collingwood is also discussed, idem, "The Historical Imagination and the New Hermeneutic: Collingwood and Pannenberg," in **The Pedagogy of God's Image: Essays on Symbol and the Religious Imagination**, ed. Robert Masson (Chico, CA: Scholars Press, 1982), 9-30; and Ian G. Nicol, "Facts and Meanings: Wolfhart Pannenberg's Theology as History and the Role of the Historical-Critical Method," **RS** 12 (1976): 129-139.

[2]Pannenberg thinks that God's self-revelation takes place indirectly through history ("Introduction," 13-16). He explains more fully what he means by his claim that the totality of history shows who God is in an indirect way by stating that he rejects "the conception of a direct self-revelation of God through his name, his Word, or through Law and gospel. What has finally emerged in contrast is the thought of an indirect self-revelation of God as a reflex of his activity in history. . . . Direct communication has in an immediate way just that content that it intends to communicate, whereas indirect communication initially has some other content than that which is actually to be communicated. Direct communication transmits content without a break from the sender to the receiver. In indirect communication, the path is broken: the content first reveals its actual meaning by being considered from another perspective" (Pannenberg, "Introduction," 13-14). According to Pannenberg the theories of inspiration had in mind a direct communication. On the other hand, indirect communication can very easily be unmediated and received without a middleman and for Pannenberg is "on a higher level" (ibid., 14-15). In order to avoid an infinite number of revelations, because there are an infinite number of events in the course of history, it is only the *whole* of history in its unity and totality that reveals God. Hence Pannenberg's emphasis of universal history. On the indirect character of revelation, see Pannenberg, **SyTh/E**, 1:227, 230-257, especially 243; idem, "Introduction," 8-19; idem, "Response to the Discussion," 230-241; cf. also Tupper, 84-86; Kurt Koch, 69-70; Greiner, 97-101; Polk, 134-135; Denis Müller, 29-34; John B. Cobb, Jr., "Past, Present, and Future," 207-210.

and only in *anticipation* can one speak of the whole of reality.¹ With respect to God, this means that God also appears to have a history² because "the God who constitutes history has himself fully entered the process of history in his revelation."³ For Pannenberg, "the entire process of divine economy leading to that final consummation amounts to a self-demonstration of God's existence."⁴ In fact, Pannenberg says that "God actualizes himself in the world by his coming into it."⁵ Thus, "the action of God in the world is a repetition or reiteration of his eternal deity in his relation to the world."⁶

From statements like these, it appears that Pannenberg, despite his emphasis on

---

¹"The category of anticipation or prolepsis . . . thus shows itself to be a fundamental structural element . . . of the being of beings in their temporality" (Pannenberg, "Response to the Discussion," 260). On Pannenberg's understanding of the concept of *anticipation*, see idem, **Metaphysics and the Idea of God**, 91-109. Philip Clayton, has commented that the notion of anticipation "is not an easy teaching" ("Anticipation and Theological Method," in **TWP**, 131), with which Pannenberg concurs (Pannenberg, "A Response to My American Friends," 320). For further critique of Pannenberg's use of anticipation, see Ernstpeter Maurer, "Metaphysik und Antizipation: Wolfhart Pannenbergs theologische Meditationen über das Ganze," **Merkur** 44/501 (1990): 1091-1095, especially 1094; see also Drumm, 235-257, especially 241; Polk, **On the Way to God**, 74-75, 80; Lothar Kugelmann, **Antizipation: Eine Begriffsgeschichtliche Untersuchung**, FSÖTh 50 (Göttingen: Vandenhoeck & Ruprecht, 1986), 52-58, shows how Pannenberg introduces the term "anticipation" into dogmatics.

²"In distinction from the idea of immutability, that of God's faithfulness does not exclude historicity or the contingency of world occurrence, nor need the historicity and contingency of the divine action be in contradiction with God's eternity. If eternity and time coincide only in the eschatological consummation of history, then from the standpoint of the history of God that moves toward this consummation there is room for becoming in God himself, namely, in the relation of the immanent and the economic Trinity, and in this frame it is possible to say of God that he himself became something that he previously was not when he became man in his Son" (Pannenberg, **SyTh/E**, 1:438). Almost twenty years earlier, in 1969, Pannenberg wrote: "Thus it is necessary to say that, in a restricted but important sense, God does not yet exist. Since his rule and his being are inseparable, God's being is still in the process of coming to be" (**Theology and the Kingdom of God**, 56). Pannenberg even went on to say that "the very essence of God implies time" (ibid., 62).

³Pannenberg, "On Historical and Theological Hermeneutic," 158. Pannenberg continues by saying that God "has done so in such a way that precisely as he is here transmitted in a process of tradition, he is at the same time the future of history, the coming God who . . . is always distinguishing himself in a new way from what happens in this history."

⁴Pannenberg, **Introduction to Systematic Theology**, 12.

⁵Pannenberg, **SyTh/E**, 1:390, 391; idem, **SyTh/G**, 2:437-438. For Pannenberg the goal of God's action in the world is twofold: it is first the creation of a creaturely reality that is distinct from God and its consummation in an encounter with the Creator, and, second, the revelation of God's deity as the Creator of the world (idem, **SyTh/E**, 1:389).

⁶Pannenberg, **SyTh/E**, 1:389. In **SyTh/G**, 2:437, he prefers the term "self-actualization of God" (Selbstverwirklichung Gottes) over against Karl Barth's expression of a "repetition of God" (Wiederholung Gottes).

history--which at times has been misunderstood by some to be in close proximity to Process Philosophy[1]--in fact, still operates within the classical concept of the timelessness of God that is based on Greek philosophy rather than on Scripture alone.[2] Pannenberg has pointed out that the relationship between time and eternity is the key problem of eschatology and has repercussions on all areas of Christian teaching.[3] How, then are we to understand Pannenberg when he speaks about the future of history, which even seems to include the concept of history in the idea of God?

David Polk has pointed out that we are accustomed to conceive the future in terms of not-yet-present. The future, in this understanding, is that which has not been decided yet, which has not entered into the concreteness of becoming yet. This is not Pannenberg's perspective at all.[4] For him, the future of history could be described as

---

[1]John B. Cobb, Jr., claims that "Pannenberg was the first German theologian to take serious interest in process theology" ("Pannenberg and Process Theology," in **TWP**, 54). David McKenzie thinks that the crucial ideas in Pannenberg's work on the issue of God and freedom are more at home in the setting of process theology than anywhere else (**Wolfhart Pannenberg and Religious Philosophy** [Lanham, MD: University Press of America, 1980], 133, 137). Cf. Lewis S. Ford, "A Whiteheadian Basis for Pannenberg's Theology," **Encounter** 38/4 (1977): 307-317. Pannenberg has admitted that he found the experience with process philosophy enriching because it made up for a certain lack in the great tradition of German idealism (Pannenberg, **Metaphysics and the Idea of God**, 113) and also because it is "this century's most significant contribution to metaphysics" (ibid., xiv). Pannenberg has emphatically criticized the atomistic ontology of process philosophy. See Wolfhart Pannenberg and Lewis S. Ford, "A Dialogue about Process Philosophy," **Encounter** 38/4 (1977): 318-324; cf. Wolfhart Pannenberg, "Der Gott der Geschichte: Der trinitarische Gott und die Wahrheit der Geschichte," **KuD** 23 (1977): 82-86; idem, "Atom, Duration, Form: Difficulties with Process Philosophy," trans. John C. Robertson, Jr., and Gérard Vallée, **PrSt** 14/1 (1984): 21-30, now reprinted in Pannenberg, **Metaphysics and the Idea of God**, 113-129; and idem, SyTh/G, 2:29-31; 91, n. 175. Already in 1973 Galloway perceived that "a marriage between Pannenberg's theology of revelation as history and a suitably modified version of Whitehead's philosophy of reality as process is not likely to be very fruitful" (**Wolfhart Pannenberg**, 138). On Pannenberg's relation to process thought, see also Lewis S. Ford, "The Nature of the Power of the Future," in **TWP** 75-94; David P. Polk, "The All-Determining God and the Peril of Determinism," in **TWP**, 152-168; and Brian J. Walsh, "Pannenberg's Eschatological Ontology," **CSR** 11 (1982): 229-249.

[2]On the technical meaning of timelessness as primordial presupposition in much of theology, see the discussion in Fernando Luis Canale, **A Criticism of Theological Reason: Time and Timelessness as Primordial Presuppositions**, AUSDDS 10 (Berrien Springs, MI: Andrews University Press, 1987); Nelson Pike, **God and Timelessness** (London: Routledge & K. Paul, 1970), 6-16; and Alan G. Padgett, **God, Eternity and the Nature of Time** (New York: St. Martin's Press, 1992), 23-37.

[3]Pannenberg, SyTh/G, 3:641. In a similar manner Galloway (**Wolfhart Pannenberg**, 99), has suggested earlier that "the relation between time and eternity is the key to most aspects of his [Pannenberg's] theological system. It wholly determines his doctrine of the Trinity."

[4]Polk, **On the Way to God**, 256.

"*that which is futural to the whole of history.*"¹ Thus, as Polk has put it, God is understood "as 'post-historical', in comparison with historical, future."² In His eternity, God is present at all times and the manifestation of His lordship over the world of creation does not make good a lack in His eternal being.³ Hence, "although the essence of God is from everlasting to everlasting the same, it does have a history in time."⁴ This everlasting sameness of God⁵ is not a timeless eternity in the Platonic sense but follows the insights of Plotinus (205-270), who incorporated the idea of the presence of the totality of life into God's eternity.⁶

> Understood thus, eternity for Plotinus was not opposed to time but was the presupposition of understanding it. **The moments of time are separate in our experience of time. We can think of them as related to one another and to the whole if we refer them to the totality of eternity.** This reference is mediated to us by the soul which experiences time. **But in time the relation to the totality of life is different from what it is in eternity.** Instead of the perfect, the infinite, and the whole, we have constant succession to infinity (*Enn. 3.7.11*). In Plotinus, then, the Platonic antithesis of eternity and time persists. But the doctrine of time as the copy of eternity is changed. Time is now seen as the dissolution of the unity of life into a sequence of separate moments, and yet it is constituted a sequence by the reference to the eternal totality.⁷

---

¹Ibid., 257. Pannenberg puts it as follows: "If the future of all creatures is a universal one, that is, if each instance of reality has the same future, then the future to which I look forward today is the same future that confronted every earlier present. My future now was also Julius Caesar's future, the future of the prehistoric saurians and the future of the first physical processes approximately ten billion years ago. Thus I come to view past events as having eventuated from the same future to which I look forward. And, of course, those past events were the **finite** future of yet earlier events" (**Theology and the Kingdom of God**, 61); emphasis is added to point out the distinction between universal/ultimate and historical/finite future.

²Polk, **On the Way to God**, 257.

³Pannenberg, **SyTh/E**, 1:389. This statement stands in clear contrast to process thought.

⁴Pannenberg, "Dogmatic Theses on the Doctrine of Revelation," 133-134.

⁵Pannenberg speaks of an "ewigen Selbigkeit Gottes," in **SyTh/G**, 2:197.

⁶Pannenberg, **SyTh/E**, 1:403. Cf. the section "Being and Time," idem, **Metaphysics and the Idea of God**, 69-90; idem, "Providence, God, and Eschatology," in **The Whirlwind in Culture: Frontiers in Theology: In Honor of Langdon Gilkey**, 177-178. Pannenberg refered to Plotinus in a lecture in 1984, printed in "Die Wahrheit Gottes in der Bibel und im Christlichen Dogma," 309. For a succinct account of Plotinus' philosophy and influence, see Philip Mertan, "Plotinus," **The Encyclopedia of Philosophy**, ed. Paul Edwards (New York: Macmillan, 1967), 6:351-359.

⁷Pannenberg, **SyTh/E**, 1:403-404 (emphasis supplied). For Plotinus "the simultaneous presence of the whole is eternity" (ibid., 406). Pannenberg concludes his extensive discussion of the concept of time by stating that "critical insight into the limitations of modern reconstructions of the conditions of our experience of time permits us to suppose that Plotinus's doctrine of eternity as the condition of an appropriate concept of time has not been superseded by modern discussion" (ibid., 407). Cf. idem, **SyTh/G**, 3:653, where Pannenberg speaks about a "Aufhebung" of time

For Plotinus, the crossing or the transition from eternity to time is perceived as "jump," as a qualitative difference that Plotinus has described as "fall."[1] This indicates that Pannenberg, who follows Plotinus' concept of eternity, has not yet fully succeeded in bridging the qualitative gap between an eternal God and human history.

This understanding of God and its ramifications has significant implications for all areas of Pannenberg's theology, including his concept of Scripture. His concept of God does not allow for a propositional form of revelation where a specific content is being revealed to humankind. Rather than conceiving God in personal terms, capable of communicating a specific content to mankind, Pannenberg defines the personhood of God in relational terms as reciprocal self-distinction of Father, Son, and Spirit as the concrete form of the Trinitarian Relations.[2] In the words of Pannenberg, "in the vital movement of such reciprocal dedication, the unity of Father, Son, and Spirit consumates itself in the historical process of the revelatory event."[3] Galloway thinks that "this points to the ontological basis of Pannenberg's doctrine of universal history as revelation."[4] Thus the reciprocal dedication and self-differenciation of the Trinity becomes the basis of his concept of "revelation as history."[5] By perceiving God as being universally present through His Spirit in His creation and in humankind, Pannenberg cuts against the role of special revelation as a source for theology and of one's knowledge of God. Scripture is not considered to be special revelation. In fact, the concept of special revelation is replaced by a new "natural theology"[6] that appears to turn theology into philosophy.

Moreover, Pannenberg's view of the indirect self-revelation of God through

---

in eternity where the different moments of time and the modi of time do not simply disappear but cannot be separated from each other either.

[1] Pannenberg, **SyTh/G**, 2:116, 114.

[2] Cf. Chuck Gutenson, "Father, Son and Holy Spirit--The One God: An Exploration of the Trinitarian Doctrine of Wolfhart Pannenberg," **AsbTJ** 49/1 (1994): 5-21.

[3] Pannenberg, **Jesus--God and Man**, 183.

[4] Galloway, **Wolfhart Pannenberg**, 112.

[5] Taking up Karl Rahners thesis of an identity between the immanent and the economic Trinity Pannenberg asserts that the doctrine of the Trinity "must constantly link the trinity in the eternal essence of God to his historical revelation, since revelation cannot be viewd as extraneous to his deity" (**SyTh/E**, 1:328). Thus, "the concept of revelation . . . is developed by the trinitarian understanding of God . . ." (ibid., 332). Cf. idem., 384-386.

[6] Cf. Georg Kraus, 349-375.

history explains why Scripture is seen as a historical document with theological orientation. This, however, excludes any supernatural authority of Scripture. It is understood as essentially historical and, therefore, as a human document. Furthermore, from his understanding of history as the transmission of traditions, it seems that Scripture not only originates within a particular religious tradition but is also a result of it. Inasmuch as the entire historical process of the divine economy amounts to a "self-actualization of God in his relation to creation,"[1] God's "action" in the world is but "a repetition or reiteration of his eternal deity in his relation to the world."[2] Hence, it could be said that the creative inspirations by which humankind participates in the divine Spirit are included in this repetition of God's eternal deity. If God's reign is understood as His self-actualization, one could even say that these "inspirations" originated, so to speak, in God's eternity. On the other hand, it seems that the question of how precisely Scripture came into being is not directly explained through Pannenberg's concept of God alone. For this, we have to turn to his anthropological presuppositions which are closely intertwined with his concept of God.

Anthropological Presuppositions

Scripture, for Pannenberg, as we have seen above, is a document that has not originated by supernatural revelation, i.e., it is not "from above." Instead, it is essentially a human document, i.e., it is originating "from below." To explain this calls for an analysis of his anthropological presuppositions.

In contrast to Karl Barth,[3] Pannenberg believes in the existence of some form

---

[1]Pannenberg, **SyTh/E**, 1:386. The German expression "Selbstverwirklichung," which is used by Pannenberg could also be rendered "self-realization." Cf. idem, **SyTh/G**, 1:418.

[2]Pannenberg, **SyTh/E**, 1:389. Pannenberg himself has put the talk about God's "actions" in italics because it "traces back to God the connections that appear in world occurence" (ibid., 388). According to Pannenberg "the three persons of Father, Son, and Spirit are primarily the subject of the divine action. By their cooperation the action takes form as that of the one God. . . . The kingdom of God in the world is certainly the kingdom of the Father. The monarchy of the Father is God's absolute lordship. The Son serves it, and so does the glorifying of the Father and the Son by the Spirit. But the monarchy of the Father is mediated by the Son, who prepares the way for it by winning form for it in the life of creatures, and also by the Spirit, who enables creatures to honor God as their Creator by letting them share in the relation of the Son the the Father. This is the action of the one God by the Father, Son, and Spirit as it may be seen in the light of the eschatological consummantion of the kingdom of God in the world" (ibid., 388-389; cf. 390).

[3]Barth's emphasis on the "infinite qualitative distinction" between God and man, which he derived from Kierkegaard is well known. Cf. Karl Barth, **The Epistle to the Romans**, 10.

of contact between God and man. The contact between man and God is made possible by man's essential openness beyond himself. Such *self-transcending*[1] openness to the world and to God[2] is characteristic of all human life. Man is open to constantly new things and fresh experiences,[3] because in his temporality "the peculiar nature of the ecstatic self-transcendence found in all living things emerges most clearly."[4]

In its ecstatic form human minds participate in the divine Spirit.[5] In Pannenberg's own words,

> the human mind can be described as a special realization of this ecstatic character of life. Man not only lives beyond himself in having experience of what is going on in his environment and relevant for his own life, but the human mind is characterized by a reflective attitude to himself and is therefore able to take his stand beyond himself and know that. **The human mind represents an intensified form of self-transcendence, i.e., of the ecstatic structure of life. . . . This ecstatic element of the life of the mind I call "spirit."**[6]

In this qualitative distinction between time and eternity God touches man's world "as a tangent touches a circle, that is without touching it" (ibid., 30). Elsewhere Barth expressed this difference in the following comparison: "It is only an appearance that the rainbow stands on the earth, in reality it arches over the earth; true, it stoops down to the earth, yet it does not stand on our earth, but is only perceived from it. So it is with divine truth; this needs no human support, as the rainbow does not need the earth. True, it shines on man and he receives it; yet it is not dependent on man. It withdraws and man remains in darkness; it returns and man walks in light. But man is not its assistant; he cannot produce the light; similarly he cannot store it" (Eduard Böhl, **Dogmatik**, 1886, xxv, quoted by Karl Barth in **CD**, I/1, 223). On Barth's concept of the "infinite qualitative distinction," see Provence, 56-67).

[1]On Pannenberg's concept of self-transcendence as participation of man in the divine spirit, see Pannenberg, **SyTh/G**, 2:48-49; 226-227; idem, **SyTh/G**, 3:19, 150-151; idem, **SyTh/E**, 1:93, 155-156; idem, "The Spirit of Life," in idem, **Faith and Reality**, trans. John Maxwell (Philadelphia: Westminster Press, 1977), 35-38.

[2]"Man's openness to the world presupposes a relation to God. Where there is no explicit clarity about this, the expression *open to the world* remains unclear. It can be misunderstood to mean that man is oriented toward the world, while it really involves the necessity that man inquire beyond everything that he comes across as his world. This peculiarity of human existence, man's infinite dependence, is understandable only as the question about God" (Pannenberg, **What Is Man?** 12). Accordingly "this unending movement into the open is directed toward God, . . . therefore openness to the world essentially means openness to God" (ibid., 54). In contrast to animals, the awareness of the future seems to be reserved to man (idem, **Theology and the Kingdom of God**, 68).

[3]Pannenberg, **What Is Man?** 7.

[4]Pannenberg, **Anthropology in Theological Perspective**, 524.

[5]Wolfhart Pannenberg, "The Working of the Spirit in the Creation and in the People of God," 19; cf. idem, "The Doctrine of the Spirit and the Task of a Theology of Nature," **Theol** 75 (1972): 8-21, republished in idem, **Faith and Reality**, trans. John Maxwell (Philadelphia: Westminster Press, 1977), 20-38.

[6]Pannenberg, "The Working of the Spirit in the Creation and in the People of God," 18

Although at one place Pannenberg rejects the idea that man creates religions by himself through his imagination,[1] he seems to stress a continuity between divine spirit and human spirit[2] to the point where pantheism "appears to lie close at hand."[3] According to Pannenberg,

> . . . the element of transcendence in spirit suggests that after all it might be neither necessary nor wise to admit a fundamental distinction between a human spirit and a divine spirit. The ecstatic, self-transcendent character of all spiritual experience brings sufficiently to bear the transcendence of God over all created beings. The spirit never belongs in a strict sense to the creature in his immanent nature, **but the creature participates in the spirit**--and I venture to say: in the divine spirit--**by transcending itself, i.e., by being elevated beyond itself in the ecstatic experience that illustrates the working of the spirit.** We remember: the spirit is not the mind, but the human mind comes to life only when he is touched by the spirit. . . . **Thus the idea of spirit allows us to do justice to the transcendence of God and at the same time to explain his immanence in his creation.**[4]

(emphasis supplied). Konrad, 647, has seen a danger of immanent thinking in Pannenberg's thought.

[1]According to Pannenberg "something else always preceded all imaginative activity in the formation of religions, and for that reason religion is more than merely a creation of man" (**What Is Man?** 9-10).

[2]This has been pointed out by Timothy Bradshaw, **Trinity and Ontology: A Comparative Study of the Theologies of Karl Barth and Wolfhart Pannenberg** (Edinburgh: Rutherford House Books, 1988), 166-168. Cf. Pannenberg's statement in **Jesus--God and Man**, 177: "The immanence of the Spirit in believers exists only through the fact that as believers they have found the ground of their life *extra se*, beyond themselves." See also ibid., n. 150, and idem, "The Working of the Spirit in the Creation and in the People of God," 19-20.

[3]Pannenberg, **Jesus--God and Man**, 176. Olson, "Trinity and Eschatology: The Historical Being of God in the Theology of Wolfhart Pannenberg," 211-219 has pointed out that by seeking to relate "Spirit" with the openness of man beyond himself, i.e., with the ecstatic structure of life itself, Pannenberg has difficulty distinguishing the Spirit from man. It even seems that "the divine spirit is identical with the unique quality of humanity as such" (Olson, 218). Olsen continues by saying that "the difference between man's spirit and God's Holy Spirit seems in this scheme to be reduced to a temporal one. What, then, will the difference be in the eschaton when the unity toward which man is oriented is reached? When anticipation becomes union, what distinction will remain between man's spirit and God's?" (ibid., 219).

[4]Pannenberg, "The Working of the Spirit in the Creation and in the People of God," 21. Pannenberg has reiterated this idea in **SyTh/G**, 2:498 where he writes: "Der Geist hebt die Menschen über ihre eigene Endlichkeit hinaus, . . . an solcher Ekstase ist nichts Unnatürliches, da vielmehr das geistige Leben des Menschen seiner Grundverfassung nach ekstatisch ist und darin in seiner besonderen Weise die Eigenart des Lebendigen überhaupt realisiert. Das menschliche Bewußtsein ist im Vollzug seiner Fähigkeit, beim andern seiner selbst zu sein, durch und durch ekstatisch strukturiert, und gerade so ist es vom Geist belebt." This unity with the Spirit, however, is not to be understood in the sense of a mystical union (Einigungsmystik) with Christ or God in which one does not perceive any difference to God and Christ any more (ibid., 499). Bradshaw has tried to describe the intricate thought of Pannenberg on this point by saying that "the human self-transcending dynamic exists because of the divine Spirit, which, being future, is transcendent but as transcendent it is immanent in the human self-transcendence" (**Trinity and Ontology**, 167). Given this intricate connection between man and God, which is made possible only through the

Part of the ecstatic structure of human life, which Pannenberg calls "spirit," are imaginative inspirations. They often open up for the first time an understanding of reality. In these imaginative inspirations, man experiences himself as simultaneously creative and dependent.[1] That is, "divine inspiration and human creativity are not in competition but, rather, work together in such a way that inspiration is the condition for human creativity."[2] In other words, "man in his contemplative nature conceives from God by means of imagination."[3]

Furthermore, through an anticipation of the future, human beings are provided with "a presentiment of eternity"[4] which "alone grasps the abiding identity of things, an identity that transcends the experience of them as changing and combines their past with their still open future in a single conception of their being."[5] For Pannenberg, "it belongs to the nature of man's openness to the world to see reality in the most objective way possible. This means to see it out of the perspective of an eternal present."[6] In other words, it appears that man's ecstatic relationship to the future is ultimately more than just a relationship to a temporal future. It seems to include some form of relationship or participation in the eternal One which is only "placed" in our future because only from a "standpoint from within the stream of events itself is time divided into past, present, and future. Seen from beyond the flow of time, all events coincide in an eternal present."[7]

Spirit, Helmut Thielicke's charge that with Pannenberg "the theology of the Holy Spirit is inevitably secondary" is difficult to sustain. Helmut Thielicke, **The Evangelical Faith**, 3 vols., ed. and trans. G. W. Bromiley (Grand Rapids, MI: Eerdmans, 1982), 3:xxvii. Thielicke is not far off, however, when he says that this "can lead only to something that was already at work at the beginning, namely a radical and rich regeneration of 'natural theology'" (ibid).

[1]Pannenberg, **What Is Man?** 26; idem, **Anthropology in Theological Perspective**, 377.

[2]Pannenberg, **Anthropology in Theological Perspective**, 377.

[3]Pannenberg, **What Is Man?** 26. Elsewhere Pannenberg has emphasized that "one must not fail to recognize the significance of the constantly new situation, or of the creative power of the imagination. . . . The imagination, however, . . . can only develop itself within the realm of a spiritual tradition, always according to the degree to which that tradition is differentiated" (Pannenberg, "What Is a Dogmatic Statement?" 206).

[4]Pannenberg, **Anthropology in Theological Perspective**, 525.

[5]Ibid., "It is from the future that the abiding essence of things discloses itself, because the future alone decides what is truly lasting."

[6]Pannenberg, **What Is Man?** 76.

[7]Ibid., 81. Hence Pannenberg can claim that "the essential nature of the future lies in the

Here one can perceive a close intertwining between Pannenberg's understanding of the nature of God as "eternal present" and a correlation in man's nature to the divine by means of his openness beyond himself and through his imaginative inspirations in which the future is anticipated. The qualitative difference between God's eternal nature and man's historical existence is indicated in Pannenberg's understanding of human language as being doxological.[1] Pannenberg follows his teacher and Doktorvater Edmund Schlink who had developed the expression in contrast to the doctrine of analogical interpretation.[2] For Pannenberg, direct analogicity between our words and the truth of God's essence seems to be impossible. For that reason, it is illegitimate to draw conclusions from doxological statements without further ado.[3] One implication of this doxological understanding of human language is that statements about God

───────────────

unpredictable new thing that is hidden in the womb of the future" (ibid., 42).

[1]Pannenberg, "Analogy and Doxology," 212-238; idem, "What Is a Dogmatic Statement?" 202-205; and idem, **SyTh/E**, 1:55. On Pannenberg's use of doxology, see the detailed study by Drumm, 191-292; and Alpern, 1-50. Pannenberg himself has defined the structure of doxological statements in contradistinction to kerygmatic statements: "Kerygmatic statements speak of definite earthly events that are understood as events that come from God, and in this sense they speak of 'God's acts.' Doxological statements, on the other hand, intend primarily to speak of God's eternal essence. They are the praise of the eternal God on the basis of his deeds. All theological language about God has such doxological character; it is essentially characterized by the structure of devotion and worship. . . . In the sense here intended, doxological statements are statements about God on the basis of events that have been experienced as having occurred from him. They speak of the way in which God has shown himself in specific occurrences. Thereby human conceptualization sacrifices itself in adoration" (Pannenberg, **Jesus--God and Man**, 184-185). In other words, doxological statements are a proleptical anticipation of an absolute future which has yet to prove itself. The worshipper in uttering doxological statements is "reduced to mystery," as he tries to express what he cannot say or know. Yet, Alpern thinks that the doxological statements have a cognitive basis both in the historical acts of God and in the confirmation provided as history unfolds and the promises of God are fulfilled (Alpern, v-iv); cf. Drumm, 233. Carl F. H. Henry, on the other hand, suggests that the concept of doxological statements scuttles the universal validity and cognitive truth status of statements about God (**God, Revelation and Authority**, 3:294).

[2]"In using this expression [i.e., doxological] we follow Edmund Schlink's distinction between kerygmatic and doxological forms of expression" (Pannenberg, **Jesus--God and Man**, 184). Cf. Edmund Schlink, "Die Struktur der dogmatischen Aussage als ökumenisches Problem," **KuD** 3 (1957): 251-306; idem, **The Coming Christ and the Coming Church**, trans. I. H. Nielson (Edinburgh: Oliver & Boyd, 1967), 16-84, especially 19-34 and 41-42. On Schlink's understanding of doxology, see Drumm, 123-190.

[3]Pannenberg, **SyTh/G**, 3:569, writes that God's own reality transcends all our concepts. See idem, "Analogy and Doxology," 217; and idem, **Jesus--God and Man**, 185. Cf. Elizabeth A. Johnson, "The Right Way to Speak about God?" 673-692; and Polk, **On the Way to God**, 248-249.

remain provisional or proleptic in character.[1] For Pannenberg, the temporal difference between our speech about God and its fulfillment by God Himself cannot be expressed by means of the concept of analogy.[2] Thus, the degree of correspondence between our words and concepts and the truth of God remains open, inasmuch as that to which they point is still ahead of us. This means that one can speak solely of the *Deus pro nobis*-- of the *Deus in se*, nothing whatsoever can be said.[3] In other words, only from our human perspective of the God *pro nobis* it appears that the future is not yet decided.[4] But in contrast and "in distinction from creatures, who as finite beings are subject to the march of time, the eternal God does not have ahead of him any future that is different from his present."[5] Eternity as the complete totality of life is thus seen from the standpoint of time only in terms of a fullness that is sought in the future.[6]

Through Pannenberg's concept of imagination, it seems, the question of a knowledge of God has moved from supernatural revelation as recorded in Scripture to the field of religious experience.[7] It is not insignificant that Pannenberg connects

---

[1] Pannenberg, "What Is a Dogmatic Statement?" 205; Polk, **On the Way to God**, 249.

[2] Pannenberg, "Analogy and Doxology," 238. On Pannenberg's understanding of Analogy, see idem, "Analogie," **RGG**, 1:350-353; idem, "Analogie," **EKL**(2), 1:133-144; and his unpublished inaugural dissertation, "Analogie und Offenbarung: Eine kritische Untersuchung der Geschichte des Analogiebegriffs in der Gotteslehre." (The latter was not available to me.)

[3] Hill, **The Three-Personed God**, 157. By denying any knowledge of God as He is in Himself, Pannenberg seems to stand within the Kantian hermeneutical circle. Cf. Gruenler, 107-108.

[4] "... futurity is fundamental to Pannenberg's understanding of history.... Against any charge of developmental pantheism Pannenberg argues that it is from our finite present that the future appears to be undecided" (Villa-Vicencio, 36). Cf. Pannenberg, **SyTh/G**, 2:20. Speaking about the coming of Jesus the Son of God, Pannenberg asserts: "Dem ewigen Gottessohn widerfährt nichts Unvorhergesehenes und Unbeabsichtigtes. Nur auf der Seite seiner menschlichen Natur ist zwischen tätigem Auftreten und Wirken einerseits, dem als Widerfahrnis zu erleidendem Geschick andererseits zu unterscheiden" (ibid., 2:489).

[5] Pannenberg, **SyTh/E**, 1:410.

[6] Ibid., 1:408.

[7] The content of the word "God" does not derive from a narrow, personal sphere of living, or any single religious experience but includes a broader view of religious experience (Pannenberg, **SyTh/E**, 1:65-67, 70). This is in accord with earlier statements of Pannenberg such as: "If we take our bearings solely from the experiences of our personal life, the decision to believe or not to believe always retains an ultimately arbitrary, emotional element. **It is the breadth of total experience of every and all reality which provides the field where we have to enquire whether the divine nature of the God of the Bible can stand up to verification; it is not the narrow bounds of an entirely personal experience of life, taken in isolation**" (**The Apostles' Creed**, 35), (emphasis supplied). Cf. Alfred Glässer, **Verweigerte Partnerschaft? Anthropologische,**

religious experience with "feeling,"[1] invoking Schleiermacher's famous proposal--that man is related initially [ursprünglich] to the totality of his life and world.[2] Pannenberg interprets this immediate self-consciousness of the yet incomplete whole of life "along religious lines as a consciousness of God, on the grounds that feeling . . . unites itself to the totality of the finite and therein knows itself to be related to the infinite as distinct from the world."[3] The aspect of Schleiermacher's interpretation of the concept of feeling that continues to be relevant for Pannenberg is that

> . . . religious feelings are not simply specific feelings that are distinguished from others by their special object or by their reference to such an object. Their particular character consists, rather, in the fact that in them the wholeness of human life which is always present in feeling as such becomes thematic.[4]

Inasmuch as feeling "grasps the relations and connections of things among themselves and relates these 'to our entire present state'," feelings accompany "the activity of the imagination."[5] As such, the concept of imaginative inspirations in which man conceives of God and is related to the infinite, plays a significant role for the origin of Scripture. To the degree that these inspirations are man's inspirations, their origin can be seen to be human. Yet, inasmuch as the human mind is not only creative but also dependent in its imaginations,[6] and in them participates in the divine

---

konfessionelle und ökumenische Aspekte der Theologie Wolfhart Pannenbergs, Est 31 (Regensburg: Verlag Friedrich Pustet, 1991).

[1]Pannenberg, **SyTh/G**, 3:192-193; 643. On p. 193, n. 211, Pannenberg refers specifically to Schleiermacher's section in **The Christian Faith**, § 3, 2. In idem, **Anthropology in Theological Perspective**, 247-248, to which Pannenberg refers in **SyTh/G**, 3:192, n. 210, and 643, n. 228, he discussed Schleiermacher's positive contribution at greater length. That Pannenberg is echoing Schleiermacher's teaching about the consciousness of God is pointed out by Avis, 86-89, 76.

[2]Cf. Schleiermacher, **The Christian Faith**, § 3, 2, p. 7, where he speaks about feeling as "the immediate presence of whole undivided Being, etc." See also ibid., § 5, 4-5.

[3]Pannenberg, **Anthropology in Theological Perspective**, 248. He adds that "in this area Schleiermacher's concept of feeling has by no means been superseded by the present state of discussion in psychology."

[4]Pannenberg, **Anthropology in Theological Perspective**, 251.

[5]Ibid., 246. Avis see's Pannenberg here echoing Schleiermacher's teaching of the consciousness of God and thinks that "the most fruitful interpretation of Pannenberg will be to see him as the executor of Schleiermacher's innovative theology that tries to face the challenge of the modern world head-on" (Avis, 86, 88).

[6]". . . as far as imagination is concerned, divine inspiration and human creativity are not in competition but, rather, work together in such a way that inspiration is the condition for human creativity" (Pannenberg, **Anthropology in Theological Perspective**, 377, 381).

Spirit, one can also speak of a divine origin of those inspirations.¹ Nevertheless, the writing down of those impressions appears to be left to man alone, because Pannenberg does not allow for the possibility of any supernatural assistance and denies supernatural inspiration. Hence, the origin of the written words of Scripture is solely in man, i.e., "from below." Again, an intimate interconnection between divine and human aspects in Pannenberg's thought is apparent where, through God's immanent Spirit, a contact with man is established which leads to the recording of these experiences and thus to the origin of the text of Scripture. Prompted by the experience of the divine in those "religious feelings," men are driven to write down their experiences with the divine, and those eventually result in a particular tradition. In other words, Pannenberg's famous proposal of "revelation as history" is not to be understood as a direct identification of revelation with general history or natural happenings in history as such.² History (Geschichte) is always the history of the transmission of traditions and,

---

¹Schleiermacher also connects the feeling of absolute dependence with the origin of Biblical writings in as much as he claims that human self-consciousness includes two inseparable interconnected levels, one sensible and the other absolute (**The Christian Faith**, § 5, 4-5). Absolute self-consciousness, which in itself is always self-identical, is able to manifest itself in time by entering into relation with the sensible self-consciousness so as to constitute a moment (ibid., § 5, 4, p. 22). Thus, since within human self-consciousness the feeling of absolute dependence (originated by a timeless God) always co-occurs with feelings of pleasure and pain (originated by sensory temporal experiences) the feeling of absolute dependence is always linked to the contents of the sensible self-consciousness through which it expresses itself. Thus, the contents of the sensible self-consciousness, to which the feeling of absolute dependence is connected in the very instance of its origination, becomes the content of its external historical manifestation. Consequently, the writing down of religious literature becomes "the attempt to translate the inward emotions into thought" (ibid., § 13, postscript, p. 67).

²"Modern history is not however divine revelation so to speak of itself. The connection between revelation and history is not to be taken in the sense that revelation is necessarily to be encountered wherever one gains entry to history. Yet the revelation of the divinity of the biblical God has to do with history as a whole. It is disclosed only in history as a whole; not uniformly in every specific event, but only--as we have seen--in an end-perspective. For history is a whole only when seen from the end and through that end" (Wolfhart Pannenberg, "Divine Revelation and Modern History," in **Faith and Reality**, 89). Cf. also the following quotation: "History [Geschichte] is never composed of so-called bare facts [bruta facta]. As human history [Menschengeschichte], events are always intertwined with understanding, in hope and remembrance, and the transformations of understanding are themselves historical events [Geschichtsereignisse]. These elements are not to be separated from the happenings of history, as they originally occurred. Thus, history [Geschichte] is always the history of the transmission of traditions; and even the events of nature, which are included in the history [Geschichte] of a people, have significance only with reference to their positive or negative relationship to the traditions and expectations in which those men live. The events of history speak their own language, the language of facts, but this language is hearable only in the context of the interpretation of the traditions and expectations in which the occurrences actually happen" (Pannenberg, "Dogmatic Theses on the Doctrine of Revelation," 152-153). We have followed

as such, is hermeneutically oriented. Natural events, like natural catastrophes, for instance, are included in this history (Geschichte) only inasmuch as they are experienced as significant for the lives of the people.[1]

Such experiences with the divine reality find expression in the different religions of this world,[2] not just the Judeo-Christian tradition. The Christian Scriptures are the human testimony of one of those religious traditions, namely, the Judeo-Christian tradition. As such, Scripture is a reflection and an expression of the experience in this particular tradition.

Because these imaginative inspirations are common to all human beings and all men share a fundamentally religious orientation,[3] there is little if any need for special illumination in Pannenberg's thought. When revelation happens as history, it does not require an illumination by the Holy Spirit or a special insight of faith in order to be known.[4] In fact, events have an inherent power to convince of their truth and are

---

here the translation as given by Tupper, 103, which reflects the thrust of the German more adequately.

[1]So Pannenberg to Hasel, January 21, 1994, 1; cf. also Pannenberg, "Geschichte/ Geschichtsschreibung/Geschichtsphilosophie: VIII," 668, 670.

[2]"For the religions have to do with the current experience of the power that supports all reality, towards which the question of man's existence is directed. . . . That applies also to the pre- and non-Christian religions, too, however. They are not merely the expression of an isolated human question and its accompanying projected answer. It is not only in Christian faith that the human question lives from the happening of a divine answer. All religions stem from particular happenings of the reality inquired after in the question of human existence" (Wolfhart Pannenberg, "The Question of God," in **BQT**, 2:226). Cf. idem, "Geschichte/Geschichtsschreibung/ Geschichtsphilosophie VIII," 668, 670-671; idem, "Religion und Religionen: Theologische Erwägungen zu den Prinzipien eines Dialogs mit den Weltreligionen," in **Dialog aus der Mitte christlicher Theologie**, BRTh 5, ed. Andreas Bsteh (Mödling: Verlag St. Gabriel, 1987), 179-196; idem, "The Religions from the Perspective of Christian Theology and the Self-Interpretation of Christianity in Relation to the Non-Christian Religions," **ModT** 9/3 (1993): 285-297. A similar version of the article appeared in 1992 under the German title "Die Religionen in der Perspektive christlicher Theologie und die Selbstdarstellung des Christentums im Verhältnis zu den nichtchristlichen Religionen," TB 23/6 (1992): 305-316. See also the rejoinder and critique by Helmut Burkhardt, "Haben alle Religionen mit einem und demselben Gott zu tun?" **TB** 24/4 (1993): 212-217; and Gary Bollinger, "Pannenberg's Theology of the Religions and the Claim to Christian Superiority," **Encounter** 43 (1982): 273-285.

[3]Man is incurably religious and has a religious disposition which makes religion constitutive for human nature. Pannenberg, **SyTh/E**, 1:155-157. Cf. idem, "Religion und menschliche Natur," 9-24; and idem, "A Response to My American Friends," 313. He says: ". . . it is only in the form of religion and *one* religion among others that the divine reality can be perceived by human beings. Religion, then, is the primary human form of perceiving the reality of God. As such, the issue of religion also belongs to anthropology."

[4]Pannenberg, **SyTh/G**, 3:538. This already has been maintained by Pannenberg:

clear to all because of the tradition-historical context in which they are recorded.[1] Hence, they need no additional boost from the outside to make them clear.[2] Thus, Pannenberg affirms the logical priority of knowledge over faith.[3] In other words, Pannenberg does not allow for noetic effects of the fall on man's cognitive faculties. It seems as if Pannenberg would qualify as a representative of what Millard J. Erickson has termed "'epistemological Pelagianism.' Sin affects humans, but not their ability to know. That ability . . . is undisturbed by the presence of sin in the unbeliever."[4] The question, therefore, remains: "How is it that some respond positively to the hearing of the report whereas others reject the message?"[5]

Being a human document,[6] Scripture is the product of human tradition. It is not the deposit of timeless truths that are revealed to human reason but a historical document that reflects the experience with the divine in one particular tradition. Inasmuch as all men are religiously oriented, Scripture reflects this anthropological orientation towards the divine and can be examined for its theological orientation. In

---

"Nothing must mute the fact that all truth lies right before the eyes, and that its appropriation is a natural consequence of the facts. There is no need for any additional perfection of man as though he could not focus on the 'supernatural' truths with his normal equipment for knowing. . . . In particular the Holy Spirit is not an additional condition without which the event of Christ could not be known as revelation" (Pannenberg, "Dogmatic Theses on the Doctrine of Revelation," 136).

[1]Wolfhart Pannenberg, "How Is God Revealed to Us?" in **Faith and Reality**, 61.

[2]Braaten, "Wolfhart Pannenberg," 644. This has been the point of contention in the debate between Pannenberg and Paul Althaus. Cf. Paul Althaus, "Offenbarung als Geschichte und Glaube," 321-330; and Pannenberg's response to Althaus in Wolfhart Pannenberg, "Insight and Faith," in **BQT**, 2:28-45. For a critique of Pannenberg's thesis that historical revelation is open to anyone who has eyes to see, cf. G. G. O'Collins, 405; Donald G. Bloesch, **EET**, 1:54; 86, n. 97; **EET**, 2:267-268.

[3]Cf. the recent discussion of the nature of faith in Pannenberg, **SyTh/G**, 3:156-196, 364; see idem, "Wahrheit, Gewißheit und Glaube," 226-264; and idem, "Die Rationalität der Theologie," 533-544. Cf. Avery Dulles, "Pannenberg on Revelation and Faith," in **TWP**, 170, who remarks that Pannenberg's attempt to base the decision to believe on intelligible grounds so that it can be defended against the charge of capriciousness "harmonizes excellently with the Catholic mentality, which has, at least until very recently, been characterized by universalism and rationality." Cf. also the survey of the role of faith in different theological approaches in idem, "Models of Faith," 405-413, and especially 408 on Pannenberg. Richard A. Rhem has suggested that what is really crucial about Pannenberg's doctrine of revelation is that it is universally available to human reason ("A Theological Conception of Reality as History--Some Aspects of the Thinking of Wolfhart Pannenberg," **RefR** 26 [1972]: 186-187).

[4]Millard J. Erickson, **Evangelical Interpretation: Perspectives on Hermeneutical Issues** (Grand Rapids, MI: Baker Book House, 1993), 45.

[5]Grenz and Olson, 197.

[6]Cf. Pannenberg, **SyTh/G**, 3:169.

other words, Scripture offers theology, the science of God, only as the science of religions,[1] that is, historic religions.[2] For one tradition, the Judeo-Christian religion, it serves as the historical resource book for theological ideas that need to be tested for their universal validity. Hence, the rivalry of the history of the different religious truth claims and religious traditions can be read as the manifestation of the divine reality, which is undisputed only at the end, i.e., in the future.[3]

Conclusion

Pannenberg as yet has not provided a systematic description of his understanding of Scripture. Even in his **Systematic Theology**, one misses a prolegomena on the role and function of Scripture in theology. This does not mean, however, that he has no concept of Scripture and its role in theology. In fact, it appears that his understanding of Scripture is derived from his understanding of God and also is coupled to anthropological presuppositions.

The strength and genius of Pannenberg can be seen in his systematic unfolding of all aspects of theology from the idea of God, including his concept of Scripture. There is a certain conceptual neatness[4] and coherence in Pannenberg's trinitarian understanding of God that is admirable and worthy of respect. It is no overstatement to say that Pannenberg is a truly *systematic* theologian, one who with much

---

[1] Joseph A. Colombo, **An Essay on Theology and History: Studies in Pannenberg, Metz, and the Frankfurt School**, AARSR 61 (Atlanta, GA: Scholars Press, 1990), 44.

[2] "Theology as a science of God is therefore possible only as a science of religion, and not as the science of religion in general but of the historic religions. *Christian* theology, on this view, would be the study of the *Christian* religion, the science of Christianity" (Pannenberg, **TPS**, 314).

[3] "If the history of religion is not just a history of human ideas and attitudes, if the issue in it is instead the truth of divine reality in the deities of the religions, this is because the history of religion can be read as that of the manifestation of divine reality and the process of criticism of inadequate human views of this reality. The increasing unity of religion in religious history, in spite of the plurality, corresponds to the unity of the divine reality which is coming to light in this history through all the changes and upheavals" (Pannenberg, **SyTh/E**, 1:171). Cf. also idem, **Gottesgedanke und menschliche Freiheit** (Göttingen: Vandenhoeck & Ruprecht, 1972), 46-47; and idem, "Toward a Theology of the History of Religions," in **BQT**, 2:65-118. It appears that Pannenberg's statement about the increasing unity of religion in religious history is too optimistic and does not do justice to the diverse character of different religions. For a critique of Pannenberg's approach of a theology of the history of religions, and the inadequacy of his reflection on the diversity of different religions, see Heinzpeter Hempelmann, **Kritischer Rationalismus und Theologie als Wissenschaft: Zur Frage nach dem Wirklichkeitsbezug des christlichen Glaubens**, 2d ed. (Wuppertal: R. Brockhaus Verlag, 1987), 170-172.

[4] Clayton, "The God of History and the Presence of the Future," 105.

determination and insight has succeeded in constructing his entire theology from one fundamental idea, the idea of God. In this endeavor, Pannenberg not only has incorporated a vast knowledge of the intricate history of theology and philosophy but also creatively appropriated new insights from the natural sciences for his theological argument. This makes him a truly comprehensive theologian, one who moves with erudition and German "Gründlichkeit" through the most complex issues.

In order to grasp Pannenberg's understanding of the role of Scripture in theology, one has first of all to comprehend his concept of God which influences his concept of revelation and has specific implications for the origin and nature of Scripture and, ultimately, for his use of Scripture as well. As we have seen in our investigation above, Pannenberg perceives the idea of God in a creative new way as a field of power that determines everything. In this rather impersonal conception, the "person" of God is defined in relational terms as the reciprocal dedication of Father, Son, and Spirit that consummates in the revelatory historical process. By perceiving God's essence in relational terms in connection with the concept of field, Pannenberg is able to bring together the concept of God's transcendence and immanence in a creative way. God's immanence is given through the fact that humankind participates in some measure in the divine life through the Spirit who is given to all at creation and who is active in everything living. Inasmuch as man is dependent on this Spirit, God is also transcendent.

Here Pannenberg's anthropological point of contact between humans and God becomes significant. Pannenberg interprets man's essential openness beyond himself, which is constitutive for all men, as an openness toward God. In this ecstatic self-transcendence, the human mind participates in the divine Spirit and brings forth imaginative inspirations. In these imaginative inspirations, man experiences himself simultaneously as creative and dependent on the Spirit and conceives of God's eternal future by means of anticipation. It seems that through this point of contact in man's essential openness to the divine, in which man participates in the divine Spirit, Pannenberg revises the upstairs-downstairs, supernatural-natural model.[1] The combination of Pannenberg's concept of God and his anthropological perspective has significant implications for his concept of Scripture.

Pannenberg's impersonal understanding of God as field of force does not allow

---

[1]Laurence W. Wood, "Above, Within, or Ahead Of?" 53, 62.

him to conceive revelation as propositional in nature where some cognitive content is supernaturally disclosed by God.[1] Instead, revelation is defined in the modern sense as God's self-revelation which, according to Pannenberg, is closely connected with the divine action in history. This means that revelation does not come from *above* but takes place indirectly *as* history. History, in the sense of "Geschichte," is essentially the history of the transmission of traditions, where human beings write down their experiences with the divine. To the extent that human beings are incorporated into the eternal fellowship of the Father through the Spirit, "the action of God in this world is a repetition or reiteration of his [God's] eternal deity in his relation to the world."[2] Given the priority of the future in Pannenberg's thought, this seems to point to what Langdon Gilkey has called "a kind of Calvinism set in temporal reverse gear."[3]

The above-mentioned theological and anthropological presuppositions impact Pannenberg's understanding of Scripture in yet several additional ways. Inasmuch as the human mind participates in the divine Spirit, and in his creative inspirations is dependent on the Spirit, those "perceptions" of the divine originate at least to some degree in God.[4] In them, however, no content is being revealed and no cognitive content is transmitted. These imaginative moments of self-transcendence, however, result in the writing down of those experiences with the divine. Hence, religious traditions are created which eventually develop into the books of Scripture. Scripture, then, serves as a source book for one religious tradition in which the human awareness of the divine is reflected.

As far as the actual writing down of those experiences is concerned, no divine influence is accounted for. The writing of Scripture takes place, to use one of Pannenberg's phrases, "from below." This means that the very words of Scripture are human words that report the divine human experience in which no cognitive content

---

[1]Pannenberg, **SyTh/E**, 1:202, 237.

[2]Ibid., **SyTh/E**, 1:389.

[3]Gilkey, "Pannenberg's **Basic Questions in Theology**," 53. Kaiser, 124, follows Gilkey's analysis and judgment. In other words, "only from our temporally finite point of view does it *appear* that God changes as God encompasses change" (Polk, **On the Way to God**, 289). It seems that Pannenberg has never addressed himself in published form to Gilkey's analysis and criticism (ibid., 314, n. 264).

[4]It should be noted, however, that any anticipation of God's ultimate future is "always ambiguous" and " as such does not guarantee the truth of its content" (Pannenberg, **Metaphysics and the Idea of God**, 96).

is being revealed. Put differently, the words of Scripture originate on the historical level alone. Hence, Pannenberg dismisses the traditional understanding of the origin of Scripture through supernatural revelation and inspiration. It is not originated directly from God as His word. This even more so because for him human language is doxological in nature; it does not "reveal" anything about God in Himself. Thus, Scripture does not carry divine authority. This might explain why Pannenberg is not interested in the question whether the words of Scripture are infallible or even inerrant or not. The words of Scripture have originated strictly on the historical level, and for this reason they remain provisional and limited and cannot guarantee the truth of their assertions. Scripture is not the basis of religion but its cognitive expression. Inasmuch as these human words reflect the religious orientation of all humans, they have a theological orientation and can be consulted for their theological ideas.

Pannenberg does not hold that an eternal truth is being revealed "objectively" to human reason and then put into writing under the influence of the Spirit. Scripture is not a deposit of divinely revealed truth. It is, rather, a historical document that reports and reflects in purely human words man's experience with the divine. As such, it is never prescriptive but only descriptive of those experiences. Inasmuch as Scripture reflects the pluralism of different strands of human traditions, it is capable to err in its statements and, therefore, the experiences recorded need to be tested and evaluated for their truth claims with rational and scientific methods from the perspective of the totality of human experience before they can be accepted. Thus, Pannenberg has distanced himself from any irreducible claims to authority and has opened historical revelation to rational discussion and investigation. Yet, Scripture is assigned a normative function by being a sign of the identity of the Christian faith through the centuries. However, the nature of Scripture has changed from a principle of immediate divine authority to a principle whereby Christianity is attached to its historic origin.

Because revelation takes place as history, in the sense of the transmission of traditions, tradition becomes an important element in Pannenberg's concept of Scripture. Scripture is the result of a particular tradition, and the history of the transmission of traditions becomes the hermeneutical key for understanding the meaning of revelatory events. Thus, the clarity of Scripture is replaced by the clarity of history. Because the words of Scripture originate strictly on the historical level, Scripture can be investigated historically-critically without any special approach or faith commitment.

The final chapter returns to the questions raised here when it compares Pannenberg's concept of Scripture with that of Bloesch and evaluates it according to its strengths' and weaknesses.

CHAPTER IV

SCRIPTURE IN D. G. BLOESCH'S SYSTEMATIC THEOLOGY

Introduction

This chapter examines Bloesch's understanding of Scripture. In order to provide a comprehensive view of his position, a brief discussion of Bloesch's personal and theological background is given here before the investigation of his understanding of the origin, nature, and role of Scripture is approached. After this more descriptive task, the second part of this chapter focuses on an analysis of some fundamental presuppositions that have influenced his concept of Scripture.

As in the previous chapter, the method used is the systematic approach rather than a merely historical description. Therefore, special consideration is given to the mature Bloesch, as he is presented in his latest systematic theology.[1] In this latest magnum opus, Bloesch brings together in a comprehensive fashion and with greater depth than before what he proposed earlier. This investigation also includes earlier statements that are pertinent to the issue under investigation.

Just as in the previous chapter, this present one is restricted primarily to Bloesch's understanding of Scripture and deals with related aspects only in as much as they are important for a better understanding of his concept of Scripture and help to clarify his position.

D. G. Bloesch: The Man and Theologian

Before considering more closely Bloesch's understanding of Scripture, a short profile of him is helpful. Such a brief outline includes biographical data,[2] the

---

[1]The first two volumes of a projected seven-volume set have appeared in print so far. They are: Donald G. Bloesch, **A Theology of Word and Spirit: Authority and Method in Theology**; and idem, **Holy Scripture: Revelation, Inspiration, and Interpretation**. Hereinafter the abbreviation **TWS** is used for the former and **HSRII** for the latter. Bloesch's earlier two-volume "systematic theology," **Essentials of Evangelical Theology**, vol. 1, **God, Authority, and Salvation**; and idem, **Essentials of Evangelical Theology**, vol. 2, **Life, Ministry, and Hope**, is also taken into consideration. Hereinafter the abbreviation **EET** is used to refer to them.

[2]Biographical data about Bloesch can be found in **Who's Who in Religion**, 2d ed. (Chicago, IL: Marquis Who's Who, 1977), s.v. "Bloesch, Donald George," 61; Robert K. Johnston, ed., **The Use of the Bible in Theology: Evangelical Options**, 249; James Emery White, "The Concept of Truth in Contemporary American Evangelical Theology" (Ph.D. dissertation, The Southern Baptist Theological Seminary, 1991), 215-220; and most extensively

intellectual influences on his thought, and a short résumé of his place in the current theological spectrum.

Donald George Bloesch was born on May 3, 1928, in Bremen, Indiana,[1] to Herbert and Adele Bloesch. His father was an ordained minister[2] of the Evangelical Synod of North America.[3] As a young man, his father drove Reinhold Niebuhr around in a horse and buggy when Niebuhr was trying to earn money by selling books.[4] A side effect of this family friendship between the Niebuhr's and Bloesch's can be seen in Donald Bloesch's later decision to write his dissertation on Reinhold Niebuhr's apologetics.[5]

The Bloesch family later moved to the Chicago suburb of Monee, Illinois. Here Bloesch accepted the Christian faith as his own.[6] After high school he went to Elmhurst College, Illinois.[7] He developed a strong interest in sociology while in College and graduated with a B.A. degree as a philosophy major in 1950.[8] Pre-ministerial students at Elmhurst usually went on to Eden Theological Seminary in St.

---

in Leslie R. Keylock, "Evangelical Leaders You Should Know: Meet Donald G. Bloesch," **ModM** 88/7 (1988): 61-63; and Donald K. McKim, "Donald G. Bloesch," in **Handbook of Evangelical Theologians**, ed. Walter A. Elwell (Grand Rapids, MI: Baker Book House, 1993), 388-400. See also Donald G. Bloesch, **Theological Notebook. Volume 1: 1960-1964** (Colorado Springs: Helmers & Howard, 1989), xi-xii. The latter is reprinted in idem, **Theological Notebook. Volume 2: 1964-1968** (Colorado Springs: Helmers & Howard, 1991), ix-x.

[1]Keylock, 61; **Who's Who in Religion**, 61.

[2]His family included pastors and missionaries. His two grandfathers, both of whom studied at evangelical mission schools in Switzerland (St. Chrischona and the Basel Mission), came to the United States as missionaries to German-speaking immigrants (Bloesch, **Theological Notebook**, 1:xi).

[3]The Evangelical Synod of North America merged in 1934 with the Reformed Church in the United States to form the Evangelical and Reformed Church. This denomination later merged with the Congregational Christian Churches to form the present-day United Church of Christ (UCC). The Evangelical Synod of North America had been established out of the Old Prussian Union in Germany--a mixture of Lutheran and Reformed traditions. The influence of these two traditions continues to be vital in Bloesch's theology (McKim, "Donald G. Bloesch," 389; cf. Keylock, 62; and Bloesch, **Theological Notebook**, 1:xi).

[4]Bloesch, **Theological Notebook**, 1:xi-xii.

[5]Donald G. Bloesch, "Reinhold Niebuhr's Re-Evaluation of the Apologetic Task" (Ph.D. dissertation, University of Chicago, 1956).

[6]Keylock, 61-62.

[7]Elmhurst College is a denominational school affiliated with the United Church of Christ, founded in 1871, and located in Chicago's western suburbs.

[8]James Emery White, 216; McKim, "Donald G. Bloesch," 389.

Louis, Missouri. Contrary to that tradition Bloesch selected Chicago Theological Seminary which had offered him a full-time scholarship.[1] He received his B.D. in 1953, and was ordained the same year to the ministry in the United Church of Christ. From 1953 to 1956 he served as pastor of St. Paul's United Church of Christ in Richton Park, Illinois.[2] After his graduation from Chicago Theological Seminary, he went directly to the University of Chicago.[3] Among his teachers were Charles Hartshorne, Daniel Jenkins, Wilhelm Pauck, Jaroslav Pelikan, and Daniel Day Williams.[4] At that time Bloesch did not perceive himself as evangelical in orientation, and he did not consider any of the leading conservative evangelical theologians in America as viable options.[5] However, during this time Bloesch actively began to participate in the InterVarsity Christian Fellowship and discovered the merits of neo-orthodox theology.[6] In 1956, he received a Ph.D. in theology from the University of Chicago; his dissertation on Reinhold Niebuhr's apologetics was written under the direction of Bernhard Meland.[7]

From 1956 to 1957 Bloesch served as a fellow in the World Council of Churches[8] and completed some post-doctoral studies at the University of Oxford.[9]

---

[1]Keylock, 62.

[2]**Who's Who in Religion**, 61. Bloesch also served as interim pastor for several churches in the Chicago area in 1952, 1953, and 1957, giving him altogether five years of pastoral experience (Donald G. Bloesch to Frank M. Hasel, December 14, 1993, 4).

[3]Bloesch characterized Chicago Theological Seminary as an institution which espoused an "extreme liberal theology" where most of the professors called themselves "neonaturalists" (Keylock, 62).

[4]Bloesch, **Theological Notebook**, 1:xi.

[5]Keylock, 62.

[6]Ibid., 62-63.

[7]McKim, "Donald G. Bloesch," 389.

[8]**Who's Who in Religion**, 61.

[9]Ibid., 61; Bloesch, **Theological Notebook**, 1:xi. During that time he visited Switzerland, France, Italy, and Germany. His study of monasticism during this period accentuated his concern for renewal in mainline denominations. Throughout his life one can see this interest for renewal for he produced such works as: **Centers of Christian Renewal** (Philadelphia: United Church Press, 1964); **The Crisis of Piety: Essays Towards a Theology of the Christian Life** (Grand Rapids, MI: Eerdmans, 1968); **The Reform of the Church** (Grand Rapids, MI: Eerdmans, 1970); **Wellsprings of Renewal: Promise in Christian Communal Life** (Grand Rapids, MI: Eerdmans, 1974); **The Invaded Church** (Waco, TX: Word Books, 1975); **Crumbling Foundations: Death and Rebirth in an Age of Upheaval** (Grand Rapids, MI:

In 1957 he received a one-year appointment at the Presbyterian University of Dubuque Theological Seminar, in Iowa.[1] That one-year appointment has turned into a more than 35-year tenure.[2]

From 1963 to 1964, Bloesch went to Switzerland and Germany were he engaged in post-doctoral research at the University of Basel and Tübingen. During this time, he studied under such noted theologians as Karl Barth, Hans Küng, and Leonard Hodgson.[3] He also received an honorary doctor of divinity degree from Doane College,[4] and from 1963-1964, he was faculty fellow of the American Association of Theological Schools. His growing theological recognition is obvious in his election as president of the Midwest Division of the American Theological Society during 1974-1975,[5] a short time before he published the widely praised two-volume work **Essentials of Evangelical Theology (EET)**.[6]

Zondervan Publishing House, 1984); and **The Struggle of Prayer** (Colorado Springs: Helmers & Howard, 1988), not to mention numerous articles.

[1]Bloesch recalls: "I later discovered that the administration hired me partly to be a liberal counterpart to a neo-orthodox theologian on the faculty. . . . They assumed that because I had gone to the University of Chicago, I would be liberal" (Keylock, 63).

[2]Except for several stints as a visiting professor at the school of religion, University of Iowa, in 1982; and Ontario Theological Seminary, Toronto, in August 1984 and in 1992, Bloesch has taught at Dubuque since 1957. He has given formal theological lectures at many more seminaries, colleges, and universities. See Donald G. Bloesch, "Curriculum Vitae," n.p., n.d., 2. According to Bloesch, the University of Dubuque Theological Seminary is one among other seminaries where neo-orthodoxy has made an impact and is, together with Western Theological Seminary the only school which continues to reflect, at least in part motifs associated with neo-orthodoxy. Theologians who taught together with Bloesch at Dubuque include Donald McKim and Arthur Cochrane, both of whom are active members of the Karl Barth Society of North America (Bloesch, **The Future of Evangelical Christianity: A Call for Unity amid Diversity**, 47, 162 n. 45).

[3]Bloesch, **Theological Notebook**, 1:xi.

[4]Ibid.

[5]**Who's Who in Religion**, 61; Bloesch, **Theological Notebook**, 1:xii.

[6]The two volumes have been praised especially by evangelical scholars as "a significant contribution to the field of systematic theology" (David S. Dockery, "Review of **Essentials of Evangelical Theology**, vols. 1 and 2, by Donald G. Bloesch," **GTJ** 2 [1981]: 152); as "two superlative books which articulate the foundational elements of historic Christian orthodoxy in a manner that attempts to be affirmative, comprehensive, irenic, and biblical" (Lewis Rambo, "Review of **Essentials of Evangelical Theology**, vols. 1 and 2, by Donald G. Bloesch," **ResQ** 25 [1982]: 179); as "a major American systematic theology from within the circle of conservative evangelicals" (Clark H. Pinnock, "Review of **Essentials of Evangelical Theology**, vols. 1 and 2, by Donald G. Bloesch," **TToday** 26 [1980]: 266); as opening up "new ground" (David Foxgrover, "Review of **Essentials of Evangelical Theology**, vol. 2, by Donald G. Bloesch," **CT** 24/9 [1980]: 40); and achieving "a highly creative and original treatment of the topics under discussion" (Paul

These biographical details of Bloesch's career, as valuable as they are, are not enough to tell about Bloesch, the theologian. One must look at his theological and intellectual contours to do that. The reading of his wide-ranging writings[1] reveals both pastoral and academic concerns. Much of his life work has been dedicated to maintaining an evangelical witness in pluralistic environments. Besides lecturing at seminaries, colleges, and church conferences, in addition to teaching at Dubuque, he is advisor to renewal groups within mainline denominations.[2] Therefore, often his treatment of a subject is not only sound academically, but at the same time it is also deeply spiritual. Richard Lovelace said, not without justification, that "Bloesch has made spiritual and theological renewal more central in his writings than any other systematic theologian in our century."[3] In seeking to balance theological with practical aspects, Bloesch is not shallow but "theologically literate."[4] He reveals a "truly

---

D. Feinberg, "An Evangelical Systematic Theology: A Review of **Essentials of Evangelical Theology**, vol. 1, by Donald G. Bloesch," CT 23/22 [1979]: 38). Not all reviews have been so favorable. Some, as R. P. Lightner, have classified them as belonging to the "left wing" of contemporary evangelicalism ("Review of **Essentials of Evangelical Theology**, vol. 1, by Donald G. Bloesch," **BSac** 136 [1979]: 181), who in a subsequent review called it "a weak and watered-down form of what is essential in evangelical theology" ("Review of **Essentials of Evangelical Theology**, vol. 2, by Donald G. Bloesch," **BSac** 137 [1980]: 279). Bloesch drew criticism especially for his understanding of Scripture and its inerrancy. Clark H. Pinnock suggests that Bloesch's use of the term is simply to retain the attention of his conservative readers ("Review of **Essentials of Evangelical Theology, Vol. 1 and 2**, TToday 36/2 [1979]: 268). Even non-Evangelical reviewers have noted that Bloesch's understanding of inerrancy will not please fellow Evangelicals (David Foxgrover, "Review of **Essentials of Evangelical Theology, Vol. 2**," CC 96 [1979]: 192).

[1]Cf. the comprehensive bibliography in Bloesch, **Theological Notebook**, 2:181-197. McKim has categorized Bloesch's books in three categories: formal theology, the church and renewal, and contemporary issues (McKim, "Donald G. Bloesch," 394-395).

[2]Bloesch, **Theological Notebook**, 1:xii.

[3][Richard Lovelace], "Renewal and the Future of Evangelicalism," **Renewal** 3/3 (1983): 12. Bloesch's concern for spiritual and theological renewal received attention in at least two recent dissertations: Michael T. Smith, "Theology as a Resource in Faith Translation for the Local Church" (D.Min. dissertation, Northern Baptist Theological Seminary, 1986); and Ronald Mark Perry, "A Holistic Model of Church Renewal in Light of a Critical Evaluation of the Contributions of D. Elton Trueblood, Donald G. Bloesch, and Leonard Boff" (Ph.D. dissertation, New Orleans Baptist Theological Seminary, 1992).

[4]Walter D. Wagoner, "Review of **The Crisis of Piety: Essays Towards a Theology of the Christian Life**, by Donald G. Bloesch," JES 7 (1970): 146.

remarkable breadth of reading,"¹ and an amazing "command of the literature in the field."²

Bloesch is well-recognized for his comprehensive knowledge of the growing evangelical movement.³ He seeks a perspective that takes into consideration evangelical theology and piety as well as the rich heritage of that tradition. This "ecumenical concern"⁴ surfaces repeatedly in Bloesch's writings when, for instance, he calls for a theology that is both evangelical and authentically catholic.⁵ Bloesch contends that the word "evangelical" needs to be deepened and expanded,⁶ in order to share "the concern in the wider catholic evangelical movement for appreciation of the church fathers and medieval reformers."⁷ He cautiously maintains "a certain critical stance toward catholicizing tendencies within Protestantism"⁸ while at the same time calling "to discover anew the catholicity of Protestantism,"⁹ referring to himself

---

¹Laurence E. Porter, "Review of **The Ground of Certainty**, by Donald G. Bloesch," **EvQ** 45 (1973): 120; cf. also A. C. M. Ahlen, "Review of **The Christian Life and Salvation**, by Donald G. Bloesch," **LQ** 20 (1968), 211; Paul D. Feinberg thinks that "the breadth of knowledge Bloesch brings to the theological task is impressive" ("An Evangelical Systematic Theology," 38). That Bloesch reveals "extraordinarily wide reading in contemporary Catholic sources" is also acknowledged by Roman Catholic theologian Monika Hellwig, "Review of **The Reform of the Church**, by Donald G. Bloesch," **TS** 32 (1971): 155, who adds however, that Bloesch does not always seem to be adequately oriented within Catholic theology to draw valid comparisons.

²Dockery, "Review of **Essentials of Evangelical Theology**, 154.

³McKim, **What Christians Believe about the Bible**, 87-89. Cf. Bloesch, "Evangelicalism," 168-173; idem, **The Future of Evangelical Christianity**; idem, **The Evangelical Renaissance** (Grand Rapids, MI: Eerdmans, 1973); and idem, "The New Evangelicalism," **RL** 41 (1972): 327-339.

⁴Bertrand de Margerie, "Review of **The Reform of the Church**, by Donald G. Bloesch," **JES** 8 (1971): 649.

⁵For a cautious evaluation of a catholic renewal in Evangelicalism, see David F. Wells, "Reservations about Catholic Renewal in Evangelicalism," in **The Orthodox Evangelical: Who They Are and What They Are Saying**, ed. Robert E. Webber and Donald G. Bloesch (Nashville, TN: Thomas Nelson, 1978), 213-224.

⁶Bloesch, **The Future of Evangelical Christianity**, 3.

⁷Ibid., 51. But Bloesch "insists that the Roman and Eastern Orthodox traditions (as well as the Reformation tradition) must be purified of unbiblical practices and ideas before any kind of church unity can become a practical reality" (ibid.).

⁸One such tendency is "to absolutize the Bible as a book," making an absolute equation between the words of the Bible and divine revelation, thus placing the Word of God "in the power of man, since words and propositions can be mastered by reason" (ibid., xxi).

⁹Ibid.

without compunction as "a catholic evangelical."[1] This open Evangelical orientation and his earnest and insistent willingness to dialogue with those of other persuasions[2] has earned Bloesch the reputation of being a bridge builder.[3]

From early on Donald Bloesch has been a theologian who has taken "the confessional position of the church seriously."[4] By a confessional church, Bloesch does not mean a merely creedal church that gives intellectual assent to the dogmatic statements of a bygone age.[5] Instead, he has in mind a church that boldly confesses

---

[1]Ibid.

[2]David F. Wells, "Review of **Essentials of Evangelical Theory** [sic], vols. 1 and 2," **RL** 49 (1980): 120.

[3]Mark Ellingsen, "Review of **A Theology of Word and Spirit: Authority and Method in Theology**, by Donald G. Bloesch," **Dialog** 32/3 (1993): 238; Foxgrover, "Review of **Essentials of Evangelical Theology**, volume 2," 40 [576]. Bloesch himself sees his task to "build bridges between the various strands of evangelicalism and also between evangelical Protestantism and the Catholic churches" (**The Future of Evangelical Christianity**, xxi). More recently Bloesch has called for a recovery of a "centrist position" that stands "thoroughly in the tradition of orthodoxy but [is] not averse to articulating the faith in new ways that relate creatively to the contemporary situation. A centrist position must not be misconstrued as a middle-of-the-road position that tries to hold opposing camps in dialectical tension; instead, its goal is to drive beyond the theological polarity to a synthesis that negates the misconceptions of both sides but at the same time fulfills their legitimate hopes and concerns" (Bloesch, **TWS**, 31).

Despite Bloesch's desire to build bridges between evangelical Protestantism and the Catholic churches, it is noteworthy that his writings have elicited hardly any responses from the Roman Catholic side and to our knowledge they have been completely ignored by the Eastern Orthodox church. The few times Roman Catholic's have reacted to his writings, they have usually voiced reservations. Brendan Rosendall, for instance, wrote that "on occasion one suspects the accuracy of his presentations. Moreover, some of B.'s suggestions for liturgical and sacramental renewal reveal a spirit of sectarianism. He is definitely working from certain doctrinal premises; in itself this is not surprising, but it does become rather disturbing when it is seen on occasion that these principles are totally incompatible with the reforms he desires" ("Review of **The Reform of the Church**, by Donald G. Bloesch," in **Worship** 44 [1970]: 506-507). Similar criticism is voiced by other Catholic scholars who think that Bloesch "leaves the reader in doubt as to the practical coherence of his position" (Hellwig, 156); cf. also P. Joseph Cahill, "Review of **The Ground of Certainty: Toward an Evangelical Theology of Revelation**, by Donald G. Bloesch," **CBQ** 34 (1972): 203. Thus, it seems that Roman Catholic theologians see Bloesch's bridge-building attempts with reservation.

[4]Ahlen, 211; Rogers, "The Search for System," 13. See also Donald G. Bloesch, "The Need for a Confessing Church Today," **RJ** 34/11 (1984):10-15; idem, **The Future of Evangelical Christianity**, 35-38; and idem, **Is the Bible Sexist? Beyond Feminism and Patriachalism** (Westchester, IL: Crossway Books, 1982), 82: "I contend for a confessional over a revisionist theology."

[5]According to Rogers "this commitment to a confessional centrist theology is not motivated by authoritarianism, antiquarianism, a desire to compromise, or a search for the lowest common denominator. It is forstered by the desire for roots, a clear identity, and a dynamic base from which to grow and develop" ("The Search for System," 13).

that Jesus Christ is Lord and that the gospel is crucial in our time and culture.[1] Through such a confessional stance, he seeks to maintain a distance (*diastasis*) from cultural movements rather than a correlation of them with the Biblical message.[2]

Coming from such a confessional perspective for Bloesch, "probably the single most important issue in a theological prolegomenon is the enigmatic relation between faith and reason."[3] In his approach to theology, he has opted unashamedly for the priority of faith over reason in the doing of theology.[4] This does not mean he eliminates reason from theology;[5] rather he sees reason as "grasped by revelation and brought into the service of revelation rather than an independent reason interpreting revelation."[6] He recognizes that "theology has its own distinct method"[7] and maintains

---

[1] "Confessional theology . . . has for its aim the overthrowing of the new world consciousness and its supplanting by fear and trust in the living, holy God revealed in the Scriptures" (Bloesch, **The Future of Evangelical Christianity**, 107); also idem, "The Need for a Confessing Church Today," 10.

[2] Bloesch, **Crumbling Foundations**, 112-115. In other words, confessional theology is returning to the roots of the faith and stands in stark contrast to revisionist theology which seeks the radical revision of the values and concepts of Christian tradition (idem, **The Future of Evangelical Christianity**, 108). Bloesch continues by saying that "at the same time, confessional theology is conservative, for it strives always to maintain the truth of Scripture **and** tradition" (ibid.), (emphasis supplied).

[3] Bloesch, **TWS**, 35.

[4] Cf. ibid., 34-61; and idem, **The Ground of Certainty: Toward an Evangelical Theology of Revelation** (Grand Rapids, MI: Eerdmans, 1971), 176-203. Roger E. Olson notes about Bloesch's earlier **EET** that "a constant theme throughout this work [**EET**] is anti-rationalism" ("Review of **Essentials of Evangelical Theology**, volumes 1 and 2, by Donald G. Bloesch," **CSR** 10/1 [1980]: 86). Carl F. H. Henry bemoans that Donald Bloesch among other things "assails as rationalism theological convictions long affirmed by evangelical orthodoxy, including revelationally based claims about the transcendent nature of God, the propositional nature of revelation, and the insistence that the object of faith be rationally credible" (**God, Revelation and Authority**, 5:356). James Emery White, 264, has accurately observed that Bloesch has "left the strict rationalism of Evangelical theology which had been characterized by such persons as Carl Henry, Ronald Nash, Kenneth Kantzer, and Gordon Clark."

[5] Says Bloesch: Our point of departure is neither faith nor reason but divine revelation, which can be apprehended to be sure only with the eyes of faith. Yet the light of faith is a light that also illumines our reason, so that a reborn reason is capable of understanding the truth of revelation, not exhaustively but adequately. Christianity does not contradict rationality, for the Word of God is also the Logos or wisdom of God, but it does oppose rationalism, which seeks to bring revelation into accord with the canons of human logic" (Bloesch, **Ground of Certainty**, 122).

[6] Bloesch, **TWS**, 190; cf. also idem, **Ground of Certainty**, 176-203.

[7] Bloesch, **TWS**, 20.

that "theology presupposes regenerate theologians."[1] Thus, he terms his theological position *"fideistic revelationalism,"* where the decision of faith is as important as the fact of revelation giving us certainty of the truth of faith.[2] It is clear that with such an approach Bloesch rules out natural theology.[3]

Here one can detect a close connection to his foremost theological mentor Karl Barth,[4] who continues to exercise a lasting influence on Bloesch's theology.[5] Besides

---

[1] Ibid., 124.

[2] Ibid., 21. According to Bloesch, his approach of *fideistic revelationalism* is not to be confounded with *revelational positivism*, nor with *presuppositionalism*, nor *foundationalism*, *evidentialism*, or *corherentism* (ibid.).

[3] ". . . we must steer clear of any natural theology that supposes valid knowledge of God on the basis of this general light in creation" (Bloesch, **The Future of Evangelical Christianity**, 121). More recently Bloesch confirmed this position: "In place of a natural theology, in which the knowledge of God is based on what we can discover on our own through reason and nature, I propose a theology of creation, in which we analyze nature and conscience in the light of God's self-revelation in Jesus Christ" (**TWS**, 173). Cf. also the extensive discussion in ibid., 141-183. Earlier Bloesch opposed natural theology in several of his writings (cf. idem, **EET**, 1:19; 2:241; idem, **The Ground of Certainty**, 43, 60, 193; idem, **Theological Notebook**, 2:173). Harry Buis correctly recognizes that in his recent systematic theology "Bloesch is vigorously opposed to natural theology" ("Review of **Theology of Word and Spirit: Authority and Method in Theology**, by Donald G. Bloesch," RefR 46 [1993]: 254).

[4] Cf. Karl Barth, **No! Answer to Emil Brunner**, in **Natural Theology**, trans. Peter Fraenkel (London: The Centenary Press, 1946), 65-128.

[5] Bloesch has said that "besides Luther and Calvin, I count Karl Barth among my principal theological mentors" (Donald G. Bloesch, "Karl Barth: Appreciation and Reservations," in **How Karl Barth Changed My Mind**, ed. Donald K. McKim [Grand Rapids, MI: Eerdmans, 1986], 126, 127; similarly idem, **TWS**, 32, and idem, **HSRII**, 12, where he also mentions Forsyth. Cf. also idem, **Freedom for Obedience: Evangelical Ethics in Contemporary Times** (San Francisco: Harper and Row, 1987), 10-12. The influence of Barth on Bloesch's thinking is not just restricted to the area of natural theology but can be perceived in much of his writings. Anthony A. Hoekema, for instance, bemoans that "in many places Bloesch reveals a basically Barthian theological orientation" ("Review of **Essentials of Evangelical Theology**, volume 1, by Donald G. Bloesch," **CTJ** 14/1 [1979]: 86); cf. also the brief evaluation of **EET** in Gordon R. Lewis and Bruce A. Demarest, **Integrative Theology**, 3 vols. (Grand Rapids, MI: Zondervan Publishing House, 1987-1994), 1:56-57. On the importance and the wide range of Barth's influence on Bloesch's theology, see Richard Albert Mohler, Jr., "Evangelical Theology and Karl Barth: Representative Models of Response" (Ph.D. dissertation, The Southern Baptist Theological Seminary, 1989), 175-197. In his book **The Evangelical Renaissance**, 80-81, Bloesch wrote that "even though not wishing to be known as Barthian or neo-Barthian, we believe that Barth must be taken with the utmost seriousness by any theologian of evangelical or Reformed persuasion. . . . First of all it should be said that Karl Barth is himself an evangelical theologian." See also Bloesch's evaluation of Karl Barth in idem, **The Christian Witness in a Secular Age: An Evaluation of Nine Contemporary Theologians** (Minneapolis, MN: Augsburg Publishing House, 1968), 36-44; idem, "The Legacy of Karl Barth," **TSF Bulletin** 9/5 (1986): 6-9; and his book on Karl Barth, **Jesus Is Victor! Karl Barth's Doctrine of Salvation** (Nashville, TN: Abingdon, 1976), 9, which was written "in order to counteract popular misunderstandings of Karl Barth's theology and also partly to show how authentically modern Barth really is." In the words of

Karl Barth, however, are a number of other influential minds that, according to Bloesch himself, have left a lasting imprint on his thought. The most influential theologians next to Karl Barth include Martin Luther, John Calvin, Augustine, Pascal, Kierkegaard, Bonhoeffer, and Forsyth.[1]

Bloesch is aware that his decision to opt for a fundamental separation of faith and reason, theology and philosophy,[2] thereby grounding theology not on philosophy but solidly in Biblical faith, goes contrary to much traditional thinking on the relationship between theology and philosophy.[3] This, however, makes him an

---

Gregory G. Bolich, Bloesch's reception of Barth has been that of an invaluable ally and useful foil (**Karl Barth and Evangelicalism** [Downers Grove, IL: InterVarsity Press, 1980], 89-91).

[1]So Donald G. Bloesch in a letter to the author, where he writes that he has appreciated those theologians "in particular because of their emphasis on the transcendence of God; their distrust of philosophical categories in articulating the mysteries of faith; their fidelity to the scriptural message that we are saved by grace alone; their high Christology, which affirms the truth of the incarnation; their commitment to the doctrine of the Trinity; their high view of Scripture as the inspired Word of God; their acknowledgement of the inseparable unity of Word and Spirit; and their emphasis on life and experience as well as doctrine" (Bloesch to Hasel, 14. December 1993, 1, 4).

Elsewhere Bloesch lists an extensive theological ancestral tree, among which he includes: "Isaiah, Jeremiah, St. Paul, Augustine, Calvin, Luther, Kierkegaard, Forsyth, and Karl Barth. It also includes, in varying degrees, Pascal, Philip Spener, Richard Sibbes, Jonathan Edwards, Zinzendorf, and Abraham Kuyper" (**EET**, 1:4, 11). He continues by saying that from his theological ancestral tree are excluded "rationalists such as Justin Martyr, Clement of Alexandria, Abelard, Socinus, Erasmus, Lord Herbert of Cherbury, John Locke, and Christian Wolff. Mystics who verge towards a monistic or panentheistic orientation are also excluded: among these are Dionysius the pseudo-Areopagite, Evagrius, John Scotus Erigena, Meister Eckhart, Angelus Silesius, Schleiermacher, Alan Watts and Gerald Heard. . . . I see evangelical theology at odds with modern existentialism . . ." (ibid., 4-5). Another list can be found in **HSRII**, 13; cf. also idem, **Theological Notebook**, 1:29-30. This extensive list is indicative of the fact that Bloesch tries to broaden the word "evangelical" to include the rich heritage of the universal church under the banner of the gospel. Cf. idem, **The Future of Evangelical Christianity**, 3. Two theologians who are often not recognized in their importance on Bloesch's thinking are Peter Taylor Forsyth and Arthur C. Cochrane. With the latter, who has been a major interpreter of Karl Barth's thought, Bloesch has enjoyed a lifelong friendship. McKim, "Donald G. Bloesch," 390. The former is quoted extensively and supportively in Bloesch's writings. Forsyth's has influenced Bloesch most obviously in the area of Christology and his understanding of the authority of Scripture. It has been noted that "Donald Bloesch probably comes as close as any modern evangelical scholar to the hermeneutical theology of Forsyth" (William Ray Rosser, "The Cross as the Hermeneutical Norm for Scriptural Interpretation in the Theology of Peter Taylor Forsyth" (Ph.D. dissertation, Southern Baptist Theological Seminary, 1990), 156.

[2]Cf. Bloesch, **TWS**. 34-66; idem, "Theology and Philosophy," **Quest** (Spring 1952): 1-10; idem, **Ground of Certainty**, 26-67; idem, **The Future of Evangelical Christianity**, 121-122.

[3]Bloesch, **The Ground of Certainty**, 7. Cf. Eugene M. Skibbe, "Review of **The Ground of Certainty**, by Donald G. Bloesch," **LQ** 24 (1972): 423-424; Edwin H. Rian, "Review of **The Ground of Certainty**, by Donald G. Bloesch," **Princ S B** 66 (1973): 146.

interesting theologian to study because he promises to develop "a post-fundamentalist, neo-Barthian evangelicalism"[1] that attempts to go beyond the short comings of both.[2]

It has been said that "Bloesch has emerged as one of the most significant theologicans in the broader evangelical movement and one of the pivotal figures in the development of evangelical consciousness."[3] Representing a refined and informed Evangelical theological view he attempts to steer a moderate course, somewhere in the middle between fundamentalism and dispensationalism on the one hand and liberalism and secularism on the other.[4] With his two-volume **EET**, he has made "an outstanding contribution"[5] to modern Evangelical thought, "signaling progressive evangelicals' entry into mainstream theological dialogue."[6] It seems that **EET** has initiated an unprecedented outpouring of recent evangelical scholarship that continues

---

[1]So Wonders, 48.

[2]One can see here certain parallels with Bernard Ramm, **After Fundamentalism: The Future of Evangelical Theology** (San Francisco: Harper and Row, 1983).

[3]Mohler, 169. This view is shared by others. According to Paul D. Feinberg ("An Evangelical Systematic Theology," 38), Bloesch "has distinguished himself as a leading spokesman for evangelical theology," and Keylock (61), maintains that he has gradually established himself as one of "the most brilliant, creative evangelical[s] working in systematic theology." As early as 1970 Scaer wrote that "Donald Bloesch is quickly emerging on the American theological scene as a genuine prophet. He combines a number of favorable features: he writes lucidly, he speaks to current issues, he is well versed in the history of the church. Like the late Edward John Carnell, he is conservative theologically, but hardly conservative in temperament" ("Review of **The Reform of the Church**, by Donald G. Bloesch," **Spfdr** 34 [1970]: 159). To our knowledge, no one has disputed this view publicly. Interestingly, however, Bloesch has received this high praise mainly from evangelical colleagues, which might indicate that his theological influence is limited to basically the evangelical community.

[4]McKim, "Donald G. Bloesch," 395; also J. F. Walvoord, "Review of **The Reform of the Church**, by Donald G. Bloesch," **BSac** 128 (1971): 159; and Robert K. Johnston, "Review of **Essentials of Evangelical Theology**, vol. 2," **JETS** 23/3 (1979): 281. According to Wonders, 48, his recent **TWS** "signals a move away from the 'standard' inerrancy position of the past, upheld by Francis Schaeffer and James Boice, towards a postfundamentalist, neo-Barthian evangelicalism."

[5]H. D. McDonald, "Review of **Essentials of Evangelical Theology**, vol. 1, by Donald G. Bloesch," **JETS** 22/3 (1979): 279; Foxgrover called it a "significant work from which evangelicals can learn much" ("Review of **Essentials of Evangelical Theology**, 192). Also more recently Ray S. Anderson, who maintains that Donald Bloesch has "made a significant contribution to the literature of contemporary evangelical theology . . ." ("Evangelical Theology," in **The Modern Theologians: An Introduction to Christian Theology in the Twentieth Century**, ed. David F. Ford [Oxford: Basil Blackwell, 1989], 2:147).

[6]Clark H. Pinnock, "Review of **Essentials of Evangelical Theology**, vol 1 and 2," **Sojourners** 8 (1979): 32. Carson, "Recent Developments in the Doctrine of Scripture," 363-364, n. 6, assigns Bloesch to the emerging "left-wing of Evangelicals."

to bring forth new systematic theologies at an amazing rate.¹ It has become an important seminary textbook and guide for evangelical Christians and has been translated into several languages.² Writing almost ten years after the first publication of **EET**, Gabriel Fackre has accurately described it as a work "with wide impact."³ In time, Bloesch has gradually established himself as "one of the English-speaking world's foremost evangelical theologians,"⁴ who through his theological contribution, has "placed the evangelical world in his debt."⁵ With the appearance of the first

---

¹Cf. Henry, **God, Revelation and Authority**; Gabriel J. Fackre, **The Christian Story: A Narrative Interpretation of Basic Christian Doctrine** (Grand Rapids, MI: Eerdmans, 1978); idem, **The Christian Story: A Pastoral Systematics**, vol. 2, **Authority: Scripture in the Church for the World**; Millard J. Erickson, **Christian Theology**, 3 vols.; Charles W. Carter, ed., **A Contemporary Wesleyan Theology: Biblical, Systematic, and Practical**, 2 vols. (Grand Rapids, MI: Zondervan Publishing House, 1983); Thomas N. Finger, **Christian Theology: An Eschatological Approach**, 2 vols. (Nashville, TN: Thomas Nelson, 1985); Richard Rice, **The Reign of God: An Introduction to Christian Theology from a Seventh-day Adventist Perspective** (Berrien Springs, MI: Andrews University Press, 1985); James William McClendon, Jr. **Ethics: A Systematic Theology**, vol. 1 (Nashville, TN: Abingdon Press, 1986); idem, **Doctrine: Systematic Theology**, vol. 2 (Nashville, TN: Abingdon Press, 1994); Charles C. Ryrie, **Basic Theology** (Wheaton, IL: Victor Books, 1986); Thomas C. Oden, **The Living God**, Systematic Theology, vol. 1 (San Francisco: Harper and Row, 1987); idem, **The Word of Life**, Systematic Theology, vol. 2 (San Francisco: Harper and Row, 1989); idem, **Life in the Spirit**, Systematic Theology, vol. 3 (San Francisco: Harper and Row, 1992); Lewis and Demarest, **Integrative Theology**, 3 vols.; J. Rodman Williams, **Renewal Theology**, 3 vols. (Grand Rapids, MI: Zondervan Publishing House, 1988-1992); Jewett, **God, Creation, and Revelation: A Neo-Evangelical Theology**; Spykman, **Reformational Theology: A New Paradigm for Doing Dogmatics**; James Leo Garrett, Jr., **Systematic Theology: Biblical, Historical, and Evangelical** (Grand Rapids, MI: Eerdmans, 1992); James I. Packer, **Concise Theology: A Guide to Historic Christian Beliefs** (Wheaton, IL: Tyndale House Publishers, 1993); Wayne A. Grudem, **Systematic Theology: An Introduction to Biblical Doctrine** (Grand Rapids, MI: Zondervan Publishing House, 1994); Alister E. McGrath, **Christian Theology: An Introduction** (Oxford: Basil Blackwell, 1994); to name but some of the more prominent ones.

²McKim, "Donald G. Bloesch," 388. It is now being translated into Russian; it will be used as textbook for the Baptist seminary in Odessa. Donald G. Bloesch, telephone interview by author, 11 October 1993.

³Fackre, **The Christian Story. Authority: Scripture in the Church for the World**, 72; McKim states that Bloesch's "work has had substantial influence as a model of evangelical theology . . ." ("Donald G. Bloesch," 388). Mohler, 169, points out that through his writings Bloesch has contributed to both the formal and material expressions of evangelical identity.

⁴Wonders, 48. Even Randy L. Maddox, who has severely criticized Bloesch on several points, has acknowledged him as "a prominent American evangelical theologian" ("The Necessity of Recognizing Distinctions: Lessons from Evangelical Critiques of Christian Feminist Theology," CSR 17 [1988]: 311). In 1970 David P. Scaer wrote that "to date the Lutheran Church in our country has not produced a like figure who combines a determined conservative stance to the Scriptures and a radical open mindedness to the church's problems" ("Review of **The Reform of the Church**," 161).

⁵McKim, "Donald G. Bloesch," 400.

volume of a new systematic theology, a writing feat which is projected to eventually comprise seven volumes, Bloesch is securing himself a permanent and leading role in Evangelical theology at the edge of the Third Millennium.[5]

Since Bloesch is recognized as one of the leading Evangelical scholars who has published widely,[6] it is not surprising that in several recent dissertations[7] different

---

[5]"Once completed, this project will likely vie with Millard Erickson's *Christian Theology* for pride of place among contemporary evangelical systematics, and it will likely find similarly wide use" (S. Mark Heim, "Review of **A Theology of Word and Spirit**, by Donald G. Bloesch," **RSR** 19/3 [1993]: 239). His **TWS** has been called "an uncompromisingly confessional theology in strongest opposition to all forms of revisionism--liberal or evangelical" (Clark H. Pinnock, "Advance Praise for **A Theology of Word and Spirit**," Front Inside Book Cover), and "a masterful reflection on the nature of scriptural authority and method" (Gary Mar, "What Evangelicalism Needs," **NOR** 61/5 [1994]: 29). It has been said that it "promises to be the evangelical *summa* of the twentieth century" (So I. John Hesselink, "Advance Praise for **A Theology of Word and Spirit**," Front Inside Book Cover). Clark H. Pinnock has compared it with the systematic theology of Wolfhart Pannenberg, "alongside which it will stand as the other major alternative for evangelicals" ("Advance Praise"). Thus, Mark Ellingsen, (Review of **A Theology of Word and Spirit**, 238) has properly called Bloesch "one of our era's most prominent Evangelical theologians."

[6]Bloesch has authored and/or edited over 27 books and some 300 published articles and book reviews. The most comprehensive list of published writings by Bloesch can be found in Bloesch, **Theological Notebook**, 2:181-197. Bloesch has contributed articles to such reference works as the **Beacon Dictionary of Theology**, ed. Richard S. Taylor (Kansas City, MO: Beacon Hill, 1983); the **Evangelical Dictionary of Theology**, ed. Walter Elwell (Grand Rapids, MI: Baker Book House, 1984); **Harper's Encyclopedia of Religious Education**, ed. Iris V. Cully and Kendig Brubaker Cully (San Francisco: Harper and Row, 1990); the **Dictionary of Christianity in America**, ed. Daniel G. Reid, Robert D. Linder, Bruce L. Shelly, and Harry S. Stout (Downers Grove, IL: InterVarsity Press, 1990); the **Holman Bible Dictionary**, ed. Trent C. Butler (Nashville, TN: Holman Bible Publishers, 1991); the **Encyclopedia of the Reformed Faith**, ed. Donald K. McKim (Louisville, KY: Westminster/John Knox, 1992); and **A New Handbook of Christian Theology**, ed. Donald W. Musser and Joseph L. Price (Nashville, TN: Abingdon, 1992).

[7]They are in chronological order: Robert McNair Price, "The Crisis of Biblical Authority: The Setting and Range of the Current Evangelical Crisis" (Ph.D. dissertation, Drew University, 1981); John Paul Nyquist, "An Evaluation of the Inroads of Process Theology into Contemporary Evangelicalism" (Th.D. dissertation, Dallas Theological Seminary, 1984); Charles Wayne Scriven, "The Transformation of Culture: Christian Social Ethics after H. Richard Niebuhr" (Ph.D. dissertation, Graduate Theological Union, 1985) (this dissertation appeared in published form as **Christian Social Ethics After H. Richard Niebuhr: The Transformation of Culture** [Scottdale, PA: Herald Press, 1988]; Sheldon Warren Sorge, "Karl Barth's Reception in North America: Ecclesiology as a Case Study" (Ph.D. dissertation, Duke University, 1987); S. Edward Baxter, Jr., "A Historical Study of the Doctrine of 'Apokatastasis'" (Th.D. dissertation, Mid-America Baptist Theological Seminary, 1988); Richard Albert Mohler, Jr., "Evangelical Theology and Karl Barth: Representative Models or Response" (Ph.D. dissertation, The Southern Baptist Theological Seminary, 1989); William Ray Rosser, "The Cross as the Hermeneutical Norm for Scriptural Interpretation in the Theology of Peter Taylor Forsyth" (Ph.D. dissertation, The Southern Baptist Theological Seminary, 1990); Stephen David Charles Corts, "Particularism as an Evangelical Response to Religious Plurality" (Ph.D. dissertation, Southern Baptist Theological Seminary, 1991); and the dissertation by James Emery White.

aspects of his theology have been investigated and compared with that of other theologians. None of those aforementioned dissertations, however, have dealt in-depth with Bloesch's understanding of Scripture,[1] although in his thought the authority of Scripture has been recognized as an enduring theme.[2] Since this is so, it seems appropriate that one should investigate more closely Bloesch's understanding of Scripture.

A Description of the Concept of Scripture in Bloesch's Systematic Theology

The first volume of Bloesch's new systematic theology, **A Theology of Word and Spirit: Authority and Method in Theology**, and especially in the second volume, **Holy Scripture: Revelation, Inspiration and Interpretation**, Bloesch has devoted himself more deeply than ever before to a new discussion of the role of Scripture in theology. In order to illumine Bloesch's understanding of Scripture in theology one must consider several factors that determine and influence his position. This includes a survey of his interpretation of the origin of Scripture as well as his understanding of the nature of Scripture. His use of Scripture also is briefly noted.

The Origin of Scripture

Bloesch ventures his theology from a perspective of faith and trust in Scripture's divine origin. To better consider the question of the origin of Scripture, then, it would seem appropriate, first of all, for one to examine statements in which Bloesch reveals how he perceives the origin of Scripture. After that, one can concentrate on his position of how Scripture did not originate.

How Scripture Is Perceived to Have Originated

A reading of Bloesch's theological writings, especially the latest two volumes of his recent systematic theology, indicates that he holds to a divine origin of Scripture. For him, the content Scripture, meaning primarily the saving purpose of God with

---

[1] James Emery White, 235-246, offers a discussion of Bloesch's understanding of Scripture that is limited, however, mainly to Bloesch's delineation of the subject in **Ground of Certainty** and **EET**. He had no access to the more in-depth treatment by Bloesch in **TWP** and **HSRII** (ibid., 220-221).

[2] McKim, "Donald G. Bloesch," 396.

humanity and the gospel of Jesus Christ,[1] is given supernaturally, "from above," so to speak. Although he speaks about a dual authorship of Scripture[2] where human authors penned divine revelation in their own mode of expression, Scripture is not a human book; it is divine in its ultimate origin[3] and theological content.[4] God's

---

[1] Donald G. Bloesch, interview by author, 10 January 1994, Elmhurst, IL, tape recording. In **HSRII**, 56, Bloesch writes: "The content of the Bible is indeed God's self-revelation in Jesus Christ. . . ."

[2] Bloesch, **HSRII**, 87, cf. 115, where he speaks of the "mystery of the dual nature of the Bible." See also idem, **EET**, 1:52.

[3] Bloesch, **HSRII**, 38. Earlier Bloesch wrote: "Because the Holy Spirit superintended the writing of the Scriptures, he has been regarded in the tradition of the church catholic as the primary author of Scripture and the prophets and apostles the secondary authors" (Donald G. Bloesch, "The Sword of the Spirit: The Meaning of Inspiration," **RefR** 33/2 [1980]: 65); and idem, **Theological Notebook**, 2:80.

[4] The content that is revealed contains salvific matters that include information about Jesus Christ and the gospel of grace. In this position Bloesch differs significantly from liberal theology and Neo-Orthodox theology, both of whom do not accept the idea that any kind of content is transmitted in revelation. Instead, revelation is perceived by them as a non-cognitive existential encounter. Cf. Rudolf Bultmann, **Existence and Faith**, sel. and trans. Schubert M. Ogden (New York: Meridian Books, 1960), 100; Emil Brunner, **Revelation and Reason: The Christian Doctrine of Faith and Knowledge**, trans. Olive Wyon (Philadelphia: Westminster Press, 1946), 8; and idem, **The Divine-Human Encounter**. H. D. McDonald has pointed out that "the view that revelation was given in propositions, that it was in any sense a communication of supernatural knowledge, was vehemently repudiated" in the modern era **(Theories of Revelation: An Historical Study 1700-1960** [Grand Rapids, MI: Baker Book House, 1979], 161); see also John Baillie, **The Idea of Revelation in Recent Thought** (New York: Columbia University Press, 1956).

Miikka Ruokanen has argued in a recent study that the concept of inspiration in Martin Luther is used exclusively "only in regard to events which took place much before writing: in the direct reception and perception of God's merciful revelation existing and communicated as the divinely inspired doctrine of Christ. But because this doctrine is inseparable from the clear text of the Bible, the term biblical inspiration can be used in the case of Luther" (112). One has to keep in mind, as Ruokanen has pointed out, that for Luther "the concept of inspiration consists of the reception and perception of divine revelation; it cannot be defined narrowly in terms of recording and preserving the divine message. Luther has no formal concept of revelation. Consequently, he does not make any theoretical distinction between revelation and inspiration, but uses often the two concepts as synonyms, both meaning the reception and perception of God's message. *This message has a cognitive content (verbum cogitatum) which Luther calls doctrine*" (Ruokanen, 63). This would allow for a certain similarity between Luther and Bloesch on the issue of revelation and inspiration. In reading Ruokanen's conclusions it should be remembered, however, that a major difficulty in understanding Luther's view on this point arises from the absence of a formal statement of the doctrine in his works and from the fact that a number of scholars have discussed the issue with varied results. An alternative reading of Luther that views the content of revelation and inspiration not restricted just to salvific matters has never lacked supporters. E.g., Rohnert, **Die Inspiration der heiligen Schrift und ihre Bestreiter**; Robert D. Preus, **The Inspiration of Scripture**; idem, "Luther and Biblical Infallibility," 99-142; idem, "The View of the Bible Held by the Church," 357-382; Klug, **From Luther to Chemnitz**, 26-38. For a sensitive and balanced overview on the debate on Luther, with further literature, see Muller,

revelation to the Biblical writers includes divine communication.[1] Thus, revelation includes both propositional and personal aspects,[2] although the propositional element is clearly in the service of the personal.[3]

In writing down divine revelation, Biblical writers were guided by the Holy Spirit in their reflection, although their articulation of this reflection is at least one step removed from the revelation itself.[4] Inspiration is understood as the divine election and superintendence of particular writers and writings.[5] In contradistinction to both

---

Post-Reformation Reformed Dogmatic, vol. 2, **Holy Scripture: The Cognitive Foundation of Theology**, 239-244.

[1]Bloesch, **HSRII**, 48, writes that he has "sought to retain the conceptual character of revelation while subordinating it to personal self-disclosure. As I see it, revelation is God's self-communication through his selected instrumentality, especially the inspired witness of his prophets and apostles. This act of self-communication entails . . . also the imparting of the knowledge of his will and purpose for humankind. This knowledge is conceptual as well as existential and can be formulated but never possessed or mastered in propositions." Elsewhere in the same chapter Bloesch writes about three facets of revelation: historical, propositional, and experiential. Thus, "the Bible is both the revelation and the means and bearer of revelation" (ibid., 63). Bloesch also offers the following comprehensive definition of revelation: "Revelation is the movement of God into a particular history--that of biblical Israel culminating in Jesus Christ--and God's self-communication through both the events that constitute this history and the inspired human witness to these events--Holy Scripture" (ibid., 309, n. 9). One has to keep in mind, however, that although "the truth in the Bible is revealed because it has a divine source . . . it is at the same time partial and broken because it has a historical matrix" (ibid., 56). The threefold aspect of revelation is mentioned already in idem, "An Evangelical Perspective on Authority," **Prism** 1/1 (1986): 7-8, 5.

[2]Bloesch, **HSRII**, 72: "The Bible is a revelation not only of God's person but of God's truth. Revelation is therefore both personal and propositional, or, better, dialogical--reminding us that we are dealing with an encounter of minds as well as of wills."

[3]Bloesch "does not wish to downplay or deny the propositional element in revelation, but this element is in the service of the personal" (ibid., 284). Bloesch confirmed this in an interview with the author (Bloesch, interview, 10 January 1994). That the propositional element in Bloesch's understanding of revelation is clearly subordinated to a personalistic understanding that sees truth as an event and that focuses preeminently on Jesus Christ is recognized by James Emery White, 239, n. 109.

[4]Bloesch, **HSRII**, 56. Thus, the propositions of Scripture are not revelation in and of themselves because revelation is speech as well as an act of God and therefore can happen again and again in the experience of the Spirit of Christ in the human heart (ibid., 50).

[5]Ibid., 119, 126. Bloesch had made similar statements elsewhere when he wrote that inspiration is "the divine selection of the writers and their writings for the purpose of instruction in salvation and training in righteousness" (idem, "The Sword of the Spirit: The Meaning of Inspiration," 67). Similarly idem, "An Evangelical Perspective on Authority," 9, where he says that inspiration "is a divine process that embraces the words as well as the writers. Inspiration might be defined as the divine election and guidance of the biblical writers in order to insure a trustworthy and potent witness to the truth." Cf. also idem, **Theological Notebook**, 2:69. One should be aware, however, that Bloesch has a rather wide ranking concept of inspiration that includes prophets, all preachers, writers, compilers and editors in Biblical history (idem, **HSRII**,

Barth and Forsyth, Bloesch earlier maintained that the "doctrine of inspiration is preeminently concerned with the written product and not just with the writers and readers of Scripture."[1] Because inspiration includes conceptual and verbal aspects, Bloesch even speaks of verbal inspiredness.[2] Bloesch maintains that inspiration "conveys the truth that the writers were guided in their selection of words and meanings so that their overall witness is reliable and trustworthy."[3] Thus, Bloesch

---

119-120). Furthermore, according to Bloesch, "inspiration is correlative with immediate or final revelation; illumination is correlative with mediate or continuing revelation" (ibid., 127). Inspiration for Bloesch also includes the inward awakening of the believing reader to the truth of these writings (idem, **Theological Notebook**, 2:69). The latter aspect, however, traditionally has been designated by the term "illumination" in contrast to "inspiration" which concerns the way in which the Holy Spirit superintended the writing of Scripture (cf. Reinhold Seeberg, "Illumination," **The New Schaff-Herzog Encyclopedia of Religious Knowledge**, ed. Samuel Macauley Jackson (New York: Funk and Wagnals, 1909), 5:450-451. Charles C. Ryrie has pointed out that illumination and revelation are confused in neo-orthodox theology, where Scripture becomes the Word of God and man's discovery of truth becomes the locus of revelation ("Illumination," **Evangelical Dictionary of Theology**, ed. Walter A. Elwell (Grand Rapids, MI: Baker Book House, 1984), 545. Recently Clark H. Pinnock has bemoaned the lack of discussion of the issue of illumination among evangelicals ("The Role of the Spirit in Interpretation," **JETS** 36/4 [1993]: 491-497).

[1]Bloesch, **EET**, 1:56. In this earlier work, Bloesch would still write that "we affirm that Scripture is not only a human witness and medium of divine revelation but also a divinely inspired witness and medium. . . . With Warfield we hold this to mean that all Scripture is breathed out by God, is a product of the creative activity of the Spirit of God. It must not be taken to mean (as in Protestant liberalism) that the writers were simply assisted and illumined by the Spirit: they were so guided by the Spirit that what was actually written had the very sanction of God himself" (ibid., 54-55). Thus, he affirms "the plenary inspiration of Scripture, meaning that Scripture in its totality is inspired" (ibid., 55). The reference to Warfield in the context of the inspiration of Scripture does not recur in his later writings, probably in an attempt to distance himself from a perceived "rationalistic" stance in Warfield which he opposes. Cf. idem, "A Christological Hermeneutic: Crisis and Conflict in Hermeneutics," in **The Use of the Bible in Theology: Evangelical Options**, ed. Robert K. Johnston (Atlanta: John Knox Press, 1985), 79.

[2]Bloesch, **HSRII**, 126. One has to keep in mind, however, that to speak of verbal inspiration or verbal inspiredness is not understood by Bloesch "in the sense of perfect factual accuracy or mechanical dictation. It means that the words of human beings are adopted to serve the purposes of God" (ibid., 120). Thus, the Bible itself is not verbal revelation. This is a typical example of how Bloesch re-defines traditional terms and concepts, thereby changing their original meaning. It seems that through this practice Bloesch obfuscates the discussion and actually hampers the dialog between different positions that he seeks so eagerly.

[3]Bloesch, **The Evangelical Renaissance**, 55. James Emery White, 239, n. 109, has correctly pointed out, however, "that this is very different for Bloesch than affirming that biblical propositions are themselves revealed, a view that he discounts, see [idem,] **Essentials, Vol. 1**, p. 76. There is a propositional element, but it is virtually subsumed under the polydimensional sense of truth as an event of God."

maintains that "God is the primary author of Scripture"[1] because the origin of the Word of God is in eternity, although its revelation and reception takes place in history.[2] The divine origin of Scripture is testified to amply in both the New and Old Testament.[3]

In the whole process of the origin of Scripture, the work of the Holy Spirit is seen as of utmost importance. It is the Spirit who guided the human writers in their reflection and writing,[4] and it is the Spirit who gives life and theological significance to Scripture.[5] The theologically significant event for Bloesch was the incarnation of Jesus Christ at a particular time and place in history. The divinely inspired "recording of this event or series of events constitutes Holy Scripture."[6] Thus, the message of Scripture is prior to the community of faith which is created by this Word, although the community of faith historically is prior to the compiling and canonizing of Scripture.[7] Put differently, Scripture is the product of the inspiring work of the Holy Spirit who verified that the Biblical writers gave a reliable testimony to God's self-revelation in Jesus Christ. Its canonization is attributed to the illumining work of the Spirit who guided the fathers of the church to what the Spirit had already authorized. Hence, Word and Spirit are always seen together.

From the references given above in Bloesch's writings, one can see that his understanding of the origin of Scripture has a definite supernatural emphasis, especially

---

[1]Bloesch, **HSRII**, 125. The apostles and prophets are only secondary authors (ibid.); idem, **Theological Notebook**, 2:80.

[2]Ibid., 150. Bloesch contends that "it is a mistake to imply that history is the source or matrix of revelation" (idem, **TWS**, 42). He is aware that his "position here stands in contrast to Pannenberg . . ." (ibid., 281, n. 30). Contra Pannenberg, he thinks that history is the occasion but not the source of revelation (idem, **HSRII**, 49).

[3]Ibid., 85.

[4]Bloesch, **TWS**, 13; idem, **HSRII**, 56.

[5]Bloesch, **TWS**, 20; Bloesch repeatedly emphasizes that it is the Spirit who makes the Bible efficacious (ibid., 14; cf. also idem, "The New Evangelicalism," 328).

[6]Bloesch, **HSRII**, 150. It seems as if Bloesch reveals here a tacit preference for the priority of the New Testament over the Old. Furthermore, his Christological approach lends itself to the danger of a "Canon within the Canon," of which Bloesch is aware. Cf. Bloesch, "A Christological Hermeneutic," 98-99. Although Bloesch wants to perceive the gospel of Jesus Christ either explicitly or implicitly in every part of Scripture, the methodological problem of a "Canon within the Canon" cannot be properly solved with his Christological starting point.

[7]Bloesch, **HSRII**, 150.

where he sees God as the ultimate author of at least the theological content of the Bible.[1] It is best here to turn to statements where Bloesch speaks about his understanding of how Scripture did not originate.

How Scripture Did Not Originate

Having affirmed a supernatural origin of the theological content of Scripture, Bloesch affirms that this content did not originate with man. The language of Scripture does not have its source in religious experience but in divine revelation that breaks into culture and religious experience from beyond.[2] The Biblical witness, then, is neither the product of the believing church nor should it be subordinated to the community of faith.[3] This means that Scripture in a decisive way is distinct from other literature, as far as the origin of its divine content is concerned.

Yet, although divine revelation enters religious experience from above, Bloesch is adamant that in Scripture one finds neither the stenographic notes of God's audible voice nor the words of Scripture as directly given by God.[4] For Bloesch, Scripture was not passively dictated.[5] Instead of dictation, he prefers to speak about an

---

[1] Interestingly, despite Bloesch's strong affirmation in the supernatural origin of Scripture, there is hardly any discussion of the Biblical self-testimony to its divine origin. This evidence from Scripture itself would have given his convictions more Biblical support. On the self-testimony of Scripture to its divine origin, see John M. Frame, "Scripture Speaks for Itself," 178-200; Grudem, "Scripture's Self-Attestation and the Problem of Formulating a Doctrine of Scripture," 19-59; Ferguson, "How Does the Bible Look at Itself?" 47-66; also the early Clark H. Pinnock, **Biblical Revelation: The Foundation of Christian Theology** (Chicago: Moody Press, 1971; reprint, Philipsburg, NJ: Presbyterian and Reformed Publishing Company, 1985), 53-106.

[2] Bloesch, **TWS**, 73. Yet, the Bible contains a palpably human and, therefore, culturally conditionedq element, which nevertheless does not make it any less the Word of God. "The revelational content of Scripture is ultimately derived from God, but it is relayed to us through human language and human interpretation" (idem, **HSRII**, 71).

[3] Bloesch, **HSRII**, 147. Nevertheless, Bloesch maintains that the church, next to the Bible, is one monument of God's revealing action who's "task is to amplify and clarify what the Spirit has already given in Holy Scripture. I would hesitate to say with R. P. C. Hanson that the Bible is completed in the church, but I would contend that the Bible is made efficacious in the church by the working of the Spirit" (ibid.).

[4] Bloesch, **HSRII**, 58. Bloesch speaks about "symbolic language of Scripture" (Bloesch, **TWS**, 73); also idem, **The Battle for the Trinity: The Debate over Inclusive God-Language** (Ann Arbor, MI: Servant Publications, 1985), 13-27.

[5] It has been suggested that if the idea of dictation is abandoned, the commitment to inerrancy must go as well. Cf. William J. Abraham, **The Divine Inspiration of Holy Scripture** (Oxford: Oxford University Press, 1981), 34. This is certainly the case with Bloesch, as we shall see below. It should be noted, however, that in the history of the Christian church there have been numerous examples where people have rejected the concept of a mechanical dictation of Scripture,

interpenetration by the Spirit,[1] where "the writers are not to be thought of as simply the pens of the Holy Spirit (as a number of seventeenth-century divines taught) but as partners with the Spirit so that the end product can be attributed to coauthorship."[2] It should be noted that Bloesch speaks about a human *coauthorship* rather than about Biblical *writers*. This seems to imply a freedom of the human authors to come up with the words of Scripture, at least in those areas that do not directly touch upon the salvific content of Scripture.[3] As such "the *human words and concepts* employed by the Holy Spirit in the formation of the Scriptures fall short of bringing to humans univocal knowledge of God . . ."[4] Instead of having originated word by word from God, the language of Scripture is perceived as "theanthropomorphic,"[5] mythopoetic,[6] or symbolic.[7] In other words, Scripture did not fall from heaven. The words of Scripture are not **directly** revealed because Scripture is at least one step removed from the original revelation, which is primarily and essentially Jesus Christ.[8] Hence, Bloesch asserts that "theological language as such remains incomplete and insufficient.

---

yet have staunchly maintained a commitment to the utter trustworthiness and unerring nature of Scripture.

[1] Bloesch, **HSRII**, 122.

[2] Bloesch, **EET**, 1:55. On the position of the seventeenth century theologians on Holy Scripture, see the more balanced assessment by Robert D. Preus, **The Theology of Post-Reformation Lutheranism**, 1:254-378; idem, **The Inspiration of Scripture: A Study of the Theology of the Seventeenth Century Lutheran Dogmaticians**; Muller, **Post-Reformation Reformed Dogmatics**, 2:86-543.

[3] Randy Maddox's charge of a "docetic view of Scripture" whereby "at times Bloesch seems to approach a dictation method of inspiration where the very words and symbols of Scripture are seen as *entirely* God's formulation" seems to be an overstatement, to say the least. If there is any legitimacy for such a claim, it has to be confined to Bloesch's particular use and understanding of language in the debate over feminist language in theology ("The Necessity of Recognizing Distinctions," 318). Cf. Bloesch, **Is the Bible Sexist?**; and idem, **The Battle for the Trinity**. See also Bloesch's response to Maddox, "Reply to Randy Maddox," **CSR** 18/3 (1989): 281-284, and Maddox's rejoinder, "Reply to Donald Bloesch," **CSR** 18/3 (1989): 285-288.

[4] Bloesch, **TWS**, 81, (emphasis supplied). Nevertheless, they "give us vital information that we neglect only at our peril" (ibid.).

[5] Ibid., 74.

[6] Bloesch, **HSRII**, 259, 265.

[7] Bloesch, **The Battle for the Trinity**, 17.

[8] Bloesch, interview, 10 January 1994.

This is why Scripture entrusts us to the Holy Spirit, 'for he is the one who takes the written text and transforms it into the Word.'"¹

It seems as if there is a definite tension if not a discrepancy in Bloesch's thought between a willingness to be open for the idea of propositional revelation and his insistence that Biblical language is only mythopoetic. Ultimately, it is the Holy Spirit who bestows meaning that is not inherent in the words themselves. Thus, in actual practice, the verbal element is clearly subordinated to a pneumatic and personalistic understanding of revelation that sees truth as an event that comes alive through the Holy Spirit and that focuses preeminently on Jesus Christ[2] who is considered to be the only real revelation of God.[3]

This leads directly to the related question of the nature of Scripture which is considered next.

The Nature of Scripture

To be aware of Bloesch's understanding of the nature of Scripture, one must first concentrate on what he perceives the nature of Scripture to be before turning to statements that illumine what he thinks Scripture is not.

What Scripture Is Perceived to Be

As an Evangelical theologian, Bloesch repeatedly appeals to the authority of Scripture.[4] He writes that "the Bible is the external standard by which we judge the truth of the church and the truth in our own experience,"[5] and that the Bible remains

---

    ¹Bloesch, **TWS**, 105. The last part of the quotation is cited from Jacques Ellul, **The Humiliation of the Word**, trans. Joyce Main Hanks (Grand Rapids, MI: Eerdmans, 1985), 108. When asked to elaborate on the precise meaning of this quotation, Bloesch explained that if he were to put it in his words he would say the "the Holy Spirit takes the written text and makes this text serve the Word of God. I would not identify the text as human language with the Word of God; I would say the Holy Spirit takes the text and makes it serve God so that it becomes part of the Word of God; so that it is taken up into the Word of God but it always remains a human text. The way Ellul takes it, it seems the text ceases to be human text and becomes a divine word" (Bloesch, interview, 10 January 1994).

    ²Cf. James Emery White, 239, n. 109.

    ³"I hold that there is only one revelation of God in Jesus Christ, but this revelation is reflected and attested in Scripture, nature, conscience and experience" (Bloesch, **TWS**, 163).

    ⁴"The divine authority of Scripture will always be fundamental in evangelical theology . . ." (Bloesch, **EET**, 1:4; 61).

    ⁵Bloesch, **TWS**, 191.

the criterion for what is true and relevant.¹ Earlier Bloesch described the nature of Holy Scripture by calling it "the infallible standard of faith."² As such, Scripture is a "trustworthy and unfailing guide because the light of God's countenance shines upon it and because the Spirit grants illumination to the community of faith."³

Yet, Scripture is not simply a divine book to the exclusion of the human writers.⁴ A dual nature of Scripture exists which can be understood in terms of a Christological analogy. The Bible has a real humanity, just as Christ.⁵ However, "neither the flesh of Jesus nor the pages of Scripture are to be identified with the very Word of God, but they both embody this Word."⁶ Hence, Bloesch does not think

---

¹Bloesch, **HSRII**, 148.

²Bloesch, **EET**, 1:x. In what later became known as the "Chicago Call," several Evangelicals, among them Bloesch, affirmed "that the Scriptures, as the infallible Word of God, are the basis of authority in the church. We acknowledge that God uses the Scriptures to judge and to purify his Body. The church, illumined and guided by the Holy Spirit, must in every age interpret, proclaim and live out the Scriptures" (Robert E. Webber and Donald G. Bloesch, eds., **The Orthodox Evangelicals: Who They Are and What They Are Saying** [Nashville, TN: Thomas Nelson, 1978], 13). The "Chicago Call," representing eight themes in its final form, resulted from a gathering of forty-five Evangelicals in Chicago, IL, in May 1977. For an account of the background and motives that led to the "Chicago Call," see Robert E. Webber, "Behind the Scenes: A Personal Account," in **The Orthodox Evangelicals**, 19-39. The "Chicago Call" is not to be confused with the "Chicago Statement on Biblical Inerrancy" (1978) or the "Chicago Statement of Hermeneutics" (1982) which were conceived by a much larger group of Evangelicals under the organizational title "The International Council on Biblical Inerrancy." It resulted in a much more explicit statement regarding the nature of Biblical inspiration and the various ramifications of such a position. The "Chicago Statement on Biblical Inerrancy" can be found in **Evangelicals and Inerrancy**, ed. Ronald Youngblood (Nashville, TN: Thomas Nelson, 1984), 230-239; the "Chicago Statement on Biblical Hermeneutics," can be found in Earl D. Radmacher and Robert D. Preus, **Hermeneutics, Inerrancy, and the Bible** (Grand Rapids, MI: Zondervan Publishing House, 1984), 881-887.

³Bloesch, **Ground of Certainty**, 74. More recently Bloesch puts it in the following words: "Scripture in itself is the *written* Word of God, comprising by virtue of its divine inspiration a reliable witness to the truth revealed by God in Jesus Christ. But it becomes the *living* Word when it actually communicates to us the truth and power of the cross of Christ through the illumination of the Spirit" (idem, **HSRII**, 25-26; cf. idem, **EET**, 1:51).

⁴See the discussion above.

⁵Bloesch, **HSRII**, 69-70. Such a Christological analogy is also present in Karl Barth's thought. Cf. Nicole, "The Neo-Orthodox Reduction," 135; Paul Ronald Wells, **James Barr and the Bible: Critique of a New Liberalism** (Philipsburg, NJ: Presbyterian and Reformed Publishing Company, 1980), 12; and Frank M. Hasel, "The Christological Analogy of Scripture in Karl Barth," 41-49.

⁶Bloesch, **HSRII**, 69. The Bible is not the incarnate Word of God (ibid., 67). "Jesus Christ is sinless, and this means that he alone is the perfect vessel for the divine plan of salvation in the world. . . . There is a hypostatic union between the eternal Christ and the Jesus of history,

primarily of a book with divine prerogatives. Scripture as such is not the basis and source of spiritual authority. Instead, the latter belongs to the divine revelation that confronts humans in Scripture,[1] i.e., Jesus Christ. While Scripture has a certain priority over other dependent norms, such as the proclamation of the church and the light of faith implanted in man by the Spirit, none of these communicate the knowledge of salvation apart from the action of the living Christ who illumines and integrates these various norms by His Spirit.[2] It is the Word **and** the Spirit, where the Spirit who points to the living Word of God, the gospel, assumes ultimate authority in Bloesch's theology.[3] Says Bloesch: "Our authority is not completely enclosed in the pages of a book, for this would reduce the truth of the Bible to law and also exclude the role of the Holy Spirit."[4] This shows that Scripture is the Word of God only in a derivatory and functional sense,[5] namely, inasmuch as it points to the material center and final norm of Scripture, Jesus Christ.[6]

In order to somehow hold together the dual nature of Scripture Bloesch proposes a "union but not a fusion between the divine content and its worldly form."[7] This union is brought about through the action of the Spirit[8] and is termed as a "sacramental

---

but there is no such union between Christ and the church or between the Word and the Bible" (ibid., **TWS**, 200).

[1]Bloesch, **TWS**, 14.

[2]Ibid., 197; and idem, **Ground of Certainty**, 74.

[3]Cf. Bloesch, **HSRII**, 158-161.

[4]Bloesch, **TWS**, 194. Earlier Bloesch "developed a reputation as an evangelical who affirmed a careful distinction between the Word of God and the words of Scripture" (Maddox, "The Necessity of Recognizing Distinctions," 314).

[5]"The Bible's authority is functional in that it is a signpost to Jesus Christ. But is it not simply functional. There is an integral and organic relation between Christ's promises and the written word. The word not only points to Christ, but it was brought into being by the Spirit of Christ acting upon the prophets and apostles" (Bloesch, **EET**, 2:272). Cf. also the above discussion p. 200.

[6]"In our view the concrete reality from which theological concepts are derived is the irreversible and incomparable act of God in Jesus Christ. Insofar as Scripture participates in this act, Scripture too is a primary and indispensable source for theological work. The task of theology is to ascertain how the text of Scripture is related to the material norm, the revelation of God's love and judgement in Jesus Christ" (Bloesch, **EET**, 2:168).

[7]Bloesch, **The Future of Evangelical Christianity**, 119.

[8]There is an "inseparable and dynamic interrelationship of Word and Spirit" (Bloesch, **TWS**, 188). However, through his particular understanding of the living Word in its inseparable

view of Scripture."¹ His sacramental understanding of the nature of Scripture is seen essentially as God in action, and therefore, he regards Scripture as the primary channel or medium of revelation. By conceiving Scripture sacramentally, i.e., as the outward and visible sign of an inward and spiritual grace, a vehicle by which the Spirit teaches Christ to us,² Bloesch apparently wants to maintain the freedom of the Word and steers away from thinking of the Bible in purely intellectual terms.³

However, since it is the Spirit who gives life and significance to Scripture, it follows that those statements where Bloesch speaks about Scripture as being the criterion and unfailing guide for theology have to be qualified. As Bloesch himself says, "The final criterion for faith is not the words of the Bible as such but the paradoxical unity of Word and Spirit, which is always a gift of grace and not a human achievement."⁴ In this sacramental view of Scripture, there is a perceivable tendency in Bloesch's thought to give the Spirit ultimate priority over the written Word of God. He writes:

> We should not empty God's will or God's word of its conceptual content. Yet this conceptual content goes **beyond** what is explicitly stated in the Bible, even though it includes

---

pneumatological unity with Scripture, Bloesch seems to take back what he had tried to affirm before, namely, the emphasis on the propositional character of divine revelation.

¹Bloesch delineated his understanding of the sacramental view of Scripture in idem, **EET**, 2:270-275; idem, **The Future of Evangelical Christianity**, 118-119; idem, "The Challenge Facing the Churches," in **Christianity Confronts Modernity: A Theological and Pastoral Inquiry by Protestant Evangelical and Roman Catholics**, ed. Peter Williamson and Kevin Perrotta (Ann Arbor, MI: Servant Books, 1981), 209; cf. also idem, **HSRII**, 120, where he speaks about Scripture as a "sacramental sign."

²"The unity between the revealed Word, Jesus Christ, and the written word lies both in the inspiration of the Spirit, whereby he guarantees a trustworthy witness to Christ, and in his revelatory action, in which he speaks through this witness to people of every age" (Bloesch, **EET**, 2:271-272).

³Clark H. Pinnock, **The Scripture Principle** (San Francisco: Harper and Row, 1984), 164.

⁴Bloesch, **HSRII**, 114. Bloesch at one place states that "the Holy Spirit is not a second criterion alongside the Word but one aspect of the sole criterion--the Word enlightened by the Spirit or the Spirit illuminating the Word" (idem, **TWS**, 203). Although Bloesch wants to hold together Spirit and Word, the written Word eventually tends to be subordinate to the work of the Spirit. In this he seems to be closer to the Reformed tradition, which spoke of a working of the Spirit *cum verbo* and tended more towards a separation of the Spirit from the Word and even an autonomous operation of the Spirit. The Lutherans, in contrast, spoke of the Spirit *per verbum*, which threatened to lead to an automatic working of the Word (Hendrikus Berkhof, **Christian Faith: An Introduction to the Study of the Faith**, rev. ed., trans. Sierd Woudstra [Grand Rapids, MI: Eerdmans, 1985], 66).

this. God's word is the light that the Spirit brings to us through the written text but related to the existential situation in which we find ourselves.¹

This means that Bloesch sees the nature of Scripture in functional terms.² But lest Bloesch is seen as someone who dissolves Scripture's authority in mere functional terms, it should be pointed out that he also claims that Scripture is more than this. The Bible has not only a functional authority but an ontological one as well, where it not only directs people to truth but also communicates truth.³ This capacity of the Bible to direct people to truth and to communicate truth is founded on the revelatory and inspiring work of the Spirit on both writers and readers.⁴ It is the Spirit alone who alone makes Scripture an "effectual sign."⁵ The ongoing activity of the Spirit means that by the action of the Spirit revelation occurs and recurs "again and again in the experience of the Spirit of Christ."⁶

Because of the ongoing revelatory activity of the Holy Spirit, Bloesch does not argue absolutely for a closed canon.⁷ The criterion for canonicity is not so much historical proximity, although this has to be taken into account, but the revelatory

---

¹Bloesch, **Freedom for Obedience**, 216, (emphasis supplied). Cf. idem, **TWS**, 14.

²"The Bible does not have infallibility within itself, but through the power of the Spirit it carries the infallibility of the very truth of God. We may also speak of the Bible as having a functional infallibility in its role as the supreme rule of faith, conduct and worship" (Bloesch, **HSRII**, 43). Bloesch seems to use the term "functional" in the sense that the practical utility of the Bible is used rather than its intrinsic quality or character and thus comes up with results very similar to the late G. C. Berkouwer who also stressed the divine function of Scripture. See the discussion in Hendrik Krabbendam, "The Functional Theology of G. C. Berkouwer," in **Challenges to Inerrancy: A Theological Response**, ed. Gordon Lewis and Bruce Demarest (Chicago: Moody Press, 1984), 305-314. On the functionalist use of Scripture, see Chang, "Crisis of Biblical Authority: A Critical Examination of Biblical Authority in Contemporary Theology with Special Reference to Functionalism;" Kelsey, **The Uses of Scripture in Recent Theology**; and Charles Manford Sharpe, "The Normative Use of Scripture by Typical Theologians of Protestant Orthodoxy in Great Britain and America," who appears to use the term "functional" for the first time (ibid., 75).

³Bloesch, **HSRII**, 133.

⁴Ibid., 117.

⁵Bloesch, "The Challenge Facing the Churches," 209.

⁶Bloesch, **HSRII**, 50. "The moment of revelation occurred then--in the history of Israel culminating in the Incarnation of Jesus Christ--and this same moment occurs now as the Spirit opens our inward eyes to the eternal significance of this event of redemption" (Bloesch, **TWS**, 197).

⁷Bloesch, **HSRII**, 150.

potential of the witness.[1] Hence, Luther's famous hermeneutical principle "Was Christum treibet,"[2] i.e., whatever points to Christ, with all its problems is taken up. The "absolute norm for Christian faith" is the "gospel of God" or the "gospel of Christ,"[3] which becomes the material norm rather than Scripture, which is the formal norm of faith.[4]

---

[1]"Does the witness drive one to Christ, does it teach the priority of grace over works, does it prepare one to trust and acclaim the Messiah of Israel? This criterion presumably rules out the apocryphal books but not possible undiscovered writings that may have been preserved by the Spirit for elevation at a future time. For example, if a writing was unearthed that could be proven to be authored by Paul or one of the apostles, it would have to be given serious consideration by the church. Yet any addition to the canon could only be made if the Christian community as a whole were directly moved towards this act by the Holy Spirit" (ibid., 150-151). Scripture is the binding witness to Jesus Christ whom Bloesch considers to be the center and apex of the Biblical writings (ibid., 90).

[2]WADB, 7, 385, 25-30. The German verb "treiben" has various shades of meaning, including "impel" and "propel."

[3]Bloesch, **TWS**, 195.

[4]"We must bear in mind that the ultimate, final authority is not Scripture but the living God himself as we find him in Jesus Christ. Jesus Christ and the message about him constitute the material norm for our faith just as the Bible is the formal norm. The Bible is authoritative because it points beyond itself to the absolute authority, the living and transcendent Word of God. . . . Just as the church is subordinate to the Bible, so the Bible in turn is subordinate to Jesus Christ" (Bloesch, **EET**, 1,62-63). Cf. also the following statement: "In evangelical theology, Scripture is the source; the atonement or message of the cross is the central content. Later Protestant orthodoxy referred to the first as the formal norm and the second as the material norm of faith" (idem, **The Future of Evangelical Christianity**, 16).

To our knowledge there is at least one instance where the terms *formal* and *material* are employed in some contradictory manner by Bloesch. In **EET**, 1:55, he refers to Jesus as the *formal* norm of Scripture. Elsewhere in the same volume, however, he writes that "the Bible is the formal norm" and that Jesus Christ constitutes the material norm (ibid., 62). The latter way of putting it seems to be in harmony with other statements like **TWS**, 186, where the Bible is again designated as *formal* norm of faith and the gospel of Jesus Christ as *material* norm. In support for his claim that Jesus is the *formal* norm, Bloesch refers to Aristotle in order to explain his use of *formal* in the sense of "goal" or "criterion" (idem, **EET**, 1:80, n. 16). One wonders, however, whether it would not be more appropriate, if at all, to say that the idea of a "goal" is expressed by Aristotle's *final cause*. In fact, it seems that the *formal cause* in the Aristotelian sense denotes the "pattern or structure which is to become embodied in the thing when it is fully realized; it is that *which the thing* essentially *is*." The *material cause* on the other hand, is that by which Aristotle "understands the crude and relatively undifferentiated stuff, that *from which* the thing in question is made" (Frank Thilly, **A History of Philosophy**, rev. Ledger Wood [New York: Henry Holt and Company, 1951], 107).

Furthermore, it should be kept in mind that the popular distinction between a formal and a material principle in Protestantism, as described by Paul Tillich, for instance (cf. Paul Tillich, **Systematic Theology**, 3 vols. [Chicago: University of Chicago Press, 1951-1963], 1:47-51), is a rather recent phenomenon, dating back no longer than 1800, as the detailed study by Albrecht Ritschl has shown, and cannot really be attributed to the Reformers themselves (Albrecht Ritschl, "Ueber die beiden Principien des Protestantismus: Antwort auf eine 25 Jahre alte Frage," **ZKG** 1 [1877]: 397-413). But even apart from that, the distinction between formal and material seems to imply that the formal is not complete without the material. Cf. Ebeling, "'Sola Scriptura' and

This distinction between a material and a formal norm is crucial in Bloesch's thought and it recurs[1] repeatedly with different formulations.[2] Thus, it is significant that Bloesch understands Scripture to be materially determined by the gospel.[3] With Johann Christoph Blumhardt, whom he quotes approvingly, he writes:

> One must have norms, even for the Bible. And in this case it is Christ, as he is presented by the apostles. Wherever in Scripture I cannot make that norm fit, then that passage is not for me until I *can* make it fit. Many times, then, I must wait until the teaching comes, until finally it is given to me.[4]

Therefore, the statement that Scripture is the standard and criterion by which one is to judge the truth of the church and/or one's experience needs to be understood in a particular way that merits closer attention. A reading of Bloesch's systematic theology and his other publications reveals that the Bible is the "written Word of God"[5] only for the following reasons.[6] First, it brings us a message from God through symbolic language.[7] As such it is the channel of the revelatory core meaning

---

Tradition," 117-119, 127. Similarly, Markus Barth, who says that "the distinction of a formal and material aspect of the Gospel and of faith bore seeds in themselves which had to lead, even within Protestantism, to the radical questioning of the formal authority of the Bible" ("Sola Scriptura," 76).

[1]"The Bible is the formal norm for faith; the gospel or the voice of the living Christ is the material norm" (Bloesch, **TWS**, 186).

[2]Jesus Christ or the gospel of God can be called "absolute norm," and "ultimate norm" (ibid., 186, 187, 191). Thus, he "affirms the interdependence of the relative norms--the Bible, the church, conscience--and the independence of the absolute norm--God's self-revelation in Jesus Christ" (ibid., 196). "These relative norms are interdependent, but they are not equal" (ibid.); cf. also ibid., 186, 191; similarly idem, **Ground of Certainty**, 74. Scripture, the church, and the faith experience can be called "instrumental norms, but they are not in themselves the definite norm of faith. The Bible might be regarded as a regulative norm as well, but it is not in and of itself the absolute norm" (idem, **TWS**, 197).

[3]Corts, 92-93. Cf. Bloesch, **EET**, 1:4.

[4]Bloesch, **TWS**, 205, emphasis in the original. The Blumhardt quotation is taken from Vernard Eller, ed. **Thy Kingdom Come: A Blumhardt Reader** (Grand Rapids, MI; Eerdmans, 1980), 63-64. The attempt to distinguish between a culturally conditioned form and a divine eternal content has led Bloesch to maintain a Christological hierarchy in Scripture.

[5]Bloesch distinguishes between the *written* Word of God and the *living* Word of God, and only the latter communicates God's truth to mankind. "Scripture in itself is the *written* Word of God, comprising by virtue of its divine inspiration a reliable witness to the truth revealed by god in Jesus Christ. But it becomes the *living* Word when it actually communicates to us the truth and power of the cross of Christ through the illumination of the Spirit" (Bloesch, **HSRII** 25-26; idem, **EET**, 1:51).

[6]For the following points, see Bloesch, **HSRII**, 70.

[7]Bloesch, **The Battle for the Trinity**, 17.

that comes from God. Second, it is the inspired witness to revelation which remains the criterion that guides as well as limits theological speculation.[1] Third, it is the vehicle and carrier of revelation, the source of continuing revelation. Finally, it is the document of the final revelation, and by the action of the Spirit, it participates in this revelation. In this understanding, one can detect that Scripture is the Word of God only in a qualified sense. For Bloesch, Scripture is one step removed from revelation.[2] The Bible only participates in the transcended Word of God in an indirect manner through the Spirit of God.[3] In other words, the text of Scripture in and of itself is not the Word of God,[4] but it can become the Word of God when the text is understood in the light of the living Word of God, Jesus Christ, as the Spirit of God works within Scripture and the mind of the reader to bring home the Christological and soteriological significance of Scripture.[5]

Thus, through an emphasis on the special action of the Holy Spirit, Bloesch wants to maintain the concept of a supernatural inspiration of Scripture and even of its infallibility[6] "without reducing its truth to a datum available to human perception."[7] It appears from the foregoing discussion that despite Bloesch's recommendable

---

[1]Ibid., 26.

[2]Bloesch, **EET**, 1:76.

[3]Bloesch, **HSRII**, 70. Thus the Biblical writings are the word of revelation only indirectly by the action of the Spirit.

[4]"One may also say that the Bible is intrinsically the Word of God in that it is encompassed by the 'Word's presence', the living reality of the Spirit of Christ. Because the sign participates in what it signifies, the Bible is included in the redemptive act of Christ as his Spirit works in the community of faith. **The Bible in and of itself is not the Word of God--divine revelation**--but it is translucent to this revelation by virtue of the Spirit of God working within it and within the mind of the reader and hearer" (ibid., 27), (emphasis supplied). "The presence of the living Word in Holy Scripture is not an ontological necessity but a free decision of God who acts and speaks" (ibid., 26).

[5]Ibid., 78.

[6]On Bloesch's revised definition of infallibility and inerrancy, see **EET**, 1:64-70; and idem, "Crisis in Biblical Authority," **TToday** 35/4 (1979): 455-462. Paul D. Feinberg has criticized Bloesch for so radically redefining theological terms that they are self-contradictory or at best lack much relationship with their historical usage ("An Evangelical Systematic Theology," 38 [1259]).

[7]Bloesch, **The Evangelical Renaissance**, 21. Speaking about the symbolic nature of the language of Scripture, Bloesch contends that it "cannot be directly comprehended by theoretical reason. A symbol points beyond itself to a reality that can only be dimly perceived by the senses or faintly understood by reason" (Bloesch, **The Battle for the Trinity**, 20). Hence, "the meaning of a symbol can only be intuitively grasped" (ibid., 17). Cf. also James Emery White, 238.

intentions to follow "a methodology that has its source of inspiration in Scripture, not in some philosophy extraneous to Scripture,"[1] he "is unable to rid himself of philosophical influences."[2]

After considering Bloesch's understanding of the nature of Scripture, one must investigate what he thinks Scripture is not.

What Scripture Is Not

Characteristically, Bloesch often affirms one position while he rejects another with the same breath. Thus, some facets that are dealt with in this section briefly were alluded to in the previous one. There are several aspects of the nature of Scripture that Bloesch clearly denies.

He repeatedly writes against a view of Scripture where the text of the Bible is identified directly with the Word of God.[3] In his opinion, a direct identity between Scripture and revelation would lead to bibliolatry.[4] This, he thinks, is the case in Fundamentalism, where the revelation of God is identified with the propositions of Scripture.[5] Bloesch tries to distance himself from what he perceives to be a "rationalistic biblicism" where "an absolute identification is made between the words

---

[1]Bloesch, **The Future of Evangelical Christianity**, 122.

[2]Ralph W. Vunderink, "Review of **The Ground of Certainty**, by Donald G. Bloesch," **CTJ** 8 (1973): 88. Vunderink, 88-89, points out that "to the extent that he is a loyal follower of Barth, one may expect to find Kantian and Platonic elements in Bloesch's future biblical or constructive theology."

[3]"The Bible in and of itself is not the Word of God--divine revelation--but is translucent to this revelation by virtue of the Spirit of God working within it and within the mind of the reader and hearer" (Bloesch, **HSRII**, 27; 57). Cf. also idem, "A Christological Hermeneutic," 83; idem, **The Evangelical Renaissance**, 57, where he writes: "The Word of God is not the letter or text by itself but the divine meaning imbedded in the text, a meaning unveiled only by the Holy Spirit." Similarly, idem, **Is the Bible Sexist?** 71, where he writes that "we do not adulate the Bible as a book, but we are called to revere the Word of God who meets us in the Bible, and who is in one sense inseparable from the Bible." The latter statement comes very close to a neo-orthodox position, where the Word of God (Jesus Christ) is to be found among the many words of Scripture.

[4]Bloesch, **EET**, 1:53. It seems that the charge of "bibliolatry" goes back at least to Heinrich Philipp Konrad Henke, **Lineamenta Institutionum Fidei Christianae Historico-Criticarum** (Helmstadii: Fleckeisen, 1795), 18-22; and Gotthold Ephraim Lessing, "Bibliolatrie," in **Lessing Werke**, ed. J. Petersen and W. von Olshausen (Berlin: Deutsches Verlagshaus Bong & Co., 1925), 23:307-312. The deficiency and unfairness of those kinds of charges has been pointed out by Carl F. H. Henry, **The Protestant Dilemma: An Analysis of the Current Impasse in Theology** (Grand Rapids, MI: Eerdmans, 1949), 77; and more recently by Helge Stadelmann, **Grundlinien eines bibeltreuen Schriftverständnisses** (Wuppertal: R. Brockhaus, 1985), 63-64; and Silva, **God, Language and Scripture**, 38.

[5]Bloesch, **HSRII**, 94-100; idem, **The Future of Evangelical Christianity**, 25, 118.

of the biblical text and the truth of revelation."[1] In contrast, Bloesch maintains that the Bible does not contain universal, unchanging truths that are waiting to be discovered[2] and, therefore, cannot be a source book for revealed truth that can be drawn out of Scripture by deductive or inductive logic.[3] Only the soteriological **message** of Scripture is infallible and inerrant.[4] Because of the human coauthorship of Scripture, Bloesch is convinced that the Biblical interpreter has to acknowledge that there are culturally conditioned ideas as well as historically conditioned language in the

---

[1] Bloesch, **The Evangelical Renaissance**, 21. In another place Bloesch had claimed that a direct identity between Scripture and revelation could lead to bibliolatry. Hence, "we do affirm an indirect identity in that by the work of the Holy Spirit the very human words of the prophets and apostles are conjoined with the Word spoken by God to them. God's Word is consequently not the Bible in and by itself but the correlation of Scripture and Spirit (Barth)" (**EET**, 1:53). This position reminds one of Karl Barth's objection to an identification of Scripture with divine revelation. According to Karl Barth, such an identification would elevate Scripture to a "paper Pope" who is given up into the hands of its interpreters, thereby loosing its ability to be a free and spiritual force (**CD**, I/2, 525). In a similar manner, Emil Brunner objects that "God is not a 'Book-God'; what matters is not the Book but the Person" (**Revelation and Reason**, 143). It has been seriously questioned whether Bloesch's account of "rationalistic biblicism" adequately and fairly portrays that particular branch of Evangelical scholarship. Nash thinks that Bloesch's "account is a caricature," 130).

[2] "I have considerable difficulty with the view, so appealing to those of a rationalist bent, that the Bible is impregnated with universal, unchanging truths that are waiting to be discovered and formulated" (Bloesch, **HSRII**, 20). Elsewhere Bloesch states that "there is no eternal moral law in the sense of unchanging principles. . . . There is no moral law in the sense of a propositional formula that is in and of itself absolute and eternal, that is there waiting to be discovered. Divine revelation provides moral direction, but it does not yield rules that are eternal and therefore directly applicable to every situation" (idem, **Freedom for Obedience**, 7); cf. also idem, "Law and Gospel in Reformed Perspective," **GTJ** 12/1 (1991): 179-188. For a critical assessment of Bloesch's position, see Terrance Tiessen, "Toward a Hermeneutic for Discerning Universal Moral Absolutes," **JETS** 36/2 (1993): 190-191.

[3] Bloesch, **EET**, 1:69. Neither is it a source book of data on Israel's history (ibid., 1:70).

[4] It appears lately that Bloesch is not comfortable with the term "inerrancy" when applied to Scripture "because it has been co-opted by a rationalistic, empiricistic mentality that reduces truth to facticity. Yet, I wish to retain what is intended by this word--the abiding truthfulness and normativity of the biblical witness. This truthfulness, however, is a property not of the human witness itself but of the Spirit who speaks in and through this witness" (Bloesch, **HSRII**, 27; 116). Biblical writers, according to Bloesch, certainly erred in their thoughts, words, and acts, although they were enabled through the superintendence of the Spirit to remain in the truth in their public acts (ibid., 298). Gabriel Fackre, in a helpful categorization of different positions on the question of Biblical authority has classified Bloesch correctly among the infallibilists, rather than among the inerrantists. Among the infallibilists he is a proponent of an essentialist infallibility (Fackre, **The Christian Story. Authority: Scripture in the Church for the World**, 69-72). See also Robert K. Johnston's classification in **Evangelicals at an Impasse**, 15-37, who does not mention Bloesch, however. It should be noted at this point that although it is now customary to distinguish between infallibility and inerrancy, historically those two terms were used interchangeably to express the conviction that Scripture is absolutely trustworthy in all that it teaches and touches upon (D. A. Carson, "Recent Developments in the Doctrine of Scripture," 31).

Bible.¹ "The Bible contains a fallible element in the sense that it reflects the cultural limitations of the writers."² The historical and cultural limitations of the Biblical writers also include "their theological and ethical ideas."³ Hence, Scripture is not absolutely trustworthy in all it teaches and touches upon.

This raises the question whether Christ, who is seen as the infallible center of Scripture,⁴ could ever contradict the Bible or the church?⁵ Bloesch is quick to assure the reader that "Christ cannot contradict himself, but his Word is not identical with the words of his servants and messengers."⁶ This means that not every part of Scripture is equally important.⁷ Since the historically conditioned and limited language of the Biblical writers contains a fallible element, it is clear that Bloesch has little interest in defending what he calls a "naive biblical literalism" where the "credibility of the Bible rests upon the edibility of Jonah."⁸ Scripture must not be treated as a dependable

---

¹Bloesch, **EET**, 1:64. It seems that those limitations extend to all the text because, as Bloesch writes, "the text when taken only by itself, apart from its theological and spiritual context, is fallible and deficient" (**HSRII**, 126).

²Bloesch, **EET**, 1:68-69.

³Ibid., 1:68. In **HSRII**, 122-123, Bloesch writes that "inspiration does not guarantee that the Bible is inerrant in the sense of being exempt from human misconceptions and limitations--even in the areas of ethics and theology." This appears to constitute a decisive move away from Evangelical theology and even traditional orthodoxy. Yet, Bloesch is reluctant to give any specifics. Instead, he claims that there are only "innocent inaccuracies" (Kuyper) in Scripture (**EET**, 1:67), and maintains that Scripture "is not mistaken in what it purports to teach, namely God's will and purpose for the world. There are no errors or contradictions in its substance and heart" (ibid., 69).

⁴Bloesch, **TWS**, 204; idem, **HSRII**, 156.

⁵It has been pointed out that faith in Jesus Christ and in God's inspired Word belong intricately together and do not stand in rivalry with each other for we do not have Jesus without the written Word of God (Stadelmann, 64). Also Martin Luther, WA, 30, III, 564, 14-16.

⁶Bloesch, **TWS**, 204. Bloesch's high respect for Scripture can be seen in his decision to better "speak of ambiguities and inconsistencies in the Bible, even imperfections, rather than error" (**HSRII**, 115). "While acknowledging innocent factual inaccuracies in the Bible, I hesitate to call these error. I readily grant that forms of expression in Scripture may conflict with science, but science is not the final norm, for scientific theories are constantly in flux. Because error does not touch what is truly divine in the Bible, it is more proper to speak of 'difficulties' than of errors, of chaff but not tares" (ibid., 117).

⁷Bloesch, **HSRII**, 97; according to Bloesch, there are "peaks and plains in the canon" (idem, "An Evangelical Perspektive on Authority," 5; idem, **EET**, 1:55). In a personal interview Bloesch was not prepared to follow through with the implication arising out of his position, namely, that Scripture is not equally inspired, either. He still wants to maintain that all Scripture is inspired (Bloesch, interview, 10 January 1994).

⁸Bloesch, **The Evangelical Renaissance**, 28.

scientific source for philology, paleontology, paleozoology, or ethnography, although its affirmations have important implications in all these areas.[1] In other words, the Bible is not a document concerning science, history, or religion as such but a divine-human encounter in which one finds above all, Jesus.

In all this "the criterion is always whether the prophet's testimony conforms to the gospel of God, which comes directly from Christ."[2] One wonders whether Bloesch thereby has not seriously put into question the clarity and perspicuity of Scripture,[3] as well as its internal unity.[4] It appears that Jesus Christ as the center of Scripture for all practical purposes becomes the substitute for the lost unity of Scripture. This Christological principle, which goes back at least until Martin Luther,[5] is burdened with an unavoidable subjectivism of the individual interpreter.[6] Gerhard Maier has pointed out that Scripture itself does not know the term nor the concept of a "center of Scripture." He thinks it is improper to substitute the inherent unity of Scripture through a proclaimed center.[7] Once the clarity and unity of Scripture are compromised, the concept of Scripture alone (*sola Scriptura*) is difficult to maintain.[8]

---

[1]Bloesch, **HSRII**, 361, n. 81; idem, "The Sword of the Spirit," 66, 67.

[2]Bloesch, **TWS**, 204.

[3]One has to keep in mind that in Lutheran theology the clarity of Scripture pertains to the language and sense and words of Scripture, not to the teachings and mysteries of faith, which can never be understood but must be accepted on faith (Preus, **The Theology of Post-Reformation Lutheranism**, 1:312). H. Østergaard-Nielsen, 24, says that Luther's notion of Biblical clarity meant that the Scriptures had the ability to make their message clear and to convince one of their assertions. On the concept of the clarity of Scripture, see Friedrich Beisser, **Claritas Scripturae bei Martin Luther**; Rothen, **Die Klarheit der Schrift, Teil 1, Martin Luther: Die wiederentdeckten Grundlagen**; and Robert Sandin, "The Clarity of Scripture," in **The Living and Active Word of God: Studies in Honor of Samuel J. Schultz**, ed. Morris Inch and Ronald Youngblood (Winona Lake, IN: Eisenbrauns, 1983), 237-253.

[4]On the Unity of Scripture, see Maier, **Biblische Hermeneutik**, 160-178; Robert D. Preus, "The Unity of Scripture," **CTQ** 54/1 (1990): 1-23.

[5]Cf. Kohls, 46-75.

[6]Robert Grant with David Tracy, 94.

[7]Maier, **Biblische Hermeneutik**, 175-176.

[8]"If we have the Bible alone--apart from the church and apart from the experience of faith--then we end in the morass of a certain kind of fundamentalism or narrow biblicism. . . . When the Reformers spoke of *sola Scriptura*, they meant the Bible illumined by the Spirit in the matrix of the church. *Sola Scriptura* is not *nuda Scriptura* (the bare Scripture). It means that the Bible is our primary authority, not our only authority" (Bloesch, **TWS**, 193). "It is fallacious to assume, as do some evangelicals, that we can neglect the branches that have sprung from the roots and begin over again with the roots alone (a false conception of *sola scriptura*)" (idem, **The Future**

This leads one to the question of the use of Scripture which deserves further consideration.

The Use of Scripture

This section of this study first investigates how Scripture is used by Bloesch, and then it moves into a study of how Scripture is not used by Bloesch.

How Scripture Is Used

When one looks at the use of Scripture in Bloesch's systematic theology, one can clearly perceive that Bloesch uses it from a confessional standpoint.[1] The truthfulness of Scripture's central message is accepted with a certain trust and confidence. Quite often it is taken as it reads. At times, one comes across a use of Bible texts in support of a particular argument or doctrine that on the surface resembles the so called "Proof-text-method."[2]

Yet, not all statements of Scripture are equally accepted.[3] While Bloesch affirms the divinity and truthfulness of its central message, which is the gospel of Jesus Christ,[4] he dismisses other things as peripheral.[5] His use of Scripture reveals that

---

of Evangelical Christianity, 120).

[1]By confessional theology we mean theology that takes its point of departure within the framework of faith and a given faith community. Cf. Martin L. Cook, "Confessional Theology," in **A New Handbook of Christian Theology**, ed. Donald W. Musser and Joseph L. Price (Nashville, TN: Abingdon, 1992), 96-98; see also idem, **The Open Circle: Confessional Method in Theology** (Minneapolis: Fortress Press, 1991).

[2]Randy Maddox contends that "the central problem with Bloesch's model of revelation is that it does not take the historical-situatedness of Scripture seriously enough. This helps explain his tendency to disregard or undervalue historical-critical perspectives on the meaning of biblical symbols, especially 'masculine' symbols" ("The Necessity of Recognizing Distinctions," 318-319). In **EET** he "even slips in a few biblical proof texts from the deutero-canonical books, no doubt a surprise to any Evangelical reader who notices them!" (Bob Price, "Review of **Essentials of Evangelical Theology**, volumes 1 and 2, by Donald G. Bloesch," **DG** 50/3 [1980]: 54).

[3]Maddox has rightly criticized Bloesch's hermeneutic which rejects one aspect of Scripture and affirms another as "subjective and arbitrary" ("The Necessity of Recognizing Distinctions," 315; and idem, "Reply to Donald Bloesch," 285).

[4]Bloesch, **HSRII**, 174.

[5]"But this does not mean that they were faultless in their recording of historical data or in their world view, which is now outdated" (Bloesch, **EET**, 1:65). Also: "We would do well to recognize that there is a Christian center (the gospel) and a Christian periphery (cultural application). There can be no center without a periphery. The center always takes precedence over the periphery, but the center will dissolve without a periphery" (idem, **Freedom for Obedience**, 160). Cf. the discussion above, 208.

Bloesch does not suggest that everything in Scripture should be treated as if it were on an equal level.[1] Instead, he proposes a thoroughly Christological use of Scripture. In an important paragraph in **TWS**, Bloesch delineates his Christological use in contrast to other theological methods. He writes:

> In the theological method I advocate, we do not adduce true insights from Scripture ([Thomas N.] Finger), nor do we deduce true propositions from Scripture (Carl [F. H.] Henry). Neither do we infer general truths from Scripture by an investigation of particulars--the way of induction (Charles Hodge). *Instead, we discover the truth within Scripture after being confronted by the One who is the Truth--Jesus Christ. We begin not with Scripture as a historical text but with the living Word of God--Jesus Christ--and then try to ascertain how Scripture bears witness to him.*[2]

In other words, Scripture is to be used functionally with regards to Jesus Christ.[3] For him there exists an integral and organic relation between Christ and Scripture,[4] to the point where Bloesch can affirm that the absolute authority of faith,

---

[1]Clark H. Pinnock apparently has missed this obvious aspect in Bloesch's theology, for he inaccurately states that "the theological method employed [by Bloesch] can only be called biblicist, the strict application of the *sola scriptura* [sic] principle" ("Review of **Essentials of Evangelical Theology**," TToday, 266).

[2]Bloesch, **TWS**, 118, (emphasis supplied). At the end of this quotation, Bloesch p. 303, n. 48, adds: "Once we see Scripture in the light of its divine center and goal, we are then free to use both induction and deduction in the task of understanding the full import of the scriptural message."

Although in Bloesch's theology there already exists an anticipatory or proleptic knowledge of Jesus Christ in the Old Testament, inasmuch as the Old Testament bears witness to Christ by pointing to His coming in the future, the question can be raised whether the people during those times could come to an adequate knowledge of their Scriptures, since Jesus Christ had not yet come, which means that they could not begin their theological quest with Him. In a private interview, Bloesch responded to this challenge by saying that Christ revealed Himself directly to many of these prophets, apart from Scripture, so that the content or matter of the Bible was present before it took written form (Bloesch, interview, 10 January 1994).

[3]Bloesch readily grants "that scriptural infallibility can legitimately be described in functional terms" (**HSRII**, 132-133). Yet, "besides infallibly directing us to Christ" Scripture also "provides[s] infallible information concerning the will and purpose of God as supremely manifested in Christ" (ibid., 133). Thus, Bloesch sees the Bible "as having an ontological as well as a functional authority. It not only brings sinners the saving message of redemption by the action of the Spirit, but its writing is filled and penetrated by the presence of the Spirit" (ibid.). From such a statement it would possible to say that it is the Holy Spirit who uses Scripture functionally, rather than human beings. A functional nature of Scripture in Bloesch's thought is recognized by Fackre, **The Christian Story. Authority: Scripture in the Church for the World**, 72. Such a functional use of Scripture with a Christological hermeneutic is quite subjective. For how is one to determine which passages effectively preach Christ and which do not, except by faith? Cf. Grant, 94; Maier, **Biblische Hermeneutik**, 174.

[4]"The Bible contains both wheat and husk. The husk is not falsehood or even what is peripheral or marginal. It has an important, even an indispensable, role, for it holds the wheat" (Bloesch, **HSRII**, 125). Earlier he wrote, consistent with the logical conclusion of his thought, that "when I say that the Bible contains chaff as well as wheat, I mean that there are parts of the

the living Christ Himself, has so bound Himself to the historical attestation in Scripture that the latter necessarily participates in the authority of its Lord.[1] Hence, the ruling criterion of the gospel must not be construed as referring only to particular sections of Scripture. It is either implicit or explicit in the whole of Scripture.[2] Thus, the whole Bible revolves around Christ, and all of Scripture constitutes a compelling witness to Him.[3] According to Robert K. Johnston, Bloesch thereby has sought to steer a middle ground between left-wing neo-orthodoxy and right-wing scholastic orthodoxy.[4] It can be questioned, however, whether Bloesch's nobel attempt to mediate between liberal and conservative understandings of Scripture is not just as inconsistent a theological position as neo-orthodoxy is, which attempts "to return to the *sola scriptura* and to specifically Christian experience as the sole source of religious authority, even while still pursuing a thoroughgoing historical approach to theological reflection."[5]

Bloesch claims that form and content are inseparable, yet they cannot be equated.[6] The climax of revelation is clearly Jesus Christ. Some light of Him exists already in the Old Testament.[7] But the truth of the Bible is available to humans only when they strive to see the text in relation to the New Testament.[8] Theological discrepancies between the Old Testament and the New Testament can be explained on

---

Bible that are marginal and peripheral--but certainly not worthless" (idem, **Theological Notebook**, 2:116-117).

[1]Bloesch, **EET**, 1:63.

[2]Ibid.

[3]Bloesch, **HSRII**, 128; 90; 59. It is for this overall message that infallibility and veracity apply to the whole Bible. Infallibility does not apply to any particular text or report in the Bible (ibid., 116).

[4]Robert K. Johnston, "Biblical Authority and Hermeneutics: The Growing Evangelical Dialogue," **CovQ** 50/3 (1992): 13; the same article appeared under the same title in **SWJT** 34/2 (1992): 22-30, here 28. But Maier has ably shown that it is not possible to substitute the unity of Scripture through a theological center (**Biblische Hermeneutik**, 174-175).

[5]Schubert M. Ogden, "Sources of Religious Authority in Liberal Protestantism," **JAAR** 44/3 (1976): 410. Wilhelm Pauck made a similar observation when he stated that "orthodox theologies give rise to more orthodoxies; liberal theologies give rise to neo-orthodoxies" (as quoted in Tracy, **Blessed Rage for Order**, 27).

[6]Bloesch, **HSRII**, 134.

[7]Ibid., 50.

[8]Ibid., 38.

the basis of levels of revelation.¹ Bloesch himself admits that "as we move on to the New Testament, we find ourselves in a *qualitatively* different situation."² In other words, one can detect a clear tendency in Bloesch's use of Scripture to give the New Testament priority over the Old Testament. This seems to be the case because his theological norm, Jesus Christ, determines the appropriateness and adequacy of Biblical passages in pointing to Him. Bloesch is aware that with such a use of Scripture he can legitimately be asked whether he is operating with a canon with the canon.³ His desire to uphold the unity of Scripture, yet have a higher criterion within the Bible,⁴ clearly stands in an unresolved tension.

Another characteristic of Bloesch's use of Scripture also is derived from his understanding of the dual nature of Scripture. Because he refuses to posit an absolute equation between the letter of the Bible and divine revelation Scripture's human side, the text of Scripture, can be investigated historically-critically, although the historical-critical method is used in a modified sense. Bloesch espouses a qualified approval of the historical-critical method, wanting to reject the naturalistic philosophy of many of the higher critics.⁵ He displays a readiness to take into account scientific discoveries and new scientific evidence, "even if this calls into question certain reputed historical facts or opinions of the world and man found in the Bible."⁶ Bloesch believes that historical criticism enables one to recapture the humanity of Scripture,⁷ but one must not lose sight of its divinity if one is to recover the Bible as an authoritative guide for

---

¹Ibid., 111.

²Bloesch, "A Christological Hermeneutic," 92.

³Ibid., 98. On the problem of a canon within the canon, see Lønning, "**Kanon im Kanon.**". Maier, **Biblische Hermeneutik**, 137-138, concludes that "die 200 jährige Suche nach einem allseits überzeugenden Kanon im Kanon erlaubt es uns heute, eine Bilanz zu ziehen. Sie lautet: Diese Suche war vergeblich."

⁴Bloesch, **EET**, 1:63, ix.

⁵Ibid., 1:16; idem, "A Christological Hermeneutic," 95.

⁶Bloesch, **EET**, 1:16.

⁷Such a statement certainly does not do justice to all those Biblical scholars who lived in pre-critical times and who engaged in serious exegetical investigations. It seems that although most of them accepted the divine origin and authority of Scripture they at the same time were very well aware of the human dimension of Scripture, too. Cf. the discussion in Frederic W. Farrar, **History of Interpretation** (New York: E. P. Dutton and Co., 1886), 307-394; Armour, "Calvin's Hermeneutic and the History of Christian Exegesis;" Heinrich Bornkamm, **Luther and the Old Testament**, trans. Eric W. and Ruth C. Gritsch, ed. Victor I. Gruhn (Philadelphia: Fortress Press, 1969); and John D. Hannah, ed., **Inerrancy and the Church** (Chicago: Moody Press, 1984).

the church today.[1] In the use of the historical-critical method, a close relationship between Bloesch and his theological mentor, Karl Barth, can be seen.[2] With Barth, Bloesch holds that the theologian may be involved in "Sach-exegesis--the delineation of the content or substance of Scripture. But we are not to engage in content criticism."[3] Bloesch also maintains that historical criticism enables one to understand

---

[1] Bloesch, **EET**, 1:56. Recent scholarship has seriously questioned whether the historical critical method is really an adequate tool for the investigation of Holy Scripture. One recalls Gerhard Maier's famous statement that "critique is not the appropriate answer to revelation" (Gerhard Maier, **The End of the Historical Critical Method**, trans. Edwin W. Leverenz and Rudolph F. Norden [St. Louis, MS: Concordia Publishing House, 1977], 22). It has been pointed out by several that a neutral concept of criticism in Biblical studies is not possible because of the naturalistic presuppositions of the historical critical method that are inevitably bound to the method itself and cannot be left aside without substantially changing the method itself. So, recently, Linnemann, **Historical Criticism of the Bible: Methodology or Ideology?**; Thomas C. Oden, **After Modernity What?**; Helge Stadelmann, **Grundlinien eines bibeltreuen Schriftverständnises**, 93; Karl-Heinz Michel, **Sehen und Glauben: Schriftauslegung in der Auseinandersetzung mit Kerygmatheologie und historisch-kritischer Forschung** (Wuppertal: R. Brockhaus Verlag, 1982); Hellmuth Frey, **Die Krise der Theologie: Historische Kritik und pneumatische Auslegung im Lichte der Krise** (Wuppertal: R. Brockhaus Verlag, 1971); Gerhard F. Hasel, **Biblical Interpretation Today** (Washington, DC: Biblical Research Institute, 1985), 78-85; Vern Sheridian Poythress, **Science and Hermeneutics: Implications of Scientific Method for Biblical Interpretation**, FCI 6 (Grand Rapids, MI: Zondervan Publishing House, 1988); and Gerhard Maier's new important study **Biblische Hermeneutik**, especially 213-270, to name but a few voices. The inadequacy of the historical-critical method is not only criticized from without, but also increasingly by practitioners from within. Cf. Walter Wink, **The Bible in Human Transformation: Toward a New Paradigm for Biblical Study** (Philadelphia: Fortress Press, 1973); Friedrich Beisser, "Irrwege und Wege der historisch-kritischen Bibelwissenschaft: Auch ein Vortrag zur Reform des Theologiestudiums," **NZSTh** 15 (1973): 192-214; Archie L. Nations, "Historical Criticism and the Current Methodological Crisis," **SJT** 36 (1983): 56-71; Eugen Drewermann, **Tiefenpsychologie und Exegese**, vol. 1, **Die Wahrheit der Formen. Traum, Mythos, Märchen, Sage und Legende** (Olten: Walter Verlag, 1984), 23-47; Jon D. Levenson, "The Bible: Unexamined Commitments of Criticism," **FiT** 30 (1993): 24-33; idem, **The Hebrew Bible, the Old Testament, and Historical Criticism: Jews and Christians in Biblical Studies** (Philadelphia: Westminster/John Knox Press, 1993); John Ziesler, "Historical Criticism and a Rational Faith," **ExpRev** 105/9 (1994): 270-274. For a Roman Catholic reaction to the historical-critical method, see Joseph Cardinal Ratzinger, "Biblical Interpretation in Crisis: On the Question of the Foundations and Approaches of Exegesis Today," in **Biblical Interpretation in Crisis: The Ratzinger Conference on Bible and Church**, ed. Richard John Neuhaus (Grand Rapids, MI: Eerdmans, 1989): 1-23.

[2] Cf. the excellent dissertation by Thomas Edward Provence, "The Hermeneutics of Karl Barth," especially 213-287, 333-361; see also David F. Ford, "Barth's Interpretation of the Bible," in **Karl Barth: Studies of His Theological Method**, ed. S. W. Sykes (Oxford: Clarendon Press, 1979), 55-87; Werner G. Jeanrond, "Karl Barth's Hermeneutics," in **Reckoning with Barth: Essays in Commemoration of the Centenary of Karl Barth's Birth**, ed. Nigel Biggar (London: Mowbray, 1988), 80-97; Ramm, **After Fundamentalism**, 101-115; and James A. Wharton, "Karl Barth as Exegete and His Influence on Biblical Interpretation," **USAQ** 28/1 (1972): 5-13.

[3] Bloesch, **HSRII**, 177. Robert Morgan has pointed out that the German term "*Sachkritik*' has been variously translated into English as 'content criticism', 'material criticism of the content', 'objective criticism'(!), 'theological criticism', 'critical interpretation', and 'critical study of the

the cultural and historical background of the text, but it cannot uncover the spiritual significance of it.¹ Therefore, it is necessary to understand that historical criticism "can only take us so far, and then we have to go on to the 'highest criticism', seeing every text in the light of the Gospel, the theological center of the Bible."² Here Bloesch obviously takes back with one hand what he wants to affirm with the other. For subjective reasons, he seems not willing to apply the historical-critical method consistently all the way.

Instead of sticking only to a historical-critical use of Scripture, Bloesch proposes that one must proceed beyond the historical-critical investigation of the text to a "theological exegesis, which means seeing the text in the light of its theological context, relating the text to the central message of Holy Scripture."³ This "highest criticism" that Bloesch has in mind is possible only with the help of the Holy Spirit because it eludes the grasp of reason. The spiritual significance[4] of the Biblical text is unclear

---

content'. It refers to the interpreter's criticism of the formulations of the text in the light of what (he thinks) the subject-matter (*Sache*) to be; criticism of what is said by what is meant" ("Introduction: The Nature of New Testament Theology," in **The Nature of New Testament Theology: The Contribution of William Wrede and Adolf Schlatter**, SBT(2) 25, ed. and trans. Robert Morgan [Naperville, IL: Alec R. Allenson, 1973], 42). See also I. Howard Marshall, "An Evangelical Approach to 'Theological Criticism'," **Themelios** 13/3 (1988): 80. In other words, Bloesch is willing to critically exegete the text of Scripture but he is not willing to criticize the content of Scripture in the light of his critical investigation, except where no immediate connection to the norm of Scripture, Jesus Christ, can be made.

¹Bloesch, **EET**, 1:72.

²Ibid.

³Ibid., 1:71. This so called "theological exegesis" has some resemblance with the *sensus plenior*, i.e., the fuller sense than that consciously intended by the human author. Generally, *sensus plenior* is used to refer to a meaning that cannot be demonstrated by means of traditional grammatical-historical exegesis. On the meaning and use of *sensus plenior*, see the important study by Raymond Edward Brown, **The Sensus Plenior of Sacred Scripture** (Baltimore, MD: St. Mary's University, 1955); idem, "The *Sensus Plenior* in the Last Ten Years," **CBQ** 25 (1963): 262-285; William Sanford LaSor, "The *Sensus Plenior* and Biblical Interpretation," in **Scripture, Tradition, and Interpretation: Essays Presented to Everett F. Harrison by His Students and Colleagues in Honor of His Seventy-Fifth Birthday**, ed. W. Ward Gasque and William Sanford LaSor (Grand Rapids, MI: Eerdmans, 1978), 260-277; Douglas J. Moo, "The Problem of *Sensus Plenior*," in **Hermeneutics, Authority, and Canon**, ed. D. A. Carson and John D. Woodbridge (Grand Rapids, MI: Zondervan Publishing House, 1986), 175-221; and the helpful survey in Henning Graf Reventlow, **Problems of Biblical Theology in the Twentieth Century**, trans. John Bowden (Philadelphia: Fortress Press, 1986), 37-47, with further literature.

⁴It seems that Bloesch is not entirely clear on the distinction between significance and meaning and confuses the two at times (**EET**, 1:73). The difference between those terms and concepts is of no minor importance. Hirsch has convincingly shown that the meaning of a text remains the same while the significance of that meaning might change. "If textual meaning itself

to the unbeliever and cannot be penetrated by reason.¹ The interpreter has to be opened up to the guidance and illumination of the Holy Spirit in order to discover what was in the mind of the Spirit who inspired the Biblical writers. It seems that Bloesch ultimately moves beyond the confines of the text to discern the essential meaning of Scripture that is given to human beings through the Spirit.² To read the Bible with the "Mind of Christ" is not something that man possesses, something that can be taken for granted; it is something that must be imparted again and again.³ It means that the interpretation of Scripture is not an art to be learned but a gift to be received, because no technique or formula can disclose the real Word of God.⁴ One consequence of this pneumatic use of Scripture is that the text can have a fluidity of meaning within certain parameters,⁵ where the "original meaning is both fulfilled and transcended."⁶ In 1978,

---

could change, contemporary readers would lack a basis for agreement or disagreement. . . . The significance of textual meaning has no foundation and no objectivity unless meaning itself is unchanging" (E. D. Hirsch, Jr., **Validity in Interpretation** [New Haven: Yale University Press, 1967], 214). Similarly Emilio Betti, **Die Hermeneutik als Allgemeine Methodik der Geisteswissenschaften**, PG 78/79 (Tübingen: J. C. B. Mohr, 1962), 28-29, who distinguishes between "Bedeutung" and "Bedeutsamkeit." Cf. also Nash's similar critique of Bloesch's confusing the difference between truth and the apprehension of truth (**The Word of God and the Mind of Man**, 131). In his latest book Bloesch touches upon the important distinction between meaning and significance in E. D. Hirsch and Walter Kaiser and comments as follows: "Though recognizing that authorial intention is of vital importance, I contend that theological relation is equally important. Part of the problem of relying on the intention of the original author is that he may not always have had a clear vision of what he was trying to say. Moreover, the community of faith may well have received the text with a different understanding from that in the mind of the author. Again, the intention **of the Spirit of God**, the divine author, may sometimes be at variance with the intention of the human author. . . . The distinction between meaning and application is artificial, for meaning does not simply reside in the words of a text or in the intention of the author but in an event in which the reader or hearer participates in the revelation of meaning given to the author" (**HSRII**, 189-190). Cf. also the recent critique of Hirsch's approach by Millard J. Erickson, **Evangelical Interpretation: Perspectives on Hermeneutical Issues** (Grand Rapids, MI: Baker Book House, 1993); and the meta-critique of Hirsch by G. B. Madison, **The Hermeneutics of Postmodernity: Figures and Themes** (Bloomington, IN: Indiana University Press, 1988), 3-24.

¹Bloesch, **EET**, 1:73.

²Bloesch, **HSRII**, 206-207.

³Ibid., 182.

⁴Ibid., 180-181; similarly already in idem, "A Christological Hermeneutic," 100. This is reminiscent of Bloesch's sacramental understanding of the nature of Scripture.

⁵Bloesch, **HSRII**, 191.

⁶Bloesch, **EET**, 1:73.

Bloesch still claimed that "this is not pneumatic exegesis,"[1] but in his recent systematic theology he writes that

> instead of the literalistic approach of fundamentalism and the historical-critical approach of liberalism I recommend the *post-critical pneumatic approach of a catholic evangelicalism*.[2]

Elsewhere in the same volume, he calls it "a historical-pneumatic hermeneutics in which Word and Spirit are joined together in dynamic unity."[3] Thus the interpreter is drawn through a "hermeneutical magnet" into the work of the Spirit on the text.[4]

This pneumatic use of Scripture at times appears to come dangerously close to an allegorical use of Scripture.[5] Bloesch is concerned to supplement the literal meaning uncovered by the historical-critical method through a "theological exegesis, in which the innermost intentions of the author are related to the center and culmination of sacred history mirrored in the Bible, namely the advent of Jesus Christ."[6] Such a deeper understanding--the perception of faith[7]--is outside the confines of a purely historical exegesis and unveils the innermost intentions of the Biblical writers of which

---

[1] Ibid. Bloesch here still claimed that "this is not pneumatic exegesis, which ignores or devalues the meaning of the witten word, but theological exegesis which tries to relate the original meaning to the central message of Scripture" (ibid.), yet only a few sentences after he gives this disclaimer Bloesch goes on the write that whereas the Reformers objected to the exegetical methods of the fathers and medieval scholastics because the literal or original sense was too often bypassed in favor of a purely subjective or mystical interpretation, "we cannot remain with the natural or literal sense, but this must be our point of departure, the basis on which we make our synthetic judgments" (ibid.). Cf. also idem, "A Christological Hermeneutic: Crisis and Conflict in Hermeneutics," 100).

[2] Bloesch, **HSRII**, 181, (emphasis supplied).

[3] Ibid., 200, also 206, 207.

[4] Ibid., 202. The Spirit is not only the ultimate author of the Bible but also the ongoing interpreter of the Biblical message to the church in every age. Although what the Spirit says to the church does not contradict what the Spirit has already revealed to the prophets and apostles of old, "it may go beyond their specific witness as the Word of God is related to a new situation" (idem, **TWS**, 14).

[5] Bernard Ramm defined allegorical interpretation as follows: "Allegorical interpretation believes that beneath the letter (rhētē) or the obvious (phanera) is the real meaning (hyponoia) of the passage" (**Protestant Biblical Interpretation: A Textbook of Hermeneutics**, 3d rev. ed. [Grand Rapids, MI: Baker Book House, 1970], 24. Similarly Andrew Louth: "Allegory is a principle of interpretation that treats the text as having a less-than-straight-forward meaning. . . . Allegorical interpretation suggests that we seek another meaning than the obvious 'surface' meaning: in contrast to such a 'surface' meaning (the so-called 'literal' meaning) the allegorical meaning is 'deeper' or 'hidden'" ("Allegorical Interpretation," **A Dictionary of Biblical Interpretation**, ed. R. J. Coggins and J. L. Houlden (London: SCM Press, 1990), 12).

[6] Bloesch, "A Christological Hermeneutic," 81; also idem, **HSRII**, 174.

[7] Bloesch, "An Evangelical Perspective on Authority," 11.

they themselves might not have been completely aware.[1] Such a "plentitude of meaning *(sensus plenior)*"[2] where the content of revelation is not self-evident in the words of Scripture, "but must be given by the Spirit of God,"[3] appears to resemble an allegorical use of Scripture.[4] Thus, it is not surprising that Bloesch approvingly quotes a number of authors who have used some form of allegorical method.[5]

Another aspect of Bloesch's use of Scripture also needs to be mentioned. In his recent writings especially, Bloesch has repeatedly emphasized that we do not read and use the Bible apart from the church.[6] If that were done, "we would end in the morass of a certain kind of fundamentalism or narrow biblicism."[7] Through this new

---

[1] Bloesch, **HSRII**, 175.

[2] Ibid., 176.

[3] Bloesch, "An Evangelical Perspective on Authority," 8.

[4] Bloesch also speaks of a "typological" or "spiritualizing" exegesis of Biblical writers (**HSRII**, 184). Cf. also Bloesch's exposition of some Biblical texts in idem, "A Christological Hermeneutics," 86-98. There he comments, for instance, on Gen 3:14-15 by saying that "our task is to discover not only the intent of the author but also the way in which the Spirit uses this text to reveal the saving work of Jesus Christ" (ibid., 87). On Gen 4:1-16, he writes: "The deepest christological significance of this story is that God's grace covers the sins of all people. . . . Unlike fundamentalist scholars whose primary concern is the historical veracity of this story rather than its christological significance, I am not troubled that the author employs a poetic narrative to convey deeper truth. . . . The intention of the author is not to convey factual information on the first murder but instead to show how murder is endemic to sin and how grace is available even to the worst of sinners" (ibid., 88-89).

[5] Bloesch mentions, among other things, a number of famous church fathers and medieval theologians like John Chrysostom, Origen, John Cassian, Augustine, Thomas Aquinas, and Nicholas of Lyra (**HSRII**, 184-186). Even the Protestant Reformers, who were highly critical of the tendency to read into the text some higher or mystical meaning, according to Bloesch, did not remain with the "natural meaning, but proceeded to give a theological treatment of the Old Testament text, which generally consisted in assessing its Christological significance" (ibid., 186). It can be questioned whether Bloesch gives an adequate picture of the Protestant Reformers on this point, especially in light of their insistence on the natural meaning of the text in contrast to any allegorical interpretation. On Luther's critical stance towards the allegorical method of his day, see Gerhard Ebeling, **Evangelische Evangelienauslegung: Eine Untersuchung zu Luthers Hermeneutik** (Darmstadt: Wissenschaftliche Buchgesellschaft, 1962); idem, "The Significance of the Critical Historical Method for Church and Theology in Protestantism," in Gerhard Ebeling, **Word and Faith**, trans. James W. Leitch (Philadelphia: Fortress Press, 1963), 17-61; Friedrich Beisser, **Claritas Scripturae**, 37-54. A similar critical stance towards allegory can be seen in John Calvin (Armour, 172-214).

[6] Bloesch, "An Evangelical Perspective on Authority," 5-6.

[7] Bloesch, **TWS**, 193; idem, "An Evangelical Perspective on Authority," 6. Bloesch has called us to look, by all means, "to the Bible **and** to the confessions, even to theological systems of the past, for indications of God's will and purpose for ourselves and for the world . . ." (ibid., 256), (emphasis supplied). Cf. also ibid., 124.

emphasis on the importance of the church, Bloesch has opted for a "confessional theology that witnesses to the claims of the gospel as presented in Scripture **and** church tradition,"[1] thereby implying that the authority of Scripture and the authority of the church are interrelated.[2] Even though the Bible alone is a supreme norm,[3] this norm is not effective apart from the church.[4] As early as 1964, Bloesch could write that

> when one has the Bible alone apart from the church, one is reading the Bible through the eyes of the culture. As evangelical Christians, we desire a biblically-oriented faith but not biblicism, which means to equate the Bible with revelation and to interpret the Bible apart from the exegetical and theological helps of the past and present.[5]

Although Bloesch does not want to subordinate Scripture to the church, his writings tend to give the impression that tradition is "to be respected and honored"[6] in such a manner that, at times, a continuation with the whole church throughout the ages is sought more than a reformation of the church.[7] The "attempt to form an amalgam

---

[1] Ibid., 267, (emphasis supplied). It seems that Bloesch uses the terms "church" and "tradition" interchangeably. A typical example is found in **HSRII**, 155: "Just as the Bible is over the church, so we must assert the other side of the dialectic: the Bible properly belongs within the church. The Bible cannot function apart from church tradition. . . . The relationship between Christ (the living Word), the Bible and the church (tradition) might be expressed by the following diagram: Jesus Christ is the center, the inner circle represents the Bible, the wider circle the tradition. In a sense the tradition includes all, but its center and norm is Jesus Christ alone, the Christ attested in Scripture."

[2] Bloesch, "An Evangelical Perspective on Authority," 5-6. Earlier Bloesch wrote that "the 'Protestant principle' needs to be united with 'catholic substance' if the church is to maintain continuity with the world wide apostolic tradition" ("The New Evangelicalism," 334).

[3] It is only "a" supreme norm, i.e., it is one norm among others but it is not **the** supreme norm, which is Jesus Christ for Bloesch.

[4] Bloesch, **HSRII**, 156; idem, "An Evangelical Perspective on Authority," 5.

[5] Bloesch, **Theological Notebook**, 1:163.

[6] Bloesch, **HSRII**, 151.

[7] Bloesch writes that a renewed evangelical theology is "catholic in the sense that it will be universal in its outreach and stand in continuity with the tradition of the whole church. It will draw on the theological commentary on Scripture in the church through the ages. The Reformers appealed not only to Scripture but also to the church fathers in support of their theses. In addition, a renewed theology will be Reformed. First, it will be anchored in the Protestant Reformation. . . . Second, it will see itself as always being reformed in the light of the Word of God" (**TWS**, 124-125). Note that Bloesch mentions first the continuation with tradition and only second the reformation according to the Word of God (i.e., Jesus Christ?). Earlier Bloesch wrote: "What are the hallmarks of a true confession of faith? Certainly it will be intent with the historic catholic faith. It will seek not to be innovative but interpretative of the tradition" (idem, "The Need for a Confessional Church Today," 11). Also: "The 'Protestant principle' needs to be united with 'catholic substance' if the church is to maintain continuity with the worldwide apostolic tradition" (idem, "The New Evangelicalism," 334). Concerning ethics, he proposes that norms are derived

between an evangelical 'heart piety' and a more broadly based and ecclesiastically centered tradition" has been criticized by others for not doing justice to all that Scripture affirms and teaches[1] and, in effect, seems to dissolve the Scripture principle of the Protestant Reformation.

The above considerations point out how Bloesch proposes to use Scripture; now it is time to briefly consider how he thinks Scripture should not be used.

How Scripture Is Not Used

From the investigation above, it is obvious that Bloesch's functional Christological-pneumatic approach to Scripture ultimately does not allow him to use Scripture as the final norm and authority for theology. Instead of Scripture, Jesus Christ is accepted as the final norm and apex of Scripture which only testifies to Him. Scripture is authoritative only as it partakes in and conveys the gospel of Jesus Christ. This means that Bloesch does not use Scripture as the starting point of his theology. He does not begin with Scripture as historical text to construct his theology; he begins with the living Christ as mediated through the Holy Spirit.[2] The genesis of his theology is the living Word of God, Jesus Christ. Yet, Christ is intricately bound up with the testimony of Scripture and should not be separated from it. Because Scripture testifies to God's special revelation in Jesus Christ and also, in a mystical way, contains it,[3] Scripture is more than just an ordinary book for Bloesch.

Yet, Bloesch does not use Scripture in a manner where its authority is based on its divine perfection in all it affirms and touches upon.[4] This is the result of a metaphysical deductive use of Scripture which he opposes. He also rejects an existentialistic use of Scripture.[5] Yet, there exists in his use of Scripture a definite

---

from "a wrestling with Scripture and the wisdom of Church tradition" (idem, **Freedom for Obedience**, 60, 191, 200).

[1]Cf. Wells, "Reservations about Catholic Renewal in Evangelicalism," 213.

[2]Cf. Bloesch, **TWS**, 118.

[3]"The revelation of God comes to us in the form not of logical axioms but of paradox and mystery. Yet this is not sheer mystery (as in mysticism) for meaning shines through mystery (Reinhold Niebuhr)" (Bloesch, "An Evangelical Perspective on Authority," 10).

[4]Bloesch, **HSRII**, 78.

[5]Although Bloesch's approach has an existential dimension, where the significance of the theological meaning of Scripture has to be personally appropriated, Bloesch resists an

existentialistic dimension. He believes that humans can know God partially, but truly when they are known by God in the event of the awakening to faith.[1] Thus, "because dogma speaks to the human heart as well as the human mind, it is best described as a propositional-existential truth."[2]

Further, his distinction between the formal and the material norm indicates that he does not use Scripture in the strict sense of *sola* Scriptura. For him Scripture is not the only source of revelation. It is only the original and primary witness to revelation.[3] Hence, Scripture is ultimately not used as its own interpreter (*scriptura scripturae interpres*). Rather, it is interpreted in light of its material center and unifying content, Jesus Christ. This means, however, that Scripture in and of itself is not sufficiently clear to function as the sole source of its own exposition,[4] which effectively compromises the sufficiency of Scripture and thereby challenges the *sola scriptura* principle. Furthermore, because no one-to-one identity exists between the words of Scripture and revelation,[5] the Bible cannot be used as a direct source book for doctrine and ethics.

In order to find out why Bloesch reaches some of his conclusions on the role of Scripture, one must investigate and an analyse some important presuppositions that seem to have influenced Bloesch's concept of Scripture.

An Analysis of Presuppositions Which Influence Bloesch's Concept of Scripture

In order to better understand why Bloesch is led to certain conclusions about his understanding of Scripture and why he argues in a particular way requires one to investigate some of his theological presuppositions and their consequences for his theology. This study first explores his understanding of God as it relates to and

---

existentialistic approach where history is dissolved into the historicity of existence ("A Christological Hermeneutic," 80-81).

[1] Bloesch, **The Battle for the Trinity**, 63.

[2] Bloesch, **TWS**, 274, n. 9.

[3] Ibid., 126. "The Bible is unique because it was written by eye-witnesses and ear-witnesses of revelation. The period of original revelation closes with the death of the last apostle or eye-witness" (idem, **Theological Notebook**, 1:63).

[4] "*Sola scriptura* is therefore the formal affirmation of the position that the Holy Scriptures are the sole source of their own interpretation" (Ebeling, "'Sola Scriptura' and Tradition," 127).

[5] Bloesch, "An Evangelical Perspective on Authority," 8.

influences his perception of Scripture. Then it concentrates on his anthropological presuppositions and, finally, considers the relationship between Word and Spirit and its impact on the role of Scripture in his thought.

Theological Presuppositions

As the writing of Bloesch's current systematic theology is still in process, the discussion of the doctrine of God has not yet received the same in-depth treatment as his understanding of Scripture.[1] For an analysis of his doctrine of God, therefore, one must rely primarily on his treatment in **Essentials of Evangelical Theology, The Battle for the Trinity**, as well as articles in journals and books.

Unfortunately, Bloesch has not yet presented his concept of God as comprehensively as is desired. As is his practice elsewhere, he presents his ideas and the survey of other positions that, at times, read more like a theological catalogue, where he affirms one particular view while rejecting another, without giving evidence of a clearly developed system according to which he organizes the material.[2] Nevertheless, a number of aspects in his concept of God stand out clearly and have repercussions for his understanding of Scripture.

Even a cursory reading of Bloesch's writings reveals a strong motif of the transcendence of God.[3] For him "biblical religion is distinguished from all forms of culture-religion in its affirmation of the utter transcendence of God."[4] Bloesch is adamant that a recovery of the concept of God's transcendence is needed in theology

---

[1] Bloesch is currently in the process of writing the third volume of his new systematic theology which deals with the doctrine of God. I had no access to the content of that forthcoming book.

[2] So the criticism by Stephen T. Franklin, "Review of **Essentials of Evangelical Theology**, Volumes 1 and 2, by Donald G. Bloesch," **JCQ** 48/4 (1982): 234; cf. also Richard Rice, "Review of **Essentials of Evangelical Theology**, volumes 1 and 2, by Donald G. Bloesch," **RSR** 7/2 (1981): 108. Anthony A. Hoekema, 85, has criticized along similar lines that although Bloesch makes copious references to the positions of other theologians and then gives his own view, the reader often "wishes that Bloesch had spent more time developing his own position and less time quoting or paraphrasing other authors."

[3] Cf. Bloesch, **The Battle for the Trinity**, 29-32. It has been noted that Bloesch's position "differs most basically with liberal theology on the level of cosmology, or ontology. The traditional concept of a supernatural realm which impinges on that of ordinary experience in various ways accounts for radical differences between the evangelical and liberal interpretations of every Christian doctrine . . . In particular, it accounts for the divergent attitudes toward the Bible which lead to contrasting concepts of the theological task" (Rice, "Review of **Essentials of Evangelical Theology**," 108).

[4] Bloesch, **EET**, 2:242.

today. Just like his theological mentor Karl Barth, Bloesch is aware of and repeatedly points to the qualitative difference between God and man. For him "the God of biblical faith transcends history"[1] and cannot be explained by historical analysis.[2] It is only by starting with God's self-revelation in Jesus Christ that theology can say anything about God.[3] Contrary to Process philosophy and Process theology, he maintains that God cannot be identified with the substance or reality of the world.[4]

This strong emphasis on the transcendent nature of God emphasizes that there exists no natural point of contact between God and man. For Bloesch, "it is crisis, not continuity, that is the hallmark of the biblical understanding of God."[5] Consequently, natural theology is strongly rejected because God lies beyond the confines of man's perception and conception.[6] What humans perceive is only the phenomenal world, not the noumenal which transcends the reach of human perception and imagination.[7] Although Bloesch is quick to affirm God's transcendence as well as His immanence, God "*is basically transcendent, whereas his immanence is a gift of grace to a fallen humanity.*"[8] The transcendent nature of God "infinitely transcends the principles and

---

[1] Bloesch, **HSRII**, 283.

[2] God "enters into history, but he is always hidden in events and actions that are illuminating only when his Spirit gives us inner eyes to see what cannot be seen directly" (ibid., 283; 289-290).

[3] God "is the One who remains hidden until he gives himself to be known in revelation" (Bloesch, **EET**, 1:25). Cf. the more recent statement: "I have been led to choose the way of Barth over that of Bultmann and Tillich because in the first I see a theology that begins with God's self-revelation in Christ rather than with the gropings and searchings of a despairing humanity" (idem, **HSRII**, 227-228; cf. idem, **TWS**, 59).

[4] Donald G. Bloesch, "Process Theology and Reformed Theology," in **Process Theology**, ed. Ronald Nash (Grand Rapids, MI: Baker Book House, 1987), 40. Elsewhere Bloesch has maintained that God "is the ruler and redeemer of the world process rather than subject to the process (as in neo-naturalism)" (idem, **EET**, 2:243). In light of Bloesch's strong opposition to process theology, it remains a mystery how John Paul Nyquist, 2, can claim that "Evangelical concessions to process thought in both the doctrines of God and the doctrine of Scriptures are evident in the writings of . . . Donald Bloesch . . . among others." In his whole dissertation, Bloesch is hardly ever quoted and when he is quoted, it is never in support of process thought.

[5] Bloesch, **EET**, 2:242. Clark H. Pinnock recently criticized Bloesch by pointing out that "Bloesch presses the point that confrontation, not correlation, is central to the engagement of theology with culture but may minimize the positive side of building bridges and finding points of contact" ("The Role of the Spirit in Interpretation," 497).

[6] Bloesch, **EET**, 1:26.

[7] Bloesch, **HSRII**, 75.

[8] Bloesch, **EET**, 2:244, (emphasis supplied). Similar ideas are present earlier: "He [God]

categories of human thought."[1] Natural reason cannot grasp the mystery of divine revelation.[2] Real, although not exhaustive, knowledge of God is not possible apart from faith.[3]

It has been pointed out that "one's understanding of God affects directly one's conception of the manner and process of the divine action in revelation and inspiration,"[4] which in turn influences one's understanding of Scripture. Therefore this study turns now to the crucial question of how God is supposed to act in time and space which impinges upon Bloesch's understanding of Scripture. The brevity with which he deals with this aspect does not provide much help, although a few statements seem to point in a certain direction. Quoting Karl Barth,[5] Bloesch affirms a spaciality and time in God. For Bloesch, "true eternity includes the potentiality of space and time."[6] God's eternity is not to be viewed as a negation of time as in Platonic and

---

is primarily and originally transcendent and secondarily and derivatively immanent" (idem, **The Battle for the Trinity**, 29). As early as 1966 he writes that "the god of deism is wholly transcendent. The god of pantheism is totally immanent. The god of panentheism is basically immanent, though open to transcendence. The god [sic] of Christian faith is basically transcendent, but he is also radically immanent" (idem, **Theological Notebook**, 2:119, 114).

[1]Bloesch, **TWS**, 41. Also: "The true God lies beyond the confines of man's perception and conception. He is to be sharply distinguished from the idols of man's vain imagination" (idem, **EET**, 1:26). Thus, although Bloesch acknowledges that God is "radically immanent," God is **ontologically** and **epistemologically** transcendent" (idem, **The Battle for the Trinity**, 30, (emphasis supplied).

[2]Bloesch, **HSRII**, 21; idem, "An Evangelical Perspective on Authority," 10; idem, **The Battle for the Trinity**, 20.

[3]Bloesch, **HSRII**, 19.

[4]Canale, "Revelation and Inspiration: The Ground for a New Approach," 92.

[5]Actually Karl Barth's understanding of eternity is somewhat complex. In a way, that is typical of Barth's "dialectical theology," he wants to say two things about divine eternity at the same time. On the one hand, Barth writes that "time has nothing to do with God" (**CD**, II/1, 608), on the other hand, he affirms that "even the eternal God does not live without time. He is supremely temporal" (**CD**, III/2, 437). For a helpful and concise discussion of Barth's concept of time and eternity, see Alan G. Padgett, **God, Eternity and the Nature of Time** (New York: St. Martin's Press, 1992), 141-146. According to Padgett, 143, "Barth refuses to define eternity as the antithesis of time, but instead argues that eternity is *the fullness of time without the defects of succession*. What is missing from eternity as God's time is the past-present-future distinction. . . . What Barth's doctrine does in effect is to call into question the reality of process." This conclusion seems to be supported by R. H. Roberts, "Karl Barth's Doctrine of Time: Its Nature and Implications," in **Karl Barth: Studies in His Theological Method**, ed. S. W. Sykes (Oxford: Clarendon Press, 1979), 88-146, and Colin Gunton, **Becoming and Being: The Doctrine of God in Charles Hartshorne and Karl Barth** (Oxford: Oxford University Press, 1978), 177-185.

[6]Bloesch, **EET**, 1:30. Note that it includes only the potentiality but not the actuality or reality of space and time.

neo-Platonic philosophy. It is not timelessness nor the endless duration of time, it is rather the "fulfillment of time."[1] Thus, God's eternity is His exaltation over time. Yet in his writings Bloesch has not yet committed himself to a precise and systematic exposition of the nature of God's eternity that is free of ambiguities.

Bloesch also writes that "revelation enters history, but it does not become bound to history. History is the vessel of Eternity **but not an aspect of Eternity.**"[2] Hence, God is "transhistorical."[3] Bloesch has also contrasted the "temporal order" with the "eternal order" saying that

> there is a chronology in both God's acts and man's responses, but God's time and man's time are not on the same level. Because of the qualitative difference between the two types of time (or between time and 'eternity'), the beginning of the plan of salvation is not to be located simply in the past, nor the consummation simply in the future. Rather, both the source and completion of the plan are to be located in God."[4]

When asked to clarify his position on this point, Bloesch repeated essentially the above position saying that God has His own history, and God's own history is not our history. Thus, there is still a qualitative distinction between God and humanity, just as God has His own time and space.[5] For Bloesch, God is not limited by the natural realm and is not part of the natural process.[6] In other words, "God becomes historical but in such a way that he remains the eternal. He is not an empirical datum in history. . . ."[7]

From these admittedly limited and perhaps preliminary statements by Bloesch, it appears that the concept of God's transcendence with its radical discontinuity rather than continuity between God and man, points to an understanding where time and history does not belong to ultimate reality but is seen as being only part of the human

---

[1]Ibid. Bloesch made reference to this also in a private interview (Bloesch, interview, 10 January 1994).

[2]Bloesch, **The Future of Evangelical Christianity**, 181, n. 26.

[3]Bloesch, **TWS**, 202.

[4]Donald G. Bloesch, **The Christian Life and Salvation** (Grand Rapids, MI: Eerdmans, 1967), 26. Cf. also his statement that "revelation enters into history, but it does not become bound to history. History is the vessel of Eternity but not an aspect of Eternity" (idem, **The Future of Evangelicalism**, 181, n. 26).

[5]Bloesch, interview, 10 January 1994.

[6]Ibid.; cf. idem, "Process Theology and Reformed Theology," 31-56.

[7]Bloesch, **HSRII**, 290.

condition.¹ Therefore, the cleavage between the divine and the human can be bridged only by a "paradoxical entry of eternity into time."² Thus, for Bloesch, the focus of faith appears to be "not on history as such, not even on biblical history, but on eternity breaking into history at a particular time and place."³ This has taken place most fully in the revelation of Jesus Christ, which makes the gospel the highest criterion for Bloesch's theology.

At the same time this ontological difference is probably the reason why the nature of human language, which is part of the historical-human realm, is symbolic or mythopoetic when it speaks about God,⁴ because God is part of the noumenal realm. Bloesch here seems to accept the Kantian dichotomy between the phenomenal world and the noumenal realm,⁵ thereby rejecting the notion that truth is a rational correspondence between the human mind and the mind of God.⁶ Thus, "the mystery

---

¹Recent studies have argued convincingly that the Biblical understanding of eternity is not timelessness but endless time. The idea of timelessness seems to be at home in Greek philosophy rather than in Biblical thought. Cf. Padgett, 23-37, and passim; Fernando Luis Canale, **A Criticism of Theological Reason: Time and Timelessness as Primordial Presuppositions**, AUSDDS 10 (Berrien Springs, MI: Andrews University Press, 1987). Oscar Cullmann's influential book, **Christ and Time: The Primitive Christian Conception of Time and History**, trans. Floyd V. Filson (Philadelphia: Westminster Press, 1950), remains the single most important book on this subject. Cullmann has been criticized by James Barr (**Biblical Words for Time**, 2d rev. ed. [Naperville, IL: Alec R. Allenson, 1969], 50-85) for over-emphasizing the difference between *kairos* and *chronos*. Yet, the force of his argument, that the New Testament knows nothing of a timeless eternity, remains intact (Padgett, 30).

²Bloesch, **TWS**, 76. Quoting Brunner he affirms the "contradictory truth that the eternal God enters time" (ibid., 77). More recently, he wrote: "The truth of God is not a timeless idea nor a wholly temporal event but the paradox of the eternal breaking into time. The truth of faith is both an event of the superhistorical entering time and a metaphysical presupposition that directs out reflection on this event. This presupposition is not at our disposal, however, but is available to us only as we go forward in obedience and faith. It is a truth that is grasped only in the passion of inwardness and is therefore not generally accessible to human understanding" (idem, **HSRII**, 290).

³Bloesch, **TWS**, 42; idem, **HSRII**, 264.

⁴Bloesch, **HSRII**, 121-122, 259, 265, 274; idem, **TWS**, 70; idem, **The Battle for the Trinity**, 13-28.

⁵Bloesch bemoans that modern Fundamentalism "has yet to come to terms with Kant's insightful observation that human reason by itself can yield knowledge only of the phenomenal world, not of the noumenal realm, which concerns God, freedom and immortality" (**TWS**, 254-255).

⁶Cf. Gruenler, 36. Bloesch repeatedly has stated that in his understanding, the object of faith is beyond criticism. "Historical criticism pertains only to the form, not to the divine content (*Sache*), of the Bible" (**HSRII**, 205). Gruenler has pointed out that "the biblical interpreter who accepts the Kantian dichotomy will confine religious experience to the domain of personal,

of revealed truth is not encapsulated in any human language, not even the language of sacred Scripture,"¹ but is bestowed as a gift by the Holy Spirit.² This explains why for Bloesch Scripture cannot be a direct source book for revealed truth.³ It also indicates the need for Bloesch's emphasis on the Holy Spirit.⁴ The Spirit is the divine agent by whose action the gap between the transcendent God and the reader of Scripture is bridged. It is the Spirit who makes the Bible efficacious⁵ by somehow clarifying things left unclear in the text itself because of the inadequacy of all human language.⁶ Thus, the Spirit becomes the giver of a theological meaning that is

---

transcendental faith (which cannot be touched by historical criticism) and confine the historical-critical method to analysis of natural cause and effect without recourse to matters of faith and supernatural revelation" (ibid., 38). This would certainly apply to Bloesch for whom "faith lies beyond criticism" (**HSRII**, 203).

¹Bloesch, **TWS**, 75; Bloesch thinks that Biblical propositions inevitably fall short of the truth they want to express (ibid., 104).

²Ibid., 75; idem, **HSRII**, 114, 206. Natural reason cannot grasp the mystery of divine revelation (ibid., 21).

³"I do not share the vision of much traditional orthodoxy that the Bible is impregnated with universal, unchanging truths that are waiting to be discovered and formulated" (Bloesch, **HSRII**, 207). "It is inadmissible to treat the Bible as though it were a source book of revealed truths that can be drawn out of Scripture by deductive or inductive logic. The truth of the Bible can only be known as the Spirit makes it known in the event of revelation, yet even here there is no direct perception of truth but only a submission and reception which are adequate for salvation but not for comprehension. The truth in the Bible is enveloped in mystery and therefore can only be dimly perceived (1 Cor. 13:9, 12). Indeed mystery and revelation often seem to go together (cf. Mark 13:11; 1 Cor. 2:7; Rom. 16:25). This does not mean that the Word of God is basically unknowable but that it cannot be known exhaustively and that it remains mysterious even to faithful reason (Rom. 11:33)" (idem, **EET**, 1:69-70).

⁴The writings of Bloesch reveal clearly that he assigns the Holy Spirit an important role in his understanding of Scripture. Donald A. D. Thorsen bemoans that Bloesch wrote the two-volume work **EET** without explicitly devoting a single chapter to the doctrine of the Holy Spirit (**The Wesleyan Quadrilateral: Scripture, Tradition, Reason, and Experience as a Model of Evangelical Theology** [Grand Rapids, MI: Zondervan Publishing House, 1990], 250). It seems, however, that in his later writings, Bloesch brings the role of the Spirit more to the forefront than he did earlier. Thus, already the title of his new systematic theology points to the importance of the Spirit in his theology: **A Theology of Word and Spirit: Authority and Method in Theology**. In fairness to Bloesch, it should be pointed out, however, that one can find significant references to the Holy Spirit already in his earlier writings. See for instance the numerous references in the index in **EET**, s.v. "Holy Spirit," in **EET**, 1:263, and **EET**, 2:312.

⁵Bloesch, **TWS**, 13, 14.

⁶For Bloesch, "the capacity of the human language to bear meaning lies in the action of the Spirit of God who opens the inner eyes of faith to the significance of what God has done for us in Christ" (**TWS**, 73). Thus, "the truth of the gospel must finally be taught to us by the Spirit of God himself" (ibid., 24). In other words, "the meaning of a biblical text is revealed only in the act of disclosure between the ultimate author, the Holy Spirit, and the reader or hearer who comes

ultimately independent from the (historical) text of Scripture.¹ Such a stance closely resembles a pneumatic use of Scripture.²

Bloesch also affirms the personal nature of God.³ In harmony with such a personal dimension of God, he sees revelation as having both a conceptual and a personal dimension. The personal aspect of revelation, however, definitely has priority over the conceptual for Bloesch thinks that religious language was originally symbolic and only "brokenly reflects what it is intended to signify."⁴ This skepticism with regards to the capability of the human language to speak adequately about God seems to be adopted by Bloesch from neo-orthodox theology,⁵ although Bloesch is willing to

---

to the Scriptures in faith. Meaning in this ultimate sense is therefore a gift, not an achievement" (ibid., 103). Kurt E. Marquart, in a manner that is characteristic for the Lutheran tradition, thinks that "there can be no appeal to the Spirit *from* the biblical text, as though He needed to supply missing arguments, but only an appeal to Him *in* the text that He Himself has given. We are left, then, finally with the inspired text itself. It can and must alone (*sola scriptura*) adjudicate the basic issues of hermeneutics" ("A Response to Adequacy of Language and Accommodation," in **Hermeneutics, Inerrancy, and the Bible**, ed. Earl D. Radmacher and Robert D. Preus [Grand Rapids, MI: Zondervan Publishing House, 1984], 402); see also Christian Gremmels, "Der Heilige Geist als Ausleger der Schrift," in **Sola Scriptura: Ringvorlesung der theologischen Fakultät der Philipps-Universität**, ed. Carl-Heinz Ratschow (Marburg: N. G. Elwert Verlag, 1977), 153-177.

¹Bloesch displays here some similarities to Karl Barth who also stressed the inadequacy of human language and, instead, recurred to an actualistic understanding of revelation. Cf. Gordon H. Clark, **Karl Barth's Theological Method** (Philadelphia, PA: Presbyterian and Reformed Publishing Company, 1963), 136-145; and Runia, 196-209.

²Bloesch himself calls his approach "a historical-pneumatic hermeneutics" (**HSRII**, 206, 207), because "the revelatory meaning of the text cannot be produced by any technique, including existential analysis. It can only be conveyed by the action of the Spirit upon the text and within our hearts" (idem, "A Christological Hermeneutics," 100). Hence, "Christ himself is the final interpreter of Scripture" because "he tells us through his Spirit what Scripture says" (idem, **HSRII**, 206). This is necessary because "at times a simple historical reconstruction of the text may falsify the overall message of the Bible" (ibid., 342, n. 103). On the pneumatic interpretation of Scripture, see the discussion in Gerhard Maier, **Heiliger Geist und Schriftauslegung**, TuD 34 (Wuppertal: R. Brockhaus, 1983), 21-29; idem, **Biblische Hermeneutik**, 37-52; Stadelmann, 78-82; F. L. Arrington, "Hermeneutics, Historical Perspectives on Pentecostal and Charismatic," in **Dictionary of Pentecostal and Charismatic Movements**, ed. Stanley M. Burgess and Gary B. McGee (Grand Rapids, MI: Zondervan Publishing House, 1988), 376-389, especially 382-384; and Friedrich Mildenberger, **Biblische Dogmatik: Eine Biblische Theologie in dogmatischer Perspektive**, 3 vols. (Stuttgart: W. Kohlhammer, 1991-1993), 1:48, n. 48.

³Bloesch, **The Battle for the Trinity**, 30.

⁴Ibid., 17. Hence, "the meaning of a symbol can only be intuitively grasped" (ibid.); and idem, **HSRII**, 121.

⁵Cf. Karl Barth, **CD**, II/1, 188. It has been pointed out that for Barth the inadequacy of human language is related to his view of God's radical transcendence (Paul D. Feinberg, "A Response to Adequacy of Language and Accommodation," in **Hermeneutics, Inerrancy, and the**

allow for some reliable communication, at least as far as the salvific content of the gospel of Jesus Christ is concerned. Because revelation is limited to the self-revelation of God in and through Jesus Christ, true knowledge of God can come only through Jesus Christ, who is the apex and center of revelation.

In addition to the above discussed theological presuppositions, Bloesch also has a number of anthropological presuppositions that impact his understanding of Scripture; therefore they need to be explored more fully.

Anthropological Presuppositions

One dominant idea that runs through Bloesch's theology is the qualitative difference between man and God. Following his theological mentor Karl Barth, Bloesch affirms that there exists no natural point of contact between man and God. The concept of God as a transcendent being, together with the affirmation of man's total depravity,[1] prohibits Bloesch to affirm any natural disposition or inclination toward God in sinful man, at least on the rational-cognitive level. It is helpful here to concentrate on a couple of different aspects that are present in Bloesch's thought.

Building on the idea of the total depravity of humankind, Bloesch affirms that "there is no longer any way from man to God, since sin has blinded man's perception as well as shackled his will."[2] Part of the manifestation and consequence of sin is a "spiritual blindness"[3] as well as "the impairment of man's reasoning" powers.[4] In other words, man's depravity has negative epistemological side effects because sin has "serious noetic implications"[5] that blind humankind to the truth about God[6] so that man no longer can come to a valid knowledge of God on his own.[7] From these

---

Bible, ed. by Earl D. Radmacher and Robert D. Preus [Grand Rapids, MI: Zondervan Publishing House, 1984], 385-386).

[1]Bloesch, **EET**, 1:88-119.

[2]Ibid., 1:89.

[3]Ibid., 1:98.

[4]Ibid., 1:101.

[5]Ibid.

[6]Ibid., 1:102.

[7]"Prior to faith our reasoning is distorted by sin" (Bloesch, **TWS**, 58). "Because of sin, our inward eyes are blinded to the objective glory of God reflected in nature. . . . The natural knowledge of God is sufficient neither for a valid understanding nor for salvation but only for

statements, it is clear that Bloesch opposes natural theology[1] and calls for a return to divine revelation which gives a knowledge of personal acquaintance.[2]

In addition to humankind's sinfulness, with its restrictions on human knowledge and cognition, another aspect seems to be present in Bloesch's thought that influences his understanding of human language. It appears that Bloesch also holds to an ontological difference between God and man that may account for his view of the inadequacy of all human language to perfectly describe divine realities. Inasmuch as the Biblical languages share in the limitations of all human languages, Holy Scripture also reflects a diastasis between the original Word of God and its witness in the written text.[3] Thus, "the human words and concepts employed by the Holy Spirit in the formation of the Scriptures fall short of bringing us univocal knowledge of God . . ."[4] Instead they are for the most part "symbolic"[5] or "mythopoetic."[6] It seems that Bloesch arrives at such a view of the limitation of human language in describing divine realities because he accepts Kant's distinction between the phenomenal world and the noumenal realm.[7] Since human language is not part of the divine realm, it suffers a diffraction whereby it reflects a diastasis between the original Word of God and its witness to Him in the written text. Yet, Bloesch affirms that humankind can have a

---

condemnation" (idem, **The Future of Evangelical Christianity**, 121). With this position, Bloesch stands in sharp contrast to some Evangelical thinkers like Carl F. H. Henry, who not only believes God's revelation is essentially rational or cognitive, but also maintains that sin did not destroy the categories of human reason and that the rational capacity of man was not affected by the fall (Walter E. Johnson, "A Critical Analysis of the Nature and Function of Reason in the Theology of Carl F. H. Henry" [Th.D. dissertation, New Orleans Baptist Theological Seminary, 1989], 225, and passim); for an analysis of Evangelical rationalism, see also Gier, **God, Reason, and the Evangelicals**.

[1]". . . we must steer clear of any natural theology that supposes valid knowledge of God on the basis of this general light in creation" (Bloesch, **The Future of Evangelical Christianity**, 121).

[2]Bloesch, **TWS**, 178. "In place of a natural theology, in which the knowledge of God is based on what we can discover on our own through reason and nature, I propose a theology of creation, in which we analyze nature and conscience in the light of God's self-revelation in Jesus Christ" (ibid., 173).

[3]"Even the language of . . . the Bible is not exempt from the crisis of the limitation of all human language in conveying real knowledge of God" (ibid., 69).

[4]Ibid., 81.

[5]Ibid., 70-71; idem, **The Battle for the Trinity**, 20-27.

[6]Bloesch, **TWS**, 70; idem, **HSRII**, 259, 265, 274.

[7]Cf. Bloesch, **TWS**, 254-255.

real knowledge of God and His saving purpose that goes beyond the unknowability of God that is bound up with Kant's philosophy.¹

Bloesch seems to allow for some form of "contact" where a valid knowledge of God can be gained through the work of the Holy Spirit. Here theological and anthropological presuppositions more or less merge into one. This "point of contact" is not natural; it is initiated and made possible by God alone through His Spirit and, thus, is always a divine gift.² That way Bloesch safeguards his premise that "there is no material point of contact, that is, a power of light resident in humanity that enables us to apprehend the truth that God reveals to us."³ The Spirit "implants faith within us, thereby enabling us to understand and believe."⁴ Through this "pneumatic dimension"⁵ in which the Spirit of God imparts wisdom, man is made a partaker of God's redeeming action in this world.⁶ In other words, through the work of the Holy Spirit, faith is created within man that makes it possible to attain a direct intuition of the truth as it is in Jesus and to come to a knowledge of the transcendent God. Yet, this truth cannot be expressed in human language which belongs to a different realm. Scripture, then, which does not belong to the divine realm shares in the same limitations as all human language, even though it it is used by God to point to Jesus Christ, and even though God is not necessarily bound to the text of Scripture in revealing His will.⁷

Just as Bloesch affirms a sacramental understanding of Scripture, where Scripture cannot function as the Word of God without the Spirit and its theological meaning could not be discerned without the work of the Spirit, so Bloesch sees the

---

¹Karl-Heinz Michel, **Immanuel Kant und die Frage der Erkennbarkeit Gottes**, 220-248; idem, "Erkenntnis und Idee Gottes in der Philosophie Immanuel Kants," 107-119; and idem, "Kants Vernunftkritik und ihre Folgen für die Theologie," 370-375.

²Bloesch, **HSRII**, 76.

³Ibid.

⁴Ibid.

⁵Bloesch, **The Battle for the Trinity**, 66.

⁶Bloesch, **HSRII**, 191.

⁷According to Bloesch, "faith is discriminating. It distinguishes between the kernel and the husk, what is central and what is peripheral in the Bible" (**HSRII**, 204), for "faith is not directed to the text but to the living Christ to whom the text points" (ibid., 203). "At times a simple historical reconstruction of the text may falsify the overall message of the Bible" (ibid., 342, n. 103).

Spirit as the decisive agent that makes possible a knowledge of Christ in the believer that otherwise would not be possible. Hence, the human element is subsumed under the divine, giving the Holy Spirit ultimate priority in providing a knowledge of God as well as providing a correct interpretation of Scripture. At one place, Bloesch has called the close interpenetration of the Word with the Spirit and the participation of the believer in the transcendent Word of God through the Spirit "an immanentism of the Holy Spirit."[1]

Conclusion

The discussion about the role of Scripture, especially in Evangelical theology, has received new impulses from the work of Donald Bloesch. His concern about the erosion of Biblical authority in contemporary theology has led him to affirm the centrality of the Word of God in theology. In his understanding of Scripture, he distances himself not only from Liberalism, and to some degree from Neo-Orthodoxy, but also from rationalistic Fundamentalism. By reacting to and interacting with contrasting positions, Bloesch has attempted to avoid their pitfalls. With his irenic spirit, he consistently tries to build bridges by incorporating insights gained from either side of the debate. Despite a wide recognition of Bloesch's significance and his impact (especially on Evangelical theology), discussions of his position (particularly his position on Scripture) are generally brief and rather limited in scope.

Bloesch is to be commended for his high respect of Scripture and his genuine desire to uphold its special status in the church. He is one of few recent Evangelical theologians who have seriously reflected on the role of the Holy Spirit. Bloesch has provided a discussion of the Holy Spirit as it impinges upon the process of the origin of Holy Scripture as well as in its application to the life and experience of the believer. Moreover, the work of the Holy Spirit is crucially important for Bloesch's sacramental understanding of Scripture. It is only the Holy Spirit who brings out the theological meaning of Scripture, a meaning that is not available through a historical-critical investigation of the Biblical text and, in fact, seemingly at times to be independent from

---

[1] Bloesch, "The New Evangelicalism," 332. It seems that through this pneumatic dimension "all people have an immediate awareness of God in that God may and does speak to people in a direct as well as indirect manner" (idem, **TWS**, 50). It has been pointed out that "Barthian theology elevated the long neglected role of the Holy Spirit to new significance in its exposition of divine revelation" (Henry, **God, Revelation, and Authority**, 4:256). Bloesch certainly follows this route that Barth had begun.

it. Through the Holy Spirit who originates faith in man, the believer is able to perceive the theological meaning of Scripture that is not readily available in the text itself nor through historical investigation. It might very well be that Bloesch's emphasis on the importance of the Holy Spirit for Holy Scripture and theology sends an important signal for the need of a renewed reflection of the relationship between Scripture and Spirit.

In a time when Evangelical theology is being criticized for not having "adequately explained the dynamics between the use of reason and the noetic effects of the fall,"[1] and theologians across the theological spectrum have elevated logic above God and personal encounter to a point where rationalistic criteria determine the truthfulness of theological assertions, Bloesch stands out with a different perspective.[2] He has repeatedly pointed to the limited use of fallen, unregenerate human reason in arriving at a valid knowledge of God. Taking seriously the noetic effects of sin, Bloesch's emphasis on God's transcendence and the qualitative difference between God and man has taken up a significant theme of Scripture that has been marginalized in much of modern theology. The acceptance of a strong view of God's transcendence ultimately leads Bloesch to reaffirm the epistemological priority of special revelation as testified to in Scripture which is construed to include a propositional element.

It is obvious that Bloesch has developed an understanding of Scripture "from above," one that takes into consideration a supernatural dimension. With classical Protestant theology but in opposition to Liberal theology and even Neo-Orthodoxy, Bloesch maintains that a conceptual content is supernaturally originated and given by God to man in faith.[3] He also affirms the guidance of the Biblical writers by the Holy Spirit in the transmission of this salvific message. Thus, the nature of Scripture encompasses more than being a purely historical document like any other human book.

Despite the sincerity of Bloesch's effort to maintain or regain a view of Scripture that functions authoritatively and that allows for the revelation of a special content, his attempt to do so raises a number of questions that are explored in the following chapter. It appears that "on the important issue of scriptural authority Bloesch

---

[1]James Emery White, 270.

[2]It has been noted that on this point Bloesch represents a view that is somewhat out of line with mainstream Evangelical theology (ibid., 256-257, n. 6).

[3]"Bloesch wishes clearly to distinguish his position from all 'non-cognitive' views of revelation. While revelation is not primarily propositional, it does have cognitive import and significance" (Olson, "Review of **Essentials of Evangelical Theology**," 86).

repeatedly takes away with one hand what he wants to maintain with the other."[1] Bloesch, for instance, wants to maintain the authority of Scripture as well as its human limitations. These limitations, however, and the cultural conditioning of Scripture affect even theological points. This has implications for his understanding of the nature of Scripture. Bloesch's sacramental view of Scripture eventually leads him to a position where the nature of Scripture is seen in functional terms. Scripture in and of itself is not enough for theology. This raises the question of theological authority. For Bloesch, the Holy Spirit ultimately becomes the highest norm and final authority whereby everything else, including Scripture, must be tested. Consequently, the infallible standard and norm is not Scripture in and of itself but the Spirit who is united with the Bible and testifies to the gospel of Jesus Christ.

It seems that a fundamental issue that is not satisfactorily solved by Bloesch is the relationship between the divine and human aspect of Scripture and its implications for theology. One can clearly detect a tension, if not a discrepancy, in his concept of Scripture that is raised by his desire to uphold a divine aspect of the Bible as foundational for theology and by his simultaneous employment of the historical-critical investigation of Scripture.[2] It seems that the implications and consequences of the

---

[1] Bob Price, "Review of **Essentials of Evangelical Theology**," 57.

[2] The question needs to be raised whether critical methods and conclusions, as used by Bloesch, are free from bias or can be used in a "modified form?" Here the famous proposal of a "hermeneutics of consent" by Peter Stuhlmacher comes to mind, where Stuhlmacher calls for a new listening to the claims of tradition in addition to and beyond the historical critical method (**Historical Criticism and Theological Interpretation of Scripture: Towards a Hermeneutics of Consent**, trans. Roy A. Harrisville [Philadelphia: Fortress Press, 1977], 83-87; and idem, **Vom Verstehen des Neuen Testaments: Eine Hermeneutik**, 2d rev. and enl. ed. [Göttingen: Vandenhoeck & Ruprecht, 1986], 222-256). Stuhlmacher has drawn a lot of criticism on his fourth principle of "consent," and its compatibility with the other three principles of historical-criticism and appears to have abandoned it again in his latest writings. In his recent tome **Biblische Theologie des Neuen Testaments**, vol. 1, **Grundlegung von Jesus zu Paulus** (Göttingen: Vandenhoeck & Ruprecht, 1992), 10, he affirms that "there is only one scientifically proven method available [for exegesis], [that is] the historical-critical method used by all historical sciences. In its usage it consists of a whole ensemble of single methods, which are integrated in a process of totality which follows certain principles. Ernst Troeltsch called them 'criticism', 'analogy' and 'correlation'." On Stuhlmacher's hermeneutical approach, see the unpublished dissertation by Christian Stawenow, "Historische und Geistliche Hermeneutik bei Peter Stuhlmacher. Eine Untersuchung seines Entwurfes einer 'Hermeneutik des Einverständnisses' hinsichtlich der von ihm selbst benannten hermeneutik-geschichtlichen Voraussetzungen" (Th.D. dissertation, Kirchliches Oberseminar, Naumburg, 1986). Lutheran systematic theologian Ted Peters has pointed out that the "very structure of historical criticism undermines the scripture principle. The Bible cannot serve as authority for one whose very method of interpretation presupposes alienation from its message" ("Sola Scriptura and the Second Naivete," **Dialog** 16 [1977]: 273).

historical-critical method and the relationship between Scripture and theology, between Biblical theology and systematic theology, are not adequately developed by Bloesch. This problematic relationship is hinted at when he writes that "Biblical study, however valuable in its own right, cannot replace theology, which involves both the exposition of the biblical text and its application to the modern world."[1] This indicates that Bloesch lives with an approach to Scripture that conflicts with other aspects that he tries to uphold. The final chapter returns to the questions raised here.

---

[1]Bloesch, **TWS**, 111.

CHAPTER V

EVALUATION AND CONCLUSION

Introductory Remarks

The previous discussion has sought to provide a clearer comprehension of the role of Scripture in Pannenberg's and Bloesch's theologies as well as a discussion of important presuppositions and assumptions that are at the foundation of their respective understandings of Scripture. Only after a careful delineation of Pannenberg's and Bloesch's understanding of Scripture has been provided, as attempted in chapters 3 and 4, is it possible to venture into an effective comparison and evaluation of their respective positions.

Thus, the purpose of this chapter is to compare and evaluate Pannenberg's and Bloesch's views of Scripture and to close with a few suggestions for the role of Scripture in systematic theology. For the sake of greater clarity, I first look at the contrast between the two authors, as far as their understanding of the origin, nature, and use of Scripture are concerned, before I compare similarities between the two. In the second part of the chapter, I will then evaluate their views primarily on the basis of their inner consistency or inconsistency. In other words, the criticisms made of each position are intended as internal criticisms.[1] They deal with the relation of the actual procedure employed to the avowed method, the internal consistency of the method, as well as the kinds of ultimate assumptions upon which the whole position rests. This kind of analysis and evaluation should help to point out implications of their approaches. A brief outlook on what remains to be done concludes the chapter.

Pannenberg's and Bloesch's Concept of Scripture
A Comparison

From what we have seen so far, there seems to be a definite relationship between Pannenberg's and Bloesch's understanding of the origin and nature of Scripture and the role it plays in their theologies.[2] Their answers to the question of

---

[1] Cf. John B. Cobb, Jr., **Living Options in Protestant Theology: A Survey of Methods** (Philadelphia: Westminster Press, 1962), 14.

[2] This observation stands in contrast to James Barr's thesis that the question of the origins of the Bible is "actually of marginal theological importance" (**The Bible in the Modern World**,

the origin of Scripture seems to determine, to a considerable extent, their notions of the nature of Scripture, which in turn has ramifications for their use of Scripture.

The Origin of Scripture

The question of the origin of Scripture is an area where one can detect some of the most significant differences between Pannenberg and Bloesch. The decision about the elementary Christian doctrine of revelation and inspiration, which itself is influenced by extra-Scriptural assumptions, shapes their formulations concerning the nature of the Bible.[1] Pannenberg is clearly a modern theologian[2] who operates within the Enlightenment tradition with its rejection of all external authority and dismissal of supernatural revelation. He believes in the power of reason to conceive a unified whole. For him the origin of Scripture is seen "from below." Posting a universal religious disposition of man towards the infinite, the cognitive contents of Scripture ultimately originate from human imagination which makes anthropology foundational for theology in general, and, for the origin of Scripture in particular. In other words, the Christian Bible originated, together with other religious texts, as an expression of religious experience. As such, Scripture is part of the history of the transmission of traditions. It is a human history book, reflecting one particular religious tradition. Written by human authors, it does not contain eternal, unchanging truths that can be universally applied or deduced from its pages. Hence, there is no need for a special guidance of the Biblical writers in the process of writing down their "experiences with the divine," because in them no content is communicated. In this, Pannenberg clearly falls in the "typology" where Scripture is originated "from below." With Schleiermacher, he rejects the idea that some specific content is being communicated

---

23-24). Edwin E. Scott, has pointed out, however, that "the problem of the nature of the Bible influences the use of the Bible" ("The Nature and Use of Scripture in the Writings of Clark H. Pinnock and James Barr" [Th.D. dissertation, New Orleans Baptist Theological Seminary, 1989], 58).

[1]Cf. Scott, 139, who comes to similar conclusions with regard to James Barr and Clark H. Pinnock.

[2]According to Jürgen Moltmann, one decisive principle of the modern world "is the unprejudiced application of modern science and technology to the comprehension of life in the modern world. Faith does not depend on the Bible's worldview but rather liberates reason to its own reasonableness. That includes the application of the historical sciences to the Bible and to church dogma. Historical criticism does not destroy the foundations of the faith but, rather, unveils faith's transcendental foundation" ("Christianity in the Third Millennium," **TToday** 51/1 [1994]: 80-81). In this sense, Pannenberg certainly qualifies as a modern theologian.

from God to humankind and with his concept of imagination, Pannenberg creatively appropriates Schleiermacher's stance where the origin of one's knowledge of God is part of one's religious experience.

In contrast to Pannenberg's modern point of departure, Bloesch approaches the question of the origin of Scripture from a confessional standpoint which in some sense reminds one of a pre-modern position. For Bloesch, Scripture is given "from above," deriving from divine revelation and coming into existence under divine inspiration. Thus, contrary to Pannenberg, Bloesch rejects a natural point of contact between man and God.[1] Nevertheless, he acknowledges a "dual authorship" of God and the human writers in Scripture where divine communication is included in revelation, although this aspect is clearly subservient to the personal dimension of it. It appears, however, that Bloesch focuses on the theological content of Scripture which for him is infallibly revealed. In other words, revelation includes verbal aspects[2] inasmuch as they relate to Christ and the gospel. Still, despite the superintendence of the Spirit in the process of inspiration, all human words and concepts fall short of giving univocal knowledge of God. Instead, Biblical language is symbolic or mythopoetic and remains incomplete and insufficient. From this it appears that Bloesch tries to combine two distinct positions: that of the pre-modern and pre-Kantian Protestant Reformers, who maintained the cognitive revelation of divine truths in Scripture and Kant's observation that human reason by itself can yield knowledge only of the phenomenal world but has no access to the noumenal realm, which includes God.[3]

Furthermore, the role of the Holy Spirit in the process of the origin of Scripture

---

[1]Bloesch states that he is closer to the position of Karl Barth than to Emil Brunner, who posited a capacity within the human person for revelation. Bloesch readily acknowledges "that outwardly there is a point of contact. . . . But this is a sociological, not a theological, point of contact. The meaning or truth of revelation can be discerned only through the power of the Spirit. . . . There is a formal point of contact, which is best seen as sociological or psychological, not theological. But there is no material point of contact, that is, a power or light resident in humanity that enables us to apprehend the truth that God reveals to us" (**HSRII**, 76).

[2]Cf. pp. 187ff.

[3]Bloesch, **TWS**, 254-255. Writes Bloesch: "It is, of course, a mistake to remain with this Kantian dichotomy as much as liberal and existential theology has done; knowledge of the noumenal realm is then reduced to symbolic awareness or mystical insight, which eludes conceptual articulation. As Christians we must affirm that the noumenal has entered into the phenomenal in the person of Jesus Christ and confronts us on the plane of the phenomenal, bringing us real knowledge of transcendent reality previously hidden from human sight and understanding" (ibid., 325, n. 11).

is important for both authors, although in different ways. Pannenberg, for instance, understands the Spirit in general, universal, and impersonal terms. Perceived as a comprehensive field,[1] the Spirit is the place, so to speak, where all human beings participate in God. As this general force, the Spirit is the source for imaginative inspirations in all humans.

Bloesch, on the other hand, understands the Holy Spirit more in personalistic terms. He is active on the individual level. Revelation is the special work of the Holy Spirit in the lives of selected individuals where divine truths are communicated from God to man, which results in the writing down of the received revelation under the inspiration of the Holy Spirit. At the same time, Bloesch understands the Spirit to be active in the lives of the readers of Scripture, making true understanding of the theological message possible. Thus, the origin as well as the receiving of the theological message is seen as a divine gift, through the Spirit, which cannot be presupposed in every human being.

Although both authors start out from fundamentally different premises in their understanding of revelation, both agree, interestingly enough, that the actual words of Scripture are not to be directly identified with divine revelation. This is to be expected in Pannenberg's case, given the modern starting point of his approach, and is made possible in Bloesch's theology because of his decision to limit revelation to Jesus Christ. Thus, Bloesch sees Scripture as a witness to revelation rather than being revelation itself.[2]

---

[1] Pannenberg has found the noncorporal field theory, which developed in physics in the nineteenth century, and the Stoic concept of pneuma of great theological importance. Pannenberg relates the field phenomenon, in which every created reality exists, to the dynamic presence of the Spirit in all of creation (**SyTh/G**, 2:99-105). Ted Peters recently aptly describes that "Pannenberg rushes in where two-language angels have feared to tread. . . . There is a directness and a literalness here that seems to throw caution to the wind. One can admire his scholarly courage, but perhaps this assertion should retain its hypothetical status for a period to await confirmation or disconfirmation. Historians of science are quick to point out the dangers of trying to float a theological assertion aboard a scientific ship, because the intellectual weather can change suddenly. . . . How long will field theory stay afloat? If someday it should sink, will Pannenberg's theology of spirit sink with it?" ("Editor's Introduction: Pannenberg on Theology and Natural Science," 14). A similar concern is voiced by Hudson, 48.

[2] The influence of Karl Barth on Bloesch's thought on this point is obvious and it seems that for all practical purposes Bloesch follows his theological mentor in regarding Scripture as a witness to revelation rather than revelation in and of itself. On Barth's view of Scripture as witness to divine revelation, see Klaas Runia, 18-56. Runia has pointed out that for Barth there is not merely a quantitative distinction but an essentially qualitative distinction between the Bible and revelation (ibid., 33). The same could be said of Bloesch. After having carefully investigated the

The comparison between Pannenberg's and Bloesch's understanding of Scripture becomes even more interesting when one considers their positions on the nature of Scripture.

The Nature of Scripture

The position that Pannenberg and Bloesch have adopted in their understanding of the origin of Scripture has some definite bearings on their perception of the nature of Scripture. Conceiving the origin of Scripture basically "from below," Pannenberg sees the Bible essentially as a collection of historical documents in which the human awareness of the divine is reflected. However, because he assumes that the reality of God is *co-given* to experience in other objects,[1] he perceives the Biblical texts as theologically oriented history of religions.[2] Consequently, the Bible is only the cognitive expression of religious experience. As a consequence it follows that the special status of Scripture in Christianity is derived from its particular place in history and the historical proximity to certain important events.[3] In other words, it is the church which decides to accept certain documents as Scripture, serving as point of reference and norm for Christian identity. As such, Scripture does not possess inherent authority, much less divine authority.

Biblical material, Runia concludes: "There is, therefore, but one conclusion possible: These witnesses are *revelatory witnesses*. They are not only witnesses to revelation, in a limiting and distinct way, but they themselves *belong to the revelation*. Their speaking and writing *is* revelation" (ibid., 35).

[1]Pannenberg, **TPS**, 301.

[2]Ibid., 379.

[3]Pannenberg frankly states that the catch-word "Word of God" is "no longer understood in the classical Protestant sense as the divinely inspired--insofar as spoken by God himself--word of the Bible, but instead as either the whole process of Christian tradition (understood in a Protestant light) from Jesus Christ to Scripture and proclamation, or else, preferably, as the last of these alone" ("On Historical and Theological Hermeneutics," in **BQT**, 1:146). Even a scholar like James Barr has pointed out, however, that "there is an important distinction between the 'authority' of a historical source and the 'authority' of a theological norm or criterion. . . . Status as a historical source, or nearness to the events reported, does not mean the same thing as theological normativeness" **(The Bible in the Modern World**, 80). Barr concludes by saying that "the possession of proximity to the historical events is an ambiguous quality; and it does not of itself validate the status of the existing Bible as theological norm for today" (ibid., 81). It should be pointed out, however, that Pannenberg does not assign some normative function to Scripture on the fact of historical priority alone. Rather, the appropriateness of its message is to be evaluated on the horizon of the present human experience of reality (Pannenberg, **TPS**, 380-381).

In contrast to Pannenberg's perception of the nature of Scripture as a theologically oriented human document of a particular history of religion, Bloesch sees the nature of Scripture in sacramental terms. This allows him to perceive Scripture as a trustworthy and unfailing guide and as an external standard and criterion for faith which carries divine authority. Such an affirmation is made possible because Bloesch proposes a sacramental understanding of the nature of Scripture. God is seen in action through the work of His Spirit so that the fallible human words are taken up and used by God to become the Word of God and a channel of revelation. As such, Scripture is an inspired witness to and a carrier of revelation. In other words, it carries divine authority because of its sacramental union with the material norm, Jesus Christ. This is accomplished through the work of the Holy Spirit on a continuous basis.

Despite these differences, one can also perceive a number of areas where the two theologians seem somewhat closer. Pannenberg, as well as Bloesch, does not directly identify the words of Scripture with divine revelation. Therefore, both do not see Scripture as a source book for doctrine or revealed truth. Furthermore, both agree that as a human document Scripture is questionable in its reliability and is principally capable to err. In this, both display common characteristics that are typical for a view of Scripture "from below." Yet, both respond differently to such questions as the unity, clarity, and sufficiency of Scripture, all of which are challenged by the application of a historical-critical approach to Scripture.

Pannenberg maintains that there is doctrinal plurality in Scripture and perceives contradictions and antithesis in Biblical statements. Nevertheless, Pannenberg perceives in the history of Jesus Christ, Who is the anticipation and prolepsis of the end of history, a central and unifying motif of Scripture. Thus, he can speak of a "unity of Scripture relative to its central content,"[1] i.e., Jesus Christ, who is undoubtedly "the focal point of revelation."[2] In this latter aspect, there is some similarity with Bloesch, who also tries to maintain a unity within Scripture by elevating Jesus Christ as its unifying center. Bloesch, however, emphasizes in stronger terms than Pannenberg that Jesus Christ is the center and apex of Scripture and that **all** of Scripture testifies to Him.

---

[1]Pannenberg, **SyTh/E**, 1:14.

[2]Ibid., 212, my translation of the German word "Brennpunkt."

As far as the clarity of Scripture is concerned, Pannenberg seems to have replaced it with the clarity of history where the context of the transmission of traditions provides the meaning of an event that is clear to all, not just the believer. Bloesch, in contrast, understands the clarity of Scripture not as pertaining to the text but as a result of the special work of the Holy Spirit.[1] Scripture in itself appears to be unclear.[2]

This means, moreover, that for both, Scripture alone is no longer sufficient.[3] While Pannenberg attempts to take the Biblical record with historical seriousness, he does not view it as the self-authenticating Word of God.[4] Instead, common human experience and the rationality and coherency of the Biblical message with modern scientific understanding of reality seem to determine the adequacy of Biblical statements for Pannenberg.[5] Bloesch, on the other hand, supplants the Scriptures by the Holy Spirit in order to come up with a valid theological meaning. In both cases, however, Scripture alone is insufficient to determine its own correct theological meaning because it is not the sole source of its own exposition. Theology is not developed from

---

[1] Luther distinguished between, what he called, "external clarity" (*claritas externa*) and the "internal clarity" (*claritas interna*) of Scripture. The internal clarity of Scripture has to do with the "knowledge of the heart" that is darkened through sin, and needs the Spirit to understand Scripture properly. The external clarity of Scripture on the other hand is comparable to a philosophical principle that needs no further demonstration and is independent from all subjective experience, for it can be communicated and examined. According to Bernhard Rothen, both, that is, external and internal clarity, are dependent upon Scripture, for the words of Scripture alone can build and substantiate the truth of faith (**Die Klarheit der Schrift. Teil 1: Martin Luther. Die wiederentdeckten Grundlagen**, 90-91, 83-95); cf. also Hermann, 32-65, and passim; and Beisser, **Claritas Scripturae bei Martin Luther**, especially 82-97.

[2] It seems as if Bloesch's understanding of the role of the Holy Spirit goes beyond the need of the Holy Spirit in illumination, which has traditionally been affirmed in Protestant theology. The classical statement for the need of the Holy Spirit in understanding and accepting Holy Scripture can be found in John Calvin, **Institutes of the Christian Religion**, I. vii. 4-5; III. i. 1; III. ii. 33-36. Cf. Niesel, **The Theology of John Calvin**, 30-39. For Calvin and other Protestant theologians the need for the Holy Spirit has always been acknowledged as necessary. Yet, the evidences of Scripture and the evidence of the Spirit are "identical" (Paul Althaus, **Die Prinzipien der deutschen reformierten Dogmatik im Zeitalter der aristotelischen Scholastik**, 212). In other words, the testimony of the Spirit never contradicts the clear meaning of Scripture. Cf. Calvin, **Institutes**, I. vii. 2, at the conclusion on p. 76.

[3] On the interrelationship between the notion of the clarity and the sufficiency of Scripture, see Preus, **The Theology of Post-Reformation Lutheranism: A Study of Theological Prolegomena**, 1:311.

[4] Gilbert W. Stafford, "Frontiers in Contemporary Theology," in **A Contemporary Wesleyan Theology: Biblical, Systematic, and Practical**, 2 vols., ed. Charles W. Carter (Grand Rapids, MI: Zondervan, 1983), 1:39.

[5] Cf. for instance Pannenberg, SyTh/G, 2:99, 184; idem, **The Apostles' Creed in the Light of Today's Questions**, 97, 104.

Scripture alone. This leads us to the question of the use of Scripture in Pannenberg and Bloesch, to which we turn now.

The Use of Scripture

To no one's surprise, the understanding of the origin and nature of the Bible has some definite implications for the role of Scripture in Pannenberg's and Bloesch's theology. In the case of Pannenberg, for instance, one practical result from his understanding of the origin and nature of Scripture seems to be his assertion that Scripture should be used descriptively because Scripture is essentially a historical document that describes and reflects a particular religious tradition. In harmony with this understanding, Pannenberg uses no special approach towards Scripture. He is convinced that the historical investigation of Scripture gains an eminent theological significance because it arrives at the theological meaning. A theological interpretation is not added to the historical as something totally new. Rather, for the theological interpretation there is only one method and that is the historical-critical.[1] Because Scripture is essentially a historical document of human origin, it can and should be investigated historically-critically just like any other historical document would be.[2] Furthermore, since God reveals Himself only indirectly through history, the content of Christian faith can be appropriated only in connection with its tradition, and here only from its end.[3] Hence, one finds a curious parallelism in Pannenberg's theology between exegetical arguments and the history of the transmission of philosophical and theological traditions as they touch upon a particular issue under discussion. It is crucial to notice that Pannenberg does not move directly from Biblical assertions to systematic conclusions but "first seeks to establish, by general rational criteria, the

---

[1] Reinhardt, 323, 328. Gerhard Sauter thinks that the historical-critical method "einstens der Teufelei verdächtigt, ist zum Organon der Apologie Gottes geworden" (**Vor einem neuen Methodenstreit in der Theologie**, ThExH 164 [Munich: Chr. Kaiser, 1970], 18).

[2] The phrase that Scripture should be interpreted "just like any other book" seems to go back to Benjamin Jowett's famous essay "On the Interpretation of Scripture," in **Essays and Reviews** (London: John W. Parker and Sons, 1886), 330-433, especially 375, 377. On Jowett's approach, cf. David C. Steinmetz, "The Superiority of Precritical Exegesis," **TToday** 37 (1980): 27-38; and James Barr, "Jowett and the Reading of the Bible "Like Any Other Book," **HBT** 4 (1982): 1-44.

[3] Here the influence of Wilhelm Dilthey can be seen. For a concise introduction to Dilthey's historicism, cf. Richard E. Palmer, **Hermeneutics: Interpretation Theory in Schleiermacher, Dilthey, Heidegger, and Gadamer** (Evanston, IL: Northwestern University Press, 1969), 98-123.

extent to which Biblical views are valid for our day."¹ Thus, Pannenberg uses Scripture functionally,² and tests the adequacy of Biblical and theological assertions by extra-Biblical criteria.

Bloesch, in contrast, endorses a prescriptive use of Scripture.³ The trustworthiness and infallibility of at least the theological message of Scripture is accepted by him in faith. Although he, too, supports a historical-critical investigation of Scripture, he insists, contrary to Pannenberg, that such an exercise does not lead to theological truth because it deals only with the human text of Scripture and not with its theological meaning. In fact, rather than starting with the historical text to arrive at theological truth, Bloesch moves towards a pneumatological use of Scripture where the theological meaning is given to the eyes of faith alone. He acknowledges a certain fluidity of meaning of the written text and seems to come quite close to a new allegorical use of Scripture where the Holy Spirit may use any particular text to point to Christ. In this Bloesch definitely moves beyond the position of the Protestant Reformers, with whom he feels closely connected, because they all were critical of an allegorical use of Scripture. Instead they emphasized the literal meaning of the text, even in their Christological interpretation. It seems that the role of tradition becomes increasingly significant for Bloesch, possibly in order to safeguard an excessive individualism in a pneumatological use of Scripture. This pneumatological use of Scripture is also closely connected with his Christological approach where all of Scripture is believed to revolve around Christ, thus maintaining the hermeneutical priority of the New Testament over the Old.

Despite the above mentioned differences, there are a number of surprising similarities between Pannenberg's and Bloesch's use of Scripture. Both would agree that ultimately Scripture in itself cannot be used as final norm and authority. Scripture is not to be used as a direct sourcebook for doctrine and ethics. Both, it seems, use Scripture functionally, not authoritatively. In addition, for both, tradition ultimately seems indispensable for a proper reading and reception of Scripture. Despite important

---

¹Finger, **Christian Theology: An Eschatological Approach**, 1:206.

²Cf. Kelsey, **The Uses of Scripture in Recent Theology**, 53, n. 84, where Kelsey compares Pannenberg's use of Scripture to that of G. E. Wright.

³For Bloesch "theology is fundamentally *prescriptive*, for its case rests upon truth claims that have metaphysical import" (**TWS**, 23).

differences in their presuppositions, one can see significant similarities between Pannenberg's and Bloesch's position inasmuch as both depend upon other sources than Scripture in their interpretation of Scripture. Thus, the classical Protestant Scripture principle[1] has been changed on the one hand from a principle of immediate divine authority to a principle whereby Christianity is attached to its historic origin, as in Pannenberg, or it has lost its critical function to the Holy Spirit who ultimately becomes the highest norm and final authority by which everything else, including Scripture, must be tested, as in Bloesch.

Last but not least, both theologians see Jesus Christ and the gospel as **the** authority by which Scripture has to be measured and which regulates its use. The authority of Scripture is an indirect authority that is dependent upon the authority of the gospel. Only inasmuch as Scripture testifies to this central content does Scripture have authority. This last point seems to be especially significant in light of their different starting points and methodologies. Furthermore, it raises the question whether such an approach is indicative of some presuppositions and commitments that are at work in their particular understanding of Scripture that are not immediately obvious. Therefore, we now turn to an evaluation of Pannenberg's and Bloesch's view of Scripture.

Pannenberg's and Bloesch's Concept of Scripture: An Evaluation

The contrasting views of Wolfhart Pannenberg and Donald G. Bloesch on their understanding of Scripture invite careful evaluation of their strengths and weaknesses. In order to do justice to the particular approach employed by each of them I have chosen to evaluate their respective positions on the basis of the internal consistency of their views. I also take into consideration the style of their presentation as well as examine some of their assumptions and presuppositions upon which their respective positions seem to rest.

Pannenberg's View of Scripture

This evaluation of Pannenberg's position begins by focusing on his strengths before turning to some of his weaknesses.

---

[1]Cf. Gloege, "Schriftprinzip," in **RGG**, 5:1540-1541.

Strengths

Even a casual reader of Pannenberg's writings will admire his intricate knowledge of the issues involved and will be impressed by the profoundness of his ideas. Not without reason, many consider Pannenberg as one of the most outstanding and most creative Protestant theologians of this century.[1] It has been said that his "theological orientation cannot simply be . . . dismissed as a passing fad," but promises to exercise a lasting influence throughout the theological world.[2] With his encyclopedic knowledge, which regularly broadens the discussion beyond the strictly theological realm,[3] he is truly a master of his field, one who intimately knows the subject and comes up with novel interpretations. Through his expertise and personal engagement in scientific and ecumenical dialogue,[4] he succeeds in bringing together different traditions for a mutually enriching discussion. In general, his presentations and discussions of different positions strike me as accurate and fair.

From another perspective, the strength of Pannenberg's view of Scripture can be seen in the elegance and coherence of his approach. Pannenberg consistently applies to Scripture what he assumes at the outset. Sparked by his acceptance of modern epistemological approaches, Pannenberg rejects any posting of an external authority as well as the possibility of supernatural communication between God and man in Scripture. Instead, he envisions the revelatory character of history, where history as a whole is the place of God's indirect self-revelation. In line with his understanding

---

[1] Richard John Neuhaus thinks "that Pannenberg's [theological thought] is the single most ambitious and impressive project in constructing theology in the Christian world today" ("Theology for Church and Polis," in **TWP**, 227).

[2] Grenz, **Reason for Hope**, 4.

[3] Cf. Peters, "Editor's Introduction: Pannenberg on Theology and Natural Science," 1-14.

[4] Pannenberg has been the director of the institute for Fundamental-theology and Ecumenism at the Ludwig-Maximilians-University Munich and has been for several years a member of the "World Council of Churches' Faith and Order Commission," as well as directing the ecumenical work group of Protestant and Catholic theologians in the Federal Republic of Germany (Steck, "Von Personen: Laudatio Wolfhart Pannenberg," 887). Through his theological work he has given the ecumenical work in Germany and beyond important impulses and opened up new perspectives. Cf. Karl Lehmann and Wolfhart Pannenberg, eds., **Glaubensbekenntnis und Kirchengemeinschaft: Das Modell des Konzils von Konstantinopel (381)**, DdK 1 (Freiburg: Herder, 1982); idem, **Lehrverurteilungen--kirchentrennend? Rechtfertigung, Sakramente und Amt im Zeitalter der Reformation und heute**, DdK 4 (Freiburg: Herder, 1986); the English trans. of the latter is idem, **The Condemnations of the Reformation Era: Do They Still Divide?** trans. Margaret Köhl (Minneapolis: Fortress Press, 1990); and Wolfhart Pannenberg and Theodor Schneider, eds., **Verbindliches Zeugnis: Kanon--Schrift--Tradition**, DdK 7 (Freiburg: Herder, 1992).

of revelation as history, Pannenberg sees Scripture as a historical document,[1] that retains its significance for the church because it binds Christianity to its historical origin.[2]

Pannenberg logically and consistently unfolds his understanding of revelation and the derivatory concept of Scripture from his trinitarian concept of God and his corresponding understanding of anthropology. God, as the all-determining power over everything, who is universally present through His Spirit, has His counterpart in the openness of humankind to the divine. Consistent with his modern starting point, Pannenberg seeks to establish the basis of religion in a philosophical anthropology where humankind inevitably raises the question of God,[3] thereby linking "natural knowledge and revelation."[4] Thus, Pannenberg attempts to do away with the division between the supernatural and the natural, God's transcendence and His immanence.[5] Given the assumptions with which Pannenberg starts, his conclusions properly reflect the inherent thrust of his presuppositions. As such, they deserve to be taken seriously. As far as Pannenberg's concept of Scripture is concerned, it seems that there is no recognizable shift in his position.[6] This does not mean that there are no other areas where a modification in his theological perspective can be perceived.[7] But as far as

---

[1]Wolfhart Pannenberg, "Frage und Antwort--Das Normative in Christlicher Überlieferung und Theologie," in **Text und Applikation: Theologie, Jurisprudenz und Literaturwissenschaft im Hermeneutischen Gespräch**, ed. Manfred Fuhrmann, Hans Robert Jauß, and Wolfhart Pannenberg (Munich: Wilhelm Fink Verlag, 1981), 416.

[2]Pannenberg, **TPS**, 380-381; idem, "Gibt es Prinzipien des Protestantismus, die im ökumenischen Dialog nicht zur Disposition gestellt werden dürfen?" 80. It is obvious that the classical Protestant Scripture principle is no longer maintained in its original form. Pannenberg himself speaks of "the dissolution of the Scripture principle" ("The Crisis of the Scripture Principle," 4). Reinhardt, 426, also maintains that "die historisch-kritische Erforschung der Schrift machte es unmöglich, an dem Schriftprinzip im herkömmlichen Sinn festzuhalten, daß nämlich die Schrift als ein in sich klarer Text alleiniges Erkennungsprinzip der Theologie sei." According to Laurence Wood, what is normative for valid theological statements, for Pannenberg, "is not the Biblical texts themselves, but the historically verifiable events which the texts report" ("History and Hermeneutics: A Pannenbergian Perspective," 16).

[3]O'Donnell, "Pannenberg's Doctrine of God," 78-79.

[4]McKenzie, **Wolfhart Pannenberg and Religious Philosophy**, 14.

[5]Cf. Bradshaw, **Trinity and Ontology**, 176.

[6]Already in some of his early writings Pannenberg maintains the same view that he reiterates in his **Systematic Theology**. Cf. Pannenberg, "Schriftautorität und Lehrautorität," 5-10; idem, "The Crisis of the Scripture Principle," 1-14; idem, "What Is a Dogmatic Statement?" in **BQT**, 1:182-210.

[7]When Pannenberg was asked in 1981 to reflect on the question of how his mind had

his view of Scripture is concerned, one can say there is definitely a continuity in his thought.

Furthermore, through his emphasis on the historical aspect of reality and of revelation, Pannenberg can be credited to have taken seriously again the historical dimension of Scripture, at least over against a kerygmatic de-historization of theology. It should be noted, however, that his "recovery" of the historical character of Scripture went hand in hand with a devaluation of the supernatural dimension of Scripture. Although the category of history is an essential part in a theology of Scripture, Braaten has sounded "a word of caution when a single category assumes control of the whole of theology and becomes the sole explanatory principle."[1] Thus, it seems that an area of Pannenberg's strength is at the same time a weakness. Despite the elegance and stringency that characterize many of Pannenberg's arguments in his understanding of God and of Scripture, there are a number of questions that need to be raised against his position.

Weaknesses

The overall coherence of an approach is not necessarily an indication of its correctness and truth. While there is a general consistency in Pannenberg's approach, there are nevertheless some areas where Pannenberg's proposal borders on internal

---

changed over the years, he wrote that "when I [Pannenberg] search my memories and other evidence, I find it difficult to discern any fundamental change in my theological perspective since 1959, when I published an article on 'Redemptive Event and History'" (Pannenberg, "God's Presence in History," 260).

One can see some development in Pannenberg's understanding of God. It seems that it was not until the early 1980s that he began "to feel solid ground under [his] feet in this area" (Pannenberg, "An Autobiographical Sketch," in **TWP**, 16). Writing in 1981, Pannenberg revealed that now he felt "much more confident to develop a doctrine of God and to treat the subjects of Christian dogmatics in that perspective. That doctrine will be more thoroughly trinitarian than any example I know of" (idem, "God's Presence in History," 263). Such a trinitarian development of the idea of God in its own right was first given in his books on metaphysics (idem, **Metaphysics and the Idea of God**, and his **Systematic Theology**.

One other noteworthy development should be mentioned. It appears that "Pannenberg sees more clearly now the brokenness of the knowledge of revelation in the era before the consummation" (Grenz, **Reason for Hope**, 42). In comparison to the third thesis of **Revelation as History**, where he wrote that "the historical revelation is open to anyone who has eyes to see" (Pannenberg, "Dogmatic Theses on the Doctrine of Revelation," 135), he now admits that it did not adequately deal with the aspect of "a brokenness of the knowledge of revelation in the context of ongoing debatability and of the power of doubt that constantly assails the believers" (idem, **SyTh/E**, 1:250); cf. also Avery Dulles, "Pannenberg on Revelation and Faith," in **TWP**, 184-186.

[1] Carl E. Braaten, "Revelation," in **A New Handbook of Christian Theology**, ed. Donald W. Musser and Joseph L. Price (Nashville, TN: Abingdon Press, 1992), 413.

inconsistency. For instance, it would seem that Pannenberg's emphasis on the importance of Jesus Christ and the Christian gospel as authority for Christian faith as well as for Scripture is in conflict with the historical character of theology and its proposed scientific and hypothetical nature, where the truth of something can be confirmed or falsified only at the end.[1] Thus, for example in his **Systematic Theology**,[2] Pannenberg writes that the authority of Scripture is grounded in the authority of the gospel and that Scripture has to be measured by the gospel. Pannenberg told the author that he understands this passage to describe the function of Scripture in the context of the life of the church and especially for the teaching of the church but not for the general problem of the relationship between authority and reason.[3] Nevertheless, it is not entirely clear how Pannenberg can avoid, even with the above made qualification, a subtle faith commitment or at least a tacit preference for the Christian tradition in which he stands.[4] It is doubtful how one can legitimately arrive at an authoritative understanding of Christ from a purely historical investigation.[5] Even a functional authority of Christ, as assigned by the church, seems

---

[1]Wainwright, "Method in Theology," 372-373. On the scientific character of Pannenberg's theology, see Wentzel van Huyssteen, **Theology and the Justification of Faith: Constructing Theories in Systematic Theology**, trans. H. F. Snijders (Grand Rapids, MI: Eerdmans, 1989), 71-100; Philip Hefner, "The Role of Science in Pannenberg's Theological Thinking," **Zygon** 24/2 (1989): 135-151; and Daniel Winthrop Hackmann, "Validation and Truth: Wolfhart Pannenberg and the Scientific Status of Theology" (Ph.D. dissertation, University of Iowa, 1989), 57-239.

[2]Pannenberg, **SyTh/G**, 2:509-511.

[3]"Wenn ich in [SyTh/G,] 2:509ff. von der im Evangelium begründeten Autorität der Schrift spreche, dann handelt es sich um die Funktion der Schrift im Zusammenhang des Lebens der Kirche und insbesondere für die Lehre der Kirche, nicht um das allgemeinere Problem von Autorität und Vernunft" (Pannenberg to Hasel, 21 January 1994, 2).

[4]Carl E. Braaten has raised a similar question when he asks whether the normative role of the Christ event and the principle of justification by faith alone are received as gifts from the tradition in which Pannenberg stands or whether they are products of theological work? ("The Place of Christianity Among the World Religions: Wolfhart Pannenberg's Theology of Religion and the History of Religions," in **TWP**, 308). Cf. the comment made by Polk, **On the Way to God**, 113, on another aspect: "A considerable circularity of argument is at work here, in that the universal significance of what comes to expression in the tradition of Christianity is largely grounded in its capacity for providing the ultimate answer to our common human dilemma which has actually been defined within the context of that tradition. Conversely the motif of, say, the Hindu and Buddhist traditions emphasizing a goal of futurelessness is dismissed as erroneous *from the perspective of a definition of human existence informed by Christian thinking*."

[5]The shadow of Ernst Troeltsch looms over any such attempt as Van Harvey has shown. Van Austin Harvey, 3-9. Langdon Gilkey calls into question Pannenberg's entire approach that looks to history for the basis for a theological system. To see history as "theological" is an optical

to be at variance with the general trend of his theology and specific statements made by Pannenberg, where he endorses the rationality of theology as a science.[1] He explicitly states that the development of the historical consciousness has led to the relativity of **all** historical testimonies and their interpretation.[2] Furthermore, in a letter to the author, Pannenberg admits that the function of Scripture as authority for church doctrine does not rule out the fact that the statements of Scripture are open to rational examination in every respect. He continues by saying that the relativity of historical documents and interpretation is not touched by the authoritative function of Scripture in the church.[3] How and why, even as functional authority Christ should be exempt from historical relativity, Pannenberg does not tell.[4]

---

illusion for Gilkey. The jump from humanist categories to historical inquiry and then from the interpretation of history to theological categories is as difficult in historical inquiry as it is in science. "And probably for most of us who accept an historical explanation of events, the possibility of divine activity within historical events is as difficult, not to say incredible, a conception as is that of the divine activity within the forces of nature" (**Reaping the Whirlwind: A Christian Interpretation of History** [New York: Seabury Press, 1976], 336, n. 4).

[1]It should be noted that "science" in English has overtones of natural science, while "Wissenschaft" in German signifies something like "rational, academic discipline" and "field of knowledge" and therefore does not necessarily denotes natural science. Peter C. Hodgson observes that the German use of "Wissenschaft" corresponds with "scientia" in Latin, which is, however, a false cognate in English, at least insofar as it is much broader in scope, meaning something like "disciplined, methodological knowledge in any realm of human inquiry" ("Review of **Theology and the Philosophy of Science**," **RSR** 3 [1977]: 216). Pannenberg's understanding of theology as a science is put forth most stringently in **TPS**. See also van Huyssteen, **Theology and the Justification of Faith**, 77-92; Hackmann, 140-239; and Nancey C. Murphy, **Theology in the Age of Scientific Reasoning**, 19-34, 176-178.

[2]Pannenberg, **SyTh/G**, 3:177. For Wilhelm Dilthey (1833-1911), "the father of modern conceptions of historicality," a consequence of historicality is that man does not escape from history, which results in historical relativism (Palmer, 117). This is significant because Pannenberg claims that the thoughts of Dilthey have had a much greater influence on him than Hegel (Pannenberg to Hasel, 21 January 1994, 1).

[3]"Die Funktion der Schrift als Autorität für kirchliche Lehre schließt nicht aus, daß die Aussagen der Schrift in jeder Hinsicht vernünftiger Prüfung zugänglich sind, und ebensowenig ist die Relativität aller geschichtlichen Zeugnisse und Interpretationen davon berührt" (Pannenberg to Hasel, 21 January 1994, 2).

[4]Ernst Troeltsch perceptively recognized that "once the historical method is applied to Biblical science and church history, it is a leaven that alters everything and, finally, bursts apart the entire structure of theological methods employed until the present" ("Ueber historische und dogmatische Methode in der Theologie," 2:730). Troeltsch knew that "whoever had lend it the little finger must also give it his whole hand" (ibid., 734). This fact is recognized today by scholars within as well as without the historical-critical tradition. Cf. Manfred Oeming, "Unitas Scripturae? Eine Problemskizze," in **Einheit und Vielfalt Biblischer Theologie**, JBT 1, ed. Ingo Baldermann et al. (Neukirchen-Vluyn: Neukirchener Verlag des Erziehungsvereins, 1986), 53;

Furthermore, one wonders about the consistency in a related aspect of Pannenberg's thought. If history as a whole constitutes the self-revelation of God, as Pannenberg claims, how can one particular event in history, i.e., the resurrection of Jesus Christ, possess absolute revelatory significance? If history as a whole is revelation, can the event of Jesus Christ be superseded? This problem is not satisfactorily solved even when Pannenberg employs the concept of anticipation. Either every anticipation is only provisional, as Pannenberg himself admits, or the final end has already been decided from the perspective of the ultimate future and therefore can be anticipated. In the latter case, however, the contingency of historical events seems to be jeopardized, yet Pannenberg strongly emphasizes the contingent character of historical events.

With respect to Scripture, one could raise the related question whether Scripture can and should be superseded by new religious documents because the tradition-forming activity of human imagination continues and Scripture is necessarily an incomplete reflection of the process of revelation as history.[1] Given Pannenberg's affirmation that there is divine revelation in all the religions, I raise with Braaten the question "whether Pannenberg has found a clear enough way to speak of the distinction between God's revelation in the religions and God's unique revelation in Jesus Christ, which the New Testament calls 'the gospel.'"[2] If there is divine revelation in other religions, why is Scripture necessary and are other religions also "ways of salvation?"[3]

John J. Collins, "Is a Critical Biblical Theology Possible?" in **The Hebrew Bible and Its Interpreters**, BJSUCSD 1, ed. William Henry Propp, Baruch Halpern, and David Noel Freedman (Winona Lake, IN: Eisenbrauns, 1990), 5, 14; Michael Weinrich, "Grenzen der Erinnerung: Historische Kritik und Dogmatik im Horizont Biblischer Theologie: Systematische Vorüberlegungen," in **Wenn nicht Jetzt, Wann Dann? Aufsätze für Hans-Joachim Kraus zum 65. Geburtstag**, ed. Hans-Georg Geyer, Johann Michael Schmidt, Werner Schulider and Michael Weinrich (Neukirchen-Vluyn: Neukirchener Verlag, 1983), 333; and Noller.

[1]Inasmuch as Pannenberg supports the idea of an open canon of Scripture he seems to follow the internal logic of his proposal. From this openendedness it is also understandable why for Pannenberg Scripture cannot interpret itself, because only from the final end is it possible to determine the ultimate meaning of an individual event or passage. It has been correctly observed by Carl E. Braaten that Pannenberg's method calls for a suspension of the *sola Scriptura* principle ("The Place of Christianity among the World Religions," 307).

[2]Braaten, "The Place of Christianity Among World Religions," 309.

[3]Ibid., 310. Braaten has pointed out that universalistic features permeates Pannenberg's thought from beginning to end and has claimed that Pannenberg's theology of universal history would seem to lead to universalism (ibid., 311-312). Recently Pannenberg made some statements that seem to confirm Braaten's observation. According to Pannenberg, there is room for the idea that "in other religions God is worshipped under different names and in variously refracted forms

Why does Pannenberg place the Judeo-Christian Scripture at the top of all religious literature? It seems that the reason Pannenberg prefers it over other (religious) literature is because it presents reality most adequately as historical.[1] But does that not betray a subtle philosophical preference and a prior commitment on the part of Pannenberg to his own theological tradition?

It seems that "Pannenberg should recognize more clearly that the movement of faith is already operative in the very perception of historical fact."[2] Harder and Stevenson have pointed out that "in Pannenberg's theology, the first logical step is the a priori assumption that God reveals himself in history. This is nothing less than an assertion of faith without which one could not follow his arguments."[3] Wilhelm Weischedel was not far off when he observed that even in the case of Pannenberg, where Protestant theology tried the hardest to escape a purely fideistic grounding of faith, he remains trapped in it.[4]

---

and even in forms of perversion," yet, "these religions are still related to the reality of the one God" ("The Religions from the Perspective of Christian Theology and the Self-Interpretation of Christianity in Relation to Non-Christian Religions," 290). Furthermore, Pannenberg asks: "Do the Christians have to say that non-Christian religions in each and every case lead their adherents astray, turn them away from the true God, to the effect that people living in non-Christian cultures can have a change of participating in the final salvation only in spite of their religious adherence, not through it? It is hardly possible to give a general answer to this question. However, if it belongs to the created existence of human beings to be related in some way or other to their creator a relationship to the one God that is a subject of contemplation in all cultures and especially in their religious life, then one must not exclude the possibility that even religious institutions of non-Christian religions may in fact contribute to encourage their people in their quest for ultimate salvation, even if the institutions of those religions may appear from a Christian point of view to be mixed with many elements that turn people away from the truth of God" (ibid., 295); also idem, "Religion und Religionen: Theologische Erwägungen zu den Prinzipien eines Dialoges mit den Weltreligionen," 179-196. For a critical interaction with Pannenberg's ideas on this point, see Helmut Burkhardt, "Haben alle Religionen mit einem und demselben Gott zu tun?" 212-217.

[1]"The fact that history is the sphere of the self-revelation of the deity of God was a discovery of Israel, into whose inheritance Christianity stepped" (Pannenberg, **SyTh/E**, 1:171). Earlier, Pannenberg, had written that "today there is widespread consent to the view that the specific consciousness of universal history has its origin in the Jewish and Christian theology of history. . . . Israelite thought is thereby characteristically distinguished from other sorts of understanding of history" ("Response to the Discussion," in **TaH**, 245).

[2]Harder and Stevenson, 51.

[3]Ibid., 50-51.

[4]Weischedel, 2:86-87; cf. also Eberhard Jüngel, "Das Dilemma der natürlichen Theologie und die Wahrheit Ihres Problems: Überlegungen für ein Gespräch mit Wolfhart Pannenberg," 434-437.

There is another aspect of Pannenberg's thought that requires critical assessment. It seems that his crucially important concept of history (Geschichte), in the sense of history as the transmission of traditions, is not without ambiguities. Colin Gunton has raised the question whether Pannenberg's concept of universal history is not an imposition of a philosophical pattern on Old Testament history.[1] He has further criticized Pannenberg's conception of the history of transmission of traditions (*Überlieferungsgeschichte*) as elusive and as essentially ambiguous where attention is focused on a linguistic tradition rather than on reality itself.[2] It should be kept in mind that Pannenberg's clarion call that "history is the most comprehensive horizon of Christian theology"[3] was issued over against de-historicizing tendencies in dominant schools in modern theology.[4] Yet, Pannenberg never intended to create a stark contrast between word(s) and event(s).[5] Although he is adamant that God did not

---

[1] Gunton, **Yesterday and Today**, 77-78.

[2] Ibid., 78. Gunton thinks that Pannenberg thereby avoids "ontological commitment where possible" (ibid.). It seems to us, however, that Gunton is overstating the case because Pannenberg appears to be interested not just in a linguistic tradition but also in the facticity of real events. See for instance Pannenberg's critical remarks with regard to the non-historical perspective of "narrative theology" which groups together all the events recorded in Scripture unter the category of "story" (Pannenberg, **SyTh/E**, 1:231-232); similarly idem, "Geschichte/Geschichtschreibung/ Geschichtsphilosophie," **TRE**, 12:668, where Pannenberg states that "der Begriff von Geschichte nicht ausschließlich von der Struktur des Erzählens, der Narrativität, her zu bestimmen ist. Nicht jede Erzählung ist historisch im spezifischen Sinne der Geschichtserzählung, sondern nur diejenige, die den Gang tatsächlichen Geschehens wiederzugeben beansprucht." Thus, there is truth in Anthony C. Thiselton's observation that "Pannenberg is more deeply concerned with *the extra-linguistic realities of history,* and with *the interaction and intertwining of language and patterns of events in the context of historical traditions*" (**New Horizons in Hermeneutics** [Grand Rapids, MI: Zondervan Publishing House, 1992], 337). Yet, Pannenberg's understanding of the relationship between events and historical traditions is not entirely clear and some have bemoaned that there is "a lack of sufficient clarity with regard to the 'eventful' character of history as *Überlieferungsgeschichte*" (Polk, **On the Way to God**, 78); similarly James Barr has criticized that "the formula 'revelation in history' has proved to be a highly ambiguous one" leaving unclear such crucial questions as "the nature of the revelatory events . . . the sense of 'history' . . . the relation between revelation and history . . . [and] the relation between revelation and the biblical text itself" ("Revelation in History," **IDBSup**, 746-747).

[3] Pannenberg, "Redemptive Event and History," 15.

[4] Pannenberg's proposal can be seen specifically in contrast to the existentialist kerygmatic theology, on the one side, which dissolves history into the historicity of existence, and the "salvation history" theology, on the other side, which depreciates real history by its thesis that the real content is suprahistorical. Cf. Pannenberg, "Redemptive Event and History," 15-16; see also the perceptive analysis by Braaten, "The Current Controversy on Revelation: Pannenberg and His Critics," 225-226.

[5] Already in the postface to the second German edition of **Offenbarung als Geschichte**, Pannenberg reacted strongly against such a false interpretation of his position especially through

reveal Himself directly or anything about Himself in the words of Scripture,[1] his concept of revelation as history, in the sense that history is the transmission of traditions, is intricately connected with human words. Pannenberg's concept of "Revelation as History" is not to be interpreted in the sense of a direct identification of revelation with (every event that occurs in) history.[2] He acknowledges that "history is never composed of raw or so-called brute facts. As the history of man, its happening is always bound up with understanding, in hope and remembrance."[3]

Thus, we are faced with the perplexing situation that on the one hand Pannenberg denies that the words of Scripture reveal God or information about him directly, yet, on the other hand words are important because they are instrumental in forming religious traditions and as such are foundational for his concept of revelation as history (Geschichte) where God is revealed indirectly through history.[4] This raises the question about what precisely constitutes the "eventful" character of history,

---

Günter Klein (**Theologie des Wortes Gottes und die Hypothese der Universalgeschichte: Zur Auseinandersetzung mit Wolfhart Pannenberg** BEvTh 37 [Munich: Chr. Kaiser, 1964]) and Steiger (88-113); Pannenberg, "Nachwort zur zweiten Auflage," 132-148 (Göttingen: Vandenhoeck & Ruprecht, 1965), 132-139. Unfortunately this important postface has never been translated into English. Pannenberg also referred to the "original unity of event and meaning" in idem, "The Revelation of God in Jesus of Nazareth," 127; and recently reiterated his position in **SyTh/E**, 1:227-228.

[1]Pannenberg, **SyTh/E**, 1:240-244.

[2]Pannenberg has clearly stated that "modern history is not however divine revelation so to speak of itself. The connection between revelation and history is not to be taken in the sense that revelation is necessarily to be encountered wherever one gains entry to history. Yet the revelation of the divinity of the Biblical God has to do with history as a whole. It is disclosed only in history as a whole; not uniformly in every specific event, but only--as we have seen--in an end-perspective" ("Divine Revelation and Modern History," 89). On the understanding of the relationship between revelation and history, see the helpful overview and discussion of diverse positions in Peter Eicher, "Geschichte und Wort," 321-354.

[3]Pannenberg, "Dogmatic Thesis on the Doctrine of Revelation," 152 (my translation). Unfortunately the English translation of this important section is very unreliable and misleading. Pannenberg continues in the same context by stating that "history is always also the history of the transmission of traditions and even natural events that are involved in the history of a people have their meaning not apart from the positive or negative connection with the traditions and expectations in which men live." It is in this sense that the events of history speak their own language, the language of facts. Cf. also idem, "The Revelation of God in Jesus of Nazareth," 125-127.

[4]Pannenberg has admitted that "it is a very difficult task to understand how it is possible for human words--even though they are spontaneous and freely formed--to express the essence of the objects with which we have to do. I will discuss this fully in my *Theologie der Vernunft (Theology of Reason)*" ("Response to the Discussion," 238, n. 26). To my knowledge, Pannenberg has not yet taken up his promise and written a "Theology of Reason," nor has he told us how to solve the indeed difficult task of the relation of human words to the essence of the objects.

understood as history of the transmission of traditions (*Überlieferungsgeschichte*). In some sense it seems that Pannenberg wants to maintain that an understanding of the reality of history encompasses not only the transmission but also the origins of traditions. Here David Polk has raised the important question whether these origins are ever anything more fundamental than initial moments in the chain of linguistic transmission?[1]

> If that were so, there would be no essential difference between Pannenberg and those who accent the 'linguisticality of reality.' If it is not so, what is the meaning of event vis-à-vis *Überlieferung*? It would appear that Pannenberg's understanding here requires a more adequate grounding in an ontology that does justice to the whole of reality as a process of events interlaced with the transmissions of their meanings. What we have is a theology in search of a metaphysics, of an ontology of events.[2]

When recently asked to clarify the difficult question of the relationship between an event vis-à-vis its transmission in his concept of history and whether his concept of history adequately encompasses "nature" and "natural happenings," Pannenberg responded by saying that

> natural happenings are included in the concept of history inasmuch as they are experienced as significant for the lives of people, which is the case especially with natural disasters. Whether one can speak of a history of nature as such is quite a different matter. Such a use of language, however, would of course go beyond the concept of history as history of the transmission of traditions (Überlieferungsgeschichte).[3]

One wonders, however, whether this really solves the problem? For "if natural history stands outside of tradition history, how is the latter the most adequate concept for

---

[1]Polk, **On the Way to God**, 78.

[2]Ibid., 78-79. Cf. also Carl E. Braaten's observation that "Pannenberg agrees that the historical events of revelation are not brute facts in the sense of positivistic historicism. The pure facts of positivistic historicism were the result of an abstraction. The facts were abstracted from their historical context, and they were selected from the point of view of positivistic assumptions. If Pannenberg rejects such an approach to the events of biblical history (or any history), Kähler did so too and at a much more difficult time. If the revelatory facts are not intelligible as isolated bare facts, but must be interpreted within the original context of their place in the historical process and the history of their transmission in the tradition (*Überlieferungsgeschichte*), then I do not understand Kähler to have been saying anything else--with this qualification. For Kähler such realities as personal faith, the Holy Spirit, the living Christ, the *viva vox evangelii*, the reality of the church, the apostolic confession of Christ, the biblical witness are all *conditions sine qua non* in our knowledge of historical revelation. They are all essential elements in the hermeneutical arch that spans both the objective occurrence of revelation and the on-going mediation and reception of that revelation. This mediation and reception cannot be reduced to historical reason and the historico-scientific method. This is all the more impossible as long as the professional historians continue to operate with a hidden positivistic world view in their reconstructions of history" ("The Current Controversy on Revelation," 234-235).

[3]Pannenberg to Hasel, January 21, 1994, 1 (translation mine).

embracing reality as history?"¹ The relationship between history and natural event still awaits an adequate clarification by Pannenberg.²

Another problem that arises in this context is the question of the truth status of those words that originate in human imagination. They may be true but they could also be deceptive. Hence they cannot establish why and by what right the content of such imaginative inspirations should be understood as an act of God, much less as a revelation of God.³ This forces Pannenberg to maintain that an inspiration only allows someone to perceive it as God's dealing "if the divinity of God is already proven and evident as reality from another context."⁴ In other words, "immediate religious experience cannot *by itself alone* establish the certainty of the truth of its content."⁵ This means, however, that even though Christian theology begins with the Christian tradition, it must proceed to confirmation of that data vis-à-vis a reality external to the tradition, i.e., contemporary sorts of data, if it is to be scientific.⁶ Thus, taking Scripture as "historical texts"⁷ that reflect a particular tradition, Pannenberg's approach

---

¹Polk, **On the Way to God**, 91, n. 108.

²Nancey C. Murphy recently criticized Pannenberg's theory of revelation for not providing what it claims to do, namely providing an "objective" starting point for theology. Murphy has shown that an entirely different interpretation of history than Pannenberg's is possible. Whereas Pannenberg sees history as a series of acts of God it is also possible to conceive the course of history as devoid of Providence. "Pannenberg claimed that what is needed to settle disputes . . . is for the historians to get straight about the facts: was Jesus raised from the dead or not? But getting straight about this fact led to disputes about the proper method for historians to use, and the choice of method seemed to depend in the end on abstruse views about the meaning of history and whether or not one could account for it without assuming a transcendent ground or the unity of history--which brings us full circle" (**Theology in the Age of Scientific Reasoning**, 49).

³It should be pointed out, however, as David A. Pailin has done, that "although Pannenberg agrees that 'deeper psychological understanding of religious consciousness' cannot by itself show that its 'intensive feeling of reality' is not 'completely erroneous', he argues that a study of 'the fundamental anthropological structure of human behavior' can show that religious experience is not wholly deceptive. It does this by revealing that the structure of human existence both presupposes and finds its fulfillment in 'a mystery of reality transcending its finitude'" (David A. Pailin, **The Anthropological Character of Theology: Conditioning Theological Understanding** [Cambridge: Cambridge University Press, 1990], 108).

⁴Pannenberg, "Response to the Discussion," 237. To hold that inspirations can establish why and by what right an event should be understood as an act of God "would lead once again to an authoritarian claim of revelation" (ibid.), which is absolutely unacceptable for Pannenberg.

⁵Pannenberg, "Response to the Discussion," 239.

⁶Murphy, **Theology in the Age of Scientific Reasoning**, 87.

⁷Ibid., 170.

leads "to a study that seeks its data beyond the confines of Scripture."[1] In that sense history is not the last or ultimate horizon for Pannenberg's theology. In fact, it is understandable why for Pannenberg neither individual human experience, nor tradition which results out of it, nor Scripture as a reflection and testimony of a particular tradition, has final authority. Instead the rationality and coherence of events become normative criteria for Pannenberg that function authoritatively.[2] Not without reason this approach has been recognized by many as being rationalistic in its orientation.[3] It is rationalistic not in the sense that reason brings forth the content of Scripture or revelation, but reason and universal human experience seem to determine the validity and truth of those imaginative inspirations that result in religious traditions.

It appears that the question of the role of Scripture in Pannenberg's theology is ultimately determined largely by his presuppositions and the epistemological basis of it.[4] This raises the question of the relationship between philosophy and theology in

---

[1] Ibid., 87.

[2] Pannenberg stresses that "no tradition can be accepted as true without examination. That would be contrary to reason" (idem, "Jesus' History and Ours," in **Faith and Reality**, trans. John Maxwell [Philadelphia: Westminster Press, 1977], 70). Thus, even faith must be "open to the judgments of reason" (ibid.). Elsewhere Pannenberg writes that "all momentary certainty stands in need of further confirmations and interpretation, and it is only by reference to the unity of all our experience and of all our knowledge that we can determine what is true. Coherence provides the final criterion of truth, and it can serve as such a criterion because it also belongs to the nature of truth: Whatever is true must finally be consistent with all other truth, so that truth is only one, but all-embracing, closely related to the concept of the one God" (idem, **An Introduction to Systematic Theology**, 6, 8). Cf. also idem, **TPS**, 315, where Pannenberg writes: "The traditional claims of a religion may therefore be regarded as hypotheses to be tested by the full range of currently accessible experience. They are to be judged by their ability to integrate the complexity of modern experience into the religion."

[3] Pannenberg himself states that "the result of my reflections was not a surrender of my claim to the rationality of faith but a revision of its form. . . . To the degree that there was a change in my attitude, however, it meant an increase in critical rationality, rather than its limitation in order to make room for faith. I could never understand the argument that faith was in danger if it was in agreement with the judgement of true reason. I rather suspect that the real danger for faith lurks in its estrangement from rationality" ("God's Presence in History," 263).

[4] David H. Kelsey has pointed out that the way a theologian will construe and use Scripture "is itself determined by a logical prior imaginative judgement in which he characterizes in one of several different possible ways the basic *discrimen* of any theology that appeals to scripture, i.e., the conjunction of God's presence among the faithful and their use of scripture" (**The Uses of Scripture in Recent Theology**, 183). In a similar manner it has been pointed out that "the central problem for twentieth century theology is its own epistemological basis. From what fountainhead does theology acquire her information with which she creates her doctrinal models and tests her hypothesis? What is the great *principium theologiae* which provides and authenticates the subject matter for preaching the Gospel? The very weight of this crucial question has kept the debate about Biblical authority at the center of the theological arena in our era, and

Pannenberg's thought. It is well known that for Pannenberg the concerns of theology and philosophy overlap[1] in that both attempt to speak about the whole of reality or about universal truth.[2] The "close connection between theology and philosophy"[3] is especially evident in the necessity of theology to unite with the philosophical idea of God.[4] Thus, Pannenberg states that "Christian theology is dependent upon the conversation with philosophy, especially for the clarification of its discourse about God, but also for its work on the relationship between God and created reality."[5]

Since Pannenberg's concept of God is the foundational idea that guides the structure of his entire systematic theology, it also shapes his understanding of Scripture. Yet, his definition of God "as the all-determining reality"[6] raises a number of questions with regard to Scripture. If God is indeed conceived of in these terms, then "everything must be shown to be determined by this reality and to be ultimately unintelligible without it."[7] Here we touch upon a tension in Pannenberg's understanding of divine causality and the question of the compatibility of human

---

properly so. No endeavor in theology can begin until some answer is given" (Clark H. Pinnock, **A Defense of Biblical Infallibility** [Philadelphia: Presbyterian and Reformed Publishing Company, 1967], 1). James I. Packer similarly writes that *"when you encounter a present-day view of Holy Scripture, you encounter more than a view of Scripture. What you meet is a total view of God and the world, that is, a total theology, which is both an ontology, declaring what there is, and an epistemology, stating how we know what there is"* (Packer, "Encountering Present-Day Views of Scripture," 61).

[1]On the relationship between theology and philosophy in Pannenberg, see the discussion in Tupper, **The Theology of Wolfhart Pannenberg**, 50-54; Polk, **On the Way to God**, 21-27; Georg Kraus, 369-371; Grenz, **Reason for Hope**, 18-21; and Harald Schützeichel, "Das Verhältnis von Theologie und Philosophie in der Sicht Karl Rahners und Wolfhart Pannenbergs," **Renovatio** 43/1 (1987): 19-22. Roger E. Olson thinks that on the one hand Pannenberg seems to reduce theology to philosophy while on the other hand one could also argue that he considers philosophy essentially theologically ("Trinity and Eschatology: The Historical Being of God in the Theology of Wolfhart Pannenberg," 18-19).

[2]Pannenberg has developed his thesis of the complementary nature of theology and philosophy in several places, particularly in "Christian Theology and Philosophical Criticism," in **BQT**, 3:116-143; cf. **TPS**, 303-305.

[3]Pannenberg, **TPS**, 303.

[4]Cf. Pannenberg, "The Appropriation of the Philosophical Concept of God as a Dogmatic Problem of Early Christian Theology," 139. Thus, "Christian faith has to become involved in the philosophical question about the true God and has to give an account of its answer right down to the present time" (ibid., 136).

[5]Pannenberg, **Metaphysics and the Idea of God**, xiii.

[6]Pannenberg, **TPS**, 302.

[7]Pannenberg, **TPS**, 302.

freedom[1] over against God as the power of the future.[2] It seems that Pannenberg's comments about the action of God in the world, as being a repetition or reiteration of his eternal deity,[3] essentially reflects "a continuity with notions of efficient causation, though now viewed somewhat in reverse."[4] The question that arises at this point is whether what comes into momentary existence in history, and here we are specifically interested in the origin of Scripture, is also traceable to any additional agents or efficient causes.

A number of statements make it quite plausible that Pannenberg conceives God ultimately as the One who fully constitutes what emerges in history.[5] This gives the distinct impression that Pannenberg is finally unable to avoid the conclusion of some of his critics that the "openness" of the future is merely epistemological but not ontological. Even his concept of the anticipation of an ultimate unity seems to turn the

---

[1]Pannenberg has tried throughout his theology to affirm the contingent character of history and the freedom of God which establishes creaturely freedom and thus is seen in contrast to the traditional concept of predestination. For a helpful presentation of Pannenberg's thought on this issue, see Polk, **On the Way to God**, 270-280; and idem, "The All-Determining God and the Peril of Determinism," in **TWP**, 152-168.

[2]The compatibility of Pannenberg's idea of God as the power of the future with the experience of human freedom has been questioned by several scholars, such as Gilkey, **Reaping the Whirlwind**, 234-236; Kaiser, 123-124; and David Zedic Nowell, "Futurity and Contingency: An Alternative Paradigm" (Ph.D. dissertation, Baylor University, 1991), 76-77. Even critics normally sympathetic to Pannenberg have expressed concern that this understanding of God does not leave any role for human will. Cf. Philip Hefner, "Theological Reflections: Questions for Moltmann and Pannenberg," **Una Sancta** 25 (1968): 32-51; Roger E. Olson, "Pannenberg's Theological Anthropology: A Review Article," **PRS** 13 (1986): 164; David McKenzie, "Pannenberg on God and Freedom," **JR** 60 (1980): 325-326; and Arthur H. Jentz, Jr., "Personal Freedom and the Futurity of God: Some Reflections on Pannenberg's 'God of Hope'," **RefR** 31 (1977): 151.

[3]Pannenberg, **SyTh/E**, 1:389-391; idem, **SyTh/G**, 2:437-438; idem, **Introduction to Systematic Theology**, 12.

[4]Polk, **On the Way to God**, 286.

[5]Cf. Pannenberg's provocative but somewhat underdeveloped concession in **TPS**, 302: "If 'God' is to be understood as the all-determining reality, everything must be shown to be determined by this reality and to be ultimately unintelligible without it." In an interview with David Polk Pannenberg responded to the question whether there is any degree of self-expression that is not determined by God by saying: "No, I don't think so. . . . Even everything we do in shaping our lives is an effect of God's creative action. They don't work on the same level, and therefore they can't possibly be in competition. If the human person is a *creature* of God, so everything that belongs to that creature, including its self-creative, self-determining potential, is already an effect of the work of the Creator" (as quoted in Polk, **On the Way to God**, 313, n. 262).

openness of the future into a sham.¹ In other words, what happens on the historical plane is decided out of God's eternity or ultimate future which is not yet known to us.² Gilkey has aptly pointed out that if God *does* determine all events from the future then what arises as contingent novelty in *our* midst is that to which God is eternally related. Hence, "contingency is *only* our ignorance of the determining divine will, freedom only our subjective ignorance of God's overwhelming influence over us."³ The end result is that "Pannenberg has merely substituted for the unpalatable tradition of divine pre-determinism an equally odious divine *post-determinism*,"⁴ or what Gilkey has described as "a kind of Calvinism set in temporal reverse gear."⁵ Thus, it seems that Pannenberg has not really been able to overcome the gap between God's (future) eternity and historical reality of which Scripture is a part. His understanding of the nature of God is informed and shaped more by philosophical thought, and here particularly by the Neo-Platonist philosopher Plotinus, than by Scripture itself, and remains at several crucial points unclear and inconsistent.⁶

Last, but not least, is a word on Pannenberg's style of writing. It seems that one factor that contributes significantly to the difficulty in comprehending Pannenberg's ideas, causing a "relative neglect (relative, that is, to what is warranted) of

---

¹Polk, **On the Way to God**, 81, 115.

²Gilkey, "Pannenberg's **Basic Questions in Theology**," 46, 53. On the concept of "the future" in Pannenberg see the discussion on pp. 149f.

³Gilkey, "Pannenberg's **Basic Questions in Theology**," 53. In the words of Polk, the "conclusion seems inescapable that human openness *to* the future is nothing more than a process of discovery of what will come to be but is actually already decided (in God's future)" (**On the Way to God**, 287).

⁴Polk, **On the Way to God**, 287; cf. also 114-115.

⁵Gilkey, "Pannenberg's **Basic Questions in Theology**," 53. Kaiser, 124, follows Gilkey's analysis and judgement. William J. Hill's conclusion, that the future as the mode of being for God implies for Pannenberg that God has not yet achieved his deity can hardly be sustained from Pannenberg's publications (**The Three-Personed God**, 157, 159). In fact, Pannenberg objects strongly to such an idea (**SyTh/E**, 1:390; idem, **SyTh/G**, 2:74, 437).

⁶According to Gilkey, some of those unresolved questions are "*ontological* problems, problems of understanding God in terms of the structure of his reality and of his action--in relation both to time and to history's structure and modes of interaction. These problems involve, therefore, issues concerning the nature of time, space, causality and substance, issues of the reality of beings and their forms of interrelations, and so of God's being and his interrelations. What we have found is a deep unclarity if not confusion on these issues" (Gilkey, "Pannenberg's **Basic Questions in Theology**, 54).

Pannenberg's work to date"[1] is the difficult style of his writings. As a sympathetic interpreter of Pannenberg has said:

> He is--it is commonly said and can hardly be protested--hard to read. Not only are the ideas demanding, but the style is, as they say, 'Germanic'--heavy, ponderous, lumbering, persistently winding in its interconnectedness. In some instances he has been poorly served by translators, but it cannot be denied that his German is rigorous and his written English not felicitous. Given the relaxed standards of contemporary theological education, that explains in large part why Pannenberg is not the rage in seminaries and divinity schools.[2]

This perceptive description of Pannenberg's writing style explains why Pannenberg generally appears to be more respected than read.[3] While his writing style in some way reflects the complexity of his ideas and neither constitutes an inconsistency in his approach nor questions the validity of what he claims, it certainly is not always helpful in the presentation and distribution of his thought, and in this sense can be seen as a weakness in the propagation of his ideas.

Despite the above perceived weaknesses one has to give credit to Pannenberg for his brilliant attempt to structure and develop his entire theology in a truly systematic fashion from the idea of God. With regard to Scripture, this has demonstrated that one's concept of God does indeed significantly shape and influence one's understanding of Scripture. The degree of conceptual consistency with which Pannenberg remains true to his own fundamental principles of theological understanding is remarkable. His erudition and scientific rigor have made him one of the giants of modern theology.

Bloesch's View of Scripture

As in Pannenberg's case, this evaluation of Bloesch's view of Scripture begins with the strengths of his presentation before turning to some of his weaknesses.

Strengths

A reader of Bloesch's writings will appreciate his lucid style and irenic spirit. He demonstrates a forthrightness in his discussion of theological issues and shows a desire to be relevant to current issues. Bloesch engages a wide variety of different positions and demonstrates a genuine interest to enter into dialogue with those of different persuasions. His writings are characterized by a genuine desire to build

---

[1] Neuhaus, "Theology for Church and Polis," 228.

[2] Ibid.

[3] Ibid., 227.

bridges, wherever possible, between various parties in the church.[1] Through his publications Bloesch has exerted a considerable influence among evangelical scholars and thereby contributed significantly to modern evangelical theology.

Consistent with his confessional approach, Bloesch firmly believes "that Scripture can be an authoritative and credible guide for faith and practice even in our day."[2] Bloesch is to be commended for trying to take Scripture's own claim to its divine authority seriously, thereby following up on his professed approach to seek to develop a theological methodology that is informed by the Biblical material.[3] In harmony with this perspective, Bloesch acknowledges the existence, in at least some form, of cognitive revelation and maintains that inspiration encompasses not only the divine election and superintendence of particular writers but also of their writings.[4] By affirming both conceptual and verbal aspects in inspiration[5] and revelation, Bloesch appears to advance somewhat beyond the Neo-Orthodox position of his theological mentor Karl Barth,[6] for whom the reality of a cognitive element in revelation and a verbal dimension in inspiration are certainly not as clearly present, if at all. Bloesch, who wishes "to defend the orthodox evangelical faith"[7] and sees himself as standing in continuity with the position of the Protestant Reformers, rather than following the liberal wing of modern Protestant theology, has endeavored to go beyond a liberal understanding of Scripture[8] by affirming a sacramental view of it that takes seriously a "meaning-content"[9] that is conveyed in Scripture which transcends both culture and

---

[1]Cf. Bloesch, **HSRII**, 14-15.

[2]Ibid., 11.

[3]Bloesch, **The Ground of Certainty**, 22.

[4]Bloesch, **HSRII**, 119-121. According to Bloesch inspiration entails not only the aspects of divine election and guidance of the writers and the superintendence in the process of their writing but also "the inward illumination of hearers and readers, and the communication of the truth of revelation" as well as "the providential preservation of these writings as the unique channel of revelation" (ibid., 119-120). By including the aspect of illumination under the general category of inspiration, one can see an influence of Karl Barth's thought on Bloesch's position.

[5]Ibid., 120.

[6]For a succinct reaction of Bloesch on Barth's view of Scripture, see ibid., 101-103.

[7]Ibid., 11.

[8]Ibid., 103-105.

[9]By this Bloesch has in mind God's self-revelation in Jesus Christ (ibid., 56).

history.¹ In this sacramental understanding of Scripture, however, Bloesch demonstrates a greater affinity with Karl Barth's position than with the Protestant Reformers. Although Bloesch and Luther both have a Christological emphasis in their approach to Scripture, Bloesch differs significantly from Luther, Calvin, and Zwingli in that he does not identify Scripture with the Word of God whereas the Protestant Reformers regarded this identification as self-evident.² Even in his Christological emphasis, Bloesch appears closer to Karl Barth than to Luther.

Bloesch can also be credited with having emphasized again the aspect of God's transcendence, an aspect that appears to have been prominent among the Protestant Reformers but which has been rather marginalized in modern theology. Consistent with this assumption of God's transcendence, Bloesch develops a view of man that is characterized by an awareness of the noetic effects of sin on human reason and man's utter inability to come to a true knowledge of God by himself. Hence, he strongly emphasizes the need for supernatural revelation and the work of the Holy Spirit because there is no natural point of contact between humankind and God. The prominence of the idea of God's transcendence and his allegiance to the Protestant Reformation and fidelity to the historic tradition of the church³ ensure that Scripture is not perceived as a purely human document.

Still, one cannot help but note several weaknesses in Bloesch's view of Scripture which deserve closer attention.

Weaknesses

One of those weaknesses is the tension, if not inconsistency, that exists in Bloesch's understanding of the origin and nature of Scripture. On the one hand, he repeatedly stresses his conviction in an ultimately divine origin of Scripture.⁴ On the other, however, he maintains a particular understanding of the human dimension of Scripture that tends to negate some of the characteristics usually associated with a

---

¹Ibid., 115.

²McGrath, **The Genesis of Doctrine**, 123.

³Bloesch, **HSRII**, 13.

⁴"Both Testaments amply testify to the divine origin of Scripture" (ibid., 85); "The Bible is God-breathed in the sense that it is a production of the creative breath of God. The breath of the Holy Spirit accounts for both the Bible's origin and its viability through the ages" (ibid., 120); "we can say with catholic and evangelical tradition that God is the primary author of Scripture, and the prophets and apostles secondary authors" (ibid., 125).

divine origin of Scripture, such as its utter trustworthiness in all it affirms and touches upon, its clarity and perspicuity, as well as its sufficiency. Despite Bloesch's affirmation of the divine superintendence by the Holy Spirit on the writers and their writings,[1] "the text when taken only by itself, apart from its theological and spiritual context, is fallible and deficient."[2] The fallibility and deficiency of Scripture is not restricted to historical information, as some might expect, but extends even to "the areas of ethics and theology."[3] It is readily apparent, as Bloesch himself admits, that his "stand is in contradiction to a biblicism that bases the authority of the Bible on its divine perfection as a supernatural book."[4] One wonders about the consistency[5] of

---

[1] Bloesch states that he "prefer[s] to think of inspiration mainly in connection with the biblical writings, which constitute the primary witness to divine revelation" (ibid., 119) and therefore writes that "inspiration is both conceptual and verbal. It is permissible to speak of verbal inspiration or verbal inspiredness, but not in the sense of perfect factual accuracy or mechanical dictation" (ibid., 120).

[2] Ibid., 126.

[3] Ibid., 122. For a list of examples of what Bloesch considers cultural conditioning, historical inaccuracies, and internal contradictions in Scripture, see ibid., 108-110. Bloesch acknowledges "innocent factual inaccuracies in the Bible," but he hesitates "to call these errors. I readily grant that forms of expression in Scripture may conflict with science, but science is not the final norm, for scientific theories are constantly in flux. Because error does not touch what is truly divine in the Bible, it is more proper to speak of 'difficulties' than errors, or chaff but not tares" (ibid., 117).

[4] Ibid., 78.

[5] As far as the question of a change or development in his thinking on this point is concerned one can attest to a general consistency in Bloesch's thought over the years. As far as the understanding and the role of Scripture is concerned one cannot speak of an "evolution," or a change in Bloesch's theology, where he shifted from one position to another. In fact some of his earliest statements on the issue under investigation (cf. Bloesch, **Theological Notebook**, vol. 1, **1960-1964**, 58, 68-69, 163, 174, 184); idem, **Theological Notebook**, vol. 2, **1964-1968**, 17, 63, 69, 76, 80, 93, 105, 116-117, 130-131, 143-144), are repeated almost verbatim in his recent writings. Rather than speaking about a change in Bloesch's concept of Scripture one could speak of a more explicit emphasis on the Role of the Holy Spirit in his later writings. While in 1985 Bloesch was still hesitant to call his approach to Scripture "pneumatic" (Bloesch, "A Christological Hermeneutic: Crisis and Conflict in Hermeneutics," 100), he now is willing to term his approach "a historical-pneumatic hermeneutics" (idem, **HSRII**, 206-207). At the same time it seems that Bloesch has distanced himself more from the position of Benjamin Warfield, even though he never subscribed to it in toto. Thus, in **EET**, 1:54-55, he affirmed that "with Warfield we hold this [i.e., the inspiration of Scripture] to mean that all Scripture is breathed out by God, is a product of the creative activity of the Spirit of God. It must not mean (as in Protestant liberalism) that the writers were simply assisted and illumined by the Spirit: they were so guided by the Spirit that what was actually written had the very sanction of God himself." More recently, however, one can notice a subtle nuance in his appreciation of Warfield when he writes: "In my opinion Warfield was correct in his contention that inspiration means something more than 'breathed into' in the sense of illumination (as liberals often describe it). Yet he sometimes spoke as if the Bible were directly divine, thereby failing to acknowledge its human, fallible character . . . Scripture thus

Bloesch's assertion that Scripture contains a fallible and deficient account, even in matters of ethics and theology, and his simultaneous affirmation that the Bible is nevertheless "not mistaken in what it purports to teach."[1] If the potential for error is grounded in Scripture's humanity, as Bloesch seems to hold, how can it not be mistaken in what it purports to teach?[2] There seems to be a tension if not an inconsistency in what Bloesch wants to affirm about the nature of Scripture and what he repudiates.[3]

---

becomes transparent to its object, with the result that God's Word is readily accessible to human perception and conception" (idem, **HSRII**, 88).

[1]Bloesch, **HSRII**, 115. Bloesch does not explain why language can function as a reliable guide in matters that pertain to Jesus Christ and the salvation through him but is misleading in other areas. Nor has he dealt with the phenomenon that in Scripture statements that pertain to such theological issues as salvation through Jesus Christ are often closely linked with historical statements that assume the historical reliability of the Scriptural account. Cf. John T. Baldwin, "Progressive Creationism and Biblical Revelation: Some Theological Implications," **JATS** 3/1 (1992): 105-119. It appears that Bloesch's contention about language's reliability in matters of salvation but its unreliability in other areas is somewhat arbitrary. While he affirms that the Bible "contains both wheat and husk," where "the authority of Scripture rests finally not on the inspired record but on God speaking to us through this record" (**HSRII**, 125), in his debate over the Feminist revision of the language about God he maintains that we have the divine content only in the cultural form in which it is given to us. Hence, he argues, it is wrong to think that the church is no longer bound to the mythological garment in which the faith is enclosed (Bloesch, **Is the Bible Sexist?** 33-34); cf. the critique by Maddox, "The Necessity of Recognizing Distinctions," 311-323; and idem, "Reply to Donald Bloesch," 285-288.

[2]D. A. Carson has pointed out the difficulties in the argument that error is essentially human. "The question is whether it is error that is essential to humanness, or finitude. If the latter, it is difficult to see why Scripture would be any less 'human' if God so superintended its writing that no error was committed. Human beings are always finite; but it does not follow they are always in error. Error does not seem to be essential to humanness. But if someone wishes to controvert the point, then to be consistent that person must also insist that between the Fall and the new heaven and the new earth, not only error but *sinfulness* is essential to humanness. No writer of Scripture escaped the sinfulness of his fallen nature while composing what came to be recognized as Holy Writ: does this mean that the humanness of Scripture entails not only error but sinfulness? And if not, why not? Who wishes to say that Scripture is sinful? This is not mere *reductio ad absurdem*: rather, it is a way of showing that human beings who in the course of their lives inevitably err and sin do not necessarily err and sin in any particular circumstance. Their humanness is not compromised when they fail to err or sin. By the same token, a God who safeguards them from error in a particular circumstance--namely, the writing of Scripture--has not thereby vitiated their humanness" ("Recent Developments in the Doctrine of Scripture," 27-28).

[3]Nash has questioned the logic behind claiming an absolute qualitative difference between God and man and at the same time making some valid statements about God. "If there is absolutely no point of contact between the divine logic and a so-called human logic, then what passes as human 'reasoning' can never be valid. And, of course, if this were so, then the putative reasoning in Bloesch's own book would be invalid" (Ronald H. Nash, 96). A similar critique has been voiced about Bloesch's fideistic alternative by P. Joseph Cahill. "The very effort to explain the option [i.e., fideism over against rationalism] involves so much rationalism that one wonders if the author is doing anything more than reviewing the Kierkegaardian option with a bit of

This predicament is not satisfactorily solved even with Bloesch's sacramental view of Scripture whereby he tries to combine and hold together the qualitative transcendence of divine truth and the fallibility of the human element of Scripture. While there is an inescapable relation between the divine and the human elements in Scripture, it appears that Bloesch falls short of affirming an absolute identity between God's Word and Scripture.[1] Rather than conceiving Scripture in terms of a union of the human and the divine elements, Bloesch's "own preference is to speak of a *conjunction* between the Word of God and sacred Scripture by the action of the Spirit."[2] One wonders why the divine aspect, which Bloesch affirms, has hardly any direct influence on the human dimension. Is there truly a union of the human and divine in Scripture, that makes it fully human and fully divine at the same time, or rather, do the two remain separate and are conjoined only in a dialectical and paradoxal manner through the Holy Spirit?[3]

It seems that the difficulty that one encounters at this point in Bloesch's thinking is intricately connected to his understanding of language and revelation and the manner in which one can gain a true knowledge of God. It is here that we come across another set of inconsistencies that deserve our attention. Although Bloesch seems to

---

rationalism that perhaps Kierkegaard himself would have found objectionable" ("Review of **The Ground of Certainty**, 203).

[1] Bloesch, **HSRII**, 57.

[2] Ibid., 58. Earlier Bloesch wrote in a similar manner: "While we must resist the temptation to posit a direct identity between Scripture and revelation (since this could lead to bibliolatry), we do affirm an indirect identity in that by the work of the Holy Spirit the very human words of the prophets and apostles are conjoined with the Word spoken by God to them. God's Word is consequently not the Bible in and of itself but the correlation of Scripture and Spirit (Barth)" (idem, **EET**, 1:53); cf. also a similar statement made in 1963 where Bloesch writes: "The relation between the divine and the human in the Bible and the church is only analogous, not identical, to the relation between God and man in Jesus Christ. The reason is that the Bible and the church are not exempt from the stain of sin; consequently there can be only an intimate association or conjunction, not a substantial union, between the Word of God on the one hand and the Bible and the church on the other. Neither the Bible nor the church is to be identified with the Word of God, as is Jesus Christ; but they become the Word of God when they are made vehicles of the outreach and presence of Jesus Christ" (idem, **Theological Notebook**, 1:68-69).

[3] If one wanted to correlate Bloesch's understanding of the nature of Scripture to the early Christological controversies, it would seem that its greatest affinities are neither with the Ebionite nor with the Docetic point of view but with the Nestorian understanding of the nature of Christ. Nestorius, who although affirming that Christ was two persons, one human, one divine, denied any real organic union between the two.

want to maintain some form of propositional revelation,[1] he repeatedly stresses the fact that "even the language of . . . the Bible is not exempt from the crisis of the limitation of all human language in conveying real knowledge of God."[2] This means not only that human language is rather limited in its capability to effectively communicate a true knowledge of God and His salvific will but that "our propositional statements are at least one step removed from the revelation itself and therefore always stand under the judgment of revelation."[3] Furthermore, the content of such a propositional revelation is limited to salvific matters and the gospel of Jesus Christ. Bloesch does not question only the limitations of human language to fully express all the dimensions of divine revelation. To this hardly anyone appears to object. But more than that, one gets the impression that Bloesch doubts that what is being reported in Scripture is trustworthy in all it affirms. Furthermore, the theological meaning is not dependent on the text at all but is a gift of the Spirit. One wonders how he can affirm that there is propositional revelation if it cannot be discerned and if it is not connected to the text. Thus, there is a pervasive skepticism on the part of Bloesch about the adequacy of human language to effectively communicate God's will to mankind, for he is convinced that "the human words and concepts employed by the Holy Spirit in the formation of the Scriptures fall short of bringing us univocal knowledge of God."[4] Instead he conceives Biblical language for the most part as being "symbolic"[5] or "mythopoetic"[6] in nature. For him, the mystery of revealed truth cannot be encapsulated in any human language, "not even the language of sacred Scripture."[7] How Bloesch can consistently maintain at the

---

[1]Bloesch writes that "language is the vehicle by which the truth of God is communicated to the human subject. . . . Meaning will *eo ipso* be expressed in propositions" (**TWS**, 104).

[2]Ibid., 69.

[3]Bloesch, **Theological Notebook**, 2:105. Similarly, Bloesch stated more recently that "we need to acknowledge that the holy Spirit guided the prophets in their reflection, but their articulation of this reflection is at least one step removed from the revelation itself" (**HSRII**, 56).

[4]Bloesch, **TWS**, 81.

[5]Ibid., 70-71; idem, **The Battle for the Trinity: The Debate over Inclusive God-Language** (Ann Arbor, MI: Servant Publications, 1985), 20-27.

[6]Bloesch, **TWS**, 70; idem, **HSRII**, 259.

[7]Bloesch, **TWS**, 75; idem, **EET**, 1:69-70, where he states: "It is inadmissible to treat the Bible as though it were a source book of revealed truths that can be drawn out of Scripture by deductive or inductive logic. The truth of the Bible can only be known as the Spirit makes it known in the event of revelation, yet even here there is no direct perception of truth but only a submission and reception which are adequate for salvation but not for comprehension. The truth

same time "that our knowledge of God is neither clear and distinct"[1] and yet claim that it gives "us vital information that we neglect only at our peril"[2] will be difficult for some to understand.

It seems that Bloesch's position on the inadequacy of human language and knowledge about divine things stems at least from two different aspects in his thought. On the one hand, the depravity of humankind is responsible for the limited capability of human beings to speak about God and to know Him exhaustively. On the other hand, there seems to be an ontological difference between God and humankind that is responsible for this limitation. Even though man is able to grasp some cognitive truths about God and His salvific will in faith, this knowledge still cannot be adequately expressed in human language because it remains on the historical plane, whereas God appears to be beyond it.[3] Although Bloesch at times appears to be aware of the

---

in the Bible is enveloped in mystery and therefore can only be dimly perceived (1 Cor. 13:9, 12). Indeed mystery and revelation often seem to go together (cf. Mark 13:11; 1 Cor. 2:7; Rom. 16:25). This does not mean that the Word of God is basically unknowable but that it cannot be known exhaustively and that it remains mysterious even to faithful reason (Rom. 11:33)." According to Bloesch, he has been influenced on this point by "Søren Kierkegaard, who teaches that the mystery of divine revelation comes to us in the form of the Absolute Paradox--God becoming man in Jesus Christ, which cannot be fully assimilated or comprehended by human reason. But it is not irrational, for we can state true propositions about this mystery, though we cannot resolve the mystery in a rational system" (Bloesch to Hasel, 14 December 1993, 1). It should be pointed out, however, that a mystery in the Biblical sense could be more adequately described as "something that can be known--indeed, that to some extent *must be* known--but cannot be fully or exhaustively understood. A mystery in the Christian sense is neither an enigma nor a secret but a truth to be proclaimed" (Harold O. J. Brown, "On Method and Means in Theology," in **Doing Theology in Today's World: Essays in Honor of Kenneth S. Kantzer**, ed. John D. Woodbridge and Thomas Edward McComiskey [Grand Rapids, MI: Zondervan Publishing House, 1991], 148). In a similar fashion, James I. Packer has stated that "a dimension of *mystery* is inescapable and must be acknowledged whenever we set ourselves to think about God. By this I mean, not that there is anything necessarily and intrinsically unclear in what God has revealed in the Bible, but that we must always proceed on the basis that there is more to God's being, work, and purposes than we have been told, or could grasp if we were told" ("Is Systematic Theology a Mirage? An Introductory Discussion," in ibid., 29-30). It has been pointed out that in "Lutheran theology the clarity of Scripture pertains to the language and sense and words of Scripture, not to the teachings and mysteries of faith, which can never be understood but must be accepted on faith. . . . The clarity of Scripture is an intrinsic and objective clarity of its words and sense. If read according to its literal sense, i.e., its native and intended sense, Scripture is clear to anyone, also the unregenerate" (Preus, **The Theology of Post-Reformation Lutheranism**, 1:312-313). Cf. also Slenczka, "Schriftautorität und Schriftkritik," 328-329.

[1]Bloesch, **TWS**, 80.

[2]Ibid., 81.

[3]Thus, Bloesch can say that "the focus of faith is not on history as such, not even on biblical history, but on eternity breaking into history at a particular time and place" (ibid., 42).

difficulty in establishing a relationship between an eternal (timeless) God with historical creation,[1] he also speaks of the "contradictory truth that the eternal God enters time."[2] Could it be that Bloesch has not yet sufficiently clarified his understanding of the nature of God and here especially the question of God's relationship to His creation and God's action in history, so that a conclusive position on this point can be reached?[3]

Furthermore, is Bloesch's distinction between the message or truth of Scripture, which is infallible, and its (fallible) words, in the sense of human witness to the divine revelation in Jesus Christ, truly warranted? The difficulty with such a position is that the infallible meaning is not only removed from the words but also from the realm of the text because the theological meaning is a gift that is given to the eyes of faith by the Spirit.[4] D. A. Carson has pointed out that this constitutes nothing less than a transfer of the locus of authority from Scripture to the Spirit-illumined knower[5] which is hardly warranted by the Scriptural material itself.[6]

---

[1] Cf. Bloesch, **EET**, 1:25-31.

[2] Bloesch, **TWS**, 77, 78.

[3] It is hoped that Bloesch will be able to address some of these questions with greater clarity and rigor in the third volume of his Systematic Theology. In a personal interview with the author Bloesch indicated that he considers his treatment of the doctrine of God in many respects as the most important of all.

[4] "In biblical perspective meaning is the intent given to a word by the Spirit of God. . . . The meaning of a biblical text is revealed only in the act of discourse between the ultimate author, the Holy Spirit, and the reader or hearer who comes to the Scriptures in faith. Meaning in this ultimate sense is therefore a gift, not an achievement" (Bloesch, **TWS**, 103).

[5] Carson, "Recent Developments in the Doctrine of Scripture," 37-38.

[6] Cf. Grudem, "Scripture's Self-Attestation and the Problem of Formulating a Doctrine of Scripture," 19-59. A number of recent studies have ably demonstrated that human language can be an effective carrier of divinely revealed content. See for example the excellent studies by Jack Barentsen, "The Validity of Human Language: A Vehicle for Divine Truth," in **GTJ** 9/1 (1988): 21-43; Eckhard Schnabel, **Inspiration und Offenbarung: Die Lehre vom Ursprung und Wesen der Bibel** (Wuppertal: R. Brockhaus Verlag, 1986), 130-137; William J. Larkin, Jr. **Culture and Biblical Hermeneutics: Interpreting and Applying the Authoritative Word in a Relativistic Age** (Grand Rapids, MI: Baker Book House, 1988), 242-251; John M. Frame, "God and Biblical Language: Transcendence and Immanence," in **God's Inerrant Word: An International Symposium on the Trustworthiness of Scripture**, ed. John Warwick Montgommery (Minneapolis, MN: Bethany Fellowship, 1974), 159-177; James I. Packer, "The Adequacy of Human Language," in **Inerrancy**, ed. Norman L. Geisler (Grand Rapids, MI: Zondervan Publishing House, 1980), 197-226; Vern S. Poythress, "Adequacy of Language and Accommodation," in **Hermeneutics, Inerrancy, and the Bible**, ed. Earl D. Radmacher and Robert D. Preus (Grand Rapids, MI: Zondervan Publishing House, 1984), 351-376; Heinzpeter Hempelmann, "Veritas Hebraica als Grundlage christlicher Theologie: Zur systematisch-theologischen Relevanz der biblisch-hebräischen Sprachgestalt," in **Hebraica Veritas: Die hebräische Grundlage der biblischen Theologie als exegetische und systematische Aufgabe**,

Moreover, by accepting the Barthian premise that revelation takes place only in Jesus Christ, Bloesch seems to separate divine revelation, which is beyond the historical realm,[1] from the human words of Scripture, which belong to the historical realm. By creating a *diastasis* between the written Word of God and the personified Word of God, Bloesch in effect tends to separate the theological aspect from its historical dimension, although he tries to keep the two together through the paradoxical work of the Spirit. In the final analysis, however, Bloesch does not seem to have so much a high view of Scripture, as a cognitive source of theology, but appears to hold a high view of the revelatory sacramental function of Scripture which is made possible through the Spirit.

Bloesch at times acknowledges that he does not develop his understanding of Scripture directly from the Bible itself but rather starts out with the living Christ as mediated to man by the Holy Spirit. Thus, it appears that Bloesch's view of the inadequacy of human language to effectively communicate God's will to humankind depends upon some deeper philosophical presuppositions that are at work in his thought. This brings us to another inconsistency in his approach, namely the relationship between philosophy and theology. Although he has repeatedly advocated a position where "true theology necessarily excludes philosophy"[2] and where "the relation between theology and philosophy is not one of synthesis or correlation but one of conflict and contradiction,"[3] the question remains whether he has been able to entirely rid himself of philosophical influences.[4] Here I have in mind especially the

---

ed. Klaus Haacker and Heinzpeter Hempelmann (Wuppertal: R. Brockhaus, 1989), 39-78; idem, **Gott--Ein Schriftsteller! J. G. Hamann über die End-Äußerung Gottes ins Wort der Heiligen Schrift und ihre hermeneutischen Konsequenzen** (Wuppertal: R. Brockhaus, 1988); cf. also Oswald Bayer, **Autorität und Kritik: Zu Hermeneutik und Wissenschaftstheorie** (Tübingen: J. C. B. Mohr, 1991), 51-58.

[1]"The arena of revelation and salvation is not the world, understood as either nature or history, but the life, death and resurrection of Jesus Christ. The Incarnation of God in Christ as well as the resurrection of Christ to God occurred in history but at the same time beyond history (in superhistory). These events are not to be subsumed under *Historie*, objective, recorded history as such, but under *Geschichte*, the eternal significance of a particular history, which cannot be uncovered by historical research or investigation" (Bloesch, **TWS**, 183).

[2]Ibid., 43.

[3]Ibid.; cf. also idem, **The Ground of Certainty**, 7, 26-50, 78-104.

[4]Vunderink, 88-89, points out that "to the extent that he is a loyal follower of Barth, one may expect to find Kantian and Platonic elements in Bloesch's future biblical or constructive theology."

influence of Kierkegaard's philosophy, whose impact can also be seen on Karl Barth's thought.[1] Kierkegaard appears to have exercised a significant influence on Bloesch's theology[2] as well as Kant's distinction between the realm of the phenomena and the noumena.

Kierkegaard's emphasis on the paradoxal[3] nature of truth is repeatedly reflected in Bloesch's theology.[4] The counterpart to Kierkegaard's emphasis on the theme of the paradox is his doctrine that truth is subjectivity.[5] What Kierkegaard insisted on was that it is wrong to think of religious truth as acquired in the same way as one obtains information. In a similar manner, Bloesch maintains that "the revelatory meaning of the text cannot be procured by any technique" but "can only be conveyed by the action of the Spirit upon the text and within our hearts."[6] Here the danger of personal subjectivism becomes quite real.

It should be noted that the premise--that no one can have a saving understanding of the Bible apart from the illuminating work of the Holy Spirit--does not necessarily

---

[1] Cf. Wilhelm Anz, "Zur Wirkungsgeschichte Kierkegaards in der deutschen Theologie und Philosophie," **ZTK** 79 (1982): 452-460; Alastair McKinnon, "Barth's Relation to Kierkegaard: Some Further Light," **CJT** 13 (1967): 31-41; J. Heywood Thomas, "The Christology of Soren Kierkegaard and Karl Barth," **HibJ** 53 (1955): 280-288; William Walter Wells, "The Influence of Kierkegaard on the Theology of Karl Barth" (Ph.D. dissertation, Syracuse University, 1970), 215-265; and idem, "The Reveille That Awakened Karl Barth," **JETS** 22/3 (1979): 223-233.

[2] Kierkegaard's affirmation of the qualitative distance between God and humankind, his emphasis on the priority of faith over reason, his use of the concept of paradox, his view that man can never expect to be able to complete a system which will explain reality, as well as his emphasis on the existential dimension of truth are some areas where Kierkegaard's influence on Bloesch's thought becomes apparent. Bloesch mentions Kierkegaard repeatedly as belonging to his theological ancestral tree (**EET**, 1:4; idem, **HSRII**, 12; idem to Frank M. Hasel, December 14, 1993, 1); cf. also idem, **TWS**, 61-66.

[3] For a brief presentation of the idea of paradox in Kierkegaard, see Livingston, 316-320; Sylvia I. Walsh, "Paradox," in **A New Handbook of Christian Theology**, ed. Donald W. Musser and Joseph L. Price (Nashville, TN: Abingdon, 1992), 347; and E. Herbert Nygren, "Existentialism: Kierkegaard," in **Biblical Errancy: An Analysis of Its Philosophical Roots**, ed. Norman L. Geisler (Grand Rapids, MI: Zondervan Publishing House, 1981), 119-124. It has been pointed out that Kierkegaard "never took the question of the nature of contradiction seriously, and hence he never explained the difference, if any, between paradox (in his sense of the word) and mere inconsistency. But without such a clarification, the notion is fatally unclear" (Alasdair MacIntyre, "Kierkegaard, Søren Aabye," **The Encyclopedia of Philosophy**, ed. Paul Edwards (New York: Macmillan, 1967), 4:339.

[4] Bloesch, **TWS**, 62-63, 65-66, 76-81, 199-200; idem, **HSRII**, 41, 77, 79, 87, 119, 266, 271, 290, 295.

[5] Livingston, 320.

[6] Bloesch, "A Christological Hermeneutic," 100.

warrant Bloesch's conclusion that the Spirit has to supplant something that is not present in Scripture itself. If the words of Scripture are obscure in themselves and insufficient, the teaching of the Holy Spirit becomes clearer than Scripture and consequently more authoritative too.[1] This, strangely enough, is indicated even by Bloesch himself, when he writes that the "Spirit takes precedence over the Bible."[2] Consequently, the Reformation principle of the clarity of Scripture, and with it the *sola Scriptura* principle, can no longer be upheld because Scripture cannot be obscure and remain the sole authority for faith.[3] If Scripture alone ultimately is not the criterion (*Scriptura iudex*) by which and with which to judge man and church,[4] the critical and correcting function of Scripture over against non-Scriptural ideas and traditions is endangered. What normative standard is there to decide whether it is indeed the Holy Spirit which is speaking and whether the Spirit's teaching is true and in harmony with God's will?[5]

The problematic relationship between the human and the divine, the historical and the eternal aspects in Bloesch's understanding of Scripture finds another expression in his willingness to use historical-critical methods on the one hand and his refusal on the other to pursue the logical-consistent course of an intrinsically naturalistic or a-

---

[1] In my opinion, the work of the Spirit, among other aspects, consists in the illumination of the believer and redirects the reader of Scripture to Scripture so that Scripture, which is inspired by the Spirit of God, can explain Scripture, and be the sole source of its own exposition. Cf. Slenczka, "Schriftautorität und Schriftkritik," 325-326.

[2] Bloesch, **TWS**, 13.

[3] Pinnock, **Biblical Revelation: The Foundation of Christian Theology**, 96-101, especially 99: "The theological issue runs deep. . . . An obscure book could not perform the functions Scripture would perform. A denial of perspicuity is a denial of the *sola scriptura* principle itself. The clarity of Scripture is denied by every man-centered theology in interest of promoting another source of 'clearer revelation.'" Cf. Robert T. Sandin, "The Clarity of Scripture," 244; and Duchrow, 1-17. Martin Luther, in his exchange with Erasmus was adamant in his insistence on the clarity of Scripture (LW, 33, 94). On Luther's understanding of the clarity of Scripture, see also Kohls, 46-75; Hermann, **Von der Klarheit der Heiligen Schrift**; Beisser, **Claritas Scripturae**; and Rothen, **Die Klarheit der Schrift**.

[4] Slenczka, "Schriftautorität und Schriftkritik," 323-324.

[5] Susan Foh has pointed out this problem in Bloesch's argument. Commenting on Bloesch's understanding of human language she writes: "The Bible is not the final authority but the Spirit in the believers. The problem with this view is the loss of an objective standard. What happens if the Spirit apparently says different things to different Christians?" (Review of **The Battle for the Trinity: The Debate Over Inclusive God-Language**, by Donald G. Bloesch," **WTJ** 48 [1986]: 408).

theistic method.¹ In order to avoid the historical dissolution of the supernatural aspect of Scripture, Bloesch opts for what he calls "theological" reading of Scripture, which is not strictly dependent upon the historical meaning of the text and must be given supernaturally by the Holy Spirit. Since divine truth is not dependent on historical investigation and cannot be determined by it, one wonders why Bloesch still upholds the need for a historical-critical investigation of the Biblical text? Why engage in exegesis and theology at all if the meaning is not dependent on the text and its historical-critical investigation is given as a gift by the Spirit? It seems that Bloesch wants to have it both ways, eat the (Biblical) cake by means of historical-critical scholarship and at the same time keep it (i.e., the theological meaning of Scripture).

Bloesch demonstrates a genuine desire to know God's will and to do it, and firmly believes that the Spirit of God will instruct us today. Through his acceptance of some cognitive element in revelation he tries to recover a divine dimension of Scripture that is missing in much of neo-orthodox theology. But although he is earnestly trying to overcome the limitations and ambiguities of previous positions, especially that of Karl Barth's theology² and of rationalistic Fundamentalism,³ in the final analysis Bloesch's understanding of Scripture falls short of being a satisfactory advance over against the shortcomings of both. In fact, his approach "stands in danger of becoming a rather worn-out Barthian way that looks back into the decades of the fifties and sixties rather than into the future."⁴

Finally, in trying to describe and evaluate Bloesch's position, one is faced with the notorious difficulty that he often radically redefines the theological terms and concepts that he uses so that "at worst they are self-contradictory and at best lack much relationship to their historic usages."⁵ Such an inflation of the content of common

---

¹Cf. Adolf Schlatter, **Atheistische Methoden in der Theologie** (Gütersloh: Bertelsmann, 1909). The problematic if not incompatible relationship between historical-critical scholarship and dogmatics has been recognized by many. Cf. Fritz Buri, **Dogmatik als Selbstverständnis des Christlichen Glaubens**, 2 vols. (Bern: Verlag Paul Haupt, 1956), 1:315-325; Hermann Diem, **Dogmatics**, trans. Harold Knight (Philadelphia: Westminster Press, 1959), 4-9; and more recently Noller.

²Bloesch, **Jesus Is Victor**, 31.

³Cf. Bloesch, **HSRII**, 94-100; idem, **The Future of Evangelical Christianity**, 24-29.

⁴Richard A. Muller, "Review of **A Theology of Word and Spirit: Authority and Method in Theology**, by Donald G. Bloesch," **CTJ** 29/1 (1994): 307.

⁵Bloesch argues, for example, for the infallibility and even inerrancy of Scripture but then

terms and concepts not only makes problematic Bloesch's claim and desire to stand in continuity with the vision of the great Protestant Reformers, but also inhibits an effective dialogue between different theological positions and makes a meaningful discussion of the latter less than satisfactory. Thus, one of his strengths, namely his desire to build bridges wherever possible, makes a certain eclecticism almost unavoidable[1] and at times leaves an ambivalent impression in the name of mediation.[2] It has been noted that on the important issue of Scriptural authority, Bloesch repeatedly seems to "take away with one hand what he wants to maintain with the other."[3] This discrepancy in Bloesch's thought seems to stem from two different understandings of Scripture, each of which was originally intended to explain the Bible to the exclusion of the other.[4]

Conclusion and Final Suggestions

This investigation into the nature and role of Scripture in two prominent contemporary systematic theologians has led to a description, analysis, comparison, and

---

goes on to qualify those terms by stating that this does not leave us with a totally inerrant Bible (cf. **HSRII**, 107-117). Paul D. Feinberg lists another example from Bloesch's earlier work **EET**, vol. 1, by pointing to Bloesch's treatment of irresistible grace. "He believes the idea of irresistible grace is theologically correct, yet goes on to qualify the concept. Although grace is given to all and not to just a select group of the elect, this does not mean that all are saved. Grace is seen as triumphing even in the unsaved 'in the form of wrath and judgment.' Is God then drawing them irresistibly to wrath and judgment? Clearly, Bloesch wants to say no, but it is not easy to see how he can" (Feinberg, "An Evangelical Systematic Theology, 38, 41 [1259, 1262]).

[1]"In short, our approach to metaphysics and philosophy must be utilitarian" (Bloesch, **TWS**, 49).

[2]According to Mark A. Noll, "the most important conviction of evangelical scholars is that the Bible is true. Those who in America call themselves evangelicals usually affirm that truthfulness instinctively, simply, and unequivocally. Moreover, evangelicals hold that the Bible is true not just as religion but also as fact. While Scripture certainly portrays accurately the nature and dimensions of religious experience, it is [sic] also provides a true record of character (whether human or divine), cosmologies, historical actions, and states of personal being" (**Between Faith and Criticism**, 143). According to Noll's description, Bloesch would not fall under the term "Evangelical." Interestingly, Noll does not even mention Bloesch in his book, although he is widely recognized as a leading Evangelical theologian. Could it be that Bloesch's effort to define the term "Evangelical" as relating to the gospel message and the Catholic heritage, which upholds an openness under the Word, is an attempt to broaden the term to such a degree that he can comfortably be included under it? Cf. Bloesch, **The Future of Evangelical Christianity**, 4; and idem, **EET**, 1:12, 15, for a definition of "Evangelical" along those lines. More recently Bloesch has termed his approach as "progressive evangelical theology" (**HSRII**, 276).

[3]Bob Price, "Review of **Essentials of Evangelical Theology**, 57.

[4]Ibid.

evaluation of their understanding of Scripture. The time has come to draw some final conclusions and to end with a brief outlook on what remains to be done. We have seen that there exists on the one hand a broad difference of opinions as to what the nature and the role of Scripture is supposed to be. In general, the divergent approaches of Pannenberg and Bloesch exemplify some of the diversity that currently exists in contemporary systematic theology, especially with respect to the question of methodology.[1] On the other hand, however, despite their significant difference, we have noticed that they have a number of surprising similarities.

Particularly noteworthy is their common rejection of any identification of revelation with the words of Scripture and an emphasis on the centrality of Christ as focal point of revelation. For both, Scripture is not understood as being the Word of God, and both do not see Scripture to be authoritative in a direct sense. Instead, a functional use of Scripture is advanced, where the concepts of the clarity and sufficiency of Scripture need to be supplemented by other sources. In short, both have modified or changed the Protestant Scripture principle, so that Scripture alone is no longer the sole source of its own exposition and thereby the final norm for faith and practice.

It has become clear that the relationship between Scripture and other sources of theology depends in large measure on the question where one places the locus of revelation. In other words, the issue of the origin and nature of Scripture must be settled before one can begin thinking about the role of Scripture in theology.[2] Here the relationship between the human and the divine element plays a crucial role. Neither of these two theologians succeeds in uniting these two aspects adequately in their concept of Scripture. Pannenberg exalts the human dimension of Scripture, especially as far as its written origin is concerned, to the detriment of any direct influence of the divine, thus making Scripture a historical document.[3] Bloesch, on the other hand, acknowledges both the humanity of Scripture as well as its divine origin, yet has not

---

[1] Gabriel Fackre recently has spoken of an *aggiornamento* in systematics that is characterized by a striking diversity of frameworks ("In Quest of the Comprehensive: The Systematic Revival," **RSR** 20/1 [1994]: 11, 10).

[2] Grant R. Osborne, **The Hermeneutical Spiral: A Comprehensive Introduction to Biblical Interpretation** (Downers Grove, IL: InterVarsity Press, 1991), 299.

[3] Since revelation occurs indirectly as history, Scripture can be investigated in search of its theological orientation.

been able to harmoniously unite both but, keeps them in dialectical conjunction. Ultimately for him the divine aspect is independent from and unaffected by the historical. Thus, both do not arrive at an understanding of Scripture that eventually goes beyond the shortcomings and limitations of previous positions. One question that still awaits an adequate answer is how the normative authority of Scripture can be posited in the face of its alleged historical and cultural limitations.[1] What still remains to be done is the development of an understanding of Scripture where the role of the human and divine agents is allowed to be developed from Scripture itself rather than from extra-scriptural premises.[2] This leads us to the next point.

One had wished, Bloesch and Pannenberg had devoted a careful analysis and in depth investigation of the Biblical material in order to develop an understanding of the origin, nature, and possible use of Scripture that is derived from Scripture itself.[3] In light of Bloesch's expressed desire to develop an approach that is derived from Scripture rather than from philosophy one does not feel free to assume that he has not given careful attention to the claims of Scripture. This raises the question of why he does not deal in depth with those passages that explicitly speak about the origin and nature of Scripture. Apparently he must have been influenced by a set of

---

[1] Cf. J. Christiaan Beker, "The Authority of Scripture: Normative or Incidental?" **TToday** 49/3 (1992): 380.

[2] Such an attempt has recently been made by Canale who has proposed that Scripture is "historically constituted" rather than historically conditioned, thereby attempting to give full credit to the human as well as the divine dimension in the origin of Scripture because the historical side of Scripture is not just external and incidental to its theological content but belongs to the very essence of its divinely revealed and inspired contents (Canale, "Revelation and Inspiration: The Ground for a New Approach," 98). The idea that Scripture is historically constituted is also found in Frank M. Hasel, "Reflections on the Authority and Trustworthiness of Scripture," in **Issues in Revelation and Inspiration**, ATSOP 1, ed. Frank Holbrook and Leo Van Dolson (Berrien Springs, MI: Adventist Theological Society Publications, 1992), 208-209.

[3] Although some claim that the Bible makes no internal claims about itself (James Barr, **Fundamentalism**, 78), a significant segment of contemporary scholarship provides strong evidence to the contrary (cf. Wayne A. Grudem, "Scripture's Self-Attestation and the Problem of Formulating a Doctrine of Scripture," 19-59; John M. Frame, "Scripture Speaks for Itself," 178-200; Sinclair B. Ferguson, "How Does the Bible Look at Itself?" 47-66; Howard I. Marshall, **Biblical Inspiration** (Grand Rapids, MI: Eerdmans, 1982), 19-30; Maier, **Biblische Hermeneutik**, 79-125; Stadelmann, **Grundlinien eines bibeltreuen Schriftverständnisses**, 22-32; Eckard Schnabel, **Inspiration und Offenbarung: Die Lehre vom Ursprung und Wesen der Bibel**; Jacob van Bruggen, **Wie maakte de Bijbel? Over afsluiting en gezag van het Oude en Nieuwe Testament** (Kampen: Kok, 1986); Slenczka, **Kirchliche Entscheidung in theologischer Verantwortung: Grundlagen--Kriterien--Grenzen**, 38-62.

presuppositions that have priority over the Biblical text itself and which decisively influence and determine his use of the Biblical material.

Something similar could be said about Pannenberg. His interest in the texts of a given tradition, which form an integral part of the hypothesis that this tradition is making about the whole of reality,[1] causes us to assume that he is well aware of the claims of Scripture and the Christian tradition about the supernatural origin and nature of Scripture. The fact, however, that a close examination of the question of the origin and nature of Scripture in the Biblical materials itself is practically absent leads us to the conclusion that other presuppositions must be at work in his thinking that determine the selection and interpretation of the Biblical materials. It would seem appropriate, however, even from a scientific point of view, that the data best qualified to shed light on the exploration of the question of the origin and nature of Scripture is Scripture itself.[2] It seems reasonable to think that in order to arrive at an adequate understanding of the role of Scripture in theology, the Bible itself should be allowed to inform and form the presuppositions with which the quest for its proper role in theology must proceed.[3] The decision that is taken on this point is crucial. It seems, however, that the concept of Scripture is determined for both theologians ultimately by presuppositions that are derived and shaped *extra scripturam*. This is not a new phenomenon, and can be seen as somewhat typical for large segments of Protestant theology.[4]

---

[1]Cf. Hackmann, 218.

[2]German Lutheran theologian Reinhard Slenczka has pointed out that "a decisive criterion for a science is . . . not the universality of its procedure, but its proper procedure according to its object [Sachgemäßheit]. The dilemma of theology, however, results from the fact that God's revelation claims universal validity but does not encounter universal approval" ("Was heißt und was ist schriftgemäß?" 310, our translation); similarly also Horst Seebaß: "Die Theologie des Wortes Gottes muß, wie immer sie auch gefaßt sein mag, nach ihrer eigenen Logik Auslegerin der Schrift sein" (**Biblische Hermeneutik** (Stuttgart: W. Kohlhammer, 1974), 83); cf. also Martin Kähler, **Die Wissenschaft der christlichen Lehre von dem evangelischen Grundartikel aus im Abrisse dargestellt** (Neukirchen-Vluyn: Neukirchener Verlag des Erziehungsvereins, 1966), 5; and F. Traub, "Kirchliche und Unkirchliche Theologie," **ZTK** 13 (1903): 65.

[3]Rolf Knierim points out that "it is clear that Pannenberg's point of departure leads from the outset to a critical separation between texts that are suitable and unsuitable for the theme [of revelation]" (206, n. 1); cf. also the criticism of Rolf Rendtorff, one of the original members of the Pannenberg circle, in "Offenbarung und Geschichte--Partikularimus und Universalismus im Offenbarungsverständnis Israels," 37-49; and Franz Hesse, "Wolfhart Pannenberg und das Alte Testament," 191-195, 182.

[4]Edgar V. McKnight succinctly states that "theologians use the Bible within a framework that is not derived from the Bible" (**Postmodern Use of the Bible: The Emergence of Reader-**

We have seen that both Pannenberg and Bloesch have not developed a consistent view of Scripture where the questions of its origin, nature, and use are developed from Scripture alone. The challenge that is before us is to do precisely this. Such a task will not come easily and requires a determined willingness to be open to the Biblical material itself, so that Scripture is allowed to actively shape what Graham Cole has called the "micro," "macro," and "mega level"[1] of our thinking. To take Scripture seriously as being the sole source of its own exposition calls for a fresh rethinking of a number of issues, among them (1) the old question of the relationship between Scripture and the other traditional sources in theology (tradition, experience, and reason); (2) the question of the legitimacy of a normative center in theology,[2] a canon within the canon[3]--be that Jesus Christ[4] or some other organizing center or focal point; (3) the question of how to arrive at a more integrative relationship[5] between Biblical

---

Oriented Criticism [Nashville, TN: Abingdon, 1988], 98). Paul Avis simply declares that "it is a truism that Christian theology has drawn on non-Christian philosophical resources very extensively. . . . Philosophical thinking is vital for both the systematization and the formulation of theology" (**The Methods of Modern Theology**, 220). John Jefferson Davis has pointed out that the "very variety of theological systems within the evangelical tradition alone, all claiming an equally high regard for the authority of Scripture, is in itself an indication that there are factors beyond the text itself which shape the gestalt of the system" ("Contextualization and the Nature of Theology," in **The Necessity of Systematic Theology**, ed. John Jefferson Davis [Grand Rapids, MI: Baker Book House, 1980], 177). Eginhard Peter Meijering has stated that the Protestant principle of *sola scriptura* has in actual fact never enjoyed great popularity in Protestantism ("'Sola Scriptura' und die historische Kritik," 56); and Jürgen Henkys observed that in many places it is easier to access Scripture through a discovery of *et scriptura* rather than *sola scriptura* ("Sola Scriptura im gegenwärtigen kirchlichen Handeln," in **Sola Scriptura: Das reformatorische Schriftprinzip in der säkularen Welt**, ed. Hans Heinrich Schmid and Joachim Mehlhausen [Gütersloh: Gerd Mohn, 1991], 84). Cf. also the recent discussion in Haacker, "Sola Scriptura: Zur Bedeutung der Bibel für die Kirche heute," 130-138.

[1]Cole, 26. Under the "mega level" Cole includes the "Christian world view or metaphysics."

[2]On the problem of a center in the Bible, see Gerhard F. Hasel, **Old Testament Theology: Basic Issues in the Current Debate**, 4th ed. (Grand Rapids, MI: Eerdmans, 1991), 139-171; idem, "The Problem of the Center in the OT Theology Debate," **ZAW** 86 (1974): 65-82; cf. also Vern S. Poythress, **Symphonic Theology: The Validity of Multiple Perspectives in Theology** (Grand Rapids, MI: Zondervan Publishing House, 1987), 82-88.

[3]Lønning, 16-30, 108-115, 269-272; and Gerhard Maier, **Biblische Hermeneutik**, 135-138, who draws the conclusion that the 200-year-long search for a canon within the canon was in vain (ibid., 137-138).

[4]It goes without saying that any view of Scripture "without Christ is empty, but Christ without Scripture, whose son is he?" (Cole, 31).

[5]"Das tatsächliche Auseinanderbrechen der beiden theologischen Hauptdisziplinen Exegese und Dogmatik dürfte die entscheidende Krise unserer heutigen Theologie darstellen" (Werner

theology¹ and systematic theology² that under the circumstances of the post-Reformation period³ has become so problematic.⁴ The actual task of developing such

---

Wiesner, "Exegese und Dogmatik," **TLZ** 79 [1954]: 449). For a fresh attempt of defining the relationship between Biblical theology and systematic theology anew, see Gerhard F. Hasel, "The Relationship between Biblical Theology and Systematic Theology," 113-120.

¹The process of separating and distinguishing between Biblical theology, as an essentially historical study of the Bible, and systematic theology, which is of necessity concerned with coherence and program appears to have been initiated by J. P. Gabler in 1787. Cf. Wallace, "Historicism and Biblical Theology," 223, 225. For a helpful English translation and analysis of Gabler's influential inaugural address *De justo discrimine theologiae biblicae et dogmaticae regundisque recte utriusque finibus*, see Sandys-Wunsch and Eldredge, 133-158. With William Wrede, this splitting between Biblical and systematic theology had led to a thorough separation between the two. According to Wrede "Biblical theology has to investigate something from given documents. . . . It tries to grasp it as objectively, correctively, and sharply as possible. That is all. How the systematic theologian gets on with its results and deals with them--that is his own affair. Like every other real science, New Testament theology has its goal simply in itself and is totally indifferent to all dogma and systematic theology. What could dogmatic offer it? Could dogmatics teach New Testament theology to see the facts correctly? At most, it could color them. Could it correct the facts that were found? To correct facts is absurd. Could it legitimize them? Facts need no legitimation" ("The Task and Methods of 'New Testament Theology'," In **The Nature of New Testament Theology**, ed. Robert Morgan [Naperville, IL: Alec R. Alleson, 1973], 69-70).

²The traditional systematic approach is dependent on philosophical methods, contents, and traditions that are alien to Scripture itself (cf. Gerhard Ebeling, **The Study of Theology**, trans. Duane A. Priebe (Philadelphia: Fortress Press, 1978), 53-58; John Macquarrie, **Principles of Christian Theology**, 21-25; and Lonergan, 335-340) and normally uses Scripture only to confirm a particular theological agenda that is derived independently from it. Otto Weber maintains that "dogmatics cannot tie itself down to one set of concepts. This means that it cannot permit its structure to be dictated to it by the given structure of any one philosophical system and thus it cannot find its own realm of expression limited by such a system. If this were to happen, then the self-understanding which is behind every philosophical system would become the criterion of dogmatics, and this would mean that substantive heresy would have emerged. . . . To bind dogmatics logically into one system would be to integrate its message into an already given exclusive totality of interpretations of being and existence. In such a total system, God would then occupy the place which had been foreseen for him in the spirit of that system. This God could not be the One who revealed himself in Jesus Christ" (**Foundations of Dogmatics**, 1:49). Weber continues by raising the question of "whether a *system* can be the fitting structure of dogmatics? We understand by 'system' the totality of an intellectual structure which is based upon a fundamental concept (a 'principle') and which develops it logically and methodically. The presupposition is, accordingly, that the 'principle' contains potentially the one and total content which is then explained in greater detail in the systematic exposition. This means in turn that in its exposition the system cannot contain elements which are not already given in the 'principle.' The 'principle' is, therefore, the intellectual condensation of an all-embracing totality. . . . The general result was that the 'principle' evolved into the universal idea, that is, a conception of the whole in one single idea. However, this idea was a human one. . . . Even if a concept of God is found at the pinnacle of such a system, which is generally the case, this concept must fit into the system without any dislocation. The god of a system designed on the basis of a 'principle' is in a profound sense always the god of man" (ibid., 51-52).

³"Only in recent times was biblical work emancipated from dogmatics. Initially this took place under the banner of a biblical-theological critique of the dominating school-dogmatics and of particular church dogmas, and then under the banner of a historical-critical investigation of the

an understanding of the role of Scripture goes beyond the scope of this dissertation and still remains before us.¹ One can only pose the challenge of such a task. In a time when the need for a paradigm change in theology is being voiced in many corners,²

---

biblical tradition. That led to a methodological dualism that seemed to coincide with the association and contrast of historical and systematic disciplines, but which in fact never really coincided" (Ebeling, **The Study of Theology**, 8). Friedrich Mildenberger recently also pointed out that behind the dividing up of theology in different disciplines is concealed a highly problematic methodological dualism which reveals a problem of orientation **(Biblische Dogmatik: Eine Biblische Theologie in dogmatischer Perspektive**, 1:33, 35). Edward Farley, **Theologia: The Fragmentation and Unity of Theological Education** (Philadelphia: Fortress Press, 1983), 39-44, 50-54, 77-80, 89-90, says that the distinction between Scripture interpretation and dogmatics happened quite naturally under the circumstances subsequent to the post-Reformation period. Eventually a fourfold encyclopedic division developed out of this fundamental distinction between the exegetical/historical and dogmatic/practical: Bible, church history, dogmatics, and practical theology, a pattern which, according to Farley, ultimately departs from the material unity of theology. See also Eberhard Jüngel, Karl Rahner, and M. Seitz, "Das Verhältnis der theologischen Disziplinen untereinander," in **Unterwegs zur Sache. Theologische Bemerkungen**, ed. Eberhard Jüngel (Munich: Chr. Kaiser, 1972), 34-59.

⁴Horace D. Hummel has called the relationship between Biblical and systematic theology agonizing ("Biblical or Dogmatic Theology," **LTJ** 16/1 [1982]: 3); similarly Gerhard Ebeling: "Mit der Frage nach dem Verhältnis von Dogmatik und Exegese assoziiert man heute weithin Krise und Mißstimmung," ("Dogmatik und Exegese," **ZTK** 77 [1980]: 267); cf. also Karl Rahner, "Exegesis and Dogmatic Theology," in **Dogmatic vs Biblical Theology**, ed. Herbert Vorgrimmler (Baltimore: Helicon Press, 1964), 31; and Henning Graf Reventlow, who has concluded his survey on the problematic relationship between the two by saying that "the exact way in which biblical theology is to be distinguished from dogmatic theology remains an open problem" **(Problems of Biblical Theology in the Twentieth Century**, 176).

¹There have been some modest attempts in that direction, for instance, by Thomas N. Finger, who has pointed out that Scripture itself contains forms of presentations, discussions, and argument which are compatible with more "systematic" elaboration ("Biblical and Systematic Theology in Interaction: A Study on the Atonement," in **So Wide a Sea: Essays on Biblical and Systematic Theology**, TRS 4, ed. Ben C. Ollenburger (Elkhart, IN: Institute of Mennonite Studies, 1991], 1-17, especially 3-5; cf. also idem, "Is 'Systematic Theology' Possible from a Mennonite Perspective?" in **Explorations of Systematic Theology from Mennonite Perspectives**, ed. Willard M. Swartley [Elkhart, IN: Institute of Mennonite Studies, 1984], 37-55; idem, **Christian Theology: An Eschatological Approach**, 1:31-60; Donald A. Carson, "Unity and Diversity in the New Testament: The Possibility of Systematic Theology," in **Scripture and Truth**, ed. D. A. Carson and John D. Woodbridge [Grand Rapids, MI: Zondervan Publishing House, 1983], 65-95); and Gerhard F. Hasel, "The Relationship Between Biblical Theology and Systematic Theology," 113-120; and idem, "Scripture and Theology," **JATS** 4/2 (1993): 76-86.

²Richard A. Rhem, "Theological Method: The Search for a New Paradigm in a Pluralistic Age," **RefR** 39/3 (1986): 242-254; Paul Wiebe, "Search for a Paradigm," **JR** 64 (1984): 348-368; Howard John Loewen, "The Mission of Theology: Reflections on the Structure of Theology from a Believers' Church Perspective," in **Explorations of Systematic Theology from Mennonite Perspectives**, ed. Willard M. Swartley (Elkhart, IN: Institute of Mennonite Studies, 1984), 85-86. Cf. also the discussion in Hans Küng and David Tracy, eds., **Paradigm Change in Theology: A Symposium for the Future**, ed. Hans Küng and David Tracy, trans. Margaret Köhl (New York: Crossroad, 1989); Hans Küng, **Theology for the Third Millennium**, 123-226; and J. Mouton, A. G. van Aarde, and W. S. Vorster, eds., **Paradigms and Progress in Theology** ([South Africa]: Human Science Research Council, 1988).

it seems appropriate, however, to challenge theology to engage in such a foundational task and to develop a theology that allows Scripture in its entirety (*tota Scriptura*) to be the ultimate authority and norming norm for theology and the sole source for its own exposition. An approach to theology that arises out of Scripture does not necessarily rule out other disciplines that open up options which might not otherwise be available to the interpreter.[1] However, such a Scriptural theology will evaluate all other options and sources on the basis of Scripture *alone* and develop its theological proposals in accordance with Scripture. It is in this sense[2] that Scriptural criticism is needed--not a human criticism of Scripture but the critical examination of ourselves, the church, and all other options by Scripture, for which the Biblical text alone is divinely fitted. Thereby Scripture is allowed to be the controlling principle and final authority for theology.

---

[1] E. Edward Zinke, "A Conservative Approach to Theology," Supplement to the **Ministry: International Journal for Clergy** 50/10 (1977): 240.

[2] Reinhard Slenczka has pointed out that under the assumption of the authority of Scripture, Scriptural criticism ("Schriftkritik") can only be understood in the sense of a subjective genitive: scriptura iudex, where Scripture judges all else ("Schriftautorität und Schriftkritik," 323-324). Cf. Martin Luther in his lectures on Genesis, WA 42, 116, 18-19: "Est autem haec omnis tentationis origo et caput, cum de verbo et Deo ratio per se iudicare conatur sine verbo." LW 1, 154: "This is the beginning and the main part of every temptation, when reason tries to reach a decision about the Word of God on its own without the Word."

SELECTED BIBLIOGRAPHY

Abba, Raymond. **The Nature and Authority of the Bible.** London: James Clarke, 1958.

Abraham, William J. **The Divine Inspiration of Holy Scripture.** Oxford: Oxford University Press, 1981.

— **Divine Revelation and the Limits of Historical Criticism.** New York: Oxford University Press, 1982.

— "Oh God, Poor God: The State of Contemporary Theology." **The Reformed Journal** 40 (1990): 18-23.

Ahlen, A. C. M. "Review of **The Christian Life and Salvation**, by Donald G. Bloesch." **The Lutheran Quarterly** 20 (1968): 211.

Alpern, Barbara Delp. "The Logic of Doxological Language: A Reinterpretation of Aquinas and Pannenberg on Analogy and Doxology." Ph.D. dissertation, University of Pittsburgh, 1980.

Althaus, Paul, "Offenbarung als Geschichte und Glaube: Bemerkungen zu Wolfhart Pannenbergs Begriff der Offenbarung." **Theologische Literaturzeitung** 87 (1962): 321-330.

— **Die Prinzipien der deutschen reformierten Dogmatik im Zeitalter der aristotelischen Scholastik.** Leipzig: A. Deichertsche Verlagsbuchhandlung, 1914, reprint Darmstadt: Wissenschaftliche Buchgesellschaft, 1967.

— **The Theology of Martin Luther.** Translated by Robert C. Schultz. Philadelphia: Fortress Press, 1966.

Anderson, Bernhard W. "Editorial: The Bible in the Church Today." **Theology Today** 37/1 (1980): 1-6.

Anderson, Ray S. "Evangelical Theology." In **The Modern Theologians: An Introduction to Christian Theology in the Twentieth Century.** 2 vols. Edited by David F. Ford, 2:131-151. Oxford: Blackwell, 1989.

Aner, Karl. **Die Theologie der Lessingzeit.** Halle: Verlag von Max Niemeyer, 1929.

Anz, Wilhelm. "Zur Wirkungsgeschichte Kierkegaards in der deutschen Theologie und Philosophie." **Zeitschrift für Theologie und Kirche** 79 (1982): 452-460.

Armour, Michael Carl. "Calvin's Hermeneutic and the History of Christian Exegesis." Ph.D. dissertation, University of California, Los Angeles, 1992.

Arrington, F. L. "Hermeneutics, Historical Perspectives on Pentecostal and Charismatic." **Dictionary of Pentecostal and Charismatic Movements.** Edited by

Stanley M. Burgess and Gary B. McGee. Grand Rapids, MI: Zondervan Publishing House, 1988. 376-389.

Ashcraft, Morris. "The Strengths and Weaknesses of Fundamentalism." In **The Proceedings of the Conference on Biblical Inerrancy 1987**, 531-541. Nashville, TN: Broadman Press, 1987.

— "The Theology of Fundamentalism." **Review and Expositor** 79/1 (1982): 31-44.

Asmussen, Hans. **Die Heilige Schrift: Sechs Kapitel zum Dogma von der Bibel**. Berlin: Verlag "Die Spur" Herbert Dorbandt KG, 1967.

Avis, Paul. **The Methods of Modern Theology: The Dream of Reason**. Hants: Marshall Pickering, 1986.

Ayers, Robert Hyman. "A Study of the Problem of Biblical Authority in Selected Contemporary American Theologians." Ph.D. dissertation, Vanderbilt University, 1958.

Baillie, John. **The Idea of Revelation in Recent Theology**. New York: Columbia University Press, 1956.

Bainton, Roland H. "The Bible in the Reformation." In **The Cambridge History of the Bible**, ed. S. L. Greenslade, 3:1-37. Cambridge: University Press, 1963.

Baldwin, John T. "Progressive Creationism and Biblical Revelation: Some Theological Implications." **Journal of the Adventist Theological Society** 3/1 (1992): 105-119.

Barbour, Ian G. **Myths, Models and Paradigms: A Comparative Study in Science and Religion**. New York: Harper and Row, 1974.

— **Religion in an Age of Science**. The Gifford Lectures 1989-1991, vol. 1. San Francisco: Harper and Row, 1990.

Barentsen, Jack. "The Validity of Human Language: A Vehicle for Divine Truth." **Grace Theological Journal** 9/1 (1988): 21-43.

Barr, James. **The Bible in the Modern World**. London: SCM Press, 1973.

— **Biblical Words for Time**. 2d rev. ed. Naperville, IL: Alec R. Allenson, 1969.

— **Fundamentalism**. Philadelphia: Westminster Press, 1977.

— "Fundamentalismus." **Evangelisches Kirchenlexikon**. 3d ed. Edited by Erwin Fahlbusch, Jan Milič Lochman, John Mbiti, Jaroslav Pelikan, and Lukas Vischer. Göttingen: Vandenhoeck & Ruprecht, 1986. 1:1404-1406.

— **Holy Scripture: Canon, Authority, Criticism**. Philadelphia: Westminster Press, 1983.

— "Jowett and the Reading of the Bible 'Like any other Book.'" **Horizons in Biblical Theology: An International Dialogue** 4 (1982): 1-44.

— "Revelation in History." **The Interpreter's Dictionary of the Bible. Supplementary Volume.** Edited by Keith Crim. Nashville, TN: Abingdon Press, 1976. 746-749.

— "Revelation Through History in the Old Testament and in Modern Theology." **Interpretation** 17 (1963): 193-205.

Barth, Hans-Martin. **Atheismus und Orsen und Modelle christlicher Apologetik im 17. Jahrhundert.** Forschungen zur systematischen und ökumenischen Theologie, no. 26. Göttingen: Vandenhoeck & Ruprecht, 1971.

Barth, Karl. "The Christian Understanding of Revelation." In **Against the Stream: Shorter Post-War Writings 1946-1952**, trans. E. M. Delacour and Stanley Godman, ed. Ronald Gregor Smith, 205-240. London: SCM Press, 1954.

— **Church Dogmatics.** 13 vols. Edited by G. W. Bromiley and T. F. Torrance. Edinburgh: T. & T. Clark, 1936-1969.

— **The Epistle to the Romans.** 6th ed. Translated by Edwyn C. Hoskyns. Oxford: University Press, 1933.

— "Das Erste Gebot als theologisches Axiom." **Zwischen den Zeiten** 11 (1933): 297-314.

— **No! Answer to Emil Brunner.** In **Natural Theology**, trans. Peter Fraenkel, 65-128. London: Centenary Press, 1946.

— "Parergon: Karl Barth über sich selbst." **Evangelische Theologie** 8 (1948/49): 268-282

— **Protestant Thought: From Rousseau to Ritschl.** Translated by Brian Cozens. New York: Simon and Schuster, 1969.

— "Das Schriftprinzip der Reformierten Kirche." **Zwischen den Zeiten** 3 (1925): 215-245.

Barth, Markus. "Sola Scriptura." In **Scripture and Ecumenism: Protestant, Catholic, Orthodox and Jewish.** Duquesne Studies Theological Series, no. 3, ed. Leonard J. Swidler, 75-94. Pittsburgh, PA: Duquesne University Press, 1965.

Barth, Peter. **Das Problem der natürlichen Theologie bei Calvin.** Theologische Existenz Heute, no. 18. Munich: Chr. Kaiser, 1935.

Bartlett, David L. **The Shape of Scriptural Authority.** Philadelphia: Fortress Press, 1983.

Barton, John. **People of the Book? The Authority of the Bible in Christianity**. Louisville, KY: Westminster/John Knox Press, 1988.

— "Verbal Inspiration." **A Dictionary of Biblical Interpretation**. Edited by R. J. Coggins and J. L. Houlden. London: SCM Press, 1990. 719-722.

Bartsch, Hans-Werner. "Geschichte/Historie." **Historisches Wörterbuch der Philosophie**. Edited by Joachim Ritter. Basel: Schwabe & Co. Verlag, 1974. 3:398-399.

Basinger, David. "Middle Knowledge and Classical Christian Thought." **Religious Studies** 22 (1986): 407-422.

Bauman, Michael. **Roundtable: Conversations with European Theologians**. Grand Rapids, MI: Baker Book House, 1990.

Baur, Jörg. "Sola Scriptura--historisches Erbe und bleibende Bedeutung." In **Sola Scriptura: Das reformatorische Schriftprinzip in der säkularen Welt**, ed. Hans Heinrich Schmid and Joachim Mehlhausen, 19-43. Gütersloh: Gerd Mohn, 1991.

Baxter, S. Edward, Jr. "A Historical Study of the Doctrine of 'Apokatasis.'" Th.D. dissertation, Mid-America Baptist Theological Seminary, 1988.

Baxter, Christina A. "Barth--a Truly Biblical Theologian?" **Tyndale Bulletin** 38 (1987): 3-27.

— "The Nature and Place of Scripture in the Church Dogmatics." In **Theology beyond Christendom: Essays on the Centenary of the Birth of Karl Barth May 10, 1886**, ed. John Thompson, 33-62. Allison Park, PA: Pickwick Publications, 1986.

Bayer, Oswald. **Autorität und Kritik: Zu Hermeneutik und Wissenschaftstheorie**. Tübingen: J. C. B. Mohr, 1991.

Beacon Dictionary of Theology. Edited by Richard S. Taylor. Kansas City, MO: Beacon Hill, 1983.

Beck, W. David. "Agnosticism: Kant." In **Biblical Errancy: An Analysis of Its Philosophical Roots**, ed. Norman L. Geisler, 53-78. Grand Rapids, MI: Zondervan Publishing House, 1981.

Becker, Gerhold. **Theologie in der Gegenwart: Tendenzen und Perspektiven**. Regensburg: Verlag Friedrich Pustet, 1978.

Becker, Siegbert W. **The Foolishness of God: The Place of Reason in the Theology of Martin Luther**. Milwaukee, WI: Northwestern Publishing House, 1982.

Beisser, Friedrich. **Claritas Scripturae bei Martin Luther**. Forschungen zur Kirchen- und Dogmengeschichte, no. 18. Göttingen: Vandenhoeck & Ruprecht, 1966.

— "Irrwege und Wege der historisch-kritischen Bibelwissenschaft: Auch ein Vortrag zur Reform des Theologiestudiums." **Neue Zeitschrift für Systematische Theologie** 15 (1973): 192-214.

Beker, J. Christiaan. "The Authority of Scripture: Normative or Incidental?" **Theology Today** 49/3 (1992): 376-382.

Berkhof, Hendrikus. **Christian Faith: An Introduction to the Study of the Faith**. Rev. ed. Translated by Sierd Woudstra. Grand Rapids, MI: Eerdmans, 1985.

Berkhof, Louis. **Introduction to Systematic Theology**. Grand Rapids, MI: Baker Book House, 1979.

Berkouwer, G. C. **Holy Scripture**. Translated and edited by Jack Rogers. Grand Rapids, MI: Eerdmans, 1975.

Berten, Ignace. **Geschichte, Offenbarung, Glaube: Eine Einführung in die Theologie Wolfhart Pannenbergs**. Munich: Claudius Verlag, 1970.

— "Openbaring in de Geschiedenis: De Theologie van Wolfhart Pannenberg." **Tijdschrift voor Theologie** 9/2 (1969): 151-177.

Betti, Emilio. **Die Hermeneutik als Allgemeine Methodik der Geisteswissenschaften**. Philosophie und Geschichte 78/79. Tübingen: J. C. B. Mohr, 1962.

Beumer, Johannes. "Die Inspiration der Heiligen Schrift." In **Handbuch der Dogmengeschichte**, ed. Michael Schmaus, Alois Grillmeier and Leo Scheffczyk, vol. I, fasc. 3b. Freiburg: Herder, 1968.

Bevans, Stephen. "Reaching for Fidelity: Roman Catholic Theology Today." In **Doing Theology in Todays World: Essays in Honor of Kenneth S. Kantzer**, ed. John D. Woodbridge and Thomas Edward McComiskey, 321-338. Grand Rapids, MI: Zondervan, 1991.

Birkner, Hans-Joachim. **Protestantismus im Wandel: Aspekte--Deutungen--Aussichten**. Munich: Claudius Verlag, 1971.

Bizer, Ernst. **Frühorthodoxie und Rationalismus**. Theologische Studien, no. 71. Zurich: EVZ Verlag, 1963.

Black, Max. **Models and Metaphors**. Ithaca: Cornell University Press, 1962.

The Blackwell Encyclopedia of Modern Christian Thought. Edited by Alister E. McGrath. Oxford: Basil Blackwell, 1993.

Blaisdell, Charles R. **Conservative, Moderate, Liberal: The Biblical Authority Debate**. St. Louis, MO: CBP Press, 1990.

Blanke, Fritz. **Brüder in Christo. Die Geschichte der ältesten Täufergemeinde**. Zurich: Zwingli Verlag, 1955.

Bloesch, Donald G. **The Battle for the Trinity: The Debate over Inclusive God-Language**. Ann Arbor, MI: Servant Publications, 1985.

— **Centers of Christian Renewal**. Philadelphia: United Church Press, 1964.

— "The Challence Facing the Churches." In **Christianity Confronts Modernity: A Theological and Pastoral Inquiry by Protestant Evangelicals and Roman Catholics**, ed. Peter Williamson and Kevin Perrotta, 205-223. Ann Arbor, MI: Servant Books, 1981.

— "The Charismatic Revival: A Theological Critique." **Religion in Life** 35/3 (1966): 364-380.

— **The Christian Life and Salvation**. Grand Rapids, MI: Eerdmans, 1967.

— **The Christian Witness in a Secular Age: An Evaluation of Nine Contemporary Theologians**. Minneapolis, MN: Augsburg Publishing House, 1968.

— "A Christological Hermeneutic: Crisis and Conflict in Hermeneutics." In **The Use of the Bible in Theology: Evangelical Options**, ed. Robert K. Johnston, 78-102. Atlanta: John Knox, 1985.

— "The Constitution of Divine Revelation." **Journal of Ecumenical Studies** 4/3 (1967): 550-551.

— "Crisis in Biblical Authority." **Theology Today** 35/4 (1979): 455-462.

— **The Crisis of Piety: Essays Towards a Theology of the Christian Life**. Grand Rapids, MI: Eerdmans, 1968.

— **Crumbling Foundations: Death and Rebirth in an Age of Upheaval**. Grand Rapids, MI: Zondervan Publishing House, 1984.

— "Curriculum Vitae." n.p., n.d.

— "Encountering Systematics as an Evangelical." **Catalyst** 2/2 (1982): 1-3.

— **Essentials of Evangelical Theology**, vol. 1, **God, Authority, and Salvation** . San Francisco: Harper and Row, 1978.

— **Essentials of Evangelical Theology**, vol. 2, **Life, Ministry, and Hope**. San Francisco: Harper and Row, 1978.

— "An Evangelical Perspective on Authority." **Prism: A Theological Forum for the United Church of Christ** 1/1 (1986): 4-21.

— **The Evangelical Renaissance**. Grand Rapids, MI: Eerdmans, 1973.

— "Evangelicalism." In **A New Handbook of Christian Theology**, ed. Donald W. Musser and Joseph L. Price, 168-173. Nashville, TN: Abingdon Press, 1992.

— **Freedom for Obedience: Evangelical Ethics in Contemporary Times**. San Francisco: Harper and Row, 1987.

— **The Future of Evangelical Christianity: A Call for Unity Amid Diversity**. New York: Doubleday, 1983. Reprint with Foreword by Mark A. Noll. Colorado Springs: Helmers & Howard, 1988.

— **The Ground of Certainty: Toward an Evangelical Theology of Revelation**. Grand Rapids, MI: Eerdmans, 1971.

— **Holy Scripture: Revelation, Inspiration and Interpretation**. Downers Grove, IL: InterVarsity Press, 1994.

— **The Invaded Church**. Waco, TX: Word Books, 1975.

— **Is the Bible Sexist? Beyond Feminism and Patriarchalism**. Westchester, IL: Crossway Books, 1982.

— **Jesus Is Victor! Karl Barth's Doctrine of Salvation**. Nashville, TN: Abingdon, 1976.

— "Karl Barth: Appreciation and Reservations." In **How Karl Barth Has Changed My Mind**, ed. Donald K. McKim, 126-130. Grand Rapids, MI: Eerdmans, 1986.

— "Law and Gospel in Reformed Perspective." **Grace Theological Journal** 12/1 (1991): 179-188.

— "The Legacy of Karl Barth." **Theological Students Fellowship Bulletin** 9/5 (1986): 6-9.

— "The Need for a Confessing Church Today." **The Reformed Journal** 34/11 (1984): 10-15.

— "The New Evangelicalism." **Religion in Life** 41 (1972): 327-339.

— "Process Theology and Reformed Theology." In **Process Theology**, ed. Ronald Nash, 31-56. Grand Rapids, MI: Baker Book House, 1987.

— **Publications of Donald G. Bloesch 1953-1980**. Dubuque, IA: Privately printed, 1980.

— **The Reform of the Church**. Grand Rapids, MI: Eerdmans, 1970.

— "Reinhold Niebuhr's Re-Evaluation of the Apologetic Task." Ph.D. dissertation, University of Chicago, 1956.

— "Reply to Randy Maddox." **Christian Scholars Review** 18/3 (1989): 281-284.

— **The Struggle of Prayer**. Colorado Springs: Helmers & Howard, 1988.

— "The Sword of the Spirit: The Meaning of Inspiration." **Reformed Review** 33/2 (1980): 65-72. First published in **Themelios** 5/3 (1980): 14-19.

— **Theological Notebook.** Vol. 1, **1960-1964**. Colorado Springs: Helmers & Howard, 1989.

— **Theological Notebook.** Vol. 2, **1964-1968**. Colorado Springs, Helmers & Howard, 1991.

— "Theology and Philosophy." **Quest**, Spring (1952): 1-10.

— **A Theology of Word and Spirit: Authority and Method in Theology**. Downers Grove, IL: InterVarsity Press, 1992.

— To Frank M. Hasel. December 14, 1993.

— To Frank M. Hasel. October 14, 1994.

— "Toward the Recovery of Our Evangelical Heritage." **Reformed Review** 39 (1986): 192-198.

— **Wellsprings of Renewal: Promise in Christian Communal Life**. Grand Rapids, MI: Eerdmans, 1974.

Blumhofer, Edith L., and Joel A. Carpenter, eds. **Twentieth-Century Evangelicalism: A Guide to the Sources**. New York: Garland, 1990.

Boff, Clodovis. **Theology and Praxis: Epistemological Foundations**. Translated by Robert R. Barr. Maryknoll, NY: Orbis Books, 1987.

Bohlmann, Ralph A. "Principles of Biblical Interpretation in the Lutheran Confessions." In **Crisis in Lutheran Theology: The Validity and Relevance of Historic Lutheranism vs. Its Contemporary Rivals**, ed. John Warwick Montgomery, 2:139-168. Minneapolis, MN: Bethany Fellowship, 1967.

Bolich, Gregory G. **Karl Barth and Evangelicalism**. Downers Grove, IL: InterVarsity Press, 1980.

Bollinger, Gary. "Pannenberg's Theology of the Religions and the Claim to Christian Superiority." **Encounter** 43 (1982): 273-285.

Bornkamm, Heinrich. **Luther and the Old Testament**. Translated by Eric W. Gritch and Ruth C. Gritch. Edited by Victor I. Gruhn. Philadelphia: Fortress Press, 1969.

— **Das Wort Gottes bei Luther**. Schriftenreihe der Luthergesell-schaft, no. 7. Munich: Chr. Kaiser Verlag, 1933.

Braaten, Carl F. "Can We Still Hold to the Principle 'Sola Scriptura'?" **Dialog** 20 (1981): 189-194.

— "The Current Controversy on Revelation: Pannenberg and His Critics." **Journal of Religion** 45 (1965): 225-237.

— "The Gospel and the Crisis of Authority." **Dialog** 31/4 (1992): 302-310.

— **History and Hermeneutics**. New Directions in Theology Today. Vol. 2. Philadelphia: Westminster Press, 1966.

— "Introduction: Revelation, History, and Faith in Martin Kähler." In Martin Kähler, **The Socalled Historical Jesus and the Historic-Biblical Christ**, trans. and ed. Carl E. Braaten, 1-38. Philadelphia: Fortress Press, 1964.

— "The Place of Christianity Among the World Religions: Wolfhart Pannenberg's Theology of Religion and the History of Religions." In **The Theology of Wolfhart Pannenberg: Twelve American Critiques, with an Autobiographical Essay and Response**, ed. Carl E. Braaten and Philip Clayton, 287-312. Minneapolis, Augsburg Publishing House, 1988.

— "Revelation." In **A New Handbook of Christian Theology**, ed. Donald W. Musser and Joseph L. Price, 408-413. Nashville, TN: Abingdon Press, 1992.

— "Wolfhart Pannenberg." In **A Handbook of Christian Theologians**, enl. ed., ed. Dean G. Peerman and Martin E. Marty, 639-659. Nashville, TN: Abingdon Press, 1984.

Braaten, Carl E., and Philip Clayton, eds. **The Theology of Wolfhart Pannenberg: Twelve American Critiques, with an Autobiographical Essay and Response**. Minneapolis: Augsburg Publishing House, 1988.

Bradshaw, Timothy. "God's Relationship to History in Pannenberg." In **Issues in Faith and History: Papers Presented at the Second Edinburgh Conference on Dogmatics, 1987**, ed. Nigel M. de S. Cameron, 48-67. Edinburgh: Rutherford House Books, 1989.

— **Trinity and Ontology: A Comparative Study of the Theologies of Karl Barth and Wolfhart Pannenberg**. Edinburgh: Rutherford House Books, 1988.

Brandt, Richard B. **The Philosophy of Schleiermacher: The Development of His Theory of Scientific and Religious Knowledge**. New York: Harper and Brothers, 1941.

Brecht, Martin. "Zu Luthers Schriftverständnis." In **Die Autorität der Schrift im ökumenischen Gespräch**. Beihefte zur Ökumenischen Rundschau, no. 50. Edited by Karl Kertelge, 9-29. Frankfurt am Main: Verlag Otto Lembeck, 1985.

Brena, Gian Luigi. "La Theologia di Wolfhart Pannenberg." **Civiltà Cattolica** 126 (1975): 368-386.

— **La Theologia di Wolfhart Pannenberg: Christianesimo e Modernità**. Casale Monferrato: Edizioni Piemme, 1993.

Bromiley, Geoffrey W. "The Authority of Scripture in Karl Barth." In **Hermeneutics, Authority, and Canon**, ed. D. A. Carson and John D. Woodbridge, 271-294. Grand Rapids, MI: Zondervan Publishing House, 1986.

— **Historical Theology: An Introduction**. Grand Rapids, MI: Eerdmans, 1978.

Brown, Colin. "Enlightenment, The." **Evangelical Dictionary of Theology**, ed. Walter A. Elwell. Grand Rapids, MI: Baker Book House, 1984. 355-357.

Brown, Harold O. J. "On Method and Means in Theology." In **Doing Theology in Today's World: Essays in Honor of Kenneth S. Kantzer**, ed. John D. Woodbridge and Thomas Edward McComiskey, 147-169. Grand Rapids, MI: Zondervan Publishing House, 1991.

— "Romanticism and the Bible." In **Challenges to Inerrancy: A Theological Response**, ed. Gordon R. Lewis and Bruce Demarest, 49-65. Chicago: Moody Press, 1984.

Brown, Raymond Edward. "The *Sensus Plenior* in the Last Ten Years." **Catholic Biblical Quarterly** 25 (1963): 262-285.

— **The *Sensus Plenior* of Sacred Scripture**. Baltimore, MD: St. Mary's University, 1955.

Brunner, Emil. **The Divine-Human Encounter**. Translated by Amadeus W. Loos. Philadelphia: Westminster Press, 1943.

— **Nature and Grace**. In **Natural Theology**, trans. Peter Fraenkel, ed. John Baillie, 15-64. London: Centenary Press, 1946.

— **Revelation and Reason: The Christian Doctrine of Faith and Knowledge**. Translated by Olive Wyon. Philadelphia: Westminster Press, 1946.

— **Theology of Crisis**. New York: Charles Scribner's Sons, 1929.

Bryant, Robert Harry. "The Authority of the Bible." Ph.D. dissertation, Yale University, 1956.

— **The Bible's Authority Today**. Minneapolis: Augsburg Publishing House, 1968.

Bsteh, Andreas, ed. **Dialog aus der Mitte christlicher Theologie**. Beiträge zur Religionstheologie, no. 5. Mödling: Verlag St. Gabriel, 1987.

Buis, Harry. "Review of **Theology of Word and Spirit: Authority and Method in Theology**, by Donald G. Bloesch." **Reformed Review** 46 (1993): 254.

Bultmann, Rudolf. **Existence and Faith**. Selected and Translated by Schubert M. Ogden. New York: Meridian Books, 1960.

Burhenn, Herbert. "Pannenberg's Argument for the Historicity of the Resurrection." **Journal of the American Academy of Religion** 50/3 (1972): 368-379.

— "Pannenberg's Doctrine of God." **Scottish Journal of Theology** 28 (1975): 535-549.

Buri, Fritz. **Dogmatik als Selbstverständnis des Christlichen Glaubens**. 2 vols. Bern: Verlag Paul Haupt, 1956.

Burkhardt, Bernd. "Bibliographie der Veröffentlichungen von Wolfhart Pannenberg 1953-1987." In **Vernunft des Glaubens: Wissenschaftliche Theologie und kirchliche Lehre. Festschrift zum 60. Geburtstag von Wolfhart Pannenberg**, ed. Jan Rohls and Gunther Wenz, 693-718. Göttingen: Vandenhoeck & Ruprecht, 1988.

— "Pannenberg." In **Argumente für Gott. Gott-Denker von der Antike bis zur Gegenwart: Ein Autoren-Lexikon**, ed. Karl-Heinz Weger, 270-272. Freiburg: Herder, 1987.

Burkhardt, Helmut. "Haben alle Religionen mit einem und demselben Gott zu tun?" **Theologische Beiträge** 24/4 (1993): 212-217.

Burnham, Frederick B., ed. **Postmodern Theology: Christian Faith in a Pluralist World**. San Francisco: Harper and Row, 1989.

Buss, Martin J. "The Meaning of History." In **Theology as History**, New Frontiers in Theology: Discussions Among Continental and American Theologians, ed. James M. Robinson and John B. Cobb, Jr., 3:135-154. New York: Harper and Row, 1967.

Butler, Trent C., ed. **Holman Bible Dictionary**. Nashville, TN: Holman Bible Publishers, 1991.

Cahill, P. Joseph. "Review of **The Ground of Certainty: Toward an Evangelical Theology of Revelation**, by Donald G. Bloesch." **The Catholic Biblical Quarterly** 34 (1972): 203-204.

Calvin, John. **Commentaries on the Second Epistle of Peter**. Translated by John Owen. Grand Rapids, MI: Eerdmans, 1948.

— **Commentaries on the Second Epistle to Timothy**. Translated by William Pringle. Grand Rapids, MI: Eerdmans, 1948.

— **Institutes of the Christian Religion**. Translated by Ford L. Battles. Philadelphia: Westminster Press, 1960.

Camino, Juan A. Martínez. "La 'Teología Sistemática' de W. Pannenberg." **Estudios Eclesiásticos** 65 (1990): 215-225.

Canale, Fernando Luis. **A Criticism of Theological Reason: Time and Timelessness as Primordial Presuppositions**. Andrews University Seminary Doctoral Dissertation Series, vol. 10. Berrien Springs, MI: Andrews University Press, 1983.

— "Revelation and Inspiration: Method for a New Approach." **Andrews University Seminary Studies** 31/3 (1993): 171-194.

— "Revelation and Inspiration: The Ground for a New Approach." **Andrews University Seminary Studies** 31/2 (1993): 91-104.

Carroll, Robert P. **Wolf in the Sheepfold: The Bible as a Problem for Christianity**. London: SPCK, 1991.

Carson, Donald A. "Recent Developments in the Doctrine of Scripture." In **Hermeneutics, Authority, and Canon**, ed. D. A. Carson and John Woodbridge, 5-48, 336-374. Grand Rapids, MI: Zondervan Publishing House, 1986.

— "Unity and Diversity in the New Testament: The Possibility of Systematic Theology." In **Scripture and Truth**, ed. D. A. Carson and John D. Woodbridge, 65-95, 368-375. Grand Rapids, MI: Zondervan Publishing House, 1983.

Carter, Charles W., ed. **A Contemporary Wesleyan Theology: Biblical, Systematic, and Practical**. 2 vols. Grand Rapids, MI: Zondervan Publishing House, 1983.

Cauthen, Kenneth. **Systematic Theology: A Modern Protestant Approach**. Toronto Studies in Theology, no. 25. Lewiston: Edwin Mellen Press, 1986.

Chang, Andrew Dooman. "Crisis of Biblical Authority: A Critical Examination of Biblical Authority in Contemporary Theology with Special Reference to Functionalism." Th.D. dissertation, Dallas Theological Seminary, 1985.

Childs, James M., Jr. "The Significance of Wolfhart Pannenberg for Contemporary Theology." **Trinity Seminary Review** 13/2 (1991): 61-68.

Clark, Gordon H. **Karl Barth's Theological Method**. Philadelphia: Presbyterian and Reformed Publishing Company, 1963.

Clarke, William Newton. **The Use of the Scriptures in Theology**. Edinburgh: T. & T. Clark, 1907.

Clayton, Philip. "A Pannenberg Bibliography." In **The Theology of Wolfhart Pannenberg: Twelve American Critiques, With an Autobiographical Essay and Response**, ed. Carl E. Braaten and Philip Clayton, 337-352. Minneapolis: Augsburg Publishing House, 1988.

— "Anticipation and Theological Method." In **The Theology of Wolfhart Pannenberg: Twelve American Critiques, With an Autobiographical Essay and Response**, ed. Carl E. Braaten and Philip Clayton, 122-150. Minneapolis: Augsburg Publishing House, 1988.

— "The God of History and the Presence of the Future." **Journal of Religion** 65 (1985): 98-108.

Clements, Keith W. "Schleiermacher, Friedrich Daniel Ernst." **The Blackwell Encyclopedia of Modern Christian Thought**. Edited by Alister E. McGrath. Oxford: Blackwell, 1993. 589-592.

Cobb, John B., Jr. **Living Options in Protestant Theology: A Survey of Methods**. Philadelphia: Westminster Press, 1962.

— "Pannenberg and Process Theology." In **The Theology of Wolfhart Pannenberg: Twelve American Critiques, with an Autobiographical Essay and Response**, ed. Carl E. Braaten and Philip Clayton, 54-74. Minneapolis: Augsburg Publishing House, 1988.

— "Past, Present, and the Future." In **New Frontiers in Theology: Discussion Among Continental and American Theologians**, ed. James M. Robinson and John B. Cobb, Jr., 3:197-220. New York: Harper and Row, 1967.

— "Theologie in den Vereinigten Staaten: Woher und Wohin." **Evangelische Theologie** 48/2 (1989): 200-213.

Cochlovius, Joachim. "Ist die 'historisch-kritische Methode' reformatorisch? Kritische Fragen and Gerhard Ebelings Programmaufsatz." In **Evangelische Schriftauslegung: Ein Quellen- und Arbeitsbuch für Studium und Gemeinde**, ed. Joachim Cochlovius and Peter Zimmerling, 228-234. Wuppertal: R. Brockhaus Verlag, 1987

Cole, Graham. "Sola Scriptura: Some Historical and Contemporary Perspectives." **Churchman** 104/1 (1990): 20-34.

Collins, John J. "Is a Critical Biblical Theology Possible?" In **The Hebrew Bible and Its Interpreters**, Biblical and Judaic Studies from the University of California, San Diego, no. 1, ed. William Henry Propp, Baruch Halpern, and David Noel Freedman, 1-17. Winona Lake, IN: Eisenbrauns, 1990.

Colombo, Joseph A. **An Essay on Theology and History: Studies in Pannenberg, Metz, and the Frankfurt School**. American Academy of Religion Studies in Religion, no. 61. Atlanta, GA: Scholars Press, 1990.

Come, Arnold B. **An Introduction to Barth's *Dogmatics* for Preachers**. Philadelphia: Westminster Press, 1963.

Cook, Martin L. "Confessional Theology." In **A New Handbook of Christian Theology**, ed. Donald W. Musser and Joseph L. Price, 96-98. Nashville, TN: Abingdon Press, 1992.

— **The Open Circle: Confessional Method in Theology**. Minneapolis: Fortress Press, 1991.

Cook, Peter, C. A. "Pannenberg: A Post-Enlightenment Theologian." **Churchman** 90 (1976): 245-264.

Corner, Mark. "Fundamentalism." **A Dictionary of Biblical Interpretation**. Edited by R. J. Coggins and J. L. Houlden. London: SCM Press, 1990. 243-247.

Corts, Stephen David Charles. "Particularism as an Evangelical Response to Religious Plurality." Ph.D. dissertation, Southern Baptist Theological Seminary, 1991.

Countryman, William. **Biblical Authority or Biblical Tyranny?** Philadelphia: Fortress Press, 1981.

Cragg, Gerald R. **Reason and Authority in the Eighteenth Century**. Cambridge: At the University Press, 1964.

Craig, William Lane. "On Doubts about the Resurrection." **Modern Theology** 6 (1989): 53-75.

— "Pannenbergs Beweis für die Auferstehung Jesu." **Kerygma und Dogma** 34 (1988): 78-104.

Cremer, H. "Inspiration." **The New Schaff-Herzog Encyclopedia of Religious Knowledge**. Edited by Samuel Macauley Jackson. New York: 1910. 6:12-17.

Crossley, John P., Jr. "Liberalism." In **A New Handbook of Christian Theology**, ed. Donald W. Musser and Joseph L. Price, 285-287. Nashville, TN: Abingdon, 1992.

Crutsinger, G. C. "The Bible as Moral Authority: Its Use by Contemporary American Evangelical Theologians." Ph.D. dissertation, Fuller Theological Seminary, 1988.

Cully Iris V., and Kendig Brubacker Cully, eds. **Encyclopedia of Religious Education**. San Francisco: Harper and Row, 1990.

Cullmann, Oscar. **Christ and Time: The Primitive Christian Conception of Time and History**. Translated by Floyd V. Filson. Philadelphia: Westminster Press, 1950.

Davis, John Jefferson. "Contextualization and the Nature of Theology." In **The Necessity of Systematic Theology**, ed. John Jefferson Davis, 169-190. Grand Rapids, MI: Baker Book House, 1980.

— **Foundations of Evangelical Theology**. Grand Rapids, MI: Baker Book House, 1984.

Davies, Rupert E. **The Problem of Authority in the Continental Reformers: A Study in Luther, Zwingli, and Calvin**. London: Epworth Press, 1946.

Dayton, Donald W., and Robert K. Johnston, eds. **The *Variety* of American Evangelicalism**. Downers Grove, IL: InterVarsity Press, 1991.

Demarest, Bruce. "The Bible in the Enlightenment Era." In **Challenges to Inerrancy: A Theological Response**, ed. Gordon Lewis and Bruce Demarest, 11-47. Chicago: Moody Press, 1984.

Diem, Hermann. **Dogmatics**. Translated by Harold Knight. Philadelphia: Westminster Press, 1959.

Diestel, Ludwig. **Geschichte des Alten Testaments in der Christlichen Kirche**. Jena: Mauke, 1869.

Dillenberger, John, and Claude Welch. **Protestant Christianity Interpreted Through Its Development**. New York: Charles Scribner's Sons, 1954.

Dillistone, F. W. "Systematic Theology Today." **Theology Today** 37/3 (1980): 306-314.

Dobbin, Edmund J. "Seminar on Foundations: Pannenberg on Theological Method." **The Catholic Theological Society of America Proceedings** 32 (1977): 202-220.

— "Revelation as History: A Study of Wolfhart Pannenberg's Theology of Revelation." Th.D. dissertation, University of Louvain, 1971.

Dockery, David S. "Review of **Essentials of Evangelical Theology**. Vols. 1 and 2, by Donald G. Bloesch." **Grace Theological Journal** 2 (1981): 152-154.

Doolan, Leonard W. "Scripture: The Supreme Court of Divine Authority." Ph.D. dissertation, The Southern Baptist Theological Seminary, 1901.

Doran, John. "A New Reformation." **Faith and Freedom** 44/3 (1991): 119-121.

Dowey, Edward A. **The Knowledge of God in Calvin's Theology**. New York: Columbia University Press, 1952.

Drewermann, Eugen. **Tiefenpsychologie und Exegese**. Vol. 1, **Die Wahrheit der Formen. Traum, Mythos, Märchen, Sage und Legende**. Olten: Walter Verlag, 1984.

Drumm, Joachim. **Doxologie und Dogma: Die Bedeutung der Doxologie für die Wiedergewinnung theologischer Rede in der evangelischen Theologie**. Beiträge zur Ökumenischen Theologie, no. 22. Paderborn: Ferdinand Schöningh, 1991.

Duchrow, Ulrich. "Die Klarheit der Schrift und die Vernunft." **Kerygma und Dogma** 15 (1969): 1-17.

Dulles, Avery. **The Craft of Theology: From Symbol to System**. New York: Crossroad, 1992.

— "Models of Faith." In **Fides Quaerens Intellectum. Beiträge zur Fundamentaltheologie**, ed. Michael Kessler, Wolfhart Pannenberg, and Hermann Josef Pottmeyer, 405-413. Tübingen: Francke Verlag, 1992.

— **Models of Revelation**. Garden City, NY: Image Books, 1985.

— **Models of the Church**. Garden City, NY: Doubleday, 1974.

— "Pannenberg on Revelation and Faith." In **The Theology of Wolfhart Pannenberg: Twelve American Critiques, With an Autobiographical Essay and Response**, ed. Carl E. Braaten and Philip Clayton, 169-187. Minneapolis: Augsburg Publishing House, 1988.

— **The Reshaping of Catholicism: Current Challenges in the Theology of Church**. San Francisco: Harper and Row, 1988.

— "Response to Krister Stendahl's 'Method in the Study of Biblical Theology.'" In **The Bible in Modern Scholarschip**, ed. J. Philip Hyatt, 210-219. Nashville, TN: Abingdon, 1965.

— "Scripture: Recent Protestant and Catholic Views." **Theology Today** 37/1 (1980): 7-26.

Ebeling, Gerhard. "Church History Is the History of the Exposition of Scripture." In Gerhard Ebeling, **The Word of God and Tradition: Historical Studies Interpreting the Divisions of Christianity**, trans. S. H. Hooke, 11-31. Philadelphia: Fortress Press, 1968.

— **Dogmatik des christlichen Glaubens**. 3 vols. Tübingen: J. C. B. Mohr, 1979.

— "Dogmatik und Exegese." **Zeitschrift für Theologie und Kirche** 77 (1980): 269-286.

— "Erwägungen zu einer evangelischen Fundamentaltheologie." **Zeitschrift für Theologie und Kirche** 67 (1970): 479-524.

— **Evangelische Evangelienauslegung: Eine Untersuchung zu Luthers Hermeneutik**. Darmstadt: Wissenschaftliche Buchgesellschaft, 1962.

— **Luther: An Introduction to His Thought**. Translated by R. A. Wilson. Philadelphia: Fortress Press, 1970.

— "Luther und die Bibel." In **Lutherstudien**, ed. Gerhard Ebeling, 1:286-301. Tübingen: J. C. B. Mohr, 1971.

— "The Significance of the Critical Historical Method for Church and Theology in Protestantism." In Gerhard Ebeling, **Word and Faith**, trans. James W. Leitch, 17-61. Philadelphia: Fortress Press, 1963.

— "'Sola Scriptura' and Tradition." In Gerhard Ebeling, **The Word of God and Tradition: Historical Studies Interpreting the Divisions of Christianity**, trans. S. H. Hooke, 102-147. Philadelphia: Fortress Press, 1968.

—— **The Study of Theology**. Translated by Duane A. Priebe. Philadelphia: Fortress Press, 1978.

Eberts, Harry William, Jr. "'Sola Scriptura': Then and Now." **Reformed Liturgy and Music** 18 (1984): 64-69.

Egli, Emil, et al., eds. **Huldreich Zwinglis Sämtliche Werke**. Corpus Reformatorum, vol. 88-. Zurich: Theologischer Verlag, 1905-.

Eicher, Peter. "Geschichte und Wort Gottes: Ein Protokoll der Pannenbergdiskussion von 1961-1972." **Catholica** 32 (1978): 321-354.

—— **Offenbarung: Prinzip neuzeitlicher Theologie**. Munich: Kösel, 1977.

Elert, Werner. **The Structure of Lutheranism**. Vol. 1, **The Theology and Philosophy of Life of Lutheranism Especially in the Sixteenth and Seventeenth Centuries**. Translated by Walter A. Hansen. St. Louis, MO: Concordia Publishing House, 1962.

Eller, Vernard, ed. **Thy Kingdom Come: A Blumhardt Reader**. Grand Rapids, MI: Eerdmans, 1980.

Ellingsen, Mark. **The Evangelical Movement: Growth, Impact, Controversy, Dialog**. Minneapolis: Augsburg Publishing House, 1988.

—— "Review of **A Theology of Word and Spirit: Authority and Method in Theology**, by Donald G. Bloesch." **Dialog** 32/3 (1993): 238-239.

Ellul, Jacques. **The Humiliation of the Word**. Translated by Joyce Main Hanks. Grand Rapids, MI: Eerdmans, 1985.

Elwell, Walter, ed. **Evangelical Dictionary of Theology**. Grand Rapids, MI: Baker Book House, 1984.

Erickson, Millard J. **Christian Theology**. 3 vols. in one. Grand Rapids, MI: Baker Book House, 1983-1985.

—— **Evangelical Interpretation: Perspectives on Hermeneutical Issues**. Grand Rapids, MI: Baker Book House, 1993.

—— "Evangelicalism: USA." **The Blackwell Encyclopedia of Modern Christian Thought**. Edited by Alister E. McGrath. Oxford: Blackwell, 1993. 187-192.

—— "Immanence, Trancendence, and the Doctrine of Scripture." In **The Living and Active Word of God: Studies in Honor of Samuel J. Schultz**, ed. Morris Inch and Ronald Youngblood, 193-205. Winona Lake, IN: Eisenbrauns, 1983.

—— "Pannenberg's Use of History as a Solution to the Religious Language Problem." **Journal of the Evangelical Theological Society** 17 (1974): 99-105.

Ernst, Wilton Donald. "The Place of the Scriptures in the Lutheran Churches in America from the End of the First World War to the Middle of the Twentieth Century." Ph.D. dissertation, Temple University, 1962.

Evangelical Dictionary of Theology. Edited by Walter Elwell. Grand Rapids, MI: Baker Book House, 1984.

Evans, Christopher. **Is 'Holy Scripture' Christian? And Other Questions**. London: SCM Press, 1971.

Fackre, Gabriel. **The Christian Story: A Narrative Interpretation of Basic Christian Doctrine**. Grand Rapids, MI: Eerdmans, 1978.

— **The Christian Story: A Pastoral Systematics. Vol. 2, Authority: Scripture in the Church for the World**. Grand Rapids, MI: Eerdmans, 1987.

— "In Quest of the Comprehensive: the Systematics Revival." **Religious Studies Review** 20/1 (1994): 7-12.

— "The State of Systematics: Research and Commentary." **Dialog** 31 (1992): 54-61.

— "The Surge in Systematics: A Commentary on Current Works." **The Journal of Religion** 73/2 (1993): 223-237.

Farley, Edward. **Theologia: The Fragmentation and Unity of Theological Education**. Philadelphia: Fortress Press, 1983.

Farley, Edward, and Peter C. Hodgson. "Scripture and Tradition." In **Christian Theology: An Introduction to Its Traditions and Tasks**, 2d ed., ed. Peter C. Hodgson and Robert H. King, 61-87. Philadelphia: Fortress Press, 1985.

Farrar, Frederic W. **History of Interpretation**. New York: E. P. Dutton and Co., 1886.

Feinberg, Paul D. "A Response to Adequacy of Language and Accommodation." In **Hermeneutics, Inerrancy, and the Bible**, ed. Earl D. Radmacher and Robert D. Preus, 379-390. Grand Rapids, MI: Zondervan Publishing House, 1984.

— "An Evangelical Systematic Theology: A Review of **Essentials of Evangelical Theology**, Volume 1, by Donald G. Bloesch." **Christianity Today** 23/22 (1979): 38-41 [1259-1262].

— "The Meaning of Inerrancy." In **Inerrancy**, ed. Norman L. Geisler, 267-304, 468-471. Grand Rapids, MI: Zondervan Publishing House, 1979.

Ferguson, Sinclair B. "How Does the Bible Look at Itself?" In **Inerrancy and Hermeneutic: A Tradition, A Challenge, A Debate**, ed. Harvie M. Conn, 47-66. Grand Rapids, MI: Baker Book House, 1988.

Fichte, Johann Gottlob. "Über den Grund unseres Glaubens an eine göttliche Weltregierung." **Philosophisches Journal** 8 (1798): 1-20.

Finger, Thomas N. "Biblical and Systematic Theology in Interaction: A Case Study on the Atonement." In **So Wide A Sea: Essays on Biblical and Systematic Theology**. Text-Reader Series, no. 4, ed. Ben C. Ollenburger, 1-17. Elkhart, IN: Institute of Mennonite Studies, 1991.

— **Christian Theology: An Eschatological Approach**. 2 vols. Nashville, TN: Thomas Nelson Publishers, 1985.

— "Is 'Systematic Theology' Possible from a Mennonite Perspective?" In **Explorations of Systematic Theology from Mennonite Perspectives**, ed. Willard M. Swartley, 37-55. Elkhart, IN: Institute of Mennonite Studies, 1984.

Fischer, Hermann. "Fundamentaltheologische Prologomena zur theologischen Anthropologie: Anfragen an W. Pannenbergs Anthropologie." **Theologische Rundschau** 50 (1985): 41-61.

— **Systematische Theologie: Konzeptionen und Probleme im 20. Jahrhundert**. Stuttgart: W. Kohlhammer, 1992.

Fischer, Johannes. "Wie wird Geschichte als Handeln Gottes offenbar? Zur Bedeutung der Anwesenheit Gottes im Offenbarungsgeschehen." **Zeitschrift für Theologie und Kirche** 88 (1991): 211-231.

Flückiger, Felix. **Theologie der Geschichte: Die biblische Rede von Gott und die neuere Geschichtstheologie**. Wuppertal: Brockhaus Verlag, 1970.

Foh, Susan. "Review of **The Battle for the Tinity: The Debate Over Inclusive God-Language**, by Donald G. Bloesch." **Westminster Theological Journal** 48 (1986): 407-409.

Ford, David F. "Barth's Interpretation of the Bible." In **Karl Barth: Studies of His Theological Method**, ed. S. W. Sykes, 55-87. Oxford: Clarendon Press, 1979.

— "Introduction to Modern Christian Theology." In **The Modern Theologians: An Introduction to Christian Theology in the Twentieth Century**, ed. David F. Ford, 1:1-19. Oxford: Basil Blackwell, 1989.

Ford, David F., ed. **The Modern Theologians: An Introduction to Christian Theology in the Twentieth Century**. 2 vols. Oxford: Basil Blackwell, 1989.

Ford, Lewis S. "The Nature of the Power of the Future." In **The Theology of Wolfhart Pannenberg: Twelve American Critiques, With an Autobiographical Essay and Response**, ed. Carl E. Braaten and Philip Clayton, 75-94. Minneapolis: Augsburg Publishing House, 1988.

— "A Whiteheadian Basis for Pannenberg's Theology." **Encounter** 38/4 (1977): 307-317.

Forstman, H. Jackson. **Word and Spirit: Calvin's Doctrine of Biblical Authority.** Stanford, CA: Stanford University Press, 1962.

Foxgrover, David. "Review of **Essentials of Evangelical Theology.** Vol. 2, by Donald G. Bloesch," **The Christian Century** 96 (1979): 192.

— "Review of **Essentials of Evangelical Theology.** Vol. 2, by Donald G. Bloesch." **Christianity Today** 24/9 (1980): 38-40 [574-576].

Frame, John M. "God and Biblical Language: Transcendence and Immanence." In **God's Inerrant Word: An International Symposium on the Trustworthiness of Scripture**, ed. John Warwick Montgomery, 159-177. Minneapolis, MN: Bethany Fellowship, 1974.

— "Scripture Speaks for Itself." In **God's Inerrant Word: An International Symposium on the Trustworthiness of Scripture**, ed. John Warwick Montgomery, 178-200. Minneapolis, MN: Bethany Fellowship, 1974.

— "The Spirit and the Scriptures." In **Hermeneutics, Authority, and Canon**, ed. D. A. Carson and John D. Woodbridge, 213-235. Grand Rapids, MI: Zondervan Publishing House, 1986.

— "Uses of Scripture in Recent Theology." **The Westminster Theological Journal** 39 (1977): 328-358.

Franklin, R. L. "A Science of Pure Consciousness?" **Religious Studies** 19/2 (1983): 185-204.

Franklin, Stephen T. "Review of **Essentials of Evangelical Theology**, Volumes 1 and 2, by Donald G. Bloesch." **The Japan Christian Quarterly** 48/4 (1982): 232-236.

Frei, Hans W. "Conflicts in Interpretation." **Theology Today** 49/3 (1992): 344-356.

— **The Eclipse of Biblical Narrative: A Study in Eighteenth and Nineteenth Century Hermeneutics.** New Haven: Yale University Press, 1974.

— **Types of Christian Theology.** Edited by George Hunsinger and William C. Placher. New Haven: Yale University Press, 1992.

Frey, Hellmuth. **Die Krise der Theologie: Historische Kritik und pneumatische Auslegung im Lichte der Krise.** Wuppertal: R. Brockhaus Verlag, 1971.

Führer, Werner. **Das Wort Gottes in Luthers Theologie.** Göttinger Theologische Arbeiten, no. 30. Göttingen: Vandenhoeck & Ruprecht, 1984.

Fuller, Daniel P. "A New German Theological Movement." **Scottish Journal of Theology** 19 (1966): 160-175.

The Fundamentals: A Testimony to the Truth. 12 vols. Chicago: Testimony Publishing Co., 1910-1915.

Furnish, Victor Paul. "The Historical Criticism of the New Testament: A Survey of Origins." **Bulletin of the John Rylands University Library of Manchester** 56 (1974): 336-370.

Gäbler, Ulrich. **Huldrych Zwingli im 20. Jahrhundert: Forschungsbericht und annotierte Bibliographie 1897-1972**. Zurich: Theologischer Verlag, 1975.

Gaffin, Richard B. "Systematic Theology and Biblical Theology." **Westminster Theological Journal** 38 (1976): 281-299.

Galloway, Allan D. "Nineteenth and Twentieth Century Theology." In **The History of Christian Theology**, vol. 1, **The Science of Theology**, ed. Paul Avis, 233-352. Grand Rapids, MI: Eerdmans, 1986.

— **Wolfhart Pannenberg**. London: George Allen & Unwin, 1973.

Garrett, Graeme. "Scripture, Inspiration and the Word of God." **Pacifica: Australian Theological Studies** 6/1 (1993): 81-99.

Garrett, James Leo, Jr. **Systematic Theology: Biblical, Historical, and Evangelical**. Grand Rapids, MI: Eerdmans, 1992.

Gay, Peter. **The Enlightenment: An Interpretation: The Rise of Modern Paganism**. New York: Alfred A. Knopf, 1966.

Gaybba, Brian. *The* **Tradition: An Ecumenical Breakthrough?** Rome: Herder, 1971.

Geldard, M. D. "Kant, Immanuel." **New Dictionary of Theology**, ed. Sinclair B. Ferguson and David F. Wright. Downers Grove, IL: InterVarsity Press, 1988. 361-363.

Gennrich, Paul. **Der Kampf um die Schrift in der Deutsch-Evangelischen Kirche des neunzehnten Jahrhunderts**. Berlin: Verlag von Reuther and Reichard, 1898.

George, Timothy. "'A Right Strawy Epistle': Reformation Perspectives on James." **Review and Expositor** 83 (1986): 369-382.

— **Theology of the Reformers**. Nashville, TN: Broadman Press, 1988.

Gerrish, Brian A. "Biblical Authority and the Continental Reformation." **Scottish Journal of Theology** 10 (1957): 337-360.

— "From 'Dogmatik' to 'Glaubenslehre': A Paradigm Change in Modern Theology?" In **Paradigm Change in Theology: A Symposium for the Future**, ed. Hans Küng and David Tracy, 161-173. Translated by Margaret Köhl. New York: Crossroad, 1989.

— **Grace and Reason: A Study in the Theology of Luther**. Oxford: Clarendon Press, 1962.

— A Prince of the Church: Schleiermacher and the Beginnings of Modern Theology. Philadelphia: Fortress Press, 1984.

Gestrich, Christof. Zwingli als Theologe: Glaube und Geist beim Zürcher Reformator. Studien zur Dogmengeschichte und systematischen Theologie, no. 20. Zurich: Zwingli Verlag, 1967.

Geyer, Hans-Georg. "Geschichte als theologisches Problem: Bemerkungen zu W. Pannenbergs Geschichtstheologie." Evangelische Kommentare 22 (1962): 92-104.

Gier, Nicholas F. God, Reason, and the Evangelicals: The Case Against Evangelical Rationalism. Lanham, MD: University Press of America, 1987.

Gilkey, Langdon. "Neoorthodoxy." In A New Handbook of Christian Theology, ed. Donald W. Musser and Joseph L. Price, 334-337. Nashville, TN: Abingdon, 1992.

— "Pannenberg's Basic Questions in Theology: A Review Article." Perspective: A Journal of Pittsburgh Theological Seminary 14 (1973): 34-55.

— Reaping the Whirlwind: A Christian Interpretation of History. New York: Seabury Press, 1976.

— "The Roles of the 'Descriptive' or 'Historical' and of the 'Normative' in Our Work." Criterion: A Publication of the Divinity School of the University of Chicago 20/1 (1981): 10-17.

Girgensohn, Karl. Der Schriftbeweis in der evangelischen Dogmatik einst und jetzt. Leipzig: A. Deichertsche Verlagsbuchhandlung, 1914.

Glässer, Alfred. Verweigerte Partnerschaft? Anthropologische, konfessionelle und ökumenische Aspekte der Theologie Wolfhart Pannenbergs. Eichstätter Studien, Neue Folge, no. 31. Regensburg: Verlag Friedrich Pustet, 1991.

Glenn, A. A. "Criteria for Theological Models." Scottish Journal of Theology 25 (1972): 296-308.

Gloede, Günter. Theologia naturalis bei Calvin. Tübinger Studien zur systematischen Theologie, no. 5. Stuttgart: Kohlhammer, 1935.

Gloege, Gerhard. "Schriftprinzip." In Die Religion in Geschichte und Gegenwart: Handwörterbuch für Theologie und Religionswissenschaft. 3d ed. Edited by Kurt Galling. Tübingen: J. C. B. Mohr, 1961. 5:1540-1543.

— "Zur Geschichte des Schriftverständnisses." In Verkündigung und Verantwortung. Theologische Traktate, vol. 2. Göttingen: Vandenhoeck & Ruprecht, 1967.

Gnuse, Robert. The Authority of the Bible: Theories of Inspiration, Revelation and the Canon of Scripture. New York: Paulist Press, 1985.

Goebel, Hans-Theodor. **Wort Gottes als Auftrag: Zur Theologie von Rudolf Bultmann, Gerhard Ebeling und Wolfhart Pannenberg.** Neukirchen-Vluyn: Neukirchener Verlag des Erziehungsvereins, 1972.

Goldingay, John. "Models for Scripture." **Scottish Journal of Theology** 44/1 (1991): 19-37.

— **Models for Scripture.** Grand Rapids, MI: Eerdmans, 1994.

— **Models for Interpretation of Scripture.** Grand Rapids, MI: Eerdmans, 1995.

González, Jafet Mencía. "Das Göttliche als Begriff und als Wirklichkeit: Begrifflichkeit und Bewährung beim theologischen Ansatz Wolfhart Pannenbergs." Ph.D. dissertation, Ludwig-Maximilians-University, Munich, 1981.

Góźdź, Krzysztof. **Jesus Christus als Sinn der Geschichte bei Wolfhart Pannenberg.** Eichstätter Studien. Neue Folge, no. 25. Regensburg: Verlag Friedrich Pustet, 1988.

— "Das theologische Verständnis der Geschichte bei Wolfhart Pannenberg." **Collectanea Theologica** 54 (1984): 70-82.

Grant Robert M., with David Tracy. **A Short History of the Interpretation of the Bible.** 2d ed., rev. and enl. Philadelphia: Fortress Press, 1984.

Greiner, Sebastian. **Die Theologie Wolfhart Pannenbergs.** Bonner Dogmatische Studien, no. 2. Würzburg: Echter Verlag, 1988.

Gremmels, Christian. "Der Heilige Geist als Ausleger der Schrift." In **Sola Scriptura: Ringvorlesung der theologischen Fakultät der Philipps-Universität,** ed. Carl-Heinz Ratschow, 153-177. Marburg: N.G. Elwert Verlag, 1977.

Grenz, Stanley J. "The Appraisal of Pannenberg: A Survey of the Literature." In **The Theology of Wolfhart Pannenberg: Twelve American Critiques, With an Autobiographical Essay and Response,** ed. Carl E. Braaten and Philip Clayton, 19-52. Minneapolis: Augsburg Publishing House, 1988.

— "The Irrelevance of Theology: Pannenberg and the Quest for Truth." **Calvin Theological Journal** 27 (1992): 307-311.

— "Pannenberg and Evangelical Theology: Sympathy and Caution." **Christian Scholar's Review** 20/3 (1990): 272-285.

— **Reason for Hope: The Systematic Theology of Wolfhart Pannenberg.** New York: Oxford University Press, 1990.

— "Reasonable Christianity: Wolfhart Pannenberg Turns 60." **Christianity Today** 32/12 (1988): 32-34.

— "Wolfhart Pannenberg: Reason, Hope and Transcendence." **The Asbury Theological Journal** 46/2 (1991): 73-90.

Grenz, Stanley J., and Roger E. Olson. **20th Century Theology: God and the World in a Transitional Age**. Downers Grove, IL: InterVarsity Press, 1992.

Grobel, Kendrick. "Biblical Criticism." **The Interpreter's Dictionary of the Bible**. Edited by George Arthur Buttrick. Nashville, TN: Abingdon Press, 1962. 1:407-413.

— "Revelation and Resurrection." In **Theology as History**. New Frontiers in Theology: Discussions among Continental and American Theologians, 3:155-175. Edited by James M. Robinson and John B. Cobb, Jr. New York: Harper and Row, 1967.

Grudem, Wayne A. "Scripture's Self-Attestation and the Problem of Formulating a Doctrine of Scripture." In **Scripture and Truth**, ed. D. A. Carson and John D. Woodbridge, 19-59. Grand Rapids, MI: Zondervan Publishing House, 1983.

— **Systematic Theology: An Introduction to Biblical Doctrine**. Grand Rapids, MI: Zondervan Publishing House, 1994.

Gruenler, Royce Gordon. **Meaning and Understanding: The Philosophical Framework for Biblical Interpretation**. Foundations of Contemporary Interpretation Series, no. 2. Grand Rapids, MI: Zondervan Publishing House, 1991.

Gunneweg, Antonius H. J. "Sola Scriptura. Theologische und methodologische Erwägungen zu einem aktuellen Problem." In **Sola Scriptura: Beiträge zu Exegese und Hermeneutik des Alten Testaments**, ed. Peter Höffken, 184-198. Göttingen: Vandenhoeck & Ruprecht, 1983.

Gunton, Colin E. **Becoming and Being: The Doctrine of God in Charles Hartshorne and Karl Barth**. Oxford: Oxford University Press, 1978.

— "Using and Being Used: Scripture and Systematic Theology." **Theology Today** 47/3 (1990): 248-259.

— **Yesterday and Today: A Study of Continuities in Christology**. Grand Rapids, MI: Eerdmans, 1983.

Gutenson, Chuck. "Father, Son and Holy Spirit--The One God: An Exploration of the Trinitarian Doctrine of Wolfhart Pannenberg." **The Asbury Theological Journal** 49/1 (1994): 5-21.

Gutwenger, E. "Offenbarung und Geschichte." **Zeitschrift für Katholische Theologie** 88 (1966): 393-410.

Haaker, Klaus. "Sola Scriptura: Zur Bedeutung der Bibel für die Kirche heute." **Theologische Beiträge** 24/3 (1993): 130-139.

Hackmann, Daniel Winthrop. "Validation and Truth: Wolfhart Pannenberg and the Scientific Status of Theology." Ph.D. dissertation, University of Iowa, 1989.

Hagen, Kenneth. "The History of Scripture in the Church." In **The Bible in the Churches: How Different Christians Interpret the Scriptures**, ed. Kenneth Hagen, 3-34. New York: Paulist Press, 1985.

Hagen, Kenneth, ed. **The Bible in the Churches: How Different Christians Interpret the Scriptures**. New York: Paulist Press, 1985.

Hägglund, Bengt. **Die Heilige Schrift und ihre Deutung in der Theologie Johann Gerhards: Eine Untersuchung über das altlutherische Schriftverständnis**. Lund: CWK Gleerup, 1951.

Hagner, Donald A. "What Is Distinctive about 'Evangelical' Scholarship?" **Theological Students Fellowship Bulletin** 7/3 (1984): 5-7.

Haight, Roger, S.J. **Dynamics of Theology**. New York: Paulist Press, 1990.

Hall, Douglas John. **Thinking the Faith: Christian Theology in a North American Context**. Minneapolis: Augsburg, 1989.

Hall, Thor. "Does Systematic Theology Have a Future?" **The Christian Century** 93 (1976): 253-256.

—— **Systematic Theology Today: The State of the Art in North America**. Part I. Washington, DC: University Press of America, 1978.

Hamel, Martin. **Bibel--Mission--Ökumene: Schriftverständnis und Schriftgebrauch in der neueren ökumenischen Missionstheologie**. Giessen: Brunnen Verlag, 1993.

Hamilton, William. "The Character of Pannenberg's Theology." In **Theology as History**, New Frontiers in Theology: Discussions among Continental and American Theologians, ed. James M. Robinson and John B. Cobb, Jr., 3:176-196. New York: Harper and Row, 1967.

Hannah, John D., ed. **Inerrancy and the Church**. Chicago: Moody Press, 1984.

Hanratty, Gerald. "Enlightenment." **The New Dictionary of Theology**. Edited by Joseph A. Komonchak, Mary Collins, and Dermot A. Lane. Wilmington, DE: Michael Glazier, 1987. 323-324.

Harder, Helmut. "Continuity Between Method and Content in Contemporary Theology: The Achievement of Wolfhart Pannenberg." Th.D. dissertation, Toronto School of Theology, 1971.

Harder, Helmut G., and W. Taylor Stevenson. "The Continuity of History and Faith in the Theology of Wolfhart Pannenberg: Toward an Erotics of History." **Journal of Religion** 51 (1971): 34-56.

Härle, Wilfried, and Eilert Herms. "Deutschsprachige protestantische Dogmatik nach 1945. II. Teil." **Verkündigung und Forschung** 28 (1983): 1-87.

Harnack, Adolph von. **History of Dogma**. 7 vols. Translated by William M'Gilchrist. London: Williams & Northgate, 1894-1899.

Harvey, Van Austin. **The Historian and the Believer: The Morality of Historical Knowledge and Christian Belief**. New York: Macmillan Publishing Company, 1966.

Hasel, Frank M. "The Christological Analogy of Scripture in Karl Barth." **Theologische Zeitschrift** 50 (1994): 40-49.

— "Reflections on the Authority and Trustworthiness of Scripture." In **Issues in Revelation and Inspiration**, ed. Frank Holbrook and Leo Van Dolson, 201-220. Adventist Theological Society Occasional Papers, vol. 1. Berrien Springs, MI: Adventist Theological Society Publications, 1992.

— "Scientific Revolution: An Analysis and Evaluation of Thomas Kuhn's Concept of Paradigm and Paradigm Change for Theology." **Journal of the Adventist Theological Society** 2/2 (1991): 160-177.

Hasel, Gerhard F. **Biblical Interpretation Today**. Washington, DC: Biblical Research Institute, 1985.

— **Old Testament Theology: Basic Issues in the Current Debate**. 4th ed., rev. and enl. Grand Rapids, MI: Eerdmans, 1991.

— "The Problem of History in Old Testament Theology." **Andrews University Seminary Studies** 8 (1970): 23-50.

— "The Problem of the Center in the OT Theology Debate." **Zeitschrift für die alttestamentliche Wissenschaft** 86 (1974): 65-82.

— "The Relationship between Biblical Theology and Systematic Theology." **Trinity Journal** 5NS (1984): 113-120.

— "Scripture and Theology." **Journal of the Adventist Theological Society** 4/2 (1993): 47-94.

Haudel, Matthias. **Die Bibel und die Einheit der Kirchen: Eine Untersuchung der Studien von 'Glauben und Kirchenverfassung'**. Kirche und Konfession: Veröffentlichungen des Konfessionskundlichen Institus des Evangelischen Bundes, no. 34. Göttingen: Vandenhoeck & Ruprecht, 1993.

Hayes, John H., and Frederick Prussner. **Old Testament Theology: Its History and Development**. Atlanta: John Knox Press, 1985.

Hearn, Arnold Withrow. "The Problem of Biblical Authority: A Critical Study of Some Recent and Contemporary American Protestant Theologians Representative of Evangelical Liberalism, Contemporary Orthodoxy, and Neo-Reformationism." Ph.D. dissertation, Columbia University, 1961.

Hefner, Philip. "The Role of Science in Pannenberg's Theological Thinking." **Zygon** 24/2 (1989): 135-151.

— "Theological Reflections: Questions for Moltmann and Pannenberg." **Una Sancta** 25 (1968): 32-51.

Heim, Karl. **Das Gewißheitsproblem in der systematischen Theologie bis zu Schleiermacher.** Leipzig: J. C. Hinrich'sche Buchhandlung, 1911.

Heim, S. Mark. "Review of **A Theology of Word and Spirit, by Donald G. Bloesch.**" **Religious Studies Review** 19/3 (1993): 239.

Hell, Silvia. **Die Dialektik des Wortes bei Martin Luther: Die Beziehung zwischen Gott und dem Menschen.** Innsbrucker theologische Schriften, no. 35. Innsbruck: Tyrolia Verlag, 1992.

Hellwig, Monika. "Review of **The Reform of the Church**, by Donald G. Bloesch." **Theological Studies** 32 (1971): 155-156.

Helm, Paul. "Understanding Scholarly Presuppositions: A Crucial Tool for Research?" **Tyndale Bulletin** 44/1 (1993): 143-154.

Hempelmann, Heinzpeter. **Gott--Ein Schriftsteller! J. G. Hamann über die End-Außerung Gottes ins Wort der Heiligen Schrift und ihre hermeneutischen Konsequenzen.** Wuppertal: R. Brockhaus, 1988.

— **Kritischer Rationalismus und Theologie als Wissenschaft: Zur Frage nach dem Wirklichkeitsbezug des christlichen Glaubens.** 2d ed. Wuppertal: R. Brockhaus Verlag, 1987.

— "Veritas Hebraica als Grundlage christlicher Theologie: Zur systematisch-theologischen Relevanz der biblisch-hebräischen Sprachgestalt." In **Hebraica Veritas: die hebräische Grundlage der biblischen Theologie als exegetische und systematische Aufgabe**, ed. Klaus Haacker and Heinzpeter Hempelmann, 39-78. Wuppertal: R. Brockhaus, 1989.

Henke, Heinrich Philipp Konrad. **Lineamenta Institutionum Fidei Christianae Historico-Criticarum.** Helmstadii: Fleckeisen, 1795.

Henkys, Jürgen. "Sola Scriptura im gegenwärtigen kirchlichen Handeln." In **Sola Scriptura: Das reformatorische Schriftprinzip in der säkularen Welt**, ed. Hans Heinrich Schmid and Joachim Mehlhausen, 79-98. Gütersloh: Gerd Mohn, 1991.

Henry, Carl F. H. **God, Revelation and Authority.** 6 vols. Waco, TX: Word Books, 1976-1983.

— The Protestant Dilemma: An Analysis of the Current Impasse in Theology. Grand Rapids, MI: Eerdmans, 1949.

Heppe, Heinrich. **Reformed Dogmatics: Set Out and Illustrated from the Sources**, rev. and ed. Ernst Bizer. Translated by G. T. Thomson. London: George Allen & Unwin, 1950.

Hermann, Rudolf. **Von der Klarheit der Heiligen Schrift: Untersuchungen und Erörterungen über Luthers Lehre von der Schrift in** De servo arbitrio. Berlin: Evangelische Verlagsanstalt, 1958.

Hesse, Franz. "Wolfhart Pannenberg und das Alte Testament." **Neue Zeitschrift für Systematische Theologie** 7 (1965): 174-199.

Hesse, Mary. "Action at a Distance and Field Theory." **The Encyclopedia of Philosophy**. Edited by Paul Edwards. New York: The Macmillan Company and the Free Press, 1967. 1:8-15.

— Models and Analogies in Science. Notre Dame: University of Notre Dame Press, 1966.

Hesselink, I. John. "Advance Praise for **A Theology of Word and Spirit**." Front Inside Book Cover.

Hilberath, Bernd Jochen. **Theologie zwischen Tradition und Kritik: Die philosophische Hermeneutik Hans-Georg Gadamers als Herausforderung des theologischen Selbstverständnisses**. Düsseldorf: Patmos Verlag, 1978.

Hill, William J. **The Three-Personed God: The Trinity as a Mystery of Salvation**. Washington, DC: The Catholic University of America Press, 1982.

Hinton, Rory A. A. "Pannenberg on the Truth of Christian Discourse: A Logical Response." **Calvin Theological Journal** 27 (1992): 312-318.

Hirsch, E. D., Jr. **Validity in Interpretation**. New Haven: Yale University Press, 1967.

Hirsch, Emanuel. **Geschichte der neueren Evangelischen Theologie im Zusammenhang mit den allgemeinen Bewegungen des europäischen Denkens**. 5 vols. Gütersloh: Gerd Mohn, 1964.

Hodgson, Peter C. "Review of **Theology and the Philosophy of Science**." **Religious Studies Review** 3 (1977): 215-218.

Hodgson, Peter, and Robert H. King, ed. **Christian Theology**. 2d ed. Philadelphia: Fortress Press, 1985.

Hoekema, Anthony A. "Review of **Essentials of Evangelical Theology**, volume 1, by Donald G. Bloesch." **Calvin Theological Journal** 14/1 (1979): 85-87.

Hoenecke, Adolf. **Evangelisch-Lutherische Dogmatik**. 4 vols. Milwaukee, WI: Northwestern Publishing House, 1909.

Hogan, John P. **Collingwood and Theological Hermeneutics**. College Theology Society Studies in Religion, no. 3. Lanham, MD: University Press of America, 1989.

——— "The Historical Imagination and the New Hermeneutic: Collingwood and Pannenberg." In **The Pedagogy of God's Image: Essays on Symbol and the Religious Imagination**, ed. Robert Masson, 9-30. Chico, CA: Scholars Press, 1981.

Holl, Karl. **Gesammelte Aufsätze zur Kirchengeschichte: Luther**. Vol. 1. Tübingen: J. C. B. Mohr, 1932.

Holmer, Paul L. **The Grammar of Faith**. San Francisco: Harper and Row, 1978.

Holmes, Arthur F. "Ordinary Language Analysis and Theological Method." **Journal of the Evangelical Theological Society** 11 (1968): 131-138.

Holte, Ragnar. "Rationality and the Christian Tradition." In **Belief in God and Intellectual Honesty**, ed. Ruurd Veldhuis, Andy F. Sanders, and Heine J. Siebrand, 83-93. Assen/Maastricht: Van Gorcum, 1990.

Holwerda, David. "Faith, Reason and the Resurrection in the Theology of Wolfhart Pannenberg." In **Faith and Rationality**, ed. A. Plantinga and N. Woltersdorff. Notre Dame: University of Notre Dame Press, 1983.

Holzhey, Karl. **Die Inspiration der Heiligen Schrift in der Anschauung des Mittelalters: Von Karl dem Grossen bis zum Konzil von Trient**. Munich: J. J. Lentner'sche Buchhandlung, 1895.

Hornig, Gottfried. **Die Anfänge der historisch-kritischen Theologie: Johann Salomo Semlers Schriftverständnis und seine Stellung zu Luther**. Forschungen zur Systematischen Theologie und Religionsphilosophie, no. 8. Göttingen: Vandenhoeck & Ruprecht, 1961.

Horst, Ulrich. "Das Offenbarungsverständnis der Hochscholastik." In **Handbuch der Dogmengeschichte**, ed. Michael Schmaus, Alois Grillmeier and Leo Scheffczyk, vol. I, fasc. 1a, 116-143. Freiburg: Herder, 1971.

Hudson, W. D. "God Revealed in Creation: Review Article." **The Expository Times** 104/2 (1992): 47-48.

Hübner, Hans. **Biblische Theologie des Neuen Testaments**. Vol. 1, **Prolegomena**. Göttingen: Vandenhoeck & Ruprecht, 1990.

Hummel, Horace D. "Biblical or Dogmatic Theology?" **Lutheran Theological Journal** 16/1 (1982): 3-15.

Hunsinger, George. **How to Read Karl Barth: The Shape of His Theology**. New York: Oxford University Press, 1991.

Hunter, James Davidson. **American Evangelicalism: Conservative Religion and the Quandary of Modernity**. New Brunswick, NJ: Rutgers University Press, 1983.

— **Evangelicalism: The Coming Generation**. Chicago: University of Chicago Press, 1987.

Hyslop, Anita Marie. "The Theology of Image and Imagination in the Theology of Wolfhart Pannenberg." Ph.D. dissertation, Marquette University, 1977.

Idinopolis, Thomas A. **The Erosion of Faith: An Inquiry into the Origins of the Contemporary Crisis in Religious Thought**. Chicago: Quadrangle Books, 1971.

Jackson, Minus Baskin. "An Investigation of Wolfhart Pannenberg's Theory of Knowledge as Creative Subjectivity." Th.D. dissertation, Union Theological Seminary, 1973.

Jacobs, Manfred. "Liberale Theologie." **Theologische Realenzyklopädie**. Edited by Gerhard Müller. Berlin: Walter de Gruyter, 1991. 21:47-68.

Jammer, Max. "Feld, Feldtheorie." **Historisches Wörterbuch der Philosophie**. Edited by Joachim Ritter. Basel: Schwabe & Co. Verlag, 1972. 2:923-926.

Jeanrond, Werner G. "Karl Barth's Hermeneutics." In **Reckoning with Barth: Essays in Commemoration of the Centenary of Karl Barth's Birth**, ed. Nigel Biggar, 80-97. London: Mowbray, 1988.

— **Theological Hermeneutics: Development and Significance**. New York: Crossroad, 1991.

Jenson, Robert W. "God." **The Blackwell Encyclopedia of Modern Christian Thought**. Edited by Alister E. McGrath. Oxford: Blackwell, 1993. 234-246.

Jentz, Arthur H., Jr. "Personal Freedom and the Futurity of God: Some Reflections on Pannenberg's 'God of Hope.'" **Reformed Review** 31 (1977): 148-154.

Jewett, Paul King. **Emil Brunner's Concept of Revelation**. London: James Clarke & Co., 1954.

— "Emil Brunner's Doctrine of Scripture." In **Inspiration and Interpretation**, ed. John F. Walvoord, 210-238. Grand Rapids, MI: Eerdmans, 1957.

— **God, Creation, and Revelation: A Neo-Evangelical Theology**. Grand Rapids, MI: Eerdmans, 1991.

Jodock, Darrell. **The Church's Bible: Its Contemporary Authority**. Minneapolis: Fortress Press, 1989.

— "The Reciprocity Between Scripture and Theology: The Role of Scripture in Contemporary Theological Reflection." **Interpretation** 44 (1990): 369-382.

Joest, Wilfried. "Fundamentalismus." **Theologische Realenzyklopädie**. Edited by Gerhard Krause and Gerhard Müller. Berlin: Walter de Gruyter, 1983. 11:732-738.

Johnson, Elizabeth Ann. "Analogy/Doxology and Their Connection with Christology in the Thought of Wolfhart Pannenberg." Ph.D. dissertation, Catholic University of America, 1981.

— "The Right Way to Speak about God? Pannenberg on Analogy." **Theological Studies** 43 (1982): 673-692.

Johnson, J. F. "Lutheran Tradition, The." **Evangelical Dictionary of Theology**. Edited by Walter A. Elwell. Grand Rapids, MI: Baker Book House, 1984. 667-670.

Johnson, Walter E. "A Critical Analysis of the Nature and Function of Reason in the Theology of Carl F. H. Henry." Th.D. dissertation, New Orleans Baptist Theological Seminary, 1989.

Johnston, Robert K. "Biblical Authority and Hermeneutics: The Growing Evangelical Dialogue." **The Covenant Quarterly** 50/3 (1992): 3-19.

— "Biblical Authority and Hermeneutics: The Growing Evangelical Dialogue." **Southwestern Journal of Theology** 34/2 (1992): 22-30.

— **Evangelicals at an Impasse: Biblical Authority in Practice**. Atlanta, GA: John Knox Press, 1978.

— "Review of **Essentials of Evangelical Theology**, vol. 2." **Journal of the Evangelical Theological Society** 23/3 (1979): 281-282.

Johnston, Robert K., ed. **The Use of the Bible in Theology: Evangelical Options**. Atlanta, GA: John Knox Press, 1985.

Jowett, Benjamin. "On the Interpretation of Scripture." In **Essays and Reviews**, 330-433. London: John Parker and Sons, 1860.

Jüngel, Eberhard. "Das Dilemma der natürlichen Theologie und die Wahrheit ihres Problems: Überlegungen für ein Gespräch mit Wolfhart Pannenberg." In **Denken im Schatten des Nihilismus. Festschrift für Wilhelm Weischedel zum 70. Geburtstag**, ed. Alexander Schwan, 419-440. Darmstadt: Wissenschaftliche Buchgesellschaft, 1975.

— "Nihil divinitatis, ubi non fides: Ist Christliche Dogmatik in rein theoretischer Perspektive möglich? Bemerkungen zu einem theologischen Entwurf von Rang." **Zeitschrift für Theologie und Kirche** 86 (1989): 204-235.

Jüngel, Eberhard, Karl Rahner, and M. Seitz. "Das Verhältnis der theologischen Diszilininen untereinander." In **Unterwegs zur Sache. Theologische Bemerkungen**, ed. Eberhard Jüngel, 34-59. Munich: Chr. Kaiser, 1972.

Kähler, Martin. **Geschichte der protestantischen Dogmatik im 19. Jahrhundert**. 2d enl. ed. Wuppertal: R. Brockhaus Verlag, 1989.

— **The So-Called Historical Jesus and the Historic, Biblical Christ**. Translated and edited by Carl E. Braaten. Philadelphia: Fortress Press, 1964.

— **Der sogenannte historische Jesus und der geschichtliche biblische Christus**. Leipzig: A. Deichert, 1896.

— **Die Wissenschaft der christlichen Lehre von dem evangelischen Grundartikel aus im Abrisse dargestellt**. Neukirchen-Vluyn: Neukirchener Verlag des Erziehungsvereins, 1966.

Kaiser, Christopher B. **The Doctrine of God: An Historical Survey**. Westchester, IL: Crossway, 1982.

Kant, Immanuel. **Critique of Pure Reason**. Translated by J. M. D. Meiklejohn. London: J. M. Dent & Sons, 1959.

— **Critique of Practical Reason**. Translated by Lewis White Beck. Indianapolis: Bobbs-Merrill, 1956.

— **What Is Enlightenment?** Translated and edited by Lewis White Beck. Indianapolis: Bobbs-Merrill, 1959.

Kantzenbach, Friedrich Wilhelm. **Programme der Theologie: Denker, Schulen, Wirkungen von Schleiermacher bis Moltmann**. Munich: Claudius Verlag, 1978.

Kantzer, Kenneth S. "Calvin and the Holy Scriptures." In **Inspiration and Interpretation**, ed. John F. Walvoord, 115-155. Grand Rapids, MI: Eerdmans, 1957.

Kantzer, Kenneth S., and Carl F. H. Henry, eds. **Evangelical Affirmations**. Grand Rapids, MI: Zondervan Publishing House, 1990.

Karpp, Heinrich. "Bibel IV. Die Funktion der Bibel in der Kirche." **Theologische Realenzyklopädie**. Edited by Gerhard Krause and Gerhard Müller. Berlin: Walter de Gruyter, 1980. 6:49-70.

— **Schrift, Geist und Wort Gottes: Geltung und Wirkung der Bibel in der Geschichte der Kirche--von der Alten Kirche bis zum Ausgang der Reformationszeit**. Darmstadt: Wissenschaftliche Buchhandlung, 1992.

Kasper, Walter. **The Methods of Dogmatic Theology**. Translated by John Drury. New York: Paulist Press, 1969.

Kaufman, Gordon D. "Doing Theology from a Liberal Christian Point of View." In **Doing Theology in Today's World: Essays in Honor of Kenneth S. Kantzer**, ed. John D. Woodbridge and Thomas Edward McComiskey, 397-415. Grand Rapids, MI: Zondervan Publishing House, 1991.

— **An Essay on Theological Method**. Missoula, MT: Scholars Press, 1975.

— "What Shall We Do with the Bible?" **Interpretation** 25 (1971): 95-112.

Kehm, G. H. "Pannenberg's Theological Program." **Perspective** 9 (1968): 245-266.

Kelsey, David H. "Appeals to Scripture in Theology." **Journal of Religion** 48 (1968): 1-21.

— "The Bible and Christian Theology." **Journal of the American Academy of Religion** 48 (1980): 385-402.

— "Method, Theological." **The Westminster Dictionary of Christian Theology**. Edited by Alan Richardson and John Bowden. Philadelphia: Westminster Press, 1983. 363-368.

— **The Uses of Scripture in Recent Theology**. Philadelphia: Fortress Press, 1975.

Kensinger, Wilmer Roy. "Certain Outstanding Theological and Philosophical Movements of the Past Two Centuries in Relation to Their Bearing upon the Doctrine and Use of the Scriptures." Ph.D. dissertation, New York Theological Seminary, 1941.

Kent, J. H. S. "The Socinian Tradition." **Theology** 78 (1975): 131-140.

Keylock, Leslie R. "Evangelical Leaders You Should Know: Meet Donald G. Bloesch." **Moody Monthly** 88/7 (1988): 61-63.

Kienzler, Klaus. **Logik der Auferstehung: Eine Untersuchung zu Rudolf Bultmann, Gerhard Ebeling und Wolfhart Pannenberg**. Freiburger Theologische Studien, no. 100. Freiburg: Herder, 1976.

Kim, Kyuun-Jin. "Offenbarung Gottes und die Geschichte bei W. Pannenberg und J. Moltmann." In **Gottes Zukunft--Zukunft der Welt. Festschrift für Jürgen Moltmann zum 60. Geburtstag**, ed. Hermann Deuser, Gerhard Marcel Martin, Konrad Stock, and Michael Welker, 481-490. Munich: Chr. Kaiser, 1986.

Klein, Günter. **Theologie des Wortes Gottes und die Hypothese der Universalgeschichte: Zur Auseinandersetzung mit Wolfhart Pannenberg**. Beiträge zur evangelischen Theologie, no. 37. Munich: Chr. Kaiser, 1964.

Kliever, Lonnie D. **The Shattered Spectrum: A Survey of Contemporary Theology**. Atlanta: John Knox Press, 1981.

Klooster, Fred H. "Historical Method and the Resurrection in Pannenberg's Theology." **Calvin Theological Journal** 11 (1976): 5-33.

Klug, Eugene F. **From Luther to Chemnitz: On Scripture and the Word.** Grand Rapids, MI: Eerdmans, 1971.

——— "Word and Scripture in Luther Studies Since World War II." **Trinity Journal** 5NS (1984): 3-46.

Knierim, Rolf. "Offenbarung im Alten Testament." In **Probleme biblischer Theologie**, ed. Hans Walter Wolff, 206-235. Munich: Chr. Kaiser, 1971.

Knitter, Paul. "What Is German Protestant Theology Saying about the Non-Christian Religions?" **Neue Zeitschrift für Systematische Theologie** 15 (1973): 38-64.

Koch, Klaus. **The Rediscovery of Apocalyptic.** Studies in Biblical Theology, 2d series, no. 22. Translated by Margaret Köhl. Naperville, IL: A. R. Allenson, 1972.

Koch, Kurt. **Der Gott der Geschichte: Theologie der Geschichte bei Wolfhart Pannenberg als Paradigma einer philosophischen Theologie in ökumenischer Perspektive.** Tübinger Theologische Studien, no. 32. Mainz: Matthias Grünewald Verlag, 1988.

Köhler, O. "Geschichte." **Lexikon für Theologie und Kirche.** Edited by Josef Höfer and Karl Rahner. Freiburg: Herder, 1960. 4:777-780.

Koehler, Walther. **Dogmengeschichte als Geschichte des christlichen Selbstbewusstseins: Das Zeitalter der Reformation.** 2 vols. Zurich: Max Niehans Verlag, 1951.

Kohls, Ernst-Wilhelm. "Luthers Aussagen über die Mitte, Klarheit und Selbsttätigkeit der Heiligen Schrift." **Lutherjahrbuch** 40 (1973): 46-75.

König, Adrio. **Here Am I: A Christian Reflection on God.** Grand Rapids, MI: Eerdmans, 1982.

Körtner, Ulrich H. J. "Schrift und Geist: Über Legitimität und Grenzen allegorischer Schriftauslegung." **Neue Zeitschrift für Systematische Theologie** 36 (1994): 1-17.

Kolden, Marc. "Pannenberg's Attempt to Base Theology on History." Ph.D. dissertation, University of Chicago, 1976.

Konrad, Franz. **Das Offenbarungsverständnis in der evanglischen Theologie.** Beiträge zur Ökumenischen Theologie, no. 6. Munich: Max Hueber Verlag, 1971.

Konrad, Johann Friedrich. **Abbild und Ziel der Schöpfung: Untersuchungen zur Exegese von Genesis 1 und 2 in Barths Kirchlicher Dogmatik III, 1.** Beiträge zur Geschichte der biblischen Hermeneutik, no. 5 Tübingen: J. C. B. Mohr, 1962.

Kooiman, Willem Jan. **Luther and the Bible.** Translated by John Schmidt. Philadelphia: Muhlenberg Press, 1961.

Krabbendam, Hendrik. "The Functional Theology of G. C. Berkouwer." In **Challenges to Inerrancy: A Theological Response**, ed. Gordon Lewis and Bruce Demarest, 285-316. Chicago: Moody Press, 1984.

Kraus, Georg. **Gotteserkenntnis ohne Offenbarung und Glaube? Natürliche Theologie als ökumenisches Problem.** Konfessionskundliche und Kontroverstheologische Studien, no. 50. Paderborn: Verlag Bonifatius-Druckerei, 1986.

Kraus, Hans-Joachim. **Die Biblische Theologie: Ihre Geschichte und Problematik.** Neukirchen-Vluyn: Neukirchener Verlag, 1970.

— **Geschichte der historisch-kritischen Erforschung des Alten Testaments.** 3d rev. and enl. ed. Neukirchen-Vluyn: Neukirchener Verlag des Erziehungsvereins, 1982.

Krentz, Edgar. **The Historical-Critical Method.** Philadelphia: Fortress Press, 1975.

Kropatscheck, Friedrich. **Das Schriftprinzip der lutherischen Kirche: geschichtliche und dogmatische Untersuchungen.** Vol. 1. Leipzig: A. Deichertsche Verlagsbuchhandlung, 1904.

Kruse, Heinz. **Die heilige Schrift in der theologischen Erkenntnislehre: Grundfragen des Katholischen Schriftverständnisses.** Konfessionskundliche Schriften des Johann-Adam-Möhler-Instituts, no. 5. Paderborn: Verlag Bonifatius Druckerei, 1964.

Kühne, Hans-Jochen. **Schriftautorität und Kirche: Eine kontroverstheologische Studie zur Begründung der Schriftautorität in der neueren katholischen Theologie.** Berlin: Evangelische Verlagsanstalt, 1979.

Kümmel, Werner Georg. **The New Testament: The History of the Investigation of Its Problems.** Translated by S. McLean Gilmour and Howard C. Kee. Nashville, TN: Abingdon Press, 1972.

Küng, Hans. **Theology for the Third Millenium: An Ecumenical View.** Translated by Peter Heinegg. New York: Doubleday, 1988.

Küng, Hans, and David Tracy, eds. **Paradigm Change in Theology: A Symposium for the Future.** Translated by Margarete Köhl. New York: Crossroad, 1989.

Kugelmann, Lothar. **Antizipation: Eine Begriffsgeschichtliche Untersuchung.** Forschungen zur systematischen und ökumenischen Theologie, no. 50. Göttingen: Vandenhoeck & Ruprecht, 1986.

Larkin, William J., Jr. **Culture and Biblical Hermeneutics: Interpreting and Applying the Authoritative Word of God in a Relativistic Age.** Grand Rapids, MI: Baker Book House, 1988.

LaSor, William Sanford. "The *Sensus Plenior* and Biblical Interpretation." In **Scripture, Tradition, and Interpretation: Essays Presented to Everett F. Harrison by His Students and Colleagues in Honor of His Seventy-Fifth Birthday**, ed. W. Ward Gasque and William Sanford LaSor, 260-277. Grand Rapids, MI: Eerdmans, 1978.

Latourelle, René. "Théologie Fondamentale." **Dictionnaire de Théologie Fondamentale**, ed. René Latourelle. Montréal: Éditions Bellarmin, 1992. 1352-1362.

Lau, F. "Orthodoxie, altprotestantische." **Die Religion in Geschichte und Gegenwart: Handwörterbuch für Theologie und Religionswissenschaft**. Edited by Kurt Galling. Tübingen: J. C. B. Mohr, 1960. 4:1719-1730.

Leavenworth, James L. "The Use of the Scriptures in the Works of Emil Brunner." Ph.D. dissertation, Yale University, 1950.

Lehmann, Karl, and Wolfhart Pannenberg, eds. **The Condemnations of the Reformation Era: Do They Still Divide?** Translated by Margaret Köhl. Minneapolis: Fortress Press, 1990.

— **Glaubensbekenntnis und Kirchengemeinschaft: Das Modell des Konzils von Konstantinopel (381)**. Dialog der Kirchen. Veröffentlichungen des Ökumenischen Arbeitskreises evangelischer und katholischer Theologen, no. 1. Freiburg: Herder, 1982.

— **Lehrverurteilungen--kirchentrennend? Rechtfertigung, Sakramente und Amt im Zeitalter der Reformation und heute**. Dialog der Kirchen. Veröffentlichungen des Ökumenischen Arbeitskreises evangelischer und katholischer Theologen, no. 4. Freiburg: Herder, 1986.

Leith, John H. "The Bible and Theology." **Interpretation** 30 (1976): 227-241.

— "John Calvin--Theologian of the Bible." **Interpretation** 25 (1971): 329-344.

Leonard, Bill J. "The Origin and Character of Fundamentalism." **Review and Expositor** 79/1 (1982): 5-17.

Lessing, Gotthold Ephraim. "Bibliolatrie." **Lessings Werke**. Edited by J. Petersen and W. von Olshausen. Berlin: Deutsches Verlagshaus Bong & Co., 1925. 23:307-312.

— "On the Proof of the Spirit and of Power." In **Lessing's Theological Writings**, ed. and trans. Henry Chadwick, 51-56. Stanford, CA: Stanford University Press, 1957

Levenson, Jon D. "The Bible: Unexamined Commitments of Criticism." **First Things** 30 (1993): 24-33.

— **The Hebrew Bible, the Old Testament, and Historical Criticism: Jews and Christians in Biblical Studies**. Philadelphia: Westminster / John Knox Press, 1993.

Lewis, Gordon R., and Bruce A. Demarest. **Integrative Theology.** 3 vols. Grand Rapids: Zondervan, 1987-1994.

Lichtenberger, F. **History of German Theology in the Nineteenth Century.** Translated by W. Hastie. Edinburgh: T. & T. Clark, 1889.

Liebing, Heinz. "Sola Scriptura--die reformatorische Antwort auf das Problem der Tadition." In **Sola Scriptura: Ringvorlesung der theologischen Falkultät der Philipps-Universität**, ed. Carl-Heinz Ratschow, 81-95. Marburg: N. G. Elwert Verlag, 1977.

Lightner, R. P. "Review of **Essentials of Evangelical Theology.** Vol. 1, by Donald G. Bloesch." **Bibliotheca Sacra** 136 (1979): 181.

—— "Review of **Essentials of Evangelical Theology.** Vol. 2, by Donald G. Bloesch." **Bibliotheca Sacra** 137 (1980): 279.

Lindbeck, George A. **The Nature of Doctrine: Religion and Theology in a Postliberal Age.** Philadelphia: Westminster Press, 1984.

—— "Theologische Methode und Wissenschaftstheorie." **Theologische Revue** 74/4 (1978): 265-280.

Lindemann, Walter. **Karl Barth und die kritische Schriftauslegung.** Theologische Forschung, no. 54. Hamburg-Bergstedt: Evangelischer Verlag, 1973.

Linnemann, Eta. **Historical Criticism of the Bible: Methodology or Ideology?** Translated by Robert W. Yarbrough. Grand Rapids, MI: Baker Book House, 1990.

Livingston, James C. **Modern Christian Thought: From the Enlightenment to Vatican II.** New York: Macmillan Company, 1971.

Locher, Gottfried W. **Zwingli's Thought: New Perspectives.** Leiden: E. J. Brill, 1981.

Loewen, Howard John. "The Mission of Theology: Reflections on the Structure of Theology from a Believers' Church Perspective." In **Explorations of Systematic Theology from Mennonite Perspectives**, ed. Willard M. Swartley, 83-111. Elkhart, IN: Institute of Mennonite Studies, 1984.

—— "Theology in Transition: Toward a Confessional Paradigm for Theology." In **So Wide a Sea: Essays on Biblical and Systematic Theology**, ed. Ben C. Ollenburger, 79-110. Text-Reader Series 4. Elkhart, IN: Institute of Mennonite Studies, 1991.

Lohse, Bernhard. **Martin Luther: An Introduction to His Life and Work.** Translated by Robert C. Schultz. Philadelphia: Fortress Press, 1986.

— Ratio und Fides. Eine Untersuchung über die Ratio in der Theologie Luthers. Forschungen zur Kirchen- und Dogmengeschichte, no. 8. Göttingen, Vandenhoeck & Ruprecht, 1958

— "Reason and Revelation in Luther." **Scottish Journal of Theology** 13 (1960): 337-365.

Lonergan, Bernard J. F. **Method in Theology**. New York: Seabury Press, 1972.

Löser, Werner. "'Universale Concretum' als Grundgesetz der Oeconomia Revelationis." **Handbuch der Fundamentaltheologie**. Edited by Walter Kern, Hermann Josef Pottmeyer, and Max Seckler. Freiburg: Herder, 1985. 2:108-121.

Lønning, Inge. **Kanon im Kanon: Zum dogmatischen Grundlagenproblem des neutestamentlichen Kanons**. Forschungen zur Geschichte und Lehre des Protestantismus, no. 43. Munich: Chr. Kaiser, 1972.

Lotz, David W. "Sola Scriptura: *Luther on Biblical Authority*." **Interpretation** 35 (1981): 258-273.

Louth, Andrew. "Allegorical Interpretation." **A Dictionary of Biblical Interpretation**. Edited by R. J. Coggins and J. L. Houlden. London: SCM Press, 1990. 12-14.

[Lovelace, Richard.] "Renewal and the Future of Evangelicalism." **Renewal** 3/3 (1983): 1-12.

Luther, Martin. **Werke**. Kritische Gesammtausgabe. Weimar: Bohlau, 1883-1983.

MacIntyre, Alasdair. "Kierkegaard, Søren Aabye." **The Encyclopedia of Philosophy**. Edited by Paul Edwards. New York: Macmillan, 1967. 4:336-340.

Mackintosch, Hugh Ross. **Types of Modern Theology: Schleiermacher to Barth**. New York: Charles Scribner's Sons, 1937.

Macquarrie, John. **Principles of Christian Theology**. 2d ed. New York: Charles Scribner's Sons, 1977.

— "Systematic Theology." In **A New Handbook of Christian Theology**, ed. Donald W. Musser and Joseph L. Price, 469-474. Nashville, TN: Abingdon Press, 1992.

Maddox, Randy L. "The Necessity of Recognizing Distinctions: Lessons from Evangelical Critiques of Christian Feminist Theology." **Christian Scholars Review** 17 (1988): 307-323.

— "Reply to Donald Bloesch." **Christian Scholars Review** 18 (1989): 285-288.

— **Toward an Ecumenical Fundamental Theology**. American Academy of Religion Academy Series, no. 47. Chico, CA: Scholars Press, 1984.

Madison, G. B. **The Hermeneutics of Postmoderity: Figures and Themes**. Bloomington: Indiana University Press, 1988.

Magnuson, Norris A., and William G. Travis. **American Evangelicalism: An Annotated Bibliography**. West Cornwall, CT: Locust Hill Press, 1990.

Maier, Gerhard. **Biblische Hermeneutik**. 2d rev. ed. Wuppertal: R. Brockhaus Verlag, 1991.

— **The End of the Historical Critical Method**. Translated by Edwin W. Leverenz and Rudolph F. Norden. St. Louis, MO: Concordia Publishing House, 1977.

— **Heiliger Geist und Schriftauslegung**. Theologie und Dienst 34. Wuppertal: R. Brockhaus Verlag, 1984.

Mar, Gary. "What Evangelicalism Needs." **New Oxford Review** 61/5 (1994): 28-29.

Margerie, Bertrand de. "Review of **The Reform of the Church**, by Donald G. Bloesch." **Journal of Ecumenical Studies** 8 (1971): 649-650.

Marquart, Kurt E. "A Response to Adequacy of Language and Accommodation." In **Hermeneutics, Inerrancy, and the Bible**, ed. Earl D. Radmacher and Robert D. Preus, 393-405. Grand Rapids, MI: Zondervan Publishing House, 1984.

Marsden, George M. **Fundamentalism and American Culture: The Shaping of Twentieth-Century Evangelicalism: 1870-1925**. New York: Oxford University Press, 1980.

— **Reforming Fundamentalism: Fuller Seminary and the New Evangelicalism**. Grand Rapids, MI: Eerdmans, 1987.

— **Understanding Fundamentalism and Evangelicalism**. Grand Rapids, MI: Eerdmans, 1991.

Marshall, I. Howard. "An Evangelical Approach to 'Theological Criticism.'" **Themelios** 13/3 (1988): 79-85.

— **Biblical Inspiration**. Grand Rapids, MI: Eerdmans, 1982.

Marty, Martin E. **Protestantism**. New York: Holt, Rinehart and Winston, 1972.

— "Tensions Within Contemporary Evangelicalism: A Critical Appraisal." In **The Evangelicals: What They Believe, Who They Are, Where They Are Changing**, ed. David F. Wells and John D. Woodbridge, 170-188. Nashville, TN: Abingdon, 1975.

Maurer, Ernstpeter. "Metaphysik und Antizipation: Wolfhart Pannenbergs theologische Meditationen über das Ganze." **Merkur** 44/501 (1990): 1091-1095.

McBrien, Richard P. **Catholicism**. Minneapolis, MN: Winston Press, 1981.

McClendon, James William, Jr. **Doctrine: Systematic Theology** Vol. 2. Nashville, TN: Abingdon Press, 1994.

— **Ethics: A Systematic Theology**. Vol. 1. Nashville: TN: Abingdon Press, 1986.

McDermott, Brian. "Pannenberg's Resurrection Christology: A Critique." **Theological Studies** 35 (1974): 711-721.

McDonald, H. D. "Review of **Essentials of Evangelical Theology**, vol. 1, by Donald G. Bloesch." **Journal of the Evangelical Theological Society** 23/3 (1979): 279-281.

— **Theories of Revelation: An Historical Study 1700-1960**. Grand Rapids, MI: Baker Book House, 1979.

McFague, Sallie. **Metaphorical Theology: Models of God in Religious Language**. Philadelphia: Fortress Press, 1982.

— **Models of God: Theology for an Ecological Nuclear Age**. Philadelphia: Fortress Press, 1987.

McGlasson, Paul Charles. "Karl Barth and the Scriptures: A Study of the Biblical Exegesis in *Church Dogmatics* I and II." Ph.D. dissertation, Yale University, 1986.

McGrath, Alister E. **Christian Theology: An Introduction**. Oxford: Basil Blackwell, 1994.

— "Enlightenment." **The Blackwell Encyclopedia of Modern Christian Thought**. Edited by Alister E. McGrath. Oxford: Basil Blackwell, 1993. 150-156.

— "Evangelicalism." **The Blackwell Encyclopedia of Modern Christian Thought**. Edited by Alister E. McGrath. Oxford Basil Blackwell, 1993. 183-184.

— **The Genesis of Doctrine: A Study in the Foundations of Doctrinal Criticism**. Oxford: Basil Blackwell, 1990.

— **The Intellectual Origins of the European Reformation**. Oxford: Basil Blackwell, 1987.

— **Reformation Thought: An Introduction**. Oxford: Basil Blackwell, 1988.

— ed. **The Blackwell Encyclopedia of Modern Christian Thought**. Oxford: Basil Blackwell, 1993.

McIntire, C. T. "Fundamentalism." **Evangelical Dictionary of Theology**. Edited by Walter A. Elwell. Grand Rapids, MI: Baker Book House, 1984. 433-436.

McKenzie, David. "Pannenberg on God and Freedom." **Journal of Religion** 60 (1980): 307-329.

— **Wolfhart Pannenberg and Religious Philosophy**. Lanham, MD: University Press of America, 1980.

McKim, Donald K. "Calvin's View of Scripture." In **Readings in Calvin's Theology**, ed. Donald K. McKim, 43-68. Grand Rapids, MI: Baker Book House, 1984.

— "Donald G. Bloesch." In **Handbook of Evangelical Theologians**, ed. Walter A. Elwell, 388-400. Grand Rapids, MI: Baker Book House, 1993.

— **What Christians Believe about the Bible**. Nashville, TN: Thomas Nelson Publishers, 1985.

McKim, Donald K., ed. **Encyclopedia of the Reformed Faith**. Louisville, KY: Westminster/John Knox, 1992.

McKinnon, Alastair. "Barth's Relation to Kierkegaard: Some Further Light." **Canadian Journal of Theology** 13 (1967): 31-41.

McKnight, Edgar V. **Postmodern Use of the Bible: The Emergence of Reader-Oriented Criticism**. Nashville, TN: Abingdon, 1988.

McLelland, Joseph C. "Calvin and Philosophy." **Canadian Journal of Theology** 11 (1965): 42-53.

McNally, Robert E. **The Bible in the Early Middle Ages**. Westminster, MD: Newman Press, 1959, reprint: Atlanta, GA: Scholars Press, 1986.

Meijering, Eginhard Peter. "'Sola Scriptura' und die historische Kritik." In **Sola Scriptura: Das reformatorische Schriftprinzip in der säkularen Welt**, ed. Hans Heinrich Schmid and Joachim Mehlhausen, 44-60. Gütersloh: Gerd Mohn, 1991.

Merrigan, Terrence. "Models in the Theology of Avery Dulles." **Bijdragen, Tijdschrift voor Filosofie en Theologie** 54 (1993): 141-161.

Mertan, Philip. "Plotinus." **Encyclopedia of Philosophy**. Edited by Paul Edwards. New York: Macmillan, 1967. 6:351-359.

Michalson, Gordon E., Jr. "Pannenberg on the Resurrection and Historical Method." **Scottish Journal of Theology** 33 (1980): 345-359.

Michel, Karl-Heinz. "Erkenntnis und Idee Gottes in der Philosophie Immanuel Kants." In **Wer ist das--Gott? Christliche Gotteserkenntnis in den Herausforderungen der Gegenwart**, ed. Helmut Burkhardt, 107-119. Wuppertal: R. Brockhaus Verlag, 1982.

— **Immanuel Kant und die Frage der Erkennbarkeit Gottes: Eine kritische Untersuchung der 'Transzendentalen Ästhetik' in der 'Kritik der reinen Vernunft' und ihrer theologischen Konsequenz**. Wuppertal: R. Brockhaus Verlag, 1987.

— "Kants Vernunftkritik und ihre Folgen für die Theologie." In **Evangelische Schriftauslegung: Ein Quellen- und Arbeitsbuch für Studium und Gemeinde**, ed. Joachim Cochlovius and Peter Zimmerling, 370-375. Wuppertal: R. Brockhaus Verlag, 1987.

— **Sehen und Glauben: Schriftauslegung in der Auseinandersetzung mit Kerygmatheologie und historisch-kritischer Forschung**. Wuppertal: R. Brockhaus Verlag, 1982.

Mickelsen, Berkeley. "The Bible's Own Approach to Authority." In **Biblical Authority**, ed. Jack Rogers, 77-105. Waco, TX: Word Books, 1977.

Micskey, Koloman N. **Die Axiom-Syntax des evangelisch-dogmatischen Denkens: Strukturanalysen des Denkprozesses und des Wahrheitsbegriffs in den Wissenschaftstheorien (Prologomena) zeitgenössischer systematischer Theologen**. Forschungen zur systematischen und ökumenischen Theologie, no. 35. Göttingen: Vandenhoeck & Ruprecht, 1976.

Mildenberger, Friedrich. **Biblische Dogmatik: Eine Biblische Theologie in dogmatischer Perspektive**. 3 vols. Stuttgart: W. Kohlhammer, 1991-1993

— To Frank M. Hasel. Erlangen, June 26, 1992.

Miller, Donald E. "Liberalism." **The Westminster Dictionary of Christian Theology**. Edited by Alan Richardson and John Bowden. Philadelphia: Westminster Press, 1983. 324-325.

Mirbt, Carl. "Semler, Johann Salomo." **Realencyklopädie für protestantische Theologie und Kirche**. 3d enl. ed. Edited by Albert Hauck. Leipzig: J. C. Hinrichsche Buchhandlung, 1906. 18:203-209.

Mohler, Richard Albert, Jr. "Evangelical Theology and Karl Barth: Representative Models of Response." Ph.D. dissertation, The Southern Baptist Theological Seminary, 1989.

Moltmann, Jürgen. "Christianity in the Third Millennium." **Theology Today** 51/1 (1994): 75-89.

— **Theology of Hope: On the Ground and the Implications of a Christian Eschatology**. Translated by James W. Leith. London: SCM Press, 1967.

— "Die Zukunft als neues Paradigma der Transzendenz." **Internationale Dialog Zeitschrift** 2 (1969): 2-13.

Montgommery, John Warwick. "The Theologian's Craft: A Discussion of Theory Formation and Theory Testing in Theology." In **The Suicide of Christian Theology**, 267-313. Minneapolis: Bethany Fellowship, 1970.

Moo, Douglas J. "The Problem of *Sensus Plenior*." In **Hermeneutics, Authority, and Canon**, ed. D. A. Carson and John D. Woodbridge, 175-221. Grand Rapids, MI: Zondervan Publishing House, 1986.

Morgan, Robert. "Introduction: The Nature of New Testament Theology." In **The Nature of New Testament Theology: The Contribution of William Wrede and Adolf Schlatter**, ed. and trans. Robert Morgan, 1-67. Studies in Biblical Theology. Second Series, no. 25. Naperville, IL: Alec R. Allenson, 1973.

Morgan, Robert, and John Barton. **Biblical Interpretation**. Oxford: Oxford University Press, 1988.

Mostert, Walter. "Scriptura sacra sui ipsius interpres. Bemerkungen zum Verständnis der Heiligen Schrift durch Luther." **Lutherjahrbuch** 46 (1979): 60-96.

Mouton, J., A. G. van Aarde, and W. S. Vorster, eds. **Paradigms and Progress in Theology**. [South Africa]: Human Sciencies Research Council, 1988.

Moxter, Michael, and Ingolf U. Dalfert. "Protestant Theology: Germany." **The Blackwell Encyclopedia of Modern Christian Thought**. Edited by Alister E. McGrath. Oxford: Blackwell, 1993. 489-511.

Mühlenberg, Ekkehard. "Gott in der Geschichte: Erwägungen zur Geschichtstheologie von W. Pannenberg." **Kerygma und Dogma** 24 (1978): 244-261.

Mueller, David L. "The Contributions and Weaknesses of Karl Barth's View of the Bible." In **The Proceedings of the Conference on Biblical Inerrancy 1987**, 423-447. Nashville, TN: Broadman Press, 1987.

Mueller, J. J. **What Are They Saying about Theological Method?** New York, Paulist Press, 1984.

Mueller, Theodore. "Luther and the Bible." In **Inspiration and Interpretation**, ed. John F. Walvoord, 87-114. Grand Rapids, MI: Eerdmans, 1957.

Muether, John R. "Evangelicals and the Bible: A Bibliographic Postscript." In **Inerrancy and Hermeneutic: A Tradition, A Challenge, A Debate**, ed. Harvie M. Conn, 253-264. Grand Rapids, MI: Baker Book House, 1988.

Müller, Denis. **Parole et Histoire: Dialogue avec W. Pannenberg**. Geneva: Labor et Fides, 1983.

Müller, Gerhard Ludwig. "Pannenbergs Entwurf einer systematischen Theologie." **Theologische Revue** 86/1 (1990): 1-8.

— "Pannenbergs Entwurf einer systematischen Theologie (II)." **Theologische Revue** 88/5 (1992): 353-360.

Muller, Richard A. "The Debate over the Vowel Points and the Crisis in Orthodox Hermeneutics." **Journal of Medieval and Renaissance Studies** 10/1 (1980): 53-72.

— **Dictionary of Latin and Greek Theological Terms: Drawn Principally from Protestant Scholastic Theology**. Grand Rapids, MI: Baker Book House, 1985.

— "The Foundation of Calvin's Theology: Scripture as Revealing God's Word." **Duke Divinity School Review** 44/1 (1979): 14-23.

— **Post-Reformation Reformed Dogmatics**. Vol. 1, **Prolegomena to Theology**. Grand Rapids, MI: Baker Book House, 1987.

— **Post-Reformation Reformed Dogmatics**. Vol. 2, **Holy Scripture: The Cognitive Foundation of Theology**. Grand Rapids, MI: Baker Book House, 1993.

— "Review of A **Theology of Word and Spirit: Authority and Method in Theology**, by Donald G. Bloesch." **Calvin Theological Journal** 29/1 (1994): 307.

Murphy, C. Nancey. **Theology in the Age of Scientific Reasoning**. Ithaca: Cornell University Press, 1990.

Murphy, Roland E., and Carl J. Peter. "The Role of the Bible in Roman Catholic Theology." **Interpretation** 25 (1971): 78-94.

Muschalek, Georg, and Arnold Gamper. "Offenbarung in Geschichte." **Zeitschrift für katholische Theologie** 86 (1964): 180-196.

Musser, Donald W., and Joseph L. Price, eds. **A New Handbook of Christian Theology**. Nashville, TN: Abingdon, 1992.

Nagel, Ernst. **Zwinglis Stellung zur Schrift**. Freiburg: J. C. B. Mohr, 1896.

Nash, Ronald H. **The Word of God and the Mind of Man: The Crisis of Revealed Truth in Contemporary Theology**. Grand Rapids, MI: Zondervan Publishing House, 1982.

Nations, Archie L. "Historical Criticism and the Current Methodological Crisis." **Scottish Journal of Theology** 36 (1983): 59-71.

Neie, Herbert. **The Doctrine of the Atonement in the Theology of Wolfhart Pannenberg**. Berlin: Walter de Gruyter, 1979.

Neuhaus, Richard John. "Theology for Church and Polis." In **The Theology of Wolfhart Pannenberg: Twelve American Critiques, with an Autobiographical Essay and Response**, ed. Carl E. Braaten and Philip Clayton, 226-238. Minneapolis: Augsburg Publishing House, 1988.

— "Wolfhart Pannenberg: Profile of a Theologian." In Wolfhart Pannenberg, **Theology and the Kingdom of God**, 9-50. Philadelphia: Westminster Press, 1969.

Newlands, George. "Systematische Theologie in Großbritannien in den siebziger Jahren." **Kerygma und Dogma** 27 (1981): 309-317.

Neve, J. L. **A History of Christian Thought**. 2 vols. Philadelphia, PA: Muhlenberg Press, 1946.

Neville, Robert Cummings. **A Theology Primer**. Albany, NY: State University of New York Press, 1991.

Nicklaus, Peter. "Geschichtstheologischer Auszug aus der Geschichte? Wolfhart Pannenberg, **Systematische Theologie**, vol. 1." **Reformatio: Evangelische Zeitschrift für Kultur, Politik, Kirche** 37 (1988): 481-485.

Nicol, Ian G. "Facts and Meanings: Wolfhart Pannenberg's Theology as History and the Role of the Historical-Critical Method." **Religious Studies** 12 (1976): 129-139.

Nicole, Roger. "The Neo-Orthodox Reduction." In **Challenges to Inerrancy: A Theological Response**, ed. Gordon Lewis and Bruce Demarest, 121-144. Chicago: Moody Press, 1984.

Niebuhr, Richard R. **Schleiermacher on Christ and Religion**. London: SCM Press, 1965.

Niesel, Wilhelm. **The Theology of John Calvin**. Translated by Harold Knight. London: Lutterworth Press, 1956.

Nineham, Dennis E. "The Use of the Bible in Modern Theology." **Bulletin of the Journal of the John Rylands Library** 52 (1969): 178-199.

Nnamdi, Reginald. **Offenbarung und Geschichte: Zur hermeneutischen Bestimmung der Theologie Wolfhart Pannenbergs**. Würzburger Studien zur Fundamentaltheologie, no. 13. Frankfurt/Main: Peter Lang, 1993.

Noll, Mark A. **Between Faith and Criticism: Evangelicals, Scholarship, and the Bible in America**. 2d ed. Grand Rapids, MI: Baker Book House, 1991.

— "Evangelicals and the Study of the Bible." **The Reformed Journal** 34/4 (1984): 11-22.

Noller, Gerhard. **Metaphysik und theologische Realisation: das Ende der metaphysischen Grundstellung der Neuzeit und die Neubesinnung auf die theologische Wirklichkeit der Bibel**. Zürich: TVZ Verlag, 1990.

Nowell, David Zedic. "Futurity and Contingency: An Alternative Paradigm." Ph.D. dissertation, Baylor University, 1991.

Nuovo, Victor L. "Calvin's Theology: A Study of Its Sources in Classical Antiquity." Ph.D. dissertation, Columbia University, 1964.

Nygren, Anders. **Meaning and Method: Prolegomena to a Scientific Philosophy of Religion and a Scientific Theology**. Translated by Philip S. Watson. Philadelphia: Fortress Press, 1972.

Nygren, E. Herbert. "Existentialism: Kierkegaard." In **Biblical Errancy: An Analysis of Its Philosophical Roots**, ed. Norman L. Geisler, 105-129. Grand Rapids, MI: Zondervan Publishing House, 1981.

Nyquist, John Paul. "An Evaluation of the Inroads of Process Theology into Contemporary Evangelicalism." Th.D. dissertation, Dallas Theological Seminary, 1984.

Oberman, Heiko Augustinus. **The Harvest of Medieval Theology: Gabriel Biel and Late Medieval Nominalism**. Cambridge, MA: Harvard University Press, 1963.

— **Luther: Man between God and the Devil**. Translated by Eileen Walliser-Schwarzbart. New Haven: Yale University Press, 1989.

— "Quo Vadis, Petre? The History of Tradition from Irenaeus to *Humanis Generis*." **The Harvard Divinity Bulletin** 26/4 (1962): 1-25.

O'Collins, G. G. "Revelation as History." **Heythrop Journal** 7 (1966): 394-406.

Oden, Thomas C. **After Modernity What? Agenda for Theology**. Grand Rapids, MI: Zondervan Publishing House, 1990.

— **Life in the Spirit**. Vol. 3. Systematic Theology. San Francisco: Harper and Row, 1992.

— **The Living God**. Vol. 1. Systematic Theology. San Francisco: Harper and Row, 1987.

— **The Word of Life**. Vol. 2. Systematic Theology. San Francisco: Harper and Row, 1989.

O'Donnell, John. "Pannenberg's Doctrine of God." **Gregorianum** 72/1 (1991): 73-98.

— "Wolfhart Pannenberg, **Systematische Theologie**, Band II." **Gregorianum** 73/3 (1992): 552-554.

Oeming, Manfred. "Unitas Scripturae? Eine Problemskizze." In **Einheit und Vielfalt Biblischer Theologie**. Jahrbuch für Biblische Theologie, vol. 1. Neukirchen-Vluyn: Neukirchener Verlag des Erziehungsvereins, 1986, 1:48-70.

Oey, Thomas Geoffrey. "Wyclif's Doctrine of Scripture Within the Context of His Doctrinal and Social Ideas." Ph.D. dissertation, Vanderbilt University, 1991.

Ogden, Schubert M. "The Authority of Scripture for Theology." **Interpretation** 30 (1976): 242-261.

— "Sources of Religious Authority in Liberal Protestantism." **Journal of the American Academy of Religion** 44/3 (1976): 403-416.

Olive, Don H. **Wolfhart Pannenberg**. Makers of the Modern Theological Mind. Edited by Bob E. Patterson. Waco, TX: Word Books, 1973.

Ollenburger, Ben C. "Biblical and Systematic Theology: Constructing a Relation." In **So Wide a Sea: Essays on Biblical and Systematic Theology**, ed. Ben C. Ollenburger, 111-145. Text-Reader Series, no. 4. Elkhart, IN: Institute of Mennonite Studies, 1991.

— "What Krister Stendahl 'Meant'--A Normative Critique of 'Descriptive Biblical Theology.'" **Horizons in Biblical Theology: An International Dialogue** 8/1 (1986): 61-98.

Olson Roger E. "Pannenberg's Theological Anthropology: A Review Article." **Perspectives in Religious Studies** 13 (1986): 161-169.

— "Review of **Essentials of Evangelical Theology**, vols. 1 and 2, by Donald G. Bloesch." **Christian Scholars Review** 10/1 (1980): 85-86.

— "Trinity and Eschatology: The Historical Being of God in the Theology of Jürgen Moltmann and Wolfhart Pannenberg." **Scottish Journal of Theology** 36 (1983): 213-227.

— "Trinity and Eschatology: The Historical Being of God in the Theology of Wolfhart Pannenberg." Ph.D. dissertation, Rice University, 1984.

— "Wolfhart Pannenberg's Doctrine of the Trinity." **Scottish Journal of Theology** 43 (1990): 175-206.

Olthuis, James H. "God as True Infinite: Concerns about Wolfhart Pannenberg's *Systematic Theology*, vol. 1." **Calvin Theological Journal** 27 (1992): 318-325.

Oosterbaan, J. A. "The Reformation of the Reformation: Fundamentals of Anabaptist Theology." **Mennonite Quarterly Review** 51 (1977): 171-195.

Osborn, Robert T. "Pannenberg's Programme." **Canadian Journal of Theology** 13/2 (1967): 109-122.

Osborne, Grant R. **The Hermeneutical Spiral: A Comprehensive Introduction to Biblical Interpetation**. Downers Grove, IL: InterVarsity Press, 1991.

Østergaard-Nielsen, H. **Scriptura Sacra et Viva Vox: Eine Lutherstudie**. Forschungen zur Geschichte und Lehre des Protestantismus, no. 10. Munich: Chr. Kaiser, 1957.

Packer, James I. "The Adequacy of Human Language." In **Inerrancy**, ed. Norman L. Geisler, 197-226. Grand Rapids, MI: Zondervan Publishing House, 1980.

— "Calvin's View of Scripture." In **God's Inerrant Word: An International Symposium on the Trustworthiness of Scripture**, ed. John Warwick Montgomery, 95-114. Minneapolis, MN: Bethany Fellowship, 1974.

— **Concise Theology: A Guide to Historic Christian Beliefs**. Wheaton, IL: Tyndale House Publishers, 1993.

— "Encountering Present-Day Views of Scripture." In **The Foundation of Biblical Authority**, ed. James Montgomery Boice, 61-82. Grand Rapids, MI: Zondervan Publishing House, 1978.

— **'Fundamentalism' and the Word of God: Some Evangelical Principles**. Grand Rapids, MI: Eerdmans, 1958; reprint, 1990.

— "Is Systematic Theology a Mirage? An Introductory Discussion." In **Doing Theology in Today's World: Essays in Honor of Kenneth S. Kantzer**, ed. John D. Woodbridge and Thomas Edward McComiskey, 17-37. Grand Rapids, MI: Zondervan, 1991.

— "John Calvin and the Inerrancy of Holy Scripture." In **Inerrancy and the Church**, ed. John D. Hannah, 143-188. Chicago: Moody Press, 1984.

— "Liberalism and Conservatism in Theology." **New Dictionary of Theology**, ed. Sinclair B. Ferguson and David F. Wright, 384-386. Downers Grove, IL: InterVarsity Press, 1988.

— "Scripture." In **New Dictionary of Theology**, ed. Sinclair B. Ferguson and David F. Wright, 627-631. Downers Grove, IL: InterVarsity Press, 1988.

— "'Sola Scriptura' in History and Today." In **God's Inerrant Word: An International Symposium on the Trustworthiness of Scripture**, ed. John Warwick Montgomery, 43-62. Minneapolis, MN: Bethany Fellowship, 1974.

Padgett, Alan G. **God, Eternity, and the Nature of Time**. New York: St. Martin's Press, 1992.

Pailin, David A. **The Anthropological Character of Theology: Conditioning Theological Understanding**. Cambridge: Cambridge University Press, 1990.

— "Enlightenment." **The Westminster Dictionary of Christian Theology**. Edited by Alan Richardson and John Bowden. Philadelphia: Westminster Press, 1983. 179-180.

— "Revelation." **The Westminster Dictionary of Christian Theology**. Edited by Alan Richardson and John Bowden. Philadelphia: Westminster Press, 1983. 503-506.

Palmer, Richard E. **Hermeneutics: Interpretation Theory in Schleiermacher, Dilthey, Heidegger, and Gadamer**. Evanston, IL: Northwestern University Press, 1969.

Pannenberg, Wolfhart. "A Response to My American Friends." In **The Theology of Wolfhart Pannenberg: Twelve American Critiques, with an Autobiographical Essay and Response**, ed. Carl E. Braaten and Philip Clayton, 313-336. Minneapolis: Augsburg Publishing House, 1988.

— "An Autobiographical Sketch." In **The Theology of Wolfhart Pannenberg: Twelve American Critiques, with an Autobiographical Essay and Response**, ed. Carl E. Braaten and Philip Clayton, 11-18. Minneapolis: Augsburg Publishing House, 1988.

— "Analogie." **Die Religion in Geschichte und Gegenwart**. 3d ed. Edited by Kurt Galling. Tübingen: J. C. B. Mohr, 1957. 1:350-353.

— "Analogie." **Evangelisches Kirchenlexikon. Kirchlich-theologisches Handwörterbuch**. 2d ed. Edited by Heinz Brunotte and Otto Weber. Göttingen: Vandenhoeck & Ruprecht, 1961. 1:133-144.

— "Analogie und Offenbarung: Eine kritische Untersuchung der Geschichte des Analogiebegriffs in der Gotteserkenntnis." Ruprecht-Karls-University, Heidelberg, 1955.

— "Analogy and Doxology." In **Basic Questions in Theology**, trans. George H. Kehm, 1:211-238. Philadelphia: Westminster Press, 1970.

— "Anthropology and the Question of God." In **Basic Questions in Theology**, trans. R. A. Wilson, 3, 80-98. London: SCM Press, 1973.

— **Anthropology in Theological Perspective**. Translated by Matthew J. O'Connell. Philadelphia: Westminster Press, 1985.

— "Anthropologie in theologischer Perspektive: Philosophisch-theologische Grundlinien." In **Sind wir von Natur aus religiös?**, ed. Wolfhart Pannenberg, 87-106. Schriften der Katholischen Akademie in Bayern, no. 120. Düsseldorf: Patmos Verlag, 1986.

— **The Apostles' Creed in the Light of Today's Questions**. Translated by Margaret Köhl. Philadelphia: Westminster Press, 1972.

— "The Appropriation of the Philosophical Concept of God as a Dogmatic Problem of Early Christian Theology." In **Basic Questions in Theology**, trans. George H. Kehm, 2:119-183. Philadelphia: Fortress Press, 1970.

— "Atom, Duration, Form: Difficulties with Process Philosophy." Translated by John C. Robertson, Jr., and Gérard Vallée. **Process Studies** 14/1 (1984): 21-30.

— "The Biblical Understanding of Reality." In **Faith and Reality**, trans. John Maxwell, 8-19. Philadelphia: Westminster Press, 1977.

— "Central Themes in Christian Theology." 24 April 1992, Richmond, IN. Tape recording. Earlham School of Religion Classroom Building, Earlham College.

— **Christentum in einer säkularisierten Welt**. Freiburg: Herder, 1988.

— **Christian Spirituality**. Philadelphia: Westminster Press, 1983.

— "Christian Theology and Philosophical Criticism." In **Basic Questions in Theology**, trans. R. A. Wilson, 3:116-143. London, SCM Press, 1973.

— "The Christian Vision of God: The New Discussion on the Trinitarian Doctrine." **The Asbury Theological Journal** 46/2 (1991): 27-36.

— "The Christian Vision of God: The New Discussion on the Trinitarian Doctrine." **Trinity Seminary Review** 13/2 (1991): 53-60.

— "Christianity, Marxism, and Liberation Theology." **Christian Scholars Review** 18/3 (1989): 215-226.

— **Christianity in a Secularized World**. Translated by John Bowden. New York: Crossroad, 1989.

— "Constructive and Critical Functions of Christian Eschatology." **Harvard Theological Review** 77/2 (1984): 119-139.

— "The Crisis of the Scripture Principle." In **Basic Questions in Theology**, trans. George H. Kehm, 1:1-14. Philadelphia: Fortress Press, 1970.

— "Divine Revelation and Modern History." In **Faith and Reality**, trans. John Maxwell, 87-104. Philadelphia: Westminster Press, 1977.

— "The Doctrine of the Spirit and the Task of a Theology of Nature." **Theology** 75 (1972): 8-21.

— "Dogmatic Theses on the Doctrine of Revelation." In **Revelation as History**, ed. Wolfhart Pannenberg, 123-158. Translated by David Granskou. London: Macmillan, 1968.

— "Dogmatische Erwägungen zur Auferstehung Jesu." **Kerygma und Dogma** 14 (1968): 105-118.

— "Eine philosophisch-historische Hermeneutik des Christentums." In **In Verantwortung für den Glauben leben: Beiträge zur Fundamentaltheologie und Ökumenik. Festschrift für Heinrich Fries**, ed. Peter Neuner and Harald Wagner, 35-46. Freiburg: Herder, 1992.

— **Ethics**. Translated by Keith Crim. Philadelphia: Westminster Press, 1981.

— **Faith and Reality**. Translated by John Maxwell. Philadelphia: Westminster Press, 1977.

— "Faith and Reason." In **Basic Questions in Theology**, trans. George H. Kehm, 2:46-64. Philadelphia: Fortress Press, 1971.

— "Frage und Antwort--Das Normative in Christlicher Überlieferung und Theologie." In **Text und Applikation: Theologie, Jurisprudenz und Literaturwissenschaft im Hermeneutischen Gespräch**, ed. Manfred Fuhrmann, Hans Robert Jauß and Wolfhart Pannenberg, 413-421. Munich: Wilhelm Fink Verlag, 1981.

— "Geschichte/Geschichtsschreibung/Geschichtsphilosophie: VIII, Systematisch-Theologisch." **Theologische Realenzyklopädie**. Edited by Gerhard Krause and Gerhard Müller. Berlin: Walter de Gruyter, 1984. 12:658-674.

— "Gibt es Prinzipien des Protestantismus, die im ökumenischen Dialog nicht zur Disposition gestellet werden dürfen?" In **Protestantische Existenz Heute**, ed. Friedrich Wilhelm Graf and Klaus Tanner, 79-86. Gütersloh: Gerd Mohn, 1992.

— "The God of Hope." In **Basic Questions in Theology**, trans. George H. Kehm, 2:234-249. Philadelphia: Fortress Press, 1971.

— "God's Presence in History." **The Christian Century** 98 (1981): 260-263.

— "God's Presence in History." In **Theologians in Transition: The Christian Century 'How My Mind Has Changed' Series**, ed. James M. Wall, 93-99. New York: Crossroad, 1981.

— "Der Gott der Geschichte: Der trinitarische Gott und die Wahrheit der Geschichte." **Kerygma und Dogma** 23 (1977): 76-92.

— "Der Gott der Hoffnung." In **Ernst Bloch zu Ehren: Beiträge zu seinem Werk**, ed. Siegfried Unseld, 209-225. Frankfurt: Suhrkamp Verlag, 1965.

— **Gottesgedanke und menschliche Freiheit**. Göttingen: Vandenhoeck & Ruprecht, 1972.

— "Hermeneutic and Universal History." In **Basic Questions in Theology**, trans. George H. Kehm, 1:96-136. Philadelphia: Fortress Press, 1970.

— "How Is God Revealed to Us?" In **Faith and Reality**, trans. John Maxwell, 50-67. Philadelphia: Westminster Press, 1977.

— **Human Nature, Election, and History**. Philadelphia: Westminster Press, 1977.

— "Insight and Faith." In **Basic Questions in Theology**, trans. George H. Kehm, 2:28-45. Philadelphia: Fortress Press, 1971.

— "Introduction." In **Revelation as History**, ed. Wolfhart Pannenberg, 1-21. London: Macmillan, 1968.

— **An Introduction to Systematic Theology**. Grand Rapids, MI: Eerdmans, 1991.

— **Jesus--God and Man**. 2d ed. Translated by Lewis L. Wilkins and Duane A. Priebe. Philadelphia: Westminster Press, 1968.

— "Jesus' History and Ours." In **Faith and Reality**, trans. John Maxwell, 68-77. Philadelphia: Westminster Press, 1977.

— "Kerygma and History." In **Basic Questions in Theology**, trans. George H. Kehm, 1:81-95. Philadelphia: Fortress Press, 1971.

— "Kerygma und Geschichte." In **Studien zur Theologie der alttestamentlichen Überlieferungen**, ed. Rolf Rendtorff and Klaus Koch, 129-140. Neukirchen: Neukirchener Verlag der Buchhandlung des Erziehungsvereins, 1961.

— **Metaphysics and the Idea of God**. Translated by Philip Clayton. Grand Rapids: Eerdmans, 1990.

— "Nachwort zur zweiten Auflage." In **Offenbarung als Geschichte**. 3d ed. Edited by Wolfhart Pannenberg, 132-148. Göttingen: Vandenhoeck & Ruprecht, 1965.

— "Natürliche Theologie: Im ev. Verständnis." **Lexikon für Theologie und Kirche**. Edited by Josef Höfer and Karl Rahner. Freiburg: Herder, 1962. 7:816-817.

— "Offenbarung und 'Offenbarungen' im Zeugnis der Geschichte." **Handbuch der Fundamentaltheologie**. Edited by Walter Kern, Hermann Josef Pottmeyer, and Max Seckler. Freiburg: Herder, 1985. 2:84-107.

— "On Historical and Theological Hermeneutic." In **Basic Questions in Theology**, trans. George H. Kehm, 1:137-181. Philadelphia: Fortress Press, 1970.

— "Person." **Die Religion in Geschichte und Gegenwart. Handwörterbuch für Theologie und Religionswissenschaft**. 3d ed. Edited by Kurt Galling. Tübingen: J. C. B. Mohr, 1961. 5:230-235.

— **Die Prädestinationslehre des Duns Scotus im Zusammenhang der scholastischen Lehrentwicklung**. Göttingen: Vandenhoeck & Ruprecht, 1954.

— "Preface to the American Edition." In **Revelation as History**, ed. Wolfhart Pannenberg, ix-x. Translated by David Granskou. London: Macmillan, 1968.

— "Problems of a Trintarian Doctrine of God." **Dialog** 26/4 (1987): 250-257.

— "Providence, God, and Eschatology." In **The Whirlwind in Culture: Frontiers in Theology: In Honor of Langdon Gilkey**, ed. Donald W. Musser and Joseph L. Price, 171-182. Bloomington, IN: Meyer-Stone Books, 1988.

— "The Question of God." In **Basic Questions in Theology**, trans. George H. Kehm, 2:201-233. Philadelphia: Fortress Press, 1971.

— "Die Rationalität der Theologie." In **Fides Quaerens Intellectum: Beiträge zur Fundamentaltheologie**, ed. Michael Kessler, Wolfhart Pannenberg, and Hermann Josef Pottmeyer, 533-544. Tübingen: Francke Verlag, 1992.

— "Redemptive Event and History." In **Basic Questions in Theology**, trans. George H. Kehm, 1:15-80. Philadelphia: Fortress Press, 1970.

— **Reformation zwischen gestern und morgen**. Gütersloh: Gütersloher Verlagshaus Gerd Mohn, 1969.

— "Religion und menschliche Natur." In **Sind wir von Natur aus religiös?** ed. Wolfhart Pannenberg, 9-24. Schriften der Katholischen Akademie in Bayern, no. 120. Düsseldorf: Patmos Verlag, 1986.

— "Religion und Religionen: Theologische Erwägungen zu den Prinzipien eines Dialoges mit den Weltreligionen." In **Dialog aus der Mitte christlicher Theologie**, ed. Andreas Bsteh, 179-196. Beiträge zur Religionstheologie, no. 5. Mödling: Verlag St. Gabriel, 1985.

— "Die Religionen in der Perspektive christlicher Theologie und die Selbstdarstellung des Christentums im Verhältnis zu den nichtchristlichen Religionen." **Theologische Beiträge** 23/6 (1992): 305-316.

— "The Religions from the Perpective of Christian Theology and the Self-Interpretation of Christinaity in Relation to the Non-Christian Religions." **Modern Theology** 9/3 (1993): 285-297.

— "Response to the Discussion." In **Theology as History**, New Frontiers in Theology, ed. James M. Robinson and John B. Cobb, Jr., 3:221-276. New York: Harper and Row, 1967.

— "The Revelation of God in Jesus of Nazareth." In **Theology as History**, New Frontiers in Theology, ed. James M. Robinson and John B. Cobb, Jr., 3:101-133. New York: Harper and Row, 1967.

— "Schöpfungstheologie und moderne Naturwissenschaft." In **Gottes Zukunft-- Zukunft der Welt. Festschrift für Jürgen Moltmann zum 60. Geburtstag**, ed. Hermann Deuser, Gerhard Marcel Martin, Konrad Stock and Michael Welker, 276-297. Munich: Chr. Kaiser, 1986.

— "Schriftautorität und Lehrautorität." **Mainzer Universitätsgespräche** (Sommersemester, 1962): 5-10.

— "The Significance of Christianity in the Philosophy of Hegel." In **Basic Questions in Theology**, trans. R. A. Wilson, 3:144-177. London: SCM Press, 1973.

— "Speaking about God in the Face of Atheist Criticism." In **Basic Questions in Theology**, trans. R. A. Wilson, 3:99-115. London: SCM Press, 1973.

— "The Spirit of Life." In Wolfhart Pannenberg, **Faith and Reality**, trans. John Maxwell, 20-38. Philadelphia: Westminster Press, 1977.

— "Die Subjektivität Gottes und die Trinitätslehre: Ein Beitrag zur Beziehung zwischen Karl Barth und der Philosophie Hegels." **Kerygma und Dogma** 23 (1977): 25-40.

— Systematic Theology. Vol. 1. Translated by Geoffrey W. Bromiley. Grand Rapids, MI: Eerdmans, 1991.

— Systematische Theologie. Vols. 1-3. Göttingen: Vandenhoeck & Ruprecht, 1988-1993.

— "A Theological Conversation with Wolfhart Pannenberg." **Dialog** 11 (1972): 286-295.

— "Theology and Philosophy in Interaction with Science: A Response to the Message of Pope John Paul II on the Occasion of the Newton Tricentennial in 1987." In **John Paul II on Science and Religion: Reflections on the New View from Rome**, ed. Robert John Russell, William R. Stoeger, and George V. Coyne, 75-79. Vatican City State: Vatican Observatory Publications, 1990.

— "Theology and Science." **The Princeton Seminary Bulletin** 13/3 (1992): 299-310.

— **Theology and the Kingdom of God**. Philadelphia: Westminster Press, 1969.

— **Theology and the Philosophy of Science**. Translated by Francis McDonagh. London: Darton, Longman and Todd, 1976.

— "Theta Phi Talkback Session with Wolfhart Pannenberg." **The Asbury Theological Journal** 46/2 (1991): 37-41.

— To Frank M. Hasel. Munich, June 23, 1992.

— To Frank M. Hasel. Munich, January 21, 1994.

— **Toward a Theology of Nature: Essays on Science and Faith**. Edited by Ted Peters. Louisville, KY: Westminster/John Knox Press, 1993.

— "Toward a Theology of the History of Religions." In **Basic Questions in Theology**, trans. George H. Kehm, 2:65-118. Philadelphia: Fortress Press, 1971.

— "Types of Atheism and Their Theological Significance." In **Basic Questions in Theology**, trans. George H. Kehm, 2:184-200. Philadelphia: Westminster Press, 1971.

— "Wahrheit, Gewißheit und Glaube." In **Grundfragen systematischer Theologie**, 2:226-264. Göttingen: Vandenhoeck & Ruprecht, 1980.

— "Die Wahrheit Gottes in der Bibel und im Christlichen Dogma." In **Wahrheitsansprüche der Religion heute**, Kolloquium Religion und Philosophie, ed. Willi Oelmüller, 2:271-310. Paderborn: Ferdinand Schöningh, 1986.

— "Weltgeschichte und Heilsgeschichte." In **Probleme biblischer Theologie**, ed. Hans Walter Wolff, 349-366. Munich: Chr. Kaiser, 1971.

— "What Is a Dogmatic Statement?" In **Basic Questions in Theology**, trans. George H. Kehm, 1:182-210. Philadelphia: Fortress Press, 1970.

— **What Is Man? Contemporary Anthropology in Theological Perspective.** Translated by Duane A. Priebe. Philadelphia: Fortress Press, 1970.

— "What Is Truth?" In **Basic Questions in Theology**, trans. George H. Kehm, 2:1-27. Philadelphia: Fortress Press, 1970.

— "The Working of the Spirit in the Creation and in the People of God." In **Spirit, Faith, and Church**, ed. Wolfhart Pannenberg, Avery Dulles, and Carl E. Braaten, 13-31. Philadelphia: Westminster Press, 1970.

— **Revelation as History**. Translated by David Granskou. London: Macmillan, 1968.

— ed. **Offenbarung als Geschichte**. 3d. ed. Göttingen: Vandenhoeck & Ruprecht, 1965.

Pannenberg, Wolfhart, and Lewis S. Ford. "A Dialogue about Process Philosophy." **Encounter** 38/4 (1977): 318-324.

Pannenberg, Wolfhart, and Theodor Schneider, eds. **Verbindliches Zeugnis: Kanon--Schrift--Tradition**. Dialog der Kirchen. Veröffentlichungen des Ökumenischen Arbeitskreises evangelischer und katholischer Theologen, no. 7. Freiburg: Herder, 1992.

Parker, T. H. L. **Calvin's Doctrine of the Knowledge of God**. Grand Rapids, MI: Eerdmans, 1959.

Partee, Charles. **Calvin and Classical Philosophy**. Leiden: E. J. Brill, 1977.

Pasquariello, Ronald David. "Pannenberg's Philosophical Foundations." **Journal of Religion** 56 (1976): 338-347.

— "Reality as History: An Investigation of Wolfhart Pannenberg's Understanding of Reality." Ph.D. dissertation, Fordham University, 1972.

Pelikan, Jaroslav. **The Christian Tradition: A History of the Development of Doctrine**. Vol. 4, Reformation of Church and Dogma (1300-1700). Chicago: University of Chicago Press, 1984.

— **Luther's Works**. Companion Volume: Luther the Expositor. St. Louis, MO: Concordia Publishing House, 1959.

— "Luther's Works on the New Testament." In **Luther's Works**, ed. Jaroslav Pelikan, 21:ix-xv. St. Louis, MO: Concordia Publishing House, 1956.

Perry, Ronald Mark. "A Holistic Model of Church Renewal in Light of a Critical Evaluation of the Contributions of D. Elton Trueblood, Donald G. Bloesch, and

Leonard Boff." Ph.D. dissertation, New Orleans Baptist Theological Seminary, 1992.

Pesch, Christian. **De Inspiratione Sacrae Scripturae**. Freiburg: Herder, 1906.

Peter, Nicklaus. "Geschichtstheologischer Auszug aus der Geschichte? Wolfhart Pannenberg's **Systematische Theologie**, vol. 1. **Reformatio. Evangelische Zeitschrift für Kultur, Politik, Kirche** 37 (1988): 481-485.

Peters, Ted. "Editor's Introduction: Pannenberg on Theology and Natural Science." In Wolfhart Pannenberg, **Toward a Theology of Nature: Essays on Science and Faith**, ed. Ted Peters, 1-14. Lousville, KY: Westminster/John Knox Press, 1993.

— "Editorials: Seven Pressing Theological Issues." **Dialog** 33/2 (1994): 82-84.

— "Methode und System in der heutigen amerikanischen Theologie." **Kerygma und Dogma** 29/1 (1983): 2-46.

— "Sola Scriptura and the Second Naivete." **Dialog** 16 (1977): 268-280.

Peters, Theodore Frank. "Method and Truth: An Inquiry into the Philosophical Hermeneutics of Hans-Georg Gadamer and the Theology of History of Wolfhart Pannenberg." Ph.D. dissertation, University of Chicago, 1973.

Petzoldt, Matthias. "Sola Scriptura--brauchbares Prinzip zur Rechenschaft über den Glauben?" In **Sola Scriptura: Das reformatorische Schriftprinzip in der säkularen Welt**, ed. Hans Heinrich Schmid and Joachim Mehlhause, 292-303. Gütersloh: Gerd Mohn, 1991.

Peukert, Helmut. **Science, Action, and Fundamental Theology: Toward a Theology of Communicative Action**. Translated by James Bohman. Cambridge, MA: MIT Press, 1984.

Pfenningsdorf, Emil. **Das Problem des theologischen Denkens: Eine Einführung in die Fragen, Aufgaben und Methoden der gegenwärtigen Theologie**. Leipzig: A. Deichertsche Verlagsbuchhandlung, 1925.

Pfürtner, Stephan H. "Das reformatorische 'Sola Scriptura'--Theologischer Auslegungsgrund des Thomas von Aquin?" In **Sola Scriptura: Ringvorlesung der theologischen Fakultät der Philipps-Universität**, ed. Carl-Heinz Ratschow, 48-80. Marburg: N. G. Elwert Verlag, 1977.

Piepmeier, Rainer. "Aufklärung: I. Philosophisch." **Theologische Realenzyklopädie**. Edited by Gerhard Krause and Gerhard Müller. Berlin: Walter de Gruyter, 1979. 4:575-594.

Pierard, R. V. "Evangelicalism." **Evangelical Dictionary of Theology**. Edited by Walter A. Elwell. Grand Rapids, MI: Baker Book House, 1984. 379-382.

— "Liberalism, Theological." **Evangelical Dictionary of Theology**. Edited by Walter A. Elwell. Grand Rapids, MI: Baker Book House, 1984. 631-635.

Pike, Nelson. **God and Timelessness**. London: Routledge & K. Paul, 1970.

Pinnock, Clark H. **A Defense of Biblical Infallibility**. Philadelphia: Presbyterian and Reformed Publishing Company, 1967.

— "Advance Praise for **A Theology of Word and Spirit**. Front Inside Book Cover.

— **Biblical Revelation: The Foundation of Christian Theology**. Chicago: Moody Press, 1971. Reprint, Philipsburg, NJ: Presbyterian and Reformed Publishing Company, 1985.

— "Pannenberg's Theology: Part 1: Reasonable Happenings in History: Part 2: No Nonsense Theology: Pinnock Reviews Pannenberg." **Christianity Today** 21 (1976): 147-150, 218-220.

— "Review of **Essentials of Evangelical Theology**. Vols. 1 and 2, by Donald G. Bloesch." **Sojourners** 8 (1979): 31-33.

— "Review of **Essentials of Evangelical Theology**. Vols. 1 and 2, by Donald G. Bloesch." **Theology Today** 36/2 (1980): 266-268.

— "The Role of the Spirit in Interpretation." **Journal of the Evangelical Theological Society** 36/4 (1993): 491-497.

— **The Scripture Principle**. San Francisco: Harper and Row, 1984.

— **Tracking the Maze: Finding Our Way through Modern Theology from an Evangelical Perspective**. San Francisco: Harper and Row, 1990.

Placher, William Carl. "History and Faith in the Theology of Wolfhart Pannenberg." Ph.D. dissertation, Yale University, 1975.

— "Pannenberg on History and Revelation." **Reformed Review** 30 (1976): 39-47.

— "Revealed to Reason: Theology as 'Normal Science.'" **The Christian Century** 109/6 (1992): 192-195.

Pöhlmann, Horst Georg. **Abriß der Dogmatik: Ein Kompendium**. 4th rev. and enl. ed. Gütersloh: Gerd Mohn, 1985.

— **Gottesdenker: Prägende evangelische und katholische Theologen der Gegenwart, 12 Porträts**. Hamburg: Rowohlt Verlag, 1984

Polk, David P. "The All-Determining God and the Peril of Determinism." In **The Theology of Wolfhart Pannenberg: Twelve American Critiques, with an Autobiographical Essay and Response**, ed. Carl E. Braaten and Philip Clayton, 152-168. Minneapolis: Augsburgs Publishing House, 1988.

— On the Way to God: An Exploration into the Theology of Wolfhart Pannenberg. Lanham, MD: University Press of America, 1989.

Popkin, Richard H. **The History of Scepticism from Erasmus to Descartes**. Rev. ed. Assen: Van Gorcum & Comp., 1964.

Porter, Laurence E. "Review of **The Ground of Certainty**, by Donald G. Bloesch." **The Evangelical Quarterly** 45 (1973): 119-120.

Postema, Gerald. "Calvin's Alleged Rejection of Natural Theology." **Scottish Journal of Theology** 24 (1971): 423-434.

Poythress, Vern Sheridian. "Adequacy of Language and Accomodation." In **Hermeneutics, Inerrancy, and the Bible**, ed. Earl D. Radmacher and Robert D. Preus, 351-376. Grand Rapids, MI: Zondervan Publishing House, 1984.

— **Science and Hermeneutics: Implications of Scientific Method for Biblical Interpretation**. Foundations of Contemporay Interpretation Series, no. 6. Grand Rapids, MI: Zondervan Publishing House, 1988.

— **Symphonic Theology: The Validity of Multiple Perspectives in Theology**. Grand Rapids, MI: Zondervan Publishing House, 1987.

Preus, Robert D. **The Inspiration of Scripture: A Study of the Theology of the Seventeenth Century Lutheran Dogmaticians**. 2d ed. Edinburgh: Oliver and Boyd, 1957.

— "Luther and Biblical Infallibility." In **Inerrancy and the Church**, ed. John D. Hannah, 99-142. Chicago: Moody Press, 1984.

— **The Theology of Post-Reformation Lutheranism: A Study of Theological Prolegomena**. 2 vols. St. Louis, MO: Concordia Publishing House, 1970-1972.

— "The Unity of Scripture." **Concordia Theological Quarterly** 54/1 (1990): 1-23.

— "The View of the Bible Held by the Church: The Early Church through Luther." In **Inerrancy**, ed. Norman L. Geisler, 357-382. Grand Rapids, MI: Zondervan Publishing House, 1979.

Preuss, Johannes. **Die Entwicklung des Schriftprinzips bei Luther bis zur Leipziger Disputation**. Leipzig: Chr. Herm. Tauchnitz, 1901.

Price, Bob. "Review of **Essentials of Evangelical Theology**, volumes 1 and 2, by Donald G. Bloesch." **The Drew Gateway** 50/3 (1980): 54-58.

Price, Robert McNair. "The Crisis of Biblical Authority: The Setting and Range of the Current Evangelical Crisis." Ph.D. dissertation, Drew University, 1981.

Provence, Thomas Edward. "The Hermeneutics of Karl Barth." Ph.D. dissertation, Fuller Theological Seminary, 1980.

Prust, Richard C. "Was Calvin a Biblical Literalist?" **Scottish Journal of Theology** 20 (1967): 312-328.

Quanbeck, Warren A. "The Confessions and Their Influence upon Biblical Interpretation." In **Studies in Lutheran Hermeneutics**, ed. by John Reumann, 177-187. Philadelphia: Fortress Press, 1979.

Radford Ruether, Rosemary. **Sexism and God-Talk: Toward a Feminist Theology**. Boston, MA: Beacon Press, 1983.

Radmacher, Earl D., and Robert D. Preus, eds. **Hermeneutics, Inerrancy, and the Bible**. Grand Rapids, MI: Zondervan Publishing House, 1984.

Rahner, Karl. "Exegesis and Dogmatic Theology." In **Dogmatic vs Biblical Theology**, ed. Herbert Vorgrimmler, 31-65. Baltimore: Helicon Press, 1964.

Rambo, Lewis. "Review of **Essentials of Evangelical Theology**. Vols. 1 and 2, by Donald G. Bloesch." **Restoration Quarterly** 25 (1982): 179-180.

Ramm, Bernard. **After Fundamentalism: The Future of Evangelical Theology**. San Francisco: Harper and Row Publishers, 1983.

—— **The Evangelical Heritage**. Waco, TX: Word Books, 1973.

—— "The Fortunes of Theology from Schleiermacher to Barth to Bultmann." In **Tensions in Contemporary Theology**. 2d ed. Edited by Stanley N. Gundry and Alan F. Johnson, 15-41. Grand Rapids, MI: Baker Book House, 1983.

—— "Is 'Scripture Alone' the Essence of Christianity?" In **Biblical Authority**, ed. Jack Rogers, 107-123. Waco, TX: Word Books, 1977.

—— **The Pattern of Religious Authority**. Grand Rapids, MI: Eerdmans, 1968.

—— **Protestant Biblical Interpretation: A Textbook of Hermeneutics**. 3d rev. ed. Grand Rapids, MI: Baker Book House, 1970.

Ramsey, Ian. **Models and Mystery**. London: Oxford University Press, 1956.

Ratschow, Carl-Heinz. "Einleitende Analzse der Themenfrage." In **Sola Scriptura: Ringvorlesung der theologischen Fakultät der Philipps-Universität**, ed. Carl-Heinz Ratschow, 1-21. Marburg: N. G. Elwert Verlag, 1977.

—— **Lutherische Dogmatik zwischen Reformation und Aufklärung**. 2 vols. Gütersloh: Gütersloher Verlagshaus Gerd Mohn, 1964.

Ratzinger, Joseph Cardinal. "Biblical Interpretation in Crisis: On the Question of the Foundations and Approaches of Exegesis Today." In **Biblical Interpretation in Crisis: The Ratzinger Conference on Bible and Church**, ed. John Neuhaus, 1-23. Grand Rapids, MI: Eerdmans, 1989.

Reid, Daniel G., Robert D. Linder, Bruce L. Shelly, and Harry S. Stout, eds. **Dictionary of Christianity in America**. Downers Grove, IL: InterVarsity Press, 1990.

Reid, John Kelman Sutherland. **The Authority of Scripture: A Study of the Reformation and Post-Reformation Understanding of the Bible**. London: Methuen and Company, 1957.

Reinhard, Johannes. **Die Prinzipienlehre der lutherischen Dogmatik von 1700 bis 1750: Beitrag zur Geschichte der altprotestantischen Theologie und zur Vorgeschichte des Rationalismus**. Leipzig: A. Deichertsche Verlagsbuchhandlung, 1906.

Reinhardt, Klaus. **Der dogmatische Schriftgebrauch in der Katholischen und Protestantischen Christologie von der Aufklärung bis zur Gegenwart**. Munich: Verlag Ferdinand Schöningh, 1970.

Rendtorff, Rolf. "Offenbarung und Geschichte--Partikularimus und Universalismus im Offenbarungsverständnis Israels." In **Offenbarung im Jüdischen und Christlichen Glaubensverständnis**, Quaestiones Disputatae 92, ed. Jakob J. Petuchowski and Walter Strolz, 37-49. Freiburg: Herder, 1981.

Rendtorff, Trutz. "Überlieferungsgeschichte als Problem der systematischen Theologie: Anmerkungen zu den Möglichkeiten der Theologie." **Theologische Literaturzeitung** 90/2 (1965): 81-98.

Reu, M. **Luther and the Scriptures**. Columbus, OH: Wartburg Press, 1944.

Reventlow, Henning Graf. **The Authority of the Bible and the Rise of the Modern World**. Translated by John Bowden. Philadelphia: Fortress Press, 1984.

— **Problems of Biblical Theology in the Twentieth Century**. Translated by John Bowden. Philadelphia: Fortress Press, 1986.

Rhem, Richard A. "A Theological Conception of Reality as History--Some Aspects of the Thinking of Wolfhart Pannenberg." **Reformed Review** 26 (1972): 178-223.

— "Theological Method: The Search for a New Paradigm in a Pluralistic Age." **Reformed Review** 39/3 (1986): 242-254.

Rian, Edwin H. "Review of **The Ground of Certainty**, by Donald G. Bloesch." **The Princeton Seminary Bulletin** 66 (1973): 146.

Rice, Richard. **Reason and the Contours of Faith**. Riverside, CA: La Sierra University Press, 1991.

— **The Reign of God: An Introduction to Christian Theology from a Seventh-day Adventist Perspective**. Berrien Springs, MI: Andrews University Press, 1995.

— "Review of **Essentials of Evangelical Theology**, Volumes 1 and 2, by Donald G. Bloesch." **Religious Studies Review** 7/1 (1981): 107-115.

Ritschl, Albrecht. "Über die beiden Principien des Protestantismus. Antwort auf ein 25 Jahre alte Frage." **Zeitschrift für Kirchengeschichte** 1 (1877): 397-413.

Ritschl, Otto. **Dogmengeschichte des Protestantismus: Grundlagen und Grundzüge der theologischen Gedanken- und Lehrbildung in den protestantischen Kirchen. vol. I: Prologomena: Biblicismus und Traditionalismus in der altprotestantischen Theologie.** Leipzig: J. C. Hinrichs'sche Buchhandlung, 1908.

— "Literarhistorische Beobachtungen über die Nomenklatur der theologiachen Disziplinen im 17. Jahrhundert." In **Studien zur systematischen Theologie. Festschrift für Theodor Haering zum 70. Geburtstag**, ed. Friedrich Traub, 76-85. Tübingen: J. C. B. Mohr, 1918.

— **System und systematische Methode in der Geschichte des wissenschaftlichen Sprachgebrauchs und der philosophischen Methodologie.** Bonn: A. Marcus and E. Webers Verlag, 1906.

Ro, Bong Rin. "The Inspiration of Scripture Among the Seventeenth-Century Reformed Theologians." In **The Living and Active Word of God: Studies in Honor of Samuel J. Schultz**, ed. Morris Inch and Ronald Youngblood, 207-224. Winona Lake, IN: Eisenbrauns, 1983.

Roberts, R. H. "Karl Barth's Doctrine of Time: Its Nature and Implications." In **Karl Barth: Studies of His Theological Method**, ed. S. W. Sykes, 88-146. Oxford: Clarendon Press, 1979.

Robinson, James M. "The Historicity of Biblical Language." In **The Old Testament and Christian Faith**, ed. Bernhard W. Anderson. New York: Herder, 1969.

— "Revelation as Word and as History." In **Theology as History**. New Frontiers in Theology: Discussions among Continental and American Theologians, ed. James M. Robinson and John B. Cobb, Jr., 3:1-100. New York: Harper and Row, 1967.

— ed. **The Beginnings of Dialectical Theology**. Translated by Keith R. Crim and Louis De Grazia. Richmond, VA: John Knox Press, 1968.

Robinson, James M., and John B. Cobb, Jr. "Editor's Preface." In **Theology as History**. New Frontiers in Theology: Discussions among Continental and American Theologians, ed. James M. Robinson and John B. Cobb, Jr., 3:ix-x. New York: Harper and Row, 1967.

Robinson, Robert Bruce. **Roman Catholic Exegesis since *Divino Afflante Spiritu*: Hermeneutical Implications.** Society of Biblical Literature Dissertation Series, no. 111. Atlanta, GA: Scholars Press, 1982.

Rogers, Jack. "The Search for System: Theology in the 1980s." **Journal of Religious Thought** 37 (1980): 5-15.

Rogers, Jack B., and Donald K. McKim. **The Authority and Interpretation of the Bible: An Historical Approach**. San Francisco: Harper and Row, 1979.

Rohls, Jan. "Die Persönlichkeit Gottes und die Trinitätslehre." **Evangelische Theologie** 45 (1985): 124-139.

Rohls, Jan, and Gunther Wenz, eds. **Vernunft des Glaubens: Wissenschaft-liche Theologie und kirchliche Lehre. Festschrift zum 60. Geburtstag von Wolfhart Pannenberg, mit einem bibliographischen Anhang**. Göttingen: Vandenhoeck & Ruprecht, 1988.

Rohnert, Wilhelm. **Die Inspiration der heiligen Schrift und ihre Bestreiter: Eine biblisch-dogmengeschichtliche Studie**. Leipzig: Verlag von Georg Böhme, 1889.

Rosendall, Brendan. "Review of **The Reform of the Church**, by Donald G. Bloesch." **Worship** 44 (1970): 506-507.

Rosser, William Ray. "The Cross as the Hermeneutical Norm for Scriptural Interpretation in the Theology of Peter Taylor Forsyth." Ph.D. dissertation, Southern Baptist Theological Seminary, 1990.

Rothen, Bernhard. **Die Klarheit der Schrift. Teil 1: Martin Luther. Die wiederentdeckten Grundlagen**. Göttingen: Vandenhoeck & Ruprecht, 1990.

— **Die Klarheit der Schrift. Teil 2: Karl Barth. Eine Kritik**. Göttingen: Vandenhoeck & Ruprecht, 1990.

Rückert, Hans. "Calvin." In Hans Rückert, **Vorträge und Aufsätze zur historischen Theologie**, 165-173. Tübingen: J. C. B. Mohr, 1972.

Ruh, Ulrich. "Den Glauben denken: Zu Wolfhart Pannenbergs 'Systematischer Theologie.'" **Herder Korrespondenz** 42 (1989): 180-184.

Runia, Klaas. **Karl Barth's Doctrine of Holy Scripture**. Grand Rapids, MI: Eerdmans, 1962.

Ruokanen, Miikka. **Doctrina Divinitus Inspirata: Martin Luther's Position in the Ecumenical Problem of Biblical Inspiration**. Publications of Luther-Agricola Society, no. 14. Helsinki: Luther-Agricola Society, 1985.

Ryrie, Charles C. **Basic Theology**. Wheaton, IL: Victor Books, 1986.

— "Illumination." **Evangelical Dictionary of Theology**. Edited by Walter A. Elwell. Grand Rapids, MI: Baker Book House, 1984. 544-545.

Sand, Alexander. "Die biblischen Aussagen über die Offenbarung." **Handbuch der Dogmengeschichte**. Edited by Michael Schmaus, Alois Grillmeier and Leo Scheffczyk, vol. I, fasc. 1a, 1-26. Freiburg: Herder, 1971.

Sandin, Robert T. "The Clarity of Scripture." In **The Living and Active Word of God: Studies in Honor of Samuel J. Schultz**, ed. Morris Inch and Ronald Youngblood, 237-253. Winona Lake, IN: Eisenbrauns, 1983.

Sandys-Wunsch, John, and Laurence Eldredge. "J. P. Gabler and the Distinction between Biblical and Dogmatic Theology: Translation, Commentary, and Discussion of his Originality." **Scottish Journal of Theology** 33 (1980): 133-158.

Sasse, Hermann. **In Statu Confessionis: Gesammelte Aufsätze und kleine Schriften von Hermann Sasse**. 2 vols. Edited by Friedrich Wilhelm Hopf. Berlin: Verlag die Spur, 1976.

—— **Sacra Scriptura: Studien zur Lehre von der Heiligen Schrift**. Edited by Friedrich Wilhelm Hopf. Erlangen: Verlag der Ev.-Luth. Mission, 1981.

Saucy, Robert L. "Review of **Essentials of Evangelical Theology**, Volumes 1 and 2, by Donald G. Bloesch." **Journal of Psychology and Theology** 7 (1979): 221-222.

Sauter, Gerhard. **Vor einem neuen Methodenstreit in der Theologie?** Theologische Existenz Heute, no. 164. Munich: Chr. Kaiser, 1970.

Scaer, David P. "Review of **The Reform of the Church**, by Donald G. Bloesch." **The Springfielder** 34 (1970): 159-160.

—— "How Do Lutheran Theologians Approach the Doing of Theology Today?" In **Doing Theology in Today's World: Essays in Honor of Kenneth S. Kantzer**, ed. John D. Woodbridge and Thomas Edward McComiskey, 197-225. Grand Rapids, MI: Zondervan, 1991.

—— "Theology of Hope." In **Tensions in Contemporary Theology**. 2d ed. Edited by Stanley N. Gundry and Alan F. Johnson, 197-234. Grand Rapids, MI: Baker Book House, 1983.

Scally, John. "Faith at the Frontiers: Pannenberg's Theology of Faith." **Irish Theological Quarterly** 58 (1992): 129-140.

Scharlemann, Robert P. "Theological Models and Their Construction." **The Journal of Religion** 53 (1973): 65-82.

Scheel, Otto. **Luthers Stellung zur Heiligen Schrift**. Tübingen: J. C. B. Mohr, 1902.

Schempp, Paul. **Luthers Stellung zur Heiligen Schrift**. Forschung zur Geschichte und Lehre des Protestantismus, no. 3. Munich: Chr. Kaiser, 1929.

Schlatter, Adolf. **Atheistische Methoden in der Theologie**. Gütersloh: Bertesmann, 1909.

Schleiermacher, Friedrich D. E. **The Christian Faith**. Edited by H. R. Mackintosh and J. S. Stewart. Philadelphia: Fortress Press, 1976.

— Kurze Darstellung des theologischen Studiums zum Behuf einleitender Vorlesungen. Edited by Heinirich Scholz. Hilesheim: Verlagsbuchhandlung Georg Olms, 1961.

— On Religion: Speeches to Its Cultured Despisers. With an Introduction and translated by Richard Crouter. Cambridge: Cambridge University Press, 1988.

Schlichting, Wolfhart. **Biblische Denkform in der Dogmatik: Die Vorbildlichkeit des biblischen Denkens für die Methode der Kirchlichen Dogmatik Karl Barths.** Zurich: Theologischer Verlag, 1971.

Schlink, Edmund. **The Coming Christ and the Coming Church.** Translated by I. H. Nielson. Edinburgh: Oliver & Boyd, 1967.

— "Die Struktur der dogmatischen Aussage als ökumenisches Problem." **Kerygma und Dogma** 3 (1957): 251-306.

Schmid, Heinrich. **The Doctrinal Theology of the Evangelical Lutheran Church, Exhibited and Verified from the Original Sources.** Translated by Charles A. Hay and Henry E. Jacobs. Philadelphia: Lutheran Publication Society, 1876.

Schmidt, Martin. "Aufklärung: II. Theologisch." **Theologische Realenzyklopädie.** Edited by Gerhard Krause and Gerhard Müller. Berlin: Walter de Gruyter, 1979. 4:594-608.

Schmitz, Josef. "Die Fundamentaltheologie im 20. Jahrhundert." In **Bilanz der Theologie im 20. Jahrhundert: Perspektiven, Strömungen, Motive in der christlichen und nichtchristlichen Welt,** ed. Herbert Vorgrimmler and Robert Vander Gucht, 2:197-245. Freiburg: Herder, 1969.

Schnabel, Eckhard. **Inspiration und Offenbarung: Die Lehre vom Ursprung und Wesen der Bibel.** Wuppertal: R. Brockhaus Verlag, 1986.

Scholder, Klaus. **The Birth of Modern Critical Theology: Origins and Problems of Biblical Criticism in the Seventeenth Century.** Translated by John Bowden. London: SCM Press, 1990.

Scholz, Heinrich. "Wie ist eine evangelische Theologie als Wissenschaft möglich?" **Zwischen den Zeiten** 9 (1931): 8-53.

Schreiner, Susan Elizabeth. "The Theater of His Glory: Nature and the Natural Order in the Thought of John Calvin." Ph.D. dissertation, Duke University, 1983.

Schultz, W. "Schleiermachers Theorie des Gefühls und ihre theologische Bedeutung." **Zeitschrift für Theologie und Kirche** 53 (1956): 75-103.

Schüssler Fiorenza, Elizabeth. **In Memory of Her: A Feminist Theological Reconstruction of Christian Origins.** New York: Crossroad, 1983.

Schüssler Fiorenza, Francis. "The Crisis of Scriptural Authority: Interpretation and Reception." **Interpretation** 44 (1990): 353-368.

— "Systematic Theology: Task and Methods." In **Systematic Theology: Roman Catholic Perspectives**, ed. Francis Schüssler Fiorenza and John P. Galvin, 1:3-87. Minneapolis: Fortress Press, 1991.

Schüssler, Hermann. **Der Primat der Heiligen Schrift als Theologisches und kanonistisches Problem im Spätmittelalter**. Veröffentlichungen des Instituts für Europäische Geschichte Mainz, no. 86. Wiesbaden: Franz Steiner Verlag, 1977.

Schützeichel, Harald. "Das Verhältnis von Theologie und Philosophie in der Sicht Karl Rahners und Wolfhart Pannenbergs." **Renovatio: Zeitschrift für das interdisziplinäre Gespräch** 43/1 (1987): 15-24.

Schwarzwäller, Klaus. **Theologie oder Phänomenologie: Erwägungen zur Methodik theologischen Verstehens**. Beiträge zur evangelischen Theologie, no. 42. Munich: Chr. Kaiser, 1966.

Schwöbel, Christoph. "Wolfhart Pannenberg." In **The Modern Theologians: An Introduction to Christian Theology in the Twentieth Century**, ed. David F. Ford, 1:257-292. Oxford: Basil Blackwell, 1989.

Scott, Edwin E. "The Nature and Use of Scripture in the Writings of Clark H. Pinnock and James Barr." Th.D. dissertation, New Orleans Baptist Theological Seminary, 1989.

Scott, J. J., Jr. "Biblicism, Bibliolatry." **Evangelical Dictionary of Theology**. Edited by Walter A. Elwell. Grand Rapids, MI: Baker Book House, 1984. 152.

Scriven, Charles Wayne. **Christian Social Ethics after H. Richard Niebuhr: The Transformation of Culture**. Scottdale, PA: Herald Press, 1988.

— "The Transformation of Culture: Christian Social Ethics after H. Richard Niebuhr." Ph.D. dissertation, Graduate Theological Union, 1985.

Seckler, Max. "Fundamentaltheologie: Aufgaben und Aufbau, Begriff und Namen." **Handbuch der Fundamentaltheology**. Edited by Walter Kern, Hermann J. Pottmeyer, and Max Seckler. Freiburg: Herder, 1988. 4:451-514.

— "Zur Diskussion um das Offenbarungsverständnis W. Pannenbergs." **Münchner Theologische Zeitschrift** 19 (1968): 132-134.

Seckler, Max, and Michael Kessler. "Die Kritik der Offenbarung." **Handbuch der Fundamentaltheologie**. Edited by Walter Kern, Hermann J. Pottmeyer, and Max Seckler. Freiburg: Herder, 1988. 2:29-59.

Seebaß, Horst. **Biblische Hermeneutik**. Stuttgart: W. Kohlhammer Verlag, 1974.

Seeberg, Reinhold. "Illumination." **The New Schaff-Herzog Encyclopedia of Religious Knowledge**. Edited by Samuel Macauley Jackson. New York: Funk and Wagnals, 1909. 5:450-451.

— **Text-Book of the History of Doctrines** 2 vols. Translated by Charles E. Hay. Grand Rapids, MI: Baker Book House, 1952.

Semler, Johann Salomo. **Abhandung von freier Untersuchung des Canon** (1771-1776). Edited by Heinz Scheible. Texte zur Kirchen- und Theologieschichte, no. 5. Gütersloh: Gerd Mohn, 1967.

Seybold, Michael."Die Offenbarungsthematik in der Spätpatristik und Frühscholastik." **Handbuch der Dogmengeschichte**. Edited by Michael Schmaus, Alois Grillmeier, and Leo Scheffczyk. Freiburg: Herder, 1971. 1, fasc. 1a:88-115.

Sharpe, Charles Manford. "The Normative Use of Scripture by Typical Theologians of Protestant Orthodoxy in Great Britain and America." Ph.D. dissertation, The University of Chicago, 1912.

Shuster, Robert D., et al. **Researching Modern Evangelicalism: A Guide to the Holdings of the Billy Graham Center, with Information on Other Holdings**. Westport, CT: Greewood, 1990.

Silva, Moisés. **God, Language and Scripture: Reading the Bible in the Light of General Linguistics**. Foundations of Contemporary Interpretation Series, no. 4. Grand Rapids, MI: Zondervan Publishing House, 1990.

— **Has the Church Misread the Bible? The History of Interpretation in the Light of Current Issues**. Foundations of Contemporary Interpretation Series, no. 1. Grand Rapids, MI: Zondervan Publishing House, 1987.

Skibbe, Eugene M. "Review of **The Ground of Certainty**, by Donald G. Bloesch." **The Lutheran Quarterly** 24 (1972): 422-424.

Skydsgaard, Kristen Ejner. "Schrift und Tradition: Bemerkungen zum Traditionsproblem in der neueren Theologie." **Kerygma und Dogma** 1 (1955): 161-179.

Slenczka, Reinhard. "Die Auflösung der Schriftgrundlage und was daraus folgt." **Theologische Rundschau** 60/1 (1995): 96-107.

— **Kirchliche Entscheidung in theologischer Verantwortung: Grundlagen--Kriterien--Grenzen**. Göttingen: Vandenhoeck & Ruprecht, 1991.

— "Schriftautorität und Schriftkritik." In **Verbindliches Zeugnis: Kanon--Schrift--Tradition**. Dialog der Kirchen. Veröffentlichungen des Ökumenischen Arbeitskreises evangelischer und katholischer Theologen, no. 7, ed. Wolfhart Pannenberg and Theodor Schneider, 315-334. Freiburg: Herder, 1992.

— "Was heißt und was ist schriftgemäß?" **Kerygma und Dogma** 34 (1988): 304-320.

Smalley, Beryl. **The Study of the Bible in the Middle Ages**. Oxford: Basil Blackwell, 1952.

Smart, James D. **The Strange Silence of the Bible in the Church: A Study in Hermeneutics**. Philadelphia: Westminster Press, 1970.

Smart, Ninian, and Steven Konstantine. **Christian Systematic Theology in a World Context**. Minneapolis: Fortress Press, 1991.

Smith, David L. **A Handbook of Contemporary Theology**. Wheaton, IL: Victor Books, 1992.

Smith, Michael T. "Theology as a Resource in Faith Translation for the Local Church." D.Min. dissertation, Northern Baptist Theological Seminary, 1986.

Sorge, Sheldon Warren. "Karl Barth's Reception in North America: Ecclesiology as a Case Study." Ph.D. dissertation, Duke University, 1987.

Spitz, Lewis W. "Luther's *Sola Scriptura*." In **Crisis in Lutheran Theology: The Validity and Relevance of Historic Lutheranism vs. Its Contemporary Rivals**, ed. John Warwick Montgomery, 2:123-129. Minneapolis, MN: Bethany Fellowship, 1967.

Sproul, R. C. "Sola Scriptura: Crucial to Evangelicalism." In **The Foundation of Biblical Authority**, ed. James Montgomery Boice, 103-119. Grand Rapids, MI: Zondervan Publishing House, 1978.

Spykman, Gordon J. **Reformational Theology: A New Paradigm for Doing Dogmatics**. Grand Rapids, MI: Eerdmans, 1992.

Stadelmann, Helge. **Grundlinien eines bibeltreuen Schriftverständnisses**. Wuppertal: R. Brockhaus Verlag, 1985.

Stafford, Gilbert W. "Frontiers in Contemporary Theology." In **A Contemporary Wesleyan Theology: Biblical, Systematic, and Practical**, ed. Charles W. Carter, 1:15-50. Grand Rapids, MI: Zondervan, 1983.

Stauffer, Richard. **Dieu, la Creation et la Providence dans la Predication de Calvin**. Berne: Peter Lang, 1978.

Stawenow, Christian. "Historische und geistliche Hermeneutik bei Peter Stuhlmacher. Eine Untersuchung seines Entwurfes einer 'Hermeneutik des Einverständnisses' hinsichtlich der von ihm selbst benannten hermeneutik-geschichtlichen Voraussetzungen," Th.D. dissertation, Kirchliches Oberseminar, Naumburg, 1986.

Steck, Wolfgang. "Von Personen: Laudatio Wolfhart Pannenberg." **Theologische Literaturzeitschrift** 118/10 (1993): 887-888.

Steiger, Lothar. "Offenbarungsgeschichte und theologische Vernunft: Zur Theologie W. Pannenbergs." **Zeitschrift für Theologie und Kirche** 59 (1962): 88-113.

Stein, Alois von der. "Der Systembegriff in seiner geschichtlichen Entwicklung." In **System und Klassifikation in Wissenschaft und Dokumentation**, ed. A. Diemer, 1-13. Meisenheim am Glan: Verlag Anton Hain, 1968.

Steinmetz, David C. "The Superiority of Pre-Critical Exegesis." **Theology Today** 37 (1980): 27-38.

Stendahl, Krister. "Biblical Theology, Contemporary." **The Interpreter's Dictionary of the Bible**. Edited by George Arthur Buttrick. Nashville, TN: Abingdon, 1962. 1:418-432.

Stephan, Horst, and Martin Schmidt. **Geschichte der evangelischen Theologie in Deutschland seit dem Idealismus**. 3d ed. Berlin: Walter de Gruyter, 1973.

Stephens, W. P. **The Theology of Huldrych Zwingli**. Oxford: Clarendon Press, 1986.

Stirnimann, Heinrich. "Erwägungen zur Fundamentaltheologie: Problematik, Grundfragen, Konzept." **Freiburger Zeitschrift für Philosophie und Theologie** 24 (1977): 291-365.

Stockmeier, Peter. "'Offenbarung' in der frühchristlichen Kirche." **Handbuch der Dogmengeschichte**. Edited by Michael Schmaus, Alois Grillmeier and Leo Scheffczyk. Freiburg: Herder, 1971. 1, fasc. 1a:27-87.

Stork, T. **Luther and the Bible**. Philadelphia: Lutheran Board of Publication, 1873.

Stuhlmacher, Peter. **Biblische Theologie des Neuen Testaments**. Vol. 1, **Grundlegung von Jesus zu Paulus**. Göttingen: Vandenhoeck & Ruprecht, 1992.

— **Historical Criticism and Theological Interpretation of Scripture: Toward a Hermeneutics of Consent**. Translated by Roy A. Harrisville. Philadelphia: Fortress Press, 1977.

— **Vom Verstehen des Neuen Testaments: Eine Hermeneutik**. 2d rev. and enl. ed. Göttingen: Vandenhoeck & Ruprecht, 1986.

Swartley, Willard, ed. **Essays on Biblical Interpretation: Anabaptist-Mennonite Perspectives**. Text-Reader Series, no. 1. Elkhart, IN: Institute of Mennonite Studies, 1984.

Sweet, Leonard I. "The Evangelical Tradition in America." In **The Evangelical Tradition in America**, ed. Leonard I. Sweet, 1-86. Macon, GA: Mercer University Press, 1984.

Sykes, Norman. "The Religion of Protestants." In **The Cambridge History of the Bible: The West from the Reformation to the Present Day**, ed. S. L. Greenslade, 175-198. Cambridge: University Press, 1963.

Tavard, George H. **Holy Writ or Holy Church: The Crisis of the Protestant Reformation**. New York: Harper and Brothers, 1959.

Taylor, Mark C. **Erring: A Postmodern A/theology**. Chicago: University of Chicago Press, 1984.

Taylor, Richard S., ed. **Beacon Dictionary of Theology**. Kansas City, MO: Beacon Hill, 1983.

Thielicke, Helmut. **The Evangelical Faith**. 3 vols. Edited and translated by G. W. Bromiley. Grand Rapids, MI: Eerdmans, 1982.

Thilly, Frank. **A History of Philosophy**. Revised by Ledger Wood. New York: Henry Holt and Company, 1951.

Thimme, Karl. **Luthers Stellung zur Heiligen Schrift**. Gütersloh: C. Bertelsmann Verlag, 1903.

Thiselton, Anthony C. **New Horizons in Hermeneutics**. Grand Rapids, MI: Zondervan Publishing House, 1992.

Thomas, J. Heywood. "The Christology of Soren Kierkegaard and Karl Barth." **The Hibbert Journal** 53 (1955): 280-288.

Thorsen, Donald A. D. **The Wesleyan Quadrilateral: Scripture, Tradition, Reason, and Experience as a Model of Evangelical Theology**. Grand Rapids, MI: Zondervan Publishing House, 1990.

Tice, Terrence Nelson. "Schleiermacher's Theological Method with Particular Attention to His Production of Church Dogmatics." Ph.D. dissertation, Princeton, 1961.

Tiessen, Terrance. "Toward a Hermeneutic for Discerning Universal Moral Absolutes." **Journal of the Evangelical Theological Society** 36/2 (1993): 189-207.

Tillich, Paul. **A History of Christian Thought: From Its Judaic and Hellenistic Origins to Existentialism**. Edited by Carl E. Braaten. New York: Simon and Schuster, 1968.

— **Systematic Theology**. 3 vols. Chicago: University of Chicago, 1951-1963.

Toulmin, Stephen. "The Historicization of Natural Science: Its Implications for Theology." In **Paradigm Change in Theology: A Symposium for the Future**, ed. Hans Küng and David Tracy, 233-241. Translated by Margaret Köhl. New York: Crossroad, 1989.

Tracy, David. **Blessed Rage for Order: The New Pluralism in Theology**. New York: Seabury Press, 1975.

— **Plurality and Ambiguity: Hermeneutics, Religion, Hope.** San Francisco: Harper and Row, 1989.

Traub, F. "Kirchliche und unkirchliche Theologie." **Zeitschrift für Theologie und Kirche** 13 (1903): 39-76.

Trillhaas, Wolfgang. "Die evangelische Theologie im 20. Jahrhundert." In **Bilanz der Theologie im 20. Jahrhundert: Perspktiven, Strömungen, Motive in der christlichen und nichtchristlichen Welt**, ed. Herbert Vorgrimmler and Robert Vander Gucht, 2:101-124. Freiburg: Herder, 1970.

Troeltsch, Ernst. "Die Dogmatik der 'religionsgeschichtlichen Schule.'" In **Gesammelte Schriften**. Tübingen: J. C. B. Mohr, 1913. 2:500-524.

— "Geschichte und Metaphysik." **Zeitschrift für Theologie und Kirche** 8 (1898): 1-69.

— "Über historische und dogmatische Methode in der Theologie." In **Gesammelte Schriften**. Tübingen: J. C. B. Mohr, 1913. 2:729-759.

Trollinger, William Vance, Jr. "Fundamentalism." In **A New Handbook of Christian Theology**, ed. Donald W. Musser and Joseph L. Price, 194-198. Nashville, TN: Abingdon, 1992.

Tupper, E. Frank. **The Theology of Wolfhart Pannenberg**. Philadelphia: Westminster Press, 1973.

Van Bemmelen, Peter Maarten. **Issues in Biblical Inspiration: Sanday and Warfield**. Andrews University Seminary Doctoral Dissertation Series, vol. 13. Berrien Springs, MI: Andrews University Press, 1988.

Van Bruggen, Jacob. **Wie maakte de Bijbel? Over afsluiting en gezag van het Oude en Nieuwe Testament**. Kampen: Kok, 1986.

Van Huyssteen Wentzel. **Theology and the Justification of Faith: Contructing Theories in Systematic Theology**. Translated by H. F. Snijders. Grand Rapids, MI: Eerdmans, 1989.

Vanhoozer, Kevin J. "The Semanitcs of Biblical Literature: Truth and Scripture's Diverse Literary Forms." In **Hermeneutics, Authority, and Canon**, ed. D. A. Carson and John D. Woodbridge, 53-104. Grand Rapids, MI: Zondervan Publishing House, 1986.

Vawter, Bruce. **Biblical Inspiration**. Philadelphia: Westminster Press, 1972.

Viladesau, Richard. "**Systematic Theology** 1: by Wolfhart Pannenberg." **Theological Studies** 54 (1993): 171-173.

Villa-Vicencio, Charles. "The Theology of Wolfhart Pannenberg." **Journal of Theology for Southern Africa** 16 (1976): 28-41.

Volf, Miroslav. "The Challenge of Protestant Fundamentalism." **Concilium** (1992/3): 97-106.

Vooght, Paul de. **Les sources de la Doctrine Chrétienne d'après les Théologiens du XIVe Siècle et du Début du XVe Avec le Texte Integral des XII Premieres Questions de la Summa Inedite de Gerard de Bologne.** Bruges: Desclée de Brouwer, 1954.

— "Wyclif et la *scriptura sola.*" **Ephemerides Theologicas Lovanienses** 39 (1963): 50-86.

Vries, S. J. de. "Biblical Criticism, History of." **The Interpreter's Dictionary of the Bible: An Illustrated Encyclopedia.** Edited by George Arthur Buttrick. Nashville, TN: Abingdon Press, 1962. 1:413-418.

Vunderink, Ralph W. "Review of **The Ground of Certainty**, by Donald G. Bloesch." **Calvin Theological Journal** 8 (1973): 84-89.

Wagner, Falk. "Religiöser Inhalt und logische Form: Zum Verhältnis von Religionsphilosophie und 'Wissenschaft der Logik' am Beispiel der Trinitätslehre." In **Die Flucht in den Begriff: Materialien zu Hegels Religionsphilosophie**, ed. Friedrich Wilhelm Graf and Falk Wagner, 196-228. Stuttgart: Klett-Cotta, 1982.

Wagner, Harald. "Fundamentaltheologie." **Theologische Realencyclopädie.** Edited by Gerhard Krause and Gerhard Müller. Berlin: Walter de Gruyter, 1983. 11:738-752.

Wagoner, Walter D. "Review of **The Crisis of Piety: Essays Towards a Theology of the Christian Life**, by Donald G. Bloesch." **Journal of Ecumenical Studies** 7 (1970): 145-146.

Wainwright, Geoffrey. "Method in Theology." **The Blackwell Encylopedia of Modern Christian Thought.** Edited by Alister E. McGrath. Oxford: Basil Blackwell, 1993. 369-373.

— "Pannenberg's Ecumenism." In **The Theology of Wolfhart Pannenberg: Twelve American Critiques, with an Autobiographical Essay and Response**, ed. Carl E. Braaten and Philip Clayton, 207-223. Minneapolis: Augsburg Publishing House, 1988.

Wallace, D. H. "Historicism and Biblical Theology." **Studia Evangelica** 3/2 (1964): 223-227.

Walsh, Brian J. "Introduction." **Calvin Theological Journal** 27 (1992): 304-306.

— "Pannenberg's Eschatological Ontology." **Christian Scholars Review** 11 (1982): 229-249.

Walsh, Sylvia I. "Paradox." In **A New Handbook of Christian Theology**, ed. Donald W. Musser and Joseph L. Price, 346-348. Nashville, TN: Abingdon, 1992.

Walther, Wilhelm. **Die normale Stellung zur heiligen Schrift.** Leipzig: A. Deichertsche Verlagsbuchhandlung, 1917.

Walvoord, J. F. "Review of **The Reform of the Church,** by Donald G. Bloesch." **Bibliotheca Sacra** 128 (1971): 159.

Webber, Robert E. "Behind the Scenes: A Personal Account." In **The Orthodox Evangelicals: Who They Are and What They Are Saying,** ed. Robert E. Webber and Donald G. Bloesch, 19-39. Nashville, TN: Thomas Nelson, 1978.

Webber, Robert E., and Donald G. Bloesch, eds. **The Orthodox Evangelicals: Who They Are and What They Are Saying.** Nashville, TN: Thomas Nelson, 1978.

Weber, Hans Emil. **Der Einfluss der protestantischen Schulphilosophie auf die orthodox-lutherische Dogmatik.** Darmstadt: Wissenschaftliche Buchgesellschaft, 1969.

— **Die analytische Methode der lutherischen Orthodoxie.** Naumburg a. S.: Lippert & Co., 1907.

— **Die philosophische Scholastik des deutschen Protestantismus im Zeitalter der Orthodoxie.** Leipzig: Quelle & Meyer, 1907.

— **Historisch-kritische Schriftforschung und Bibelglaube: Ein Versuch zur theologischen Wissenschaftslehre.** 2d enl. ed. Gütersloh: Bertelsmann, 1914.

— **Reformation, Orthodoxie und Rationalismus.** 3 vols. Gütersloh: Bertelsmann, 1937-51.

Weber, Otto. **Foundations of Dogmatics.** 2 vols. Translated by Darrell L. Guder. Grand Rapids, MI: Eerdmans, 1981.

Weber, Timothy P. "The Two-Edged Sword: The Fundamentalist Use of the Bible." In **The Bible in America: Essays in Cultural History,** ed. Nathan O. Hatch and Mark A. Noll, 101-120. New York: Oxford University Press, 1982.

Weborg, C. John. "Of the Making of Theologies There Is No End: A Bibliographic Report." **Covenant Quarterly** 44/4 (1986): 25-39.

Weinrich, M. "Grenzen der Erinnerung: Historische Kritik und Dogmatik im Horizont Biblischer Theologie. Systematische Vorüberlegungen." In **Wenn nicht jetzt, wann dann? Festschrift für H.-J. Kraus zum 65. Geburtstag,** ed. Hans-Georg Geyer, Johann Michael Schmidt, Werner Schneider, and Michael Weinrich, 327-338. Neukirchen-Vluyn: Neukirchener Verlag, 1983, 327-338.

Weischedel, Wilhelm. **Der Gott der Philosophen: Grundlegung einer philosophischen Theologie im Zeitalter des Nihilismus.** 2 vols. Darmstadt: Wissenschaftliche Buchgesellschaft, 1971.

Wells, David F. "Reservations about Catholic Renewal in Evangelicalism." In **The Orthodox Evangelicals: Who They Are and What They Are Saying**, ed. Robert E. Webber and Donald G. Bloesch, 213-224. Nashville, TN: Thomas Nelson, 1978.

— "Review of **Essentials of Evangelical Theory** [sic], vol. 1 and 2." **Religion in Life** 49 (1980): 119-120.

Wells, Paul Ronald. **James Barr and the Bible: Critique of a New Liberalism**. Phillipsburg, NJ: Presbyterian and Reformed Publishing Company, 1980.

Wells, William Walter. "The Influence of Kierkegaard on the Theology of Karl Barth." Ph.D. dissertation, Syracuse University, 1970.

— "The Reveille That Awakened Karl Barth." **Journal of the Evangelical Theological Society** 22/3 (1979): 223-233.

Wenger, John C. "The Biblicism of Anabaptists." In **The Rediscovery of the Anabaptist Vision: A Sixtieth Anniversary Tribute to Harold S. Bender**, ed. Guy F. Hershberger, 167-179. Scottdale, PA: Herald Press, 1957.

Wenz, Armin. **Das Wort Gottes--Gericht und Rettung. Untersuchungen zur Autorität der Heiligen Schrift in Bekenntnis und Lehre der Kirche**. Göttingen: Vandenhoeck & Ruprecht, forthcoming.

Wenz, Gunther. "Sola Scriptura? Erwägungen zum reformatorischen Schriftprinzip." In **Vernunft des Glaubens: Wissenschaftliche Theologie und kirchliche Lehre. Festschrift zum 60. Geburtstag von Wolfhart Pannenberg**, ed. Jan Rohls and Gunther Wenz, 540-567. Göttingen: Vandenhoeck & Ruprecht, 1988.

Wharton, James A. "Karl Barth as Exegete and His Influence on Biblical Interpretation." **Union Seminary Quarterly Review** 28/1 (1972): 5-13.

White, James Emery. "The Concept of Truth in Contemporary American Evangelical Theology." Ph.D. dissertation, The Southern Baptist Theological Seminary, 1991.

Whitehead, Alfred North. **Religion in the Making**. New York: Macmillan, 1926.

Who's Who in Religion. 2d ed. Chicago, IL: Marquis Who's Who, 1977. S.v. "Bloesch, Donald George."

Wiebe, Paul. "Search for a Paradigm." **Journal of Religion** 64 (1984): 348-362.

Wiesner, Werner. "Exegese und Dogmatik." **Theologische Literaturzeitung** 79 (1954): 447-454.

Wiles, Maurice. "**Systematic Theology**: Vol. 1, Wolfhart Pannenberg." **Theology** 96/769 (1993): 57-59.

— "The Uses of 'Holy Scripture.'" In **What about the New Testament? Essays in Honour of Christopher Evans**, ed. Morna Hooker and Colin Hickling, 155-164. London: SCM Press, 1974.

Wilken, Robert L. "Who Is Wolfhart Pannenberg?" **Dialog** 4 (1965): 140-142.

Willi, Hans-Peter. "Dogmatik als Lehre von Gott: Ein Bericht über den ersten Band der 'Systematischen Theologie' von Wolfhart Pannenberg." **Theologische Beiträge** 22-2 (1991): 102-110.

— "Theologie der Menschwerdung: Ein Bericht über den zweiten Band der 'Systematischen Theologie' von Wolfhart Pannenberg." **Theologische Beiträge** 22/6 (1991): 332-339.

Williams, George Hunston. **The Radical Reformation**. Philadelphia: Westminster Press, 1962

Williams, J. Rodman. **Renewal Theology**. 3 vols. Grand Rapids, MI: Zondervan Publishing House, 1988-1992.

Williams, Robert R. **Schleiermacher the Theologian: The Construction of the Doctrine of God**. Philadephia: Fortress Press, 1978.

Willis, E. David. **Calvin's Catholic Christology: The Function of the So-Called Extra Calvinisticum in Calvin's Theology**. Leiden: E. J. Brill, 1966.

Wink, Walter. **The Bible in Human Transformation: Toward a New Paradigm for Biblical Study**. Philadelphia: Fortress Press, 1973.

Wirsching, J. "Ein neues theologisches System? Randbemerkungen zur Theologie Wolfhart Pannenbergs." **Deutsches Pfarrerblatt** 64 (1964): 601-609.

Wiswedel, Wilhelm. "Bible." **The Mennonite Encyclopedia**. Edited by Harold S. Bender and C. Henry Smith. Hillsboro, KS: Mennonite Brethren Publishing House, 1955. 1:322-328.

— "The Inner and the Outer Word: A Study in the Anabaptist Doctrine of Scripture." **Mennonite Quarterly Review** 26 (1952): 171-191.

Wobbermin, Georg. **Geschichte und Historie in der Religionswissenschaft: Über die Notwendigkeit in der religionswissenschaft zwischen Geschichte und Historie strenger zu unterscheiden**. Tübingen: J. C. B. Mohr, 1911.

Wolf, Ernst. "Über 'Klarheit der Heiligen Schrift' nach Luthers 'De Servo Arbitrio.'" **Theologische Literaturzeitung** 92 (1967): 721-730.

Wonders, Lance A. "Review of **A Theology of Word and Spirit: Authority and Method in Theology**, by Donald G. Bloesch." **The Covenant Quarterly** 51/2 (1993): 48-50.

Wood, A. Skevington. **Captive to the Word. Martin Luther: Doctor of Sacred Scripture**. Grand Rapids, MI: Eerdmans, 1969.

Wood, Laurence W. "Above, Within or Ahead of? Pannenberg's Eschatologicalism as a Replacement for Supernaturalism." **The Asbury Theological Journal** 46/2 (1991): 43-72.

— "History and Hermeneutics: A Pannenbergian Perspective." **Wesleyan Theological Journal** 16/1 (1981): 7-22.

Woodbridge, John D. **Biblical Authority: A Critique of the Rogers/McKim Proposal**. Grand Rapids, MI: Zondervan Publishing House, 1982.

Woodbridge, John D., and Thomas Edward McComiskey, eds. **Doing Theology in Today's World: Essays in Honor of Kenneth S. Kantzer**. Grand Rapids, MI: Zondervan Publishing House, 1991.

Wrede, William. "The Task and Methods of 'New Testament Theology.'" In **The Nature of New Testament Theology**, ed. Robert Morgan, 68-116. Naperville: Alec R. Allenson, 1973.

Wrzecionko, P. "Vernunft und Wahrheit im Denken der Sozinianer und der altprotestantischen Orthodoxie." **Neue Zeitschrift für systematische Theologie und Religionsphilosophie** 14 (1972): 172-196.

Yarbrough, Robert W. "Evangelical Theology in Germany." **Evangelical Quarterly** 65/4 (1993): 329-353.

Young, William. "The Inspiration of Scripture in Reformation and in Barthian Theology." **Westminster Theological Journal** 8 (1946): 1-38.

Youngblood, Ronald, ed. **Evangelicals and Inerrancy**. Nashville, TN: Thomas Nelson, 1984.

Ziesler, John. "Historical Criticism and a Rational Faith." **The Expository Times** 105/9 (1994): 270-274.

Zinke, E. Edward. "A Conservative Approach to Theology." Supplement to the **Ministry: International Journal for Clergy** 50/10 (1977): 24A-24P.